May '7 725 mon
10:15
8 9-10 ~~thurs~~
Tues

Antique Trader
POTTERY
&
PORCELAIN
CERAMICS

PRICE GUIDE
3RD EDITION

EDITED BY
KYLE HUSFLOEN

CONTRIBUTING EDITOR
SUSAN N. COX

Published by
Antique Trader Books, A Division of

krause
publications

700 E. State Street • Iola, WI 54990-0001
Telephone: 715/445-2214
Web: www.krause.com

Please, call or write us for our free catalog of antiques and collectibles publications.
To place an order or receive our free catalog, call 800-258-0929.
For editorial comment and further information,
use our regular business telephone at (715) 445-2214.

Library of Congress Catalog Number: 99-68141
ISBN: 0-87341-888-3

Printed in the United States of America

Introduction

For over twenty-five years The Antique Trader has been producing general price guides covering all types of antiques and collectibles. Since the founding of our new Antique Trader Books & Price Guides division in 1994, we have greatly expanded our offerings in the category of price guides as well as other specialized references for the collecting field.

Our first product for our expanded price guide coverage was *Antique Trader Books Pottery & Porcelain — Ceramics Price Guide,* released in early 1994. This well-illustrated reference covered all major categories of pottery and porcelain, foreign and domestic, and was well received by the collecting community. Now we are bringing you a completely new Second Edition. Similar in size and format to our first edition, we have gathered all-new and updated data for the numerous categories included and have increased the number and size of our photographs to add to their usefulness and eye-appeal. As in the first volume, this edition covers ceramics produced as far back as the eighteenth century in Europe, but also includes expanded sections on popular twentieth century American chinawares and pottery. Whatever segment of the vast ceramics market you find most appealing, we'll have information included here.

As with our earlier book, we pride ourselves on providing the most accurate and detailed descriptions possible for each item included. These authoritative listings are highlighted by an abundance of fine black and white photographs since these are so important to a better understanding and appreciation of particular pieces and categories.

Ceramics, like most collecting specialties, has a vocabulary all its own. To give you a better understanding of terms used throughout this guide we begin with a general introduction to the collecting of ceramics followed by several pages of sketches showing a wide variety of pieces and forms you will find listed. The sketches include brief notes on the forms and body parts which will make it easier to study and use our guide. As an additional reference source we are including, at the conclusion of our price listings, a Glossary of Selected Ceramics Terms followed by several special Appendices covering individual collecting groups, museums of interest and references to pottery and porcelain marks. Since English ceramics of the nineteenth and early twentieth century make up quite a large portion of collectible ceramic wares found in this country, we also include an appendix explaining the unique system of English registry Marks.

My staff and I have put many hours of effort into producing an attractive and useful guide and it took many hands and hearts to produce the volume you now hold. A special note of thanks goes to our Contributing Editor Susan N. Cox for preparing a variety of categories covering some of today's most popular and collectible twentieth century American ceramics. Her special expertise has helped us present a well rounded and comprehensive guide. I sincerely hope that all who add *Antique Trader Books Pottery & Porcelain—Ceramics Price Guide* to their library will find it handy, easy to use and authoritative. Use it as a guide in your collecting pursuits and it should serve you well. If you have special comments or questions, we'll be happy to answer your inquiries. Enjoy this guide and may it bring you new knowledge and appreciation of your ceramic treasures and those waiting your discovery.

Kyle Husfloen, Editor

Photography Credits

Photographers who have contributed to this volume include: Edward Babka, East Dubuque, Illinois; Stanley L. Baker, Minneapolis, Minnesota; Dorothy Beckwith, Platteville, Wisconsin; Rodney L. Bourdeau, Danbury Connecticut; Susan N. Cox, El Cajon, California; J.D. Dalessandro, Cincinnati, Ohio; Loretta DeLozier, Bedford, Iowa; Jim Martin, Monmouth, Illinois; Louise Paradis, Sparta, Wisconsin; Joyce Roerig, Waltersboro, South Carolina; and Tom Wallace, Chicago, Illinois.

For other photographs, artwork, data or permission to photograph in their shops, we sincerely express appreciation to the following autcioneers, galleries, museums, individuals and shops.

Bell Tower Antique Mall, Covington, Kentucky; Brown Auctions, Mullinville, Kansas; Butterfield & Butterfield, San Francisco, California; The Cedars - Antiques, Aurelia, Iowa; Norm and Diana Charles, Hagerstown, Indiana; Christie's, New York, New York; Christie's South Kensington, England; Cincinnati Art Galleries, Cincinnati, Ohio; Collector's Sales & Services, Pomfret Center, Connecticut; D & L Antiques, North Berwick, Maine; DuMouchelles, Detroit, Michigan; Dunning's Auction Service, Elgin, Illinois; T. Ermert, Cincinnati, Ohio; The Galena Shoppe, Galena, Illinois; Garth's Auctions, Delaware, Ohio; Morton M. Goldberg Auction Galleries, New Orleans, Louisiana; Robert Gordon, San Antonio, Texas; Grunewald Antiques, Hillsborough, North Carolina; Vicki Harman, San Marcos, California; Gene Harris Antique Auction Center, Marshalltown, Iowa; Leslie Hindman Auctioneers, Chicago, Illinois; Jackson's Auctions, Cedar Falls, Iowa; Doris Johnson, Rockford, Illinois; Bev Kubesheski, Dubuque, Iowa; Joy Luke Gallery, Bloomington, Illinois; J. Martin, Mt. Orab, Ohio; Dave Rago, Lambertville, New Jersey; Jane Rosenow, Galva, Illinois; Skinner, Inc., Bolton, Massachusetts; Sotheby's, New York, New York; Michael Strawser, Wolcottville, Indiana; Temples Antiques, Eden Prairie, Minnesota; Town Crier Auction Service, Burlington, Wisconsin; Treadway Gallery, Cincinnati, Ohio; Lee Vines, Hewlett, New York; Bruce & Vicki Waasdorp, Clarence, New York; Wolf's Fine Arts & Auctioneers, Cleveland, Ohio; Woody Auctions, Douglass, Kansas; and Yesterday's Treasures, Galena, Illinois.

ON THE COVER:

Front: Left back - Florence Ceramics "Fair Lady" figure, $1,400-1,500, Courtesy of Rita Bee; back right - Rookwood Pottery 9" h. Black Iris glaze vase, $7,700, Courtesy of Treadway Gallery, Cincinnati, Ohio; front center - Blue & White stoneware bowls in th Grape Ware pattern, 8" d., $225, 10" d., $175, Courtesy of Steve Stone.

Back: Upper right - a McCoy Pottery cameo design jardiniere and pedestal, 21" h., $250-300, Courtesy of Craig Nissen; rare George Ohr red pitcher, 10" h., $44,000, Courtesy of Dave Rago, Lambertville, New Jersey. Lower left: Lefton China "Bossie the Cow" sugar bowl, came with matching creamer, the pair, $35, Courtesy of Loretta DeLozier.

Collecting Guidelines

Whenever I'm asked about what to collect, I always stress that you should collect what you like and want to live with. Collecting is a very personal matter and only you can determine what will give you the most satisfaction. With the wide diversity of ceramics available, everyone should be able to find a topic they will enjoy studying and collecting.

One thing that every collector should keep in mind is that to get the most from their hobby they must study it in depth, read everything they can get their hands on, and purchase the best references available for their library. New research material continues to become available for collectors and learning is an ongoing process.

It is also very helpful to join a collectors' club where others who share your enthusiasm will support and guide your learning. Fellow collectors often become your best friends and sources for special treasures to add to your collection. Dealers who specialize in a ceramics category are always eager to help educate and support collectors and many times they become a mentor for a novice who is just starting out on the road to the 'advanced collector' level.

With the very ancient and complex history of ceramic wares, it's easy to understand why becoming educated about your special interest is of paramount importance. There have been collectors of pottery and porcelain for centuries, and for nearly as long collectors have had to be wary of reproductions or 'reissues.' In Chinese ceramics, for instance, it has always been considered perfectly acceptable to copy as closely as possible the style and finish of earlier ceramics and even mark them with period markings on the base. The only problem arises when a modern collector wants to determine whether their piece, 'guaranteed' antique, was produced over two hundred years ago or barely a century ago.

With European and, to some extent, American wares, copying of earlier styles has also been going on for many decades. As far back as the mid-nineteenth century, 'copies' and 'adaptions' of desirable early wares were finding their way onto the collector market. By the late nineteenth century, in particular, revivals of eighteenth century porcelains and even some early nineteenth century earthenwares were available, often sold as decorative items and sometimes clearly marked. After a hundred years, however, these early copies can pose a real quagmire for the unwary.

Again, education is the key. As you're building your store of knowledge and experience, buy with care from reliable sources.

Another area that calls for special caution on the part of collectors, especially the tyro, is that of damaged and repaired pieces. A wise collector will always buy the best example they can find and it is a good policy to save up to buy one extra fine piece rather than a handful of lesser examples. You never want to pass up a good buy. But, in the long run, a smaller collection of choice pieces will probably bring you more satisfaction (and financial reward) than a large collection of moderate quality.

Purchasing a damaged or clearly repaired piece is a judgment only the collector can make. In general I wouldn't recommend it unless the piece is so unique that another example is not likely to come your way in the near future. For certain classes of expensive and rare ceramics, especially early pottery that has seen heavy use, a certain amount of damage may be inevitable and more acceptable. The sale price, however, should reflect this fact.

Restoration of pottery and porcelain wares has been a fact of life for many decades. Even in the early nineteenth century before good glues were available, 'make-do' repairs were sometimes done to pieces using small metal staples and today some collectors seek out these quaint examples of early recycling. Since the early twentieth century glue and repainting have been methods used to mask damages to pottery and porcelain and these repairs can usually be detected today with a strong light and the naked eye.

The problem in recent decades has been the ability of restorers to completely mask any sign of previous damages using more sophisticated repair methods. There is nothing wrong with a quality restoration of a rare piece as long as the eventual purchaser is completely aware such work has been done.

It can take more than the naked eye and a strong light to detect some invisible repairs today and that's where the popular 'black light,' using ultraviolet rays, can be of help. Many spots of repair will fluoresce under the 'black light.' I understand, however, that newer glues and paints are becoming available which won't show up under the black light. The key then, especially for the beginner, is know your ceramic or your seller and be sure you have a money-back guarantee when making a major purchase.

I certainly don't want to sound too downbeat and discourage anyone from pursuing what can be a wonderfully fun and fulfilling hobby, but starting from a position of strength, with confidence and education, will certainly pay-off in the long run for every collector.

Ceramics, in addition to their beauty and charm, also offer the collecting advantage of durability and low-maintenance. It's surprising how much pottery and porcelain from two centuries ago is still available to collect. There were literally train-cars full of it produced and sold by the late nineteenth century, and such wares are abundantly available and often reasonably priced. Beautiful dinnerwares and colorful vases abound in the marketplace and offer exciting collecting possibilities. They look wonderful used on today's dining tables or gracing display shelves.

A periodic dusting and once-a-year washing in mild sudsy, warm water is about all the care they will require. Of course, it's not recommended you put older pottery and porcelains in your dishwasher where rattling and extremely hot water could cause damage. Anyway, it's more satisfying to hold a piece in your hand in warm soapy water in a rubber dishpan (for added protection) and caress it carefully with a dishrag. The tactile enjoyment of a ceramic piece brings a new dimension to collecting and this sort of T.L.C. can be nearly as satisfying as just admiring a piece in a china cabinet or on a shelf.

Whatever sort of pottery or porcelain appeals to you most, whether it be eighteenth century Meissen or mid-twentieth century California-made pottery, you can take pride in the fact that you are carrying on a collecting tradition that goes back centuries when the crowned heads of Europe first began buying for the finest and rarest ceramics with which to accent their regal abodes.

Kyle Husfloen

Typical Ceramic Shapes

The following line drawings illustrate typical shapes found in pottery and porcelain pitchers and vases. These forms are referred to often in our price listings.

Pitcher - Barrel-shaped

Pitcher - Jug-type

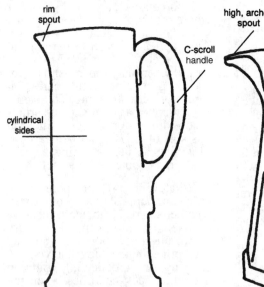

Pitcher - Tankard-type with cylindrical sides, C-scroll handle, and rim spout.

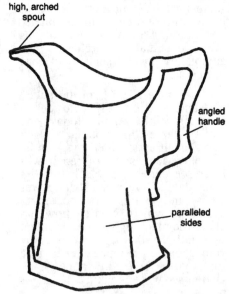

Pitcher - Tankard-type with panelled (octagonal) sides, angled handle and high, arched spout.

Vases

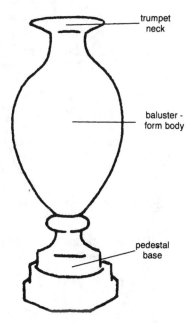

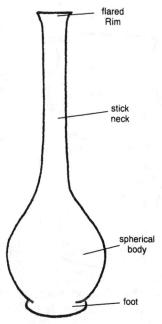

Vase - Baluster-form body with trumpet neck on a pedestal base.

Vase - Bottle-form — Spherical footed body tapering to a tall stick with flared rim.

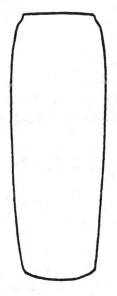

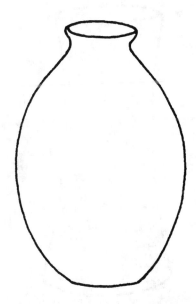

Vase - Cylindrical

Vase - Ovoid body, tapering to a short, flared neck.

Vases (Continued)

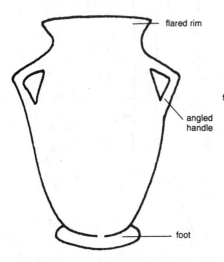

Vase - Ovoid, footed body with
flared rim & angled handles.

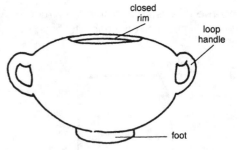

Vase - Pillow-shaped with molded rim;
on knob feet.

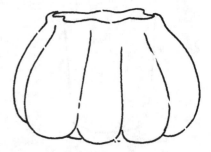

Vase or bowl vase - Spherical, footed
body with closed rim and loop
handles.

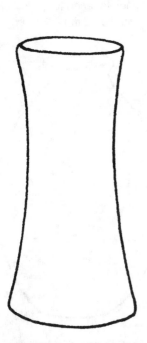

Vase - Waisted cylindrical form.

Vase - Squatty bulbous body
with lobed sides.

CERAMICS

ABINGDON

From about 1934 until 1950, Abingdon Pottery Company, Abingdon, Illinois, manufactured decorative pottery, mainly cookie jars, flowerpots and vases. Decorated with various glazes, these items are becoming popular with collectors who are especially attracted to Abingdon's novelty cookie jars.

Abingdon Mark

Book ends, model of a sea gull, No. 305, ivory glaze, 6" h., pr.................................... **$168**

Book ends, model of Scottie dog, No. 650, 7 1/2" h., pr....................................... **200**

Book ends/planters, figural dolphin, No. 444D, blue glaze, 5 3/4" h., pr....................... **65**

Candleholder, double, No. 479, Scroll patt., 4 1/2" h... **15**

Bamboo Pattern Candleholders & Plate

Candleholders, Bamboo patt., No. 716, pr. (ILLUS.)...................................... **30**

Console bowl, No. 532, Scroll patt., 14 1/2" l....................................... **20**

Console plate, Bamboo patt., No. 715, 10 1/2" d. (ILLUS. w/candleholders)............. **125**

Cookie jar, Baby, No. 561, 11" h. **750-1,000**

Cookie jar, Bo Peep, No. 694D, 12" h. **425**

Cookie jar, Choo Choo, No. 651D, 7 1/2" h....................................... **100**

Cookie jar, Clock, No. 563, 9" h...................... **100**

Cookie jar, Daisy, No. 677, 8" h........................ **50**

Cookie jar, Fat Boy, No. 495, 8 1/4" h. **650**

Cookie jar, Floral/Plaid, No. 697 8 1/2 h... **350-550**

Cookie jar, Hippo, No. 549, plain & decorated, 8" h... **350-550**

Cookie jar, Humpty Dumpty, No. 663, 10 1/2" h....................................... **208**

Cookie jar, Little Girl, No. 693, 9 1/2" h. **225**

Little Ol' Lady Cookie Jars

Cookie jar, Little Ol' Lady, No. 471, 9" h., various decorations, each (ILLUS.)....... **200-300**

Cookie jar, Miss Muffet, No. 662D, 11" h......... **350**

Cookie jar, Money Bag, No. 588D, 7 1/2" h. **40**

Cookie jar, Mother Goose, No. 695D, 12" h. **550**

Cookie jar, Pineapple, No. 664, 10 1/2" h. **150**

Cookie jar, Pumpkin, No. 674D, 8" h. **550**

Cookie jar, Three Bears, No. 696D, 8 3/4" h. (light hairline in lid)......................... **40**

Cookie jar, Windmill, No. 678, 10 1/2" h. **500**

Cookie jar, Witch, No. 692, 11 1/2" h........... **1,000**

Wigwam Cookie Jar

Cookie jar, Wigwam, No. 665D, 11" h. (ILLUS.).. **750-1,000**

Abingdon Display Sign

Display sign, marked "Abingdon" (ILLUS.)...... **300**

Scarf Dancer Figure

Figure, Scarf Dancer, No. 3902, 13" h.
(ILLUS.)... **800 up**

Various Flowerpots

Flowerpots, Nos. 149 to 152, floral decora-
tion, 3 to 6" h., each (ILLUS. of three)....... **15-30**
Lamp base, No. 254, draped shaft, 13" h. **200**
Model of a heron, No. 574, tan glaze,
5 1/4" h. **68**
Model of a peacock, No. 416, turquoise
glaze, 7" h. **96**
Model of a swan, No. 661, 3 3/4" h. **150**

Grecian Pitcher & Vase

Pitcher, 15" h., Grecian patt., No. 613
(ILLUS. right)... **150**
Planter, model of a Dutch shoe, No. 655,
5" l. **100**
Planter, model of a puppy, No. 652D,
6 3/4" l. **50**

String holder, Chinese head, No. 702,
5 1/2" h. **500**
Vase, 10" h., No. 114, Classic line **25**
Vase, 3 1/2" h., No. A1, what-not type............. **100**
Vase, 4 1/2" h., No. C1, what-not type **100**
Vase, 5" h., No. B1, what-not type................... **100**

Fern Leaf Pattern Vase

Vase, 8 1/2" h., No. 424, Fern Leaf patt.,
medium size (ILLUS.)................................... **100**
Vase, 5 1/2" h., No. 142, Classic line **40**
Vase, 7" h., No. 171, Classic line **40**

Figural Blackamoor Vase

Vase, 7 1/2" h. figure of Blackamoor, No.
497D (ILLUS.) **150**
Vase, 8" h., No. 132, Classic line **40**
Vase, 9" h., No. 513, Swirl patt., medium **20**

Boyne Pattern Vase

Vase, 9" h., No. 534, Boyne patt. (ILLUS.)......... **35**

Lung Pattern Vase

Vase, 11" h., Lung patt., No. 302 (ILLUS.) 225
Vase, 15" h., floor-type, Grecian patt., No.
603 (ILLUS. left, previous page) 150
Wall pocket, figural butterfly, No. 601,
8 1/2" h. 150
Wall pocket, figural Dutch boy, No. 489,
10" h. 150
Wall pocket, figural Dutch girl, No. 490,
10" h. 150

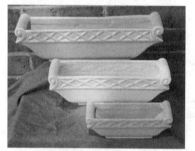

Various Size Window Boxes

Window boxes, No. 477, 13 1/2" l., No.
476, 10 1/2" l., No. 475, 7" l., each
(ILLUS.) 25-35

AMERICAN PAINTED
PORCELAIN

*During the late Victorian era American artisans
produced thousands of hand-painted porcelain
items, including tableware, dresser sets, desk sets,
and bric-a-brac. These pieces of porcelain were
imported and usually bear the marks of foreign factories and countries. To learn more about identification, evaluation, history, and appraisal, the
following books and newsletter by Dorothy Kamm
are recommended: American Painted Porcelain:
Collector's Identification & Value Guide, Comprehensive Guide to American Painted Porcelain, and
Dorothy Kamm's Porcelain Collector's Companion.*

Berry spoon holder, pierced handles, decorated w/two clusters of blackberries,
light blue border, burnished gold rim &
handles, marked "Bavaria," ca. 1894-
1914, 4 5/8 x 10" **$35**

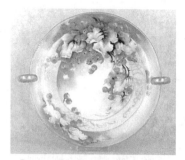

Bonbon Decorated with Currants

Bonbon, round w/gold upright ring handles, decorated w/clusters of currants on
a multicolored ground, an inner border
band w/gilded outlines of spider webs &
currant clusters, burnished gold rim,
signed "I.A. Johnson, 1915" & marked
"UNO-IT - Favorite - Bavaria," 6 3/8" d.
(ILLUS.) 40
Bouillon cup & saucer, decorated w/a cur-
vilinear geometric design in burnished
gold outlined in dark blue, burnished
gold rims & handles, marked "T & V -
Limoges - France," ca. 1892-1907 30
Bowl, 7 1/2" d., cereal, decorated w/a border design of daisy clusters on an ivory
ground, light blue border & burnished
gold rim, marked "HR - Hutschenreuther
- Selb - Bavaria," ca. 1905-18 22
Bowl, 8 3/4" w., square fruit-type, decorated on the interior w/geraniums on a
polychrome ground, on the exterior
w/scrolls on a graduated green ground,
burnished gold rim, ca. 1880-1900 70

Early Painted Butter Dish

Butter dish, cover & liner, decorated on
the domed cover & dished base w/clus-
ters of pink roses & greenery on a pale
pink & green ground, burnished gold rim
& handle, signed "R.O. BRIGGS, AUS-
TIN, IL (?)," marked w/crowned double-
headed eagle & "MZ - Austria," 1884-
1909 (ILLUS.) 75
Butter tub, round, decorated w/forget-me-
nots on an ivory ground, burnished gold
rim & handles, signed "Tossy," marked
"T & V - Limoges - France," ca. 1892-
1917 (no pierced insert) 45

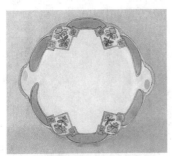

Cake Plate with Floral Panels

Cake plate, pierced rim handles, scalloped edge, decorated w/a four-panel design w/conventional-style flowers in each panel, burnished gold border outlines, dotted grounds & rim, signed w/illegible cipher & marked "HR - Charlotte - Bavaria," ca. 1887+, 9 1/8" d. (ILLUS.) 55

Chocolate cup & saucer, decorated w/yellow primrose on a shaded yellow brown ground, burnished gold rims, cup base & handle, signed "A. Brown," marked "Haviland - Limoges - France," ca. 1894-1931 30

Chocolate pot, cov., decorated w/cluster of pink roses on a pastel polychrome ground, burnished gold knob & handle, signed "M.H. Dorothy," marked "GDA - France," ca. 1900-41 150

Coffeepot, cov., decorated w/a conventional-styled dandelion design, burnished gold rims, spout interior, upper lip & handles, signed "M. Lamour," marked "J. & C. Bavaria," ca. 1902, 10" h. 175

Cracker & cheese dish, decorated w/a conventional Chinese-style floral design, an opal lustre ground, burnished gold borders & rims, illegible signature, marked w/a wreath & star & "R.S. Tillowitz - Silesia," ca. 1920-38, 8 1/2" d. 105

Cracker jar, cov., decorated w/white wild roses on a pastel polychrome ground w/burnished gold handles, signed "A.S.S.," marked "Royal" & wreath w/"O. & E.G.," 1898-1918 62

Creamer & open sugar bowl, decorated w/yellow roses on a light green border band, burnished gold borders, rims, base rims & handles, creamer marked w/a bird & "C. T. - Altwasser - Silesia," marked marked "KPM," ca. 1909-1930, pr. 35

Breakfast Cup & Saucer with Clover

Cup & saucer, breakfast-size, decorated w/a clover design on a light blue ground, burnished gold rims & handle, signed "A. H. h.," ca. 1880s-90s (ILLUS.) 45

Cup & saucer, decorated w/pink roses on a pastel polychrome ground, opal lustre interior, burnished gold rims & handle, marked "Favorite - Bavaria," ca. 1908-18, the set 25

Fern pot, decorated w/pink wild roses on a graduated green ground, signed "B.E. Miehling 99," marked "Elite" in a shield & "Limoges - France," 1899, 7 1/2" d., 4 3/4" h. 175

Gold-decorated Hair Receiver

Hair receiver, cov., squatty round form on three gold curved legs, decorated w/a conventional rose design in burnished gold, burnished gold rim & feet, signed "Ferver," ca. 1900-10, 3 7/8" d., 3 1/4" h. (ILLUS.) 50

Handkerchief box, cov., decorated w/peach-tinged yellow roses on a pastel polychrome ground, signed "WSO - 1913," marked "D. & Co. - France," 5 1/4" sq., 3" h. 65

Honey dish, on three ball feet, decorated w/pink clover & wheat sheaves, light grey border, white enamel trim, burnished gold rim, marked "Bavaria," ca. 1891-1914, 7 1/8" d. 35

Ice cream bowl, decorated w/a winter scene w/burnished gold border & rim, signed "F.L. Hey," marked "CFH - GDM," ca. 1920-30, 6 3/4 x 10 5/8", 2 3/16" h. 112

Luncheon set: 7 1/2" d. plate & cup & saucer; decorated in a conventional style floral border w/white enameled flower centers & burnished gold rims & handle, marked "Germany," ca. 1914-18, the set 35

Mug, decorated w/colorful yellow & yellowish red gooseberries on a polychrome ground, marked w/a crown & two shields w/"Vienna - Austria," ca. 1900-15, 4 3/4" h. 55

Mustard jar w/attached underplate & cover, decorated w/conventional style waterlilies on a light blue & burnished gold ground, burnished gold handle & rims, marked "D. & Co. - France," ca. 1879-1900, 3" h. 40

Napkin ring, half moon-shape, decorated w/a purple columbine on an ivory ground, ca. 1880-1915, 2 1/2" w. 15

Pin tray, rectangular w/pointed ends w/pierced handles, a border design of clusters of conventional blue & yellow flowers, connected by a burnished gold border, burnished gold rim, signed "G G Williamson," marked w/a crowned double-headed eagle & "MZ Austria," 1884-1909, 3 3/4 x 6 3/4" 45

Pitcher, 9 3/4" h., claret-type, decorated w/a conventional Art Nouveau-style floral design outlined in gold, burnished gold handle & edges, signed "V.B. Chase," ca. 1890-1914................................... 50

Pitcher, 5 3/4" h., lemonade-type, decorated w/clusters of purple grapes on an ivory ground, antique green beaded handle & border band at top, ca. 1900-16.......... 200

Pitcher & underplate, 3 3/8" h. pitcher, 5 1/4" d. plate, milk-type, decorated w/conventionalized orange blossoms w/burnished gold borders, rims, spout & handle, signed "J.M. Cliffe, 11/28" & marked "Japan," the set 30

Tulip-decorated Plate

Plate, 8 1/4" d., decorated w/large red tulips & green leaves on a shaded rust to cream ground w/burnished gold rim, marked w/a bird & "Altwasser - Germany," ca. 1909-34 (ILLUS.).................... 45

Plate, 8 3/4" d., decorated w/large orange poppies & green leaves on a shaded green ground, burnished gold rim, stamped on bottom "J. Lycett - St. Louis, Mo. - The Odean," ca. 1900-15 50

Plate, 5 1/4 x 9 1/2", salad-type, crescent-shaped, decorated w/multicolored sweet peas on a pale violet & green ground, burnished gold rim, ca. 1900-24.................... 42

Hand-painted Pomade Jar

Pomade jar, cov., small cylindrical form, decorated w/a conventional geometric design in baby blue & burnished gold outlined in brown, marked "W. G. & Co. - Limoges - France," ca. 1901, 2 1/2" d., 1 1/2" h. (ILLUS.)................................... 35

Punch cups, decorated w/clusters of forget-me-nots, opal lustre interiors, burnished gold stems & rims, marked w/"Royal," a wreath & "O. & E.G.," 1898-1918, 4" h., set of 5 112

Salt dips, cauldron-shaped, decorated w/pink roses on a pale blue & yellow ground, burnished gold rims & ball feet, signed "P. Putzki," marked w/a crown double-head eagle & "MZ - Austria," ca. 1884-1909, set of 6 105

Decorated Nippon Porcelain Shakers

Salt & pepper shakers, decorated w/delicate panels of conventional-style hawthorne berries & leaves on an opal lustre ground, burnished gold tops & branch-shaped borders, signed "A.E.F.," marked "Noritake Nippon," 1914-21, 2 1/2" h., pr. (ILLUS.)... 35

Sherbet, decorated w/daisies on an ivory ground, mother-of-pearl lustre interior, burnished gold border, rim & foot, signed "M. Paddock," marked "Epiag - Czechoslovakia," ca. 1920-39, 3 1/8" h.......... 30

Soup plates, flanged rim decorated w/three clusters of seashells & seaweeds on a very pale polychrome ground, burnished gold rims, signed "ALB," marked "H. & Co. - Haviland - Limoges - France," 1876 - 1879, 9" d., pr. 40

Sugar shaker, decorated w/Art Nouveau-style florals & squiggling border band in burnished gold, burnished gold pierced top, signed "E.C.R.," ca. 1905-15, 2 3/4" d., 4 1/2" h... 35

Syrup jug, cov., decorated w/pink & ruby roses on a polychrome ground, burnished gold handle, knob & rims, opal lustre spout interior, marked "ADK - France," ca. 1891-1910, 4" h. (missing underplate) 30

Table top centerpiece, decorated w/a cluster of daisies on a pastel polychrome ground, burnished gold rim, signed "E. Miller," marked "T & V - Limoges - France," ca. 1892-1907, 11 5/8" d. 90

Toast set: plate & cup; 9 3/16 w. plate decorated w/conventional-style strawberries on an ivory ground, opal lustre cup interior, burnished gold borders, rims & handle, ca. 1925-30, 2 pcs............................ 40

Toothpick holder, decorated w/double violets on a pastel ivory & green ground, burnished gold rim, signed "Wats" & "Pitkin & Brooks Studio," marked "T & V - Limoges - France," 1903-10, 2 3/4" h............ **25**

Tumbler, decorated w/ruby roses on a polychrome ground, burnished gold rim, illegible signature, marked "La Seynie - PP - Limoges - France," ca. 1903-17, 3 3/8" h. **22**

Vase, 7" h., bulbous base tapering to a tall slender neck, two-handled, decorated w/pink & yellow roses on a pastel polychrome ground, burnished gold rim, accents & handle, ca. 1900-20...................... **45**

AUSTRIAN

Numerous potteries in Austria produced good-quality ceramic wares over many years. Some factories were established by American entrepreneurs, particularly in the Carlsbad area, and other factories made china under special brand names for American importers. Marks on various pieces are indicated in many listings.

Austrian Marks

Cake plate, open-handled, portrait of woman w/flowing hair, Imperial, 11" d.......... **$13**

Cracker jar, cov., Kauffmann scene on cobalt blue ground, 20th c., beehive mark **165**

Dessert set: 8 1/2" plate & four matching 6" plates; Kauffmann transfers, cobalt w/gold borders, the set (Victoria, Austria)....... **72**

Dish, figural, Art Nouveau style, flaring oblong shallow form w/a shoulder-length model of a lady w/flowing hair along one edge, her arms spread clutching an applied flower among large waterlilies, creamy tan & pale green, impressed & stamped mark, 8" l. (minor rim roughness) **209**

Figurine, porcelain figure of a woman w/raised arms in a black lace evening gown & cranberry-colored cape, marked "Victoria - Carlsbad - Austria," 13" h............ **460**

Fish set: 18" platter & eight 8 1/2" d. plates; decorated w/different colorful fish centers, shell & floral raised Rococo borders, 9 pcs. (Imperial - Austria Crown China).. **500**

Mug, scuttle-shaped, cobalt blue w/floral decoration **88**

Plate, 8" d., decorated w/sprays of pink roses (M.Z. Austria)...................................... **48**

Plate, 8 1/2" d., portrait scene of shepherd & woman, blue & gold border....................... **17**

Vase, 9 3/4" h., footed, rose painted w/cobalt, yellow, green & brown background, artist-signed, marked "Vienna, Austria".. **83**

Vase, 12" h., simple cylindrical body, h.p. w/large pink, red & yellow roses & green leaves on a shaded ground, artist-signed, base marked "Vienna Austria"......... **173**

Vase, 18" h., pedestal base, swan handles, much openwork, decorated w/purple, green & yellow flowers ("R.H." Austria) **285**

Vase, 25" h., Art Nouveau style, tall ovoid body w/slender cylindrical neck & flared rim w/portrait of young woman in oval reserve surrounded by floral decoration, flared foot on square base w/bronze mounts, artist-signed "Wagner," 20th c. ... **3,680**

Austrian Portrait Vases

Vases, cov., 21" h., Art Nouveau style two-handled ovoid body w/enamel decorated half portraits of nude woman surrounded by raised gilt floral decoration on ruby red ground, flared foot on a square base w/gilt floral decoration, ca. 1900, pr. (ILLUS.)... **5,463**

BAUER

The Bauer Pottery was moved to Los Angeles, California from Paducah, Kentucky, in 1909, in the hope that the climate would prove beneficial to the principal organizer, John Andrew Bauer, who suffered from severe asthma. Flowerpots, made of California adobe clay, were the first production at the new location, but soon they were able to resume production of stoneware crocks and jugs, the mainstay of the Kentucky operation. In the early 1930s, Bauer's colorfully glazed earthen dinnerwares, especially the popular Ring-Ware pattern, became an immediate success. Sometimes confused with its imitator, Fiesta Ware (first registered by Homer Laughlin in 1937), Bauer pottery is collectible in its own right and is especially popular with West Coast collectors. Bauer Pottery ceased operation in 1962.

Bauer Mark

Baby mug, Plainware, yellow, 8 oz. $60

Baking dish, cov., individual, Ring-Ware patt., green or yellow, 4" d., each 40

Baking dish, cov., individual, Ring-Ware patt., orange/red, 4" d. 55

Batter bowl, Ring-Ware patt., green, 1 qt. 125

Ring-Ware Beater Pitcher

Beater pitcher, Ring-Ware patt., red, 1 qt. (ILLUS.) 85

Bowl, berry, 4" d., Ring-Ware patt., burgundy 50

Bowl, cereal, 4 1/2" d., Ring-Ware patt., jade green 55

A Variety of Bauer Ring-Ware Pieces

Bowl, berry, 5 1/2" d., Ring-Ware patt., delphinium (ILLUS. far left) 30

Bowl, berry, 5 1/2" d., Ring-Ware patt., yellow 25

Bowl, soup, cov., 5 1/2" d., lug handles, Ring-Ware patt., orange, green, ivory or cobalt blue, each 90

Bowl, 8" d., Cal-Art line, Swirl patt., yellow 45

Bowl, 12" d., Ring-Ware, yellow 65

Bowl, 13" d., Cal-Art line, green 35

Bowl, 15" d., wide low sides, white & brown speckled glaze, No. 149 95

Butter dish, cov., round, Ring-Ware patt., delph blue (light blue) 225

Butter dish, cov., round, Ring-Ware patt., red 155

Cake plate, Monterey patt., yellow 185

Candleholders, spool-shaped, Ring-Ware patt., jade green, pr. 130

Carafe w/original cap, Plainware, jade glaze 75

Casserole, cov., individual, Ring-Ware patt., cobalt blue, 5 1/2" d. 300

Casserole, cov., individual, Ring-Ware patt., ivory, 5 1/2" d. 300

Casserole, cov., individual, Ring-Ware patt., orange/red, 5 1/2" d. 200

Coffee carafe, cov., Ring-Ware patt., copper handle, delph blue 250

Coffee carafe, cov., Ring-Ware patt., copper handle, orange/red 150

Coffee server, cov., Plain Ware, green 75

Console set: bowl & pr. of three-light candlesticks; Cal-Art line, pink, semi-matte finish, 3 pcs. 145

Cookie jar, cov., Monterey Moderne patt., chartreuse 100

Cookie jar, cov., Ring-Ware patt., red or yellow, each 995

Monterey Midget Creamer

Creamer, midget, Monterey patt., orange/red (ILLUS.) 20

Creamer, Plain Ware, green 65

Creamer, Ring-Ware patt., jade green, small 55

Creamer, Ring-Ware patt., yellow, small 45

Creamer & cov. sugar bowl, Monterey patt., white, pr. 75

Creamer & cov. sugar bowl, Ring-Ware patt., ivory, pr. 150

Creamer & cov. sugar bowl, Ring-Ware patt., orange, pr. 75

Creamer & cov. sugar bowl, Ring-Ware patt., orange/red, small, pr. 95

Cup & saucer, demitasse, Ring-Ware patt., yellow 125

Cup & saucer, Ring-Ware patt., yellow (ILLUS. third from right w/bowl!) 45-50

Flowerpot, Ring-Ware patt., cobalt blue 45

Flowerpot, Speckleware, flesh pink, 8 1/4" d., 6 1/2" h. 40

Gravy boat, Monterey Moderne patt., pink 40

Gravy boat, Ring-Ware patt., burgundy 145

Mixing bowl, Atlanta line, No. 24, cobalt blue 100

Mixing bowl, nesting-type, Ring-Ware patt., No. 18, chartreuse 75

Mixing bowl, nesting-type, Ring-Ware patt., No. 18, jade green 75

Mixing bowl, nesting-type, Ring-Ware patt., No. 36, ivory 55

Model of duck, w/head up, white, 3 x 4 1/2" 45

Model of hippo, Cal-Art line, white glaze, ca. 1941 375

Mug, barrel-shaped, Ring-Ware patt., jade green or yellow, each 150

Nappy, Ring-Ware patt., green, No. 8 55

Bauer Oil Jar

Oil jar, No. 100, orange, 16" h. (ILLUS.) **1,000**
Oil jar, No. 100, cobalt blue, 22" h. **1,700**
Oil jars, No. 100, white, 12" h., pr. **3,000**
Pie plate, Ring-Ware patt., green....................... **45**
Pitcher, Ring-Ware patt., orange, 1 qt. **85**
Pitcher, Ring-Ware patt., delph blue, 2 qt. **200**
Pitcher, cov., jug-type, ice water, Monterey
patt., turquoise **325**
Pitcher, water, w/ice lip, Monterey patt.,
green **125**
Planter, model of a swan, chartreuse,
medium **95**
Planter, model of a swan, white, 2 1/2 x 6" **110**
Planter, model of swan, white, 3 x 9" **120**
Plate, butter, 4 1/2" d., Plain Ware, yellow **80**
Plate, 5" d., bread & butter, Ring-Ware
patt., green (ILLUS. center front w/bowl) **15**
Plate, salad, 7 1/2" d., Ring-Ware patt., yel-
low (ILLUS. center front w/bowl) **30**
Plate, 9" d., Ring-Ware patt., black **85**
Plate, 9" d., Ring-Ware patt., grey **65**
Plate, 10 1/2" d., dinner, Ring-Ware patt.,
cobalt or delph blue, each **95**
Plate, 10 1/2" d., dinner, Ring-Ware patt.,
jade green, orange or yellow, each **85**
Plate, chop, 12" d., Ring-Ware patt., bur-
gundy **150**
Plate, chop, 12" d., Ring-Ware patt., green........ **75**
Plate, chop, 12" d., Ring-Ware patt., white....... **230**
Plate, chop, 12" d., Ring-Ware patt., yellow **75**
Plate, chop, 13" d., Monterey patt., deco-
rated **175**
Plate, chop, 14" d., Ring-Ware patt., yellow **125**
Plate, chop, Monterey Moderne patt., yel-
low **45**
Plate, grill, Monterey Moderne patt., char-
treuse **35**
Plate, luncheon, Ring-Ware patt., yellow
(ILLUS. center back w/bowl) **40**
Platter, 12" oval, Ring-Ware patt., green,
No. 8.. **70**
Pudding cup, No. 3, jade glaze **65**
Pumpkin bowl, No. 513, matte pink w/gold
trim, ca. 1950s, Tracy Irwin, 6 1/2 x 10" **125**
Punch bowl, Ring-Ware patt., three-
footed, cobalt blue, 14" d.............................. **850**

Punch bowl, Ring-Ware patt., three-
footed, jade green, 14" d. **550**
Punch cup, Ring-Ware patt., delph, cobalt
blue, green, yellow or burgundy, each **35**
Relish dish, divided, Ring-Ware patt.,
cobalt blue **195**
Salt box, w/wooden cover, white w/straw-
berry decoration **240**
Salt & pepper shakers, beehive-shaped,
Ring-Ware patt., orange/red, pr. **60**
Salt & pepper shakers, Ring-Ware patt.,
black, pr. (ILLUS. back, second from left
w/bowl) **85**
Soup bowl, lug-handled, Ring-Ware patt.,
cobalt blue, 5 1/2" d...................................... **85**
Sugar bowl, cov., demitasse, Ring-Ware
patt., burgundy **60**
Sugar shaker, Ring-Ware patt., jade green..... **350**
Syrup pitcher, Ring-Ware patt., cobalt
blue **285**

Bauer "Aladdin Lamp" Teapot

Teapot, cov., Aladdin Lamp-shape, yellow,
large (ILLUS.)... **250**
Teapot, cov., individual size, Plain Ware,
yellow **85**
Teapot, cov., Ring-Ware patt., burgundy,
2-cup size **325**
Teapot, cov., Ring-Ware patt., yellow, 2-
cup size **125**
Teapot, cov., Ring-Ware patt., yellow, 6-
cup size **185**
Tumbler, Ring-Ware patt., green, large
(ILLUS. second from right w/bowl) **45-65**
Tumbler, Ring-Ware patt., delphinium,
small (ILLUS. far right w/bowl) **40**
Vase, 4 1/4" h., bulbous, Fred Johnson Art-
ware line, jade green...................................... **65**
Vase, 8" h., Hi-Fire line, deep trumpet-
shaped form w/widely flaring sides fluted
on the exterior, yellow **90**

Matt Carlton Line Vase

Vase, 8" h., ovoid base w/widely flared rim, twist shoulder handles, orange, Matt Carlton Artware line (ILLUS. previous page) **650**

Vase, 10 1/2" h., cylindrical, Ring-Ware patt., delph blue.............. **95**

Vase, 13" h., ovoid base w/widely flared rim, twist shoulder handles, jade green, Matt Carlton Artware line.......... **1,200**

Large Rebekah Vase

Vase, 24" h., Rebekah, tall slender baluster-form w/loop handles near the short flaring neck, jade green, Matt Carlton Artware line (ILLUS.).............. **2,500**

Vegetable bowl, oval w/end handles, yellow, 5" l........... **85**

BAVARIAN

Ceramics have been produced by various potteries in Bavaria, Germany, for many years. Those appearing for sale in greatest frequency today were produced in the 19th and early 20th centuries. Various company marks are indicated with some listings here.

Bowl, 9" d., ribbed mold decorated w/tulips on green & gold ground, marked "R.C. Bavaria, Claire" **$28**

Bowl, 10" d., center portrait of woman on cobalt blue w/gold border, marked "RC Alice Bavaria".......... **220**

Box, cov., the lid depicting a figural female nude reclining on a sofa, marked "Bavaria," 6" l.......... **66**

Bavarian Cake Plate

Cake plate, slightly scalloped round form w/pierced rim handles, decorated w/h.p. pink roses & green leaves on green tinted center, gold trim on rim & gold scrolls near handles, 11" d. (ILLUS.)......... **70-80**

Dinner service: service for 12 including 9 1/2" dinner plates, 7 1/2" salad plates, 6" bread & butter plates, fruit bowls, soup plates, two-handled bouillon cups & saucers, 18 cups & saucers, 12 demitasse sets, cov. coffeepot, cov. teapot, creamer & sugar bowl sets, various platters & serving pieces; "Empress Dresden Flowers" patt., floral borders & a central bouquet & scattered blossoms, marked "Bavaria Schumann, Arzberg, Germany," 20th c., 147 pcs....... **4,600**

Dresser set: cov. box, cov. powder jar, cov. hair receiver, two hatpin holders, a pair of candlesticks & a pin tray; each w/a simple form & h.p. w/poppies on a peach ground, late 19th - early 20th c., the set **316**

Game plates, decorated w/center scene of various ground fowl on burgundy background w/gold scrolled border, marked "S.T.W. Bavaria Germany" & blue beehive mark, 11" d., set of 3........... **110**

Pitcher, tankard, 11" h., decorated w/h.p. strawberries, gold trim....... **265**

Toothpick holder, figural shell, pearlized finish, marked "Bavaria"........... **143**

Vase, 14" h., footed ovoid body tapering to tall cylindrical neck w/flared rim, Bird of Paradise decoration, marked "C.T. Hutchenreuther, Bavaria, Germany" **33**

BELLEEK

Belleek china has been made in Ireland's County Fermanagh for many years. It is exceedingly thin porcelain. Several marks were used, including a hound and harp (1865-1880), and a hound, harp and castle (1863-1891). A printed hound, harp and castle with the words "Co. Fermanagh Ireland" constitutes the mark from 1891. Belleek-type china also was made in the United States last century by several firms, including Ceramic Art Company, Columbian Art Pottery, Lenox Inc., Ott & Brewer and Willets Manufacturing Co. Also see LENOX.

AMERICAN BELLEEK

BASKETS AND BOWLS

Lenox (palette mark), bowl, h.p. Art Deco cameos of tulips accented w/heavy gold, artist-signed "Clara May," dated "22," 10 1/2" d., 3" h. **$160**

Ott and Brewer (crown & sword mark), basket, applied floral & leaf decoration, 6 x 8", 3" h.......... **325**

Ott and Brewer (crown & sword mark), bowl, h.p. flowers on a cream ground w/gilded thistle handles **325**

Ott and Brewer (crown, sword & O.B. mark), tazza, hand-decorated w/twig feet & gilt paste ferns, 8" d. **900**

Willets (serpent mark), bowl, handled, h.p. apple blossoms, leaves &

twigs accented w/heavy gold, artist-
signed "ES James," 6 1/4" d., 5" h. **600**

Willets (serpent mark), bowl,
handled, h.p. delicate floral sprays, ruffled top trimmed w/gold, gilt shaped han-
dles... **350**

CANDLESTICKS & LAMPS

Lenox (palette mark), candlestick lamps,
hexagonal inverted tulip shaped
shades, h.p. roses joined by green
swags & gilding, artist-signed "Trezisc,"
shades 6" d., overall 18" h., pr. **560**

Lenox (palette mark), candlesticks, black
w/Art Deco-style enameled flowers
accented w/raised gold, 8 1/4" h., pr. **225**

CUPS AND SAUCERS

Ceramic Art Company Cabinet Cup

**Ceramic Art Company (CAC palette
mark),** cabinet cup, no saucer, delicately
enameled fretwork on footed base,
3 3/4" h. (ILLUS.).. **75**

CAC Tridacna Shape Cup and Saucer

**Ceramic Art Company (CAC palette
mark),** cup & saucer, "Tridacna" body
shape, cream-colored exterior, blue lustre interior w/gold handle & rim, saucer
5 1/4" d. (ILLUS.).. **350**

**Ceramic Art Company (CAC palette
mark),** demitasse cup & saucer, decorated w/scenes of elves & pixies inspired
by illustrator Palmer Cox, saucer 4" d. **700**

Coxon Belleek, cup & saucer, h.p. "Boule-
vard" patt. gold around the rim of the cup
& saucer, saucer 5" d. **175**

Lenox (palette mark), bouillon cup & saucer, cream-colored body w/gold banding
around top of cup & saucer, saucer 6" d. **95**

Lenox (palette mark), demitasse cup &
saucer, filigree sterling silver overlay on
two sides of the cup & around the rim of
the cup & saucer, saucer 1 1/2" d. **125**

Lenox (palette mark), demitasse cup &
saucer, sterling silver overlay in an Art
Deco design w/orange & green enameling, silver overlay around rim of cup &
saucer, saucer 4 1/2" d. **140**

Morgan (urn mark), cup & saucer, h.p. in
the "Orient" patt., saucer 5 1/4" d. **250**

Ott and Brewer (crown & sword mark),
cup & saucer, "Tridacna" body shape,
cream-colored exterior, blue lustre inte-
rior w/gold handle & rim, saucer 5 1/4" d. **300**

Willets (serpent mark), bouillon cup &
saucer, h.p. flowers w/gold trim, saucer
5 1/2" d. **350**

Willets (serpent mark), bouillon cup &
saucer, "Tridacna" shape, pearlized
cream exterior & yellow interior, saucer
6 1/2" d. **225**

Willets (serpent mark), cup & saucer, cof-
fee-size, cream-colored fluted body
w/gold handle & trim, saucer 5 1/2" d. **175**

Willets (serpent mark), cup & saucer, "Tridacna" shape, cream-colored exterior,
pink lustre interior w/gold handle & trim,
saucer 5 1/4" d. **250**

Willets (serpent mark), demitasse cup &
saucer, fluted white body w/purple
monogram "W," outlined in gold w/gold-
flecked purple dragon-shaped handle,
saucer 4" d. **95**

JARS

**Ceramic Art Company (CAC palette
mark),** dresser jar, hand-decorated
w/gold paste roses & stripes, 3 1/2" d.,
5" h. **150**

Lenox Condiment Jar

Lenox (palette mark), condiment jar &
cover, tapering hexagonal form
w/domed cover, white ground w/blue
jewel beading w/gold paste swags, ster-
ling finial, 4 1/2" w., 5 1/2" h. (ILLUS.).......... **270**

Ott and Brewer (sword & crown mark),
cracker jar & cover, hand-decorated
w/gold paste flowers & gold handles,
5" d., 7" h... **400**

MUGS

Ceramic Art Company (CAC palette mark), mug, Art Deco design w/heavy gold accents, 7" h............................... 295

Ceramic Art Company (CAC palette mark), mug, h.p. portrait of a Native American Chief, 6" h. 1,100

Ceramic Art Company (CAC palette mark), mug, portrait-type, h.p. "Colonial Drinkers," artist-signed by Fred Little, 5" h.. 325

Ceramic Art Company (CAC palette mark), mug, portrait-type, h.p. portrait of an old man w/a stein seated at a table, artist-signed "E.D. Westphal," 5 3/4" h. 300

Lenox (palette mark), mug, h.p. bird decoration, 4 1/4" h... 85

Lenox (palette mark), mug, h.p. heavy enameled flowers in the Art Deco style, artist-signed "HRM," 7" h............................ 140

Lenox (palette mark), mug, h.p. off-white & multicolored poppies on a soft cream matte ground accented w/gold & a gold curved handle, 7" h. 200

Lenox (palette mark), mug, h.p. w/intense green leaves on a rust & brown ground of berries, 5" h. 112

Lenox Belleek Mug w/Roosters

Lenox (palette mark), cylindrical w/incurved rim & C-form handle, decorated w/a frieze of parading roosters on pink & black mirrored ground, artist-signed, Lenox - Belleek stamp, ca. 1909, 5 1/2" d., 7" h. (ILLUS.) 165

Willets (serpent mark), goblet, toasting-type, "Aforetone," hand-painted, artist-signed "E.S. Wright," dated "1903," 5" d., 11" h.. 350

Willets (serpent mark), mug, h.p. blackberries & foliage on a pastel ground, 4 1/2" h. 85

Willets Belleek Mug with Monk

Willets (serpent mark), mug, h.p. scene of a monk w/a wine cask, deep maroon base & handle, 6" h. (ILLUS.)...................... 275

Willets (serpent mark), cylindrical w/incurved rim & C-form handle, overglaze decoration of desert scene w/men wearing a fez & red uniform & holding onto a rope attached to a frantic camel which is racing around pyramids, handle, shoulder & base chased w/fired-on gold, marked w/Willets Belleek transfer logo, 5 3/8" h. 165

PITCHERS AND JUGS

Ceramic Art Company (CAC palette mark), cider pitcher, h.p. w/large red apples & leaves, accented w/gold w/a gold beaded handle, 5 3/4" w., 9" h............. 450

Ceramic Art Company (CAC palette mark), creamer, footed swan-form, gold highlights, artist-signed "ES," dated "1903," 3 1/2" h... 225

Lenox (palette mark), cider set: pitcher & six cups; h.p. red apples, leaves & stems in an overall design, cups 5" h., pitcher 6" h., the set 950

Lenox (palette mark), creamer, cream-colored body w/silver overlay, 4" h. 100

Lenox (palette mark), creamer, cream-colored body w/swags of silver overlay, 5 1/4" h.. 110

Ott and Brewer (crown & sword mark), ewer, shaped form w/raised gold paste stylized leaf decoration on a matte ground, cactus-shaped handle, 7 1/2" d., 8" h.. 1,500

Willets Jug with Cavalier

Willets (serpent mark), jug, handle, wide ovoid form w/short neck, h.p. scene of a bearded cavalier seated at a table w/a wine jug & goblet, 8" h. (ILLUS.) 420

Willets (serpent mark), pitcher, jug-shaped, h.p. large poppies w/soft gold-accented foliage & handle, artist-signed "A.B. Julia," dated "1910," 7" h. 750

PLATES

Lenox (palette mark), plate, cream-colored w/sterling silver overlay of festoons of ribbons, silver around outer rim, 7 1/2" d. 36

Lenox (palette mark), plate, h.p. medallions surrounded & connected by heavy silver overlay by the Rockwell Silver Company, 7 1/2" d.. 55

Lenox (palette mark), plate, h.p. w/a few flowers, 8" d. 50

Lenox (palette mark), platter, Art Deco design w/h.p. border & solid handles w/gold trim, 16 1/2" l.................................... 125

Ott and Brewer (crown & sword mark), plate, scalloped rim w/h.p. ferns in pink, dark green, mauve & light green, 8 1/2" d.. 120

SALT DIPS

Ceramic Art Pottery (CAC palette mark), salt, h.p. violets & leaves, scalloped gold rim, 1 1/2" d.. 96

Floral-decorated Lenox Salt Dip

Lenox (palette mark), salt dips, h.p. w/a soft pink ground & small purple blossoms & green leaves w/gold trim, 1 1/4" d., set of 12 (ILLUS. of one).............. 500

Artist-signed Lenox Salt Dip

Lenox (palette mark), salt, h.p. w/a stylized band & blossom design, signed by E. Sweeny, 1 1/2" d. (ILLUS.) 55

Lenox (palette mark), salt & pepper shakers, h.p. w/small sprays of flowers, 2 1/2" h., pr.. 120

Footed Willets Salt Dip

Willets (serpent mark), salt, three-footed, lustre exterior w/gold rim & feet, 3" d. (ILLUS.).. 60

SETS

Lenox (palette mark), coffee set: pedestal-based cov. coffeepot, cov. sugar &

creamer; h.p. flowers in gold shields w/heavy gold accents, artist-signed "Kaufman," the set...................................... **1,450**

Lenox Creamer & Sugar Bowl

Lenox (palette mark), creamer & cov. sugar bowl, pedestal base, urn-form bodies, cream ground w/hand-decorated Art Deco design of enameled beading & gold paste, 7" h., pr. (ILLUS.)...................... **600**

Lenox Teapot with Roses Decoration

Lenox (palette mark), teapot, cov., pedestal base on square foot, boat-shaped body w/angled handle, h.p. sprays of pink & white roses w/green leaves, gold band trim, 10" l., 8" h. (ILLUS.)..................... **450**

TANKARDS

Ceramic Art Company (CAC palette mark), tankard, h.p. grapes, leaves & vines w/heavy gold accents, artist-signed "Nosek," dated "1905," 14 1/2" h. **900**

Lenox (palette mark), tankard, h.p. grapes, leaves & vines, embossed handle trimmed in gold, 14" h............................. **625**

Willets (serpent mark), tankard, h.p. grapes, leaves & vines on light green matte ground, artist-signed "Fisher," 11 1/4" h.. **625**

Willets (serpent mark), tankard, h.p. scene of a monk holding a pipe, brown matte ground, artist-signed "AST," 13 3/4" h.. **800**

TOOTHPICK HOLDERS

Lenox (palette mark), toothpick holder, h.p. ravens sitting on pine branches, straight sides, 2 1/4" h. **140**

VASES

Ceramic Art Company Vase

Ceramic Art Company (CAC palette mark), compressed bulbous body w/wide shoulder centered by a tiny trumpet-form neck, decorated w/orange & white nasturtiums on a gold & black ground, 4 1/2 x 7" (ILLUS.) 110

Ceramic Art Company (CAC palette mark), vase, ovoid body w/short neck & flared rim, h.p. chrysanthemums on a light green matte ground w/gold trim & gold on neck & neck rim, artist-signed "DeLan," 7 1/2" h. 725

Ceramic Art Company (CAC palette mark), vase, ovoid body tapering to a small neck w/fluted & flared rim, h.p. w/large open roses on a pale pink ground, some gold trim, 8 1/2" h. 635

Knowles, Taylor and Knowles Lotus Ware, vase, front h.p. w/a scene of a Victorian lady standing by a beehive looking up at two flying cherubs, the back w/a bouquet of flowers, applied "fishnet" work on body, 5" d., 8" h. **1,400**

Lenox (early wreath mark), vase, urn-shaped on a flaring pedestal & square foot, swan's-neck handles, white ground h.p. w/a central floral medallion on the front & back, 8" h. 265

Lenox (palette mark), vase, bud-type, h.p. & artist-signed, 2" d., 6" h. (mild crazing) 86

Lenox Vase with Blossom Seeds

Lenox (palette mark), vase, h.p. flowers w/fine gilding, signed "Valborg, 1905," fluted top w/attached handle to side of tilted bowl, 3" d., 8" h. 650

Lenox (palette mark), vase, bulbous body, h.p. floral decoration in mint condition, 5" d., 8" h. 500

Lenox (palette mark), vase, cylindrical, h.p. bird on branch w/flowers, 3" d., 9 1/2" h. 250

Lenox (palette mark), vase, tapering cylindrical body w/a short wide flared neck, h.p. w/open seed pods w/white & brown seeds & green leaves, shaded brown to cream ground, 10 1/4" h. (ILLUS.) 550

Lenox (palette mark), vase, cylindrical, decorated w/a stylized bird highlighted in gold, artist-signed "E.R. Martin," 3" d., 10 1/4" h. 300

Lenox (palette mark), vase, painted overall w/a floral design accented w/soft gold, 5" d., 10 1/4" h. 800

Lenox (palette mark), vase, impressionistic h.p. decoration w/gold trim, 5 1/2" d., 11 1/2" h. 475

Lenox (palette mark), vase, ovoid body tapering to a short flared neck, h.p. w/large chrysanthemums w/soft gold highlights, 12 1/2" h. 895

Lenox Vase with Landscape Band

Lenox (palette mark), vase, cylindrical w/slightly incurved rim, a wide rim band h.p. w/a stylized country landscape & gold border, the lower body w/a pale ground h.p. overall w/diamond devices, 13" h. (ILLUS.) 350

Lenox (palette mark), vase, cylindrical, h.p. Oriental women, trees & foliage, 15 1/2" h. 350

Ott & Brewer (sword & crown mark), bulbous base w/sides folded to form three openings w/slightly ruffled rim, decorated w/embossed blue & red forget-me-nots, a few shallow flakes to ruffled rim, 4 x 5 3/4" 825

Willets (serpent mark), vase, h.p. chrysanthemums accented w/gold on a white ground, 8" h.................................. 625

Willets Vase with a Tiger

Willets (serpent mark), vase, balusterform w/flared foot & rim, dark green ground decorated w/a h.p. tiger on one side, 4" d., 9" h. (ILLUS.)........................... 600

Willets (serpent mark), vase, cylindrical, h.p. design of three Japanese women in kimonos on a pale green ground, 3" d., 10" h. 450

Willets (serpent mark), vase, bulbous body w/a short pinched neck & fluted rim, h.p. overall w/large pastel roses & foliage, 8" d., 10" h. 500

Willets (serpent mark), vase, h.p. Pickard decoration of a full-length Art Nouveau lady w/flowing hair & gown on a pink lustre ground, 6" d., 10 1/2" h. 1,600

Willets (serpent mark), vase, bulbous shape w/a short, small neck w/fluted rim, h.p. w/flowers & heavy gold paste accents, 6 1/2" d., 11" h. 900

Willets (serpent mark), vase, bulbous shape w/a short pinched neck w/fluted rim, h.p. overall w/pink, red & white roses, 9" d., 13" h. 1,850

Willets (serpent mark), vase, undecorated, urn-shaped w/curved applied handles, 8" d., 13 3/4" h. 125

Willets (serpent mark), vase, waisted cylindrical form, h.p. overall w/hyacinths w/gold accents, artist-signed "E. Miler," 15 1/2" h..................................... 1,050

IRISH BELLEEK

Irish Belleek Mark

Bowl, 4 3/4" d., 4" h., six-scallop rim, Shells & Seaweed patt., lustre interior, green mark 60

Bread plate, Shamrock patt., green handles, 3rd green mark, 10 5/8" d. 130

Creamer, Fishscale patt., 4 1/4" h., green mark 55

Creamer & open sugar bowl, Shamrock-Basketweave patt., creamer 3" h., sugar 2 1/2" h., green mark, pr...................... 100

Cup & saucer, demitasse, Shamrock patt., cup 3" d., saucer 4 1/2" d., green mark.......... 65

Cup & saucer, Neptune patt., 2nd black mark 225

Cup & saucer, Shell patt., 3rd black mark 85

Cup & saucer, Tridacna patt., pink-trimmed, 2nd black mark 85

Dish, leaf-shaped, 5 x 5 1/4", green mark 30

Model of a swan, 2nd green mark, 4 3/4 x 5 3/4" 80

Mug, coffee, Shamrock-Basketweave patt., 4" h., green mark.............................. 60

Plate, 5 7/8" d., Grass Tea Ware, 1st black mark 200

Plate, 8" d., Shell patt., 3rd black mark 85

Plate, 10 1/2" d., Shamrock-Basketweave patt., green mark 38

Spill, Shamrock patt., 3rd black mark, 5 1/4" h....................................... 100

Tea set: cov. teapot, open sugar bowl, creamer, two cups & saucers & undertray; Neptune patt., pink-trimmed, 2nd black mark (tiny chip on rim of teapot spout opening, worn mark on one saucer) 1,700

Teapot, cov., Limpet patt., 3rd black mark 310

BENNINGTON

Bennington wares, which ranged from stoneware to parian and porcelain, were made in Bennington, Vermont, primarily in two potteries, one in which Captain John Norton and his descendants were principals, and the other in which Christopher Webber Fenton (also once associated with the Nortons) was a principal. Various marks are found on the wares made in the two major potteries, including J. & E. Norton, E. & L. P. Norton, L. Norton & Co., Norton & Fenton, Edward Norton, Lyman Fenton & Co., Fenton's Works, United States Pottery Co., U.S.P. and others.

The popular pottery with the mottled brown on yellowware glaze was also produced in Bennington, but such wares should be referred to as "Rockingham" or "Bennington-type" unless they can be specifically attributed to a Bennington, Vermont factory.

Bennington Marks

Book flask, binding embossed "Life of Kos-
suth" w/impressed "J," Flint Enamel
glaze, 5 3/4" h. (very minor hairline)........... **$489**

Book flask, binding marked "Departed
Spirits," Flint Enamel glaze, 5 5/8" h.
(minor edge wear) **468**

Bottle, figural, barrel-shaped standing Mr.
Toby, mottled Flint Enamel glaze, ca.
1849-58, 10 3/4" h. (minor chips) **1,610**

Butter churn, stoneware, w/molded rim &
eared handles, large slip-quilled stylized
floral design, bright Bennington blue, "J.
& E. Norton, Bennington, VT," ca. 1859,
3 gal., 15 1/2" h. (restoration to age line
but not in blue) **715**

Cake crock, stoneware, cylindrical
w/molded rim & eared handles, thick
blue & large stylized flower design fills
the entire front, "J. Norton & Co., Bennington, VT," ca. 1859, 1 1/2 gal.,
7 1/4" h. (short hairline & rim chip in front
& full length tight line on side) **770**

Flint Enamel Candlestick

Candlestick, ringed columnar form
w/heavy socket ring & flaring round
base, overall motted brown Flint Enamel
glaze, hairline in foot & line around
flange of base, probably manufacturing
defect, 7 3/4" h. (ILLUS.) **385**

Crock, stoneware, cylindrical w/molded rim
& eared handles, slip-quilled stylized floral design, "E & LP Bennington, VT," ca.
1870, 2 gal., 9" h. (surface chip on rim in
back) **165**

Crock, stoneware, cylindrical w/molded rim
& eared handles, slip-quilled thick blue
double flower design, "J. & E. Norton,
Bennington, VT," ca. 1859, 3 gal., 10" h.
(long J-shaped tight hairline from rim to
right of flower) **358**

Crock, stoneware, ovoid w/molded rim &
eared handles, brilliant slip-quilled thick
cobalt blue flower design, "J. & E.
Norton, Bennington, VT," ca. 1859, 2
gal., 10 1/2" h. (grease stain spot on
back) **853**

Crock with Double Flower

Crock, stoneware, ovoid w/molded rim &
eared handles, large slip-quilled cobalt
blue double flower design, bold cobalt
blue, "J. & E. Norton, Bennington,
VT," ca. 1855, professional restoration to
long j-shaped line in front, through blue
& long straight line from rim on back, 4
gal., 13 3/4" h. (ILLUS)................................. **413**

Crock, stoneware, cylindrical w/molded rim
& eared handles, slip-quilled cobalt blue
decoration of a recumbent stag in a
landscape w/shrubs, fences & a tree,
impressed "J. & E. Norton - Bennington
VT - 2," mid-19th c., 2 gal., 10 3/4" d.,
9 1/4" h. **5,460**

Cuspidor, squatty waisted paneled form,
mottled brown Rockingham glaze,
impressed "1849" mark, 9" d. **110**

Jug, stoneware, ovoid w/brushed cobalt
blue triple flower design, "Norton & Fenton, Bennington, VT," ca. 1845, glued
chip at spout & some clay discoloration,
appears to be in making, 2 gal.,
12 1/2" h. **385**

Jug, stoneware, semi-ovoid w/bright blue
stylized floral design, "J. & E. Norton,
Bennington, VT," ca. 1859, 3 gal., 15" h.
(some stains from use)................................. **385**

Jug, stoneware, semi-ovoid w/slip-quilled
cobalt blue large dotted peacock on
stump, "J. & E. Norton, Bennington,
VT," ca. 1859, 3 gal., 15" h. (profes-
sional restoration to handle)...................... **2,970**

Jug, stoneware, cobalt decorated,
impressed mark "L. Norton Co., Bennington, Vermont," double-feather deco-
ration, mid-19th c., 15" h. (minor chip) **230**

Bennington Pie Plate

Pie plate, wide flat bottom w/flaring rim, mottled brown Rockingham glaze, impressed "1849," 11 7/8" d. (ILLUS. previous page) 963

Pitcher, 9 3/4" h., Parian, Wild Rose patt., applied molded label "Fenton's Works, Bennington, Vermont" 605

Toby bottle, overall mottled brown Rockingham glaze, marked on base, 10 1/2" h. 460

Toby jar, seated Mr. Toby w/an overall light green sponging w/brownish amber interior, impressed "1849" mark, 4 1/2" h. (hat has chips on inner flange) 660

BERLIN (KPM)

The mark, KPM, was used at Meissen from 1724 to 1725, and was later adopted by the Royal Factory, Konigliche Porzellan Manufaktur, in Berlin. At various periods it has been incorporated with the Brandenburg sceptre, the Prussian eagle or the crowned globe. The same letters were also adopted by other factories in Germany in the late 19th and early 20th centuries. With the end of the German monarchy in 1918, the name of the firm was changed to Staatliche Porzellan Manufaktur and though production was halted during World War II, the factory was rebuilt and is still in business. The exquisite paintings on porcelain were produced at the close of the 19th century and are eagerly sought by collectors today.

Basket, fruit, pierced flaring rim w/enameled floral design on pink ground, late 19th c., Germany, 7 3/4" h. $288

Charger, round, enameled floral decoration w/a scrolled gilt rim, "K.P.M." back mark, late 19th c., 15 3/4" d. 1,725

Coffee service: 10 1/2" h. cov. coffeepot, cov. sugar bowl, creamer & 6 cups & saucers; each decorated w/an armorial crest & gilt details, late 19th c., printed marks, the set.. 920

Berlin Topographical Cup & Saucer

Cup & saucer, gilt banded borders & foliate trim w/h.p. center panel depicting a stately home, titled under base "Blieniche bei Potsdam," 19th c., Germany, gilt wear, KPM marks (ILLUS.) 403

Figure group, white-glazed, two scantily-clad children, mounted on a scrolled oval base, underglaze-blue "K.P.M." mark, ca. 1900, 5 1/4" h. 489

Lamp, figural, tripod base formed as three winged griffins, the cone shaped shade w/pierced circular motifs, printed marks, 19" h. 1,725

Plaque, oval, three-quarter length portrait of the Madonna & Child, back impressed w/"KPM" & sceptre marks, 19th c., 17" h... 5,462

Plaque, rectangular, a group portrait in three-quarters length, two young ladies in Renaissance dress in the foreground w/a gentleman centered behind them, after Titian, impressed "KPM" & sceptre marks, 19th c., 10 x 12 1/2"...................... 4,312

Plaque, rectangular, a colorful scene of a lovely winged angel & infant w/cherubs descending on a village, mounted in an ornate hand-carved giltwood frame, German inscription on the back & a "KPM" & sceptre mark, plaque 6 1/4 x 9 1/4".......... 4,600

Plaque, rectangular, polychrome enamel interior scene of a sailor & family sitting around a table entitled "Return from His First Voyage," impressed "K.P.M." mark, 19th c., giltwood frame, 10 x 12 1/2" 9,200

Plaque, rectangular, porcelain, full figure portrait of young dark-haired girl in field of flowers, after Marowsky, titled "Ophelie" ornate scrolled leafy frame, early 20th c., impressed "KPM" sceptre mark & dimensions, 8 x 13 1/4"................ 6,900

Plaque, oval, porcelain three quarter portrait of young girl w/long dark hair pulled to one side & over her shoulder, floral background, artist-signed, late 19th c., impressed "KPM - 6" & sceptre mark, 13 1/2" h. 13,800

Berlin Plaque of the Virgin Mary

Plaque, oval, three-quarter length portrait of the Virgin Mary flanked by the heads of angels, after Murrillo, framed, 17" (ILLUS.)... 6,160

Portrait plates, 10 3/4" d., each depicting Napoleon or ladies or gentlemen of his court, gilt-beaded borders w/gilt & cobalt band, ca. late 19th c., artist-signed & titled in red enamel, underglaze-blue beehive mark, set of 12 7,475

Berlin Urn

Urns, cov., square base w/flared foot below wide ovoid body, two ring handles w/lion's head masks, decorated w/h.p. & gilded multicolored foliage, domed cover w/blossom finial, late 19th c., 8 1/2" h., pr. (ILLUS. of one)................................... **1,035**

Vase, 14" h., double gourd form, one side decorated w/figural reserves, reverse w/foliate spray, turquoise ground **633**

BISQUE

Bisque is biscuit china, fired a single time but not glazed. Some bisque is decorated with colors. Most abundant from the Victorian era are figures and groups, but other pieces from busts to vases were made by numerous potteries in the U.S. and abroad. Reproductions have been produced for many years so care must be taken when seeking antique originals

Bust of a young boy, holding a letter, 8" h.... **$138**

Bisque Bust of Young Boy

Bust of a young boy, on a cobalt blue base, after Houdon, France, 16" h. (ILLUS.)... **173**

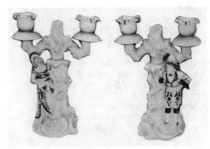

Bisque Candlesticks

Candlesticks, two-light, figural, each w/a tan & white tree trunk-form shaft w/a pair of curved arms near the top each ending in a candlecup, one w/a figure of a young girl in a long blue & white dress & bonnet standing to one side of the base, the other w/a figure of a young boy in a blue & white hat, jacket & kneebreeches, gilt trim, tops separate from base, overall 8 1/2" h., facing pr. (ILLUS.)........................ **325**

Figure group, a late Victorian gentleman & lady each wearing a bicycle club uniform & riding their safety bicycles, fine hand-decoration, probably France or Germany, late 19th c., 9 1/4" h.......................... **303**

Figure group, a young lady & gentleman in early 19th c. country-style costume walking under a large greyish blue umbrella, naturalistic coloring, 3 3/8" d., 6" h. **145**

Bisque Seated Boy

Figure of a boy, seated w/one hand on knee, dressed orange jacket, yellow pants, grey hat & shoes, black & white neck scarf, unmarked, 3 1/2 x 5 1/2", 6" h. (ILLUS.)... **195**

Figure of a Dutch girl, seated pose w/hands on her knees, wearing a white bonnet over light brown hair, tinted face & arms, blue dress w/white bodice & trim on sleeves & at waist, unmarked, 3 1/2 x 5", 6 1/2" h. **195**

Figure of moon-headed man, a seated figure w/his legs straight out to the sides, the large crescent moon head w/a smiling expression & pale yellow tint, his arms holding a tan mandolin, wearing a white suit w/black collar & brown shoes, probably Schafer & Vater, Germany, late 19th - early 20th c., 4" w., 4 1/2" h. 145

Figure of young girl, w/cat on a swing, 5 3/4" h. 110

Figures, a male & female w/gilt & yellow enamel trim, he standing holding a fishing net, she holding a small keg, Germany, late 19th c., 28" h., pr. 920

Figures, nodders, a seated Chinese Mandarin man & matching woman, gilt & enamel-decorated, Germany, late 19th - early 20th c., 6 3/4" h., pr. 633

Figures, man w/grapes & woman w/rake, 8 3/4" h., pr. 49

Figures of a boy & girl, seated in cream, tan & green chairs & each dressed in green & white attire w/large green hats, gold shoes & raised gold dot trim on dress, pants & vest, 6 1/4" h., pr. 145

Bisque Victorian Figures

Figures of a boy & girl, each dressed in Victorian attire w/yellow hats & jackets w/white floral-decorated skirt or vest, trimmed in gold, blue & brown, each holding a badminton racket, on a round base, facing pr., 2 3/4" d., 9 1/4" h., pr. (ILLUS.) 218

French Skating Figures

Figures of a lady & man, each in 18th c. costume, wearing ice skates & depicted in skating pose, each on a shaped platform base, France, late 19th c., facing pair, minor restorations, 28" h., pr. (ILLUS.) 2,070

Bisque Steinbach Dog

Model of a dog, seated small white Spitz-like dog w/curly coat & a bit of tan around the eyes, orange tongue, marked "Steinbach," 5 1/2" h. (ILLUS.) 135

Model of dog, Dachshund, 7 x 9 1/2" 300

Piano baby, crawling, 9 1/2" l., 6 1/4" h. 425

Snow baby, seated atop red airplane, Germany 225

Vase, 6 1/2" h., fan-form leafy background behind the figures of a Victorian man in a bicycle outfit helping a lady wearing a similar outfit & carrying a basket of flowers who is climbing onto a safety-style bicycle, finely colored, Germany, ca. 1890s 193

BLUE RIDGE DINNERWARES

The small town of Erwin, Tennessee was the home of the Southern Potteries, Inc., originally founded by E.J. Owen in 1917 and first called the Clinchfield Pottery.

In the early 1920s Charles W. Foreman purchased the plant and he revolutionized the company's output, developing the popular line of hand-painted wares sold as "Blue Ridge" dinnerwares. Free-hand painted by women from the surrounding hills, these colorful dishes in many patterns, continued in production until the plant's closing in 1957.

Blue Ridge Dinnerwares Mark

Ashtray, individual, Tralee Rose patt. $15

Bonbon, shell-shaped, flat, Nove Rose patt. 65

Bowl, berry, Bountiful patt., large 17

Butter pat/coaster, Lyonnaise patt., 4" d. 45

Cake tray, French Peasant patt., Maple Leaf shape 135

Cake tray, Verna patt., Maple Leaf shape 61

Candy box, cov., Rose Marie patt. 185

Character jug, American Indian.................... 525

Cigarette box, cov., French Peasant patt........ 150

Creamer, Mardi Gras patt. 10

Creamer & cov. sugar bowl, Ridge Daisy patt., pr. 19
Cup, Crab Apple patt. 9
Cup, Square Dance patt. 69
Cup & saucer, demitasse, china, Rose Marie patt. 75
Mug, child's, Chanticleer patt. 150
Pie plate, Cassandra patt., wine-colored border 25
Pie plate & server, Cross Stitch patt., 2 pcs. 45
Pie server, blue & white lattice design 24
Pitcher, 5" h., china, Annett's Wild Rose patt., Antique shape 75
Pitcher, 6 1/4" h., earthenware, Fairmede Fruits patt., Alice shape (small smear on red line trim) 90
Pitcher, 7" h., Sculptured Fruit patt., ... 75
Pitcher, china, decorated w/grapes, Helen shape 80
Pitcher, Milady patt. 195
Plate, 6" d., Bluebell Bouquet patt. 4
Plate, 6" sq., "Milkmaid," Provincial Farm Scene, Candlewick shape 50
Plate, dinner, Chanticleer patt. 30
Relish dish, deep shell-shaped, French Peasant patt. 150
Salt & pepper shakers, Dogtooth Violet patt., pr. 65
Salt & pepper shakers, figural Mallard hen & drake, pr. 450
Sugar bowl, cov., Nocturne patt. 12
Teapot, cov., Ball shape, Bluebelle Bouquet patt. 200
Tray, Trellis shape, Daffodil patt. 149
Vase, 5 1/2" h., china, Hampton patt., Hibiscus shape 80
Vase, 9 1/4" h., ruffle-top style, Delphine patt. 95
Vegetable bowl, cov., Mardi Gras patt. 95
Vegetable bowl, open, round, Ridge Daisy patt. 19
Wall sconce, Rose Marie patt. 250

BLUE & WHITE POTTERY

The category of blue and white or blue and grey pottery includes a wide variety of pottery, earthenware and stoneware items widely produced in this country in the late 19th century right through the 1930s. Originally marketed as inexpensive wares, most pieces featured a white or grey body molded with a fruit, flower or geometric design and then trimmed with bands or splashes of blue to highlight the molded pattern. Pitchers, butter crocks and salt boxes are among the numerous items produced but other kitchenwares and chamber sets are also found. Values vary depending on the rarity of the embossed pattern and the depth of color of the blue trim; the darker the blue, the better. Some entries refer to several different books on Blue and White Pottery. These books are: Blue & White Stoneware, Pottery & Crockery *by Edith Harbin (1977, Collector Books, Paducah, KY);* Stoneware in the Blue and White *by M.H. Alexander (1993 reprint, Image Graphics, Inc., Paducah, KY); and* Blue & White Stoneware *by Kathryn McNerney (1995, Collector Books, Paducah, KY).*

Baking dish, embossed Peacock patt., round w/heavy egg-and-dart-molded rim over gently curved sides, 9" d. .... **$800+**
Basin, embossed Apple Blossom patt., 9" d. 185
Batter jar, cov., printed Wildflower patt., 7" d., 8" h. .... 300+
Bean pot, cov., marked "Boston Bean Pot," 10" d., 9" h. 450

Miniature Bean Pot and Coffeepot

Bean pot, miniature, cov., wide blue band, souvenir-type (ILLUS. left) 225
Beer cooler, cov., embossed Elves patt., includes spigot, 14" d., 18" h. 725
Bowl, 3" d., miniature, heavy dark blue rim band .... 40+
Bowl, 4" d., 2" h., berry/cereal, plain w/pale blue rim band 55
Bowl, 4" d., 2" h., embossed Flying Bird patt., w/advertising 450
Bowl, 4" d., 2" h., miniature, heavy blue rim band .... 50+
Bowl, 4 1/2" d., 2 1/4" h., berry, embossed Peacock patt. 325
Bowl, 4 1/2" d., 2 1/2" h., berry, plain w/pale blue rim band 55
Bowl, 4 1/2" d., 2 1/2" h., embossed Reverse Pyramids patt. 65-75
Bowl, 4 1/2" to 14" d., embossed Pineapple patt., ten sizes, price ranges .... **174 up**
Bowl, 6" to 12" d., embossed Greek Key patt., ranges .... **100-170+**
Bowl, 7" d., embossed Beaded Rose patt. 150
Bowl, 7 1/2" d., 2 3/4" h., embossed Apricot with Honeycomb patt. 135
Bowl, 7 1/2" d., 5" h., embossed Reverse Pyramids patt. 90-100

Grape Ware Pattern Bowls

Bowl, 8" d., embossed Grape Ware patt. (ILLUS. left) 225
Bowl, 9 1/2" d., 3 3/4" h., embossed Apricot with Honeycomb patt. 185
Bowl, 9 1/2" d., 4 1/2" h., embossed Gadroon Arches or Petal Panels patt. 175
Bowl, 10" d., embossed Grape Ware patt., (ILLUS. right) 230
Bowls, embossed Ringsaround (Wedding Ring) patt., six sizes, ranges **85-225**

Bowls, nesting type, embossed Scallop patt., 6" d., 3 1/2" h., 8" d., 3 1/2" h., 9 1/2" d., 5" h., depending on size, each **85-125**

Bowls, nesting-type, embossed Cosmos patt., depending on size, each **65-275**

Bowls, nesting-type, printed Wildflower patt., 4" to 14" d., the set .... **350+**

Bow Tie Blue-banded Brush Vase

Brush vase, embossed Bow Tie (Our Lucile) patt., w/narrow blue bands, 5 1/2" h. (ILLUS.).. **225**

Brush vase, embossed Bow Tie (Our Lucile) patt., w/rose decal, 5 1/2" h. **115**

Brush vase, printed Wildflower patt., tapering cylindrical form, printed designs inside, 5" h. **300**

Butter crock, cov., embossed Cow and Fence patt., 7 1/4" d., 5" h.......................... **625+**

Butter crock, cov., embossed Cows and Columns patt., 2 lbs. to 10 lbs., ranges .... **425-650+**

Butter crock, cov., embossed Daisy and Basketweave patt., 7" d., 6 3/4" h. .... **300+**

Two Blue & White Butter Crocks

Butter crock, embossed Daisy patt., Red Wing, 3 1/2" h. (ILLUS. right) **395**

Butter crock, cov., embossed Diffused Blue with Blocks patt., 7 1/2" d., 5 1/2" h...... **125**

Butter crock, cov., embossed Diffused Blue with Inverted Pyramid Bands patt., 6" d., 4" h.. **125+**

Butter crock, cov., embossed Dragonfly and Flower patt., large, 8" d., 5" h. **345**

Butter crock, cov., embossed Dragonfly and Flower patt., small, rare **500**

Eagle Butter and Salt Crocks

Butter crock, cov., embossed Eagle patt., 6" d., 6" h. (ILLUS. right) **700**

Butter crock, cov., embossed Good Luck (Swasitka) patt., 6 1/4" d., 5 1/4" h.............. **150**

Butter crock, cov., embossed Peacock patt., w/bail handle, 1 lb., 4" h. **1,000**

Butter crock, cov., plain **125**

Butter crock, cov., printed Cows patt., 6 1/2" d., 5" h.. **195**

Butter crock, cov., Western Stoneware Co., advertising "Compliments of J. Mueller," 4 1/4" h. (ILLUS. left w/Daisy patt. crock) **295**

Butter pot, cov., printed Wildflower patt., four sizes, each .... **150+**

Canister, cov., Diffused Blues patt., 5 3/4" d., 6 1/2" h... **175**

Canister, cov., embossed Basketweave & Morning Glory (Willow) patt., "Beans," average 5 1/2" to 6 1/2" h.......................... **325+**

Basketweave & Morning Glory Canisters

Canister, cov., embossed Basketweave & Morning Glory (Willow) patt., "Coffee," average 5 1/2 to 6 1/2" h. (ILLUS. top left) .... **325+**

Canister, cov., embossed Basketweave & Morning Glory (Willow) patt., "Crackers" or "Raisins," average 5 1/2 to 6 1/2" h., each. .... **625+**

Canister, cov., embossed Basketweave & Morning Glory (Willow) patt., "Salt," "Rice," or "Cereal," average 5 1/2 to 6 1/2" h., each (ILLUS. of Salt, upper right w/Coffee)... **475+**

Canister, cov., embossed Basketweave & Morning Glory (Willow) patt., "Sugar," average 5 1/2 to 6 1/2" h. (ILLUS. bottom with Coffee & Salt previous page .... **325+**

Canister, cov., embossed Basketweave & Morning Glory (Willow) patt., "Tea," average 5 1/2 to 6 1/2" h. .... **325+**

Printed Dutch Scene Sugar Canister

Canister, cov., printed Dutch Scene patt., Sugar, 5 1/2 to 6" h. (ILLUS.) **450-650**

Barley & Blank Wildflower Canisters

Canister, cov., printed Wildflower patt., Barley, Cornstarch or Grape Nuts, Barley 5 3/4" h., each (ILLUS. of Barley, left)..... **500**

Canister, cov., printed Wildflower patt., Beans, Oatmeal or Peas, 5 1/2 to 6 1/2", each **325**

Canister, cov., printed Wildflower patt., blank title (ILLUS. right w/Barley) **475**

Canister, cov., printed Wildflower patt., Butter, tall w/flared rim, 5 3/5" h. **350**

Robinson Sugar Canister

Canister, cov., printed Wildflower patt., Crackers or Tobacco, 5 1/2 to 6 1/2" h., each **600**

Canister, cov., printed Wildflower patt., Sugar, 5 1/2 to 6 1/2" **250**

Canister, cov., wooden cover, printed Snowflake patt., six various in set, 5 3/4" d., 6 1/2" h., each **235**

Canister, cov., embossed Robinson patt., Sugar (ILLUS. previous column) **275**

Embossed Flying Bird Casserole

Casserole, cov., embossed Flying Bird patt., 9 1/2" d. (ILLUS.)................................. **600**

Chamber pot, cov., embossed Beaded Rose patt., two sizes made, large 9 1/2" d., 6" h... **250**

Chamber pot, cov., embossed Open Rose and Spearpoint Panels patt., 9 1/2" d., 6" h. **300**

Chamber pot, cov., printed Wildflower patt., 11" d., 6" h... **250+**

Chamber pot, open, embossed Bead & Rose patt., 9 1/2" d., 6" h. .... **250+**

Chamber pot, open, embossed Bowtie (Our Lucile) patt., 11" d., 6" h....................... **165**

Cider cooler, cov., w/spigot, 13" d., 15" h........ **425**

Diffused Blue & Bull's-eye Coffeepot

Coffeepot, cov., Diffused Blue patt., oval design,11" h. (ILLUS.) **1,700**

Coffeepot, cov., embossed Bull's-eye patt. .... **2,000+**

Coffeepot, miniature, cov., wide blue band, souvenir-type **300**

Cold fudge crock, w/tin lid & ladle, marked "Johnson Cold Fudge Crock," 12" d., 13" h. **300**

Red Wing Lily Pattern Combinette

Combinette, embossed Lily patt., Red
Wing (ILLUS.).. **250-300**
Cookie jar, cov., Brickers patt., 8" d., 8" h. **475**
Cookie jar, cov., embossed Basketweave
& Morning Glory (Willow) patt., marked
"Put Your Fist In," 7 1/2" h............................ **625**

Love Bird Cookie Jar

Cookie jar, cov., embossed Love Bird patt.,
6 3/4" d., 9" h. (ILLUS.) .... **1,250+**

Rare Anchovies Storage Crock

Crock, anchovies storage-type, swelled
cylindrical form, three blue bands around
top & bottom, stenciled on the side "A.
Rensch & Co. - Anchois (sic) Mustard

(over a fish) - Toledo, O.," impressed on
the bottom "Burley, Winter & Co. -
Crooksville, O.," 10 1/2" h. (ILLUS.)............. **575**
Cup, embossed Paneled Fir Tree patt.,
3" d., 3 1/2" h.. **175**
Cuspidor, embossed Basketweave &
Morning Glory (Willow) patt., 7 1/2" d.,
5 1/2" h.. **185**
Cuspidor, embossed Sunflowers patt.,
9 3/4" d., 9" h... **200**
Custard cup, embossed Fishscale patt.,
2 1/2" d., 5" h... **100**
Custard cup, embossed Peacock patt.,
2 7/8" h. **545**

Blue & White Ewer & Pitchers

Ewer, embossed Apple Blossom patt.,
large,12" h. (ILLUS. lower right) .... **450+**
Ewer, embossed Banded Scroll patt., 7" h. .... **275+**
Ewer, embossed Bow Tie (Our Lucile)
patt., w/rose decal, 11" h. **175**
Ewer, printed Wildflower patt., 10 1/2" h. **325**
Ewer, printed Wildflower patt., 6 1/2" h. **225**
Ewer, printed Wildflower patt., 8 1/2" h. **295**
Ewer, Small Floral Decal (Memphis patt.),
7" h. .... **365+**
Ewer & basin, embossed Apple Blossom
patt., the set .... **700+**
Ewer & basin, embossed Feather & Swirl
patt., ewer 8 1/2" d., 12" h., basin 14" d.,
5" h., the set **550**

Wildflower Ewer and Basin Set

Ewer & basin, printed Wildflower patt.,
stenciled designs inside the ewer & the
basin, basin 15" d., ewer 11" h., the set
(ILLUS.)... **650**
Foot warmer, signed by Logan Pottery Co. **250**
Iced tea cooler, cov., w/spigot, Maxwell
House, 13" d., 15" h. **325**
Jardiniere, embossed Apple Blossom
patt., 6" h. **495**

Embossed Cosmos Jardiniere

Jardiniere, embossed Cosmos patt., 6" h.
(ILLUS.).. **800**

Tulip Pattern Jardiniere & Pedestal

Jardiniere & pedestal base, embossed
Tulip patt., jardiniere 7 1/2" h., pedestal
7" h., the set (ILLUS.).............................. **1,500+**
Match holder, model of a duck, 5 1/2" d.,
5" h. **250**
Measuring cup, embossed Spearpoint and
Flower Panels patt., 6 3/4" d., 6" h. **450**
Meat tenderizer, printed Wildflower patt.,
3 1/2" d. at face **370**
Milk crock, cov., w/bail handle, embossed
Lovebird patt., 9" d., 5 1/2" h...................... **600+**
Mixing bowl, embossed Flying Bird. patt.,
8" d... **340+**
Mouth ewer, embossed Bow Tie (Our
Lucile) patt., 8" h. .... **275+**

Printed Dutch Scene Mug

Mug, Diffused Blue patt., banded design,
w/advertising .... **300+**
Mug, embossed Apple Blossom patt., 5" h....... **275**
Mug, embossed Cattail patt., 3" d., 4" h. .... **130+**
Mug, embossed Columns and Arches patt.,
rare, 4 1/2" h.. **350+**
Mug, embossed Flying Bird patt., 3" d.,
5" h. **225**
Mug, embossed Grape Cluster in Shield
patt., 12 oz. **195**
Mug, printed Dutch Scene mug, boy on one
side, girl on the other, 4 1/4" h. (ILLUS.) **275**
Mug, printed Wildflower patt., 4 1/2" h............ **200+**
Mustard jar, cov., 3" d., 4" h. .... **200+**
Pitcher, embossed American Beauty Rose
patt., 10" h., 7" d.. **425**

Apricot Pattern Pitcher

Pitcher, embossed Apricot patt., 5 pt., 8" h.
(ILLUS.).. **265**
Pitcher, embossed Bands and Rivets patt.,
1 gal. .... **275+**
Pitcher, embossed Bands and Rivets patt.,
1 pt. .... **285+**
Pitcher, embossed Basketweave & Morn-
ing Glory (Willow) patt., tankard-type,
9" h., 6 1/2" d. .... **255+**
Pitcher, embossed Beaded Rose patt.,
large, 10" h.. **425**
Pitcher, embossed Butterfly patt., 4 3/4" h. **600**
Pitcher, embossed Butterfly patt., 9" h............. **345**

Capt. John Smith & Other Pitchers

Pitcher, embossed Capt. John Smith & Pocahontas patt., 6 1/4" h., 6 3/4" d. (ILLUS. bottom right) 350

Pitcher, embossed Castle patt., 8" h. (ILLUS. bottom left w/Capt. John Smith pitcher) .... 325+

Pitcher, embossed Cherry Band patt., w/advertising, various sizes, ranges 375-475

Pitcher, embossed Cherry Cluster with Basketweave patt., 10" h., 8 1/2" d. .... 325+

Pitcher, embossed Chrysanthemum patt., 8" h. 225

Pitcher, embossed Chrysanthemum patt., 9 1/2" h. 275

Pitcher, embossed Columns & Arches patt., 9" h. .... 600+

Pitcher, embossed Cosmos patt., 9" h., 6 1/2" d. 415

Daisy and Nautilus Pitchers

Pitcher, embossed Daisy patt., Brush-McCoy, 7" h. (ILLUS. left) 425

Pitcher, embossed Daisy Cluster patt., 8" h., 8" d. 700

Dutch Boy & Girl Kissing Pitcher

Pitcher, embossed Dutch Boy & Girl Kissing patt., Brush-McCoy Pottery Co., 9" h. (ILLUS.) 265

Pitcher, embossed Eagle patt., 8" h. 650

Pitcher, embossed Flying Bird patt., 9" h., 6" d. (ILLUS. top next column) 825

Pitcher, embossed Grape Cluster in Shield patt., 4 pt. .... 450+

Pitcher, embossed Grape Cluster in Shield patt., 5 pt. .... 475+

Pitcher, embossed Grape Cluster on Trellis patt., four sizes, 5" to 9 1/2" h., depending on size, each 165-245

Pitcher, embossed Grape Cluster on Trellis patt., squat body, 2 pt. 400

Pitcher, embossed Grape Cluster on Trellis patt., squat body, 3 pt. 425

Embossed Flying Bird Pitcher

Pitcher, embossed Lincoln Head patt., several sizes, depending on size 900

Lovebirds Pattern Pitcher

Pitcher, embossed Lovebirds patt., 8 1/2" h., 5 1/2" d. (ILLUS.) .... 450+

Pitcher, embossed Old Fashioned Garden Rose patt., 7" h., 7" d. .... 400+

Pine Cone Pattern Pitcher

Pitcher, embossed Pine Cone patt., 9 1/2" h., 5 3/4" d. (ILLUS.) 625

Pitcher, embossed Plume patt. .... 350+

Rare Remember Pitcher

Pitcher, embossed Remember patt., molded figure of Columbia standing beside an American shield, "Remember" on the interior rim (ILLUS.) **1,500**

Pitcher, embossed Rose on Trellis patt., 8 3/4" h. **375**

Scroll & Leaf Pitcher with Advertising

Pitcher, embossed Scroll and Leaf patt., w/advertising, 7" h. (ILLUS.) **410**

Pitcher, embossed Shield patt., 8 1/2" h., 6" d. .... **475+**

Embossed Stag Pattern Pitcher

Pitcher, embossed Stag patt., 9" h. (ILLUS.) **650-850**

Pitcher, embossed Standing Deer with Fawn patt., 8 1/2" h., 6" d. **275**

Pitcher, embossed Tulip patt., 8" h., 4" d. **350**

Pitcher, embossed Windmill & Bush patt., 9" h. .... **400+**

Pitcher, embossed Windmill patt., 7 1/4" h. **200**

Embossed Windy City Pitcher

Pitcher, embossed Windy City patt., 8 1/2" h. (ILLUS.) **300**

Miniature Advertising Pitchers

Pitcher, miniature, Diffused Blues w/souvenir markings in gold lettering, each (ILLUS.) **325**

Pitcher, printed Acorn patt., 8" h. **300**

Pitcher, printed Cattail patt., 5 3/4" h. **275**

Pitcher, printed Conifer Tree patt., 5" h. **250**

Pitcher, printed Dutch Farm patt., 9" h., 8" d. .... **250+**

Pitcher, printed Nautilus patt., 8 1/2" h. **325**

Pitcher, printed Wildflower patt., tall w/long spout, five stencils per side, 8 1/2" h. **400**

Pitcher, printed Wildflower patt., bulbous body, 10 3/4" h. **425**

Blue & White Stupid Pattern Pitcher

Pitcher, printed Wildflower patt., 7 1/2" h., 4" d., ... **275**

Pitcher, Stupid patt., Diffused Blues, 8" h., 6" d. (ILLUS. bottom previous page) **475**

Pitcher, side-pour, molded bands, w/advertising, Western Stoneware, each **400**

Ramekin or nappy, embossed Peacock patt., 4" d. **300**

Roaster, cov., printed Wildflower patt., 12" d., 8 1/2" h. **345**

Roaster bowl, embossed Daisy, 9" d., 4" h. .... **250+**

Rolling pin, printed Wildflower patt., large **300**

Rolling pin, printed Wildflower patt., small **375**

Salt box, cov., embossed Apricot patt., 5 3/4" d., 5" h. **250**

Salt box, cov., embossed Blocks patt., 6 1/2" d., 6 3/4" h. **175**

Salt box, cov., embossed Butterfly patt., 5 3/4" d., 5 3/4" h. **275**

Salt box, cov., embossed Flying Bird patt., 6 1/2" d., 6" h. (ILLUS. left w/Lovebird butter crock) .... **550+**

Salt box, cov., embossed Raspberry patt., 5 1/2" d., 5 1/2" h. **200**

Salt box, cov., embossed Waffleweave patt. .... **230+**

Salt box, cov., printed Wildflower patt., hinged wooden cover, 6" d., 4 1/2" h. .... **170+**

Salt box, cov., plain **100**

Salt crock, cov., hanging-type, embossed Eagle patt., 6" d., 4" h. (ILLUS. left w/butter crock) **600**

Wildflower Advertising Salt Crock

Salt crock, open, hanging-type, printed Wildflower patt., printed advertising "Your Credit Is Good - Freed Furniture & Carpet Co.," 6" d., 4 1/2" h. (ILLUS.) **450**

Salt jar, embossed Polar patt., 11" d., 13 1/2" h. .... **750+**

Slop jar, miniature, souvenir-type, one side inscribed "Mar. 29.05," other side inscribed "J.A. Wells" **425**

Soap dish, embossed Beaded Rose patt., 4 3/4" d. **150**

Soap dish, printed Wildflower patt., 3 5/8" w., 5 1/4" l. .... **275+**

Stein, embossed Grape with Leaf Band patt., 5" h. .... **125+**

Stein, embossed Windy City patt., 5 1/2" h. **165**

Stewer, cov., embossed Basketweave & Morning Glory (Willow) patt., 4 qt. .... **275+**

Stewer, cov., printed Wildflower patt., 4 qt. .... **285+**

Teapot, cov., spherical body w/row of relief-molded knobs around the shoulder, inset cover w/knob finial, swan's-neck spout, shoulder loop brackets for

wire bail handle w/turned wood grip, blue Swirl patt., 6" d., 6" h. ((ILLUS.) .... **800+**

Rare Blue Swirl Teapot

Tobacco jar, cov., embossed Berry Scrolls patt., 5" d., 6 1/2" h. **300**

Umbrella stand, embossed Two Stags patt., solid blue, 21" h. .... **1,000+**

Wicker Basket and Bouquet Vase

Vase, 11" h., embossed Wicker Basket and Bouquet patt. (ILLUS.)` **300**

Waste jar, cov., embossed Basketweave & Morning Glory (Willow) patt., 9 1/2" d., 12 1/2" h. .... **350+**

Water cooler, cov., barrel-shaped w/slightly oversized domed cover, the front w/an embossed panel of polar bears surrounded by ornate scrolls highlighted in dark blue, grotesque head at bung hole & spigot near base, the back w/embossed flowers, 13 3/4" h. plus cover (small cover chips) **495**

Water cooler, cov., embossed Apple Blossom patt., w/spigot, 13" h. **1,000**

Water cooler, cov., embossed Cupid patt., w/spigot, 5 gal. **725**

Water cooler, cov., embossed Elk and Polar Bear patt., w/spigot, 9 1/2" d., 14" h. **825**

Wildflower Water Cooler and Base

Water cooler, cov., printed Wildflower patt., w/spigot & base, 3 gal. (ILLUS.)....... **2,225**
Water cooler, embossed Polar Bear in Medallion patt. w/"Ice Water," cylindrical w/molded rings at the rim & base, bung hole near base, 15 1/4" h. (no cover or spigot) **385**

Blue & White Polar Jug

Water jug, Polar jug, footed flat-sided moon-shape w/short cylindrical top spout, 9 3/4" d., 10" h. (ILLUS.) **650**

OTHER COLORS

Yellowware Pitchers

Pitcher, embossed Grape patt., 10" h. (ILLUS. left) **395**
Pitcher, embossed Willow patt., yellow-ware, 9" h. (ILLUS. right)............................ **300**

BRAYTON LAGUNA POTTERY

Durlin Brayton was ahead of other California upstart companies of the 1940s when he began Brayton Laguna Pottery in Laguna Beach, California in 1927. Collectors need to familiarize themselves with the various lines created by Brayton during their more than forty years in business. Hand-turned pieces were the first to be made but there were many other lines: Children, the mark usually including the name of the child; White Crackle; White Crackle with a small amount of brown stain; Brown Stain with some White Crackle which is not as popular among today's collectors as is the overall White Crackle or the White Crackle with some brown stain; Calasia, an Art Deco line, mostly vases and planters; Gay Nineties; Circus, Provincial, which was a brown stain with gloss glazes in an assortment of colors; African-American; Animals; Walt Disney sanctioned items which are much sought after and treasured; Webton Ware, popular today as it represents a country theme; and there are others.

Just as Brayton had numerous lines, the company also had various marks, no less than a dozen. Stickers were also used, sometimes in combination with a mark. Designers incised their initials on some regular sized items and many times their initials were the only mark on a piece that was too small for Brayton's other marks.

Foreign imports were instrumental in the failure of many United States companies and Brayton was no exception. Production ceased in 1968.

Bowl, 10" d., 2" h., Calasia line, feather design in bottom, scalloped rim w/raised circles on inner rim, pale green **$75**
Bust of woman's head & shoulders, White Crackle glaze, 12" h. **450**
Candleholder, figural, three choirboys............ **145**
Candleholders, figural Blackamoor, pr........... **215**
Cookie jar, cov., light brown matte body w/overall honeycomb texture, dark brown straight tree branches w/five partridges around body in pale blue, yellow & orange, glossy white interior, pale blue lid, Model No. V-12, Mark 2, 7 1/4" h. **185**
Cookie jar, figural Mammy, burgundy base & turquoise bandanna, rare early version.. **1,300**
Cookie jar, figural Provincial Lady, textured woodtone stain w/high gloss white apron & scarf tied around head, red, green & yellow flowers & hearts motif on clothing, being reproduced so must be marked, "Brayton Laguna Calif. K-27," 13" h. **455**
Cookie jar, figure of Swedish Maid (Christina), produced 1941, incised mark, 11" h. **600**
Creamer, figural cat.. **45**
Cup w/tea bag holder, Provincial line, brown bisque stain w/white & yellow flowers & green leaves outside, gloss yellow inside, marked "Brayton Laguna Calif. K-31," 1 3/4" h. (ILLUS.)........................ **16**

Provincial Line Cup with Tea Bag Holder

Figure, African-American baby w/diaper, seated, green eyes, 3 3/4" h. **115**

Figure, baby on all fours **95**

Figure, baby sitting up...................................... **95**

Figure, Blackamoor, kneeling & holding open cornucopia, heavily jeweled w/gold trim, 10" h. **215**

Figure, Blackamoor, kneeling, jeweled trim, 15" h. **275**

Figure, Blackamoor, walking & carrying a bowl in his hands, glossy gold earrings, white bowl & shoes burgundy scarf, shirt & pantaloons, 8 1/4" h. **195**

Figure, boy, Alice in Wonderland, not Walt Disney, marked "R" designer Frances Robinson, 3 3/4" h. **300**

Figure, boy wearing swimming trunks, Hillbilly Shotgun Wedding series, marked, produced 1938, designed by Andy Anderson, 4 1/4" h...................................... **165**

Figure, Children's Series, "Ann," girl seated w/legs apart, knees bent, 4" h. **95**

Figure, Children's Series, "Ellen," girl standing w/pigtails & a hat tied at neck, arms bent & palms forward, one leg slightly twisted, 7 1/2" h. **95**

Figure, Children's Series, "John," boy w/horn **95**

Figure, Children's Series, "Jon," boy standing & carrying a basket in one hand, rooster in other, 8 1/4" h............................... **95**

Figure, peasant woman w/basket at her side in front & basket at her left in back, blue dress, yellow vest, incised mark "Brayton Laguna Pottery," 7 1/2" h. **90**

Figure, sailor boy holding a gun **295**

Figure, woman w/two wolfhounds, one on each side, woman w/red hair & wearing a long yellow dress, 9 1/2" h. **145**

Figure, woman wearing a blue dress & bonnet & holding a book **135**

Figure group, African-American boy & girl, boy holding basket of flowers in each hand, black shoes, yellow socks, barefoot girl, created by L. A. Dowd, early 1940s, paper label, 4 1/4" base, boy 7" h., girl 5 1/2" h. (ILLUS. top next column)... **375**

Figure group, Bride & Groom, the bride standing on the left w/white dress & pink flowers w/green leaves & pink hat, bouquet in left hand, her right hand on the groom's shoulder, man seated wearing striped trousers, black jacket, brown shoes & brown hat in left hand, black hair & mustache, stamp mark, 4 3/4" l., 8 1/2" h. **165**

African-American Boy & Girl

Figure group, "One Year Later," Mother seated on left w/green dress holding baby in white dress, man standing w/striped trousers, black hair, mustache, jacket & shoes, stamp mark, 4" l., 8 1/4" h.. **160**

Figures, African-American boys on hands & knees playing dice, w/original die, 4 3/4" l., 3 1/2" h., 3 pcs. **195**

Figures, Children's Series, "Eric" & "Inger," Swedish boy & girl, pr. **225**

Figures, Hillbilly Shotgun Wedding series, 8 pcs... **1,250**

Flower holder, figural, "Francis," girl standing & holding small planter in front, White Crackle glossy glaze dress, yellow pot, brown hair w/blue ribbon, brown-stained face & arms, bluebird on right arm, 6 1/2" h.. **35**

Model of Carousel horse, rearing position, 16" h. **145**

Model of cat, "Kiki," seated on oval base, tail wraps around to hide back legs and paws, socks on front paws, hat perched on head & tied at front, eyes closed, colorful sweater, assorted colors of pink, blue, black & white, marked on unglazed bottom, "Brayton Laguna" above a line & "Kiki" below the line, 6" l. base, 9 1/4" h. **125**

Brayton-Laguna Cat

Model of cat, lying down, head up, yellow body w/brown accents, green eyes, stamp mark, "Copyright 1941 by Brayton Laguna Pottery," 6 1/2" l., 4 1/4" h. (ILLUS.)... **55**

Model of cat, seated on oval base, socks on front paws w/left paw over right paw, head turned to left looking back, blue eyes open, hat perched on head between ears, bluebird on front of hat, colorful colors of blue, pink, white & black, unglazed, bottom w/no marks, 6 1/4" l. base, 9" h. **115**

Model of dog, sniffing, "Pluto," Walt Disney, 6" l., 3 1/4" h. **165**

Model of duck, standing w/head down, Provincial line, brown overall stain w/glossy yellow bill, 6 1/2" h. **50**

Model of fawn, standing, ears up, brown & white spots, unmarked, 6 1/2" h. **75**

Model of fox, seated, No. H-57 .... **110**

Model of owl, brown & white, 7" h. **55**

Model of Purple Cow, original sticker **95**

Model of quail standing on base, turquoise, black & grey, underglaze mark "Brayton's Laguna Beach, Calif.," 10 3/4" h. **125**

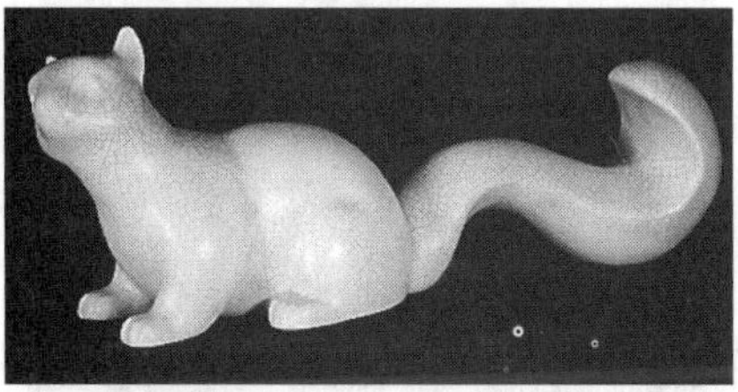

Brayton-Laguna White Squirrel

Model of squirrel, crouched w/tail behind & curving slightly upward on end, head & ears up, nondescript face, White Crackle glaze, incised mark, "Brayton's Laguna Calif. T-15," 12 3/4" l, 6" h. (ILLUS.) **125**

Models of monkeys, male & female, White Crackle w/brown stain faces, unmarked, 13" h., pr. **370**

Pencil holder, figural, Gingham Dog **75**

Pitcher, cream-size, model of a Calico kitten, high glaze white body w/pink, light blue & mauve flowers & brown stitching, pale blue ribbon around neck, black nose & eyes, stamp mark "Copyright 1942 by Brayton Laguna Pottery," 6 1/2" h. **55**

Salt & pepper shakers, figural, Gingham Dog & Calico Cat, pr. **71**

Salt & pepper shakers, figural Mammy & Chef, 5 1/2" h., pr. **85**

Salt & pepper shakers, figural peasant couple, Provincial patt., pr. **65**

Teapot & cover on stand, Provincial patt., tulip stand, the set **125**

Tile, chartreuse & yellow bird, turquoise, yellow & white flowers, black background incised mark, "Laguna Pottery," 7 x 7" **125**

Vase, 7 1/4" h., 7" w., 7" l., pillow-shape w/feather design on each side & raised circles on recessed short base, fern green **85**

Sea Horse Vase

Vase, 8 1/2" h., model of a sea horse, white body w/pink, yellow & turquoise accents, stamp mark underglaze "Brayton Calif. U.S.A.," (ILLUS.) **155**

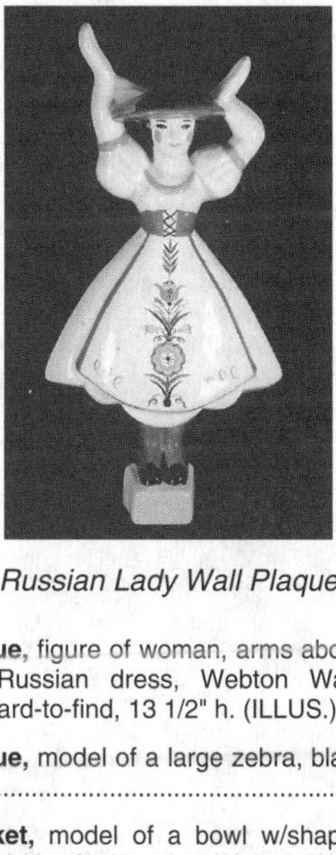

Russian Lady Wall Plaque

Wall plaque, figure of woman, arms above head, Russian dress, Webton Ware mark, hard-to-find, 13 1/2" h. (ILLUS.) **200**

Wall plaque, model of a large zebra, black & gold **95**

Wall pocket, model of a bowl w/shaped rim, two holes for hanging, Webton Ware mark on unglazed back, 2 3/4" w., 4 1/4" h. **65**

BUFFALO POTTERY

Buffalo Pottery was established in 1902 in Buffalo, New York, to supply pottery for the Larkin Company. Most desirable today in Deldare Ware, introduced in 1908 in two patterns, "The Fallowfield Hunt" and "Ye Olden Days," which featured central English scenes and a continuous border. Emerald Deldare, introduced in 1911, was banded with stylized flowers and geometric designs and had varied central scenes, the most popular being from "The Tours of Dr. Syntax." Reorganized in 1940, the company now specializes in hotel china.

Buffalo Pottery Mark

DELDARE

Chamberstick, Arlington Lodge, Lake Arrowhead, CA, ca. 1923 .... **$595**

Charger, "Fallowfield Hunt," M. Snea, 13 3/4" d. **374**

Mugs, "Fallowfield Hunt," black stamp, 5" d., 4 1/4" h., set of 4 .... **489**

Pitcher, 9" h., octagonal, 18th c. scene, "With a cane Superior air," from "The Vicar of Wakefield" **495**

Plate, 10" d., "Fallowfield Hunt," signed "H. Sheehan" **220**

EMERALD DELDARE

Chamberstick, Art Nouveau geometric banded & paneled design w/white & celadon green flowers on an olive brown ground, ink stamp mark, 6" d., 7" h. (very small edge chip) **990**

Emerald Deldare Chocolate Pot

Coffee/chocolate pot, cov., tall tapering hexagonal form w/pinched spout & angled D-form handle, inset lid w/blossom finial, stylized symmetrical designs highlighted w/white flowers on body & lid, band just under spout w/stylized moths & large butterfly, decorated by L. Newman, ca. 1911, artist's name in green slip, ink stamp logo & "7," 10 1/2" h. (ILLUS.) **1,980**

Pitcher, black stamp, decorated by Newman, 6 1/2" d., 7" h. **316**

Dr. Syntax Emerald Deldare Plate

Plate, 7 1/4" d., h.p. floral border & center scene, "Dr. Syntax Soliloquizing," by E. Missel, marked w/Emerald Deldare logo, "1911" & "4," pinhead size glaze nick off edge of rim (ILLUS.) **303**

MISCELLANEOUS

"Holland" Pitcher

Pitcher, jug-type, 5 3/4" h., "Holland," decorated w/three colorful h.p. scenes of Dutch children on the body w/band near the rim decorated w/a rural landscape, ca. 1906, marked w/Buffalo transfer logo & date, "Holland" & "9," overall consistent staining (ILLUS.) **468**

Cinderella" Pitcher

Pitcher, 6" h., jug-type, "Cinderella," ca. 1907, marked w/Buffalo transfer logo & date, "Cinderella" & "1328" (ILLUS. previous page).. 440

"Gloriana" Pitcher

Pitcher, 9" h., "Gloriana," blue on white, ca. 1908 (ILLUS.)... 550

CANTON

This ware has been decorated for nearly two centuries in factories near Canton, China. Intended for export sale, much of it was originally inexpensive blue-and-white hand-decorated ware. Late 18th and early 19th century pieces are superior to later ones and fetch higher prices.

Bowl, 9 1/4" d., 4 3/4" h., round w/notched corners, 19th c. (minor area of restoration, hairline)... $431

Bowl, 9 1/2" d., footed deep rounded sides below the squared cut-corner rim, 19th c. (minor interior glaze imperfections)......... 920

Bowl, 10" d., 2 3/4" h., round w/scalloped edge, orange peel glaze (minor chips)........ 495

Bowl, 10 1/4" d., 3" h., round w/scalloped rim, orange peel glaze (small chips & spider crack).. 385

Cider pitcher, cov., jug-form, wide ovoid body w/an applied entwined strap handle, mismatched low domed cover w/foo dog figural finial, 19th c., 8" h. 1,265

Fruit basket & undertray, oval upright reticulated sides w/a flared rim, on a conforming reticulated undertray w/a Chinese landscape in the center, orange peel glaze, 19th c., 9 1/8" l., 2 pcs. 1,540

Pitcher, 4 1/4" h. 220

Platter, 11 1/4" l.. 303

Platter, 13 3/4" l., oval w/deep sides, 19th c. (very minor chips).. 374

Platter, 14 3/4" l., oblong w/angled corners, orange peel glaze, 19th c. 385

Platter, 15 7/8" l., oval, typical blue landscape design, 19th c. (very minor rim chips).. 259

Platter, 17" l., 19th c. (very minor rim chips)..... 518

Platter, 17 1/2" l., octagonal 550

Platter, 18" l., oval w/well-and-tree in bottom, 19th c. (very minor rim chips)............. 690

Platter, 18 3/4" l., large wide oblong shape w/angled corners, large landscape scene in center, 19th c. 1,430

Punch bowl, painted in underglaze-blue, the interior & exterior w/pavilions, pagodas & figures in an island landscape, the inner trelliswork border w/pendant band of arrowheads, outer border reserved w/panels of precious objects, 19th c., 14 3/4" d... 1,610

Syllabub cups, footed, 19th c., set of 8 (two w/minor chips, two w/hairlines)............. 863

Canton Tea Caddy

Tea caddy, cov., octagonal, 19th c., China, 5 1/2" h. (ILLUS.)...................................... 2,645

Teapot, cov., barrel-shaped, cover w/figural foo dog finial, 19th c., 6 1/2" h. (mismatched cover, chips) 690

Teapot, cov., oval cylindrical form w/angled spout & entwined strap handle, inset cover w/fruit finial, worn gilt trim, 19th c., 5 1/2" h. 770

Tray, oval, 10" l... 165

Vegetable bowl, cov., w/pine cone finial, 9" l... 275

Vegetable bowl, cov., w/pine cone finial, 9 1/2" l... 193

Vegetable bowl, cov., w/pine cone finial, orange peel glaze, 10" l.............................. 330

Vegetable dish, cov., almond-shaped w/flanged rim, low domed cover w/pine cone finial, 19th c., 10 1/2" l. 220

Warming dish, oval, 19th c., 15 7/8" l............. 403

Water bottle, wide short cylindrical base below the tall waisted neck w/small rim spout, 19th c., 9 7/8" h. (chips).................... 275

CAPO-DI-MONTE

Production of porcelain and faience began in 1736 at the Capo-di-Monte factory in Naples. In 1743 King Charles of Naples established a factory there that made wares with relief decoration. In 1759 the factory was moved to Buen Retiro near Madrid, operating until 1808. Another Naples pottery was opened in 1771 and operated until 1806 when its molds were acquired by the Doccia factory of Florence, which has since made reproductions of original Capo-di-Monte pieces with the "N" mark beneath a crown. Some very early pieces are valued in the thousands of dollars but the subsequent productions are considerably lower.

Capo-di-Monte Casket

Casket, cov., rectangular, high cover w/metal hinge & pierced trellis edging w/spired finial at each end, paneled sides of gilt & enamel relief-decorated Bacchic scenes, Italy, 19th c., 13 3/4" l, 13 1/4" h. to finial (ILLUS.) **$4,029**

Dishes, oval, each molded in high-relief w/a large group of nude & semi-nude classical figures along the lower half & a wide upper flanged border w/further, small relief-molded classical figures, all w/colorful enamel decoration, late 19th c., 18" l., pr. **1,955**

Stein, cov., tapering cylindrical body decorated w/relief-molded bacchanalian figures, figural female nude handle, domed hinged cover w/figural finial of young bacchante on a goat, late 19th c., 17 1/2" h. **1,725**

Capo-di-Monte Stein

Stein, cov., cylindrical body w/classical relief enamel & gilt decorated continuous scene of bacchanalian figures, figural female nude handle, gilt bronze mounted thumb rest to hinged lid w/lion finial, underglaze-blue mark, 19th c., 9 1/4" h. (ILLUS.).. **805**

Urns, cov., painted porcelain, each w/lion finial, body decorated w/a band of classical sea-gods & nymphs, 19th c., 16 1/2" h., pr.. **2,300**

Urns, cov., tall slender trumpet-form body w/domed flaring foot & cover w/crown finial, decorated w/relief-molded bac-

canalian figures in colored enamel, 19 1/2" h., pr. **1,725**

Vases, cov., 9 5/8" h., scrolled handles terminating at female masks, the sides decorated w/a frieze band of classical figures in relief, 20th c., pr........................... **489**

Vases, cov., bulbous baluster-form body w/a wide shoulder to the small, short flaring neck w/a pierced rim supporting a low domed cover w/a pair of semi-nude figures, large C-scroll scroll-molded handles from neck to mid-body, the mid-body molded in high-relief w/a continuous band of color classical mermaids, tridents & hippocampus, a lobed lower ring over the pedestal molded w/figural fish over a round socle molded w/seaweed on a square gilt-trimmed foot, 19th c., 18" h., pr.. **2,875**

CATALINA ISLAND POTTERY

The Clay Products Division of the Santa Catalina Island Co. produced a variety of wares during their brief ten-year operation. The brainchild of chewing-gum magnate, William Wrigley, Jr., owner of Catalina Island at the time, and his business associate D. M. Retton, the plant was established at Pebbly Beach, near Avalon in 1927. Its two-fold goal was to provide year-round work for the island's residents and building material for Wrigley's ongoing development of a major tourist attraction at Avalon. Early production consisted of bricks and roof and patio tiles. Later, art pottery, including vases, flower bowls, lamps and home accessories were made from a local brown-based clay and, about 1930, tablewares were introduced. These early wares carried vivid glazes but had a tendency to chip readily and a white-bodied, more chip-resistant clay, imported from the mainland, was used after 1932. The costs associated with importing clay eventually caused the Catalina pottery to be sold to a California mainland competitor in 1937. These wares were molded and are not hand-thrown but some pieces have hand-painted decoration.

Catalina Island Pottery Mark

Ashtray, Model No. 657, green glaze **$95**

Ashtray, model of a cowboy hat, Descanso green or blue glaze, each............................ **195**

Ashtray, figural fish, decorated, Model No. 550, Toyon red glaze, 4 1/2" l. **150**

Book ends, figural monk, pearly white glaze, 4 x 5", pr. **1,200**

Bowl, fruit, 13" d., footed, blue glaze............... **175**

Bowl, 9 1/2 x 14", flared sides, white glaze...... **150**

Bowl, 17 1/2" l., oval, flared, pearly white glaze... **200**

Candelabra, No. 382, Descanso green glaze, pr. **950**

Candleholders, Descanso green, pr. 150
Candleholders, No. 380, sea foam glaze,
   pr. 200
Carafe, cov., handled, Toyon red glaze 125
Carafe, cov., handled, turquoise glaze 95

Charger with Marlin

Charger, relief-molded marlin, Monterey
   brown glaze, 14" d. (ILLUS.) 1,500
Charger, rolled edge, Toyon red glaze,
   14 1/2" d. 225
Compote, footed, w/glass liner, Toyon red
   glaze 225
Flask, model of a cactus, Descanso green,
   6 1/4" h. 600
Flowerpot, Toyon red, 4 1/2" h. 65
Lamp base, basketweave design, Des-
   canso green glaze.................................... 1,200
Oil jar, No. 351, Toyon red glaze, 18" h. 1,200
Pipe holder/ashtray, figural napping peon,
   Descanso green or blue glaze, each............ 450
Pitcher, 7 1/2" h., Toyon red glaze................... 350
Plate, chop, 11" d., Descanso green glaze 65
Plate, chop, 12 1/2" d., Toyon red glaze 70
Relish tray, handled, clover-shaped,
   seafoam glaze 650
Salt & pepper shakers, figural Senorita &
   Peon, Toyon red & yellow glaze, pr. 150
Salt & pepper shakers, model of cactus,
   tall, pr. 65
Salt & pepper shakers, model of tulip,
   blue glaze, pr.. 85

Tile Plaque with Macaw

Tile plaque, depicting green macaw,
   12 x 18" (ILLUS.)...................................... 2,000

Tortilla Warmer

Tortilla warmer, cov., Monterey brown
   glaze (ILLUS.) 1,500
Tumbler, blue glaze 35
Vase, 5" h., handled, Model No. 612, Man-
   darin yellow glaze...................................... 125
Vase, 5" h., stepped form, blue glaze.............. 275
Vase, bud, 5" h., Model No. 300, Descanso
   green glaze 100
Vase, stepped, handled, turquoise glaze,
   5" h.. 350
Vase, 5 1/2" h., Model No. 503, tan glaze 100
Vase, 5 1/2" h., Model No. 600, tan glaze 135
Vase, 6" h., ribbed body, blue glaze 65
Vase, 7" h., Model No. 636, turquoise glaze..... 145
Vase, 7 1/4" h., sawtooth edge on each
   side, Model No. 601, turquoise glaze........... 200
Vase, 7 1/2" h., trophy-form, handled,
   Toyon red glaze 350
Vase, 7 1/2" h., trophy-form, orange glaze 325
Vase, 7 3/4" h., Model No. 627, blue glaze 135

CERAMIC ARTS
STUDIO OF MADISON

During their 15 years of operation, Ceramic Arts Studio of Madison, Wisconsin was one of the nation's largest producers of figurines, shakers, and other decorative wares. Their originality and high production standards make them highly collectible works of art. In 1940, the artistic talent of Lawrence Rabbitt merged with the business acumen of Reuben Sand to start Ceramic Arts Studio. Their partnership was successful. Rabbitt remained artist in residence, and the Studio produced hand thrown bowls, pots and vases exploring the potential of Wisconsin clay. After Rabbitt's departure in 1942, a serendipitous meeting between Sand and Betty Harrington brought her artistic talents to the Studio. Under her artistic direction, the focus was changed to the finely sculpted decorative wares, including figurines of people, animals and fantasy figures. Metal Art accessories to compliment the ceramic pieces were assembled at the Studio under the direction of Zona Liberace (step-mother to the famous pianist) who also functioned as the Studio's decorating director.

From 1942 to 1948, the Studio's business flourished while imports from Europe and the Far East were suspended as a result of World War II. Annual production of 500,000 pieces and employment of 100 people were typical for these years. Harrington, although not the only designer on staff, is credited with the creation of the vast majority of the 800+ put into production. This level of output and quality helped to solidify the Studio's reputation as one of the most original and enduring ceramic producers in America.

The popularity of the Studio's work drew many poor quality imitations and outright copies. After World War II, lower-priced decorative imports began to flood the market forcing the Studio's eventual close in 1955. Attempts to continue the enterprise in Japan resulted in products bearing the name Ceramic Arts Studio - Japan and/or Mahana Imports. Some of the original molds were taken there and many of the models were produced with little or no design change, but with wide variations in quality. The ink stamp on these Japanese Studio wares is in red or blue, and the clay color is bright white. In contrast, the semi-circle mark, Ceramic Arts Studio, Madison, WI is always in black and the clay is ivory and heavier. But since only one out of four Madison Ceramic Arts Studio works were ink-stamped, other clues to authenticity are the decoration and clarity of the glaze.

Ceramic Arts Studio Marks a)First ink-stamped mark for Rabbitt's hand thrown wares, also found incised with "Ceramic Arts Studio, Rabbitt;" b)early paper label; c & d) ink-stamped marks for 1944 throu

Madonna with Child

Figure group, Madonna with Child, 6 1/2" h., 1 pc. (ILLUS.) **$120**

Love Trio: Lover Boy, Bashful Girl & Willing Girl

Figurine, Bashful Girl, dark hair, 4 1/2" h. (ILLUS. center) 75
Figurine, Berty w/ball, 4 1/2" h. 650
Figurine, Betty, sleeping, 5 1/2" l. 650
Figurine, Bo Peep, 5 1/4" h. 30
Figurine, Bobby, sitting, 3 1/4" h. 750
Figurine, Burmese Chinthe, 4" h. 225

Indian Group: Birch Bark Canoe, Bunny, Chipmunk, Fawn, Hiawatha, Indian Boy, Indian Girl, Minnehaha & Sea Gull

Figurine, Hiawatha, Indian group, 3 1/2" h. (ILLUS. second from right) 150
Figurine, Indian Boy, Indian group, 3" h. (ILLUS. center front, left) 30
Figurine, Indian Girl, Indian group, 3 1/4" h. (ILLUS. center front, right) 30
Figurine, Katrinka, 6 1/4" h. 35
Figurine, Lady Rowena on charger, 8 1/2" h. 190
Figurine, Little Boy Blue, reclining, 5 3/8" l. 25
Figurine, Lover Boy, 4 1/2" h. (ILLUS. left) 75
Figurine, Mary, 6" h. 65
Figurine, Minnehaha, Indian group, 6 1/2" h. (ILLUS. back left) 275
Figurine, Rose, part of Ballet Group, stooping, 5" h. 200
Figurine, Running Boy, Nursery Rhyme Group, 3 1/2" h. 65
Figurine, Running Girl, Nursery Rhyme Group, 3 1/4" h. 50
Figurine, Saint George on charger, 8 1/2" h. 190
Figurine, Spring Sue, 5 1/8" h. **65-75**
Figurine, Summer Sally, 3 3/8" h. **60-70**
Figurine, "Toadstool Pixie," elf on mushroom, 3 7/8" h. 40
Figurine, Violet, Ballet Group, sitting, 3" h. 150

Figurine, Willing Girl, blonde, 4 1/2" h.
(ILLUS. right) **120**
Figurine, Winter Willie, 4" h. **50-70**
Figurine, shelf-sitter, girl w/banjo **60**
Figurines, Alice & March Hare, 4 7/8" h. &
6" h., pr. **450**
Figurines, Aphrodite & Adonis, 7 3/4" h. &
9" h., pr. **748**
Figurines, Balinese Dancers, Man &
Woman, 9 1/2" h., pr. **200**

Bride & Groom Figurines

Figurines, Bride & Groom, 4 3/4" h. &
4 7/8" h., pr. (ILLUS.) **150**
Figurines, Burmese Man & Woman,
4 1/2" h., pr. **300**

Chinese Boy & Girl Figurines

Figurines, Chinese Boy & Girl, 4 1/4" h. &
4" h., pr. (ILLUS. far right & far left) **30**

Cinderella & Prince

Figurines, Cinderella & Prince, 6 3/8" h. &
6 3/4" h., pr. (ILLUS.) **150-175**
Figurines, Colonial Boy & Girl, 5 1/2" &
5" h., pr. **105**
Figurines, Colonial Man & Woman,
6 1/2" h., pr. **120**
Figurines, Gay Ninety Couple, Harry &
Lillibeth, 6 1/2" h. & 6" h., pr. **90**

Gay Ninety Man & Woman

Figurines, Gay Ninety Man & Woman,
6 3/4" h. & 6 1/2" h., pr. (ILLUS.) **125**

Gypsy Man & Woman

Figurines, Gypsy Man & Woman, 6 1/2" h.
& 7" h., pr. (ILLUS.) **120**

Rare Kabuki Man & Woman

Figurines, Kabuki Dancers, Man &
Woman, 8 1/2" h. & 6" h., pr., rare
(ILLUS.) **2,000**
Figurines, Mary & her lamb, Mary 6" h., pr. **85**
Figurines, Mop-Pi & Smi-Li, 6" h. &
6 1/4" h., pr. **120**
Figurines, Pioneer Sam & Pioneer Susie,
5 1/8" h. & 5 5/8" h., pr. **95**
Figurines, Rhumba Dancers, Man & Lady,
7 1/4" h., & 7 1/8" h., pr. **125**
Figurines, Ting-A-Ling & Sung-Tu,
5 1/2" h., 4" h., pr. **85**

Figurines, Wee Chinese Boy & Girl, 3" h.,
pr. (ILLUS. center).. **20**
Figurines, Wee Dutch Boy & Girl, 3" h., pr. **30**
Figurines, Zulu Man & Woman, 5 1/2" h. &
7" h., pr.. **650**
Figurines, shelf-sitters, Colonial Boy &
Girl, 5 1/2" h. & 5" h., pr. **150**

Farmer Boy & Girl Shelf-sitters

Figurines, shelf-sitters, Farmer Boy & Girl,
4 3/4" h., 4 1/2" h., pr. (ILLUS.) **90**
Figurines, shelf-sitters, Grace & Greg,
6 1/4" & 7", pr. **80**
Figurines, shelf-sitters, Nip & Tuck, pr. **82**
Figurines, shelf-sitters, Young Love Cou-
ple, 4 7/8" h., pr. **50**
Head vase, Barbie, 7" h. **195**
Head vase, Becky, 5 1/4" h. **125**
Head vases, Lotus & Manchu, 7 3/4" h., pr...... **250**
Lamp, table model, Zorina, original tags **285**
Model of Archibald the Dragon, 8" h. **200-225**
Model of baby bear, brown, 1 3/4" h. **50**
Model of Baby Boy Skunk, Dinky, 2" h. **45**
Model of birch bark canoe, Indian group,
8" l. (ILLUS. in background) **150**
Model of birds, Lovebirds, 2 1/2" h. **35**
Model of Budgie, parrot, turquoise.................... **95**
Model of bunny, Indian group, 1 3/4" h.
(ILLUS. front left).. **50**
Model of chipmunk, Indian group, 2" h.
(ILLUS. far right).. **60**
Model of Daisy Donkey **150**
Model of dog, Collie pup **35**
Model of dog, Scottie, Sooty, black, 3" h......... **129**
Model of dog, Scottie, Taffy, brown, 3" h. **129**
Model of dog, shelf-sitter, Collie Dog,
5 1/8" h.. **76**
Model of elephant, trunk down, "Tembino,"
2 1/2" h... **150**
Model of Elsie Elephant, 4 3/4" h. **136**
Model of fawn, Indian group, 4 1/4" h.
(ILLUS. far left, front)...................................... **90**
Model of goat, standing, w/horns, 4 1/8" h. **69**
Model of horse, Modern colt, 7 1/2" h. **250**
Model of leopard, upright **125**
Model of Little Lamb, 3 5/8" h. **30**
Model of modern panther, 6 1/2" h. **200**
Model of Mr. Skunk, 2 7/8" h............................ **55**
Model of sea gull, Indian group, (hooks
onto side of canoe), 3 3/4" w. wing span
(ILLUS. center back on canoe) **1,000**
Model of Tom Cat, standing **125**
Model of tortoise with cane, 3 1/4" h. **150**
Models of elephant, Tembo w/trunk up &
Tembino w/trunk down, 6 3/4" h &
2 1/2" h., pr.. **750**

Models of fighting leopards, pr...................... **235**
Models of fox & goose, 2" & 3 1/4" h., pr. **250**
Models of Mother Bear & Baby Bear,
nesting-type, white glaze, pr. **50**
Models of Mr. & Mrs. Monkey, pr. **200**
Models of Pete & Polly Parrot, shelf-sit-
ters, mauve, pr. **175**
Models of skunk family, Mr. & Mrs.
Skunk, 2 7/8" h., Baby Boy Skunk (Din-
key), 2 3/8" h. & Baby Girl Skunk
(Inkey), 2" h., unmarked, the set **185**
Models of stylized lions, 1 3/4 x 5 1/4 &
3 1/4 x 7 1/4, pr. **550**
Mug, figural Mr. Toby, seated, holding mug,
2 3/4" h... **125**

Adam & Eve Miniature Pitcher

Pitcher, 3" h., miniature, relief-molded
Adam & Eve decoration, branch handle
(ILLUS.) **55**
Salt & pepper shakers, figural Chinese
Boy & Girl, 4 1/4" h. & 4" h., pr...................... **40**
Salt & pepper shakers, figural Clown &
Dog, nesting-type, 3 3/4" h. & 2 1/2" h.,
pr **135**
Salt & pepper shakers, figural Fighting
Leopards, 2 3/4 x 6" & 3 1/4 x 4", pr.
(large leopard repaired).................................. **210**
Salt & pepper shakers, figural frog & toad-
stool, 2" & 2 3/8" h. pr..................................... **63**
Salt & pepper shakers, figural Mother &
Baby Donkey, 3 1/4" h. & 3" h., pr................ **350**
Salt & pepper shakers, figural Mother &
Baby Spaniel dog, 2 1/4" h. & 2" h., pr........ **175**
Salt & pepper shakers, figural Native
Riding Alligator, 2 5/8" h., 4 1/4" l., pr............. **45**
Salt & pepper shakers, figural ox & cov-
ered wagon, 2 3/8" & 3 1/2" h., pr. **90**
Salt & pepper shakers, figural Paul Bun-
yan & evergreen tree, 3 7/8" h.,
2 1/8" h., pr. **175-225**
Salt & pepper shakers, figural Pete &
Polly Parrot, red 7 7/8" h. & 8 1/2" h., pr.
(small chip on one wing) **100**

Running Mother & Baby Bunny

Salt & pepper shakers, figural Running Mother & Baby Bunny, 4 1/2" & 3 1/2" h., pr. (ILLUS.).. **250**

Salt & pepper shakers, figural Sambo & Tiger, tiger 2 5/8 x 5 1/4", Sambo 3 1/4" h., pr... **775**

Santa Claus
w/Evergreen Tree Shakers

Salt & pepper shakers, figural Santa Claus & evergreen tree, 2 1/4" h. & 2 1/2" h., pr. (ILLUS.) **400**

Salt & pepper shakers, figural stylized Mother & Baby Cat, brown, 4 1/4" h. & 2 5/8" h., pr.. **250**

Salt & pepper shakers, figural Thai & Thai-Thai, 2 1/8 x 4 3/8" & 2 x 5 1/4", pr. **115**

Salt & pepper shakers, figural Wee Pig Boy & Girl, 3 1/4" h., & 3 1/2" h., p.r............... **50**

Vase, 4 1/4" h., Comedy & Tragedy, snuggle for Encore man or lady (double sided), 1 pc... **150**

Wall plaque, pierced to hang, Grace, 8 3/4" h... **60**

Wall plaque, pierced to hang, Greg, 9 1/4" h... **60**

CHINESE EXPORT

Large quantities of porcelain have been made in China for export to America from the 1780s, much of it shipped from the ports of Canton and Nanking. A major source of this porcelain was Ching-te-Chen in the Kiangsi province but the wares were also made elsewhere. The largest quantities were blue and white. Prices fluctuate considerably depending on age, condition, decoration, etc.

CANTON and ROSE MEDALLION export wares are listed separately

Bowl, 10" d., 5" h., blue Nanking patt., cut corners, 19th c. (minute rim chips)............. **$978**

Coffeepot, cov., blue Nanking patt., footed bulbous ovoid body tapering to a small neck fitted w/a domed flanged cover w/fruit finial, short shaped rim spout & applied entwined strap handle, gilt trim, 9 1/8" h. (small flakes on cover)............... **1,045**

Dish, Famille Rose palette, irregular wide rounded & lobed form, shallow w/flared rim, floral-decorated rim band, interior w/scattered designs of figures, fish, Chinese characters, etc., 19th c., 11 1/4" l. **825**

Figures of hawks, each bird perched on open blue rockwork & looking slightly to its right & left respectively, covered in a rich apple green glaze & w/iron-red beaks & black eyes, late 19th c., 8 1/2" h.. **460**

Plate, 9" d., scalloped edge, made for the Continental market w/polychrome & gilt armorial decoration, late 18th c. (minor edge chips).. **633**

Platter, 11 1/2" l., oval, blue Fitzhugh patt., 19th c. **385**

Platter, 13 7/8" l., rectangular w/deeply angled corners, blue Nanking patt., orange peel glaze, 19th c............................. **770**

Platter, 14 1/2" l., oval, flanged rim, gilded "A" in circle mark, 19th c. (spot of rim repair)... **633**

Platter, 16 1/2" l., oval, blue & white Nanking patt., w/pierced oval insert, 19th c., 2 pcs... **440**

Platter & pierced insert, blue & gilt vintage border decoration, monogrammed, 17 1/2" l. (glaze & gilt wear) **1,265**

Punch bowl, armorial, footed, rounded flared sides, decorated w/scroll band, spearhead & floral border, coat of arms & floral sprays, ca. 1790, 10 1/4" d., 4 1/4" h. **1,064**

Chinese Export Punch Bowl

Punch bowl, exterior decorated w/scene of court figures on a dragon boat surrounded by warriors, interior w/geometric border, rust & gilt scenic motifs, 19th c., glaze wear, 15 5/8" d. (ILLUS.) **2,645**

Salt & pepper shakers, on trumpet foot base w/stylized flat leaf engraving, cylindrical bodies chased & embossed w/figures in foliate landscape, each w/pierced lid, mid-late 19th c., 4" h., pr. (restorations) **575**

Teapot, cov., cylindrical w/h.p. polychrome & gilt eagle w/wings down & shield decoration, entwined strap handle, 19th c., 5 3/4" h. (chips, hairline, scratches) **690**

Teapot, cov., blue Nanking patt., lobed form w/reeded strap handles, gilt trim, late 18th - early 19th c., 5 1/2" h. (minor chips, gilt wear) **518**

Tray, blue Nanking patt., oval w/wide flared & reticulated border & shallow center w/landscape scene, 19th c., 10 3/4" l. **495**

Tureen, decorated w/spearhead band, coat of arms & floral sprays, pineapple finial & bent twig handles, 13 1/2" l., 11" h. **532**

Tureen, cov., flared pedestal foot below oval form w/rounded sides, twisted twig handles, domed cover w/blossom finial, decorated in green & gold designs on cream ground, 14" l., 11 1/2" h. **3,360**

Vases, 24" h., floor-type, Famille Rose palette, decorated w/applied kylins & foo dogs, on hardwood stands, 19th c., pr. (minor gilt & glaze wear) **633**

Vegetable bowl, cov., Famille Rose palette, footed rectangular form w/notched corners & stepped domed cover w/fruit finial, heavy gilt trim, orange peel glaze, 9 1/2" l. **1,045**

Vegetable dish, cov., blue Fitzhugh patt., rectangular w/notched corners, stepped domed cover w/large fruit finial, trimmed in gilt, 19th c., 9 1/2" l. **825**

Vegetable dish, open, blue Nanking patt., oval w/slightly scalloped flanged rim on flaring sides, orange peel glaze, 19th c., 11 1/2" l. **275**

Warming dish, cov., orange peel glaze, oval dish decorated in a Fitzhugh manner w/Mandarin & floral motifs, black & gilt highlights on white ground, in the French taste, ca. 1820-30, 15 1/2 x 10 1/4" (minor glaze wear, lid w/minor interior edge chips) **1,840**

Warming dishes, orange peel glaze, round dish decorated in a Fitzhugh manner w/Mandarin & floral motifs, black & gilt highlights on white ground, in the French taste, ca. 1820-30, 10 3/4" d. (one w/handle damage).................................. **1,150**

Wash bowl, Famille Rose palette, rim decorated w/floral devices, interior sides w/children surrounding the bowl, a seated court lady in the bottom, 11 1/2" d. **173**

CHINTZ CHINA

There are over fifty flower patterns and myriad colors from which Chintz collectors can choose. That is not surprising considering companies in England began producing these showy, yet sometimes muted, patterns in the early part of this century. Public reception was so great that this production trend continued until the 1960s.

Ashtray, Peony patt., Royal Winton................ **$45**
Ashtray, Paisley patt., Wade Heath, 3 3/4"........ **40**

Bonbon dish, Clevedon patt., Royal Winton **225**

Bowl, octagonal, Festival patt., Crown Ducal **325**

Bowl, octagonal, Ivory Chintz patt., Crown Ducal **350**

Somerset Pattern Salad Bowl

Bowl, salad, chrome rim, Somerset patt., Rheims shape, Royal Winton (ILLUS.) **550**

Bowl, Sweet Pea patt., Crown shape, Royal Winton **750**

Majestic Pattern Breakfast Set

Breakfast set: cov. teapot, cup, creamer, open sugar bowl, toast rack & oblong paneled tray w/end handles; Majestic patt., Countess shape, Royal Winton, the set (ILLUS.) **1,750**

Breakfast set, Fireglow Black patt., Royal Winton, the set **850**

Butter dish, cov., Cranstone patt., Royal Winton **375**

Butter pat, Anemone patt., Royal Winton **35**

Butter pat, Sunshine patt., Royal Winton **135**

Cake plate, Exotic Bird patt., Saville shape, Royal Winton **135**

Cake plate, Lichfield patt., James Kent, Ltd. **135**

Cake plate, open handles, Carnation patt., Royal Winton **125**

Cake plate, open handles, Shrewsbury patt., Royal Winton **295**

Cake plate, pedestal base, Cotswold patt., Royal Winton **275**

Cake plate, Royalty patt., Ascot shape, Royal Winton **350**

Cake stand, three-tier, Skylark patt., Lord Nelson Ware **155**

Cake stand, two-tier, Clyde patt., Royal Winton **75**

Cake stand w/chrome base, Lorna Doone patt., W. R. Midwinter Ltd., 3 1/4 x 9"............. **95**

Rare Stratford Pattern Candy Dish

Candy dish, cov., low round shape, pointed finial on low domed cover, Stratford patt., Royal Winton (ILLUS.) **950**

Candy dish, Mayfair patt., Royal Winton **135**

Candy dish, Peony patt., Royal Winton **50**

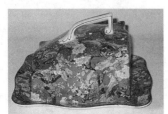

Blue Chintz Pattern Cheese Dish

Cheese dish, cov., slanted cover, Blue Chintz patt., Crown Ducal (ILLUS.) **750**

Cheese dish, cov., Summertime patt., Dane shape, Royal Winton **350**

Coaster, Paisley patt., Royal Winton **135**

Coffeepot, cov., Dorset patt., Royal Winton..... **750**

Coffeepot, cov., Hazel patt., Grecian shape, Royal Winton **1,350**

Coffeepot, cov., Pink Chintz patt., Crown Ducal **1,595**

Primula Pattern Coffeepot

Coffeepot, cov., Primula patt., Granville shape, James Kent Ltd. (ILLUS.) **1,400**

Compote, open, Blue Tulip patt., Royal Winton **75**

Compote, open, low scalloped bowl on a short scalloped pedestal base, Welbeck patt., Royal Winton (ILLUS.) **595**

Welbeck Pattern Compote

Compote, open, oblong shallow shaped bowl on a flaring rectangular pedestal base, Queen Anne patt., Royal Winton **225**

Compote, 6 1/2" h., Marguerite patt., scalloped top, ... **275**

Condiment set on tray, Delphinium Chintz patt., Royal Winton, the set **250**

Marion Pattern Cracker Jar

Cracker jar, cov., Marion patt., Rheims shape, Royal Winton (ILLUS.).................. **1,500**

Cracker jar, cov., Summertime patt., Ninevah shape, Royal Winton **1,100**

Chintz Floral Creamer

Creamer, creamy yellow background w/bunches of pink & blue flowers, green leaves, light green trim, like Unknown 5 patt. by Barker Brothers, Ltd., Sampson Smith, 3 1/4" d., 4" h. (ILLUS.) **110**

Chintz Pattern Creamer & Sugar Bowl

Creamer & cov. sugar bowl, Chintz patt., Old Cottage shape, Royal Winton, pr. (ILLUS.) 250

Creamer & cov. sugar bowl, Hazel patt., Royal Winton, pr. 110

Creamer & cov. sugar bowl, Primula patt., Crown Ducal, pr. 145

Creamer & cov. sugar bowl, Rosalynde patt., James Kent, Ltd., pr. 150

Creamer & open sugar bowl, Hazel patt., Grecian shape, Royal Winton, pr. 160

Creamer & open sugar bowl, Summertime patt., Royal Winton, pr. 169

Creamer & open sugar bowl, Sweet Pea patt., Ascot shape, Royal Winton, pr. 195

Cup & saucer, Black Beauty patt., Lord Nelson 145

Cup & saucer, Blossom patt., Oleander shape, pale green exterior, Shelley China 145

Cup & saucer, Briar Rose patt., Lord Nelson Ware, the set 85

Cup & saucer, Cheadle patt., Royal Winton, pr. 125

Hazel Cup & Saucer

Cup & saucer, Hazel patt., Ascot shape, Royal Winton (ILLUS.) 150

Cup & saucer, Heather patt., Lord Nelson 75

Cup & saucer, Merton patt., Royal Winton, the set 95

Cup & saucer, Old Cottage patt., Royal Winton 89

Cup & saucer, Petunia patt., Royal Winton 175

Cup & saucer, Primrose patt., Oleander shape, black matte exterior, Shelley China 175

Cup & saucer, Rosebud shape, yellow, Royal Winton 35

Cup & saucer, Summertime patt., Royal Winton 101

Demitasse cup & saucer, Pelham patt., Royal Winton 85

Dish, canoe-shaped, Pekin patt., Royal Winton 145

Dish, Primrose patt., 4 1/2" l 100

Dish, Spring patt., canoe-shaped, Royal Winton 200

Dish, Sweet Pea patt., rare shape, 4 1/2 x 6 1/2" 225

Dish, center-handled, Chimarita (blue paisley), James Kent, 8 1/4" 85

Egg cup, Kinver patt., Royal Winton 235

Sunshine Gravy Boat & Undertray

Gravy boat & undertray, Sunshine patt., Royal Winton, 2 pcs. (ILLUS.) 295

Hair receiver, Paisley patt., Wade Heath 75

Hot water pitcher, cov., English Rose patt., Royal Winton 750

Fireglow Hot Water Pot

Hot water pot, cov., Fireglow patt., Sexta shape, Royal Winton (ILLUS.) 700

Jam jar, cov., Lorna Doone patt., W. R. Midwinter Ltd. 100

Jam jar, cov., Peony patt., Crown Ducal 275

Jam jar, cov., Rapture patt., James Kent, Ltd. 125

Jam jar, cover & underplate, Beeston patt., Rheims shape, Royal Winton, the set 395

Triumph Pattern Mustard Jar

Jam jar, cover & underplate, Sweet Pea patt., Ascot shape, Royal Winton, the set 325
Juice reamer, Spring Blossom patt., Crown Ducal.. 450
Lily bowl, Ascot patt., Crown Ducal 145
Mustard jar, cov., footed barrel shape, Triumph patt., Royal Winton (ILLUS. previous page) 155
Mustard jar, cover & underplate, Beeston patt., Royal Winton, the set 275
Nut dish, individual, DuBarry patt., James Kent, Ltd. 95
Nut dish, individual, Eleanor patt., Royal Winton 85
Nut dish, Summertime patt., Royal Winton........ 40
Nut scoop, Floral Feast patt., Royal Winton 200
Pin tray, June Festival patt., Royal Winton 145
Pitcher, jug-form, Balmoral patt., Royal Winton 475
Pitcher, jug-form, Mauve Chintz patt., Crown Ducal.. 175
Pitcher, straight-sided, Green Tulip patt., Lord Nelson Ware 550
Pitcher, 3" h., jug-form, miniature milk-type, Chelsea patt., Globe shape, Royal Winton 110

Marguerite Milk Pitcher

Pitcher, 5" h., jug-form, Marguerite patt., Globe shape, Royal Winton (ILLUS.) 350
Pitcher, 5" h., jug-form, milk, Summertime patt., Albans shape, Royal Winton 550
Pitcher, 5" h., jug-form, milk, Sweet Pea patt., Duval shape, Royal Winton 650
Plate, 9" d., dinner, Purple Chintz patt., Crown Ducal.. 165
Plate, bread & butter, Richmond patt., Royal Winton.. 195
Plate, chop, Apple Blossom patt., James Kent, Ltd. 235
Plate, octagonal, Ivory Fruit patt., Crown Ducal 65
Plate, 8" sq., Old Cottage patt., Royal Winton 99
Plate, 8" sq., Summertime patt., Royal Winton 95
Plate, 9" d., dinner, Evesham patt., Royal Winton.. 265
Plate, 9" d., Lorna Doone patt., Broadhurst........ 80
Plate, 9" sq., dinner, Summertime patt., Ascot shape, Royal Winton 225
Plate, 9 1/4" sq., green, Royal Winton................ 50
Platter, 12" l., oval, Summertime patt., Royal Winton 325
Relish dish, Hydrangea patt., James Kent, Ltd. 150

Roll tray, ruffled edge, Rapture patt., James Kent, 7 x 13" 275
Rose bowl w/flower frog insert, Primrose patt., rectangular stepped foot supporting rectangular rounded bowl, Royal Winton 450

Florida Rose Bowl with Flower Frog

Rose bowl w/frog insert top, wide rounded urn-form bowl w/large loop shoulder handles & low domed insert flower frog top, raised on a round pedestal base, Florida patt., Crown Ducal (ILLUS.)... 2,600
Salt & pepper shakers, Summertime patt., Royal Winton, pr... 90
Salt & pepper shakers on tray, June Festival patt., Royal Winton, the set.................. 100
Salt & pepper shakers on tray, June Roses patt., Royal Winton, the set............. 295
Sandwich tray, Floral Feast patt., Royal Winton, 7 x 12"... 150
Server, center-handled, Sunnydale patt., Soho Pottery Ltd., 8" 80

Chintz Floral Pattern Server

Server, chrome center-handle w/red top, overall floral pattern in pink, blue & yellow w/green leaves, like Anemone patt. by Elijah Cotton Ltd. (Lord Nelson), Parrot & Co., 9" d. (ILLUS.) 135
Soup plate, flanged rim, Tapestry patt., James Kent, Ltd. 125
Sugar bowl, open, Old Cottage patt., Royal Winton... 69
Sugar bowl, open, round, Old Cottage patt., Royal Winton.. 59
Sugar shaker, Brama patt., Midwinter 450
Sugar w/metal cover, squared tapering sides on four small tab feet, Lorna Doone patt., Midwinter, Ltd. 375
Tea set: stacking-type, cov. creamer, sugar & teapot; Florence patt., Delamere shape, Royal Winton, the set 1,750

Tea set: stacking-type, teapot, sugar & cov. creamer; Black Beauty patt., Lord Nelson Ware, the set 950

Teapot, cov., Joyce-Lynn patt., Ascot shape, Royal Winton 1,295

Teapot, cov., Julia patt., Royal Winton, two-cup 800

Teapot, cov., Paisley patt., Wade Heath, six-cup 285

Teapot, cov., Summertime patt., Ajax shape, Royal Winton 950

Teapot, cov., Summertime patt., Ascot shape, Royal Winton 750

Teapot, cov., Tiger Lily patt., green, Royal Winton 295

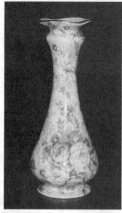

Sweet Pea Pattern Tennis Set

Tennis set: cup & oblong underplate; Sweet Pea patt., Royal Winton, 2 pcs. (ILLUS.) 165

Tennis set, Marina patt., Lord Nelson Ware, the set 100

Toast rack, Cromer patt., Royal Winton, small 165

Toast rack, Orient patt., Royal Winton 235

Tray, rectangular, Summertime patt., Royal Winton, 6 3/4 x 12" 220

Tray, rectangular, DuBarry patt., James Kent, 5 3/4 x 12 1/2" 200

Trivet, round, Silverdale patt., Royal Winton 95

Vase, bud-type, Kew patt., Royal Winton 250

Rosetime Pattern Bud Vase

Vase, bud-type, Rosetime patt., Lord Nelson Ware (ILLUS.) 225

Vase, trumpet-shaped, Marigold patt., Crown Ducal 225

Vegetable dish, oblong w/scalloped edges, Summertime patt., Royal Winton 265

Vegetable dish, open, oval, Spring patt., Royal Winton 225

CLARICE CLIFF DESIGNS

Clarice Cliff was a designer for A. J. Wilkinson, Ltd., Royal Staffordshire Pottery, Burslem, England when they acquired the adjoining Newport Pottery Company whose warehouses were filled with undecorated bowls and vases. About 1925 her flair with the Art Deco style was incorporated into designs appropriately named "Bizarre" and "Fantasque" and the warehouse stockpile was decorated in vivid colors. These hand-painted earthenwares, all bearing the printed signature of designer Clarice Cliff, were produced until World War II and are now finding enormous favor with collectors.

Note: Reproductions of the Clarice Cliff "Bizarre" marking have been appearing on the market recently.

Clarice Cliff Mark

Bone dish, Tonquin patt., black $30

Bowl, 5" d., Tonquin patt. 5

Bowl, 6 1/4" d., octagonal flanged rim on the rounded body, Woodland patt., stylized landscape w/trees in orange, green, black, blue, purple & yellow, marked 550

Bowl, 6 1/2" d., 3" h., "Bizarre" ware, footed deep slightly flaring sides, Crocus patt., the sides divided into two horizontal bands of color w/a band of small crocus blossoms along the upper half, in orange, blue, purple & green, stamped mark 550

Caprice Pattern Bowl & Vase

Bowl, 8" d., "Bizarre" ware, Caprice patt., stylized landscape w/hills, arch & tall trees in lavender, blue, yellow, green & brown (ILLUS. left) 2,800

Bowl, 8" d., 3 3/4" h., "Bizarre" ware, deep gently rounded sides tapering to a footring, Original Bizarre patt., a wide band of blocks & triangles around the upper half in blue, orange, ivory & purple, purple band around the bottom section, marked 650

Bowl, 8" d., 4 1/4" h., "Bizarre" ware, octagonal, h.p. w/Original Bizarre patt., large crudely painted bands of maroon, dark orange & dark blue diamonds above an ochre base band, ink mark **1,100**

Bowl, 9" d., deep rounded sides, the upper half w/a wide band in polychrome featuring large stylized cottages w/pointed orange roofs beneath arching trees, lime green banding, marked **800**

Bowl, 9 1/2" d., 4 1/2" h., orange, green & blue h.p. poppies **600**

Butter dish, cov., "Bizarre" ware, Crocus patt., a wide shallow base w/low, upright sides fitted w/a shallow, flat-sided cover w/a slightly domed top & flat button finial, the top decorated w/purple, blue & orange blossoms on an ivory ground, marked, 4" d., 2 3/4" h................................ **550**

A Variety of Clarice Cliff Patterns

Butter dish, cov., "Bizarre" ware, short wide cylindrical body w/an inset cover w/large button finial, Secrets patt., decorated w/a stylized landscape in shades of green, yellow & brown w/red-roofed houses on a cream ground, marked, 4" d., 2 5/8" h. (ILLUS. above left) **550**

Candleholders, figural, modeled as a kneeling woman w/her arms raised high holding the candle socket modeled as a basket of flowers, My Garden patt., orange dress & polychrome trim, marked, 7 1/4" h., facing pr. **575**

Various Clarice Cliff Items

Candleholders, Fantasque line, cylindrical form w/flared base & rim, Melon patt., decorated w/a band of overlapping fruit

in predominantly orange glaze w/yellow, bluish green & brown outline, stamped on base "Hand Painted Fantasque by Clarice Cliff Wilkinson Ltd. England," ca. 1930, minor glaze nicks, two small firing cracks to inside rim of one, 3 1/4" h., pr. (ILLUS. front) **1,380**

Candlestick, loop-handled, Tonquin patt., red **30**

Candlesticks, slender baluster-form shaft above a disk foot & w/a wide flattened rim, painted w/bold geometric designs in blue, orange & green, Delecia Citrus patt., brightly painted fruits on a cream ground pr. **2,500**

Candlesticks, squared pedestal foot supporting a tall square tapering shaft & cylindrical socket w/flared rim, decorated in bold geometric designs in orange, cream, green, blue & yellow, pr. **2,900**

Clarice Cliff Figural Centerpiece

Centerpiece, "Bizarre" ware, model of a stylized Viking longboat, raised on trestle supports & w/a frog insert, glazed in orange, yellow, brown & black on a cream ground, printed factory marks, ca. 1925, restored, 15 3/4" l., 9 5/8" h., 2 pcs. (ILLUS.) **1,500**

Charger, large round dished form, Crest patt., three large Japanese-style crests in gold, blue, rust red, black & green on a mottled green ground **12,000**

Coffee service: cov. coffeepot, creamer, open sugar bowl, five cake plates & six cups & saucers; Ravel patt., creamer & sugar w/pointed conical bodies supported by buttress legs, other serving pieces w/flaring cylindrical bodies, marked, coffeepot 6" h., the set **1,100**

Condiment set: two jars w/silver-plated lids & a small open bowl fitted in a silver-plated frame w/a looped center handle; each piece h.p. w/stylized red & blue flowers on an ivory ground, marked, tray 4 1/2 x 5, the set (small chip on one piece) **523**

Cracker jar, cov., "Bizarre" ware, Blue Chintz patt., stylized blue, green & pink blossom forms w/blue border band **1,800**

Cracker jar, cov., "Bizarre" ware, bulbous barrel shape w/large side knobs to support the arched woven wicker bail handle, wide flat mouth w/a slightly domed cover centered by a large ball finial,

Gayday patt., decorated w/a wide band of large stylized flowers in orange, rust, amethyst, blue & green above a lower band in orange on a cream ground, the cover w/an orange finial & yellow band, 5 7/8" d., 6 1/4" h. (ILLUS. right w/butter dish) **975**

Cracker jar, cov., "Bizarre" ware, squatty kettle-form w/side knobs supporting the swing bail handle, Delecia Citrus patt. **1,400**

Cup, "Bizarre" ware, tall slightly tapering cylindrical form w/D-form handle, Chintz patt., painted in orange, brown & black, stamped factory mark & gilt Lawley's stamp, ca. 1932, 3 5/8" h. **460**

Cup & saucer, "Bizarre" ware, Autumn Crocus patt., Athens shape **300**

"Bizarre" Demitasse Set

Demitasse set: cov. coffeepot, six demitasse cups & saucers, creamer & open sugar bowl; "Bizarre" ware, Fantasque patt., decorated w/a stylized tree on one side, the other w/stylized hollyhocks, small chips to one saucer, 15 pcs. (ILLUS. of part) **3,200**

Figures "Bizarre" ware, flat cut-outs, comprising two groups of musicians & two groups of dancing couples, all highly stylized & glazed in reddish orange, yellow, lime green, cream & black, printed factory marks, ca. 1925, 5 5/8 to 7" h., 4 pcs. **29,000**

Gravy boat & underplate, Tonquin patt., black, 2 pcs. **40**

Jam jar, cov., cylindrical body, Melon patt., decorated w/a band of overlapping fruit, predominantly orange w/yellow, blue & green w/brown outline, ca. 1930, restoration to rim & side, marked, 4" h. (ILLUS. top right w/candleholders) **690**

Jam pot, cov., Blue Firs patt., flat-sided round form on small log feet, domed cover w/flat round knob, stylized landscape w/trees, marked, 4 1/4" h. **900**

Jar, cov., "Bizarre" ware, a sharply tapering conical base supported on four squared buttress feet & w/a sharply inward tapering shoulder supporting the conical cover w/four small buttress tabs at the top, Canterberry Bells patt., decorated in mottled brown rim & shoulder over a stylized floral band in orange, shades of green, blue, amethyst & mottled yellow on a cream ground, 6" d., 8 1/8" h. (ILLUS.) **1,300**

Canterberry Bells Pattern Jar

Jardiniere, "Fantasque" line, Melon patt., Dover shape, deep cylindrical sides on three small tab feet, decorated w/Cubist-style fruits in orange, yellow, blue, green & amber against a cream ground, orange base & rim bands, marked, 6 1/4" d., 6 1/4" h. (minor inside paint wear) **1,900**

Lemonade set: 8" h. tankard pitcher & four cylindrical tumblers; each decorated in an abstract geometric pattern in orange, blue, purple, green & yellow, marked, the set **1,100**

Pitcher, 5 1/8" h., "Fantasque" line, squared base w/flattened spherical sides, Autumn (Balloon Trees) patt. in blue, yellow, green orange, black & purple, stamped on base "Registration Applied For Fantasque Hand Painted Bizarre by Clarice Cliff Newport Pottery England," ca. 1931, minor glaze bubbles & nicks **920**

Pitcher, 5 3/4" h., "Fantasque" line, Melon patt., wide conical body w/solid triangular handle, orange & thin black bands flanking a wide central band of stylized melons in yellow, blue, green & orange, marked, ca. 1930 (tiny glaze nicks at rim & base, faint scratch in lower orange band) **875**

Pitcher, 6 3/8" h., "Fantasque" line, footed ovoid octagonal form w/large D-form handle, Alpine patt., decorated w/trees & house in shades of orange & black w/wide border bands, marked on the base, ca. 1930 (minor glaze flakes) **1,725**

Pitcher, 7" h., 7" d., "Bizarre" ware, tapering cylindrical body w/flat rim & wide pointed spout, flattened angled handle from rim to base, Sliced Fruit patt., wide band of abstract fruit in yellow, orange & red, stamped mark **1,800**

Pitcher, 7 1/2" h., 7 1/4" d., "Bizarre" ware, My Garden patt., bulbous base below a wide cylindrical body flaring slightly at the rim, an arched bumpy branch handle in mottled purple w/long sprigs of molded green leaves at the base on the all-black matte-glazed body, ink mark (small repaired chip on handle) **413**

Pitcher, 9 3/4" h., 7 3/4" d., jug-type, "Bizarre" ware, Isis shape, Summerhouse patt., decorated w/trees & gazebos in yellow, green, purple, red & blue against an ivory ground, marked **3,900**

Pitcher, 11 1/2" h., 8 3/4" d., "Bizarre" ware, wide ringed ovoid body tapering to a wide flat round mouth, rounded C-form handle, Area patt., wide central band of stylized florals in blue, red, yellow, purple, green & black, stamped mark............. **1,050**

Pitcher, 12" h., "Bizarre" ware, Lotus shape, ringed ovoid body tapering to a wide cylindrical neck, heavy loop handle, Delecia Citrus patt., large stylized red, yellow & orange fruits around the top w/green leaves & streaky green on a cream ground **2,200**

Pitcher, 12" h., jug-form w/ovoid body w/overall fine molded banding, Lotus shape, Sunrise patt., decorated in bright yellow & orange, marked........................... **1,200**

Lotus Pitcher with Sunrise Pattern

Pitcher, 12" h., jug-form w/ovoid body w/overall fine molded banding, Lotus shape, Sunrise patt., decorated in bright yellow & orange, marked (ILLUS.) **2,800**

Plate, 8" d., "Bizarre" ware, Blue Chintz patt., stylized blue, green & pink blossom forms w/blue border band **600**

Plate, 8 3/4" d., "Bizarre" ware, Secrets patt., stylized central landscape scene w/banded borders in greens, yellow & orange, stamped mark (minor paint wear) **600**

Plate, 9" d., "Bizarre" ware, Blue Chintz patt., decorated w/stylized flowers in green, blue & pink against an ivory ground, marked **650**

Plate, 9" d., "Fantasque" line, h.p. Melon patt., a wide band of stylized fruit in yellow, orange, red, blue & green w/an orange center circle & a narrow orange rim band, ink mark (minor wear) **775**

Plate, 9 3/4" d., "Bizarre" ware, Forest Glen patt., decorated in the center w/a landscape w/cottage in green, pale blue, orange, brown & black under a marbleized streaky sky in shades of red, brown & grey on a cream ground, impressed "10/35" (ILLUS. in center w/butter dish) **600**

Plate, 10" d., "Fantasque" line, Autumn (Balloon Trees) patt. w/blue, yellow, green & purple trees & orange striped border bands, base stamped "Fantasque Hand Painted Bizarre by Clarice Cliff Newport Pottery England" (ILLUS. center left w/candleholders) **1,725**

Plate, 10 3/4" d., rounded w/four double-lobe protrusions around the sides, Sunrise patt., colorful center stylized sunrise design banded in orange & green, marked **900**

Plate, dinner, Tonquin patt., lavender **28**

Sauceboat & undertray, Tonquin patt., green, 2 pcs. **29**

Shaker, "Bizarre" ware, sharply pointed conical form, Trees and House (Alpine) patt., decorated w/orange & black borders & trees, green rooftop & grass, factory stamp on base, ca. 1930, 5 3/4" h. (minor glaze nicks, hairline in base) **1,380**

Sugar shaker, Autumn patt., sharply pointed conical form w/rows of small holes pierced around the top, decorated in pastel autumn colors, marked, 5 1/2" h. **1,200**

Sugar shaker, "Bizarre" ware, Bonjour shape, a flattened upright oval w/tiny feet across the base, Nasturium patt., stylized orange, red & yellow blossoms & pale green leaves, white at top & burnt orange at the bottom, ink mark, 1 3/4" w., 5" h. **550**

Sugar shaker, "Bizarre" ware, flattened egg-shaped body set on two tiny logform feet, Crocus patt., banded body w/a central row of stylized crocus blossoms, in yellow, blue, orange & purple, stamped mark, 2 1/2" w., 5" h. **750**

Sugar shaker, "Bizarre" ware, small footring under slender tapering ovoid body w/rounded top, Viscaria patt., stylized blossom decoration in yellow, green & brown, stamped mark, 2 3/4" d., 4 3/4" h. **850**

Banded Pattern Bonjour Shape Set

Tea for two set: cov. small teapot, creamer, open sugar, two cups & saucers & two small plates; Banded patt., Bonjour shape, brown & green bands bordering the cream body, the set (ILLUS.) **1,800**

Teapot, cov., "Bizarre" ware, inverted conical form w/angled handle & spout, glazed in shades of orange, yellow & black, stamped mark on base, ca. 1932, 4 1/4" h. (minor glaze flakes, small spout chip) **2,185**

Tumbler, Sunray patt., conical form, polychrome decoration of a stylized sun, orange banding, marked, 3" h. **600**

Vase, 5 1/4" h., "Bizarre" ware, Shape No. 341, squatty bulbous chalice-form, Delecia Citrus patt., bright fruits on a creamy ground **900**

Vase, 6 1/4" h., 3 1/4" d., "Fantasque" line, Shape No. 196, Trees and House patt., a cylindrical body w/a widely flaring & rolled rim, decorated w/a wide central landscape band in black, orange & green against an ivory ground, marked..... **1,100**

Clarice Cliff "Fantasque" Vase

Vase, 7" h., 4 1/2" h., "Fantasque" ware, slightly tapering cylindrical body w/a closed rim & thick footring, decorated w/a stylized landscape in shades of blue, green, yellow & rose on an ivory ground, marked (ILLUS.).. **770**

Vase, 7 1/2" h., 5 1/2" d., "Bizarre" ware, Inspiration patt., decorated in mottled blues, greens & purples, stamped mark **950**

Vase, 8" h., "Bizarre" ware, Isis shape, Caprice patt., stylized landscape w/hills, arch & tall trees in lavender, blue, yellow, green & brown (ILLUS. right w/bowl).. **3,800**

Vase, 8" h., "Bizarre" ware, Nasturtium patt., footed ovoid body w/a flaring rolled rim, decorated w/vivid orange, red & yellow blossoms w/black, red, yellow & green leaves atop a mottled caramel & tan ground against a white background, marked "Nasturtium - Bizarre by Clarice Cliff - Hand painted - England".................... **900**

Vase, 8" h., "Bizarre" ware, Shape No. 358, bulbous ovoid lower body tapering to a heavily ringed tapering neck, Blue Chintz patt., stylized blue, green & pink blossom forms w/blue border band **2,800**

Vase, 8" h., "Bizarre" ware, Shape No. 362, ovoid upper body above a heavy ringed & waisted base, Delecia Citrus patt., brightly painted fruits on a cream ground .. **1,200**

Vase, 8" h., "Bizarre" ware, Shape No. 386, swelled cylindrical base below the angled shoulder & tall gently flaring neck, Crocus patt., a yellow rim band & brown bottom section below a cluster of

colorful crocus blossoms on a cream ground **1,500**

Vase, 9" h., 4 1/2" d., "Bizarre" ware, baluster-shaped w/a short, wide slightly flaring neck, decorated on the upper half w/a wide band of triangles alternating w/quadrilateral blocks in blue, yellow & purple on an orange ground, Shape No. 14D, marked.. **1,800**

Vase, 9 1/2" h., 6 1/2" d., "Bizarre" ware, Isis shape, ovoid body tapering to a wide, flat rim, decorated in the Melon patt., bold stylized abstract fruits in dark red, blue, orange, green & yellow around the middle flanked by wide dark orange bands, ink mark.............................. **3,200**

Vase, 10 7/8" h., "Bizarre" ware, My Garden patt., cylindrical form tapering to flared foot decorated w/h.p. relief-molded orange & yellow flowers & black leaves on golden mushroom ground, shape No. 664, Wilkinson, Ltd. **650**

Vase, 11 3/4" h., 10" d., "Bizarre" ware, Lotus shape, Geometric patt., urn-form, handled, decorated w/a wide maroon base band & wide green neck band flanking a wide central band of triangular devices in a row in cream, purple, blue, maroon & green, blue & cream rim bands & cream handles, marked **2,900**

Vase, 12 1/4" h., gently flaring conical body on a wide round foot, molded in bold relief w/green & yellow budgie birds on a leafy branch against a light blue shaded to cream ground **410**

Clarice Cliff Crocus Vase

Vases, 8" h., "Bizarre" ware, footed ovoid body w/flared rim, Crocus patt., orange, blue & purple crocuses, green, brown & yellow bands, small glaze chip, marked, pr. (ILLUS. of one)..................................... **690**

CLEWELL WARES

Though Charles W. Clewell of Canton, Ohio, didn't operate a pottery, he is responsible for a category of fine art pottery through his development of a unique metal coating placed on pottery blanks obtained from Owens, Weller and others. By encasing objects in a thin metal shell, he produced cop-

per- and bronze-finished ceramics. Later experiments led him to chemically treat the metal coating to attain the bluish green patinated effect associated with copper and bronze. Although he produced metal-coated pottery from 1902 until the mid-1950s, Clewell's production was quite limited for he felt no one else could competently recreate his artwork and, therefore, operated a small shop with little help.

Clewell Wares Mark

Vase, 5 1/4" h., 4 1/4" d., ovoid egg-shaped body w/a wide flat mouth, raised on three small peg feet, fine verdigris & bronze patina, incised "Clewell - 411-2-6" **$550**

Vase, 5 1/2" h., 7 1/2" d., footed squatty bulbous body, the wide shoulder tapering to a cylindrical neck w/slightly flaring rim flanked by loop handles, rich deep orange to verdigris patina, etched mark **880**

Vase, 6" h., simple ovoid body w/molded rim, original green, blue & orange patina, signed "Clewell 320-24" **2,200**

Vase, 6" h., 7" w., footed squatty bulbous oblong body tapering to a short flared neck w/integral handles from the rim to the shoulders, fine verdigris & bronze patina, incised "Clewell - 408-2-6" **1,540**

Vase, 6 1/2" h., 4" d., simple ovoid form, fine verdigris & bronze patina, incised "Clewell - 32142" **715**

Vase, 7" h., footed bulbous ovoid body w/a narrow shoulder & wide flaring rim, verdigris & dark bronze patina, incised "Clewell" **1,760**

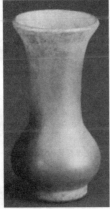

Clewell Vase

Vase, 7 1/2" h., 4 1/4" d., footed bulbous base w/trumpet form neck, copper-clad w/verdigris & bronze patina, incised "Clewell - 250-29" (ILLUS.) **605**

Vase, 9" h., urn-shaped body w/flaring rim flanked by small angled handles from shoulder to rim, rich verdigris patina, etched mark **1,210**

Vase, 9 1/2" h., 4" d., tapering cylindrical body raised on a flaring footed pedestal base, decorated w/embossed Egyptian designs under a rich brown patina, probably on an Owens Pottery blank, unmarked **495**

Vase, 11" h., simple tall ovoid body w/a rounded shoulder centered by a short rolled neck, original orange to green to blue patina, incised "Clewell 272-2-6" **1,430**

Vase, 11 1/2" h., slender ovoid body w/a short flaring neck, original drippy orange, green & blue patina, signed "Clewell 302-2-6"... **1,430**

Vase, 11 1/4" h., 8" d., large slightly flaring cylindrical body w/a narrow angled shoulder to the wide closed rim, crisp verdigris & bronze patina, incised "Clewell - 485-215".................................. **1,650**

Vase, 14 1/2" h., footed ovoid body tapering to a cylindrical neck w/flat rim, covered in a rich orange to green patina, etched mark **1,980**

Vase, 17" h., floor-type, shouldered ovoid body tapering to a short wide cylindrical neck, deep green patina, etched mark...... **1,540**

Vase, 17" h., wide bulbous ovoid body w/a narrow shoulder to the wide, short cylindrical neck w/flaring rim, original orange, brown, green & blue patina, signed "Clewell 460-26" **9,350**

Vase, 19" h., tall footed baluster-form body w/widely flared rim, original orange, green & blue patina, signed "Clewell 430-2-6"... **6,600**

COOKIE JARS

All sorts of charming and whimsical cookie jars have been produced in recent decades and these are increasingly collectible today. Many well known American potteries such as McCoy, Hull and Abingdon produced cookie jars and they are included in those listings. Below we are listing cookie jars produced by other companies. Current reference books for collectors include: The Collectors Encyclopedia of Cookie Jars *by Fred and Joyce Roerig (Collector Books, 1991);* Collector's Encyclopedia of Cookie Jars, Book II *by Fred and Joyce Roerig (Collector Books, 1994); and* The Complete Cookie Jar Book *by Mike Schneider (Schiffer, Ltd. 1991).*

AMERICAN BISQUE

Animal Crackers **$40**

Blackboard Boy (ILLUS.) **425**

Blackboard Clown **283**

Blackboard Girl (ILLUS.)............................... **288**

Blackboard Hobo **100**

Boots **120**

Bow Bear **50**

Candy Baby **80**

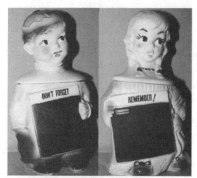

Blackboard Boy Cookie and
Blackboard Girl Cookie Jars

Carousel 50
Cat in Basket 30

Cheerleaders Cookie Jar

Cheerleaders, flasher-type (ILLUS.) 300
Chef 70
Chick with Tam 45
Churn Boy 160
Clown on Stage, flasher, green curtains 375
Collegiate Owl 45
Collegiate Owl, gold trim 150
Cookie Truck 30
Davy Crockett 245
Deer, log finial 60
Dog in Basket 40
Dutch Boy 70
Fire Chief 50
Horse, sitting position 948
Jack in Box 60
Kitten, on quilted base 145
Kitten & Beehive 30
Lady Pig, unmarked 150
Magic Bunny 80
Modern Rooster 30
Mr. Rabbit 130
Pig Dancer 133
Pirate 50
Poodle 60
Puppy 50
Rabbit with Hearts 250
Ring for Cookies, bell in lid 30
Rooster 55
Sack of Cookies 30
Sandman Cookies, kids watching TV,
   w/flasher 375
School House 40

Soldier 80
Teddy Roosevelt 80
Toothache Dog 300
Wilma on Telephone 675

BRAYTON LAGUNA POTTERY

Brayton Laguna Plaid Dog Cookie Jar

Dog, white w/yellow trim, yellow & brown
   plaid design, unmarked (ILLUS.) 450
Swedish Maiden 450

BRUSH - MCCOY

Cheerleaders, "Corner Cookie Jar, 802
   USA," flasher 400
Cinderella Pumpkin 120
Circus Horse, 1950s 875
Clown, blue pants & tie 220
Clown, brown pants 265
Clown Bust 250
Cookie House 90
Cookie House, blue & grey 65
Crock w/Cat finial 40
Davy Crockett, gold-decorated 850
Dog with Basket 250
Donkey and Cart 250
Elephant, wearing baby hat 275
Formal Pig, green hat, coat & tie 325
Granny, white w/pink apron & yellow trim 120
Happy Bunny, matte finish, white w/pink &
   yellow trim 178
Happy Bunny, white & grey w/blue neck
   scarf 140
Hen on Basket 80
Hillbilly Frog 3,900

Brush Hobby Horse Cookie Jar

Hobby Horse (ILLUS.) 950
Humpty Dumpty, brown trim 130
Lantern 50

Laughing Hippo Cookie Jar

Laughing Hippo, w/Monkey (ILLUS.) 585
Nite Owl 100
Old Shoe 100
Panda 150
Peter Pan, large 700
Pumpkin with Lock on Door 375
Siamese Cat 290
Smiling Bear 215
Squirrel on Log 90
Squirrel with Top Hat 260
Teddy Bear, feet apart 80
Three Bears 70

CALIFORNIA ORIGINALS

"Bambi" 600
Circus Wagon 50
Cookie Crocodile 90
Cookie Monster 50
Cookie Time Clock 50
Cupcake 30
Elephant 30
Elf School House 10
Ernie 60
Gum Ball Machine 50

Oscar The Grouch Cookie Jar

Oscar the Grouch (ILLUS.) 80
Pelican 50
Pinocchio (w/flake) 400

Rabbit on Safe 30
Santa Claus 200

Scarecrow Cookie Jar

Scarecrow with pumpkins, "871 USA"
   (ILLUS.) 50
Sheriff 30
Sitting Turtle 50
Small Squirrel on Stump, #2620 23
Superman 250
The Tortoise and the Hare 20
Tigger 190

METLOX

Brownie Scout Cookie Jar

Brownie Scout (ILLUS.) 750

REGAL

Churn Boy 140
Davy Crockett 350
Diaper Pin Pig 400
Dutch Girl (ILLUS.next page) 675
French Chef 375
Hobby Horse 275
Humpty Dumpty 275
Old MacDonald Barn 385

Regal Dutch Girl Cookie Jar

ROBINSON RANSBOTTOM

Chef 70
Dutch Girl 170
Hi Diddle Diddle, gold trimmed 230
Hootie Owl 50
Oscar 40
Peaches, embossed on white ground 30
Sheriff Pig 80

SIERRA VISTA

Davy Crockett Cookie Jar

Davy Crockett (ILLUS.) 900
Elephant 90
Squirrel 75

TREASURE CRAFT

Big Al, marked "Walt Disney Productions"
  around base 50
Cookie Trolley 60
Hobby Horse 50
Jackpot 50
Monk 20
Noah's Ark 70
Puppy in Basket 40
Sitting Clown 40

TWIN WINTON

Buddha, standing, brown glaze 60

Grandma Cookie Jar

Grandma (ILLUS.) 35
Hotei 45
Jack-in-the-Box 495
Ole King Cole 260

VANDOR

"Cowmen Mooranda"Cookie Jar

"Cowmen Mooranda," 1852 (ILLUS.) 260
Crocagator, head w/sunglasses 95

MISCELLANEOUS

Apple, Franciscan 295
Apple & pear, Puriton 65
Aunt Jemima, F & F Mold & Die Works 485
Bear, Gilner 30
Bear on Blocks, unmarked, Starnes of
  California 160
C3PO, original box, marked "Star Wars TM
  (c) 1977 Twentieth Century-Fox Film
  Corporation," Roman Ceramics 550
Cafe Royal, Franciscan USA 225
Cloth Doll, green polka dot dress,
  unmarked, Starnes of California................... 160
Clown, DeForest of California 40
Dove, Fredericksburg Art Pottery Co................. 30
Dutch girl (Katrina), marked "Red Wing,"
  bl. 135

Eskimo, Starnes of California 300
Hobby Horse, Gilner Pottery 120
Little Red Riding Hood, Pottery Guild 125

Mammy With Watermelon Cookie Jar

Mammy, w/watermelon, Weller (ILLUS.) 1,800
Mammy Look-A-Like National Silver 200
Mickey Mouse on Drum, Roman Ceramics 350
Monk, marked: "1964 (c) DeForest of California" 80
Monk, marked "Wm. H. Hirsch Mfg. Co. L.A. Calif. USA (c) 58" 50
Pierre chef, Red Wing, bl. 135
Pumpkin, orange, 6420 40
R2-D2, marked: "Star Wars TM (c) 1977 Twentieth Century-Fox Film Corporation," Roman Ceramics, (tiny no show chip) 185
Rabbit on cabbage, unmarked 150
Rolls Royce, Fitz & Floyd 175
Sitting pig, F & F 90
Tar Baby Shirley Corl's Kiln 320
Three Geese, Christmas decoration, B & D 45
Turkey, white 50

COORS

It was in 1908 that John J. Herold, formerly of the Owens and Roseville potteries, relocated to Golden, Colorado and, together with the Adolph Coors family, founded the Herold Pottery Company. Mr. Herold remained with the company for just two years but the firm's name didn't change until 1920 when it became the Coors Porcelain Company. One of Coors' most popular patterns, Rosebud, is widely sought by collectors today and there are several variations available but generally collectors seek them all. Original glaze colors included green, orange, rose, white (ivory), yellow and blue and today the ivory glaze seems hardest to find.

Still operating today, the Coors Ceramic Division produces items for use in chemical laboratories.

Coors Marks

Apple baker, cov., Rosebud patt., blue, 4 3/4" d., 12 oz. $70
Ashtray, square, w/advertising "COORS, GOLDEN, MALTED MILK," w/bull heads & barley decoration on corners, beige 140
Ashtray, triangular, Anholtz design 3
Bank, figural clown head, sitting or hanging-type, white, each 175
Cake plate, Rosebud patt., orange, 11" d. 65
Cake plate, thermo-porcelain, Hawthorne decal, 11 1/4" d. 75
Cake server, Rosebud patt., yellow, 10" 160
Cake server, thermo-porcelain, Floree patt., 10" 130
Casserole, cov., individual, Coorado line, orange, 2 x 2 45
Casserole, cov., Rosebud patt., blue, 2 pt. 50
Coffee maker, percolator-type, thermo-porcelain, Tulip patt., four-part w/brewing insert 250
Creamer, Rosebud patt., orange, 3" d., 7 1/2 oz. 30
Creamer & sugar bowl, porcelain w/h.p. "Herold, Gem of the Rockies," pre-1920, pr. 300
Cup & saucer, Rosebud patt., white, cup 8 oz. 65
Custard cup, Rosebud patt., maroon, 4" d., 7 oz. 15
Custard cup, thermo-porcelain, Gazebo patt., 4" d. 25
Egg cup, Rosebud patt., orange, 3" d., 6 oz. 45
Figure of monk, laughing or crying, orange, 6" h., each 325
Gravy boat, Rockmount line, red 50
Honey pot, cov., Rosebud patt., yellow, no spoon 300
Honey pot spoon/ladle, Rosebud patt., turquoise 150
Loaf pan, Rosebud patt., blue, 2 x 5 x 9 65
Malted milk crock, cylindrical w/aluminum lid, reads "COORS PURE MALTED MILK" 250
Mixing bowl w/spout & handle, Rosebud patt., yellow, 3 1/2 pt. 65
Muffin plate, cov., Rosebud patt., turquoise, 5 1/2" d. 350
Pie plate, Coorado line, yellow 60
Pitcher, cov., Rosebud patt., turquoise, 14 oz. 175
Pitcher, cov., Rosebud patt., maroon, 3 pt. 225
Pitcher, cov., jug-type, thermo-porcelain, Open Window decal, 3/4 pt. 75
Pitcher, cov., jug-type, thermo-porcelain, Chrysanthemum patt., 3 1/4 pt. 110

Plate, dessert, 6 1/4" d., Rosebud patt.,
   orange 15
Plate, 9 1/4" d., Mello-tone line, all colors,
   each 9
Plate, dinner, small, 9 1/4" d., Rosebud
   patt., yellow 28
Plate, dinner, large, 10 1/4" d., Rosebud
   patt., blue 36
Platter, 12" l., Rosebud patt., yellow 45
Ramekin, handled, Rosebud patt., maroon,
   4 1/4" d., 9 oz. 35
Refrigerator set, Rosebud patt., two bases
   w/lid, 2 x 5 x 5" 250
Salt & pepper shakers, Rosebud patt.,
   blue, 2 1/2" h., pr. 50
Salt & pepper shakers, thermo-porcelain,
   Tulip patt., 4 1/4" h., pr. 75
Salt & pepper shakers, Rosebud patt.,
   orange, 4 1/2" h., pr. 60
Salt shaker, beer bottle shape w/decal
   advertising Coors 22
Sauce dish, Rosebud patt., yellow, 5" d. 18
Soup plate w/flanged rim, Rosebud patt.,
   yellow, 8" d. 45
Sugar bowl, cov., Rosebud patt., maroon,
   4" d. 45
Teapot, cov., Rosebud patt., orange, 2-cup 275
Teapot, cov., thermo-porcelain, Open Win-
   dow decal, 5-cup 175
Teapot, cov., Rosebud patt., blue, 6-cup 225
Tumbler, footed, Rosebud patt., yellow,
   3" d., 12 oz. 225
Utility jar, w/rope handles, Rosebud patt.,
   4 1/2" d., 2 1/2 pt. 85
Vase, 6" h., grapevine design, marked
   "Coors Beer, Colorado State Fair, 1939,"
   matte white 75
Vase, 6" h., Greek key design 55
Vase, bud, 8" h., bulbous shouldered base
   w/tall slender cylindrical neck & flared
   rim 30
Vase, 10" h., Golden shape, handles form
   circle from rim to base 75
Vase, 12" h., classic form w/rope handles 125
Vase, 12" h., two-handled, Art Deco style 160

COPELAND & SPODE

W. T. Copeland & Sons, Ltd., have operated the Spode Works at Stoke, England, from 1847 to the present. The name Spode was used on some of its productions. Its predecessor, Spode, was founded by Josiah Spode about 1784 and became Copeland & Garrett in 1843, continuing under that name until 1847. Listings dated prior to 1843 should be attributed to Spode.

Copeland & Spode Mark

Bust of Music, parian, a young woman w/a
   laurel wreath in her hair, waisted circular

socle, impressed title & Copeland
   mark, ca. 1874, 13 1/2" h. (shallow chip
   to flower in her hair) **$518**

Copeland & Spode Compote

Compotes, reticulated dish on figural putti
   form standard, late 19th c., one w/dam-
   age to rim, 10" h., pr. (ILLUS. of one) **1,265**
Cups & saucers, demitasse, gilt-trimmed
   enamel floral design on pink ground, ca.
   1900, six sets 690
Dinner service: sixteen 10" d. plates, eight
   7" d. plates, ten 6" plates, ten 5" d.
   bowls, sixteen cups & saucers & one
   extra saucer, 13" l. platter, 10" l. oval
   vegetable dish (hairline); "India Tree"
   patt., each piece marked "Copeland
   Spode England India Tree," 20th c., the
   set 690
Pitcher, 9" h., ironstone, underglaze-blue
   transfer-printed floral design w/poly-
   chrome enamel, impressed "Greek 12,"
   Spode (minor wear & crazing, tip of
   spout is broken off at hinge & needs to
   be reattached) 110

Indian Tree Pattern Plate

Plate, 8 1/2" octagon, Indian Tree patt., ca.
   1890, England (ILLUS.) 140
Plates, dinner, 9 3/4" d., h.p. in iron-red
   underglaze-blue & gilt w/a central urn
   brimming w/flowers within a border of
   dense floral scrolls, fans & arched panels within a shaped brown-edged
   rim, 1815-30, "2283" pattern number
   in iron-red, set of 12 (one w/minor hairline to center, small rim chips & surface
   wear) 1,150
Tea set: cov. 8 3/4" h. teapot, cov. 5" h.
   sugar bowl & 4" h. creamer; Shanghai
   patt., the set 146

COWAN

R. Guy Cowan opened his first pottery studio in 1912 in Lakewood, Ohio. The pottery operated almost continuously, with the exception of a break during the war, at various locations in the Cleveland area until it was forced to close in 1931 due to financial difficulties.

Many of this century's finest artists began with Cowan and its associate, the Cleveland School of Art. This fine art pottery, particularly the designer pieces, are highly sought after by collectors.

Many people are unaware that it was due to R. Guy Cowan's perseverance and tireless work that art pottery is today considered an art form and found in many art museums.

One Cowan Mark

Ashtray, model of a ram, green, designed by Elizabeth Eckhardt, 5 1/4" l., 3 1/2" h. (ILLUS. lower left with ashtray/nut dish)..... **$250**

Ashtray, three section base w/figural leaping gazelle & foliage on edge, Oriental Red glaze, designed by Waylande Gregory, 5 3/4" h. 400

Cowan Ashtrays, Flower Frog & Vase

Ashtray/nut dish, model of a chick, green glaze, Shape No. 768, 3 1/2" h. (ILLUS. bottom center).. 70

Book end, model of a stylized horse, back legs raised in kicking position, black,

designed by Waylande Gregory, Shape No. E-1, 9" h. 900

Book ends, figural, model of a fish, Oriental Red glaze, Shape No. 863, 4 5/8" h., pr. 750

Book ends, figural, a nude kneeling boy & nude kneeling girl, each on oblong bases, creamy white glaze, designed by Frank N. Wilcox, Shape No. 519, Marks 8 & 9, ca. 1925, 6 1/2" h., pr. 610

Variety of Cowan Animal Pieces

Book ends, figural, model of a unicorn, front legs raised on relief-molded foliage base, orange glaze, designed by Waylande Gregory, Shape No. 961, mark No. 8, 7" h., pr. (ILLUS. left) 800

Book ends, figural, model of a ram, black, thick rectangular base w/slanted top, Shape No. E-3, designed by Waylande Gregory, 7 1/2" h., pr.................................. 2,500

Book ends, figural, a little girl standing wearing a sunbonnet & full ruffled dress, on a thick rectangular base, ivory semi-matte glaze, Shape No. 521, impressed mark & "Z," ca. 1925, 4" w., 7 1/4" h., pr. 550

Bowl, miniature, 2" d., footed, flared body, Shape No. 514, Mark No. 5, orange lustre... 45

Bowl, w/drip, 3 x 9 1/2", blue lustre finish, Shape No. 701-A.. 80

Bowl, 10" d., 2 1/2" h., Egyptian blue, Shape No. B-12... 75

Bowl, 2 1/4 x 10 1/4", blue pearl finish............. 140

Bowl, 3 x 10 x 11 1/2", leaf design, ivory & green, designed by Waylande Gregory......... 75

Bowl, 3 x 9 1/4 x 12 1/4", copper crystal glaze, Shape No. B-785-A 150

Bowl, 3 x 6 x 12 1/2" oblong, caramel w/light green glaze, Shape No. 683 50

Bowl, 3 x 8 1/2 x 16 1/4", footed shallow form, flaring scalloped sides & rim, down-curved side handles, ivory exterior w/blue interior glaze, Shape No. 743-B 120

Bowl-vase, green & gold, Shape No. B-4, 11".. 300

Buttons, decorated w/various zodiac designs, by Paul Bogatay, 50 pcs. 500

Candelabrum, "Pavlova," porcelain, two-light, Art Deco style, a footed squatty tapering central dish issuing at each side a stylized hand holding an upturned cornucopia-form candle socket, the center fitted w/a figure of a nude female dancer standing on one leg w/her other leg raised, her torso arched over & holding a long swirled drapery, Special Ivory glaze, stamped mark, 10" l., 7" h. (chip under rim of one bobeche) **248**

Candleholders, Etruscan, Oriental Red glaze, Shape No. S-6, 1 3/4" h., pr **60**

Candleholders, footed, designed by R. G. Cowan, ivory, Shape No. 811, 2 3/8" h., pr **50**

Candleholders, blue lustre finish, Shape No. 528, 3 1/2" h., pr. **35**

Candleholders, semi-circular wave design, white glaze, Shape No. 751, 4 3/4" h., pr. **90**

Various Cowan Pieces

Candlestick, flared base below twisted column, blossom-form cup, green & orange drip glaze, Shape No. 625-A, 7 3/4" h. (ILLUS. far right) **50**

Byzantine Angel Candlesticks

Candlestick, figural, Byzantine figure flanked by angels, salmon glaze, designed by R.G. Cowan, 9 1/4" h. (ILLUS. right) **400**

Candlestick, figural, Byzantine figure flanked by angels, golden yellow glaze, designed by R.G. Cowan, 9 1/4" h. (ILLUS. left) **350**

Candlestick, two-light, large figural nude standing w/head tilted & holding a swirling drapery, flanked by blossom-form candle sockets supported by scrolled leaves at the base, matte ivory glaze, designed by R.G. Cowan, Shape No. 745, 7 1/2" w., 9 3/4" h. (ILLUS.) **1,000-1,300**

Candlestick/bud vase, tapering cylindrical shape w/flared foot & rim, blue lustre, Shape 530-A, 7 1/2" h. **80**

Cowan Figural Nude Candlestick

Candlestick/bud vase, tapering cylindrical shape w/flared foot & rim, rainbow blue finish, Shape 530-A, 7 1/2" h. **50**

Candlesticks, curled form, royal blue, 1 1/2" h., pr. **45**

Candlesticks, figural grape handles, ivory glaze, 4" h., pr. **50**

Candlesticks, w/loop handle, green, Shape No. 781, 4" h., pr. **40**

Candlesticks, figural sea horse w/flared base, green, Shape No. 716, 4 3/8" h., pr. **45**

Candlesticks, "The Girl Reserve," designed by R. G. Cowan, medium blue, Shape No. 671, 5 1/2" h., pr. **300**

Candlesticks, model of a marlin on waveform base, verde green, designed by Waylande Gregory, 8" h., pr. **2,000**

Charger, "Polo" plate, incised scene w/polo players & flowers under a blazing sun, covered in a rare glossy brown & cafe-au-lait glaze, designed by Victor Schreckengost, mark Nos. 8 & 9, Shape No. X-48, impressed "V.S. - Cowan," 11 1/4" d. (grinding chips to retaining ring) **770**

Charger, wall plaque, yellow, 11 1/4" d. **150**

Charger, octagonal, hand-decorated by Thelma Frazier Winter, 13 1/4" **1,800**

Cigarette/match holder, sea horse decoration, pink, No. 726, 3 1/2 x 4" **65**

Clip dish, green, 3 1/4" d. (part of Shape PB-1) **20**

Comport, footed, square, green & white glaze, Shape No. 951, 4 1/2" sq., 2 1/4" h. **40**

Console bowl, footed, low rounded sides w/incurved rim, orange lustre, Shape No. 567-B, 2 3/4 x 9 3/4" **45**

Console bowls, 3 3/4 x 4 1/2 x 11", two-handled, footed, widely flaring fluted sides, verde green, Shape No. 538, pr. **300**

Console set: 6 1/2 x 10 1/2 x 17" bowl & pr. of candleholders; footed bowl w/figural bird handles, lobed sides, designed by Alexander Blazys, Shape No. 729, mottled blue glaze, the set **400**

Decanter w/stopper, figural King of Clubs, a seated robed & bearded man w/a large crown on his head & holding a scepter, black glaze w/gold, designed by Waylande Gregory, Shape E-4, 10" h. **1,000**

Decanter w/stopper, figural Queen of Hearts, seated figure holding scepter & wearing crown, Oriental Red glaze, designed by Waylande Gregory, Shape No. E-5, 10 1/2" h. **800**

Desk set, w/paperclip dish, Oriental Red glaze, Shape PB-1, 2 1/2 x 5 1/2", the set **125**

Cowan Figurines & Flower Frog

Figurine, "Spanish Dancer," female, white, designed by Elizabeth Anderson, Shape No. 793, 8 1/2" h. (ILLUS. right) **900**

Figurine, "Spanish Dancer," male, white, designed by Elizabeth Anderson, Shape No. 793, 8 3/4" h. (ILLUS. left) **900**

Russian Tambourine Player Figurine

Figurine, Russian peasant, "Tambourine Player," white crackle glaze, designed by Alexander Blazys, Shape No. 757-760, 9" h. (ILLUS.) **1,000**

Figurine, "Nautch Dancer," female w/a flaring pleated skirt on rectangular base, semi-matte ivory glaze w/silver accents, incised "Waylande Gregory," impressed mark, 6 3/4 x 9 1/4", 17 3/4" h. **10,450**

Figurines, "Spanish Dancer," male & female figures h.p. in polychrome glazes, the male mark No. 9, Shape No. 794-D, 8 1/4" h. & the female, mark No. 8, Shape No. 793-D, 8 1/2" h., designed by Elizabeth Anderson, impressed marks, pr. **2,530**

Flower frog, figure of a nude female, one leg kneeling on thick round base, head bent to one side & looking upward, one arm resting on knee of bent leg w/the other hand near her foot, ivory glaze, designed by Walter Sinz, 6" h. (ILLUS. left with Diver flower frog) **450**

Flower frog, figural, Art Deco nude scarf dancer, No. 35, ivory glaze, signed, 7 1/4" h. **400**

Flower frog, figural, an Art Deco dancing nude lady leaning back w/one leg raised & the ends of a long scarf held in her outstretched hands, overall white glaze, impressed mark, 7 1/2" h. **201**

Cowan Female Form Flower Frogs

Flower frog, "Diver," wave-form base w/tall wave supporting nude female figure, back arched & arms raised over head, ivory glaze, designed by R. G. Cowan, Shape No. 683, 8" h. (ILLUS. right) **900**

Flower frog, model of a deer, designed by Waylande Gregory, ivory glaze, Shape No. F-905, 8 1/4" h. (ILLUS. right with unicorn book ends) **550**

Flower frog, model of a leaping stag, relief-molded ribbed leaves in center & around base, designed by Waylande Gregory, mark Nos. 8 & 9, Shape No. 905, 1929, 8 1/2" h. **413**

Flower frog, figural Pan sitting on large toadstool, ivory glaze, designed by W. Gregory, Shape No. F-9, 9" h. (ILLUS. with ram ashtray) **1,100**

Flower frog, figural, "Swirl Dancer," Art Deco nude female dancer standing & leaning to the side, w/one hand on hip & the other holding a scarf which swirls about her, on a round lobed base w/flower holes, glossy white glaze, impressed mark, 4 1/4" d., 9 1/2" h. **1,100**

"Swirl Dancer" Flower Frog

Flower frog, figural, "Swirl Dancer," Art Deco nude female dancer standing & leaning to the side, w/one hand on hip & the other holding a scarf which swirls about her, on a round lobed base w/flower holes, ivory glaze, designed by R.G. Cowan, Shape No. 720, 10" h. (ILLUS.)..................................... **1,500**

Flower frog, "Wreath Girl," figure of a woman standing on a blossom-form base & holding up the long tails of her flowing skirt, ivory glaze, designed by R. G. Cowan, Shape No. 721, 10" h. (ILLUS. center with Diver flower frog) **900**

Flower frog, figural, modeled as a slender, leaping female dancer w/long flowing dress, curved backwards above open scrolls on a molded plinth base, ivory semi-matte glaze, stamped mark, 6 1/2" d., 10" h. (glazed over very tight crazing line to base) **2,200**

Flower frog, fluted flower-form base centered by relief-molded stalk & leaves supporting the figure of a female nude standing w/one leg bent, knee raised, leaning backward w/one arm raised overhead & the other resting on a curved leaf, ivory glaze, designed by R. G. Cowan, Shape No. F-812-X, 10 1/2" h. (ILLUS. center with Spanish Dancers) **900**

Flower frog, model of a reindeer, designed by Waylande Gregory, polychrome finish, Shape No. 903, 11" h. (ILLUS. center with unicorn book ends) **1,000**

Flower frog, figural nude w/long flowing scarf, ivory, designed by R.G. Cowan, Shape No. 687, 11 3/4" h. **900**

Flower frog, model of a flamingo, orange glaze, designed by Waylande Gregory, Shape No. D2-F, 11 3/4" h. (ILLUS.)......... **1,400**

Ginger jar, cov., orange lustre, Shape No. 583, 10" h. **500**

Cowan Flamingo Flower Frog

Lamp, candlestick-form, a disk foot & spiral-twist standard w/a flaring molded socket fitted w/an electric bulb socket, overall marigold lustre glaze, impressed mark, 11" h. **52**

Lamp, w/fittings, moth decoration, blue, 13" h., overall 22" h. **350**

Lamp base, Art Deco style, angular, green, designed by Waylande Gregory, Shape No. 821, 8 3/8" h. **195**

Cowan Lamp Base

Lamp base, round domed base below modernist teardrop-shaped body decorated w/nude female figure, ivory & brown glaze, designed by Waylande Gregory, 11" h. (ILLUS.)............................ **1,500**

Model of a bird on wave, Egyptian blue, designed by Alexander Blazys, Shape No. 749-A, 12" h. (ILLUS. next page)........ **1,500**

Model of a ram, Oriental Red glaze, designed by Edris Eckhart, 3 1/2" h. **240**

Model of elephant, standing on square plinth, head & trunk raised, rich mottled Oriental Red glaze, designed by Margaret Postgate, ca. 1930, faint impressed mark on plinth & paper label reading "X869 Elephant designed by M....et P....," 10 1/2" h. **4,620**

Bird on Wave Model

Pen base, maroon, Shape No. PB-2, 3 3/4"..... **100**
Pitcher, 8 3/4" h., foliage decoration **300**
Plaque, terradatol, designed by Alexander Blazys, Egyptian blue, Shape No. 739, 15 1/2" **1,000**
Strawberry jar w/saucer, Oriental Red glaze, designed by R.G. Cowan, Shape No. SJ-1, mark No. 8, 7 1/2" h., 2 pcs. **450**
Trivet, round, center portrait of young woman's face encircled by a floral border, white on blue ground, impressed mark & "Cowan," 6 5/8" d. (minor staining from usage) **303**

Cowan Lakeware Urn and Vases

Urn, Lakeware, blue, Shape V-102, 5 1/2" h. (ILLUS. left).................................... **100**
Vase, 4" h., bulbous ovoid tapering to cylindrical neck, Jet Black glaze, Shape No. V-5 (ILLUS. center with urn)......................... **300**
Vase, 4" h., waisted cylindrical body w/bulbous top & wide flaring rim, mottled orange glaze, Shape No. 630 (ILLUS. second from left w/No. 625-A candlestick)... **80**
Vase, 4 1/4" h., mottled green, Shape No. V-54... **75**
Vase, 4 3/4" h., bulbous body w/horizontal ribbing, wide cylindrical neck, mottled turquoise glaze, Shape No. V-30 .... **80**
Vase, 4 3/4" h., waterfall, designed by Paul Bogatay, maroon, hand-decorated, Shape No. V-77... **700**
Vase, 4 3/4" h., wide tapering cylindrical body, mottled orange, brown & rust,

Shape No. V-34 (ILLUS. second from right w/No. 625-A candlestick) **80**
Vase, 5" h., fan-shaped, designed by R.G. Cowan, golden yellow, Shape No. V-801....... **70**
Vase, 5 1/2" h., footed wide semi-ovoid body w/flaring rim, dark bluish green, Shape 575-A, mark No. 4.............................. **50**
Vase, 5 1/2" h., orange lustre, Shape No. 608 .... **40**
Vase, 6 1/4" h., six-sided w/stepped neck, blue rainbow glaze, Shape No. 546 .... **75**
Vase, 6 1/2" h., footed, squatty bulbous base w/trumpet-form neck, flattened sides w/notched corners, green glaze, Shape No. V-649-A (ILLUS. right w/urn)...... **150**
Vase, 6 1/2" h., wide bulbous body, yellow glaze, Shape V-91..................................... **650**
Vase, 7" h., fan-shaped w/scalloped foot & domed base decorated w/relief-molded sea horse decoration, pink glaze, Shape No. 715-A **60**
Vase, 7" h., footed bulbous base, the narrow shoulder tapering to tall wide cylindrical neck, Oriental Red glaze, Shape No. V-79 .... **250**
Vase, 7" h., Lakeware, bulbous base w/trumpet-form neck, Oriental Red glaze, Shape No. V-75 .... **90**
Vase, 7 1/2" h., tall slender ovoid body w/short cylindrical neck, orange lustre, Shape No. 552 (ILLUS. lower right w/ ram ashtray) **90**
Vase, 8" h., bulbous body tapering to cylindrical neck w/flaring rim, gold, Shape No. V-932 (ILLUS. far left w/No. 625-A candlestick) **200**
Vase, 8" h., footed bulbous body w/trumpet-form neck, yellow shading to green drip glaze, Shape No. 627 (ILLUS. top center w/No. 625-A candlestick) **250**
Vase, 8" h., 8" d., wide bulbous body w/narrow molded rim, embossed w/a band of stylized leaves and covered in a Persian blue crackled glaze, Shape No. V-61, impressed mark... **880**
Vase, 8 1/4" h., "Logan," footed, compressed bulbous base w/trumpet-form neck, flattened sides w/notched corners, decorative side handles, designed by R.G. Cowan, caramel glaze or Egyptian blue glaze, Shape No. 649-B, each **200**

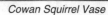

Cowan Squirrel Vase

Vase, 8 1/2" h., bulbous ovoid form decorated w/relief-molded squirrel & foliage, designed by Waylande Gregory, green, Shape No. V-19 (ILLUS.) **850**

Vase, 8 3/4" h., Lakeware, green, Shape No. V-71 .... **100**

Vase, 11 1/4" h., Chinese Bird patt., footed urn shape w/relief-molded birds at base, tan & brown crystalline glaze, impressed mark , Shape No. V-747 (small stilt pull on bottom not visible from side) **880**

Cowan Chinese Bird Vase

Vase, 11 1/4" h., Chinese Bird patt., footed urn shape w/relief-molded birds at base, green glaze, designed by R.G. Cowan, Shape No. V-747 (ILLUS.) **950**

Vase, 11 1/2" h., 6 1/2" w., Chinese Bird patt., a fanned & lightly ribbed upper body above a large stylized exotic long-tailed bird at the bottom resting on an oblong scalloped foot, covered in in a Jade Green glaze, stamped mark **495**

Vase, 11 3/4" h., blue lustre, Shape No. 691-C **250**

Vase, 11 3/4" h., two-handled, flared foot below tall slender fluted ovoid body w/cylindrical neck, orange lustre, Shape No. 652-B, Mark No. 8 .... **300**

Vase, 12 1/4" h., footed bulbous body tapering to wide cylindrical neck, green crystalline glaze, designed by Arthur E. Baggs, Shape No. V-47 .... **1,800**

Vase, 13" h., swelled cylindrical body w/a narrow shoulder to the short cylindrical wide neck covered in a lustered grey & yellow dripping glaze, mark No. 7, Shape No. 552, stamped ink mark **825**

Vase, 13 1/2" h., baluster-form body w/flaring rim, light blue glaze, Shape No. 563 ..... **275**

Wine cups, Oriental Red glaze, Shape No. X-17, 2 1/2" h., each **45**

CZECHOSLOVAKIAN

Czechoslavakia did not exist until the end of World War I in 1918. The country was put together with parts of Austria, Bohemia and Hungary as a reward for the help of the Czechs and the Slovakis in winning the war. In 1993 Czechoslovakia split and became two countries: the Czech Republic and the Slovak Republic. Items are highly collectable because the country was in existence only 75 years. For a more thorough study of the subject, refer to the following books: Made in Czechoslavakia Books 1 and 2 by Ruth A. Forsythe; Czechoslavakian Glass & Collectibles Books I and II by Dale & Diane Barta and Helen M. Rose and Czechoslovakian Perfume Bottles and boudoir Accessories by Jacquelyne Y. Jones North.

Baby plate, divided, white w/colorful nursery rhyme scene of Humpty Dumpty in each section, 7 1/4" d. **$125**

Bank, figural, model of a pear, shaded yellow & peach, green stem finial, Erphila, 5 1/4" h. **75**

Basket w/overhead handle, cream ground w/figural blue bird by handle, 4 1/2" h. **48**

Basket w/overhead handle, yellow basketweave exterior w/band of flowers at rim, 5 1/4" h. **38**

Basket w/overhead handle, purple, tan & blue, majolica, Eichwald, 7 1/2" h. **185**

Basket w/overhead handle, flared foot, center portrait decoration within narrow band of white & rust dots & similar band at rim, band of white & rust hearts on foot w/blue & rust leaf design on overhead handle & side handles, rust ground, Amphora, 12" h. **350**

Book ends, figural mountain climbers in tan, green & brown on grey rock form base, 6 1/4" h., pr. **125**

Bowl, 4'" l., oval, handled, green ground **165**

Art Deco Bowl

Bowl, 4 1/4" d., flower & fruit decoration in red, green, brown, blue on yellow ground, (Peasant Art Industries), P.A.I. (ILLUS.) **225**

Art Deco Style Covered Box

Box, cov., center band of Art Deco style painted under glaze flowers & fruit in red, blue & green on cream ground, cover decorated w/flowers & fruit, button finial, P.A.I., 5" h. (ILLUS.) **260**

Candleholder, hanging-type, flattened oblong form w/pink, blue & green floral design on black ground, bulbous base holding candle socket, black w/blue & red center medallion, orange trim, majolica, 9" h. **95**

Canister, cov., "Coffee," border design w/single pink rose & gold trim on white ground, 7 1/2" h... 45

Canister, cov., "Coffee," red ground w/slip floral decoration in yellow, blue, lavender & green & black on white ground, 7 1/2" h.. 75

Cookie jar, cov., cylindrical w/rattan-wrapped swing handle, Silhouette patt., Erphila, 7 1/2" h... 175

Creamer, footed bulbous body, blue shading to brown, figural moose head forms spout, antlers form rim, 3 1/4" h. 45

Creamer, tan & brown, 3 1/2" h.......................... 20

Creamer, figural, model of a duck, green, brown & yellow, 4" h.................................... 60

Creamer, figural, model of a parrot, orange, 4 1/2" h.. 55

Creamer, figural, model of a sitting cow, tail forms handle, brown, 4 1/2" h. 65

Creamer, figural, model of a walking cow, tail forms handle, brown, 6" h...................... 125

Creamer & cov. sugar bowl, figural, model of a strawberry, shaded red w/green handles, strawberry finial on sugar bowl cover, 4" h., pr........................... 100

Dinner set: service for eight together w/all serving pieces; Eden patt., octagonal shape w/floral border & center scene of exotic birds on branches, the set 650

Dish, cov., oval, blue w/figural tan & blue duck w/yellow bill on cover, 3" h.................... 75

Dish, cov., figural, model of a crab, red, 3 1/2".. 50

Dish, cov., figural, model of a potato, brown w/yellow butter pat-shaped finial, 4 1/4" h. 65

Egg cup, Chintz patt. 80

Dancing Couple Figure Group

Figure group, dancing couple, the woman w/blue & white dress w/gold trim, the man w/greyish blue trousers, white shirt, orange vest & brown hat w/ribbons, 5 1/2" h. (ILLUS.)... 85

Figure of woman, 1920's lady, light green, 11 1/2" h. 350

Flower frog, figural, model of a parrot on a stump, blue & yellow, 5 1/2" h. 40

Flower frog, figure of nude standing on a turtle, 10 1/2" h. 375

Jardiniere, cylindrical body w/side ring handles, decorated w/airbrushed blue & red cherries, Erphila, 4 1/4" h......................... 85

Lamp base, footed wide bulbous base w/shoulder tapering to flaring cylindrical neck w/tapering domed top, center dec-

orated w/wide tan & gold checked band flanked by narrow bands of pink roses & oval white medallion w/vase filled w/pink roses, green ground, 5 1/2" h......................... 85

Lamp base, tapering cylindrical body w/flaring foot, decorated overall w/Art Deco type blue, red & yellow flowers & fruit, wide black band at top & narrow red & black band at foot, Peasant Art Industries, 7 1/2" h. 225

Lamp base, "World," spherical body w/flaring foot, relief-molded countries in shades of blue on mottled yellow ground, Amphora, 9 1/2" h. 650

Model of a horse, blue w/white trim, 4" h. 75

Model of a parrot, blue & green, on white globe pedestal, 8 1/2" h.............................. 275

Model of Pheasant

Model of a pheasant, orange, blue, yellow & grey, on white oblong base, 4 1/2" h. (ILLUS.)... 150

Model of a zebra, standing w/neck & head thrust backward, brown & grey w/dark green curly mane & tail, 6 1/2" h. 150

Napkin ring, figural, sitting girl, pink & green w/yellow bonnet, Erphila, 4" h.............. 45

Pipe holder, figural Chinese man, yellow & brown, 4 1/4" h. 50

Pitcher, 6" h., figural woman, red & white 85

Pitcher, 6 1/2" h., decorated w/scene of couple w/sheep, brown ground 85

Pitcher, cov., 7" h., bulbous body w/flattened side w/large loop handle from rim to base, fruit & flower decoration, P.A.I........ 295

Art Deco Style Ram Goat

Pitcher, 8 1/2" h., figural Art Deco style ram goat, yellow w/red & black trim, horn forms handle (ILLUS.) 650

Plate, dinner, 9 1/2" d., red lobster & crab design on border, white ground..................... 35

Salt box, cov., border design w/single pink rose, gold trim on white ground, 6" h.............. 95

Salt & pepper shakers, figural, model of a lobster, red, 2 1/2" h., pr................................ 25

Salt & pepper shakers, figural, "Bashful Boy & Girl," brown & white, 3 1/4" h., pr. 30

Sauceboat, figural, model of a lobster, red, 3 1/4" h. 55

Snack plate w/cup, diamond-shaped, 8 1/4" plate w/cup well, blue & tan luster, the set 55

Sugar bowl, cov., figural, model of a swan, neck forms spout, C-scroll handle, button finial, white w/red bill, 3 1/4" h. 75

Teapot, creamer & cov. sugar bowl, stacking-type, decorated overall w/red, green & blue flowers on white ground, 5 1/2" h. 275

Tile, h.p. cottage scene, brown & tan, 6" sq. 45

Scenic Urn-vase

Urn-vase, bottle-form base, angled handles from shoulder to base of bulbous bowl-shaped upper section w/scalloped & flared rim, decorated w/desert scene w/camels, 5 1/2" h. (ILLUS.) 45

Urns, portrait decoration, blue & gold, 7" h., pr. 270

Vase, 5 1/2" h., slightly swelled cylindrical body w/flared rim, angled D-form shoulder handles, decorated w/bust portrait of woman on brown ground 40

Yellow Luster Vase

Vase, 5 1/2" h., tapering cylindrical form w/cupped rim, flanked by black C-form angled handles, yellow luster finish (ILLUS.) 15

Vase, 7" h., bulbous ovoid body, decorated w/multicolored flowers & geometric designs, white ground, blue rim, Amphora 200

Vase, 7 1/2" h., fan-shaped, blue, white & orange paisley type design 235

Vase, 7 1/2" h., footed bulbous base w/wide tapering neck w/flared rim, flower & fruit motif, green ground, P.A.I. 165

Vase, 8" h., footed, slender ovoid body w/flared rim flanked by scrolled handles, Silhouette patt., scene of girl w/sheep, Erphila 95

Vase, 10" h., six-sided tapering form w/flared foot & rim, slip-decorated design in orange & blue 325

Large Scenic Vase

Vase, 10 1/4" h., footed ovoid body tapering slightly to wide cylindrical neck, angled handles from shoulder to rim, decorated w/sunset scene of house w/colorful garden in foreground, brown & tan (ILLUS.) 145

Vase, 11 1/4" h., waisted cylindrical body, decorated w/scene of storks near water, tan, black, brown, orange & light blue, tan ground w/dark green C-form handles, Amphora 400

Wall pocket, figural, red, orange, white & blue bird beside brown birdhouse in tan Y-shaped branch, 6" h. 60

Wall pocket, figural white, yellow & blue bird w/white seashell, luster finish, 6" h. 70

Wall pocket with Woodpecker

Wall pocket, figural, woodpecker in tan, orange, yellow & blue on side of tan tree branch, 6 1/2" h. (ILLUS.) 70

Wall pocket, conical, decorated w/large
red flower w/yellow center, green leaves,
white ground, 7" h. 85

Wall pocket, conical, fruit & flower decoration on green ground, P.A.I., 8" h. 125

Wall pocket, Amphora portrait-type,
8 1/2" h. 250

Watering can, decorated w/lavender flowers on white ground, 4 1/2" h. 45

Watering can, orange flowers & green
leaves on white ground, 7" h. 145

DEDHAM & CHELSEA KERAMIC ART WORKS

*This pottery was organized in 1866 by Alexander
W. Robertson in Chelsea, Massachusetts, and
became A. W. & H. Robertson in 1868. In 1872, the
name was changed to Chelsea Keramic Art Works
and in 1891 to Chelsea Pottery, U.S.A. About 1895,
the pottery was moved to Dedham, Massachusetts,
and was renamed Dedham Pottery. Production
ceased in 1943. High-fired colored wares and
crackle ware were specialties. The rabbit is said to
have been the most popular decoration on crackle
ware in blue.*

*Since 1977, the Potting Shed, Concord, Massa-
chusetts, has produced quality reproductions of
early Dedham wares. These pieces are carefully
marked to avoid confusion with original examples.*

Dedham & ChelseaKeramic Art Works Marks

Boot, swan design, blue stamp, 4" w., 5" h.
....$1,093

Bowl, 4 1/2" d., swan design, blue registered stamp 460

Bowl, square, swan design, blue registered
stamp, 8 1/4 x 8 1/4" sq., 2 3/4" h. 920

Bowl, 7 1/2" d., 2 1/2" h.,Turtle patt., flat
rim, several small chips to edge, ink
stamp mark (ILLUS.) 660

Bowl w/spoon, 5 3/8" d., 2 1/8" h., cereal,
Rabbit patt., Chinese spoon w/rabbit
decoration, both w/ink stamp mark, the
set 413

Candlesticks, elephant design, blue
stamp, initials "A.R.," 2" h., the pair............. 978

Centerpiece bowl, Rabbit patt., ink stamp
mark, 3 x 12" (peppering to glaze) 523

Creamer, elephant design, blue registered
stamp, 3" w., 3" h. 1,265

Cup & saucer, grape design, blue registered stamp, 6" d., 2 3/4" h. 173

Cup & saucer, Owl patt., blue registered
stamp, 6 1/4" d., 2 1/2" h. 1,955

Dedham Turtle Pattern Bowl

Cup & saucer, snow tree design, blue registered stamp, 6" d. 173

Cup & saucer, Rabbit patt., ink stamp
mark, cup 2 1/4" h. 193

Dish, 7 1/4" d., Rabbit patt., star-shaped,
blue registered stamp, two impressed
rabbits 374

Dish, oyster shell-shaped, decorated w/a
free-hand painted blue rabbit, blue ink
stamp mark, 4 1/2" w.......................... 193

Egg cup, elephant design, blue stamp,
3 1/2" d., 3" h.............................. 1,380

Flower holder, standing bunny, hint of blue
stamp, 4 1/4" d., 6 1/4" h. 1,150

Oyster dishes, modeled as an oyster half-
shell w/a small molded blue-glazed
pearl, ink stamp mark, 4 1/2" l., pr............. 660

Paperweight, model of turtle, blue registered stamp, 2 1/4" w., 3 1/4" l. 1,035

Pitcher, 4 3/4" h., 6 1/4" d., grape design,
blue registered stamp......................... 259

Pitcher, 6" h., 6 1/4" w., Oak Block design,
blue registered stamp......................... 978

Pitcher, 6 1/4" h., 7" d., rabbit design, blue
registered stamp 575

Dedham Plates

Plate, 6" d., Horse Chestnut patt. border,
blue mark & one foreshortened rabbit,
early 20th c. (ILLUS. right) 173

Plate, 6" d., dolphin design, blue registered
stamp, two impressed rabbits, blue numbers 518

Plate, 6 1/4" d., chick design, blue stamp, one impressed rabbit................................. **2,415**

Plate, 6 1/4" d., Lily patt., central lily decoration w/"o" mark on stem, decorated by Maude Davenport, blue mark & one foreshortened rabbit, early 20th c. (ILLUS. left) **1,150**

Plate, 6 1/2" d., strawberry raised design, signed Jacob................................. **2,415**

Plate, 7 1/2" d., Crab patt. **575**

Plate, 8 1/2" d., Crab patt. **374**

Plate, 8 1/2" d., day lily design, blue stamp... **1,093**

Plate, 8 1/2" d., Duck patt................................. **230**

Plate, 8 1/2" d., Lobster patt. (rim glaze imperfection) **345**

Plate, 8 3/4" d., grouse design, blue stamp, one impressed rabbit (glaze pitting to edge surface) **2,875**

Plate, 10" d., crab design, blue stamp, one impressed rabbit................................. **1,093**

Plate, 10" d., dinner, Rabbit patt., decorated by Maude Davenport, ink stamp mark (small glaze nick on edge of rim) **303**

Plate, 10" d., Horse Chestnut patt. **86**

Plate, 10 1/4" d., Cloverleaf patt., rim w/experimental greenish glaze on molded cloverleaf design, interior blue accent band w/circular greenish glazed dots, Chelsea Keramic Art Works cipher mark, ca. 1891 .... **920**

Plate, 12" d., wolves & owl design, blue stamp (three tight hairlines, peppering)..... **2,300**

Platter, 12" d., round dished form w/wide flanged rim, Grape patt., marked **201**

Platter, 13" oval, dolphin design, blue registered mark, one impressed rabbit.......... **2,760**

Teapot, Rabbit patt., blue registered stamp, 7" w., 5 1/2" h. **920**

Toothpick holder, floral design, obscured blue stamp, 2 3/4" d., 2 3/4" h. **1,150**

Tureen, cov., Rabbit patt., blue stamp, 11" w., 8" h................................. **2,645**

Tureen, cov., Turkey patt., blue stamp, 9" d., 5 3/4" h................................. **2,300**

Azalea Pattern Tureen

Tureen, cov., Azalea patt., blue stamp, 9 1/2" d., 5 3/4" h. (ILLUS.) **920**

Vase, 5 3/4" h., terra cotta, classical urn-form w/two applied leaf-form handles, ca. 1880, impressed Chelsea Keramic Art Works cipher (firing cracks to base & handles) **633**

Vase, 6 1/4" h., iris design, cylindrical form, blue stamp, impressed "C.K.A.W."............ **1,840**

Vase, 8 1/2" h., 5" d., tapering cylindrical form, incised "Dedham Pottery," initialed "B.W."................................. **3,105**

Vase, 8 1/2" h., 9 1/2" d., spherical form w/extended raised rim & tapered base,

glossy mottled sea green glaze, modeled by Hugh Robertson, incised "Dedham Pottery 10.11.96 H.C.R. 3016B" (in-the-making glaze chips near base) **2,070**

DELFT

In the early 17th century Italian potters settled in Holland and began producing tin-glazed earthenwares, often decorated with pseudo-Oriental designs based on Chinese porcelain wares. The city of Delft became the center of this pottery production and several firms produced the wares throughout the 17th and early 18th century. A majority of the pieces featured blue on white designs, but polychrome wares were also made. The Dutch Delftwares were also shipped to England and eventually the English copied them at potteries in such cities as Bristol, Lambeth and Liverpool. Although still produced today, Delft peaked in popularity by the mid-18th century.

Bowl, 10" d., 5 3/4" h., footed, tapering sides w/wide flat rim, polychrome floral design, monogram mark, England (minor wear & chips on base) **$2,200**

Charger, round w/wide flanged rim, scattered colored floral clusters in the Fazackerly palette, Liverpool, England, 18th c., 13 1/2" d. (edge chips, spider crack) **715**

Charger, round, decorated in blue, green & yellow w/the two figures on either side of a blue-sponged tree heavily laden w/yellow fruit & w/the serpent's head appearing in the lower branches, yellow & blue border & blue-dash rim, ca 1700-10, Bristol, England, 11 3/4" d. (crack)........... **4,600**

Charger, round w/wide flanged rim, polychrome full-length portrait of King William standing in a sparse landscape & flanked by initials "W R" within a double line manganese border, ca. 1690, London, 13 1/4" d. (repaired) **5,750**

Flower brick, rectangular, h.p. blue floral decoration, England, mid-18th c., 5" l. (rim & edge chips, glaze loss) **374**

Mantel garniture set: two covered baluster-form vases w/domed covers & two trumpet-form tall vases; each w/a scallop-framed blue-decorated landscape cartouche, England, 18th c., cov. vases 10" h., other vases 8" h., the set (rim chips & glaze flakes, repaired chips throughout, glaze wear & rim restorations) **1,725**

Models of cats, each seated on a grassy mound base, wearing a yellow collar w/red spots, their white coats decorated w/red & blue markings, blue whiskers & eyes, ca. 1700, Holland, 4" h., facing pr. .. **3,450**

Pill slab, canted rectangular form, painted in blue w/arms of the Apothecary's Guild of London above a ribbon inscribed "Opiferque, Per; Orbem, Dicor," ca. 1760-80, England, 12" h. (small rim chips & glaze flaking) **9,200**

Plate, 8 5/8" d., polychrome, probably Bristol, inscribed in center w/initials "N*L*M" above date "1736" within a band of stylized plants, paneled border rim, England, 1736, (areas of glaze lost to back rim) **2,300**

Plate, 8 1/2" d., half-length portraits of King William & Queen Mary in blue & yellow flanked by initials "W M R" in center surrounded by two narrow blue bands, ca. 1690, England (restoration to rim, cracks)... **6,325**

Plate, 8 3/4" d., painted in blue w/initials "N G H" within a scrolled cartouche flanked by griffins & surmounted by a crown, dated "1693" (restored chip & small glaze flakes to rim) **977**

Lambeth Delftware Polychrome Plates

Plates, 9" d., polychrome, of Ann Gomm type, stylized plants in green, yellow, pink & blue, each inscribed within a central medallion "Mary Johnson" & dated "1793," Lambeth, England, pr. (ILLUS.) **4,312**

Posset pot, cov., bulbous body w/loop handles, domed cover, painted in red, green & blue w/dense pattern of flowers & foliage, interior & cover both inscribed "R E," ca. 1710, 9 1/4" h. (minor glaze chips to rims)... **5,750**

Punch bowl, 5 1/2 x 12 3/4," polychrome, painted in orange & blue w/stylized vases of flowers within laurel wreath borders, Holland, mid-18th c. (restored crack) **2,012**

Punch bowl, exterior densely painted in red, green & blue w/stylized flower sprigs & florets within a sawtooth border, interior painted in blue w/stylized tulips, all between narrow blue bands at rim & foot, ca. 1740, possibly England, 12 1/4" d. (restored crack to side, chips to foot) **4,887**

Tobacco jar, cov., ovoid form, inscribed "Rappe de St. Vincent No. 7" within a shaped cartouche flanked by tobacco smoking native figures, with brass 'beehive' lid, 18th c., 10 3/4" h. (restored)........ **2,587**

Water bottle, bulbous body tapering to slender cylindrical neck w/everted rim, decorated in blue w/a bird in a tree above peonies & rockwork below a diaper border, ca. 1770, probably Liverpool, England, 9 1/8" h. (restoration to neck & rim) **1,035**

DERBY & ROYAL CROWN DERBY

William Duesbury, in partnership with John and Christopher Heath, established the Derby Porcelain Works in Derby, England about 1750. Duesbury soon bought out his partners and in 1770 purchased the Chelsea factory and six years later, the Bow works. Duesbury was succeeded by his son and grandson. Robert Bloor purchased the business about 1814 and managed successfully until illness in 1828 left him unable to exercise control. The "Bloor" Period, however, extends from 1814 until 1848, when the factory closed. Former Derby workmen then resumed porcelain manufacture in another factory and this nucleus eventually united with a new and distinct venture in 1878 which, after 1890, was known as Royal Crown Derby.

A variety of anchor and crown marks have been used since the 18th century.

Derby & Royal Crown Derby Marks

Royal Crown Derby Coffee Set

Coffee set: cov. 10 3/4" h. coffeepot, hot milk pitcher, twenty large egg cups, twenty small cake plates, twenty coffee cups & saucers, a lozenge-shaped dish, a two-handled oval tray & two two-handled serving dishes; decorated w/floral reserves, blue & gilt trim borders, decorated by A. Gregory & gilt by G.W. Darlington, artist-signed, gilt printed factory marks, Royal warrant & Tiffany & Co., New York retailer's mark, impressed "DERBY," ca. 1907-09, the set (ILLUS. of part).. **$57,500**

Desk set, rectangular tray set on paw feet & mounted w/pen tray & three covered pots, domed covers w/pointed finials, floral decoration, early 19th c., red factory mark, tray 8 1/2" l., the set (ILLUS.) **1,035**

Dessert plates, eleven 9 1/4" d. plates & three footed 9 1/2" plates, each painted w/different foliate sprays, last quarter 19th c., wear, the set **2,415**

Royal Crown Derby Desk Set

Model of peacock, the colorful bird on a base w/colorful foliage, factory marks, 20th c. (minor chip) 230

Plates, 8 3/4" d., shaped scalloped rim w/a cobalt blue band & gilt floral decoration, the center h.p. w/birds in landscapes, artist-signed by Charles Harris, Royal Crown Derby, ca. 1898, set of 12 3,738

Vase, cov., footed bottle-shaped form w/tall cylindrical neck w/fitted cylindrical cap-type cover, Imari-style decoration, ca. 1800, 10 1/4" h. 728

DOULTON & ROYAL DOULTON

Doulton & Co., Ltd., was founded in Lambeth, London, about 1858. It was operated there till 1956 and often incorporated the words "Doulton" and "Lambeth" in its marks. Pinder, Bourne & Co., Burslem was purchased by the Doultons in 1878 and in 1882 became Doulton & Co., Ltd. It added porcelain to its earthenware production in 1884. The "Royal Doulton" mark has been used since 1902 by this factory, which is still in production. Character jugs and figurines are commanding great attention from collectors at the present time.

Royal Doulton Mark

ANIMALS & BIRDS

Cat, Persian Cat, seated, black & white, HN 999, 5" h. $185

Dog, Bulldog, HN 1044, small, 3 1/4" h. 350

Dog, Cocker Spaniel, large, HN 1002 325

Dog, Dalmation Ch. 'Goworth Victor,' HN 1114, 4 1/4" h. 175

Dog, French Poodle, HN 2631, white w/pink, grey & black markings, 5 1/4" h. 125

Dogs, Terrier Puppies in a Basket, three white puppies w/light & dark brown markings, brown basket, HN 2588, 1941-85, 3" h. 145

Penguin, K 23, 1 1/2" h., grey, white & black, green patches under eyes 170

CHARACTER JUGS

'Ard of 'Earing, large, D 6588, 7 1/2" h. 1,210

'Arriet, large, D 6208, 6 1/2" h. 250

Captain Henry Morgan, miniature, 2 1/4" h. 65

Captain Hook, large, D 6597, 7 1/4" h. 570

Dick Whittington, large, D 6375, 6 1/2" h. 500

Don Quixote, large, D 6455, 7 1/4" h. 85

Large Drake

Drake, large, D 6115, 5 3/4" h. (ILLUS.) 175

Fortune Teller, miniature, D 6523, 2 1/2" h. 475

Gaoler, large, D 6570, 7 1/2" h. 99

Gladiator, large, D 6650, 7 3/4" h. 508

Gondolier, large, D 6589, 8" h. 663

Granny, large, toothless, D 5521, 6 1/4" h. 880

Groucho Marx, large, D 6710, 7" h. 140

London Bobby, large, D 6744, 7" h. 93

Long John Silver, large, D 6335, 7" h. 135

Night Watchman, large, D 6569, 7" h. 135

Porthos, large, D 440, 7 1/4" h. 110

Regency Beau, large, D 6559, 7 1/4" h. 915

Robin Hood, 2nd version, large, D 6527, 7 1/2" h. 75

Sairey Gamp, large, No. 5451, 6 1/4" h. 100

Scaramouche, large, first version, D 6558, 7" h. 935

Witch (The), large, D 6893, 7" h. 245

DICKENSWARE

Bowl, 9" d., 4 1/8" h., Coaching Days series, street scenes 127

Plates, 10 3/8'" d., each w/a color scene, one titled "Alfred Jingle," the other "Sergeant Buzfuz," pr. 165

Coaching Days Series Jardiniere

Jardiniere, Coaching Days series, street scene, signed "NOKE," 10" w., 8 1/2" h. (ILLUS.) 330

FIGURINES

Abdullah, HN 2104, multicolored, 1953-62...... **480**

Anna, HN 2802, purple & white, Kate Greenaway Series, 1976-82 .... **138**

Autumn Breezes

Autumn Breezes, HN 1911, green & pink, 1939-76 (ILLUS.).. **173**

Balloon Man (The), HN 1954, black & grey, 1940 to present **200**

Belle O' the Ball, HN 1997, red & white, 1947-79 .... **275**

Blithe Morning, HN 2021, mauve & pink dress, 1949-71 .... **168**

Blithe Morning, HN 2065, blue & pink dress, 1949-71 .... **195**

Blithe Morning, HN 2065, red dress, 1950-73 .... **225**

Bonnie Lassie

Bonnie Lassie, HN 1626, red dress, 1934-53 (ILLUS.).. **350**

Boy from Williamsburg, HN 2183, blue & pink, 1969-83 .... **150**

Bridesmaid (The Little), HN 2196, white dress, pink trim, 1960-76............................. **90**

Bridget, HN 2070, green, brown & lavender, 1951-73.. **275**

Carolyn, HN 2112, white & green flowered dress, 1953-65 .... **325**

Country Lass (A), HN 1991A, blue, brown & white, 1975-81 .... **123**

Diana, HN 1716, pink & blue, 1935-49............. **350**

Ermine Coat (The), HN 1981, white & red, 1945-67 .... **230**

Fair Lady, HN 2193, green, 1963 to present **160**

Fair Lady, HN 2835, coral pink, 1977 to present **175**

Fatboy (The), HN 2096, blue & cream, 1952-67 .... **360**

Flora, HN 2349, brown & white, 1966-73 .... **425**

Friar Tuck, HN 2143, brown, 1954-65 .... **450**

Genieve and Her Ladyship

Genevieve, HN 1962, red, 1941-75 (ILLUS.)... **250**

Harlequin, HN 2186, blue, 1957-69 .... **250**

Her Ladyship, HN 1977, red & cream, 1945-59 (ILLUS.)..................................... **275**

Invitation, HN 2170, pink, 1956-75 .... **115**

Judith, HN 2089, red & blue, 1952-59 .... **295**

Lady Charmian, HN 1948, green dress, red shawl, 1940-73.................................... **185**

Lady Charmian, HN 1949, red dress w/green shawl, 1940-75 .... **195**

Lobster Man (The), HN 2317, blue, grey & brown, 1964 to present **125**

Maureen and Roseanna

Maureen, HN 1770, pink dress, 1936-59 (ILLUS.)... **250**

Midinette, HN 2090, blue dress, 1952-65 .... **258**

Miss Muffet, HN 1936, red, 1940-67.............. **165**

Noelle, HN 2179, orange, white & black, 1957-67 .... **375**

Old Meg, HN 2494, blue & grey matte finish, 1974-76 .... **250**

Omar Khayyam, HN 2247, brown, 1965-83..... **155**

Owd Willum, HN 2042, green & brown, 1949-73 .... **205**

Parson's Daughter (The), HN 564, red, yellow & green, 1923-49 .... **465**

Pensive Moments, HN 2704, blue dress, 1975-81 .... **200**

Prized Possessions, HN 2942, cream, purple & green, 1982................................... **288**

Professor (The), HN 2281, brown & black, 1965-81 157

Roseanna, HN 1926, rose shading to blue dress, 1940-59 (ILLUS.) 300

Rosemary, HN 2091, red & blue, 1952-59 350

Silks and Ribbons, HN 2017, green, red & white dress, 1949 to present 200

Skater (The), HN 2117, red & white dress, 1953-71 358

Stop Press, HN 2683, brown, blue & white, 1977-81 155

Suzette, HN 2026, 1949-59 373

Thanksgiving, HN 2446, blue overalls, 1972-76 200

Tootles, HN 1680, pink, 1935-75 75

Town Crier, HN 2119, 1953-76 285

Toymaker (The), HN 2250, brown & red, 1959-73 363

Tuppence a Bag, HN 2320, green dress, blue shawl, 1968 to present 210

Uriah Heep, HN 2101, black jacket, green trousers, 1952-67 335

Winsome, HN 2220, red dress, 1960-85 220

MISCELLANEOUS

Bowl, 8" d., The Gleaners series 185

Bowl, 8 1/2" h., Gallent Fishers series 245

Bowl, 8 7/8" d., 3 3/4" h., wide shallow rounded form, interior w/transfer-printed polychrome fox hunt scenes, green vintage border w/gilt trim, early 20th c. 138

Royal Doulton Scenic Cabinet Plates

Cabinet plates, 10 1/4" d., each w/a different English garden view within a narrow acid-etched gilt border, transfer-printed & painted by J. Price, ca. 1928, artist-signed, green printed lion, crown & circle mark, impressed year letters, painted pattern numbers "H3587," 10 1/4" d., set of 12 (ILLUS. of part) 5,750

Candlestick, "Old Moreton" series, low flaring round foot & slightly swelled cylindrical shaft below widely flaring flattened socket rim, color transfer of 16th c. gen-

tleman titled "Old Moreton," impressed "7277," 6 3/8" h. 83

Charger, Shakespeare Series, scene from "A Midsummers Night Dream," 12 5/8" d. 55

Royal Doulton Chocolate Set

Chocolate set: 8" h. cov. chocolate pot, 6 1/2" h. cov. water pot, creamer, sugar bowl & eight cups & saucers; bone china, each enamel decorated w/relief-molded fox in various poses, crop-form handles, 20th c., England, the set (ILLUS.) 748

Chop plate, round w/flanged rim, Old Moreton series, black transfer-printed design decorated in polychrome, a large center interior scene titled "Queen Elizabeth at Old Moreton 1589," early 20th c., 12 3/4" d. 110

Cracker jar, cov., Isaac Walton Ware, signed "NOKE" 251

Dish, oval, Old English scene "The Gleaners," 9 x 11 1/4, 2 1/8" h. 44

Humidor, cov., Sung Ware, flambé glaze, figural elephant finial, artist-initialed 2,400

Lamp base, slender ovoid ceramic body w/a tapering neck supporting electric lamp fittings, base decorated w/daffodils in greens, blue, white & yellow, fine brass round base mount w/a ring on the backs of four tiny figural turtles resting on a round disk on small ball feet, early 20th c., overall 28 1/2" h. (minor damage to body) 578

Loving cup, stoneware, three-handled cylindrical form w/a sterling silver rim band, a dark brown glaze band below the rim, most of the body w/a tan glaze, molded around the sides w/three white relief groups of bicycle riders, each titled either "Path," "Military," or "Road," late 19th c., base incised "8238," 5 1/2" h. 330

Mug, stoneware, tall slender & slightly tapering sides w/a sterling silver rim band, the upper third w/a dark brown glaze, the lower section w/a tan glaze, the upper band molded in relief w/a large scrolling ribbon band reading "Speed Wheel," the lower sides w/three white relief groups of bicycle racers each titled either "Path," "Military," or "Road," base incised "1957," late 19th c., 6" h. 275

Pitcher, jug-form, Kingsware, "Memories" design w/twelve faces shown, ca. 1920 600

Plate, 9 1/2" d., Izaac Walton Ware, signed "NOKE" 72

Robin Hood Series Plate

Plate, 7 1/2" sq., Robin Hood series (Friar Tuck Joins Robin Hood) natural-colored scene of Robin Hood & Friar Tuck standing & talking under large tree (ILLUS.) **85**

Plate, 10 1/4" d., Bradley Golfers, "All Fools Are Not Knaves......," **175**

Plate, 10 1/4" d., Old English scenes, "The Gleaners" ....⋮................... **44**

Plate, 10 1/4" d., "The Gypsies" **38**

Plate, 10 1/2" d., blue transfer w/center portrait of Shakespeare, border w/twelve characters from his plays **77**

Plate, 10 1/2" d., blue transfer w/central portrait of Dickens, border w/eleven of the Doulton characters used on various wares, unmarked.. **61**

Plate, 10 1/2" d., overall decoration of Aesthetic Movement florals in green & blue, marked w/lion & crown "Royal Doulton, England, Cyprus" **39**

Plate, 10 3/4" d., blue transfer w/Burns portrait in center, border shows characters such as Tam-O-Shanter, Highland Mary & others.. **49**

Plates, 10 1/4" d., series-type, color transfer-printed scenes on a tan speckled ground, one titled "The Battle," the other "The Press Gang," pr. **138**

Teapot, cov., Queen Elizabeth at Moreton Hall series **195**

Vase, 5 3/4" h., 3 3/4" d., baluster-form w/short flaring neck, slip-decorated in color w/celadon green fish & kelp on a dark brown ground, stamped "Doulton-Lambeth - 1883 - GTH - WP (?) - 593" **440**

Vase, 6" h., 3" d., Sung Ware, footed simple ovoid body tapering to a small trumpet neck, bright red & blue Flambé glaze, marked "Royal Doulton - Flambé - Sung - Noke"... **248**

Vase, 6 3/4" h., Sung Ware, tapering cylindrical body w/flared foot & incurved rim, scene of water fowl standing among tall reeds in a range of colors including Flambé reds & blues, decorated by A. Eaton & glazed by Charles Noke, Royal Doulton Flambé ink stamp mark & "No. 2836 Sung Noke" in black slip, ca. 1920s (two tight cracks at rim) **358**

Vase, 8 7/8" h., dome footed w/wide cylindrical body, the narrow shoulder tapering to wide waisted cylindrical neck decorated w/sprays of prunus & flanked by bronzed elephant head handles, flat rim, decorated in the style of Japanese lacquerwork w/wading birds among reeds between printed gilt borders of mons & ruyi-head forms in gold, platinum & red on brown ground, impressed & gilt-printed "DOULTON, BURSLEM - 863 - AP," ca. 1882 (tiny chip to underside rim of foot) **3,737**

Vase, 9" h., Welsh Ladies decoration.............. **295**

Vase, 12 1/2" h., Sung Ware, very wide bulbous ovoid body w/narrow cylindrical neck, stylized red, green & purple cherry blossoms interspersed w/lustered green, blue, red & tan drip glazes, decorated by Charles Noke, "Sung" & "Noke" in black slip & "7163," "4," & "46" impressed on bottom (restored drill hole in bottom) **1,870**

Wash bowl & pitcher set, Royal Mail series, early English coaching scenes around the sides of each, four in polychrome, early 20th c., bowl 11 7/8" d., pitcher 7 3/8" h., pr. **193**

Wash pitcher & bowl set, deep rounded wide bowl & tall slightly tapering tankard-form pitcher w/gently arched rim & angled handle, blue, white & gold-trimmed Art Nouveau-style "Aubery" patt., ca. 1910, bowl 16" d., pitcher 13 1/2" h., the set **550**

Whiskey jug w/figural stopper, 'Kingsware,' bulbous ovoid body w/a loop shoulder handle, the body in overall dark brown, the stopper in the shape of a stout 18th c. man wearing a tricorn hat & painted in polychrome, 8 1/4" h.................... **110**

Whiskey jug w/stopper, stoneware, advertising-type, bulbous ovoid body w/a wide shoulder centered by a small cylindrical neck w/tiny knobbed stopper, small loop shoulder handle, brown neck & handle shaded to tan below, the front w/applied ship & label reading "Special Highland Whiskey" in olive green & cream, stopper w/"Dewar's Whiskey," 7 1/8" h. **138**

FIESTA (HOMER LAUGHLIN CHINA CO. -HLC)

Fiesta dinnerware was made by the Homer Laughlin China Company of Newell, West Virginia, from the 1930s until the early 1970s. The brilliant colors of this inexpensive pottery have attracted numerous collectors. On February 28, 1986, Laughlin reintroduced the popular Fiesta line with minor changes in the shapes of a few pieces and a contemporary color range. The effect of this new production on the Fiesta collecting market is yet to be determined.

Fiesta Mark

Fiesta Carafe

Ashtray
chartreuse	$96
cobalt blue	55-60
ivory	55-60
red	55-60
turquoise	50-55
yellow	48

Bowl, cream soup
cobalt blue	60-65
forest green	85
ivory	56
red	65-70
turquoise	47
yellow	44

Bowl, dessert, 6" d.
ivory	45-50
turquoise	40
cobalt blue	45-50
red	55
yellow	38

Bowl, individual fruit, 5 1/2" d.
chartreuse	35
ivory	33
turquoise	25
yellow	25

Bowl, nappy, 8 1/2" d.
ivory	53-56
turquoise	42
red	55
yellow	44
cobalt blue	55-60

Bowl, nappy, 9 1/2" d.
ivory	65-70
turquoise	50-55
cobalt blue	65-75
red	70-75
yellow	50-60

Bowl, salad, large, footed
cobalt blue	375-400
red	350-375
turquoise	335-380
yellow	350-385

Candleholders, bulb-type, pr.
cobalt blue	120-125
ivory	115-120
red	115-120
turquoise	100-105
yellow	100-105

Carafe, cov.
cobalt blue	325-340
ivory	300-330
red	295-310
turquoise	280-295
yellow (ILLUS.)	270-280

Casserole, cov., two-handled, 10" d.
cobalt blue	200-210

Casserole, cov., two-handled, 10" d.
ivory	195-205
red	195-200
turquoise	130-140
yellow	155-160

Coffeepot, cov.
cobalt blue	235-245
ivory	230-240
red	225-250
turquoise	200-205
yellow	175-185

Coffeepot, cov., demitasse, stick handle
cobalt blue	475-500
ivory	500-535
red	525-575
turquoise	620-665
yellow	425-465

Compote, 12" d., low, footed
cobalt blue	170-180
ivory	165-170
red	180-190
turquoise	150-160
yellow	155-160

Compote, sweetmeat, high stand
cobalt blue	90-95
ivory	83-88
red	90-100
turquoise	75-80
yellow	75-85

Creamer
cobalt blue	35
ivory	30
red	30-35
turquoise	24
yellow	25

Cup, demitasse, stick handle
cobalt blue	75
ivory	75-80
red	80
turquoise	71-75
yellow	55-60

Cup, ring handle
cobalt blue	26-28
ivory	28-30
red	25-30
turquoise	24
yellow	23

Cup & saucer, demitasse, stick handle
cobalt blue	95
ivory	90-100
red	100-105
turquoise	90-100
yellow	75-80

Cup & saucer, ring handle
cobalt blue 35
ivory 30-35
medium green... 67
red 35-40
turquoise... 30
yellow 25-30
Egg cup
cobalt blue 74-78
ivory 72-75
red 75-80
turquoise.. 55-60
yellow.. 60-65
Fork (Kitchen Kraft)
cobalt blue 155-170
light green.. 115-125
red 145-160
yellow... 145-165
Gravy boat
cobalt blue 70-73
forest green 93
ivory 69-71
medium green.. 223
red 75-85
turquoise.. 40-45
yellow.. 40-45
Marmalade jar, cov.
cobalt blue 320-345
ivory 315-345
red 325-345
turquoise... 310-340
yellow.. 245-265
Mixing bowl, nest-type, size No. 1, 5" d.
cobalt blue 265-285
ivory 250-265
red 215-235
turquoise... 240-260
yellow.. 195-215
Mixing bowl, nest-type, size No. 2, 6" d.
cobalt blue 120-130
ivory 145-160
red 125-135
turquoise... 135-145
yellow.. 125-135
Mixing bowl, nest-type, size No. 3, 7" d.
cobalt blue 155-165
ivory 150-160
red 145-155
turquoise... 145-155
yellow.. 130-140
Mixing bowl, nest-type, size No. 4, 8" d.
turquoise... 145-155
cobalt blue 150-165
ivory 170-180
red 140-155
yellow.. 120-130
Mixing bowl, nest-type, size No. 5, 9" d.
cobalt blue 200-210
ivory 190-205
red 190-200
turquoise... 170-180
yellow.. 140-150
Mixing bowl, nest-type, size No. 6, 10" d.
cobalt blue 295-320
ivory 280-305
red 285-300
turquoise... 280-310
yellow.. 230-260

Mixing bowl, nest-type, size No. 7, 11 1/2" d.
cobalt blue 380-420
ivory 425-465
red... 410-455
turquoise... 335-370
yellow.. 355-395
Mug, Tom & Jerry style
cobalt blue 70-75
ivory/gold 75-80
red.. 75-80
turquoise.. 50-55
yellow... 57
Mustard jar, cov.
cobalt blue 290-305
ivory 270-285
light green... 293
red... 300-310
turquoise... 230-250
yellow.. 260-275

Fiesta Onion Soup Bowl

Onion soup bowl, cov. turquoise
(ILLUS.)... 11,000
Pie server (Kitchen Kraft)
cobalt blue 155-170
light green.. 140-155
red.. 175-190
yellow.. 130-145
Pitcher, water, disc-type
chartreuse.. 295
cobalt blue 155-160
forest green.. 343
ivory 155-165
medium green... 1,867
red.. 150-160
turquoise... 115-120
yellow.. 115-120
Plate, 10" d.
cobalt blue 41-42
ivory 40
light green... 29
medium green.. 168
red.. 44
turquoise.. 29
yellow.. 28-30
Plate, 6" d.
cobalt blue 8
ivory 7
red.. 7
turquoise... 7
yellow.. 7
Plate, 7" d.
cobalt blue 11
ivory 10

red	12
turquoise	9
yellow	9

Plate, 9" d.

cobalt blue	17-18
ivory	16
red	17-18
turquoise	13
yellow	13

Plate, chop, 13" d.

cobalt blue	45-50
ivory	43-47
red	45-50
turquoise	40-45
yellow	38

Plate, chop, 15" d.

cobalt blue	75-80
ivory	64-67
red	75-80
turquoise	50-55
yellow	47

Plate, grill, 10 1/2" d.

cobalt blue	45
ivory	45-50
red	60-70
rose	74
turquoise	43
yellow	40-43

Platter, 12" oval

cobalt blue	45-48
ivory	35-40
red	52
turquoise	35-40
yellow	36

Relish tray w/five inserts

cobalt blue	300-375
ivory	375-400
red	370-380
turquoise	345-365
yellow	325-350

Salt & pepper shakers, pr.

cobalt blue	32
ivory	30-35
red	30-35
turquoise	26
yellow	25

Soup plate w/flanged rim, 8" d.

ivory	54
red	55-60
turquoise	39
yellow	36

Sugar bowl, cov.

cobalt blue	55-60
ivory	55-60
medium green	265
red	55-60

Fiesta Sugar Bowl

turquoise (ILLUS.)	46
yellow	42

Teapot, cov., medium size (6 cup)

cobalt blue	215-225
ivory	200
red	195-200
turquoise	160-165
yellow	155-160

Tumbler, water, 10 oz.

cobalt blue	73-75
ivory	69-72
red	72
turquoise	62
yellow	60-65

Utility tray

cobalt blue	45-50
ivory	35-40
red	45-50
turquoise	40
yellow	42

Vase, 8" h.

cobalt blue	720-740
ivory	750-770
red	760-780
turquoise	550-600
yellow	525-585

Vase, bud, 6 1/2" h.

cobalt blue	100-105
ivory	105-110
red	90-100
turquoise	90-100
yellow	85-90

FLORENCE CERAMICS

Some of the finest figurines and artwares were produced between 1940 and 1962 by the Florence Ceramics Company of Pasadena, California. Florence Ward began working with ceramics following the death of her son, Jack, in 1939.

Mrs. Ward had not worked with clay before her involvement with classes at the Pasadena Hobby School. After study and first-hand experience, she began production in her garage, using a kiln located outside the garage to conform with city regulations. The years 1942-44 were considered her "garage" period.

In 1944 Florence Ceramics moved to a small plant in Pasadena, employing fifty-four employees and receiving orders of $250,000 per year. In 1948 it was again necessary to move to a larger facility in the area with the most up-to-date equipment and the number of employees increased to over 100. Within five years Florence Ceramics was considered one of the finest producers of semi-porcelain figurines and artwares.

Florence created a wide range of items including figurines, lamps, picture frames, planters and models of animals and birds. It was her extensive line of ladies in beautiful gowns and gentlemen in fine clothes that gave her the most pleasure and was the foundation of her business. Two of her most popular lines of figurines were inspired by the famous 1860 Godey's Ladies Book and by famous artists from the Old Master group. In the mid-1950s two bird lines were produced for several years. One of the bird lines was designed by Don Winton and the other was a line of contemporary sculptured bird and animal figures designed by the well-known sculptor, Betty Davenport Ford.

There were several unsuccessful contemporary artwares lines produced for a short time. The Driftware line consisted of modern free-form bowls and accessories. The Floraline is a rococo line with overglazed decoration. The Gourmet Pottery, a division of Florence Ceramics Company, produced accessory serving pieces under the name of Scandia and Sierra.

Florence products were manufactured in the traditional porcelain process with a second firing at a higher temperature after the glaze had been applied. Many pieces had overglaze paint decoration and clay ruffles, roses and lace dipped in slip prior to the third firing.

Florence Marks

Bank, figural, model of a dog standing w/left paw across body w/"Ford" advertising under left paw & right paw on top of head, head turned slightly to left, glossy grey w/black highlights, in-mold mark "Florence Ceramics Pasadena, California" & copyright symbol, 6 3/4" h. **$100-125**

Bell, anniversary, applied pink Dresden-type flowers on white ground w/gold trim, 4 1/2" h. **75-100**

Casserole, cov., Scandia line, satin white, w/metal frame, 2 1/2 qt. **30-40**

Chip 'n dip, leaf-shaped, Sierra patt., white, 9 1/4 x 14" h. **25-35**

Clock, mantel-type, figural, an ornate scroll-footed & scroll-cast base w/applied roses supporting a rounded embossed case enclosing the round clock dial w/Roman numerals, the scroll-molded high top decorated w/applied rose blossoms & a figural cherub finial, 11 1/2" h. **700-800**

Cornucopia-vase, pink shading to grey, w/pink rose at base, 7 3/4" h. **50-75**

Dealer sign, figural, woman dressed in pink w/left hand on top & right hand on side of a white sign inscribed "Florence Pasadena California," 7" h. **500-600**

Dish, Driftwood line, model of two leaves, pale green, marked "Florence Ceramics Inc. Pasadena, California," 3 1/2 x 9" **20-30**

"Cinderella and Prince Charming" Figure Group

Figure group, "Cinderella & Prince Charming," dancing couple on raised base, both in white Renaissance period costume, white w/gold trim & gold tiara on her blonde hair, he holds a silver slipper behind her back in his right hand, 11 3/4" h. (ILLUS.) **3,000-5,000**

Figure group, "The Christening," woman w/peacock blue dress trimmed in lace at neck, sleeves & front of dress holding an infant in a long white christening dress, articulated fingers, 8 1/2" h. **700-800**

"Grandmother and I" Figure Group

Figure group, two woman sitting at a round table covered in a white tablecloth w/a teapot on it & the older woman sitting on a white chair holding a teacup in her right hand, wearing a violet dress w/lace trimmed cuffs & collar, a young woman dressed in a pink dress w/lace trim at the neck & a bow tied in the back, holding a teacup in her left hand, 6 3/4" h. (ILLUS.) **1,500-2,000**

Figure group, "Story Hour," seated mother & girl, woman reading book held in left hand, rose dress w/lace at neck, roses in her hair, girl w/blonde hair w/right arm on bench, ruffled lace short-sleeved white dress w/blue & pink trim, small boy dressed in blue shirt & pants & standing near girl 8" l., 6 3/4" h. **800-900**

Figure of a ballerina, "Marcella," standing w/right foot pointed in front of left leg, arms w/elbows slightly bent & pointed downward, pink tutu, applied roses in brown hair, 7" h. **150-200**

Florence "Little Don" Figure

Figure of a boy, "Little Don," standing w/a grey cat at right side w/both arms extended outward, red pants & shirt w/ruffled lace trim, white cummerbund & shoes, from the Old Master group, Francisco Goya's "Don Manuel Osorio," 7 3/4" h. (ILLUS.) **750-850**

Figure of a boy, "Mike," standing w/head thrown back & arms straight up & back w/palms up, 6 1/2" h. **200-250**

Figure of a boy, "Peter," standing w/legs apart & holding a package in his right hand, white jacket, shirt & shoes, pale blue pants & hat, brown hair, 5 1/2" h. . **100-125**

Figure of a boy, "Sandy," standing w/feet slightly apart, left hand holding an inner tube, right arm bent w/hand on hip, brown hair, navy swimsuit w/polka dots, navy shoes, 7 1/2" h. **350-400**

Figure of a girl, "Tess," wearing large hat, holding up one side of skirt, 7 1/4" h. **429**

Figure of a girl, young blonde girl seated & holding a bird in her hands, white dress & shoes w/grey trim & hat, 5" h. **100-150**

Figure of a Godey woman, "Abigail," beige full-skirted dress, cape & bonnet w/green bow tied under chin, 8 1/4" h. . **150-200**

Figure of a Godey woman, "Annabelle," standing w/right arm bent & holding a white dove in hand, left arm in outward position, brown hair, white long full jacket w/gold trim, large white hat, articulated fingers, 8 3/4" h. **350-400**

Figure of a Godey woman, "Camille," standing & wearing white dress trimmed in gold, shawl over both arms made entirely of hand-dipped lace, brown hair, white triangular hat w/applied pink rose, ribbon tied to right side of neck, articulated hands, 81/2" h. **250-300**

Figure of a Godey woman, "Delia," beige dress w/long sleeves, green hat & ribbon tied under chin, holding a muff, 7 1/2" h **75-125**

Figure of a Godey woman, "Georgette," royal red dress w/full skirt, long sleeves w/lace & gold trim, large white bonnet w/lace & flower trim, holding a hatbox in left hand, articulated fingers, 10 1/4" h. **325-400**

Figure of a Godey woman, "Irene," grey dress w/gold trim, flower in upswept hair, right hand holding muff near face, 6" h. ... **50-75**

Figure of a Godey woman, "Lillian," long pink jacket, white collar, hat & purse, 7 1/4" h. **75-125**

Figure of a Godey woman, "Scarlett," violet dress & bonnet, right hand holding a muff near face, left hand holding handbag, 8 3/4" h. **150-250**

Figure of a Godey woman, "Sue Ellen," green full-skirted dress w/long sleeves, brown trim, white bodice, floral bonnet w/brown tie under chin, both hands holding a bouquet near waist, 8 1/4" h. **75-150**

Figure of a grandmother, "Memories," sitting in a white wing chair w/gold trim, reading a book, white dress w/gold trim, white lace shawl around shoulders, 6 1/2" h. **750-800**

Figure of a man, "Edward," black top hat, grey suit w/green trimmed vest, sitting in grey & purple chair, 7" h. **250-350**

Figure of a man, "Eugene," standing w/gloved hands touching the shoulders, green suit, triangular hat, 9" h. **250-300**

Figure of a man, "Leading Man," standing w/right leg in front of left, royal red kneebritches, white stockings w/gold-trimmed shoes, knee-length coat w/lacy jabot at neck, left arm bent at elbow & raised upward, left arm extended outward holding a scroll, 10 1/2" h. **250-350**

"Louis XV" & "Madame Pompadour"

Figure of a man, "Louis XV," standing wearing pink knee-length britches, royal red coat w/lacy jabot at neck, white stockings & black shoes, left arm bent at elbow & raised upward holding a gold package, scroll-molded base, 12 1/2" h. (ILLUS.)... **350-450**

Figure of a man, "Martin," white trousers & tie, rose & royal red knee-length coat w/cape & top hat, standing w/right hand on hip, left hand resting on a walking stick, 10 1/2" h. **175-225**

Figure of a man, "Rhett," standing w/right hand on vest, left hand in pocket, white ruffled shirt trimmed in red, knee-length coat & top hat, 9" h. **175-225**

Figure of a man, "Victor," holding white top hat in right hand, white trousers & shirt, royal red jacket w/tails & long swirling white cape, 9 1/2" h. **175-225**

"Adeline" Figure

Figure of a woman, "Adeline," brown hair w/applied roses in both sides of hair, green off-the-shoulder full pleated dress, holding a pink shawl wrapped around her lower arms, 9" h. (ILLUS.)............... **250-300**

Figure of a woman, "Amber," brown hair, pink ruffled long dress & large bonnet w/right arm bent & holding a pink parasol at right shoulder, left arm extended w/fingers touching her dress, articulated fingers, 9 1/4" h.................... **400-500**

Figure of a woman, "Anita," standing w/right arm bent, palm extended near waist, left arm almost straight down at side, gold brocade long dress w/short sleeves & fitted waist, articulated fingers, 15" h. **900-1,200**

Figure of a woman, "Ava," wearing a dirndl-type dress w/brown skirt & tan peasant blouse, left hand on hip & right arm raised & holding a large green basket on her head, 6" h. **250-350**

Figure of a woman, "Bea," teal w/white hat....... **95**

Figure of a woman, "Betsy," green skirt & long jacket w/tight bodice, ruffled floral trim & long sleeves, hands in muff, 7 1/2" h. **75-100**

Figure of a woman, "Carmen," dancer w/head slightly turned & tilted to left, right arm bent w/fingers touching black hair, left arm across body at waist, ruffled lace short-sleeved white dress w/red & gold trim, 12 1/2" h. **900-1,200**

Figure of a woman, "Colleen," standing w/head slightly turned to left, right hand behind back & left arm to the front, green dress w/white collar, bonnet w/ribbon tied under chin, 8" h. **150-200**

Figure of a woman, "Cynthia," standing w/left arm extended slightly backward, head turned slightly to left, right hand holding large white hat trimmed w/flowers, aquamarine overdress w/white underskirt, lacy jabot at neck & lace cuffs, articulated fingers, 9 1/4" h. **450-550**

Figure of a woman, "Darlene," standing w/head tilted, brown hair w/curls & roses at neck, green dress, white underskirt, white lace trim on bodice & extending to bottom of dress, right arm bent & holding an open parasol at right shoulder, left arm at waist, articulated fingers, 8 1/4" h. **400-500**

Figure of a woman, "Delores," royal red dress w/white collar & hat w/floral trim, holding a parasol, 8" h. **150-200**

Figure of a woman, "Denise," off-the-shoulder white dress w/gold trim extending down the dress front, violet overskirt, brown hair w/roses, both arms bent at waist w/right hand holding a closed fan, articulated fingers, 10" h. **500-600**

"Fair Lady" Figure

Figure of a woman, "Fair Lady," standing on scrolled base decorated w/roses & gold trim, rose dress w/ornate white lace trim panel in front of dress, rose trim at bodice, upswept brown hair w/roses, right hand raised, articulated fingers, 11 1/2" h. (ILLUS.).......................... **1,400-1,500**

Figure of a woman, "Gibson Girl," white dress w/gold trim, lace & gold trim at cuffs & bodice, large white hat w/gold & floral trim, 10" h. **175-225**

Figure of a woman, "Laura," pink dress w/applied roses on skirt, white collar w/gold trim, pink hat w/roses, both hands holding hat ribbons near chin, 7 1/2" h. **150-175**

Figure of a woman, "Linda Lou," green skirt & hat, dark green jacket w/peplum, holding a bouquet near her head, 7 3/4" h. **150-175**

Figure of a woman, "Louise," beige dress & hat, green trim ribbon at neck & gloves, left hand at shoulder, right arm extended & holding a green parasol, 7 1/4" h. **75-125**

Figure of a woman, "Mary," grey dress, lacy jabot at neck, seated in an armchair w/foot on small footstool, 7 1/2" h. **450-550**

"Rosalie" Figure

Figure of a woman, "Rosalie," moss green dress w/lace ruffle at the off-the-shoulder neckline, brown hair w/roses, holding skirt out at each side, articulated fingers, 9 1/2" h. (ILLUS.)...................... **350-450**

Figure of a woman, "Sarah," dress w/full skirt & peplum, white hat w/bow tied at neck, right hand holding a white purse, 7 1/2" h. **75-125**

Figure of a woman, "Tess," light green dress w/lace ruffle at neckline, large hat, holding edge of skirt up over shoe, 7" h. **350-450**

Figure of a woman, "Vivian," wearing a bonnet w/ribbon tied on left side of neck, full-skirted dress w/long sleeves, right hand holding a parasol overhead, left hand holding a lace hankie, 9 3/4" h. **175-250**

Figure of an angel, w/yellow hair, arms bent across upper body, part of angel's wings showing, white robe w/gold trimmed rope sash, cuffs & collar, gold & brown ribbon sticker, 7" h......................... **75-90**

Figures of "Blueboy" & "Pinkie"

Figures, "Blueboy" & "Pinkie," figure of man standing on base, blue pants & coat w/white trim, white stockings, holding plumed hat in right hand & woman standing on base, wearing white dress w/rose trim & hat w/loose ribbon, right

arm behind back, left arm held in front of body, 12" h., pr. (ILLUS.)...................... **650-750**

Figures of "Dot" & "Bud"

Figures, "Bud" & "Dot," standing w/legs apart, "Bud" w/hands on guns at side, brown hair, white chaps, blue shirt, red neckerchief, black hat, vest, boots & gloves, "Dot" w/right hand on gun at side, left hand holding a doll, brown hair, blue skirt, red neckerchief, black hat, vest & boots, 7 1/2" h., each (ILLUS.) **350-400**

Figures, "John Alden" & "Priscilla," he dressed in dark grey kneebritches, light grey coat, shoes & large brim hat & holds a gun, she dressed in light grey skirt & cap, white apron, gloves & bonnet tied under the chin & holds books, both w/gold trim, 9 1/4 & 7 1/4" h., pr. **375-425**

Figures of choir boys, 6 1/2" h., set of 3 .... **300**

Flower holder, figural, "Patsy," wearing tiered & ruffled white dress w/pink floral trim, pink scarf in blonde hair, standing in front of square white relief-molded rock wall flower holder, 6" h. **45-50**

Flower holder, figural, "Bee," girl wearing hat & carrying a basket, 6 1/4" h. **50**

Flower holder, figural, "June," girl in front of pleated-edge block, 7" h. **50**

Flower holder, figural, "Kay," girl standing, wearing large hat, holding skirt out to sides, 7" h.. **50**

Flower holder, figural, "Emily," lady standing, holding hat on head w/one hand, closed parasol in other hand, 8" h................. **68**

Flower holder, figural, "Jerry," white suit trimmed in blue, pink tie, holding a white bass fiddle trimmed w/gold, 8" h. **125-150**

Flower holder, figural, "Rita," ivory, 9 1/2" h... **250**

Flower holders, figural, Chinese boy & girl, boy holding a vase in left hand, the girl holding a fan in her right hand, white w/gold trim, 7 3/4" h., pr. **75-100**

Head vase, "Violet," brunette hair, moss green bodice & large hat, 7" h.............. **125-150**

Lamp base, figural, "Delia," eggshell dress, hardwood base, 7 1/2" h. **250-300**

Lamp base, figural, Oriental man & woman, polished brass base, 7 3/4" h. **250-300**

Lapel pin, figural bust of woman w/brown hair, grey hat & ribbon tied under chin, 2 1/4" h. **250-300**

Model of a bird, "Cardinal," flying position
w/head turned slightly to left, mounted
on a stump w/flowers around base,
designed by Don Winton, 4 3/4" h......... **275-350**

Model of a fox, on base, running position
w/back legs & tail up, head turned to
side, brown & white porcelain bisque,
designed by Betty Davenport Ford,
Model No. B-13, 9 x 16" **375-450**

Model of a High Button Shoe

Model of a high button shoe, white w/lace
& gold trim, small applied pink rose but-
tons, 5" h. (ILLUS.)................................ **125-150**

Picture frame, white w/lace trim, 2 x 3" **75-100**

Picture frame, white w/roses & lace trim,
4 x 5" **125-175**

Picture frame, white w/Dresden-type flow-
ers, 5 x 7" **175-225**

Planter, model of a swan, neck up & head
bent downward, designed by Don Win-
ton, 7 x 7 x 12" **225-275**

Powder box, cov., figural "Diane," brown
hair, full three-tiered ruffled lace skirt &
fitted bodice, white w/gold trim, Model
No. 71, 6 x 6".. **250-350**

Wall plaque, cameo-type, irregular dark
grey edge fading gradually to light grey
at center, relief-molded bust of man
w/black hat & tie, Model P7, 7 1/4" h..... **100-150**

Wall plaque, rectangular, pink frame
w/brown edge, 1860 "Godey's Ladies'
Book" figure holding a muff, Model P1,
6 1/4 x 9" **100-150**

FLOW BLUE

*Flow Blue ironstone and semi-porcelain was
manufactured mainly in England during the second
half of the 19th century. The early ironstone was
produced by many of the well known English potters and was either transfer-printed or hand-painted
(Brush stroke). The bulk of the ware was exported
to the United States or Canada.*

*The "flow" or running quality of the cobalt blue
designs was the result of introducing certain chemi-
cals into the kiln during the final firing. Some patterns are so "flown" that it is difficult to ascertain the
design. The transfers were of several types: Asian,
Scenic, Marble or Floral.*

*The earliest Flow Blue ironstone patterns were
produced during the period between about 1840
and 1860. After the Civil War Flow Blue went out of*

*style for some years but was again manufactured
and exported to the United States beginning about
the 1880s and continuing through the turn of the
century. These later Flow Blue designs are on a
semi-porcelain body rather than heavier ironstone
and the designs are mainly florals.*

AMERILLIA (Podmore Walker & Co., ca. 1840s-50s)
Plate, 7 1/2" d. **$70**
Platter, 16" **600**

AMOY (Davenport, dated 1844)
Creamer, 6 1/2" h. **300**
Cup & saucer, handled..................................... **195**

Amoy Water Pitcher

Pitcher, water, 12" h., rare body style
(ILLUS.).. **1,500**
Plate, 7 1/2" d. **75**
Plate, 8 1/2" d. **85**
Plate, 9 1/2" d. **120**
Plate, 10 1/2" d. **165**
Platter, 12" **250**
Platter, 16" **450**
Platter, 18" **650**
Soup plate w/flanged rim, 10" d. **200**
Sugar bowl, cov. **375**
Vegetable bowl, open, 8" l. **595**
Waste bowl, "double bulge" style..................... **325**

ANEMONE (Minton, ca. 1860)
Plate, 8 1/2" d. **95**
Plate, 9 1/2" d. **125**
Platter, 14", oval... **400**

Anemone Covered Vegetable Bowl

Vegetable bowl, cov., footed (ILLUS.)............. **400**

ARABESQUE (T.J. & J. Mayer, ca. 1845)
Creamer, Classic Gothic style, 6" h................. **500**
Plate, 7 1/2" d.. **150**
Plate, 10 1/2" d.. **195**
Soup plate w/flanged rim, 10" d. **185**
Sugar bowl, cov., Classic Gothic style **595**
Teapot, cov., Classic Gothic style **800**

ARGYLE (W.H. Grindley & Co., ca. 1896)
Butter dish, cov., w/drainer **600**
Cup & saucer, handled.................................. **110**
Gravy boat **200**
Pitcher, 1 1/2 pt.. **425**
Plate, 7" d... **65**
Plate, 8" d... **75**
Plate, 9" d... **85**
Plate, 10" d.. **95**
Platter, 14" l... **275**
Sauce dish **50**
Vegetable bowl, open, medium...................... **185**

ATHENS (C. Meigh, ca. 1845)
Cup & saucer, handleless **225**
Gravy boat **350**
Plate, 7 1/2" d.. **95**
Plate, 10 1/2" d.. **125**

Athens Punch Cup

Punch cup (ILLUS.) **145**

CARLTON (S. Alcock, ca. 1850)
Plate, 8 1/2" d.. **130**
Plate, 9 1/2" d.. **140**
Platter, 14" **300**
Soup plate w/flanged rim, 10" **150**

Carlton Vegetable Bowl

Vegetable bowl, cov., ca. 1850 (ILLUS.)......... **400**

CASHMERE (Francis Morley, ca. 1845)
Coffeepot, cov., octagonal, 9 1/2" h............. **1,925**
Cup & saucer, handleless **300**
Mug, 3 1/2" h.. **400**
Plate, 7 1/2" d.. **100**
Plate, 8 1/4" w., paneled, set of 13 (one
  w/spider crack, one w/flake)........................ **935**
Plate, 9 1/2" d.. **175**
Plate, 10 1/4" d., paneled, set of 4 .... **715**
Plate, 10 1/2" d.. **200**
Soup plate w/flanged rim, 10 3/4" w.,
  scalloped edges, set of 7 .... **1,375**
Soup plate w/flanged rim, 10" d. **235**

CASHMERE (Morley & Ashworth, ca. 1859-62)
Platter, 13 3/4 x 17", scalloped edge **880**

CHAPOO (John Wedgwood, ca. 1850)
Creamer, 6 1/2" h.. **350**
Cup & saucer, handleless **135**
Plate, 10 1/2" d.. **155**
Soup plate w/flanged rim, 10" d. **165**

CHINESE (Dimmock, ca. 1845)

Chinese Platter

Platter, 18", well & tree-type (ILLUS.) **700**

CHUSAN (J. Clementson, ca. 1840)
Creamer, 6" h... **250**
Plate, 7 1/2" d.. **125**
Plate, 9 1/2" d.. **145**
Platter, 14" l... **350**
Vegetable bowl, open, 8" l............................. **200**

COBURG (J. Edwards, ca. 1850)
Cup & saucer, handleless **150**
Plate, 8 1/2" d.. **135**
Plate, 10 1/2" d.. **155**
Platter, 16" **300**

CONWAY (New Wharf Pottery, ca. 1891)
Sauce dish **50**
Sugar bowl, cov.. **200**
Vegetable bowl, open, oval **150**

DOROTHY (Johnson Bros., ca. 1900)
Bone dish **65**
Plate, 8" d... **65**
Plate, 9" d... **75**

FLORAL (Laughlin Art China Co., ca. 1900)

Floral Tyg

Tyg, three-handled (ILLUS.)............................. 350

FLORIDA (W.H. Grindley, ca. 1891)

Cup & saucer, handled..................................... 170
Plate, 7" d.. 100
Plate, 8" d.. 125

GAUDY (Brushstroke, ca. 1850)

Gaudy Relish Dish

Relish dish, w/polychrome (ILLUS.) 195

GAUDY (Mellor Venables & Co., ca. 1840)

Creamer, Classic Gothic shape 250
Sugar bowl, cov., Classic Gothic shape 450

Gaudy Teapot

Teapot, cov., Classic Gothic shape
   (ILLUS.).. 900

GINGHAM FLOWERS (Brushstroke, ca. 1845)

Cup & saucer, handleless 220
Plate, 7 1/2" d. 175

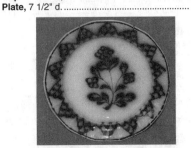

Gingham Flowers Plate

Plate, 9 1/2" d. (ILLUS.).................................... 200
Platter, 14" l... 350

GOTHIC (J. Furnival, ca. 1850)

Plate, 8 1/2" d. 145
Plate, 9 1/2" d. 165
Soup plate w/flanged rim, 10" 175

GRAPE & BLUEBELL (Brushstroke, ca. 1850)

Plate, 8" d.. 150
Soup plate w/flanged rim, 10 1/2" 175

HONG KONG (C. Meigh, ca. 1845)

Cup & saucer, handleless 165

INDIAN TREE (Unknown, probably English, probably early-Victorian, ca. 1845)

Indian Tree Plate

Plate, 8" d. (ILLUS.)... 40

IRIS (Arthur Wilkinson - Royal Staffordshire Potteries, ca. 1907)

Gravy boat 80
Plate, 5 3/4" d. 15
Plate, 9" d.. 30
Platter, 13" l.. 90
Vegetable bowl, cov., 7 1/2" d......................... 180

JAPAN (T. Fell & Co., ca. 1860)

Pitcher, 8" h. 400
Platter, 16" l.. 350

LA BELLE (Wheeling Pottery, ca. 1900)

Bowl, large, helmet-shaped 375
Cake plate 175
Celery dish 235
Cracker jar, cov., 7 1/2" h. 600

Cup & saucer, handled.................................. 195
Dessert dish, fancy... 155
Mug, chocolate 400
Pitcher, 7 1/2" h. 450

LORNE (W.H. Grindley, ca. 1900)
Cup & saucer, handled.................................. 125
Dinner service: six 10" d. dinner plates,
ten 9" d. luncheon plates, thirteen cups
& ten saucers, one each sauce dish,
gravy boat & cov. vegetable dish; each
marked, the set (minor stains, several
chips).. 1,210
Plate, 7" d. 75

Lorne Plate

Plate, 10" d. (ILLUS.)....................................... 100
Platter, 12", oval... 150

LUCERNE (New Wharf Pottery, ca. 1891)
Cup & saucer 95
Plate, 9" d... 85
Vegetable bowl, cov. 150

MANHATTAN (Johnson Bros., ca. 1895)
Creamer 195
Plate, 9" d... 90
Sugar bowl, cov... 245
Waste bowl 100

MANILLA (Podmore, Walker & Co., ca. 1845)
Creamer, Primary shape, 6" h. 350

MARGUERITE (W.H. Grindley, ca. 1891)
Bone dish 65
Plate, 7" d... 60
Plate, 9" d... 85
Sauce dish 55

MATLOCK (F. Winkle & Co., ca. 1890)

Matlock Covered Vegetable Dish

Vegetable dish, cov., 7 x 11 1/2", 5 1/2" h.
(ILLUS.)... 195

MELBOURNE (W.H. Grindley, ca. 1891)
Plate, 9" d... 95
Platter, 16" l... 200

MENTONE (Johnson Bros., ca. 1900)

Mentone Teapot

Teapot, cov. (ILLUS.)...................................... 600

NANKIN (Davenport, ca. 1850)
Cup & saucer, handleless 200
Plate, 10 1/2" d. 195
Vegetable bowl, open, rectangular, 8" l.......... 250

NON PARIEL (Burgess & Leigh, ca. 1891)
Plate, 9" d... 100
Soup plate, 8" d. 130

NORMANDY (Johnson Bros., ca. 1900)
Cup & saucer, handled.................................... 150
Gravy boat 95
Plate, 7" d... 90
Plate, 8" d... 100
Plate, 9" d... 120
Soup plate, 8" d. 135

OREGON (T.J. and J. Mayer, ca. 1845)
Creamer, pumpkin shape................................ 350
Cup plate 150
Plate, 7 1/2" d. 130
Plate, 10 1/2" d. 195
Platter, 12" l... 350
Platter, 14" l... 400
Sugar bowl, cov., pumpkin shape................... 450
Teapot, cov., pumpkin shape 650

OSBORNE (Ridgways, ca. 1905)
Egg cup, large.. 130
Gravy boat 150
Plate, 7" d... 65
Plate, 9" d... 85

PELEW (E. Challinor, ca. 1850)
Pitcher, water, 9" h... 800
Plate, 7 1/2" d. 130
Plate, 10 1/2" d. 175
Punch cup 150
Teapot, cov., pumpkin shape 650

ROSE (W.H. Grindley, ca. 1893)
Bone dish 65
Plate, 7" d... 55
Plate, 9" d... 75

ROXBURY (Ridgway, ca. 1910)
Bone dish 60
Bowl, berry 50

Gravy boat 125
Vegetable bowl, open...................................... 150

SCINDE (J&G Alcock, 1839-46)
Cup & saucer, handleless 225

Scinde Gravy Boat

Gravy boat w/undertray, Full Panel Gothic
style (ILLUS.) 375
Plate, 7 1/2" d.. 160
Plate, 10 1/2" d.. 225

Scinde Punch Cup

Punch cup (ILLUS.) 175
Relish dish, shell-shaped 175
Sugar bowl, cov., Full Panel Gothic style 450

SPINACH (Libertas, Brushstroke, ca. 1900)

Spinach Bowl

Bowl, 5" d. (ILLUS.)... 95
Plate, 9" d.. 85

STRAWBERRY (J. Furnival, Brushstroke, ca. 1850)
Cup & saucer, handleless 200
Plate, 7 1/2" d.. 150
Plate, 9 1/2" d. (ILLUS.).................................. 175
Platter, 14" l.. 450
Waste bowl 225

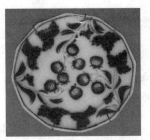

Strawberry Plate

TEMPLE (Podmore, Walker & Co.)
Cup plate 135
Relish dish, shell-shaped 300
Soup plate w/flanged rim, 10" d. 165

TONQUIN (J. Heath, ca. 1850)
Creamer, full panel Gothic style, 6" h.............. 300
Cup & saucer, handleless 195
Plate, 9 1/2" d.. 145
Soup plate, 10" d. 165
Sugar bowl, cov., full panel Gothic style.......... 450

TOURAINE (H. Alcock & Co., ca. 1898 or Stanley Pottery, ca. 1898)
Plate, 7" d... 70
Plate, 8" d... 75

TOURAINE (Henry Alcock, ca. 1898 & Stanley Pottery, ca. 1898)
Waste bowl 200

TROY (C. Meigh, ca. 1840)
Cup plate 195
Gravy boat 250
Plate, 8 1/2" d.. 175
Plate, 10 1/2" d.. 195
Soup plate w/flanged rim, 10" 200

WAVERLY (J. Maddock & Son, ca. 1891)
Plate, 7" d... 65
Plate, 8" d... 75
Vegetable bowl, open...................................... 110

WHAMPOA (Mellor Venables, ca. 1840)
Basin & ewer 1,000
Cup plate 185
Teapot, cov., Primary shape 795

FRANCISCAN WARE

Franciscan tableware was made by Gladding McBean and Co., at the Glendale plant bought from Tropico potteries in 1923. By 1934 the first dinnerware lines were produced. The first line El Patio was made in pastel colors. In 1935 it was made in Two Tone colors. In 1936 the Coronado line was introduced. The hand decorated lines were introduced in 1937, Apple pattern 1940, Desert Rose 1941, Wildflower 1942, Ivy 1948, and Franciscan Poppy in 1950. In 1962 Gladding McBean merged with Lock Joint Pipe Co. The name was changed to Interpace Co. In 1979 Franciscan was purchased by Wedgwood Ltd.. The Glendale plant was closed in October 1984.

For hand decorated patterns and Starburst use the following guide: Forget-me-not the same as Desert Rose; Meadow Rose the same as Desert Rose.

Apple +20%

Bountiful +20%

Cafe Royal -10%

Daisy -15%

Fresh Fruit +20%

Ivy +50%

October -10%

Original Small Fruit +60%

Poppy +75%

Strawberry Fruit +40%,

Strawberry Time +40%

Wildflower +200%

Franciscan Mark

Ashtray, Apple patt., 4 1/2 x 9" oval.............. $105
Ashtray, Desert Rose patt., 4 3/4 x 9" oval........ 85
Ashtray, Desert Rose patt., square 325
Ashtray, El Patio tableware, coral satin glaze.. 8
Ashtray, individual, Desert Rose patt., 3 1/2" d... 24
Ashtray, individual, Apple patt., apple-shaped, 4" w., 4 1/2" l. 19
Ashtray, individual, Ivy patt., leaf-shaped, 4 1/2" l. 27
Baking dish, Apple patt., 1 qt. 275
Baking dish, Desert Rose patt., 1 qt. 223
Baking dish, Meadow Rose patt., 9 x 14", 1 1/2 qt. 125
Bank, figural pig, Desert Rose patt. 265
Bell, Desert Rose patt., Danbury Mint, 4 1/4" h.. 130
Bell, dinner, Franciscan.................................. 150
Bowl, bouillon soup, cov., 4 1/2" d., Desert Rose patt... 275
Bowl, fruit, 5 1/4" d., Desert Rose patt. 15
Bowl, cereal, 6" d., Desert Rose patt. 18
Bowl, 7" d., Picnic patt. 8
Bowl, cereal, 7" d., October patt. 18
Bowl, salad, 10" d., Desert Rose patt. 120
Bowl, salad, 11" d., Daisy patt. 90
Bowl, fruit, Arden patt...................................... 12
Box, cov., Desert Rose patt., heart-shaped, 4 1/2" l., 2 1/2" h. 195
Box, cov., egg-shaped, 1 1/2 x 4 3/4", Desert Rose patt. 200

Box, cov., round, Desert Rose patt., 4 3/4" d., 1 1/2" h.. 195
Box, cov., Twilight Rose patt., heart-shaped 225
Butter dish, cov., Desert Rose patt. 55
Candleholders, Desert Rose patt., pr............... 95
Candleholders, Starburst patt., pr.................. 150
Casserole, cov., Desert Rose patt., 1 1/2 qt., 4 3/4" h.. 95
Casserole, cov., Desert Rose patt., 2 1/2 qt. 225
Cigarette box, cov., Desert Rose patt., 3 1/2 x 4 1/2", 2" h.................................... 150
Coaster, Apple patt., 3 3/4" d. 53
Coffee server, El Patio tableware, turquoise glossy glaze..................................... 40
Coffeepot, cov., Desert Rose patt., 7 1/2" h. 140
Coffeepot, cov., 10" h., Daisy patt. 85
Coffeepot, cov., demitasse, Coronado Table Ware, coral satin glaze...................... 90
Coffeepot, individual, cov., Desert Rose patt. 425
Compote, open, Desert Rose patt., 8" d., 4" h... 77
Compote, open, Meadow Rose patt., 8" d., 4" h... 85
Cookie jar, cov., Desert Rose patt. 325
Creamer, individual, Desert Rose patt., 3 1/2" h.. 45
Creamer, Ivy patt., 4" h. 30
Creamer, Desert Rose patt., 4 1/4" h. 28
Creamer, October patt. 24
Creamer & cov. sugar bowl, Daisy patt., pr. 58
Creamer & open sugar bowl, Tiempo patt., lime green, pr. 25
Creamer & open sugar bowl, individual, Desert Rose patt., pr. 115
Creamer & open sugar bowl, individual, El Patio Nuevo patt., orange, pr. 50

Apple Pattern Plate, Cup & Saucer

Cup & saucer, Apple patt. (ILLUS.) 9
Cup & saucer, Arden patt. 15
Cup & saucer, coffee, Desert Rose patt. 22
Cup & saucer, Desert Rose patt., jumbo size.. 75
Cup & saucer, tall, Desert Rose patt. 55
Cup & saucer, tea, Desert Rose patt............... 18
Cup & saucer, demitasse, Apple patt. 55
Cup & saucer, demitasse, Desert Rose patt. 65
Cup & saucer, demitasse, El Patio tableware, golden glow glossy glaze 20

Cup & saucer, demitasse, El Patio tableware, Mexican blue glossy glaze 20
Cup & saucer, demitasse, El Patio table-
ware, turquoise glossy glaze......................... 20
Egg cup, Desert Rose patt., 2 3/4" d.,
3 3/4" h... 48
Egg cup, Meadow Rose patt., 2 3/4 d.,
3 3/4" h... 19
Egg cup, Twilight Rose patt., 2 3/4" d.,
3 3/4" h.. 350
Egg cup, Apple patt., double............................ 32
Goblet, footed, Desert Rose patt., 6 1/2" h. 210
Goblet, Meadow Rose patt., 6 1/2" h. 85
Goblet, Picnic patt., 6 1/2" h............................ 20
Gravy boat, Desert Rose patt. 45
Hurricane lamp, Desert Rose patt.................... 325
Jam jar, cov., Desert Rose patt....................... 125
Microwave dish, oblong, Desert Rose
patt., 1 1/2 qt. 295
Mixing bowls, Desert Rose patt., 3 pc. set...... 550
Mug, Desert Rose patt., 10 oz.......................... 145
Mug, Desert Rose patt., 12 oz........................... 65
Napkin ring, Desert Rose patt. 60
Napkin ring, Meadow Rose patt. 19
Pepper mill, Duet patt...................................... 125
Pepper mill, Starburst patt............................... 165
Pickle dish, Desert Rose patt., 4 1/2 x 11"........ 42
Pickle/relish boat, Desert Rose patt., inte-
rior decoration, 4 1/2 x 11" 350
Pitcher, milk, 6 1/2" h., Desert Rose patt.,
1 qt. 110
Pitcher, milk, 8 1/2" h., Daisy patt. 78
Pitcher, water, 8 3/4" h., Apple patt., 2 qt. 98
Pitcher, water, 8 3/4" h., Desert Rose patt.,
2 1/2 qt. 140
Plate, dinner, Arden patt................................... 15
Plate, luncheon, Arden patt. 12
Plate, salad, Arden patt. 8
Plate, bread & butter, 6 1/4" d., Ivy patt............. 10
Plate, bread & butter, 6 1/2" d., Apple
patt., ca. 1940 (ILLUS. w/cup & saucer) 6
Plate, bread & butter, 6 1/2" d., October
patt. 7
Plate, bread & butter, 6 1/2" d., Wildflower
patt. 50
Plate, side salad, 4 1/2 x 8", crescent-
shaped, Apple patt. 38
Plate, side salad, 4 1/2 x 8", crescent-
shaped, Ivy patt. 49
Plate, side salad, 4 1/2 x 8, crescent-
shaped, Meadow Rose patt. 29
Plate, child's, divided, 7 1/4 x 9", Apple
patt. 169

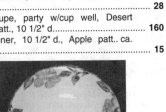

Coronado Table Ware Plate

Plate, luncheon, 9 1/2" d., Coronado Table
Ware, coral satin glaze (ILLUS.) 10

Plate, luncheon, 9 1/2" d., Desert Rose
patt. 28
Plate, coupe, party w/cup well, Desert
Rose patt., 10 1/2" d.................................... 160
Plate, dinner, 10 1/2" d., Apple patt.. ca.
1940 15

Dessert Rose Dinner Plate

Plate, dinner, 10 1/2" d., Desert Rose patt.
(ILLUS.).. 24
Plate, T.V. w/cup well, 8 x 13 1/2", Ivy patt. 85
Plate, T.V. w/cup well, 14" l., Desert Rose
patt. 144
Plate, T.V. w/cup well, 8 1/4 x 14", Star-
burst patt. 75
Plate, chop, 11 1/2" d., Desert Rose patt. 55
Plate, chop, 14" d., Desert Rose patt. 195
Plate, coupe, steak,11" l., Apple patt............... 138
Plate, coupe, steak, 11" l., Desert Rose
patt. 125
Plate, grill or buffet, 11" d., Desert Rose
patt. 96
Platter, 11" l., oval, Arden patt. 35
Platter, 11 1/4" l., Ivy patt. 65
Platter, 12 3/4" l., Apple patt. 50
Platter, 14" l., Desert Rose patt. 75
Platter, 10 1/4 x 14" oval, Apple patt. 45
Platter, 19" l., oval, Apple patt. 207
Platter, 19" l., turkey-size, Desert Rose
patt., ... 325
Relish dish, oval, Desert Rose patt................... 45
Relish/pickle dish, Wildflower patt., inte-
rior design, 4 1/4 x 12" oval.......................... 525
Salt & pepper shakers, figural rose bud,
Desert Rose patt., pr. 28
Salt & pepper shakers, October patt., pr. 35
Salt & pepper shakers, Strawberry Time
patt., 3" h., pr... 35
Salt shaker & pepper mill, Daisy patt., pr....... 135
Salt shaker & pepper mill, Desert Rose
patt., 6" h., pr. 325
Sherbet, Desert Rose patt., footed, 4" d.,
2 1/2" h. 23
Sherbet, Ivy patt., footed, 4" d., 2 1/2" h. 30
Sherbet, Coronado Table Ware, ivory
glaze.. 12
Soup bowl, footed, Desert Rose patt................ 35
Soup bowl, rimmed, Desert Rose patt.............. 35
Soup plate w/flanged rim, Arden patt.............. 15
Soup tureen, cov., Desert Rose patt............... 525
Soup tureen, cov., Fresh Fruit patt., made
in England 200
Sugar bowl, cov., Coronado Table Ware,
glossy coral glaze 14
Sugar bowl, cov., Desert Rose patt. 38
Sugar bowl, cov., Strawberry Time patt............. 30

Syrup pitcher, Desert Rose patt., 1 pt.,
6 1/2" h. 95
Tea canister, cov., Desert Rose patt. 282
Teapot, cov., Arden patt.................................... 125
Teapot, cov., Desert Rose patt., 6 1/2" h. 95
Thimble, Desert Rose patt., 1" h....................... 45
Trivet, tile, Desert Rose patt. 195
Tumbler, Desert Rose patt., 10 oz.,
5 1/4" h... 38
Vase, bud, 6" h., Meadow Rose patt. 50
Vegetable bowl, open, oval, Arden patt.,
large 45
Vegetable bowl, Daisy patt.,
6 3/4 x 13 3/4", 2 1/4" h.................................... 38
Vegetable dish, Desert Rose patt., 8" l. 35
Vegetable dish, Desert Rose patt., 9" l. 45
Vegetable dish, divided, Desert Rose
patt., 7 x 10 3/4" 55

FRANKOMA

John Frank studied at the Chicago Art Institute and was fortunate to train under two noted ceramic artists: Mrs. Myrtle Merritt French and Dr. Charles F. Binns. When a Dr. Jacobsen asked Professor French to find someone to begin a new ceramic art department at the University, she highly recommended John Frank. That position enabled him to study and formulate various glazes. From these experiments he was able to create a beautiful rutile glaze that had been used only sparingly in the past.

When he founded Frankoma Potteries in 1933 Mr. Frank almost always used the rutile technique which helped to create beautiful glazes for his pottery.

With his family, Mr. Frank moved his operation from Norman, Oklahoma to Sapulpa, Oklahoma. He felt he had come home. The family and its company have remained in Sapulpa since that time.

Over the years Frankoma products have been marked in a variety of ways. The "pot and leopard" mark was used from 1935-1938 when a fire on November 11, 1938 destroyed everything including the mark.

A creamy looking clay known as "Ada" is highly collectible today but it was discontinued in 1953. Frankoma then began using the clay from Sapulpa which resulted in a red brick color.

In May 1970 John Frank was contacted by a writer and in response to his questions Mr. Frank personally sent the writer the answers. There has been much controversy over the actual date when John Frank changed from Ada clay (which is more valuable) to Sapula clay. Below is a paragraph from John Frank's letter to the writer, signed by him, that explains the date. You can find the entire letter printed beginning on page 13 of the "Collectors Guide to Frankoma Pottery," Book II, by Susan N. Cox. "...We have always used an Oklahoma clay as the base of all our pottery. The first clay came from Ada, and we used it until 1953 when we switched over to a local brick shale that we dig right here in Sapulpa. Using this as a base we add other earths and come up with what we call our Frankoma Pottery. Peculiar in itself, and it is not available anywhere else, nor is it used by any other pottery, it

fires a brick red and we are able to temper it in the cooling so that all of our ware is guaranteed oven proof."

When Richard Bernstein purchased Frankoma in 1991 a new era began resulting in different products and glazes. True Frankoma collectors search for the products made before 1991 and certainly those made before 1953. Lucky ones can find pot and leopard-marked pieces and those marked "Frank Potteries."

Baker, Westwind patt., Model No. 6vs,
Peach Glow glaze, 1 1/2 pt. **$24**
Book ends, Bucking Bronco, Model No.
423, Prairie Green glaze, 5 1/2" h., pr......... **400**
Book ends, model of leopard, Pompeian
Bronze glaze, Model No. 431, 9" l.,
5 1/2" h., pr. **900**
Book ends, seated figure, Ivory glaze,
Model No. 425, 1934-38, 5 3/4" h., pr. **1,000**

Ocelot Book Ends

Book ends, Walking Ocelot on a two-tiered
oblong base, black high glaze, Model
No. 424, signed on reverse of tiered
base "Taylor" denoting designer Joseph
Taylor, pot & leopard mark on bottom,
7" l., 3" h., pr. (ILLUS.) **1,015**
Bottle-vase, V-1, 1969, limited edition,
4,000 created, small black foot w/Prairie
Green body, 15" h. **125**
Bottle-vase, V-7, limited edition, 3,500 created, Desert Gold glaze, body w/coffee
glazed stopper & base, signed by
Joniece Frank, 13" h. **100**
Bowl, 11" l., divided, Lazybones patt.,
Brown Satin glaze, Model No. 4qd................ **18**
Brooch, four-leaf clover-shape, Desert
Gold glaze, w/original card, 1 1/4" h.............. **40**
Catalog, 1953, unnumbered sixteen pages,
dated July 1, 1953, two versions for
color cover, one w/photograph of Donna
Frank or one w/photograph of Grace Lee
Frank, each **45**
Christmas card, figural fish tray, Woodland Moss glaze, marked, "1960 the
Franks, Frankoma Christmas
Frankoma," 4" l. **75**
Christmas card, "Statue of Liberty Torch,"
White Sand glaze, created by Grace Lee
Frank Smith for her & Dr. A. Milton
Smith's friends, 1986, 3 1/2" l. **75**

Bronze Green Cigarette Box

Cigarette box, cov., rectangular, cover w/single raised & hard-to-find curved leaf handle, Bronze Green glaze, Ada clay, marked "Frankoma," 4 x 6 3/4", 3 1/2" h. (ILLUS.).. **150**

Figure of Fan Dancer, seated, No. 113, Ivory glaze, Ada clay, 14" l., 9" h.................. **800**

Figure of farmer boy, wearing dark blue overalls, light blue short-sleeved shirt, black scarf tied around neck, yellow hair & ivory wide-brim hat w/only brim showing from front, black shoes, bisque arms, hands, face & neck, marked "Frankoma 702," 6 3/4" h... **125**

Figure of gardener girl, holding pale green apron to form a basket in front of her, light blue dress w/short puffed sleeves & scooped neckline, long yellow hair w/dark blue bow on top, bisque face, neck, arms & hands, marked "Frankoma 701," 5 3/4" h. **125**

Frankoma Indian Chief Figure

Figure of Indian Chief, No. 142, Desert Gold glaze, Ada clay, 7" h. (ILLUS.)............. **165**

Mug, 1968, (Republican) elephant, white........... **80**

Mug, 1970, (Republican) elephant **60**

Mug, 1971, (Republican) elephant **55**

Mug, 1973, (Republican) elephant **40**

Mug, 1974, (Republican) elephant **30**

Pitcher, Wagon Wheel patt., Model No. 94d, Prairie Green glaze, Ada clay, 2 qt. **45**

Plate, 8 1/2" d., Bicentennial Series, Limited Edition No. 1, "Provocations," eleven signers of the Declaration of Independence, White Sand glaze, 1972, mispelling of United States as "Staits" **155**

Plate, 7" d., Wildlife Series, Limited Edition No. 1, Bobwhite quail, Prairie Green glaze, 1,000 produced................................. **125**

Plate, 7 1/2" d., Easter 1972, "Jesus Is Not Here...He Is Risen," scene of Jesus' tomb **20**

Political chip, John Frank's profile on front surrounded by the words, "Honest, Fair, Capable," & at bottom "Elect John Frank Representative 1962," obverse w/outline of Oklahoma state w/"One Frank" inside it, around it "Oklahomans deserve outstanding leadership" & "For statesmanship vote Republican," unglazed red brick color, 1 3/4" d., 1/8" h. **25**

Postcard, color photograph of Joniece Frank sitting w/various Frankoma products used to show the current Frankoma glazes, 5 1/2 x 6 1/2"...................................... **10**

Salt & pepper shakers, model of a Dutch shoe, Desert Gold glaze, Model No. 915h, ca. 1957-60, 4" l., pr. **50**

Salt & pepper shakers, model of an elephant, Desert Gold glaze, No. 160h, produced in 1942 only, Ada clay, 3" h., pr........ **135**

Stein, footed, advertising-type, for John Frank Memorial Charity Gold Tournament, Blue, 150 created, 1973 (ILLUS.)......... **16**

Teapot, cov., Wagon Wheel patt., Model No. 94j, Desert Gold glaze, Ada clay, 2 cup **35**

Trivet, Eagle sitting on branch, large wings fill up most of the trivet, Peach Glow glaze, Model No. 2tr, 6" sq...................... **65**

Tumbler, juice, Plainsman patt., Model No. 51c, Autumn Yellow glaze, 6 oz. **7**

Vase, 3 1/2" h., round foot rising to bulbous body w/short neck & rolled lip, unusual high gloss deep blue, marked "Frank Potteries".. **550**

Vase, 4" h., small foot rising to a flat, narrow body w/tab handle on each side, Ivory glaze, marked "Frankoma" **70**

Vase, 4" h., small foot rising to a flat, narrow body w/tab handle on each side, Ivory glaze, pot & leopard mark **155**

Vase, 6" h., square-shaped w/relief-molded flying goose, relief-molded reed decoration on reverse, No. 60B **35**

Vase, 7" h., Art Deco-style w/round foot w/panel on each side at base, rising to a plain, flat body w/stepped small elongated handles, Jade Green glaze, Model No. 41, pot & leopard mark **195**

Wall masks, bust of Oriental man, No. 135 & Oriental woman, No. 133, Jade Green glaze, pot & leopard mark, Ada clay, man 5 1/2" h., woman 4 3/4" h., pr............. **385**

FULPER

The Fulper Pottery was founded in Flemington, New Jersey, in 1805 and operated until 1935, although operations were curtailed in 1929 when its main plant was destroyed by fire. The name was changed in 1929 to Stangl Pottery, which continued in operation until July of 1978, when Pfaltzgraff, a division of Susquehanna Broadcasting Company of York, Pennsylvania, purchased the assets of the Stangl Pottery, including the name.

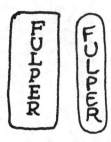

Fulper Marks

Book ends, figural, "Roman Mausoleum" model, bold classical doorway w/peaked roof over fan light above the door which stands ajar, sheer mottled ivory & white matte glaze w/clay showing through, rectangular ink mark, 5 1/2" w., 6" h., pr. (small chip & restoration to corner of one) **$605**

Book ends, square base w/figural Egyptian "Rameses" covered in a matte green glaze, ink marks, 8" h., 4" sq., pr................. **770**

Bowl, 10" d., 6" h., deep rounded sides, the slightly rounded shoulder tapering to a wide, flat molded mouth, decorated w/molded thistles & branches & covered in an ivory to Chinese blue flambé glaze, rectangular ink mark (rim chip & hairline)..... **523**

Bowl, 11 1/2" d., 6 1/2" h., footed, deep flaring sides, interior covered in Flemington green glaze, exterior in Famille Rose glaze, unmarked...................... **825**

Bowl-vase, squatty bulbous body raised on three tiny feet, the wide shoulder tapering to a short cylindrical neck, smooth matte green glaze, professional chip restoration to two feet, mark obscured by glaze, 6 3/4" d., 3 1/2" h. **413**

Candlesticks, flaring socket on a simple four-sided columnar standard above the flaring, stepped round foot, top w/a glossy ivory shading down to a streaked French blue flambé glaze, ink racetrack mark, 10 1/2" h., pr....................... **550**

Center bowl, figural, "Ibis" model, three stylized birds w/wings spread support the wide shallow bowl w/incurved sides, Flemington Green flambé exterior & brown flambé over mustard matte exterior, rectangular ink mark, 11" d., 5 3/4" h. **935**

Center bowl, Effigy-type, a wide flat-bottomed shallow bowl w/incurved sides raised on three crouching figures resting on a molded thick disk base, cat's-eye flambé, blue crystalline & speckled brown matte glaze, ink racetrack mark, 13" d., 4 1/2" h............... **715**

Doorstop, model of a cat, reclining animal facing viewer, tail curled along the body, creamy ground w/streaky brown cat's-eye flambé glaze, ink racetrack mark, 9" l., 6" h................... **1,045**

Fulper Flagon and "Mushroom" Lamp

Flagon, footed bulbous ovoid body w/three ribbed bands & upright curved neck w/square cut-out above applied braided handle, Chinese blue flambé glaze, incised racetrack mark, 11" h., 7" d. (ILLUS.)....................... **440**

Flower frog, figural, modeled as an Indian maiden seated in a canoe perched on a rocky outcrop, in green, mahogany, & brown matte glazes, unmarked, 7" l., 4" h. (small flat bottom chip, probably in the making) **550**

Flower frog, model of a medieval castle on grassy base, brown & green matte glaze, early ink mark, 5 x 5" (a few minor nicks to edges) **440**

Flower frog, figural, a penguin standing atop a large rocky outcrop base w/flower holes, the bird in cream, brown & blue matte glazes w/brown matte glaze on the base, rectangular ink mark, 7" h............ **303**

Flower frog, figural, frog on lily pad, mirrored green & caramel flambé glaze, vertical inkstamp rectangle mark, 7" d. **220**

Lamp, table model, a wide low domed mushroom-shaped pottery shade, inset around the sides w/textured amber slag glass & iridescent green jewels, raised on a tall slender waisted cylindrical base w/a widely flaring foot, two electric sockets, grey & light blue flambé glaze over mirrored lustre gunmetal, base stamped w/vertical "FULPER" in a box, circular "VASECRAFT" stamp, also stamped "Patent Pending U.S. and Canada" & "6," shade stamped "17-17-8," unobtrusive crazing, 20 1/2" h., shade 17" d. (ILLUS.).................. **21,850**

Urn, small round pedestal foot supporting a large bulbous ovoid body w/a wide rounded shoulder to a short wide flat mouth flanked by small loop handles, fine ochre, mahogany & pale blue flambé glaze over textured body, raised racetrack mark, 9" d., 9" h........................... **935**

Urn, tall slender classical form w/wide shoulders & a short neck w/widely rolled rim, upright scroll-tipped handles from the shoulder to the rim, overall Mirror Black glaze on a "hammered" body, rectangular ink mark, 5 1/2" d., 11" h. **495**

Urn, Chinese-form, footed tapering bulbous ovoid body w/a tall cylindrical neck & flared rim, small squared loop shoulder handles, overall Mirror Black glaze over a "hammered" body, raised racetrack mark, 8" d., 11" h. (reglued handle tip)...... **1,045**

Urn, footed baluster-form, shoulder tapering to cylindrical neck w/molded rim, flanked by scrolled handles, covered in a glossy & matte Chinese blue flambé glaze, rectangular ink mark, 11 1/4" h., 5 3/4" d. **715**

Vase, 3" h., miniature, a squatty bulbous base w/an angled shoulder below the conical neck flanked by arched handles from the rim to shoulder, gunmetal crystalline glaze over a caramel crystalline flambé glaze, stamped vertical mark........... **220**

Vase, 3" h., squatty bulbous body tapering gently to a closed rim, overall dark purple & mottled blue matte glaze, vertical stamped mark **176**

Fulper Miniature Vases

Vase, miniature, 3 1/2" h., 3" d., footed squatty bulbous base tapering to a rounded stepped neck w/molded rim, Copperdust crystalline glaze, ink racetrack mark (ILLUS. left) **358**

Vase, 4 1/2" h., swelled cylindrical body w/a sharply angled shoulder to the wide, short cylindrical neck, fine brown, blue & caramel drippy flambé glaze, stamped vertical mark.. **319**

Vase, 4 1/2" h., swelled cylindrical body w/an angled shoulder to a short, wide cylindrical neck, green over blue to red overall drip glaze, unmarked........................ **176**

Vase, 4 1/2" h., 4 1/2" d., footed, lobed bell pepper-shaped, w/small closed mouth, blue over Famille Rose flambé glaze, rectangular ink mark **660**

Vase, miniature, 4 3/4" h., 3 1/4" d., bulbous ovoid body w/closed mouth, covered in a fine ivory to cat's-eye flambé glaze, ink racetrack mark (ILLUS. right)....... **165**

Vase, 5" h., wide half-round lower body w/an angled center shoulder below the wide tapering neck w/flat rim, squared curled C-scroll handles from rim to shoulder, overall purple & blue mottled matte glaze, stamped vertical mark **231**

Vase, 5 1/4" h., 6 3/4" d., footed spherical body w/incurved rim, light blue to elephant's breath flambé glaze, ink racetrack mark **385**

Vase, 5 1/2" h., bulbous ovoid body tapering to a wide heavy molded rim, overall Copperdust glaze, embossed vertical mark **319**

Vase, 5 1/2" h., 4 1/2" d., bulbous ovoid body tapering to a wide short flared rim, dark mirrored green & blue flambé glaze, raised mark **330**

Vase, miniature, 5 3/4" h., 2 1/4" d., slender cylindrical form covered in cat's-eye flambé glaze, interior line does not go through, rectangular ink mark (ILLUS. center).. **275**

Vase, 6 1/4" h., 8 1/2" d., footed spherical body w/short wide cylindrical neck, three loop handles, matte Wisteria glaze, incised racetrack mark **385**

Vase, 6 1/2" h., ovoid body w/an angled shoulder at the short, widely flaring neck, three flat pierced short handles from the rim to the shoulder, green to blue to charcoal semi-gloss drip glaze over a red matte ground, vertical stamp mark........ **253**

Vase, 7" h., wide gently tapering cylindrical body w/a rounded bottom edge & closed flat rim, cat's-eye flambé glaze, impressed vertical mark (minor grinding chips to base).. **248**

Vase, 7 1/4" h., 5" d., wide gently tapering cylindrical body w/a rounded bottom edge & closed flat rim, cat's-eye flambé glaze, ink racetrack mark **385**

Vase, 8" h., 7" d., seven-sided gently tapering ovoid body, flowing matte olive flambé glaze, incised racetrack mark.......... **495**

Vase, bud, 8 1/4" h., slender slightly tapering square form raised on a low angled square foot, glossy & matte Chinese blue flambé glaze, rectangular ink mark **275**

Vase, 8 1/2" h., squatty bulbous base w/tall tapering cylindrical neck, four buttressed handles, cat's-eye flambé glaze, ink racetrack mark **440**

Vase, 8 1/2" h., wide bulbous body w/short wide cylindrical neck flanked by four buttress handles to the shoulder rim, Wisteria matte glaze, raised racetrack mark (hairline to one handle) **1,100**

Vase, 8 1/2" h., 3" d., bud-type, slender baluster-form w/very slender trumpet neck, Leopard Skin crystalline glaze in shades of green, cream & brown, rectangular ink mark **1,430**

Vase, 9 1/2" h., baluster-form, Leopard Skin crystalline glaze, incised racetrack mark **523**

Vase, 10 1/2" h., footed wide bulbous body, the wide shoulder tapering to a short cylindrical neck, Mirror Black flambé glaze, raised racetrack mark **1,870**

Vase, 11" h., tall slender slightly waisted cylindrical body w/rectangular narrow buttress handles halfway down the sides, each w/a narrow rectangular opening, unusual blue & green flambé

over red matte glaze, incised vertical
mark **1,100**

Vase, 12 1/2" h., footed bulbous ovoid body
w/short cylindrical neck w/molded rim,
loop shoulder handle, Leopard Skin
crystalline glaze, incised racetrack mark .. **2,530**

Vase, 12 3/4" h., 7 3/4" d., bullet-shaped
body w/two ring handles, covered in text-
book Cucumber & Leopard Skin crystal-
line glaze, ink racetrack mark **3,850**

Vase, 13" h., tall cylindrical form w/flat rim,
overall relief-molded cattails & long slender leaves, covered in a Matte green &
Leopard Skin crystalline glaze, the
brown clay showing through, rectangular
ink mark (restoration to lines from rim) **1,760**

Vase, 13 1/4" h., squatty bulbous base
w/tall trumpet-form neck, gunmetal &
Chinese blue flambé glaze, incised racetrack mark & remnant of paper label **1,650**

Tall Cylindrical Vase

Vase, 16 1/4" h., tall slightly expanding
cylindrical body w/short molded rim, covered in a frothy Moss to Rose glaze, ink
racetrack mark (ILLUS.) **1,540**

Vase, 17" h., tall swelled cylindrical body
tapering slightly to a short cylindrical
neck, Leopard Skin glaze w/large crystals in green & tan, impressed vertical
mark **2,530**

Vase, 17 1/2'" h., 9" d., floor-type, tall baluster-form w/a short rolled neck, mirrored Flemington Green flambé glaze,
incised racetrack mark (burst bubble
near base) **495**

GAUDY DUTCH

*This name is applied to English earthenware
with designs copied from Oriental patterns. Production began in the 18th century. These copies
flooded into this country in the early 19th century.
The incorporation of the word "Dutch" derives from
the fact that it was the Dutch who first brought the
Oriental wares into Europe. The ware was not, as
often erroneously reported, made specifically for
the Pennsylvania Dutch.*

Cup & saucer, handleless, Butterfly patt.
(wear, stains, chips, hairlines, close mis-
match) **$275**

Cup & saucer, handleless, Double Rose
patt. (wear, enamel flaking, slight color
variation) **440**

Cup & saucer, handleless, Single Rose
patt. (cup stained & crazed, saucer
w/small rim repair, wear to both) **330**

Cup & saucer, handleless, Single Rose
patt. (stains, minor wear) **534**

Gaudy Dutch Plates & Teapot

Plate, 7" d., War Bonnet patt. (ILLUS. left) **825**
Plate, 8 3/8" d., Sunflowers patt. (minor
wear & stains) **715**
Plate, 8" d., War Bonnet patt., minor wear,
green enamel flaked (ILLUS. right) **770**
Plate, 8 1/4" d., Urn patt., wear & scratches **743**

Single Rose Pattern Plate

Plate, 9 7/8" d., Single Rose patt., minor
wear & small enamel flakes (ILLUS.) **770**
Teapot, cov., War Bonnet patt., some
enamel wear, yellowed repairs, 6" h.
(ILLUS. center) **605**
Waste bowl, Double Rose patt., 5 1/2" d.,
2 3/4" h. (wear, enamel flaking, slight
hairline) **550**

GAUDY WELSH

*This is a name for wares made in England for
the American market about 1830 to 1860, with
some examples dating much later. Decorated with
Imari-style flower patterns, often highlighted with
copper lustre, it should not be confused with Gaudy
Dutch wares whose colors differ somewhat.*

Bowl, 10 1/4" d., 5 1/2" h., footed, molded
arched panel designs w/floral decoration
in underglaze-blue w/red & green
enamel & lustre trim (wear, hairline &
some enamel touch-up w/recoating) **$165**

Mug, cylindrical w/ornate C-scroll handle, Dogwood (Shanghai) patt., 3 1/8" h. **358**

Gaudy Welsh Gwent Pattern Pitcher

Pitcher, 6 1/2" h., hexagonal wide lower body below the waisted neck w/a high arched spout & angled handle, Gwent patt., rim chips (ILLUS.) **413**

Pitcher, 9" h., baluster-form w/wide squatty center, scalloped rim w/wide arched spout & ornate C-scroll handle, Centerpiece patt. w/large six-petal blossom on vine w/dark blue leaves, molded background, blue, red & green w/lustre trim, mid-19th c. (firing flaw near handle, flaking to green) **468**

Punch bowl, flared & paneled low pedestal foot supporting a wide bowl w/deep slightly flared sides, the exterior molded w/oblong panels each w/an individual fruit cluster, the interior decorated in polychrome w/the Grape IV patt., mid-19th c., 10" d., 5 7/8" h. (minor flakes w/chips on foot) **880**

Teapot, cov., Grape I patt., footed boat-shaped deep body w/a flaring upswept neck & domed fitted cover w/button finial, swan's-neck spout, upswept angled loop handle, underglaze-blue, red, green enamel & pink lustre trim, ca. 1830 (minor wear, some painted-over spout chips) **770**

Washbowl & pitcher, miniature, Tulip patt., footed 4 3/8" d. bowl w/flaring sides, baluster form 3 7/8" h. pitcher w/arched spout & ornate scrolled handle, minor wear, the set **330**

GEISHA GIRL WARES

Geisha Girl Porcelain features scenes of Japanese ladies in colorful kimonos along with the flora and architecture of turn of the century Japan. Although bearing an Oriental motif, the wares were produced for Western use in dinnerware and household accessory forms favored during the late 1800s through the early 1940s. There was minimal production during the Occupied Japan period. Less ornate wares were distributed through gift shops and catalogs during the 1960s-70s; some of these are believed to have been manufactured in Hong Kong. Beware overly ornate items with fake Nippon marks which are in current production today, imported from China. Over a hundred porcelain manufacturers and decorating houses were involved with production of these wares during their heyday.

Prices cited here are for excellent to mint condition items. Enamel wear, flaking, hairlines or missing parts all serve to lower the value of an item. Prices in your area may vary.

Over 275 Geisha Girl Porcelain patterns and pattern variations have been catalogued; others are still coming to light.

The most common patterns include:

Bamboo Tree

Battledore

Child Reaching for Butterfly

Fan series

Garden Bench series

Geisha in Sampan series

Meeting series

Parasol series

Pointing series

The rarest patterns include:

.. And They're Off

Bellflower

Bicycle Race

Capricious

Elegance in Motion

Fishing series

Foreign Garden

In Flight

Steamboat

The most popular patterns include:

Boat Festival

Butterfly Dancers

By Land and By Sea

Cloud series

Courtesan Processional

Dragonboat

Small Sounds of Summer

So Big

Temple A

A complete listing of patterns and their descriptions can be found in The Collector's Encyclopedia of Geisha Girl Porcelain. Additional patterns discovered since publication of the book are documented in The Geisha Girl Porcelain Newsletter.

References: Litts. E., Collector's Encyclopedia of Geisha Girl Porcelain, Collector Books, 1988; Gei-

sha Girl Porcelain Newsletter, P. O. Box 3394, Morris Plains, NJ 07950.

Bamboo Trellis Basket Vase

Basket-vase, 8 1/2" h., Bamboo Trellis patt., apple green around handle, brown around base, both w/gold lacing (ILLUS.) **$125**

Carp A Biscuit Jar

Biscuit jar, cov., 6" h., tri-footed, Carp A patt., orange w/gold lacing (ILLUS.) **65**
Biscuit jar, cov., Battledore patt., apple green w/gold lacing & white & yellow mums, marked "Japan," 6 1/2" h. **50**
Bonbon tray, Bow B patt., orange w/gold radiations, three large plum blossom reserves, one w/subject pattern & two scenic, backdrop of flowers, wheat & stippled highlights, 5 x 7 1/4" **28**

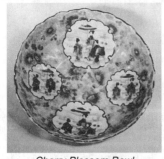

Cherry Blossom Bowl

Bowl, 7 1/2" d., Cherry Blossom patt., red edge (ILLUS.) **45**

Festival Dance Bowl

Bowl, 8" d., Festival Dance patt., pale blue w/gold lacing below (ILLUS.) **40**
Bowl, 8 5/8" d., Daikoku patt., cobalt blue extending inward to form alternating clover & scallop patterns over the lobes, pattern circles around side of bowl, center has chrysanthemum-shaped reserve of hand-painted scenery **75**
Bowl, 8 3/4" d., raised footrim, Cat, Garden Bench K & Parasol H patterns in reserves on a background diaper of butterflies & peonies, mint green w/gold lacing, red & gold leaves on exterior **65**

Boys' Processional Bowl

Bowl, 9 1/2" d., Boys' Processional patt., red-orange w/yellow lacing (ILLUS.) **55**
Cake platter, 11" d., Boat Festival patt., scalloped blue w/interior band of gold lace, plum blossom & "Japan" mark **35**

Foreign Garden Celery Tray

Celery tray, Foreign Garden patt., cobalt blue rim band (ILLUS.) **45**
Celery tray, Painting D patt., scalloped red-orange w/gold lacing, rich maroon coloring **45**

Chamberstick

Chamberstick, Courtesan Processional patt., cobalt blue w/gold lacing (ILLUS.) **70**

Battledore Chocolate pot

Chocolate pot, cov., Battledore patt., red w/gold cherry blossoms around rim & spout, handle red w/gold vines, pattern in wavy panel alternating w/linear diaper stencil covered w/apple green wash topped by pink, yellow & maroon cherry blossoms, signed in Japanese, 7 1/4" h. (ILLUS.) **75**

Chocolate Pot

Chocolate pot, cov., Battledore patt., apple green w/gold lacing, 9 1/2" h. (ILLUS.) **60**

Condensed milk jar w/drip plate, Temple B patt., red w/gold striations **55**

Garden Bench Condiment Set

Condiment set: tray, cov. mustard pot & salt & pepper shakers; Garden Bench patt., pine green, mint green & red w/gold geometrics, "TT" mark (ILLUS.) **45**

Condiment tray, Meeting A patt., scalloped red-orange outlined in gold, signed "Imai tsukuru," 4 1/4 x 6" **24**

Cracker Jar

Cracker jar, cov., low, wide body, Samurai Dance patt., red-orange w/gold (ILLUS.) **65**

Cup & saucer, chocolate, Footbridge A patt., red-orange w/yellow lacing **18**

Footbridge B Cup & Saucer

Cup & saucer, chocolate, Footbridge B patt., red-orange w/gold striations (ILLUS.) **20**

Cup & saucer, tea, Elegance in Motion patt., maroon band, subject pattern in floral reserve, lady & young boy in fan reserve, pale blue diapered background of stylized flowers comprised of tiny stenciled black circles plus two beige & white mums, marked "Hand Painted (paulownia blossom) Made in Japan" **27**

Floral Tribute Cup & Saucer

Cup & saucer, tea, Floral Tribute patt.,
edged in red, black stencil, marked
"Japan" (ILLUS.).. **24**
Cup & saucer, tea, Geisha Band patt.,
scalloped cobalt blue w/gold lacing,
marked "Made in Japan" **23**

Parasol L Dish

Dish, ovoid & scalloped w/fluting at pointed
end, Parasol L patt., red-orange w/gold
lacing outside of beige band w/cherry
blossoms & mums, then pale green
w/gold diapering; three reserves w/sub-
ject pattern & scenery alternating w/red-
orange band overlaid w/gold, centered
w/white reserve w/pale blue & pink flowers; green bands & beige form center,
7 3/8 x 8" (ILLUS.)... **60**

Hair Receiver

Hair receiver, cov., jooi head-shaped, Gift
of Food patt., wavy red-orange, chrysanthemum groupings on either side of
base, signed "Kamaki" (ILLUS.)..................... **45**

Temple A Jar

Jar, cov.,Temple A patt., red & gold bands
sandwiching band of beige w/flowers,
green "M" in wreath "Nippon" mark,
4 1/2" h. (ILLUS.).. **75**

Jewel Chest

Jewel chest, cov., Mother and Daughter
patt. in reverse, gold rim, red-orange
pomegranate finial, overall background
decoration of green & red-orange
ground, pink & yellow cherry blossoms,
violet roses, swirls of coralene & gold,
signed "Yoshi," 3 1/2 x 4 1/2" (ILLUS.)......... **125**

Lemonade set: pitcher, & five handled
mugs; Bellflower patt., brown w/green
band & beading, marked "Japan" **150**

Match holder, Garden Bench A patt., blue-
green, striker on base **37**

Match holder, Lantern B patt., red-orange
w/apple green circles, strikers on both
sides, 1 1/4 x 2 1/2 x 2 1/2" **45**

Mayonnaise set: bowl, drip plate & ladle;
Duck Watching A patt., gold border,
black stencil, yellow background,
marked "Made in Japan" (ILLUS.).................. **40**

Mug, child size, Wait for Me patt., red trim **28**

Mustard pot, cov., w/attached drip plate,
Rendezvous patt., multicolor geometric
border... **35**

Mayonnaise Set

Pancake server, cov., So Big patt., floriate-edged dish w/upward reaching rim, multi-banded border, red w/gold lacing, beige w/gold chrysanthemums, tan w/gold circles & netting, red w/gold scalloped lines & semicircles, dome cover w/squared handle & six steam holes, red & gold handle, signed "Kutani," 3 1/2 x 9 1/2" **150**

Perfume bottle w/stopper, Prayer Ribbon patt., red-orange stopper & neck overlaid by intertwined gold circles **75**

Pin tray, Kakemono patt., blue-green **22**

Temple B Pitcher

Pitcher, 8 1/2" h., Temple B patt., red-orange w/interior band of gold lace (ILLUS.)... **75**

Plate, child's, Birdcage patt., pine green w/white ribbon **15**

Plate, 6" d., Chinese Coin patt., green coins & gold cherry blossoms on red serve as backdrop for three reserves; one w/geisha, the others noting scenes from Boone Island, York, Maine & Young's Hotel, York Beach, Maine **35**

Plate, 6" d., Temple Vase patt., wavy red-orange w/yellow lacing, second border of wavy pink diaper of stylized clouds, waves & flowers, interior border of cobalt blue, red & violet w/yellow cherry blossoms **20**

Butterfly Dancers Plate

Plate, 7" d., Butterfly Dancers patt., scalloped red-orange w/gold lacing (ILLUS.)........ **25**

Plate, 7 1/4" d., Geisha in Sampan E patt., black band w/internal frame of floral striated black stencil in scalloped form w/yellow enamel wash, bright orange background wash, marked "Hand Painted - (double T in diamond) - Made in Japan" **25**

Plate, 7 1/4" d., Visitor to the Court patt., scalloped cobalt blue, marked "Japan" **25**

Plate, 8" d., scalloped & fluted, Dragonboat patt., cobalt blue w/gold lacing, signed "Kutani" **35**

Plate, 8 1/4" d., scalloped & fluted, Temple B patt. in off center reserve, cobalt blue w/gold, internal amber frame, hand-painted violet & magenta roses **55**

Bow A Pattern Platter

Platter, 12" d., Bow A patt., floral edged, red border w/gold spider mums, subject pattern & scenery alternating in reserves on floral & gold ground, signed "Kutani" (ILLUS.)... **125**

Ring tree, Garden Bench Q patt., alternating pine green, red-orange & golden brown w/gold lacing, gold hand extending up from base, signed "Kutani" **85**

Roll tray, Vantine's Blue patt., A. A. Vantine & Co.'s typical pale blue, delicate hand-decorating of geisha & scenery, Vantine's postage stamp mark **35**

Salt & pepper shakers, Parasol C patt., red, 4" swirl fluted, pr. **14**

Salt & pepper shakers, Picnic A patt., cobalt blue, gold stars around pouring holes, hexagonal tri-footed, pr...................... **25**

Salt & pepper shakers, water jar shape, Garden Bench patt., red trim, pr.............. **18**

Sauce dish, Baskets of Mums A patt., mint green w/gold interior band, pierced handle **12**

Sauce dish, Oni Dance A patt., red w/gold lacing.. **14**

Shaving mug, Samurai Dance patt., red w/gold lacing **70**

Soap dish, Garden Bench A patt., gold lacing **20**

Spooner, oblong, double handled, Geisha in Sampan B patt., maroon band **25**

Chrysanthemum Garden Stein

Stein, Chrysanthemum Garden patt., red w/gold buds, marked "Japan," 7 1/2" h. (ILLUS.).. **100**

Fan Silhouette Sugar Bowl & Creamer

Sugar bowl, cov., & creamer, Fan Silhouette of Hoo patt., blue-green w/gold lacing, singed "Tashiro," pr. (ILLUS.).................. **42**

Sugar bowl, cov., & creamer, Rivers Edge patt., geometric red & turquoise green border w/gold, handles red w/gold, spout red w/gold chrysanthemums, upper edge of body is red w/gold band, cen-

tered below which are two turquoise triangles surrounding golden form encompassing blue & yellow butterfly, forms look like miniature chocolate pot & jam jar, signed "Kutani," 4" h., pr. **50**

Sugar shaker, handled & pleated, To the Teahouse patt., beige top, red w/gold neck, multicolored floral shoulder, signature worn, 4 3/4" h. **85**

Sweetmeat set, Rivers Edge patt., gold edged, nine pieces in lacquered box **85**

Fan A Teapot

Teapot, cov., Fan A, Fan Dance A & scenic patterns in reserves on pink background w/red ribbons & large gold plum blossoms, signed "Kutani" (ILLUS.) **125**

Teapot, cov., Geisha in Cards patt., scalloped cobalt blue, advertising premium marked "Cafe Martin, New York," 3" h. **40**

Trivet, Feather Fan patt., grey w/gold lacing interrupted by red-orange outlined beige segments w/gold dots & stylized pink & gold chrysanthemums w/cobalt blue stylized leaves, marked "Royal Kaga Nippon" **55**

Vase, 3 1/2" h., Cricket Cage patt., red-orange **20**

Parasol C Bud Vase

Vase, bud, 3 1/2" h., tri-footed, Parasol C patt., red-orange w/single gold bud (ILLUS.).. **28**

Temple A Vase

Vase, 5" h., Temple A patt., red & gold edge, interior band of beige w/flowers, signed "Kutani" (ILLUS.)................................. 55

Vase, 8" h., Fan A patt., cobalt blue, five reserves; one large & three small pinched corner rectangles w/Court Lady patt., four-lobed w/Garden Bench H & stylized fan w/subject pattern backdrop of dots, phoenix, water & mums 140

Wall pocket, Waterboy patt., pine green, Torii mark 65

Water jar, child's, Pointing A patt. red-orange w/yellow beading, 2 1/4" h. 25

GOLDSCHEIDER

The Goldscheider firm, manufacturers of porcelain and faience in Austria between 1885 and the present, was founded by Freidrich Goldscheider and carried on by his widow. The firm came under the control of his sons, Walter and Marcell, in 1920. Fleeing their native Austria at the time of World War II, the Goldscheiders set up an operation in the United States. They were listed in the Trenton, New Jersey, City Directory from 1943 through 1950 and their main production seems to have been art pottery figurines.

Goldscheider Marks

Figure group, tall svelte Art Deco lady wearing a long flowered dress & wide-brimmed hat, one hand on her hip, the other holding her hat, striding beside her sleek wolf hound, printed & impressed marks, 15" h. (ILLUS. left)........................... **$575**

Two Goldscheider Figures

Figure of ballerina, wearing a lace skirt, printed marks, 17" h. 862

Figure of dancer, the tall slender young lady w/long hair posed wearing a halter top & long flowered skirt which she holds out to the sides, on a plinth base, printed marks, 17 3/4" h. (ILLUS. right).................... 747

Figure of nude lady, an Art Deco style lady standing nude except for stockings & a floral-decorated drapery, wearing a high upswept hat, on a paneled plinth, impressed, printed & painted marks, 19" h. **2,875**

Lamp base, finely detailed figure of a woman decorated in colors of green, yellow, purple & blue, on a bluish white ground & a black base, signed "Goldscheider, Wien, Made in Austria, XXVII," 32" h. overall 1,610

Plaque, molded in relief w/the head of a young woman, stamped mark, 12 1/4" h....... 460

GONDER

Lawton Gonder founded Gonder Ceramic Arts in Zanesville, Ohio in 1941 and it continued in operation until 1957.

The firm produced a higher priced and better quality of commercial art potteries than many firms of the time and employed Jamie Matchet and Chester Kirk, both of whom were outstanding ceramic designers. Several special glazes were developed during the company's history and Gonder even duplicated some museum pieces of Chinese ceramic. In 1955 the firm converted to the production of tile due to increased foreign competition and by 1957 their years of finest production were over

Increase price ranges as indicated for the following glaze colors: red flambé - 50 percent, antique gold crackle - 70 percent, turquoise Chinese crackle - 40 per cent, white Chinese crackle - 30 per cent

Ashtray, rectangular w/wavy wide edge, Chinese White Crackle glaze on edges & brown on interior, no mold number ... **$75-100**

Ashtray, oblong w/model of Trojan horse head on rim, Mold No. 548, gunmetal glaze, 6 x 6 1/2" (ILLUS.) 25-50

Ashtray, square, Mold No. 805, 9 1/4".......... 20-40

Ashtray, "S" swirl design, Mold No. a 408, 2 1/2 x 10" 25-35

Ashtray, square, Mold No. 586 20-30

Ashtray with Trojan Horse Head

Bank, figural, Sheriff, 8" h........................... **200-250**
Basket, shell shape w/overhead handle,
   Mold No. 674, 7 x 8".................................. **25-50**
Basket, Mold No. L-19, 9 x 13" **20-30**
Bell, figural "Sovereign Bonnet Lady," Mold
   No. 800, 3 1/2" h. **50-75**
Beverage set: 8" h. pitcher & six 5" h.
   mugs; LaGonda patt, Mold No. 917 &
   909, the set **50-75**
Book end, model of horse, Mold No. 582,
   10" h... **100-125**

Trojan Horse Head Book Ends

Book ends, model of Trojan horse head,
   mottled green glaze, Mold No. 220,
   7 1/2" h., pr. (ILLUS.) **100-150**
Bowl, 13" d., oak leaf design, Mold No. 591.. **40-60**
Bowl, low, scalloped tulip shape, Mold No.
   523 .... **35-50**
**Butter warmer, cover & candleholder
   base,** Mold No. 996, 2 1/2 x 4 1/2", 3
   pcs... **25-40**
Candleholders, model of dolphin, Mold
   No. 561, 2 1/4 x 5", pr. **40-60**
Console bowl, oblong shell-molded
   w/pointed ends & starfish molded at the
   sides, speckled brown on yellow glaze,
   Mold No. 500 .... **100-125**
Console bowl, lobed incurved sides, Mold
   E-12, 2 1/2 x 7"... **5-15**
Console bowl, crescent moon shape, Mold
   J-55, 5 x 12".. **15-30**
Console bowl, seashell shape, Mold No.
   521, 7 x 12".. **25-40**
Console bowl, rectangular base, body
   w/relief-molded center fan shape flanked
   by cornucopia forms, Mold K-14,
   7 1/2 x 12 1/2" **150-200**
Console set: 14" l. bowl & pr. of 5" h. candleholders; shell shape, Mold Nos. 505
   & 552, the set...................................... **100-125**
Console set: 16" l. bowl & pr. of candle-
   holders; "Banana Boat" bowl, Mold Nos.
   565 & 567, the set **75-100**
Cookie jar, Pirate, 8" h............................. **200-250**

Cookie jar, Mold No. P-24, 8 1/2" h. **15-30**
Cookie jar, Sheriff, Mold No. 950,
   12" h. **1,000-1,200**
Cornucopia-vase, ribbed, Mold No. 360,
   7" h. **20-35**
Cornucopia-vase, square base, Mold E-5,
   7" h... **15-30**
Cornucopia-vase, w/round handles, Mold
   No. 380, 7" h. **20-35**
Cornucopia-vase, leaves at base, Mold
   No. 691, 7 1/2" h. **50-75**
Cornucopia-vase, on flat square base,
   Mold No. J-66, 10" l.................................. **20-35**
Cornucopia-vase, double loop handle,
   Mold J-69, 11" h. **50-65**
Dish, flat, dog bone shape, Mold No.,
   2 x 11 1/2" **25-50**

Gonder Slant-top Ewer

Ewer, bulbous base tapering to a tall
   slanted top w/pointed spout & integral
   handle, Mold 410, Chinese Turquoise
   Crackle glaze (ILLUS.) **75-100**
Ewer, fluted, Mold No. E-60, 6" h. **5-15**
Ewer, "Z" handle, Mold No. E-65, 6 1/4" h..... **10-20**
Ewer, Mold No. H-73, 8" h........................... **15-25**

Carafe-shaped Ewer

Ewer, w/stopper, carafe-shaped, gunmetal
   glaze, Mold No. 994, 8" (ILLUS.)............. **75-100**
Ewer, Mold H-33, 9" h. **30-50**
Ewer, scrolled handle, Mold No. H-606 &
   606, 9" h.. **50-75**
Figure of Chinese peasant, kneeling &
   reaching forward, Mold No. 546,
   4 1/2 x 6 1/2"... **25-40**
Figure of Chinese peasant, standing fig-
   ure, Mold No. 545, 8" h. **15-30**
Figure of coolie, kneeling & bending for-
   ward, Mold No. 547, 5" h........................... **15-30**

Figure of Oriental male, Mold No. 773,
11" h. **40-60**
Figure of Oriental mandarin, Mold No.
755, 8 3/4" h. **50-75**
Ginger jar, cov., square, 10" h. **100-150**
Ginger jar, cov., decorated w/Oriental
dragon, pedestal base, Mold No. 533,
11" h., 3 pcs. **150-200**
Lamp, model of Trojan horse head, Mold
No. 540, 10" h. **75-100**
Lamp, driftwood design, 12" h. **25-50**
Lamp, model of two horse heads, 12" h. **40-50**
Lamp, Oriental dual figures on side,
16" h. **150-200**
Model of cat, seated "Imperial Cat," Mold
No. 521, 12" h. **200-250**

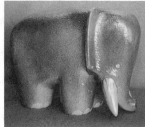

Gonder Model of an Elephant

Model of elephant, stylized standing animal w/greenish brown glaze & ivory trim,
Mold 108 (ILLUS.) **400-500**
Model of panther, recumbent, Mold No.
217, 12" l. **30-50**
Model of panther, standing, Mold No. 205,
12" h. **30-50**
Model of panther, recumbent, Mold No.
217, 15" l. **75-100**
Models of geese, one looking down & one
w/neck stretched upward, Mold Nos. B-
14 & B-15, 3 1/2 & 5 1/2" h., pr. **25-40**
Mug, swirled wood finish, Mold No. 902,
5" h. **15-30**
Pedestal base, Mold No. 533-B, 6" d. **25-50**
Pitcher, 6 1/2" h., squatty bulbous base,
cylindrical neck w/flared rim, zigzag han-
dle, Mold No. E-73 & E-373 .... **25-35**
Pitcher, 7" h., ruffled lip, Mold No. 1206 .... **25-50**
Pitcher, 5 x 8", ridged wood-tone glaze,
Mold No. 901 .... **50-75**
Pitcher, 9" h., plain lip, Mold 1205 .... **50-75**
Pitcher, 10" h., Mold No. 682 .... **50-75**
Pitcher, 12 1/2" h., water, two-handled, tan
glaze decorated w/black figures, Mold
No. 104 (ILLUS.) **350-450**
Planter, w/hole, Mold No. 738,
2 3/4 x 4 1/4" (top to Mold No. 724) **5-15**
Planter, footed, square w/hole in base,
Mold No. 706, 5" h. **10-20**
Planter, Mold No. 724, 4 x 5" (bottom to
African violet planter No. 738) **5-15**
Planter, bulbous body w/tab handles, dec-
orated w/relief-molded flowers, Mold No.
H-83, 5 1/2" h. **50-60**
Planter, model of swan, Mold No. E-44,
5 1/2" h. **5-15**
Planter, figural Madonna, Mold E-303 & R-
303, 4 x 6" **5-15**

Gonder Two-handled Water Pitcher

Planter, figural, Oriental water carriers,
gold trim, 14" **200-250**
Planter, figural, Bali girl carrying basket on
head, 14 1/2" h. **50-75**
Planter, model of large Chinese sampan
(junk), Mold No. 520, 15" l. **25-40**
Planter, two-footed w/flared top, Mold No.
716 .... **25-40**
Planters, figural Bali man & Bali woman
w/buckets, 14" h., pr. **60-80**
Plate, square, LaGonda patt. **10-20**
Relish dish, shallow, divided, six lobe-form
sections, mottled yellow glaze, Mold No.
871, 11 x 18" **90-120**

Gonder La Gonda Pattern Teapot

Teapot, cov., upright rectangular form,
LaGonda patt., creamy yellow glaze,
Mold 914 (ILLUS.) **50-75**
Teapot, cov., Mold No. P-31, 6 1/2" h. **15-25**
Tray, pillow form, flat, Mold No. 544,
7 x 10" **40-60**
Tray, rectangular, flat, Mold No. 700 .... **20-35**
TV lamp, figural "Comedy & Tragedy
Mask," Mold No. 519, 6 1/2 x 10" **75-100**
TV lamp, model of chanticleer rooster,
9 1/2 x 14" **40-60**
TV lamp, model of masted ship, 14" h. **15-25**
Vase, squared Oriental-style w/angular
neck handles, pale green glaze, Mold
537 (ILLUS. top next page) **50-75**
Vase, 5" h., cylindrical, Mold No. 710 .... **10-20**
Vase, 5 x 5" sq., flared, leaf decoration,
Mold No. 384 .... **25-35**
Vase, 5 3/4" h., square pillow form, Mold
No. 705 .... **10-20**
Vase, 6" h., bulbous base w/flared top, leaf
decoration, Mold E-66 .... **10-20**

Gonder Oriental-style Vase

Vase, 6 1/2" h., footed bulbous base w/trumpet-form neck, leaf-shaped handles, Mold No. E-67 .... **15-25**

Vase, 6 1/2" h., hourglass shape w/large applied leaf, Mold E-70 .... **15-25**

Vase, 6 1/2" h., ribbed bulbous base w/cylindrical neck, angled handles, Mold No. E-48 .... **10-25**

Vase, 6 1/2" h., ribbed, swirl design, Mold No. 381 .... **20-35**

Vase, 6 1/2" h., seashell shape, Mold No. 216 .... **70-90**

Vase, 6 1/2" h., two-handled, draped inverted bell design, Mold No. 418 .... **40-55**

Vase, 6 1/2" h., urn shape w/leaf design, single handle, Mold No. H-80 .... **20-30**

Vase, 4 1/2 x 7", ovoid body w/flared top, shoulder handles, Mold E-1 .... **5-15**

Vase, 7" h., bottle form, Mold No. 1203 .... **30-50**

Vase, 7" h., pinched leaf design, Mold No. E-372 .... **15-30**

Vase, 6 1/2 x 7 1/4", scroll footed, Mold No. E-4 or 304 .... **10-25**

Vase, 4 1/2 x 7 1/2", footed, model of single flower, Mold No. #-3 .... **10-20**

Vase, 7 1/2" h., basketweave w/knothole design, Mold No. 867 .... **30-50**

Vase, 7 1/2" h., flared foot below inverted pear-shaped body, flaring lobed top, Mold No. E-6 .... **10-20**

Vase, 7 x 7 1/2", model of seashell w/two dolphins at base, Mold No. 558 .... **50-75**

Vase, 7 x 7 1/2", two-handled, bulbous base w/wide flaring neck, Mold H-42 .... **25-35**

Vase, 7 3/4" h., two-handled, Mold No. H-49 .... **40-60**

Vase, 6 x 8", model of starfish, Mold No. H-79 .... **15-25**

Vase, 7 1/4 x 8", cuspidor top, Mold No. 559 .... **200-250**

Vase, 8 1/2" h., footed bulbous body w/flaring rim, triple loop handles, Mold No. H-75 .... **15-25**

Vase, 8 1/2" h., model of a stylized swan, Mold No. 511 .... **30-45**

Vase, 8 1/2" h., rectangular, decorated w/relief-molded crane, Mold No. H-76 .... **30-40**

Vase, 8 1/2" h., relief-molded double leaf form w/berries, Mold J-70 .... **35-50**

Vase, 8 1/2" h., six-fluted top w/raised leaf design, Mold H-11 .... **20-35**

Vase, 8 1/2" h., tapering pillow form, Mold No. 702 .... **35-50**

Vase, 8 1/2" h., triple leaf form, Mold No. H-67 .... **15-25**

Vase, 8 1/2" h., two-handled, flared foot below horizontal ribbed base & bulbous lobed top, Mold No. H-52 .... **15-30**

Vase, 4 1/4 x 8 3/4", fluted handle, Mold H-34 .... **15-30**

Vase, 6 1/2 x 9", model of stylized horse w/wings, Mold No. 553 .... **10-25**

Vase, 6 x 9", basketweave design w/flared top, Mold H-36 .... **40-50**

Vase, 6 x 9", flame shape, Mold No. H-69 ..... **25-40**

Vase, 6 x 9", tulip form, Mold No. H-68 .... **10-25**

Vase, 9" h., bottle form, Mold No. 1210 .... **25-50**

Vase, 9" h., footed, square double bulb form, Mold No. 607 & H-607 .... **75-100**

Vase, 9 1/2" h., model of fawn head, Mold No. 518 .... **75-100**

Vase, 9 1/2" h., two-handled, twisted baluster-form body, Mold No. H-62 .... **15-30**

Vase, 10" h., Art Deco free form design, Mold No. 636 .... **80-100**

Vase, 10" h., feather form, Mold No. 539 ...... **50-75**

Vase, 10" h., hooked squares design, Mold No. 512 .... **75-100**

Vase, 10" h., model of Trojan horse head, Mold No. 540 .... **75-100**

Vase, 10" h., square form w/impressed flower design, Mold No. 688 .... **50-75**

Vase, 10" h., two-handled, flared footed w/bulbous base & square neck w/flaring rim, Mold No. H-604 .... **40-55**

Vase, 7 x 10", conical w/relief-molded leaves at base, Mold J-64 .... **40-50**

Vase, 7 x 10", model of a butterfly, Mold No. 523 .... **75-150**

Vase, 7 x 10", model of leaves on branch, Mold No. 683 .... **50-75**

Vase, 9 x 10", model of angel fish on waves, Mold No. 522 .... **75-125**

Vase, model of swan, Mold No. 802, 6 x 10" **25-50**

Vase, 10 1/4" h., zig zag & buttons design, Mold No. 517 .... **75-100**

Vase, 11 1/2" h., orchid design, Mold No. 513 .... **50-75**

Vase, 12" h., swirl design w/two openings, Mold No. 862 .... **75-125**

Vase, 6 x 12", Chinese Imperial dragon handle, w/base, Mold No. 535, 2 pcs. ... **200-250**

Vase, 6 3/4 x 12 1/2", model of cactus, Mold No. K-26 or 826 .... **50-75**

Vase, 13" h., trellis w/flowers design, Mold No. 863 .... **50-75**

Vase, 6 1/2 x 13", double, tall slender cylindrical forms joined at triangular form base, slanted rim, mottled green glaze, Mold No. 868 (ILLUS.) **150-200**

Double Cylindrical Form Vase

Vase, 6 1/2 x 13", double, triangular, Mold
No. 368... **70-100**
Vase, 15 3/4" h., leaves & twigs design,
Mold No. 599....................................... **100-150**

GOUDA

While tin-enameled earthenware has been made in Gouda, Holland since the early 1600s, the productions of modern factories are attracting increasing collector attention. The art pottery of Gouda is easily recognized by its brightly colored peasant-style decoration with some types having achieved a "cloisonné" effect. Pottery workshops located in, or near, Gouda include Regina, Zenith, Plazuid, Schoonhoven, Arnhem and others. Their wide range of production included utilitarian wares, as well as vases, miniatures and large outdoor garden ornaments.

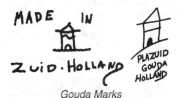

Gouda Marks

Unusual Gouda Clock

Clock, wall-type, a large flattened disk centered by a small round dial w/Arabic numerals, the front decorated in dark blue w/stylized irises & foliage in shades of green, blue, mauve, rust & yellow, glossy glaze, clock works marked "Junghans," crazing, clock not working, ca. 1900, 9" d. (ILLUS.).................................... **$805**

Toothpick holder, floral decoration on black ground, side medallion KLM logo silhouette, 208 Zenith, Gouda Fleer, 1 3/4" h.. **80**
Vase, 4" h., decorated w/glossy multicolor florals on mottled grey ground, green interior, Royal Areo 2841 House mark........ **125**

Small Gouda Vase

Vase, 4 1/8" h., 3 1/2" d., two-handled, footed bulbous form, decorated w/stylized flowers in blue, gold, rust, tan & black on off-white ground, bands in shades of green on rim, black interior, foot & handles (ILLUS.)................................. **95**
Vase, 7 3/8" h., bulbous, nearly spherical body w/shoulder tapering to short cylindrical neck w/wide flared rim, handles from shoulder to rim, decorated w/colorful Art Nouveau flowers, blue, tan & cream on dark green to black ground, marked "Made in Zuid Holland" on bottom in black slip & incised "18," also marked w/small house & "W" in black slip... **770**
Vase, 9" h., footed bulbous nearly spherical body centered by a tall slender neck w/flared rim, high slender loop handles from rim to shoulder, decorated in rust & moss & grass green w/stylized tulip blossoms & leaves swirling against a dark green ground, glossy glaze, painted marks **413**
Vase, 9" h., ovoid shouldered body w/a slender swelled neck, decorated w/stylized flowers & leaves in shades of dark green, rust, brown, pale green & white, matte glaze, signed "Made in Holland" **176**
Vase, 11" h., shouldered ovoid body, decorated w/butterflies & foliage, signed **1,092**
Vase, 12 1/2" h., tall baluster-form w/a short small cylindrical neck, a black ground decorated w/stylized florals in shades of green, cobalt blue, mustard yellow, rust, mauve & purple, glossy glaze, marked "304 - Gouda - Holland - J.B." w/a house (minor glaze imperfections) **575**
Vase, 12 1/2" h., 4 3/4" d., footed tall slender tapering cylindrical form w/a short cylindrical neck, dark green ground decorated w/a standing profile portrait of a Dutch peasant woman w/white cap, green neckerchief & purple blouse, dark blue apron & orange dress, marked

"#7052 RR Holland Gouda - #1852R" (flake on bottom) **385**

Vase, 22" h., tall slender ovoid body, decorated in colors w/an exotic bird & foliage, signed.. **2,760**

GRUEBY

Some fine art pottery was produced by the Grueby Faience and Tile Company, established in Boston in 1891. Choice pieces were created with molded designs on a semi-porcelain body. The ware is marked and often bears the initials of the decorators. The pottery closed in 1907.

GRUEBY

Grueby Pottery Mark

Bowl, 4 3/4" d., 3 3/4" h., coupe-form, the deep half-round bowl raised on a low funnel foot, mottled matte green glaze w/glossy interior, impressed flower mark ... **$495**

Bowl, 7" d., 3 1/2" h., deep flaring floriform five-lobed sides w/tooled buds on slender stems, fine curdled matte green glaze on exterior, glossy green interior glaze, circular pottery mark & "RE 339-2".. **2,750**

Bowl, 8" d., 2" h., wide shallow rounded flaring sides w/a closed rim, interior w/streaky light green glossy glaze, the exterior w/a dark green matte glaze, paper label, impressed mark (minute inside rim flake) **495**

Candlestick, tall slender corseted form w/flaring foot & bulbed neck below the flaring socket rim, tooled & applied leaves around the sides, leathery dark greenish blue matte glaze, paper label, 4" d., 8 1/2" h. **2,530**

Rare Grueby Covered Humidor

Humidor, cov., tapering cylindrical form w/waisted neck & fitted disk shape lid w/knob finial, decorated w/repeating floral band on rim, curdled matte sea-green glaze, impressed mark & incised "ER, 3 - 14," glaze bursts, 8" h. (ILLUS.) **1,093**

Paperweight, figural, oblong model of a scarab beetle, overall white curdled glaze, impressed pottery mark, 4" l., 2 3/4" h. **880**

Paperweight, figural, model of a scarab beetle, covered in a leathery mustard

matte enamel, impressed "Grueby Faience Co. - Boston USA" & paper label, 3" l., 2" h. **770**

Tile, square, cuenca, sea gulls diving in high waves, browns, green & French blue enamels, unframed, unmarked, 4" sq. **770**

Tile, square, cuenca, decorated w/a three-masted ship & rolling waves against a blue sky, browns, ivory & French blue matte enamels, "MM" in glaze, unframed, 6" sq. **660**

Tile, square, depicting the cupid Eros in red bisque clay w/a matte mustard glaze background, unmarked, unframed, 6" sq. **330**

Tile, square, sculpted & painted design of tulips in blue & green w/green stems & leaves against darker green matte ground, unframed, 6" sq. (minor flakes) **990**

Vase, 4 1/2" h., 4 1/4" d., bulbous ovoid body w/a rounded shoulder centering a short rolled neck, crisply tooled & applied wide pointed leaves alternating w/yellow buds around the shoulder, leathery matte green glaze, no visible mark (minor touch-ups to edges, restoration to small rim chips) **5,225**

Vase, 5" h., 3 1/2" d., footed bulbous body w/slightly flaring rim, semi-matte leathery green glaze, impressed mark (small chips to rim).. **880**

Vase, 5 1/2" h., 4" d., ovoid body w/a short flaring neck, incised vertical ridges, matte green enamel, impressed circular mark **1,540**

Vase, 6" h., 8 1/4" d., wide squatty tapering bulbous body, the wide shoulder centering a wide short cylindrical neck, wide applied pointed leaves alternating w/small buds around the shoulder, fine matte green glaze, impressed round pottery mark, by Florence Liley **5,500**

Grueby Vase with Crocus Buds and Grueby Vase with Buds & Leaves

Vase, 6 1/4" h., 3 1/2" d., ovoid body w/wide flat rim, tooled & applied full-height leaves alternating w/large white crocus buds, matte French blue ground, stamped mark, two paper labels (ILLUS. left) **19,800**

Vase, 7" h., footed cylindrical body, the rounded shoulder tapering to flared rim, covered in a thick honey matte glaze, stamped pottery mark **1,870**

Vase, 7 1/2" h., 8 1/2" d., wide bulbous ovoid body w/a deep rounded shoulder centered by a large cylindrical neck w/rolled rim, the body carved & applied w/a continuous band of wide, pointed overlapping leaves, two-tone green matte glaze, signed "W. Post," impressed mark (neatly restored drill hole in base).. **2,860**

Vase, 7 3/4" h., 4" d., slightly swelled cylindrical form w/a ruffled floriform rim, tooled & applied w/full-length broad pointed leaves, leathery matte green glaze, circular Faience mark **2,640**

Vase, 8" h., squatty bulbous base w/shoulder tapering sharply to tall cylindrical neck w/slightly flaring rim, tooled & applied rounded leaves at the base, covered in matte green glaze, impressed circular "Faience" mark (touch-up to minor nicks at edges of leaves)................. **2,860**

Vase, 8 1/4" h., 7 1/2" d., flat-bottomed spherical body w/horizontal ridges, tapering to a slender short trumpet neck w/flattened rim, overall matte green glaze, impressed Faience mark (rim chip restoration) **3,850**

Vase, 8 3/4" h., 7" d., bulbous ovoid body w/a wide flat molded mouth, tooled slender matte green leaves against a mustard yellow ground, by Ruth Erikson, impressed pottery mark & "RE - 9 - 22 - 37" (stilt pulls on base) **5,500**

Vase, 9 7/8" h., 4 1/4" d., cylindrical body swollen at base, decorated w/matte yellow glazed buds on elongated stems alternating w/elongated leaf blades under matte green glaze, designed by Wilhelmina Post, impressed marks & incised artist's initials (ILLUS. right) **4,888**

Vase, 11" h., simple ovoid body w/a five-sided pinched & flared rim, the sides sculpted & applied w/tall pointed leaves divided by carved stems & tiny buds, overall dark green matte glaze, impressed mark (repaired chips).............. **2,310**

Vase, 11 3/4" h., 8" d., wide cylindrical body w/round shoulder & short molded rim, decorated w/two tiers of overlapping leaf blades & alternating bud on stem, thin matte green glaze trailing & gathering at decoration edges & base, pale matte yellow glaze on buds, designed by Wilhelmina Post, No. 36, tight spider hairline in base, impressed marks & incised artist's initials **5,750**

Vase, 16" h., 8 1/2" d., squatty bulbous base w/the shoulder tapering to very tall slender cylindrical neck w/flat rim, tooled & applied leaves on the base, leathery matte green glaze, spherical pottery mark, "133A" & paper label **1,870**

Large Rare Grueby Vase

Vase, 20" h., bulbous ovoid body w/tapering neck, flat rim, decorated w/tooled & applied waterlily blossoms in yellow & red & large curled leaves under a rich thick matte green glaze, impressed circular mark, some color run (ILLUS.) **22,000**

HALL CHINA

Founded in 1903 in East Liverpool, Ohio, this still-operating company at first produced mostly utilitarian wares. It was in 1911 that Robert T. Hall, son of the company founder, developed a special single-fire, lead-free glaze which proved to be strong, hard and non-porous. In the 1920s the firm became well known for their extensive line of teapots (still a major product) and in 1932 they introduced kitchenwares followed by dinnerwares in 1936 and refrigerator wares in 1938.

The imaginative designs and wide range of glaze colors and decal decorations have led to the growing appeal of Hall wares with collectors, especially people who like Art Deco and Art Moderne design. One of the firm's most famous patterns was the "Autumn Leaf" line, produced as premiums for the Jewel Tea Company. For listings of this ware see "Jewel Tea Autumn Leaf."

Helpful books on Hall include, The Collector's Guide to Hall China *by Margaret & Kenn Whitmyer, and* Superior Quality Hall China - A Guide for Collectors *by Harvey Duke (An ELO Book, 1977).*

Hall Marks

Ashtray, triangular, deep, No. 683, turquoise.. **$15**

Ashtray w/match holder, closed sides, No. 618 1/2, cobalt **20**

Baker, fluted, French shape, Blue Bouquet patt. **25**

Baker, fluted, French shape, Silhouette patt. 30

Baker, fluted, French shape, Yellow Rose patt. 25

Batter jug, Sundial shape, Blue Garden patt. 250

Bean pot, cov., New England shape, No. 4, Blue Blossom patt. 225

Bean pot, cov., New England shape, No. 4, Crocus patt. 325

Bean pot, cov., New England shape, No. 4, Shaggy Tulip patt. 275

Bean pot, cov., New England shape, No. 488 patt. 275

Bean pot, cov., New England shape, Wild Poppy patt. 205

Bean pot, cov., one-handle, orange................. 100

Bean pot, cov., tab-handled, Pert shape, Rose Parade patt. 125

Bowl, 6" d., Medallion shape, Silhouette patt. 23

Bowl, 6" d., Radiance shape, No. 4, Crocus patt. 28

Bowl, 6" d., Radiance shape, Yellow Rose patt. 20

Bowl, 6" d., Thick Rim shape, Blue Blossom patt. 80

Bowl, 7" d., Medallion shape, Silhouette patt. 25

Bowl, 7" d., Radiance shape, Crocus patt......... 29

Bowl, 7 1/2" d., straight-sided, Rose White patt. 18

Bowl, 8 1/2" d.,Thick Rim shape, Tulip patt........ 25

Bowl, 8 3/4" d., Five Band shape, Cactus patt. 35

Bowl, 9" d., Radiance shape, Crocus patt......... 45

Bowl, 9" d., salad, Rose Parade patt. 44

Bowl, 9" d., salad, Serenade patt...................... 20

Bowl, 9" d., salad, Silhouette patt. 25

Bowl, 10" d., Medallion line, lettuce green 30

Butter dish, cov., Crocus patt., Zephyr shape, 1 lb... 1,200

Primrose Cake Plate

Cake plate, Primrose patt. (ILLUS.) 20

Canister, cov., Radiance shape, Chinese red 175

Casserole, cov., Five Band shape, Flamingo patt. 75

Casserole, cov., Medallion shape, Silhouette patt. 60

Casserole, cov., Radiance shape, Blue Bouquet patt.. 55

Casserole, cov., Radiance shape, Crocus patt. 80

Casserole, cov., Ribbed line, russet 35

Casserole, cov., round, No. 76, Wild Poppy patt., 10 1/2" d. 75

Casserole, cov., Sundial shape, No. 4, Chinese red 65

Casserole, cov., tab-handled, Rose Parade patt.. 42

Casserole, cov., tab-handled, Rose White patt. 35

Casserole with Inverted Pie Dish Lid

Casserole w/inverted pie dish lid, Radiance shape, No. 488, silver ring trim on casserole lip, pie dish edge & below tab handles, orange, red & purple flowers w/light & dark green leaves, marked in gold "Hall's Superior Quality Kitchenware" in a square w/"Made in U.S.A." below the square, 6 1/2" d., 4" h. (ILLUS.)... 38

Coffeelator, cov., cobalt blue 125

Coffeepot, cov., Drip-O-Later, Duse shape 50

Coffeepot, cov., Drip-O-Later, Sash shape, red 70

Hall Coffeepots

Coffeepot, cov., Drip-O-Later, Jerry shape (ILLUS. left) 50

Coffeepot, cov., Drip-O-Later, Scoop shape w/Wildflower patt. 40

Coffeepot, cov., Drip-O-Later, Waverly shape 35

Coffeepot, cov., drip-type, all-china, Jordan shape, Morning Glory patt..................... 275

Coffeepot, cov., drip-type, all-china, Kadota shape, Crocus patt. 350

Coffeepot, cov., drip-type, all-china, Medallion line, lettuce green 175

Coffeepot, cov., drip-type w/basket, Crocus patt.. 90

Coffeepot, cov., electric percolator, Game Birds patt. 103

Coffeepot, cov., Tricolator, Ansel shape, yellow art glaze 75

Coffeepot, cov., Tricolator, Coffee Queen, Chinese red.. 95

Coffeepot, cov., Tricolator, Coffee Queen, Ritz shape, Chinese red (ILLUS. right w/Jerry Drip-O-Later) 135

Coffee Queen Tricolator Coffeepot

Coffeepot, cov., Tricolator, Coffee Queen,
   yellow (ILLUS.) 35
Coffeepot, cov., Waverly shape, Minuet
   patt. 65
Cookie jar, cov., Five Band shape, Blue
   Blossom patt. 298
Cookie jar, cov., Five Band shape, Chi-
   nese red (marks on paint) 98

Meadow Flower Cookie Jar

Cookie jar, cov., Five Band shape,
   Meadow Flower patt. (ILLUS.) 260
Cookie jar, cov., Flareware, Gold Lace
   design 65
Cookie jar, cov., Grape design, yellow,
   gold band 60

Owl Cookie Jar

Cookie jar, cov., Owl, brown glaze
   (ILLUS.) 120
Cookie jar, cov., Red Poppy patt. 50
Cookie jar, cov., Sundial shape, Blue Blos-
   som patt. 350
Cookie jar, cov., Zeisel, gold dot design 85
Creamer, Art Deco style, Crocus patt. 25
Creamer, Medallion shape, Silhouette patt. 18
Creamer, modern, Red Poppy patt. 35

Creamer, individual, Sundial shape, Chi-
   nese red, 2 oz. 65
Creamer, Sundial shape, Chinese red, 4
   oz. 45
Creamer & cov. sugar bowl, Blue Bou-
   quet patt., pr. 40
Custard, straight-sided, Rose Parade patt. 32
Custard cup, Medallion line, lettuce green 12
Custard cup, Radiance shape, Serenade
   patt. 20
Custard cup, straight sides, Rose White
   patt. 20
Custard cup, Thick Rim shape, Meadow
   Flower patt. 35
Drip jar, cov., Radiance shape, Chinese
   red 60
Drip jar, cov., Thick Rim shape, Royal
   Rose patt. 25
Drip jar, open, No. 1188, Mums patt. 35
Gravy boat, Red Poppy patt. 110
Gravy boat, Springtime patt. 30
Leftover, cov., loop handle, Blue Blossom
   patt. 150
Leftover, cov., rectangular, Blue Bouquet
   patt. 65
Leftover, cov., square, Crocus patt. 85

Fantasy Leftover

Leftover, cov., Zephyr shape, Fantasy patt.
   (ILLUS.) 195
Mixing bowl, Thick Rim shape, Royal
   Rose patt., 8 1/2" d. 30
Mug, beverage, Silhouette patt. 60
Mug, flagon shape, Monk patt. 45
Mug, Irish coffee, footed, high gloss yellow
   exterior w/white interior, marked "Hall" in
   a circle & "Made in U.S.A. 1273" outside
   the circle & an incised " B27," 6" h. 15
Mug, Tom & Jerry, Red Dot patt. 15
Pie plate, Orange Poppy patt. 45
Pitcher, ball-shape, No. 3, Chinese Red 90
Pitcher, ball-shape, No. 3, Delphinium 35

Hall Ball-type Pitcher

Pitcher, ball-shape, No. 3, orchid (ILLUS.) 75
Pitcher, ball-shape, Royal Rose patt. 95

Pitcher, cov., jug-type, Radiance shape,
No. 488 patt., No. 4 95
Pitcher, jug-type, Doughnut shape, cobalt 65
Pitcher, jug-type, loop handle, Blue Blos-
som patt. 195
Pitcher, jug-type, loop handle, emerald
green 65
Pitcher, jug-type, Medallion line, Silhouette
patt., No. 3 35
Pitcher, jug-type, No. 628, maroon 90
Pitcher, jug-type, Nora, yellow 20
Pitcher, jug-type, Pert shape, Rose Parade
patt. 62
Pitcher, jug-type, Streamline shape,
Canary 55
Pitcher, Radiance shape, Wildfire patt.,
No. 5 45
Pitcher, Rose White patt., large 35
Pitcher, tankard-type, black 65
Plate, salad, 8 1/4" d., No. 488 patt. 15
Plate, dinner, 9" d., Silhouette patt. 15
Plate, dinner, 10" d., Wildfire patt. 45
Platter, 11 1/4" l., oval, Springtime patt. 20
Platter, 13 1/4" l., oval, Mums patt. 35
Pretzel jar, cov., Crocus patt. 223
Pretzel jar, cov., Pastel Morning Glory patt. 125
Punch set: punch bowl & 10 punch cups;
Old Crow, punch bowl reads "May YOU
always - have an eagle in your pocket
...a turkey on your table - and Old Crow
in your glass," the set 175
Salt & pepper shakers, Five Band shape,
Blue Blossom patt., pr. 90
Salt & pepper shakers, handled, range-
type, Blue Blossom patt., pr. 90
Salt & pepper shakers, handled, Royal
Rose patt., pr. 34
Salt & pepper shakers, Medallion line, let-
tuce green, pr. 55
Salt & pepper shakers, Novelty Radiance
shape, Orange Poppy patt., pr. 95
Salt & pepper shakers, Pert shape, Rose
Parade patt., pr. 45
Salt & pepper shakers, Radiance shape,
canister-style, Chinese red, pr. 120

Rose White Salt Shaker

Salt & pepper shakers, Rose White patt.,
holes form letters "S" & "P," pr. (ILLUS.
of one) 29
Salt & pepper shakers, Teardrop shape,
Blue Bouquet patt., pr. 35
Soup tureen, cov., Crocus patt., clover lid 350
Soup tureen, Thick Rim shape, Blue Bou-
quet patt. 300
Stack set, Medallion line, lettuce green 95
Stack set, Radiance shape, Carrot patt. 125

Sugar bowl, cov., Art Deco style, Crocus
patt. 35
Sugar bowl, cov., Medallion line, Silhou-
ette patt. 25
Sugar bowl, cov., Red Poppy patt., mod-
ern 40
Syrup pitcher, cov., Five Band shape,
Blue Blossom patt. 165
Tea tile, octagonal, art glaze blue & white 45
Tea tile, round, Chinese red 50
Teapot, cov., Airflow shape, Chinese red 100
Teapot, cov., Airflow shape, cobalt blue
w/gold trim, 6-cup 90
Teapot, cov., Aladdin shape, cobalt blue
w/gold trim, 6-cup 95
Teapot, cov., Aladdin shape, Crocus patt. 925
Teapot, cov., Aladdin shape, oval opening,
w/infuser, cobalt blue w/gold trim 110
Teapot, cov., Aladdin shape, round open-
ing, cadet blue w/gold trim 65

Serenade Teapot

Teapot, cov., Aladdin shape, w/infuser,
Serenade patt. (ILLUS.) 350
Teapot, cov., Aladdin shape, yellow w/gold
trim, w/infuser 58
Teapot, cov., Albany shape, emerald green
w/"special gold" decoration 50
Teapot, cov., Albany shape, mahogany
w/gold trim, 6-cup 95

Adele Teapot

Teapot, cov., Art Deco style, Adele shape,
olive green (ILLUS.) 200
Teapot, cov., Automobile shape, turquoise
w/pink 600
Teapot, cov., Automobile shape, turquoise
w/platinum 650
Teapot, cov., Baltimore shape, Gold Label
line, ivory, ... 80
Teapot, cov., Basket shape, cadet blue
w/platinum decoration 150
Teapot, cov., Basket shape, lemon yellow 150
Teapot, cov., Basketball shape, cobalt blue 750
Teapot, cov., Basketball shape, emerald
green w/gold decoration 450

Orange Poppy Teapot

Teapot, cov., Bellevue shape, Orange
Poppy patt. (ILLUS.).................................. **1,600**
Teapot, cov., Birdcage shape, burgundy **400**
Teapot, cov., Birdcage shape, burgundy
w/gold decoration, 6-cup **335**

Birdcage Teapot

Teapot, cov., Birdcage shape, yellow, "special gold" decoration (ILLUS.)...................... **500**

Blue Garden Teapot

Teapot, cov., Blue Garden patt., morning
set (ILLUS.) **400**
Teapot, cov., Boston shape, canary yellow,
2-cup **45**
Teapot, cov., Boston shape, Chinese red **195**
Teapot, cov., Boston shape, cobalt blue
w/gold Trailing Aster design, 6-cup **150**
Teapot, cov., Boston shape, Crocus patt. **225**

Bowling Ball Teapot

Teapot, cov., Bowling Ball shape, turquoise
(ILLUS.).. **375**
Teapot, cov., Cleveland shape, turquoise
w/gold decoration **45**
Teapot, cov., Cleveland shape, warm yel-
low.. **60**
Teapot, cov., Coverlet shape, white w/gold
cover, 6-cup **40**
Teapot, cov., Cube shape, emerald green **100**
Teapot, cov., Cube shape, turquoise, 2-cup..... **140**
Teapot, cov., Doughnut shape, Chinese
red **400**

Orange Poppy Doughnut Shape Teapot

Teapot, cov., Doughnut shape, Orange
Poppy patt. (ILLUS.)..................................... **400**
Teapot, cov., Flareware line, Gold Lace
design.. **60**
Teapot, cov., Football shape, maroon............. **600**
Teapot, cov., French shape, Chinese red &
white, 2-cup.. **90**
Teapot, cov., French shape, maroon
w/gold decoration, 6-cup **45**
Teapot, cov., French shape, old rose
w/gold French Flower decoration, 6-cup **50**
Teapot, cov., Globe shape, No-Drip, Addi-
son grey w/gold decoration, 6-cup **90**
Teapot, cov., Hollywood shape, Indian red **150**
Teapot, cov., Hollywood shape, silver lus-
tre decoration **325**
Teapot, cov., Hook Cover shape, cadet
blue w/gold decoration **33**

Illinois Teapot

Teapot, cov., Illinois shape, maroon w/gold
decoration (ILLUS.) **175**
Teapot, cov., Illinois shape, Stock Brown
w/gold decoration **250**
Teapot, cov., Illinois shape, yellow................... **325**
Teapot, cov., Indiana shape, warm yellow
w/gold decoration, 6-cup **308**
Teapot, cov., Kansas shape, ivory w/gold
decoration **300**
Teapot, cov., Lipton shape, maroon **45**
Teapot, cov., Lipton shape, yellow................... **60**
Teapot, cov., Los Angeles shape, emerald
green w/gold decoration, 6-cup...................... **85**

Teapot, cov., Manhattan shape, Chinese red, 8-cup 500

Teapot, cov., Manhattan shape, side handle, cobalt blue, 2-cup 95

Teapot, cov., McCormick shape, turquoise 50

Teapot, cov., Medallion shape, Crocus patt. 65-70

Teapot, cov., Medallion shape, Silhouette patt. 70

Teapot, cov., Melody shape, Chinese red 305

Teapot, cov., Melody shape, Orange Poppy patt. 370

Moderne Teapot

Teapot, cov., Moderne shape, marine blue (ILLUS.) 85

Teapot, cov., musical-type, blue, 6-cup 150

Teapot, cov., Nautilus shape, turquoise blue w/gold decoration 225

Teapot, cov., New York shape, Crocus patt. 275

Teapot, cov., Ohio shape, brown w/gold decoration 200

Ohio Teapot

Teapot, cov., Ohio shape, pink, gold dot decoration (ILLUS.) 250

Teapot, cov., Parade shape, black 65

Teapot, cov., Parade shape, warm yellow w/gold decoration 45

Teapot, cov., Pert shape, Chinese red, 4-cup 60

Teapot, cov., Pert shape, Chinese red, 6-cup 75

Teapot, cov., Pert shape, Chinese red & white, 2-cup 75

Teapot, cov., Philadelphia shape, blue w/hearth scene patt. 75

Teapot, cov., Plume shape, pink 40

Teapot, cov., Radiance shape, Acacia patt. (ILLUS.) 225

Teapot, cov., Rhythm shape, Chinese red 350

Teapot, cov., Rhythm shape, cobalt blue 110

Acacia Teapot

Teapot, cov., Rhythm shape, yellow w/gold decoration, 6-cup 125

Teapot, cov., Star shape, cobalt blue 145

Teapot, cov., Star shape, cobalt blue w/gold decoration 125

Teapot, cov., Streamline shape, Chinese Red 175

Fantasy Teapot

Teapot, cov., Streamline shape, Fantasy patt. (ILLUS.) 400

Teapot, cov., Streamline shape, Orange Poppy patt. 343

Teapot, cov., Sundial shape, ivory w/gold decoration 140

Teapot, cov., Sundial shape, yellow w/gold decoration, 6-cup 85

Teapot, cov., Surfside shape, cadet blue 263

Teapot, cov., Surfside shape, canary yellow 185

Teapot, cov., Surfside shape, emerald green w/gold decoration, 6-cup 120

Teapot, cov., T-Ball round shape, black w/gold label, 6-cup 195

Tea-for-Two Teapot

Teapot, cov., Tea-for-Two shape, pink w/gold decoration (ILLUS.) 200

Teapot, cov., Tea-for-Two shape, Stock brown w/gold decoration 100

Teapot, cov., Tea-for-Two shape, Stock green 125

Teapot, cov., Thorley series, Apple design, black w/gold decoration................................. 95

Teapot, cov., Thorley series, Starlight shape, pink w/gold & rhinestone decoration 125

Teapot, cov., Thorley series, white w/rhinestone decoration... 295

Teapot, cov., Thorley series, Windcrest shape, lemon yellow w/gold decoration 95

Teapot, cov., Tip-Pot, twinspout, emerald green... 95

Birch Teapot

Teapot, cov., Victorian series, Birch shape, blue w/gold decoration (ILLUS.).................. 175

Teapot, cov., Victorian series, Bowknot shape, pink... 50

Teapot, cov., Victorian series, Connie shape, celadon green, 6-cup......................... 42

Teapot, cov., Windshield shape, Gamebird patt. 250

Teapot, cov., Windshield shape, Gold Label line, white w/gold dots 35

Teapot, cov., Windshield shape, turquoise w/gold decoration..................................... 68

Twin-Tee set: cov. teapot, cov. hot water pot & matching divided tray; art glaze green 125

Twin-Tee set: cov. teapot, cov. hot water pot & matching divided tray; Pansy patt....... 185

Vase, Edgewater, No. 630, cobalt 25

Vase, bud, Trumpet, No. 631, Chinese red 35

Vase, bud, No. 631 1/2, maroon.......................... 15

Vase, bud, No. 641, canary 10

Blue Garden Water Bottle

Water bottle, cov., refrigerator ware line, Zephyr shape, Blue Garden patt. (ILLUS.)... 750

Water bottle, cov., refrigerator ware line, Zephyr shape, Chinese red.......................... 300

Water server, cov., Montgomery Ward refrigerator ware, delphinium blue.................. 55

Water server, Plaza shape, Chinese red......... 135

Water server w/cork stopper, Hotpoint refrigerator ware, Dresden blue 75

Water server w/hinged cover, Westinghouse refrigerator ware, Hercules shape, cobalt blue 110

HAMPSHIRE POTTERY

Hampshire Pottery was made in Keene, New Hampshire, where several potteries operated as far back as the late 18th century. The pottery now known as Hampshire Pottery was established by J. S. Taft shortly after 1870. Various types of wares, including Art Pottery, were produced through the years. Taft's brother-in-law, Cadmon Robertson, joined the firm in 1904 and was responsible for developing over 900 glaze formulas while in charge of all manufacturing. His death in 1914 created problems for the firm and Taft sold out to George Morton in 1916. Closed during part of World War I, the pottery was later reopened by Morton for a short time and manufactured white hotel china. From 1919 to 1921, mosaic floor tiles became the main production. All production ceased in 1923.

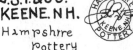

Hampshire Marks

Bowl-vase, low sides decorated w/repeating petals & leaves in low-relief, matte two-tone blue glaze highlighted w/strands of pale blue, impressed & incised marks, No.132, designed by Cadmon Robertson, 6" d., 3" h.................. $546

Bowl-vase, squatty bulbous form w/a wide rounded & flattened shoulder centered by a low, wide mouth, molded w/wide leaves up around the sides, overall dark blue matte glaze, embossed mark, 6" d., 4" h. 550

Bowl-vase, wide bulbous tapering form w/a wide rounded shoulder centering a short molded mouth, overall green matte glaze, embossed mark, 3 1/2" h.................. 308

Hampshire Ewer

Ewer, the wide squatty bulbous footed base w/a wide shoulder tapering to a cylindrical neck flaring to a long arched spout & incurved tab attached to the top of the slender C-scroll handle, matte green glaze, impressed mark, 9 3/4" h. (ILLUS.)... **440**

Inkwell, low cylindrical form, the flat top pierced w/pen holes centering the small round cap w/button finial, w/liner, smooth matte green glaze, impressed mark, 3 1/2 x 4".. **385**

Lamp, table model, a wide squatty lobed bulbous base w/wide vertical ribs & a wide shoulder tapering up to a flat rim supporting a domed metal burner, shoulder & burner fitted w/a widely flaring conical leaded glass shade composed of a stylized geometric design of green slag glass & small bands of blue & red diamonds, pink blossoms & purple top segments, base w/impressed mark, overall 22" h... **2,200**

Lamp base, ovoid form, decorated w/alternating bud on stem & lotus leaves in relief under a dark matte blue glaze, raised on a carved Oriental-style wood base, green glass & brass finial, modeled by Cadmon Robertson, impressed "Hampshire Potttery 42" w/a Robertson cipher, ca. 1910, 19 1/4" h. (minor glaze bursts)... **575**

Vase, 2 1/2" h., 5 1/2" d., squatty bulbous form tapering to a wide flat mouth, incised geometric design under a matte green glaze, marked on the base & w/the cipher of "M" as tribute to Cadmon Robertson's wife, Emoretta, early 20th c...... **345**

Vase, 2 7/8" h., flattened square form w/inverted rim, brown over green curdled matte glaze, designed by Cadmon Robertson, impressed mark, artist's cipher & No. 149 on base (glaze burst at rim).. **288**

Vase, 5" h., 6" d., wide bulbous ovoid body w/wide closed rim, fine overall dark blue & green matte glaze, impressed mark **413**

Vase, 6 1/4" h., 3 1/2" d., incised foliate design under a matte green glaze w/frothy white highlights, incised "Hampshire Pottery 52/2"....................................... **403**

Vase, 6 1/2" h., Arts & Crafts style shouldered cylindrical body w/flat rim, decorated w/relief-molded tulips & leaves, matte green glaze, impressed "Hampshire Pottery," "33" & M inside an O **605**

Vase, 7" h., expanding cylinder w/rounded shoulder, relief-molded leaf decoration, thick feathered blue & white matte glaze, impressed "Hampshire Pottery" **660**

Vase, 7" h., simple ovoid form w/a wide flat mouth, the sides molded w/stylized three-petal blossoms above pairs of leaves atop tall slender stems down the sides, good medium green matte glaze, impressed mark... **715**

Vase, 9" h., 13" d., lobed circular body, matte green glaze, designed by Cadmon

Robertson, impressed "Hampshire - M (in a circle) - 900," ca. 1908 (hairline) **863**

Vase, 9 1/2" h., squat body w/repeating stylized leaf design, extended neck w/flared rim, matte marbleized blue glaze, designed by Camdon Robertson, No. 124, impressed marks **978**

HARKER POTTERY

Harker Pottery was in business for over 100 years (1840-1972) in the East Liverpool area of eastern Ohio. One of the oldest potteries in Ohio, it advertised itself as one of the oldest in America. The pottery produced two lines that are favorites of collectors: ovenware under the BakeRite and HotOven brands and Cameoware. However, Harker also produced many other lines as well as Rockingham reproductions, souvenir items and a line designed by Russel Wright that are gaining popularity with collectors. Harker was marketed under dozens of backstamps in its history.

Harker Marks

ADVERTISING, NOVELTY & SOUVENIR PIECES

Ashtrays, w/advertising, each.................... **$10-20**

Harker 1929 Calendar Plate

Calendar plates, 1907 to 1930, later dates of lower value, each (ILLUS. of 1929 plate) **30-50**
Souvenir plates, 6" d., each **20-25**
Trivet, "Townsend Plan"................................ **35-50**

AUTUMN LEAF

Harker made some Autumn Leaf for Jewel Tea before Hall China received the exclusive contract. The design is larger than that used on later ware and no mark has been found.

Cake plate, Virginia shape **200-250**
Casserole, cov. **75-100**

BAKERITE, HOTOVEN

Harker was one of the first American potteries to produce pottery that could go from the oven to the table. Most of this ware, made from the late 1920s to 1970, features brightly colored decals that are popular with collectors today. Prices vary depending upon the decal pattern. Among the most popular designs are Amy, Colonial Lady, Countryside, red and blue Deco Dahlia, Fireplace, Ivy, Lisa, Mallow, Monterey, Oriental Poppy, Petit Point, Red Apple and Tulips.

Au gratin/casserole, cov. **25-35**
Batter bowl, w/pouring lip **40-50**
Batter jug, cov., Ohio shape **30-40**
Batter set, two batter jugs, lifter & utility
 plate, the set.. **100-150**
Bean pot, Calico Tulip patt., w/original wire
 rack **65**

Various Petit Point Pattern Pieces

Bean pot, individual, Petit Point patt.
 (ILLUS. top row, center front)..................... **8-10**
Bowl, 6" d., Red Apple I patt., Zephyr
 shape (ILLUS. front row, second from
 right w/casserole)...................................... **20**
Bowl, 9" d., Petit Point Rose patt. **15**
Butter dish, cov., Petit Point patt., 1 lb. **40**
Butter tray, cov. **30-50**
Cake/pie lifter **10-20**
Casserole, cov., Petit Point patt., Zephyr
 shape (ILLUS. top row, left w/bean pot)......... **35**

Red Apple Pattern Pieces

Casserole, cov., Red Apple I patt., Zephyr
 shape (ILLUS. far right)................................ **35**
Casserole, cov., stacking-type..................... **10-20**
Cheese bowl, cov. **30-40**
Cheese tray, Zephyr shape **15-20**
Coffeepot, cov., Petit Point patt, Zephyr
 shape, no brewer (ILLUS. top row, right
 w/bean pot) **50**
Coffeepot, cov., w/basket **65-80**

Condiment jar, cov., individual **10-15**
Condiment set, three jars in a holder, the
 set **50-60**
Cookie jar, cov., Modern Age shape **25-30**
Cookie jar, cov., Zephyr shape.................... **40-50**
Cup & saucer, jumbo size........................... **20-30**
Custard cup, individual **8-10**
Custard cup set, six cups in a rack, the set.. **60-75**
Grease jar, cov., D'Ware shape................... **20-25**
Grease jar, cov., Hi-Rise shape **15-25**
Hot plate, Petit Point Rose patt......................... **40**
Mixing bowl, medium.................................. **15-20**
Mixing bowl, Petit Point patt., large **25-50**
Mixing bowl, Petit Point patt., medium
 (ILLUS. middle row, center w/bean pot)......... **20**
Pie baker **15-25**
Pie plate, Amy patt..................................... **16**
Pie plate, Petit Point Rose patt. **15**
Pitcher, jug-type, Arches patt...................... **20-30**
Pitcher, jug-type, Hi-Rise shape **50-125**
Pitcher, jug-type, Regal shape.................... **25-40**
Plate, dinner, Petit Point patt. (ILLUS. mid-
 dle row, right w/bean pot)............................ **15**
Plate, dinner, Red Apple II patt. (ILLUS.
 back row, center w/casserole)....................... **15**
Rolling pin **75-125**
Rolling pin, Petit Point patt. (ILLUS. front
 left w/bean pot).. **125**
Rolling pin, Silhouette patt. **115**
Salad fork or spoon, Petit Point patt.,
 each (ILLUS. front row, right w/bean pot)....... **20**
Salt & pepper shakers, Hi-Rise shape, pr. .. **15-25**
Scoop **50-150**
Syrup pitcher, cov., Ohio shape.................. **15-25**
Tea tile, octagonal, Petit Point patt. (ILLUS.
 top row, center back)..................................... **25**
Teapot, cov., Red Apple II patt., Zephyr
 shape (ILLUS. far left w/casserole) **50**
Teapot, cov., w/basket **65-85**
Utility bowl, Petit Point patt., Zephyr
 shape, 3" d. (ILLUS. middle row, left).............. **8**
Utility bowl, Red Apple I patt., Zephyr
 shape, 4" d. (ILLUS. front, center) **10**
Utility plate, Calico Tulip patt., Virginia
 shape, 12" w.. **28**
Utility plate, Virginia shape........................... **10-25**

CAMEOWARE

Created in the early 1930s and based on a European process, the sky blue ware with its white design that seems to be etched into the surface is Harker's most widely collected pattern. The process was first tried by Bennett Pottery but when Bennett closed, the Cameoware line was taken over by Harker. After the blue intaglios met with great success, Harker also made pink, which was much less popular and rare today, and yellow, which never went into full production. Because of its rarity and its bright contrast to the blue engobe, the yellow ware is highly prized and highly priced today. Prices given are for pink or blue. Yellow prices are almost double or more, depending upon the item.

In addition, Harker also manufactured a line of blue and pink intaglio ware for Montgomery Ward with the name "White Rose." Not so common as the design called "Dainty Flower," White Rose has its own devoted fans.

Ashtray, Dainty Flower patt., Swirl or Zephyr shape, each 5

Cameoware Pieces

Ashtray, Modern Age shape, blue Dainty Flower patt., (ILLUS. far left) 20
Au gratin/casserole, cov., Zephyr shape 25-45
Berry/salad set, serving bowl & six individual dishes, the set 40-50
Bowl, cereal, Shellware shape 8-10
Bowl, salad, Pear patt, Swirl shape (ILLUS. center front w/ashtray) 20
Cake/pie lifter 15-20
Casserole, cov., square, blue 65
Coffeepot or teapot, cov., each 30-50
Cookie jar, cov., blue Dainty Flower patt., Zephyr shape (ILLUS. far right w/ashtray) 50
Creamer 10-25
Cup & saucer, Swirl shape, blue 16
Custard cup 8-10
Demitasse cup & saucer 25-30
Fork or spoon, each 15-20

A Variety of Dainty Flower Pieces

Fruit dish, blue Dainty Flower patt., Virginia shape (ILLUS. top, far right) 5
Gravy boat 30-35
Grease jar, cov., D'Ware shape 15-30
Grease jar, cov., Hi-Rise shape 10-25
Mixing bowl 25-45
Pitcher, jug-type, Hi-Rise shape 75-150
Pitcher, jug-type, round 30-50
Pitcher, jug-type, square 30-50
Plate, 6" d., Swirl shape 5-8
Plate, 6" sq., blue Dainty Flower, Virginia shape (ILLUS. top row, far left w/fruit dish) 8

Plate, 7" d., luncheon, blue Dainty Flower patt., Swirl shape (ILLUS. back row, left w/ashtray) 10
Plate, 7" sq., Zephyr shape 12-15
Plate, 9" d. 12-15
Platter, oval, plain 15-35
Platter, rectangular 20-40
Rolling pin, blue or pink 100-125
Salt & pepper shakers, D'Ware shape, pr. ... 20-25
Salt & pepper shakers, Dainty Flower patt., Hi-Rise shape, stained, pr. (ILLUS. top row, center front w/fruit dish) 6
Salt & pepper shakers, Hi-Rise shape, perfect, pr. 25-30
Salt & pepper shakers, Modern Age shape, pr. 10-20
Soup plate, flat rim, square 10-15
Sugar bowl, cov. 10-25
Tea tile 20-30
Utility plate, blue Dainty Flower patt., Virginia shape, 12" w. (ILLUS. back row, center w/fruit dish) 25
Vegetable bowl, blue Dainty Flower patt., Virginia shape (ILLUS. bottom w/fruit dish) 20

CHILDREN'S WARE

Harker's Kiddo sets were made in pink and blue with an occasional rare teal. Their etched classic designs of ducks, elephants, kittens and toy soldiers are loved by many collectors. Harker also made hot water feeders.

Bowl 25-30
Hot water feeder, child's 40-60

Child's Mug & Plate

Mug, toy soldier decoration, Kiddo set (ILLUS. bottom) 15
Plate, Teddy bear w/balloon decoration, Kiddo set (ILLUS. top) 30

LATER INTAGLIOS

Although highly popular during their time and thus so abundant, the later intaglios produced by Harker are not so in demand today. Therefore the prices are about half of those of Dainty Flower. Often labeled "Cameoware" by dealers, the green, pink-cocoa, yellow and robin's-egg blue ware do not carry the Cameoware backstamp. Popular designs include Brown-Eyed Susan, Cock O'Morn, Ivy Wreath, Petit Fleur, Springtime, Wild Rice and Wild Rose.

Creamer & sugar bowl, pr. 10-15
Cup & saucer 5-8
Plate, dinner 5-10
Platter 10-20

MODERN AGE/MODERN TULIP

Created to resemble and compete with Jewel Tea's Autumn Leaf, Modern Tulips' orange and brown pattern was primarily used on Harker's Modern Age shape, easily identified by its flattened oval, "Life-Saver" finials and the impressed arrow fletchings. Unfortunately, Modern Tulip has yet to be discovered by collectors.

Cake plate 15-20

Modern Tulip Pieces

Cookie jar, cov. (ILLUS. bottom) 30
Creamer, (ILLUS. top row center) 10
Custard cup (ILLUS. center row, second
   from right) 5
Pie baker (ILLUS. top row, left) 15
Pitcher, cov., square, jug-type (ILLUS. top
   row, right) 25
Plate, 6" d. (ILLUS. center row, right) 5
Sugar bowl 10-15
Teapot, cov. (ILLUS. center row, left) 20
Utility bowl, 4" d. (ILLUS. center, second
   from left) 8

ROCKINGHAM

The dark brown Rockingham glazed pieces were reproduced by Harker in the early 1960s. Because they are often impressed with the date of Harker's founding---"1840"---some confusion among collectors and dealers has arisen. Most items are marked as reproductions, but some are not. Many collectors find the honey-brown and bottle green items more desirable.

Ashtray, model of a tobacco leaf 15-20
Bread tray 20-35
Mug, figural, Daniel Boone head 20-30
Mug, figural hound handle 25-30
Mug, figural Jolly Roger head 15-25
Pitcher, jug-type w/figural hound handle
   (ILLUS.) 50
Plate, relief-molded American Eagle (Great
   Seal of the U.S.) 10-25

Hound-handled Pitcher

ROYAL GADROON/CHESTERTON (GREY) OR CORINTHIAN (TEAL)

With its distinctive scalloped edge, the Gadroon line was extremely popular. In the days of bright decals, it was a perfect foil for classic designs like Bridal Rose, Currier & Ives, Cynthia, Forget-me-not, Game Birds, Godey, Ivy, Margaret Rose, Morning Glories, Royal Rose, Violets, White Thistle and Wild Rose.

The classic grey and deep teal of Chesterton and Corinthian, create an elegant backdrop. Still popular today, these two gadroon patterns are frequently marked "Pate sur Pate."

Royal Gadroon Collection

Bowl, cereal or soup, lug handles, Vintage
   patt. (ILLUS. bottom row, center) 8
Bowl, cereal/soup, lug handles 8-10
Cake plate, Wild Rose patt., 10" d. (ILLUS.
   bottom row, left) 15
Cake set: cake plate w/six matching serv-
   ing plates & cake server; Currier & Ives
   patt., 8 pcs. 35
Cake/pie lifter 10-20
Casserole, cov. 40-50
Cup & saucer 10-15
Fork or spoon, each 15-25
Fruit dish 3-5
Fruit dish, St. John's Wort patt. (ILLUS.
   middle row, center) 3
Gravy boat 15-25

Nappy **15-20**
Party set, cup & plate, 2 pcs. **10-15**
Pickle dish **8-10**
Plate, 6" d., Game Birds patt. (ILLUS.
   middle row, right).. **6**
Plate, 6" d., luncheon, Bermuda patt.
   (ILLUS. top row, right) **8**
Plate, 9" d... **12-15**
Plate, 9" d., dinner, Magnolia patt. (ILLUS.
   top row, center) **10**
Plate, 9" d., dinner, Violets patt. (ILLUS.
   top row, left) **8**
Platter **20-25**
Platter, 15" l., oval, Vintage patt. (ILLUS.
   middle row, left).. **20**
Rolling pin **85-125**
Salt & pepper shakers, pr........................... **10-20**
Soup plate, flat...................................... **10-15**
Teapot, cov., Ivy Vine patt. (ILLUS. bottom
   row, right) **50**
Teapots, cov., each................................... **30-50**

RUSSEL WRIGHT

White Clover intaglio on green, charcoal, coral or gold.

Clock, original works **75-100**
Plate **10-20**

STONE CHINA

Made of genuine Stone China clay, this heavy ware with its pink, blue, white and yellow engobe over a grey body was manufactured in the 1950s and 1960s. The engobe (colored clay) was mixed with tiny metallic chips. Later, Harker added hand-decorated designs like Seafare and used its patented intaglio process to create many other designs.

Bowl, cereal/soup... **5-8**
Bowl, fruit **2-3**
Butter tray, cov. **10-15**
Casserole, cov. **25-30**
Coffeepot, cov. **15-25**
Cookie jar, cov. **20-30**
Creamer & sugar bowl, pr. **15-20**
Cruet set **30-45**
Cup & saucer **5-10**
Nappy **10-15**
Nappy, divided **8-12**
Pitcher, jug-type... **15-20**
Plate, 9" d.. **5-10**
Platter **15-20**
Rolling pin **100-150**
Salt & pepper shakers, D'Ware shape, pr... **10-15**
Teapot, cov. **15-25**
Tidbit tray **15-25**

HARLEQUIN

The Homer Laughlin China Company, makers of the popular "Fiesta" pottery line, also introduced in 1938 a less expensive and thinner ware which was sold under the "Harlequin" name. It did not carry the maker's trade-mark and was marketed exclusively through F. W. Woolworth Company. It was produced in a wide range of dinnerwares in assorted colors until 1964. Out of production for a number of years, in 1979 Woolworth requested the line be reintroduced using an ironstone body and with a limited range of pieces and colors offered. Collec-

tors also seek out a series of miniature animal figures produced in the Harlequin line in the 1930s and 1940s.

Ashtray, regular, maroon **$68-76**
Ashtray, regular, mauve blue....................... **48-54**
Ashtray, regular, red................................... **63-71**
Ashtray, regular, spruce green **60-69**
Ashtray, regular, yellow **38-46**
Bowl, 36s, cereal, 6 1/2" d., maroon **84-120**
Bowl, 36s, cereal, 6 1/2" d., mauve blue........... **22**
Bowl, 36s, cereal, 6 1/2" d., red **18-20**
Bowl, 36s, oatmeal, 6 1/2" d., spruce green.. **73-99**
Bowl, 36s, oatmeal, 6 1/2" d., yellow **16-18**
Bowl, individual salad, 7" d., maroon **48-53**
Bowl, individual salad, 7" d., mauve blue......... **33**
Bowl, individual salad, 7" d., red **40-45**
Bowl, individual salad, 7" d., spruce green ... **33-40**
Bowl, individual salad, 7" d., yellow **29-32**
Candleholders, maroon, pr...................... **365-390**
Candleholders, mauve blue, pr. **315-360**
Candleholders, red, pr. **300-310**
Candleholders, spruce green, pr............ **335-370**
Candleholders, yellow, pr...................... **265-285**
Cream soup, handled, maroon **36-39**
Cream soup, handled, mauve blue................. **31**
Cream soup, handled, red **33-35**
Cream soup, handled, spruce green **34-36**
Cream soup, handled, yellow **23-26**
Creamer, individual size, maroon................... **35**
Creamer, individual size, mauve blue **29**
Creamer, individual size, red...................... **28**
Creamer, individual size, spruce green........ **24-28**
Creamer, individual size, yellow **25**
Creamer, maroon **25**
Creamer, mauve blue................................ **21**
Creamer, novelty, ball-shaped, maroon **49-53**
Creamer, novelty, ball-shaped, mauve blue.. **39-42**
Creamer, novelty, ball-shaped, red **38-41**
Creamer, novelty, ball-shaped, spruce
   green **46-54**
Creamer, novelty, ball-shaped, turquoise.......... **38**
Creamer, novelty, ball-shaped, yellow **29-31**
Creamer, red **23**
Creamer, spruce green **27**
Creamer, yellow **13**
Cup & saucer, maroon **20**
Cup & saucer, mauve blue **13-17**
Cup & saucer, red **16-18**
Cup & saucer, spruce green...................... **17-19**
Cup & saucer, yellow.............................. **14-16**
Egg cup, maroon **38**
Egg cup, mauve blue **32-35**
Egg cup, red **34-36**
Egg cup, spruce green............................. **33-37**
Egg cup, yellow **27-29**
Gravy boat, maroon................................ **41-44**
Gravy boat, mauve blue **30-33**
Gravy boat, red.................................... **30-32**
Gravy boat, spruce green **41-44**
Gravy boat, yellow **23-25**
Marmalade jar, cov., maroon **335-355**
Marmalade jar, cov., mauve blue **265-300**
Marmalade jar, cov., red **285-300**
Marmalade jar, cov., spruce green **325-380**
Marmalade jar, cov., yellow **210-230**
Nappy, maroon...................................... **44-49**
Nappy, mauve blue **34-37**
Nappy, red.. **33-37**
Nappy, spruce green................................ **47-51**

ANIMALS

HAVILAND

Haviland porcelain was originated by Americans in Limoges, France, shortly before the mid-19th century and continues in production. Some Haviland was made by Theodore Haviland in the United States during the last World War. Numerous other factories also made china in Limoges. Also see LIMOGES.

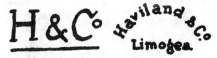

Haviland Marks

Basket, mixed floral decoration w/blue trim,
 Blank No. 1130, 5 x 7 1/2"......................... **$154**
Bone dishes, No. 146 patt., Blank No. 133,
 set of 4 66
Bouillon cups & saucers, No. 72 patt.,
 Blank No. 22, ten sets 226
Bowl, 8 3/8 x 10 3/8", 3 1/2" h., Christmas
 Rose patt., Blank No. 418 1,100
Broth bowl & underplate, No. 448, 2 pcs....... 110
Butter dish, cov., No. 133 patt....................... 110
Butter dish, cov., No. 271A patt., Blank
 No. 213.. 187
Cake plate, handled, 87C patt., Blank No.
 2, 10 1/2" d. 61
Cake plate, handled, No. 1 Ranson blank,
 patt. No. 228, 10 3/4" d. 33
Cake plate, handled, No. 72 patt., Blank
 No. 22.. 105
Cake plate, handled, Ranson blank No. 1 132
Candleholders, Swirl patt., decorated
 w/dainty roses, pr... 135
Candlesticks, Marseille blank, h.p. floral
 decoration, 6 3/4" h., pr. 193
Celery tray, Baltimore rose patt., Blank No.
 207, 5 5/8 x 12".. 110
Celery tray, Blank No. 305, titled "Her Majesty," 13" l. 66
Chocolate cup & saucer, No. 72A.................... 35
Chocolate pot, cov., scallop & scroll mold
 w/floral decoration & gold trim, marked
 "Haviland Limoges, France," 9" h................. 132

Chocolate set: cov. pot & eight cups & saucers; decorated w/pink & blue flowers w/green stems, Blank No. 1, the set **468**

Coffee set: cov. coffeepot, creamer, sugar bowl & twelve cups & saucers; Ranson blank No. 1, the set **523**

Coffeepot, cov., demitasse, Osier, Blank No. 211, impressed "Haviland & Co. - Limoges - France" & English mark **187**

Comport, divided, shell-shaped, white w/green trim, full-bodied red lobster at center, non-factory decor of red, green & black.. **550**

Compote, Meadow Visitors patt., smooth blank, 5 1/8" h., 9 7/8" d. **165**

Cracker jar, cov., floral decoration, cobalt, gold & blue bells, 1900 & decorator's marks **330**

Cracker jar, cov., Marseille blank (small repair on base rim & inner rim of cover)....... **110**

Creamer, Moss Rose patt., gold trim, 5 1/2" h. **50**

Creamer & sugar bowl, Mont Mery patt., ca. 1953 .... **94**

Cup & saucer, breakfast, Moss Rose patt. w/gold trim... **33**

Cup & saucer, demitasse, Papillon Butterfly patt., floral by Pallandre **121**

Cup & saucer, Moss Rose patt., "Haviland & Co. - Limoges - France," pr........................ **20**

Cup & saucer, Rosalinde patt........................... **50**

Papillon Butterfly Cup & Saucer

Cups & saucers, Papillon butterfly handles w/Meadow Visitors decoration, six sets (ILLUS. of part)... **1,320**

Cuspidor, smooth blank, bands of roses decorating rim & body, 6 1/2" h. **193**

Cuspidor, Moss Rose patt, smooth blank, 8" d., 3 1/4" h.. **248**

Dessert set: 8 1/2 x 15" tray & four 7 1/4" dishes; Osier Blank No. 637, fruit & floral decoration, the set.. **110**

Dessert set: 9 x 15" oblong tray w/twelve 7" square matching plates; centers decorated w/Meadow Visitors patt. & bordered in rich cobalt blue w/gold trim, commissioned for Mrs. Wm. A. Wilson, 13 pcs.. **3,520**

Dish, shell-shaped, incurved rim opposite pointed rim, h.p. scene of artist's water side studio, decorated by Theodore Davis, front initialed "D", back w/presidential seal & artist's signature, part of

Hayes presidential service, 8 x 9 1/2" (ILLUS.).. **1,925**

Haviland Scenic Dish

Dresser tray, h.p. floral decoration, 1892 mark **55**

Egg cup, footed, No. 69 patt. on blank No. 1 .... **72**

Egg cups, footed, No. 72 patt., Blank No. 22, pr. **165**

Fish set: 23" l. platter & six 9" d. plates; each w/different fish scene, dark orange & gold borders, Blank No. 1009, 7 pcs......... **495**

Haviland Hand-Painted Fish Plate

Fish set: 22" l. oval platter & twelve 8 1/2" d. plates; each piece w/a different fish in the center, the border in two shades of green design w/gold trim, h.p. scenes by L. Martin, mark of Theodore Haviland, 13 pcs. (ILLUS. of one plate) **2,750**

Fish set: 23 1/4" l. platter & twelve 7 3/8" plates; Empress Eugene patt., No. 453, Blank No. 7, 13 pcs. **413**

Gravy boat, No. 761 .... **35**

Gravy boat w/attached underplate, No. 98 patt., Blank No. 22...................................... **77**

Gravy boat w/attached underplate, No. 98 patt., Blank No. 24.................................... **116**

Hair receiver, cov., squatty round body on three gold feet, h.p. overall w/small flowers in blues & greens w/gold trim, mark of Charles Field Haviland **150**

Ice cream set: tray & 6 individual plates, Old Pansy patt. on Torse blank, 7 pcs. **303**

Haviland Rope-handled Milk Pitcher

Haviland Lemonade Pitcher

Unusual Haviland Punch Cup

Sauceboat & undertray, footed double-spouted boat-shaped sauceboat w/looped side handles w/molded rope trim, matching dished undertray, heavy gold trim on white, old Haviland & Co. mark, 2 pcs. 150

Serving dish, scalloped rectangular form w/a scalloped footring below the flaring side w/low open side handles, decorated w/pale yellowish green to dark green poppies & pale pink shadows, gold trim, variation of Schleiger No. 665, Haviland & Co. mark, 8 x 10" 175

Serving plate, blue & burgundy Art Deco decoration, black ground, "Haviland & Co. - Limoges - France," 10 1/2" d. 15

Soup bowls, No. 271A patt., Blank No. 213, set of 8 209

Soup plate w/flanged rim, No. 761 10

Soup tureen, cov., pink Drop Rose patt., on Blank No. 22 385

Large Haviland Sugar Bowl

Sugar bowl, cov., large cylindrical form w/small loop side handles & inset flat cover w/arched handle, white ground decorated w/sprays of pink daisies touched w/yellow & greyish brown leaves, variation of Schleiger No. 1311,

1 lb. size, Charles Field Haviland, marked "CFH/GDM" (ILLUS.) 75

Tea set: cov. teapot, creamer & sugar bowl, floral & leaf mold w/gold trim, 3 pcs. 204

Tea set: small cov. teapot, creamer & sugar bowl, six cups & saucers, No. 19 patt., 15 pcs. 1,320

Haviland Tea & Toast Set

Tea & toast tray & cup, Pink Drop Rose patt., gold border w/wreath, the set (ILLUS.) 165

Teacup & saucer, cup w/tapering cylindrical bowl & figural butterfly handle, h.p. grey band design on rim & border, Haviland & Co. 125

Teapot, Henri II Blank w/gold & silver decoration (inner rim restored) 138

Toothbrush box, cov., Moss Rose patt. w/gold trim, smooth blank, ca. 1860s-70s, 8" l. 110

Vegetable dish, cov., Marseille patt., Blank No. 9, 9 1/2" l. 72

Vegetable dish, cov., decorated w/small orange roses, Blank No. 24, 10" d. 61

Wash pitcher, Moss Rose patt. w/gold trim, smooth blank, 12" h. 303

HEAD VASE PLANTERS

Head Vase Planters were most popular and most abundant during the 1950s. Whereas some could be found prior to this period, the majority were Japanese imports and a direct product of Japan's post war industrial boom. Coming in all sizes, shapes, styles and quality, these factors varied according to importer. American manufacturers did produce some head vase planters during this time, but high quality standards and production costs made it hard to compete with the less expensive imports.

Ardalt, No. 6039, Madonna w/both hands holding roses, pastel coloring in glossy bisque, planter, paper label, 6" h. $22

Ardco, No. C1248, high bouffant hair, dark green dress, earrings, necklace, paper label, 5 1/2" h. 33

Brinn, No. TP2071, molded blonde hair, painted eyes, earrings, right hand near face, 6" h. 77

Inarco, King w/full grey beard, red, yellow & black w/gold trim, 4 3/4" h. (small base flake) 72

Inarco, No. E1062, 1963, head turned to the right, gold clasps on black gown, earrings, necklace, closed eyes w/big lashes, paper label & stamp, 5 1/4" h............ **44**

Inarco, No. E1062, 1963, ringlet hair, earrings, closed eyes w/big lashes, black gloved right hand holding gilt decorated fan under right cheek, paper label & stamp, 6" h. **105**

Inarco, No. E1611, 1964, closed eyes w/big lashes, earrings, gold painted bracelet, left hand under face on right, 5 1/2" h. **275**

Inarco, No. E1756, "Lady Aileen," gold & green tiara & matching painted necklace, paper label, 5 1/2" h............................ **176**

Inarco Jackie Kennedy

Inarco, No. E1852, Jackie Kennedy wearing black dress & glove w/hand to check, paper label, 6" h. (ILLUS.)............................ **253**

Inarco, No. E193/M, 1961, applied pink rose in hair, light green dress, earrings, necklace, right hand on cheek, closed eyes w/big lashes, 5 1/2" h............................. **39**

Inarco, No. E2254, black dress, pearl finish on hair, earrings, necklace, closed eyes w/big lashes, paper label, 6" h. **55**

Inarco, No. E2322, black dress, black open-edged hat w/white ribbon, gloved hand by right cheek, earrings, necklace, paper label, 7 1/4" h. **116**

Inarco, No. E2523, child w/blue scarf & dress, pigtails, painted eyes, high gloss, stamped, 5 1/2" h. **61**

Inarco, No. E2735, soldier boy w/bayonet, closed eyes, stamped, 5 3/4" h. **55**

Inarco, No. E5624, pink hat & blue dress, earrings, painted eyes, paper label & stamp, 5 1/2" h. **83**

Inarco, No. E779, 1962, applied blonde hair & peach rose, peach dress, earrings, necklace, right hand by cheek, paper label & stamp, 6" h. **44**

Inarco, No. E969/6, 1963, mint green hat & dress, painted closed eyes w/big lashes, 4 1/2" h. **25**

Japan, No. 2261, black dress w/white collar, black bow in blonde hair, painted eyes, earrings, glazed finish, 7" h. **132**

Lefton, No. 1086, white iridescent blouse, necklace, paper label, 6" h. **44**

Lefton, No. 1343A, applied flowers on large brimmed hat & collar, painted features, raised right hand, paper label, glossy finish, 6" h. **61**

Lefton, No. 2536, flower in hair, painted earrings & necklace, gloved right hand under chin, 5 1/4" h. **72**

Lefton, No. 2796, blue blouse, blue sash on head, paper label, 6" h. **61**

Lefton, No. 2796, pink blouse, pink sash on head, paper label, 6" h. **61**

Lefton, No. 4596, green hat, scarf & coat, earrings, painted eyes, black gloved hand under cheek, partial Lefton's label, 5 1/2" h. **110**

Lefton, No. 611B, Lefton paper label & Geo. Z. Lefton stamp, bird on pink floral hat, high collar, closed painted eyes, glossy finish, 6 1/4" h. **50**

Manchu, Ceramic Arts Studio of Madison, WI, 7 1/2" h.. **132**

Napco, No. A5120, large pink hat, fur trimmed pink dress w/blue daisy, closed eyes w/big lashes, paper label, 5" h............. **31**

Napco, No. A5120, orange bonnet w/bow & matching lace-trimmed dress, paper label, 5 1/4" h. **28**

Napco, No. C1775A, 1956, green striped hat w/bow on top right, jeweled green dress, hand by check, big lashes, stamped, 7 1/4" h. **77**

Napco, No. C2589A, 1956, wearing black dress & feather hat, gold painted earring, closed eyes w/big lashes, right hand under right side of chin, bracelet, paper label & stamp, 5" h. **50**

Napco No. C2632C

Napco, No. C2632C, large lavender hat w/dark trim, matching lavender dress, hand to hat, earring in exposed ear, 7" h. (ILLUS.).. **176**

Napco, No. C2633C, 1956, black hat & dress, gold dots on white hat bow, earrings, necklace, closed eyes w/big lashes, 5 1/2" h. **45**

Napco No. C2636B

Napco No. CX2708

Napco, No. C2636B, 1956, flat white hat w/gold trim, dark green dress, left hand under chin, earrings, necklace, closed eyes w/big lashes, paper label, 6" h. (ILLUS.)... 55

Napco, No. C2637C, 1956, white round flat hat, black dress, hand under left cheek, painted eyes, earrings, necklace, paper label & stamp, 7" h. 77

Napco, No. C264B, baby w/white bonnet, paper label, 5 1/2" h. 55

Napco, No. C2683C, 1956, earrings, painted eyes, molded necklace, stamped, 6" h. 330

Napco, No. C3205B, wearing crown of gold & white flowers, necklace, paper label, 5 1/2" h. 66

Napco, No. C3815, 1959, gold & white trim on blue hat, blue high collar jacket, earrings, closed eyes w/big lashes, paper label, 5 1/2" h. 44

Napco, No. C3959A, blue hat w/bow & high collar blouse, real lashes, earrings, paper label, 5 1/2" h. 55

Napco, No. C4556C, 1960, child wearing green hat, painted eyes, glossy finish, partial paper label, impressed, 5 1/4" h. 50

Napco, No. CX2707, 1957, Christmas girl, green w/red trimmed hat & dress, painted eyes, right hand under cheek, paper label & stamp, 5 1/2" h. 77

Napco, No. CX2708, 1957, Christmas girl, holly sprigs in hat, painted cross necklace, gloved right hand away from face, closed eyes w/big lashes, paper label & stamp, 6" h. (ILLUS.).................................... 176

Napco, No. CX2709A, 1957, Christmas child in fur trimmed hat & coat, holding song book, painted eyes, paper label & stamp, 3 1/2" h. (worn paint on back near base) 77

Napcoware, No. 8494, gold bow in long hair, gold dress w/white collar, left earring, painted eyes, 7 1/4" h. 110

Napcoware, No. C6428, three flowers on neck of blue gown, dark gloved hand on left cheek, earrings, closed eyes w/big lashes, stamped mark, 5 1/2" h...................... 39

Napcoware, No. C6429, molded bouffant hair, white floral collar on blue gown, closed eyes w/big lashes, earrings, dark blue glove hand by cheek, 7" h. (ILLUS.)..... 110

Napcoware No. C6429

Napcoware, No. C6985, green dress w/center jewel, closed eyes w/big lashes, earrings, necklace, 8 1/2" h. 165

Napcoware, No. C7472, dark blue blouse, necklace & earrings, paper label, 6" h............ 39

Napcoware, No. C7473, head turned to right, applied floral on right shoulder, earrings, necklace, painted eyes, 7 3/4" h.. 55

Napcoware, No. C8493, long hair off to right side, gold bow & dress w/white collar, earring in left ear, painted eyes, 6" h. (ILLUS.)... 88

Relpo, No. 2004, green dress & hair bow, painted eyes, earrings, paper label & stamp, 7" h. 165

Napcoware No. C8493

Relpo, No. 2089, Marilyn, grey bow in hair on right, black halter dress, earrings, painted eyes, open lips, paper label & stamp, 7" h. (chip on top of bow, minor paint wear on chin & left cheek) **1,100**

Relpo, No. 5634, 1965, Christmas girl, hood w/holly, fur trimmed coat, painted eyes, gloved hand near face, Sampson Import Co., impressed, 7 1/2" h. **165**

Relpo, No. K1175M, wearing hat & matching dress, w/hands folded under chin, open eyes, earrings, necklace, 5 1/2" h. **77**

Relpo, No. K1633, Japan, black dress w/white decoration, gloved right hand touching chin & cheek, earring, necklace, painted eyes, 7" h. **88**

Relpo No. K1662

Relpo, No. K1662, floral molded green & lavender hat & green dress, painted eyes, earrings, necklace, paper label & stamp, 6" h. (ILLUS.) **105**

Relpo, No. K1696, wearing green bow in hair & matching top, earrings, necklace, paper label, 5 1/2" h. **55**

Relpo, No. K1836, Japan, white hat w/blue edge & bow, blue dress w/white trim, painted eyes, right earring, 6 1/2" h. **467**

Relpo, No. K1932, black bows in hair & black high collar dress, earrings, painted eyes, paper label & stamp, 5 1/2" h. **187**

Ruben, multicolored clown in green & yellow, closed eyes, 5" h. **17**

Ruben, No. 4123, white ruffled black dress, earrings, necklace, painted eyes, impression & paper label, 7" h. **88**

Ruben, No. 4129, blonde ponytails, painted eyes, earrings, necklace, paper label, 5 1/2" h. **77**

Ruben, No. 4185, braided blonde hair w/flower, green dress w/high white collar, impressed mark, 5 1/2" h. **110**

Ruben, No. 484, heart-shaped grey hat, necklace, earrings, paper label, 5 3/4" h. **132**

Rubens "Lucy"

Rubens, No. 531, Japan, Lucy in top hat w/horse neck piece, shades of grey, stamped & painted lashes, flake in tie end, 7 1/2" h. (ILLUS.) **275**

Rubens, No. 531, Japan, Lucy in top hat w/horse neck piece, yellow & green w/glazed finish, stamped & painted lashes, 7 1/2" h. **253**

Ucagco, baby dressed in blue bonnet trimmed w/lace & blue bib, paper label, 6" h. (ILLUS. next page) **39**

Velco, No. 3688, Japan, pink hair bow & dress, w/hand at cheek, paper label, 5 1/2" h. (missing one earring) **83**

Velco, No. 3749, white bow on grey hat, black dress, rhinestone earrings, closed eyes w/big lashes, left hand near chin, paper label & stamp, 5 3/4" h. **110**

Ucagco Baby

HISTORICAL & COMMEMORATIVE WARES

Numerous potteries, especially in England and the United States, made various porcelain and earthenware pieces to commemorate people, places and events. Scarce English historical wares with American views command highest prices. Objects are listed here alphabetically by title of view.

Most pieces listed here will date between about 1820 and 1850. The maker's name is noted at the end of each entry.

Albany, New York platter, long-stemmed roses border, 16 3/4 x 20", Jackson (glaze wear) **$690**

Almshouse, New York plate, floral & scroll border, dark blue, 10" d., Andrew Stevenson (small blister, light stains, small chips on table ring) **385**

American Views, Boston and Bunker Hill platter, flowers, moss & leaves border, purple, 16" l., Thomas Godwin (crazing, glaze imperfections, minor staining) **374**

Arms of New York plate, flowers & vines border, dark blue, 10" d., T. Mayer (wear, scratches w/pinpoint flakes) **440**

Baltimore & Ohio Railroad, level (The) plate, shell border, dark blue, 10 1/8" d., E. Wood (stains, minor roughness on table ring) **990**

Baltimore & Ohio Railroad, level (The) soup plate, shell border, dark blue, 10" d. (E. Wood) **953**

Battery, New York (Flagstaff Pavilion) plate, vine leaf border, dark blue, 7 1/8" d., R. Stevenson (wear, scratches) **220**

Battle of Chapultepec plate, 9 1/2" d., Texian Campaign series, symbols of war & a "goddess-type" seated border, green, Shaw (light facial wear) **532**

Boston Mails...Ladies Cabin platter, border medallions of steamships & two views of "Acadia" & "Columbia," light

blue, 16" l., Edwards (minor staining, knife marks) **259**

Boston State House dinner service: 29 dinner plates, 19 luncheon plates, 11 soup plates, four bread & butter plates, 10 platters (one w/a pierced insert), a cov. soup tureen, ladle & undertray, four cov. sauce tureens & three undertrays, four cov. serving dishes, a square center bowl; dark blue, Rogers, the set (some w/staple & other repairs, minor cracks, chips & staining) **14,950**

Boston State House pitcher, 5 3/4" h., Rose Border series, fully opened roses w/leaves border, dark blue, Stubbs (half the spout w/old restoration, slightly discolored) **202**

Boston State House soup plate, floral border, dark medium blue, 10" d. (Wood) **364**

Boston State House tile, rectangular, floral border, dark medium blue, 6" l., Minton (several very minor flakes along rim) **190**

Capitol, Washington (The) cake plate, footed, Beauties of America series, flowers within medallions border, dark blue, 10 1/2" d., 2 1/2" h., Ridgway (few hard-to-find internal hairlines & minor stain) **3,080**

Capitol, Washington (The) plate, shell border, dark blue, 7 1/2" d. (E. Wood) **715**

Capitol, Washington (The) plate, vine border, dark blue, 10" d., Stevenson (flake on table ring) **550**

Capitol, Washington (The) plate, vine border, embossed white rim, dark blue, 10 1/8" d., Stevenson (minor wear) **413**

Castle Garden, Battery, New York platter, trefoil separated by knobs border, dark blue, 18 1/2" l., Wood (minor wear & scratches, small flake) **2,915**

Chief Justice Marshall, Troy plate, shell border, dark blue, 8 1/2" d., E. Wood (minor edge wear) **495**

City of Montreal platter, 18" l., well & tree, flowers border, light blue, Davenport (professional restoration to hairline from rim half way into center) **672**

Columbia College, New York plate, acorn & oak leaves border, medium blue, 6 3/8" d., R. Stevenson (flake at table ring & pinpoints on rim) **385**

Columbia College, New York plate, floral & scroll border, dark blue, 7 1/2" d., Andrew Stevenson (rim chip) **660**

Commodore MacDonnough's Victory plate, irregular shells border, dark blue, 10 1/8" d., Wood (minor wear, light scratches) **605**

Dam & Water Works (The), Philadelphia plate, fruit & flower border, dark blue, 9 3/4" d., Henshall, Williamson & Co. (few face scratches) **440**

Dam & Water Works (The), Philadelphia (Sidewheel Steamboat) soup plate, fruit & flowers border, dark blue, 9 3/4" d., Henshall, Williamson & Co. (wear) **660**

Entrance of the Erie Canal into the Hudson at Albany plate, floral border, dark blue, 10" d., E. Wood (minor wear, pin-point flakes, spider crack) 880

Exchange, Baltimore plate, fruit & flowers border, dark blue, 10" d. (Henshall, Williamson & Co.) 440

Fair Mount Near Philadelphia bowl, spread-eagle border, dark blue, 9 1/4" d., Stubbs (wear, light crazing, chip on table ring, several shallow chips on beaded rim) 550

Fair Mount Near Philadelphia plate, spread-eagle border, dark blue, 10 1/4" d., Stubbs (minor scratches) 275

Great Fire, City of New York, Burning of Coenties Slip plate, fire engines & eagles border, light blue, unknown maker, 8" d. (wear & small edge flakes)....... 385

Harvard College plate, acorn & oak leaves border, dark blue, minor roughness on table ring, 10" d., (Stevenson & Williams) 275

Harvard College soup plate, acorn & oak leaves border, dark blue,10" d., Stevenson & Williams (wear, scratches) 165

Hospital, Boston plate, vine border, dark blue, 8 1/2" d., Stevenson & Williams (wear & scratches) 289

Lafayette & Washington Busts plate, black transfer-print central reserve w/pair of portraits below a spread-winged American eagle, plain background w/black rim band, ca. 1825, 6 3/4" d., Wood (wear) 605

Landing of General Lafayette at Castle Garden, New York, 16 August 1824 gravy underplate, primrose & dogwood border, dark blue, 9 3/4" l., Clews 963

Landing of General Lafayette at Castle Garden, New York, 16 August 1824 pitcher, floral & vine border, jug-type, dark blue, 7 7/8" h., Clews (spider crack in foot, wear, glaze flakes) 1,100

Landing of General Lafayette Plate

Landing of General Lafayette at Castle Garden, New York, 16 August 1824 plate, primrose & dogwood border, dark blue, 8 3/4" d., Clews (ILLUS.) 310

Landing of General Lafayette at Castle Garden, New York, 16 August 1824 plate, floral & vine border, dark blue, 10 1/4" d., Clews 432

Landing of General Lafayette at Castle Garden, New York, 16 August 1824 platter, floral & vine border, dark blue, 15 1/4" l., Clews (small edge flakes) 1,760

Landing of the Fathers at Plymouth pitcher, pairs of birds & scrolls & four

medallions w/ships & inscriptions border, medium blue, 6 1/2" h., Wood (minor chips, star crack, glaze wear)...................... 345

Mitchell & Freeman's China and Glass Warehouse, Chatham Street, Boston plate, foliage border, dark blue, 9" d., Adams (wear, scratches, chip on rim back) 385

Mitchell & Freeman's China and Glass Warehouse, Chatham Street, Boston plate, foliage border, dark blue, 10 1/4" d., Adams (very minor wear)......... 1,100

Mount Vernon, The Seat of the Late Gen'l. Washington cup & saucer, large flowers border, dark blue, maker unknown, 5 1/2" d., 2 1/2" h. (light wear on saucer, small chip on foot of cup) 364

Mount Vernon, The Seat of the Late Gen'l. Washington sugar bowl, large flowers border, dark blue, 5 7/8" h., unknown maker (chips & rim hairlines, lid may be mismatched) 1,155

Near Fishkill plate, flowers & scrolls border, dark blue, 7 3/4" d. (Clews)................. 248

New York From Brooklyn Heights plate, flowers between leafy scrolls border, dark blue, 10 1/4" d., Stevenson (minor wear & chip on table ring) 1,485

New York from Brooklyn Heights Platter

New York From Brooklyn Heights platter, flowers between leafy scrolls border, dark blue, 16 1/4" l., minor wear & small rim flake, Stevenson (ILLUS.) 6,050

New York from Weehawk platter, floral border, dark blue, 18 3/4" l., Stevenson (knife scratches, hairline) 1,210

Niagara Falls From the American Side platter, shell border, dark blue, 14 7/8" l., Wood & Sons (wear, scratches)... 2,640

Octagon Church, Boston fruit bowl, footed & handled, reverse w/"Bank, Savannah" & "Exchange, Charleston," dark blue, Beauties of America series, J. & W. Ridgway, 10" d., 5" h. (minute glaze chips, very minor firing crack on one handle) 1,495

Picturesque View, Little Falls at Luzerne, Hudson River platter, floral & scroll border, black, 17 1/2" l., Clews (wear, knife scratches, small flakes) 440

President's House, Washington plate, four medallion - floral border, purple, 10 3/8" d. (E. Wood)................................... 248

Sandusky Platter

Sandusky (Ohio) platter, floral border, medium dark blue, harbor scene w/steamship "Henry Clay" & other ships, shoreline in background w/several buildings, 16 1/2" l., minor wear & short scratches, retailer's mark "I.M. Thompson & Co. Wheeling Va.," Clews (ILLUS.) **8,250**

Shepherd Boy Rescued platter, six-point star w/birds & flowers border, dark blue,12 5/8" l., Clews (staining, knife marks, glaze chips) **115**

State House, Boston gravy boat, flowers within medallions border, dark blue, 6 1/2" l., Ridgway (minor stains at interior pinpoints) **330**

State House, Boston platter, spread-eagle border, dark blue, 14 5/8" l., Stubbs (minor scratches, spider crack) **1,045**

States series pitcher, border w/names of fifteen states in festoons separated by five-point stars, center scene of castle w/flag, boats in foreground, dark blue, unmarked, 9 3/4" h. (small edge flakes on rim, handle & spout, minor wear & shallow flake on bottom) **2,530**

States series plate, two-story building w/curved drive, border w/names of fifteen states in festoons separated by five-point stars border, dark blue, 7 3/4" d., Clews (small rim bruise) **358**

States series plate, building, sheep on lawn, border w/names of fifteen states in festoons separated by five-point stars border, dark blue, 8 3/4" d., Clews (rim w/area of glaze flakes, stain)....................... **303**

Table Rock, Niagara plate, shell border - circular center, dark blue, 10 1/8" d., E. Wood (minor wear & scratches).................. **413**

Rare Texian Campaigne Compote

Texian Campaigne - Battle of Palo Alto compote, battle scene center, symbols

of war & a "goddess-type" seated border, light blue, 5 1/2" h., 10 1/4" d., Shaw (ILLUS.)................................. **2,800-3,000**

Transylvania University, Lexington plate, shell border, dark blue, 9 1/4" d., Wood (wear)... **385**

United States Hotel, Philadelphia plate, 10" d., foliage w/grotto center border, dark blue, Tams (large in-the-making spider to left of ladies) **532**

View of Governor's Island Soup Plate

View of Governor's Island soup plate, floral & scroll border, dark blue, minor wear & small flakes w/crow's foot hairline, 10 3/8" d., Stevenson (ILLUS.) **2,475**

View of Trenton Falls---Three People Rock plate, shell w/circular center w/trailing vine around outer edge of center border, dark blue, 7 3/4" d., Wood (light wear) **280**

Washington plate, flowers & scrolls border, dark blue, 7 3/4" d. (Clews).................. **385**

Washington Standing at Tomb, scroll in hand cup & saucer, dark blue, saucer 6 1/2" d., E. Wood (minor chips, staining, transfer imperfections) **454**

Water Works, Philadelphia plate, acorn & oak leaves border, dark blue, 10 1/8" d. (Stevenson & Williams) **605**

Winter View of Pittsfield, Massachusetts open vegetable dish, vignette views & flowers border, dark blue, 12 1/2" l., Clews (minor wear w/some glaze wear on edges)................................ **1,870**

Winter View of Pittsfield, Massachusetts plate, vignette views & flowers border, dark blue, 6" d. (Clews)................... **230**

HOMER LAUGHLIN CHINA COMPANY

It was after the Civil War that Homer Laughlin journeyed to East Liverpool, Ohio and set up his first short-lived stoneware pottery. In 1870 Homer and his brother Shakespeare opened another pottery which produced yellowwares and Rockingham-glazed utilitarian pieces. Some years later the firm added whiteware to the production as well as fine white ironstone china.

By the early 20th century the firm had grown tremendously and although Homer Laughlin sold out his interest in the company to the W.E. Wells family in 1898, the company name continued as the Homer Laughlin China Company. During the 1920s numerous additional production factories were opened and a wide range of dinnerwares became the main focus of their output. In the 1930s the famous Fiesta, Harlequin (which see) and Riviera lines were produced and met with great public success. Today the Homer Laughlin firm continues in operation as one of this country's longest continually running potteries.

The products of Homer Laughlin are well marked and often carry a dating code as well as the trademark. A wide range of factory-named dinnerware shapes were made by the company, however, many of the patterns they used were only given numbers, which makes collecting by pattern a little more difficult today. The following is a brief listing of Homer Laughlin dinnerware lines and patterns.

Helpful references in this field are The Collector's Encyclopedia of Homer Laughlin China by Joanne Jasper (Collector Books, 1993) and The Collector's Encyclopedia of Fiesta, Harlequin, Riviera and Kitchen Kraft, by Bob & Sharon Huxford (Collector Books, 1992). Information here was provided by the Homer Laughlin China Collectors Association. Also refer to their book Fiesta, Harlequin and Kitchen Kraft: The Homer Laughlin China Collectors Association Guide (summer 2000).

Value Guide: low end vs high end pricing is dependent on market availability and collector demand at any given moment. Generally there are harder-to-find colors in each of the lines and those would be reflected in the high end pricing. However, those colors may be different for different collectors. This is meant as a guide only. Condition of the items is representative of what prices would be without any chips, cracks, dings, scratches, etc. The smallest flaw can and does drastically lower the value accordingly.

CARNIVAL LINE
Colors: light green, red (orange), Harlequin yellow, grey, forest green, ivory, cobalt blue

Bowl, fruit	**$4-8**
Bowl, oatmeal	5-9
Plate, 6 1/2" d.	2-4
Saucer,	2-3
Tea cup	3-6
Tea cup, cobalt blue glaze	15+

OVENSERVE LINE
Colors: pink, turquoise, forest green, dark brown, rust

Baking dish, oval	6-9
Casserole, French-style	5-8
Custard cup	4-6
Pie plate, individual	9-13
Ramekin, round	6-8

RIVIERA LINE
Colors: light green, mauve blue, red (orange), Harlequin yellow & ivory.

Bowl, 7 1/4" d., nappy	**25-32**
Bowl, 5 1/2" d., fruit	10-14
Casserole, cov.	**90-145**
Plate, 10" d., dinner	45-65
Tea cup & saucer, the set	8-12

Teapot, cov.	**125-175**
Tumbler, handled	**55-80**
Tumbler, handled, ivory glaze	**140+**

WELLS ART GLAZE LINE
Colors: rust, peach, green, yellow

Bowl, 8" d., nappy	**18-24**
Creamer	15-24
Pitcher, cov., 9" h., jug-form	**90-125**
Plate, 9" d.	11-16
Platter, 11 1/2"	19-27
Syrup pitcher	75-110

HULL

This pottery was made by the Hull Pottery Company, Crooksville, Ohio, beginning in 1905. Art Pottery was made until 1950 when the company converted to utilitarian wares. All production ceased in 1986.

Reference books for collectors include Roberts' Ultimate Encyclopedia of Hull Pottery by Brenda Roberts (Walsworth Publishing Company, 1992), and Collector's Guide to Hull Pottery - The Dinnerware Lines by Barbara Loveless Gick-Burke (Collector Books, 1993).

Hull Marks

Ashtray, Ebb Tide patt., E8	**$225**
Ashtray, Butterfly patt., B3, 7" l.	55
Ashtray, Continental patt., No. A1, 8"	50
Ashtray, Serenade patt., No. S23, 10 1/2 x 13"	95
Ashtray Parchment & Pine patt., No. S-14, 14" l.	150
Bank, Corky Pig, colored	125
Bank, figural Corky Pig, pink, white & blue, 5"	100
Basket, hanging-type, Sun Glow patt., No. 99, 6" h.	65
Basket, hanging-type, Woodland Matte patt., cream & blue	400
Basket, Blossom Flite patt., No. T2, 6" h.	55
Basket, Parchment & Pine patt., No. S-3, 6" h.	75
Basket, Sueno Tulip patt., No. 102-33-6", 6" h.	350
Basket, Open Rose (Camellia) patt., No.142, 6 1/4" h.	350
Basket, Sun Glow patt., No. 84, 6 1/2" h.	75
Basket, Tokay patt., No. 6, overhead branch handle, white ground, 8" h. (ILLUS. next page)	95
Basket, Blossom Flite patt., No. T4, 8 1/2" h.	125
Basket, Royal Woodland patt., No. W9, 8 3/4" h.	50
Basket, Woodland Matte patt., fan-shaped w/center handle, pink & green, W9-8 3/4", 8 3/4" h.	143

Tokay Pattern Basket

Basket, Woodland Matte patt., fan-shaped w/center handle, yellow & green, W9-8 3/4", 8 3/4" h. **223**
Basket, Poppy patt., No. 601, 9" h. **750**
Basket, Ebb Tide patt., E5, 9 1/8" h. **125**
Basket, Wildflower patt., No. 79, 10 1/4" h.... **2,000**
Basket, Butterfly patt., three-handled, No. B17, 10 1/2" h. **350**
Basket, Magnolia Gloss patt., No. H-14, 10 1/2" h. **250**
Basket, Wildflower patt., No. W-16-10 1/2", 10 1/2" h. **375**
Basket, Poppy patt., No. 601, 12" h. **1,300**
Basket, Serenade patt., pink ground, ruffled sides, No. S14, 12" h. **313**
Basket, Serenade patt., yellow ground, ruffled sides, No. S14, 12" h. **300**
Basket, Ebb Tide patt., model of a large shell w/long fish handle, No. E-11, 16 1/2" l. **248**
Bonbon, Butterfly patt., No. B4, 6" d. **40**
Book ends, Orchid patt., No. 316, 7" h., pr... **1,200**
Bowl, cereal, 6" d., Floral patt., No. 50.............. **10**
Bowl, 6 1/2" d., low, Poppy patt., No. 602....... **295**
Bowl, 7" d., Orchid patt., No. 312.................... **135**
Bowl, 8" d., Calla Lily patt., No. 500-32.......... **135**
Bowl, fruit, 9 1/2" d., Tokay patt., No. 7........... **135**
Bowl, salad, 10" d., No. 49................................ **50**
Bowl, fruit, 10 1/2" d., Butterfly patt., No. B16.. **150**
Candleholders, Butterfly patt., No. B22, 2 1/2" h., pr...................................... **85**
Candleholders, Ebb Tide patt., No. E-13, 2 3/4" h., pr...................................... **75**
Candleholders, Woodland Matte patt., pink ground, No. W30, 3 1/2" h., pr. **105**
Candleholders, Bow-Knot patt., No. B17, 4" h., pr...................................... **225**
Candleholders, Dogwood patt., No. 512, 4" h., pr...................................... **160**
Candleholders, Parchment and Pine patt., No. S-10, 5" h., pr........................... **50**
Candleholders, Serenade patt., No. S16, 6 1/2" h., pr...................................... **105**
Candy dish, Butterfly patt., No. B6, 4 3/4 x 5 1/2" **45**
Candy dish, Continental patt., C62, 8 1/4" h...................................... **45**
Candy dish, cov., Serenade patt., No. S3C, 8 1/4" h...................................... **95**
Candy dish, cov., Tokay patt., No. 9C, 8 1/2" h...................................... **100**

Canister, cov., Little Red Riding Hood patt., "Cereal" **1,400**
Canister, cov., Little Red Riding Hood patt., "Salt" **1,100**
Casserole, cov., French handle-type & warmer, House n' Garden line, No. 979, Mirror Brown, 3 pt., 3 pcs. **125**
Casserole, oval w/figural duck cover, House n' Garden line, Mirror Brown, 2 pt. **95**
Casserole, cov., Floral patt., No. 42, 7 1/2" d.. **60**

Sun Glow Pattern Casserole

Casserole, cov., Sun Glow patt., No. 51-7 1/2", 7 1/2" d. (ILLUS.) **50**
Casserole, cov., Serenade patt., No.S20, 9" d... **125**
Coaster/spoon rest, Gingerbread Boy patt., 5" l... **39**
Compote, Tokay patt., No. 9 .... **65**
Console bowl, Wildflower patt., No. 69, 4" h., pr... **250**
Console bowl, Butterfly patt., wide-shouldered disk-form w/closed rim, raised on long curved tab feet, pebbled white ground, No. B21, 10" d............................... **163**
Console bowl, Iris patt., No. 409-12", 12" l...... **225**
Console bowl, Magnolia Gloss patt., No. H-23, 13" l... **95**
Console bowl, Orchid patt., No. 314, 13" l....... **350**
Console bowl, Royal Woodland patt., No. W29, 13" l... **75**
Consolette, Tokay patt., footed oblong form w/end branch handles, No. 14, 15 3/4" l... **113**
Cookie jar, cov., Barefoot Boy (small chip inside rim on lid, flake on rim of base).......... **280**
Cookie jar, cov., figural Duck............................. **30**
Cookie jar, cov., figural Ginger Bread Man, grey Flint Ridge line, 1980s, 12" h. **425**
Cookie jar, cov., Floral patt., No. 48, 8 1/4" h... **65**
Cookie jar, cov., Gingerbread Boy, blue w/white trim **390**
Cookie jar, cov., Gingerbread Man patt., 12" h... **550**
Cookie jar, cov., Little Red Riding Hood, open basket, gold stars on apron............... **395**
Cornucopia-vase, Butterfly patt., No. B2, 6 1/2" h... **40**
Cornucopia-vase, Water Lily, pink w/gold, L7-6 1/2", 6 1/2" h... **115**
Cornucopia-vase, Ebb Tide patt., No. E3, 7 1/2" h... **168**

Bow-Knot Cornucopia-vase

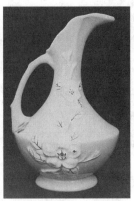

Rosella Pattern Ewer

Woodland Pattern Flowerpot & Saucer

Jardiniere, Woodland Matte patt., pink & yellow, No. W7-5 1/2", 5 1/2" h. **145**

Jardiniere, Woodland patt., dark green & blue, No. W7-5 1/2", 5 1/2" h. **96**

Jardiniere, Orchid patt., No. 310, 6" h. **225**

Jardiniere, Calla Lily patt., No. 591, 7" h. **300**

Jardiniere, Sueno Tulip patt., No. 115-33-9", 9" h. **450**

Jardiniere, Bow-Knot patt., wide bulbous body w/short & wide molded neck w/small bows at each side, B-19-9 3/8", 9 3/8" d. **963**

Lamp base, Rosella patt., No. 63-4", 4" h. **300**

Lamp base, Sueno Tulip patt., 6 1/2" h. **600**

Lamp base, Orchid patt., No. 303, 10" h. **600**

Lamp base, Iris patt., No. 414, 16" h. **750**

Lavabo & base, Butterfly patt., Nos. B24 & B25, cream & blue, overall 16" h., 2 pcs. **160**

Mug, Serenade patt., No. S22, 8 oz. **55**

Mustard jar & spoon, Little Red Riding Hood patt., 2 pcs. **463**

Pitcher, 7 1/2" h., Sun Glow patt., No. 55 .... **85**

Pitcher, 8" h., Sueno Tulip patt., No. 109-33-8" **235**

Pitcher, 8 1/2" h., Blossom Flite patt., No. T3 .... **90**

Planter, baby w/pillow, pink w/gold trim, No. 92, 5 1/2" h. **35**

Planter, model of two Siamese cats, No. 63, 5 3/4" l. **85**

Planter, model of lovebirds, pink & brown, Novelty line, No. 93, 6" h. **40**

Planter, model of a parrot pulling a flower blossom-form cart, Novelty line, No. 60, 9 1/2" l., 6" h. **50**

Planter, model of a Dachshund dog, 14" l., 6" h. **110**

Planter, bust of the Madonna, yellow, No. 24, 7" h. **35**

Basket Girl Planter

Planter, Basket Girl, No. 954, 8" h. (ILLUS.).. **40**

Planter, model of a pheasant, No. 61, 6 x 8" **50**

Planter, model of a swan, yellow glossy glaze, Imperial line, No. 69, 8 1/2 x 10 1/2", 8 1/2" h. (ILLUS.) **50**

Planter, model of Bandanna Duck, Novelty line, No. 74, 9" h. **50**

Planter, Blossom Flite patt., No. T12, 10 1/2" l. **95**

Rose bowl, Iris patt., No. 412-7", 7" l. **188**

Figural Swan Planter

Salt & pepper shakers, Sun Glow patt., No. 54, 2 3/4" h., pr. **20**

Salt & pepper shakers, Floral patt., No. 44, 3 1/2" h., pr. **25**

Sandwich tray, Gingerbread Man patt. **150**

Serving tray, three-part w/butterfly handle, Butterfly patt., gold-trimmed scalloped rim, B23, 11 1/2" l. **200**

Sugar bowl, cov., Blossom Flite patt., No. T16 .... **45**

Sugar bowl, cov., Rosella patt., No. R-4, 5 1/2" h. **60**

Tea set: cov. teapot, creamer & cov. sugar bowl; Bow-Knot patt., 3 pcs. **850**

Tea set: cov. teapot, creamer & cov. sugar bowl, Butterfly patt., Nos. B18, B19 & B20, 3 pcs. **275**

Tea set: cov. teapot No. S-11, cov. sugar bowl No. S-13 & creamer No. S-12; Parchment and Pine patt., 3 pcs. **135**

Tea set: cov. teapot W26, cov. sugar bowl W28 & creamer W27; Woodland Gloss patt., teapot 6 1/2" h., 3 pcs. **275**

Teapot, cov., Serenade patt., No. S17, 5" h., 6-cup **175**

Teapot, cov., Dogwood patt., No. 507, 5 1/2" h. **350**

Teapot, cov., Mardi Gras/Granada patt., No. 33, 5 1/2" h. **200**

Blossom Flite Pattern Teapot

Teapot, cov., Blossom Flite patt., No. T14, 8" h. (ILLUS.)... **100**

Teapot, cov., Wildflower patt., No. 72, 8" h. ... **1,200**

Teapot, cov., Royal Woodland patt., No. W26, 8-cup **95**

Tray, Mirror Brown patt., 10 x 10"...................... **75**

Vase, 4 3/4" h., Magnolia Matte patt., No. 13-4 3/4" **53**

Open Rose Vase

Woodland Gloss Pattern Wall Pocket

HUMMEL FIGURINES & COLLECTIBLES

The Goebel Company of Oeslau, Germany, first produced these porcelain figurines in 1934 having obtained the rights to adapt the beautiful pastel sketches of children by Sister Maria Innocentia (Berta) Hummel. Every design by the Goebel arti-

sans was approved by the nun until her death in 1946. Though not antique, these figurines with the "M.I. Hummel" signature, especially those bearing the Goebel Company factory mark used from 1934 and into the early 1940s, are being sought by collectors though interest may have peaked some years ago.

Hummel Marks

A Fair Measure, 4 3/4" h., Trademark 5 .... **$390**
A Stitch in Time, 6 3/4" h., Trademark 6 .... **350**
Accordion Boy, 5 1/4" h., Trademark 5 .... **300**
Accordion Boy, 5 1/4" h., Trademark 6 .... **240**
Adoration, 6 1/4" h., Trademark 3 .... **575**
Adoration, 6 1/4" h., Trademark 6 .... **420**

Adventure Bound

Adventure Bound, 7 1/4 x 8", Trademark 5
(ILLUS.) **4,200**
Angel Duet font, 2 x 4 3/4" h., Trademark
4 .... **80**
Angel Lights candleholder, 8 1/3 x 10
1/3", Trademark 6 .... **350**
Angel Serenade, angel standing, part of
Nativity scene, 3" h., Trademark 3 .... **145**
Angel Serenade, angel standing, part of
Nativity scene, 3" h., Trademark 4 .... **125**
Angel with Accordion, 2 1/2" h., Trade-
mark 4 .... **100**
Angel with Birds font, 2 3/4 x 3 1/2" h.,
Trademark 1 .... **325**
Angel with Lute, 2 1/2" h., Trademark 4 .... **100**
Angelic Sleep candleholder, 3 1/2 x 5",
Trademark 2 .... **425**
Angelic Song, 4" h., Trademark 6 .... **180**
Apple Tree Boy, 4" h., Trademark 1 .... **225**
Apple Tree Boy, 4" h., Trademark 4 .... **225**
Apple Tree Boy, 6" h., Trademark 3 .... **450**
Apple Tree Boy, 6" h., Trademark 4 .... **425**
Apple Tree Boy, 6" h., Trademark 6 .... **350**

**Apple Tree Boy & Apple Tree Girl book
ends,** 5 1/4" h., Trademark 4, pr. **425**
Apple Tree Boy table lamp, 7 1/2" h.,
Trademark 2 .... **1,000**
Apple Tree Girl, 4" h., Trademark 1 .... **500**
Apple Tree Girl, 4" h., Trademark 3 .... **250**
Apple Tree Girl, 4" h., Trademark 4 .... **225**
Apple Tree Girl, 6" h., Trademark 1 .... **900**
Apple Tree Girl, 6" h., Trademark 4 .... **425**
Artist (The), 5 1/2" h., Trademark 4 .... **1,200**
Auf Wiedersehen w/Tyrolean cap,
5 1/4" h., Trademark 2 .... **4,000**
Ba-Bee Ring plaque, 5" d., Trademark 1 .... **700**
Baker, 4 3/4" h., Trademark 4 .... **300**
Band Leader, 5" h., Trademark 1 .... **750**
Barnyard Hero, 4" h., Trademark 3 .... **300**
Be Patient, 4 1/4" h., Trademark 3.: **350**
Be Patient, 6 1/4" h., Trademark 4 .... **475**
Bird Duet, 4" h., Trademark 3 .... **230**
Birthday Serenade, 4 1/4" h., Trademark 4 ..... **260**
Birthday Serenade, reverse mold,
4 1/4" h., Trademark 4 .... **550**
Blessed Event, 5 1/4" h., Trademark 4 .... **600**
Book Worm, 4" h., Trademark 4 .... **350**
Book Worm, 5 1/2" h., Trademark 4 .... **350**
Book Worm book ends, 5 1/2" h., Trade-
mark 4, pr. **600**
Boots, 5 1/2" h., Trademark 1 .... **700**
Boots, 5 1/2" h., Trademark 3 .... **325**
Builder, 5 1/2" h., Trademark 4 .... **375**
Candlelight, 6 3/4" h., Trademark 4 .... **350**
Chef, Hello, 6 1/4" h., Trademark 3 .... **400**
Chef, Hello, 6 1/4" h., Trademark 4 .... **350**
Christ Child, from Nativity set,
1 1/2 x 3 3/4", Trademark 3 .... **95**
Congratulations, 6" h., Trademark 3, (no
socks) **325**

Congratulations

Congratulations, 8 1/4" h, Trademark 1
(ILLUS.) **8,000**
Culprits, 6 1/4" h., Trademark 1 .... **1,100**
Doctor, 4 3/4" h., Trademark 3 .... **275**
Doll Mother, 4 3/4" h., Trademark 3 .... **350**
Duet, 5 1/4" h., Trademark 3 .... **450**
Farewell, 4 3/4"' h., Trademark 1 .... **1,000**
Farewell, 4 3/4" h., Trademark 2 .... **475**
Farm Boy, 5 1/4" h., Trademark 4 .... **350**
Favorite Pet 4 1/4" h., Trademark 4 .... **450**
Favorite Pet 4 1/4" h., Trademark 6 .... **345**
Feeding Time, 5 3/4" h., Trademark 1 .... **1,000**

Feeding Time, 5 3/4" h., Trademark 2 625
Festival Harmony, angel w/flute, 8" h.,
   Trademark 3... 650
Festival Harmony, angel w/mandolin,
   8" h., Trademark 4.. 475
Festival Harmony, angel w/flute,
   10 3/4" h., Trademark 3.............................. 800
Flower Madonna, 8 1/4" h., Trademark 4,
   color 575
For Father, 5 1/2" h., Trademark 3 375
Girl with Doll, 3 1/2" h., Trademark 4.............. 100
Globe Trotter, 5" h., Trademark 3 350
Going to Grandma's, 4 3/4" h., Trademark
   1 1,000
Going to Grandma's, 6" h., Trademark 1..... 1,500
Going to Grandma's, 6" h., Trademark 3........ 800
Good Friends, 4" h., Trademark 1 750
Good Friends table lamp, 7 1/2" h.,
   Trademark 4... 475
Good Hunting, 5 1/4" h., Trademark 4 425
Good Hunting, 6 1/4" h., Trademark 3 425
Goose Girl, 4" h., Trademark 4 250
Goose Girl, 4 3/4" h., Trademark 1 800
Goose Girl, 7 1/2" h., Trademark 4 1,300
Happy Birthday, 5 1/2" h., Trademark 4.......... 450
Happy Days, 4 1/4" h., Trademark 4................ 250
Happy Days, 5 1/4" h., Trademark 3............... 475
Happy Days, 5 1/4" h., Trademark 4............... 225
Happy Days, 6" h., Trademark 1 1,550
Happy Pastime, 3 1/2" h., Trademark 3 275
Hear Ye, Hear Ye, 5" h., Trademark 1 750
Hear Ye, Hear Ye, 7 1/2" h., Trademark 3 750
Heavenly Protection, 9 1/4" h., Trademark
   3 1,200
Herald Angels candleholder, 2 14 x 4",
   Trademark 3... 275
Just Resting, 3 3/4" h., Trademark 3.............. 250
Just Resting, 5" h., Trademark 3.................... 800
Kiss Me, 6" h., Trademark 4, w/socks............. 950
Kiss Me, 6" h., Trademark 4, without socks..... 450
Latest News, 5 1/4" h., Trademark 3 500
Let's Sing, 3 1/4" h., Trademark 3................... 225
Letter to Santa Claus, 7" h., Trademark 4 ... 1,000
Little Band candleholder music box,
   4 3/4 x 5", Trademark 4............................... 500
Little Cellist, 8" h., Trademark 4...................... 650
Little Fiddler, 4 3/4" h., Trademark 1.............. 800
Little Fiddler, 4 3/4" h., Trademark 4.............. 325
Little Fiddler, 7 1/2" h., Trademark 4.............. 550
Little Fiddler, 11" h., Trademark 1................. 3,500
Little Gardener, 4 1/4" h., Trademark 1.......... 500
Little Goat Herder, 4 3/4" h., Trademark 1...... 500
Little Goat Herder, 4 3/4" h., Trademark 3..... 325
Little Guardian, 3 3/4" h., Trademark 1.......... 525
Little Hiker, 5 1/2" h., Trademark 1.................. 750
Lost Stocking, 4 3/8" h., Trademark 4 1,500
Mail Is Here (The), 4 1/4 x 6", Trademark 3.. 1,000
Max & Moritz, 5 1/4" h., Trademark 1.............. 800
Meditation, 7" h., Trademark 1 5,000
Merry Wanderer, 4 3/4" h., Trademark 1........ 700
Mountaineer, 5 1/4" h., Trademark 4.............. 400
Playmates, 4" h., Trademark 1 650
Playmates, 4 1/2" h., Trademark 4 400
Postman, 5 1/4" h., Trademark 3.................... 325
Prayer Before Battle, 4 1/4" h., Trademark
   1 650
Puppy Love, 5" h., Trademark 1 (ILLUS.) 950
Quartet plaque, 6 x 6", Trademark 3.............. 625

School Boy, 4" h., Trademark 1 600
School Boy, 5 1/2" h., Trademark 1 750

School Boys

School Boys, 10 1/4" h., Trademark 3
   (ILLUS.)... 2,250
School Boys, 10 1/4" h., Trademark 4 2,150
Sensitive Hunter, 4 3/4" h., Trademark 3........ 350
Sensitive Hunter, 4 3/4" h., Trademark 4........ 325
Sensitive Hunter, 5 1/2" h., Trademark 4........ 375
She Loves Me, 4 1/4" h., Trademark 4 290
Signs of Spring, 4" h., Trademark 2, two
   shoes on.. 1,500
Silent Night candleholder, 5 1/2" l.,
   4 3/4" h., Trademark 1............................... 1,100
Silent Night candleholder, 5 1/2" l.,
   4 3/4" h., Trademark 4................................. 475

Singing Lesson

Singing Lesson, 2 3/4" h., Trademark 1
   (ILLUS.)... 500
Sister, 5 3/4" h., Trademark 1 (ILLUS.)............ 700
Sister, 5 3/4" h, Trademark 2, ... 175
Skier, 5 1/4" h., Trademark 1 850
Skier, 5 1/4" h., Trademark 3 350
Smart Little Sister, 4 3/4" h., Trademark 4 375
Soldier Boy, 6" h., Trademark 4 650
Soloist, 4 3/4" h., Trademark 1 500
Soloist, 4 3/4" h., Trademark 4 200
Spring Cheer, 5" h., Trademark 1.................... 650
Spring Cheer, 5" h., Trademark 3.................... 325
Spring Cheer, 5" h., Trademark 4 (yellow
   dress) 300
St. Joseph, 7 1/2" h., Trademark 3 285

Stormy Weather

Stormy Weather, 6 1/4" h., Trademark 1
  (ILLUS.)... **1,350**
Street Singer, 5" h., Trademark 3..................... **350**
Strolling Along, 4 3/4" h., Trademark 1 .... **950**
Strolling Along, 4 3/4" h., Trademark 3 .... **350**
Surprise, 5 1/2" h., Trademark 1...................... **950**
Sweet Music, 5 1/4" h., Trademark 3.............. **325**

Telling Her Secret

Telling Her Secret, 5 1/4" h., Trademark 2
  (ILLUS.).. **725**
Telling Her Secret, 5 1/4" h., Trademark 4...... **450**
Telling Her Secret, 6 3/4" h., Trademark 3...... **550**
To Market, 5 1/2" h., Trademark 1 .... **1,000**
To Market, 5 1/2" h., Trademark 3 .... **450**
To Market, 5 1/2" h., Trademark 4 .... **425**
Umbrella Boy, 5" h., Trademark 4 .... **850**
Umbrella Boy, 8" h., Trademark 3................ **2,000**
Umbrella Girl, 4 3/4" h., Trademark 3.......... **1,000**
Umbrella Girl, 8" h., Trademark 3................ **2,000**
Village Boy, 6" h., Trademark 3....................... **400**
Volunteers, 5" h., Trademark 3........................ **400**
Volunteers, 5 1/2" h., Trademark 1............... **1,100**
Wash Day, 5 3/4" h., Trademark 4 .... **450**
Wayside Devotion, 7 1/2" h., Trademark 3 ..... **700**
Worship, 5" h., Trademark 3............................. **275**

IRONSTONE

The first successful ironstone was patented in
1813 by C. J. Mason in England. The body contains
iron slag incorporated with the clay. Other potters
imitated Mason's ware and today much hard, thick
ware is lumped under the term ironstone. Earlier it
was called by various names, including graniteware.
Both plain white and decorated wares were
made throughout the 19th century. Tea Leaf Lustre
ironstone was made by several firms.

GENERAL

Bowl, 7 1/4" d., 2 3/4" h., scalloped rim, all-
  white, ca. 1890s, Maddock & Co............. **$20-25**
Bowl, 7 1/2" d., 4"h., "Amherst Japan" patt.,
  pedestal-based bowl, garden scene
  w/orange flowers, blue & green leaves,
  lots of gold trim... **185**
Bowl, 8 1/2" d., 3" h., large ribs w/scalloped
  rim, all-white, ca. 1890s, J. & G. Meakin... **40-50**
Bowl, 12" d., 3" h., wide flanged rim,
  "gaudy" Imari-style decoration w/blue
  transfer design highlighted w/red enameling, printed mark "Mason's Patent Ironstone China" (interior wear, rim hairline,
  minor crazing) **220**
Bowl, 12 5/8" d., 4 3/4" h., Imari-style col-
  orful decoration, England, 19th c. (spider
  crack in base, gilt & enamel wear) **201**
Bowl, scalloped rim, all-white, ca. 1870, H.
  Burgess **95**
Bread plate, Fuchsia shape, all-white............... **18**
Bread plate, "Give Us This Day, Our Daily
  Bread" embossed on outer rim, all-white,
  unmarked, 12" l. **155-175**
Butter dish, cover & drain, Corn & Oats
  shape, all-white, ca. 1863, 6" d. **200-220**
Cake stand, scalloped apron & fluted ped-
  estal, all-white, by J.F., 9 3/4" d.,
  4 1/2" h. **245-275**
Chamberpot, cov., Prairie shape, all-white,
  J. Clementson **125**
Chamberpot, cov., Cable & Ring shape,
  all-white, 9 1/2" d.. **22**
Cheese dish, cov., "gaudy" style, molded
  C-scrolled edging trimmed in cobalt blue
  on the slant lid, decorated w/orange
  flowers, late 19th c. **204**
Cheese dish, cov., "gaudy" style, slanted
  cover & underplate in the Derby patt., S.
  Fielding & Co., England **132**

Dudson Cheese Keeper

Cheese keeper, cov., dome & stand w/high
  relief clusters of grapes, wheat & hops,
  all-white, ca. 1870s, 13" d., 10" h., Dud-
  son (ILLUS.) **550-600**
Coffeepot, cov., Fuchsia shape, all-white,
  J. & G. Meakin.. **300**
Coffeepot, cov., "gaudy," ovoid body
  raised on tab feet, wide trumpet neck
  w/inset domed cover, swan's-neck spout
  & C-scroll handle, blue transfer-printed

War Bonnet patt. trimmed in red, orange & yellow, marked "Ironstone China," 19th c., 10" h. (minor wear & hairline in spout) **220**

Compote, open, 5 3/4" d., 3 3/4" h., One Big and Two Little Ribs shape, all-white, ca. 1860s, Elsmore & Forster **135-150**

Ironstone Fruit Garden Compote

Compote, open, 12" d., 6 3/4" h., Fruit Garden patt., all-white, ca. 1860s, Jacob Furnival (ILLUS.) **235-250**
Creamer, Britannia shape, all-white, Powell & Bishop **115**
Creamer, Senate shape, all-white, Maddock & Gater **65**
Creamer, Shamrock, Thistle & Rose shape, all-white, ca. 1870s, Powell & Bishop **135**
Cup, handleless, tea, Ceres shape, all-white, Elsmore & Forster.............................. **34**
Cup plate, all-white, G. Phillips **18**
Cup plate, all-white, Longport **18**
Cup & saucer, Ceres shape, all-white, Elsmore & Forster **55**
Cup & saucer, handled, Berlin Gothic shape, all-white, ca. 1840s, T.J. & J. Mayer **80-85**
Cup & saucer, handled, Pomegranate shape, all-white, ca. 1850s, Jacob Furnival... **45-50**
Cups & saucers, handleless, red transfer scene, impressed "Pearl China W.R. & Co.," five sets (minor wear & stains) **204**
Cups & saucers, Stylized Tulip shape, handleless, all-white, E. Challinor, 5 sets (one saucer crazed) **245**

Ironstone Sauce Tureens with Underplates

Dessert service: pr. of two-handled sauce tureens, covers & underplates, one scallop-edged rectangular compote, pr. of scallop-edged rectangular serving dishes, pr. of scallop-edged oval serving dishes, pr. of oval serving dishes & twelve 9 1/8" d. dessert plates; hand-colored decoration of vase issuing flowers on a stand opposite a pierced rock issuing flowers on a blue plateau, framed with a border of floral & trelliswork panels & a shaped gilt-edged rim, impressed "Mason's Patent Ironstone China," factory marks, one sauce tureen cover w/large rim chip, one dessert plate w/central crack & two w/large rim chips, minor wear to gilding, the set (ILLUS. of part)... **3,220**
Dinner service: oval platter, eighteen 10 1/4" d. dinner plates; each printed & colored in the center w/large vase of flowers flanked by four precious objects within a cobalt & gilt scroll frame edged w/iron-red & green lappets, pale yellow ground border reserved w/flowers & foliate scrolls within a lustrous brown edged rim, aubergine printed factory marks & red painted pattern number 2240, ca. 1840-60 .... **2,587**

Ironstone Dinner Service

Dinner service: thirty-nine 9 1/2" d. plates, seventeen 8 1/8" d. plates, sixteen 9 1/2" d. soup plates, eight 6 1/8" d. plates, eleven serving platters, 9 1/4" l., & 10" l., two 12" l. platters, five platters 14 1/8" l., 18" l., 19 3/4" l., three rectangular-form cov. vegetable dishes, two cov. sauce tureens w/underplates, oval gravy boat, a bone dish, two oval serving bowls & a cov. 13 1/2" l. cov. soup tureen; polychrome decorated bird & floral design, 19th c., Davenport, the set (ILLUS. of part)... **8,625**
Ewer, Atlantic shape, all-white, ca. 1858, T. & R. Boote, 12" h................................... **195-220**
Ewer, Ceres shape, all-white, Turner & Goddard **175**
Ewer, Girard shape, all-white, ca. 1846, Ridgway, Bates & Co., 12" h. **175-190**
Ewer, Hawthorne's Fern shape, all-white, John Hawthorne **125**
Ewer, Lily of the Valley shape, all-white, J. Hughes, 12 3/4" h.. **225**
Ewer, Panelled Pod shape, all-white, J. & G. Meakin, 11 1/2" h.................................... **175**

Ewer, plain w/loop handle, all-white, ca. 1870s, Clementson Bros., 11 3/4" h...... **110-125**
Foot bath, Classic Gothic shape, all-white, ca. 1850, John Alcock........... **1,300-1,400**

Scalloped Decagon Foot Bath

Foot bath, Scalloped Decagon/Cambridge shape, all-white, ca. 1852, Davenport (ILLUS.)... **1,000-1,200**

Mayer Gravy Boat

Gravy boat, Long Octagon shape, all-white, ca. 1847, T.J. & J. Mayer (ILLUS.).. **125-140**
Honey dish, Girard shape, all-white, Ridgway Bates & Co.. **25**
Honey dish, Sharon Arch shape, all-white, ca. 1861 .... **18**
Inhaler, squatty bulbous body tapering to a cylindrical neck fitted w/a slender cylindrical glass mouthpiece, blue marbleized decoration & black shield transfer marked "Mfg. by S. Mawson & Thompson," England, 19th c., 11" h. (shallow chip on rim spout)... **275**

Grape Octagon Ladle

Ladle, Grape Octagon shape, all-white, ca. 1970s, Red Cliff (ILLUS.) **30-40**
Ladle, Hyacinth shape, all-white, unmarked, soup tureen size................... **90-100**
Mold, Grape Clusters shape, all-white, Davenport, large... **78**
Mold, Pineapple shape, all-white, oval, medium size..................................... **75**
Mold, Sheaf of Wheat shape, all-white, unmarked.. **88**
Mug, Basketweave with Band patt., all-white, Alfred Meakin................................. **65-70**
Mug, Gothic patt., all-white, ca. 1840s, James Edwards (ILLUS.) **120-130**
Mug, Gothic shape, all-rare, ca. 1847, T.J. & J. Mayer, rare..................................... **100-120**

Ironstone Gothic Mug

Mug, Laurel Wreath patt., all-white, ca. 1867, Elsmore & Forster, 4 5/8" d., 3 1/4" h... **75-85**
Pitcher, 7" h., Gothic shape, all-white............... **68**
Pitcher, 8" h., "gaudy," paneled cylindrical lower body below the tapering shoulder & flared neck w/pointed spout, looped dragon handle, printed w/an Imari-style design in underglaze-blue w/red, green & copper lustre trim, impressed "Mason's Patent Ironstone China," 19th c. (minor flaking)... **688**

Mayer Table-type Pitcher

Pitcher, 9" h., table-type, Full-Panelled Gothic shape, all-white, ca. 1847, T.J. & J. Mayer (ILLUS.) **175-185**
Pitcher, 9 3/4" h., "gaudy" blue transfer floral design w/red & green enamel, snake handle, marked "Mason's Patent Ironstone China" **275**
Pitcher, 9 3/4" h., table-type, Grape Octagon shape, all-white, Pearson & Hancock... **120-130**
Pitcher, 11 1/2" h., Memnon shape, all-white, J. Meir & Son **235**
Plate, 7 1/2" decagonal, dessert, Baltic shape, all-white, registered in1855 .... **18**
Plate, 8 3/4" d., Ceres shape, all-white, Elsmore & Forster **35**
Plate, Balanced Vine shape, all-white, J. Clementson **26**
Plate, Ceres shape, miniature, all-white, Elsmore & Forster **55**
Plate, 7" d., Boote's 1851 Octagon shape, all-white **29**
Plate 7 3/4" d., Ceres shape, all-white, Elsmore & Forster **29**
Plate, 8 1/4" d., "gaudy" free-hand Bittersweet patt. in underglaze blue w/red &

green enamel w/luster, impressed "Real Ironstone" **165**

Plate, 9 1/4" w., paneled shape, "gaudy" free-hand Morning Glory patt., underglaze-blue trimmed w/two shades of green, red & black enamel, mid-19th c. **303**

Plate, 9 1/2" d., Boote's 1851 Octagon shape, all-white **35**

Plate, 9 1/2" d., Bordered Hyacinth/Lily shape, all-white, ca. 1860, W. & E. Corn .. **25-28**

Plate, 9 1/2" w., paneled sides, "gaudy" Floral Urn free-hand patt., underglaze-blue & green & trimmed w/two shades of red enamel & copper lustre, mid-19th c. (light stains, tiny enamel flake) **330**

Plate 9 5/8" d., Ceres shape, all-white, Edward Pearson **30**

Plate, 9 5/8" d., Chinese shape, all-white **34**

Plate, 9 5/8" d., "gaudy" Blackberry patt., underglaze-blue & black trimmed w/red, yellow & copper lustre, impressed "E. Walley - Niagara Shape," 1850s **193**

Plate, 9 3/4" d., "gaudy" center floral decoration in underglaze blue w/red, pink & green enamel w/luster (stains & some wear) **275**

Plate, 9 3/4" d., Paris shape, all-white, John Alcock **26**

Plate, 10" d., center scene of chick & butterfly w/motto around rim, black transfer-printed w/polychrome enamel, marked "Staffordshire England" **138**

Plate, 10 1/4" d., New York shape, all-white, ca. 1858, J. Clementson **35-40**

Plate, 10 1/4" d., True Scallop shape, 14 sides, all-white, Edwards **36**

Plate, 10 1/4" octagonal, all-white **55**

Plate, 10 1/2" d., Fig shape, all-white, ca. 1856, Davenport/Wedgwood **50-70**

Plates, 8 1/2" d., decorated w/floral motif in blue & rust, marked "Ashworth Brothers Hanley," England, ca. 1890, set of 9 .... **134**

Plates, 10 1/2" d., scalloped flanged rim, overall Imari-style transfer decoration in polychrome trimmed w/gold, mid-19th c., pr. **303**

Platter, Columbia shape, all-white, Woolis-croft **75**

Platter, oval, 16" l., Ceres shape, all-white, Elsmore & Forster **85**

Platter, President shape, all-white **95**

Platter, oval, 10" l., President shape, all-white, John Edwards **30-40**

Platter, oval, 11" l., Tracery shape, all-white, Johnson Bros. **50**

Platter, 13 1/2" l., octagonal, "gaudy" Strawberry patt., underglaze-blue w/red, pink & green enamel & luster trim, wear, stains & some enamel flaking (ILLUS.) **770**

Platter, 13 1/2" l., rectangular w/cut corners, "gaudy" free-hand Morning Glory patt., underglaze-blue trimmed w/two shades of green, red & black, mid-19th c. (old red flaking, minor stains) **385**

Platter, 14 3/4" oval, "gaudy," blue transfer-printed War Bonnet patt. trimmed in red, orange & yellow, marked "Ironstone China," mid-19th c. (wear, scratches) **165**

Strawberry Pattern Platter

Platter, 15 3/4" l., rectangular w/cut corners, Florentine patt., light blue, T. Mayer, mid-19th c. (internal hairline) **110**

Platter, 15 3/4" l., Wheat in the Meadow shape, all-white, Powell & Bishop **112**

Platter, 16" l., Boote's 1851 Octagon shape (good condition) **150**

Platter, oval, 16" l., Rolling Star shape, all-white, James Edwards **70-80**

Platter, 16 1/4" l., oval w/lightly scalloped rim, "gaudy" free-hand Strawberry patt., underglaze black, mid-19th c. (small chips on one corner) **413**

Platter, 13 1/2 x 18 1/4", Bordered Hyacinth shape, all-white, W. Baker & Co. **135**

Platter, 18 1/2" l., Indiana patt., ca. 1880, Wedgwood **196**

Platter, 21 1/8" l., decorated w/a central scene of a pavilion & pagoda in a garden of large floral blooms, iron-red & underglaze-blue, framed within a border of angular panels & pendant flowers within a shaped rim, mid-19th c., crown & ribbon factory mark printed in brown, Mason (small rim chips & fritting to underside) **575**

Platter, 22 1/4" l., "gaudy" polychrome floral enameling w/underglaze-blue, Staffordshire (minor flaking) **770**

Large Ironstone Platter

Platter, 24" l, wide oblong form w/angled corners, well-&-tree-type, "gaudy" style, transfer-printed dark blue Imari-style floral decoration in center w/stylized floral border decorated in polychrome enamel (ILLUS.) **633**

Punch bowl, dark blue transfer-printed decoration w/lattice & scrollwork, scalloped rim, RN 298859, England, 19 1/4" d., 9 1/2" h. **605**

Relish dish, 1851 Shell shape, all-white, ca. 1851, T. & R. Boote **90-100**

Relish dish, Berlin Swirl, all-white, ca. 1856, Mayer & Elliot 65-75

Relish dish, plain, oval w/two tab handles, all-white, ca. 1870s, Wood, Son & Co 20-30

Various Red Cliff Pieces

Salt & pepper shakers, Boote's 1851 shape, all-white, ca. 1960s, Red Cliff, 4" h., pr. (ILLUS. far right & far left) 30-40

Sauce dish, Boote's 1851 shape, round, all-white 6

Shaving mug, all-white 48

Soap box, cover & liner, plain oval, all-white, ca. 1872-87, Thomas Elsmore & Son, 3 pcs. 40-45

Soap box, cover & liner, President shape, all-white, John Edwards, 3 pcs. 120-130

Soap dish, open, plain hollow rectangular body w/drain holes in well & one on side for cleaning, all-white, various potters 20-30

Soap slab, all-white, A. Shaw 35

Soup ladle, all-white, line design around handle, unmarked 150

Soup plate, flanged paneled rim, Paradise patt., purple floral transfer design w/poly-chrome trim, mid-19th c., 10 1/2" w 83

Soup plate, Mocho shape, all white, T. & R. Boote, 8 1/2" d. 14

Soup plate, Boote's 1851 shape, all-white, 9 1/4" octagonal 55

Soup plate all-white, Pankhurst, 9 3/8" d. 36

Soup plate, Sharon Arch shape, all-white, Davenport, 9 1/2" d. 28-35

Soup plate, Sydenham shape, decagon, all-white, ca. 1853, T. & R. Boote, 9 1/2" d. 50-70

Soup tureen, cov., oval body raised on scrolled feet, molded end handles, stepped & domed cover w/scrolled ring finial, decorated w/floral sprays & band-ing design, ca. 1870, 13 1/2" l., 11" h. 1,064

Soup tureen, cover, ladle & underplate, Grape Octagon shape, all-white, ca. 1960s, Red Cliff, 14 1/2" d., 13" h., 4 pcs. 140-160

Alcock Soup Covered Soup Tureen w/Ladle & Underplate

Soup tureen, cover, ladle & underplate, Stafford shape, all-white, ca. 1854, S. Alcock & Co., 4 pcs. (ILLUS.) 750-800

Wedgwood Covered Soup Tureen w/Underplate

Soup tureen, cover & underplate, Gothic Octagon shape, all-white, ca. 1840s, J. Wedgwood (ILLUS.) 700-750

Sugar bowl, cov., Athens shape, all-white, Wedgwood 135

Sugar bowl, cov., Athens Shape., black transfer w/some blue, Wm. Adams & Sons, 7 3/4" h. (stains & crazing) 193

Sugar bowl, cov., Chinese shape, all-white, ca. 1858, T. & R. Boote, 7 3/4" h. 85-95

Sugar bowl, cov., Wheat (J. F.'s), all white........ 95

Syllabub cup, 1851 shape w/loop handle, all-white, T. & R. Boote 30-35

Syllabub cup, Tulip shape, all-white, ca. 1855, Elsmore & Forster 20-25

Syrup pitcher, cov., all-white, small, J. & G. Meakin 48

Syrup pitcher, grape molding at top, gold line decoration, unmarked, 9" h 88

Tea set: child's, cov. teapot, creamer & cov. sugar bowl; Lily-of-the-Valley patt., all-white, James Edwards, the set 220-250

Tea set: child's, cov. teapot, creamer, cov. sugar bowl, waste bowl & six cups & saucers; plain, all-white, unmarked, ca. 1880s, the set 180-200

Furnival Teapot

Teapot, cov., Classic Gothic shape, all-white, ca. 1850, Jacob Furnival, 8 1/2" h. (ILLUS.) 210-230

Teapot, cov., Grape Octagon body deco-rated w/blackish purple transfer-printed design of large roses & morning glories

w/polychrome enamel trim, mid-19th c.,
9" h. (spout chips) **165**

Teapot, cov., Laurel Wreath patt., black
transfer-printed bust portrait of George
Washington inside wreath on each side,
English diamond registry mark &
"Elsmore & Forster, Tunstall," mid-19th
c., 9 3/4" h. **440**

Memnon Shape Teapot

Teapot, cov., Memnon shape, six panels
w/branch handle & bud finial, all-
white, ca. 1850s, John Meir & Son,
8 3/4" h. (ILLUS.)................................... **150-165**

Teapot, cov., octagonal, all-white, ring handle (lid has no breathing hole)...................... **115**

Panelled Grape Teapot

Teapot, cov., Paneled Grape shape, all-
white, ca. 1960s, Red Cliff, 8" h.
(ILLUS.)... **60-70**

Teapot, cov., Wheat shape, all-white, W. &
E. Corn **115**

Toddy bowl, cov., Gothic Paneled, all-
white, ca. 1860s, Elsmore & Forster,
10 1/2" d.. **250-275**

Toddy cup, all-white, three notches on
handle **25**

Toddy cup Bellflower shape, all-white,
John Edwards **35**

Toddy cup, Boote's 1851 shape, all-white......... **38**

Toddy cup, Fuchsia shape, all-white **36**

Toddy cup, Pearl Sydenham shape, all-
white... **40**

Toothbrush box, cov., Gothic Octagon
shape, all-white, ca. 1852, Davenport,
3 1/2 x 8", 3 1/4" h. **135-150**

Toothbrush box, cov., Vintage shape, all-
white, ca. 1865, E. & C. Challinor **75-85**

Toothbrush holder w/underplate, verti-
cal, all-white, unmarked **58**

Underplate, for sauce tureen, Panelled
Berry shape, all-white.................................... **38**

Undertray, for gravy boat, oval, all-white,
Clementson **36**

Undertray, for sauce tureen, Bordered
Gothic shape, all-white, Samuel Alcock......... **45**

Undertray, for soup tureen, Many Panelled
Gothic shape, all-white, "Reg. September 21, 1850," Mellor, Venables & Co.,
12 1/2 x 15 1/2" octagonal............................ **150**

Vegetable dish, cov., a flanged scalloped
foot supporting an oval flared body w/a
wide flattened flanged rim, inset high
stepped & domed cover w/a blossom finial, colorful Imari-style transfer decoration trimmed in polychrome & gilt, lion &
unicorn mark w/"Stone China LIV," mid-
19th c., 13 1/2" l. (hairline in cover)............. **303**

Cable & Ring Vegetable Dish

Vegetable dish, cov., Cable & Ring shape,
all-white, ca. 1875, J. & G. Meakin,
10 3/4" l. (ILLUS.)..................................... **60-75**

Vegetable dish, cov., Ceres shape, all-
white, Elsmore & Forster, 8 5/8" oval **170**

Vegetable dish, cov., Plain Uplift shape,
all-white, Ed. Clarke, 6 1/2 x 9" oval.............. **68**

Vegetable dish, cov., Plain Uplift shape,
all-white, J. Edwards, 7 1/2 x 9 1/4" oval........ **78**

President Shape Vegetable Dish

Vegetable dish, cov., President shape, all-
white, ca. 1856, John Edwards, 12" l.
(ILLUS.)... **165-195**

Vegetable dish, cov., Star Flower shape,
all-white, J. W. Pankhurst, 7 x 9 1/2"
oval.. **110**

Wash bowl, Athenia shape, all-white, J. T.
Close & Co., Stoke Upon Trent, 14" d.......... **145**

Wash bowl, Boote's 1851 Octagon shape,
all-white, 13" d.. **200**

Wash bowl, transfer-printed Imari-style
decoration in underglaze-blue & red
enamel, impressed "Mason's Patent
Ironstone China," 12" d. (glazed-over
chip back edge of lip) **110**

Wash bowl & pitcher, miniature, Classic Gothic shape, all-white, Red Cliff, ca. 1960s, overall 4 1/2" h. (ILLUS. second from right w/salt & pepper shakers) 30-45

Wash bowl & pitcher, miniature, Fig (registered Union shape), all-white, Red Cliff, ca. 1960s, overall 3 1/2" h. (ILLUS. second from left w/salt & pepper shakers) 30-45

Wash bowl & pitcher, miniature, Sydenham shape, all-white, Red Cliff, ca. 1960s, overall 4 1/2" h. (ILLUS. center w/salt & pepper shakers) 30-45

Wash bowl & pitcher, Paneled Grape, all-white, Jacob Furnival, 2 pcs. 180-200

Wash bowl & pitcher, Plain Berlin patt., all-white, ca. 1862-70, Liddle, Elliot & Son, 2 pcs. 150-160

Wash bowl & pitcher, President shape, all-white, 2 pcs. 375

Sydenham Wash Bowl & Pitcher

Wash bowl & pitcher, Sydenham patt., all-white, ca. 1853, T. & R. Boote, 2 pcs. (ILLUS.) 385-405

Washbowl, Fig shape, 14 sides, all white, 14 1/2" d. 145

Washbowl, Many Panelled shape, 12 sides, all-white, J. Alcock 125

Boote's Waste Bowl

Waste bowl, Sydenham shape, all-white, ca. 1853, T. & R. Boote, 5 3/8" d., 3 3/4" h. (ILLUS.) 115-125

Waste bowl, Trent shape, all-white, ca. 1855, John Alcock 85-90

TEA LEAF IRONSTONE

Bone dish, crescent-shaped, Chelsea patt., A. Meakin 40

Bone dish, plain crescent shape, A. Meakin 40

Bone dish, scalloped crescent shape, A. Meakin 25

Boston egg cup, Ruth Sayers decoration 115

Butter dish, cover & insert, Basketweave patt., A. Shaw (some glaze wear on insert) 375

Cake plate, Bamboo patt., A. Meakin 70

Cake plate, Daisy 'n Chain patt., Wilkinson 190

Cake plate, Daisy patt., A. Shaw (fine crazing, tiny edge chip) 130

Cake stand, square, low pedestal base, handled, Square Ridged patt., Red Cliff, ca. 1970 170

Chamberpot, cov., Fish Hook patt., A. Meakin 300

Chamberpot, cov., Lion's Head patt., Mellor, Taylor & Co. 175

Coffeepot, cov., Scroll patt., A. Meakin 185

Cookie jar, cov., round, Kitchen Kraft line, gold Tea Leaf, Homer Laughlin, ca. 1950s 175

Creamer, Bamboo patt., A. Meakin, 5 1/4" h. 195

Creamer, Cable patt., A. Shaw, 7" h. (manufacturing flaw on lower side) 280

Creamer, Iona patt., gold Tea Leaf, Powell & Bishop, 4 1/2" h. 70

Creamer, Lily of the Valley patt., Anthony Shaw 375

Cup & saucer, handled, child's, plain round, Wilkinson 200

Egg cup, Empress patt., Micratex by Adams, ca. 1960s 200

Gravy boat, Aladdin lamp-style, Cumbow decoration 60

Gravy boat, Basketweave patt., Anthony Shaw 140

Gravy boat, Chinese patt., A. Shaw 230

Gravy boat, Golden Scroll patt., Bishop & Stonier 45

Ladle, soup-type, large, unmarked 625

Mug, hot water-type, Daisy patt., twelve-sided, A. Shaw 275

Oyster bowl, pedestal foot, Edwards 55

Pitcher, 6 3/4" h., Plain Round patt., gold Tea Leaf, J.M. & Co. (some lustre wear) 50

Pitcher, 7" h., Empress patt., Micratex by Adams, ca. 1960s 80

Pitcher, 7 1/2" h., milk-type, Hanging Leaves patt., A. Shaw 375

Pitcher, 8" h., Fish Hook patt., Alfred Meakin 225

Pitcher, 8" h., Maidenhair Fern patt., Wilkinson 900

Relish dish, Maidenhair Fern patt., Wilkinson 250

Relish dish, mitten-style, Hawthorn patt., Wilkinson (small glaze flaw on foot rim) 275

Sauce tureen, cover & ladle, Maidenhair Fern patt., Wilkinson (hairline & chip on base, small hairline on foot) 400

Sauce tureen, cover, ladle & undertray, Square Ridged patt., Red Cliff, ca. 1960s, the set 175

Sauce tureen, cover & undertray, Basketweave patt., A. Shaw, the set (flake at ladle opening, under rim flaws) 500

Sauce tureen, cover, undertray & ladle, Cable patt., A. Shaw, the set (discoloration on handle) 500

Sauce tureen, cover, undertray & ladle, Fish Hook patt., A. Meakin, plain white ladle, the set (small inner rim chip on base) 350

Serving dish, oval, Brocade patt., A. Meakin, 7" l. (tiny discolored spot) 190

Shaving mug, Chinese patt., Anthony Shaw 110

Shaving mug, Maidenhair Fern patt., Wilkinson (professional repair to outside rim chip) 500

Soup tureen, cover, undertray & ladle, Square Ridged patt., Red Cliff, ca. 1970, the set 425

Tea set: cov. teapot, cov. sugar bowl & creamer; Empress patt., Micratex by Adams, ca. 1960s, the set 165

Teapot, cov., Bamboo patt., A. Meakin 150

Teapot, cov., Cable patt., A. Shaw 250

Teapot, cov., Daisy 'n Chain patt., Wilkinson 120

Toothbrush vase, Heavy Square patt., Clementson (some crazing, small spider crack) 350

Vegetable dish, cov., Bamboo patt., A. Meakin, 10" l. (some glaze wear) 80

Vegetable dish, cov., Iona patt., gold Tea Leaf, Bishop & Stonier, 12" l. 50

Vegetable dish, cov., oval, Basketweave patt., A. Shaw, 10 1/4" l. 230

Vegetable dish, cov., oval, Brocade patt., A. Meakin, 10" l. 150

Vegetable dish, cov., oval, Chelsea shape, A. Meakin 120

Vegetable dish, cov., rectangular, Bamboo patt., A. Meakin, 12" l. 90

Vegetable dish, cov., Square Ridged patt., Wedgwood, 10" l. 80

Wash bowl & pitcher, Brocade patt., A. Meakin (spider crack in bowl) 275

Wash pitcher, Cable patt., A. Shaw 170

Wash pitcher, Daisy 'n Chain patt., Wilkinson 130

Wash pitcher, Daisy patt., A. Shaw 160

Wash pitcher, Square Ridged patt., Wedgwood (small hairline in bottom) 210

Waste bowl, Plain Round patt., T. Hughes 40

TEA LEAF VARIANTS

Chamber pot, cov., Morning Glory patt., Portland shape, Elsmore & Forster 525

Creamer, child's, Teaberry patt., Scalloped Treasure shape, Clementson 525

Creamer, Pinwheel patt., Full Paneled Gothic shape, unmarked 450

Creamer, Pre-Tea Leaf patt., Niagara shape, E. Walley 500

Creamer, Teaberry patt., Heavy Square shape, Clementson 450

Cup & saucer, handled, child's, Teaberry patt., Plain Round shape, Clementson (minor damage) 275

Pitcher, 7 1/8" h., milk-type, Morning Glory patt., Portland shape, Elsmore & Forster 450

Pitcher, 7 1/2" h., milk-type, Teaberry patt., Heavy Square shape, Clementson 600

Pitcher, 8" h., Lustre Scallops patt., Wrapped Sydenham shape, E. Walley (slight glaze wear, manufacturing flaw) 475

Pitcher, 9 1/2" h., Teaberry patt., Heavy Square shape, Clementson (crazing, glaze hairline, small base nick) 500

Plate, 11" d., Teaberry patt., New York shape 50

Platter, 16" oval, Laurel Wreath patt., lustre trim 400

Relish dish, Laurel Wreath shape, lustre trim, Elsmore & Forster 400

Sauce tureen, cover & ladle, Laurel Wreath patt., lustre trim, plain white ladle, Elsmore & Forster, the set (ladle repair, small rim chip & spider crack) 500

Soap dish, cov., Morning Glory patt., Portland shape, Elsmore & Forster (professional repair to lower rim crack) 425

Sugar bowl, cov., Pre-Tea Leaf patt., Hyacinth shape, Cochran & Co. 550

Teapot, cov., Ceres shape, lustre trim, Elsmore & Forster 425

Teapot, cov., Chelsea Grape patt., Primary shape, unmarked, 9 1/2" h. 175

Teapot, cov., Morning Glory patt., Portland shape, Elsmore & Forster 275

Vegetable dish, cov., Pomegranate patt., Prairie Flowers shape, Powell & Bishop, 9" l. 550

Vegetable dish, cov., Pre-Tea Leaf patt., Niagara shape, E. Walley 700

Waste bowl, Pre-Tea Leaf patt., Niagara shape, E. Walley 300

Waste bowl, Teaberry patt., plain round, unmarked (some glaze wear) 195

JASPER WARE (NON-WEDGWOOD)

Jasper ware is fine-grained exceedingly hard stoneware made by including barium sulphate in the clay and was first devised by Josiah Wedgwood, who utilized it for the body of many of his fine cameo blue-and-white and green-and-white pieces. It was subsequently produced by other potters in England and Germany, notably William Adams & Sons, and is in production at the present. Also see WEDGWOOD - JASPER.

Cheese dish, cov., high cylindrical cover & matching round dished base, dark blue applied w/white relief classical figures & oak leaves, England, mid-19th c., 9 1/2" h. $516

Cheese dish, cov., very tall cylindrical cover w/flat top centered by an acorn finial, on a fitted base w/wide angled rim band, black ground w/the rim of the base & lower edge of the cover decorated in white relief w/a wide band of oak leaves & acorns, the cover w/a very wide band of white relief classical figures & trees, a white relief radiating pattern of spearpoints & leaves around the finial, England, 19th c., unmarked, 11 1/4" h. 863

German Jasper Ware Hair Receiver

Hair receiver, cov., white relief figures of three Grecian ladies around sides, one looking in mirror, one taking jewels from box & one holding a bird, white relief-molded figures of cupids on lid, blue ground, Germany, 3 1/4" d., 4" h. (ILLUS.) 95

Pitcher, 5 3/4" h., jug-form, wide ovoid body w/a cylindrical neck w/a long pointed spout, angled & pointed handle from rim to shoulder, solid blue ground applied w/white relief classical figures & foliate bands, impressed Adams & Co. mark, England, late 18th c. (restoration to handle & tip of spout) 920

Plaque, pierced to hang, scrolled free-form design w/scalloped rim, green ground decorated in white relief w/animals & female figures, Germany, ca. 1900, 12 1/2" l. 316

Plaque, round, pierced to hang, green ground w/white relief blossom & leaf decorated border around center scene depicting white relief figures of a fisher-man w/his arm around the shoulder of his lover, 6" d. 22

Sugar bowl, cov., oval, a solid blue ground applied w/white relief classical figures & foliate designs, swan finial on cover, engine-turned band at the foot, impressed Adams mark, late 18th c., England, 4 1/2" h. (slight rim chip on bowl & interior collar of cover) 1,495

Sugar bowl, cov., oval cylindrical body w/small loop end handles, dark blue ground decorated around the base in white relief w/a central continuous band of classical figures w/a large leafy flowering vine border around the bottom & a smaller similar border around the rim, the inset cover w/a raised central upright band decorated in white relief w/palmettes & centering a figural white swan finial, England, possibly Adams, early 19th c., 6 1/8" l. 1,610

Vase, 17 3/4" h., cov., three-color, the classical form w/a light blue ground applied in white relief w/fruiting grapevine festoons & oval portrait medallions w/a lav-ender ground, impressed mark of Adams and Bromley, England, ca. 1880 (cover restored, inner lid missing) 690

Vases, 7" h., handled, white relief figure of Victorian lady, green ground, Germany, pr. 44

JEWEL TEA AUTUMN LEAF

Though not antique this ware has a devoted following. The Hall China Company of East Liverpool, Ohio, made the first pieces of Autumn Leaf pattern ware to be given as premiums by the Jewel Tea Company in 1933. The premiums were an immediate success and thousands of new customers, all eager to acquire a piece of the durable Autumn Leaf pattern ware, began purchasing Jewel Tea products. Though the pattern was eventually used to decorate linens, glasswares and tinware, we include only the Hall China Company items in our listing.

HALL CHINA

Baker, Fort Pitt, 12 oz. $175

Autumn Leaf Bean Pot

Bean pot, one-handled, 2 1/4 qt. (ILLUS.) 938
Bowl, berry 9
Bowl, cream soup, two-handled 45
Bowl, 6 1/4" d. 25
Bowl, salad, 9" d. 75
Butter dish, cov., square top w/straight finial, 1/4 lb. 1,650
Cake plate 19
Cake plate, footed metal base 258
Candy dish, footed metal base 463
Casserole, round, 2 qt. 35
Coffee server, cov., 9-cup, 8 1/2" h. 55
Coffeepot, cov., all-china, electric, percolator 250
Coffeepot, cov., electric, percolator 437
Cookie jar, cov. 160
Cookie jar, cov., large eared handles, Zeisel, 1957-69 275
Cookie jar, cov., "Tootsie" 268
Creamer & cov. sugar bowl, 1930s 70
Custard cup 12
Custard cup, "Radiance," 3 1/2 oz. 7

Autumn Leaf Teapot

KAY FINCH CERAMICS

In 1930, Katherine Finch and her husband, Braden, whom she had met at Ward Belmont College moved to Corona del Mar, California. Katherine went to college to study with William Manker. After taking a worldwide trip, Katherine was certain that she should follow her instincts to work in ceramics. In 1939, Braden left his job and he and Katherine opened Kay Finch Ceramics.

From its beginning, animals were the mainstay and remained so through the twenty-five years Kay Finch Ceramics was in business. Kay created many pig figures and banks and, just a few years later, began creating wonderfully realistic dogs. Cheerfully whimsical characteristics abound on items such as skunks, donkeys, snails, elephants, and so on giving them an animated appearance.

California Country is a breakfast line including a plate, cup, saucer, cream and sugar. All the pieces in this line had a pink body with hand-decorated flower patterns of either Briar Rose, cherry blossoms or shaggy daisies. Items can be found as small as 2" or as large as 50". George, the Finch's son, received credit for planters, bowls, bath accessories, ashtrays and vases that, today, have a following of their own.

When Braden died in 1963, Kay channeled her energies toward dog breeding shows. However, in the mid-1970s, Freeman-McFarlin, another California company, hired Kay to create a set of dog figurines which were manufactured in Freeman-

McFarlin glazes. Those dogs were not as well-received by collectors as Kay Finch's own products. Kay Finch died at the age of eighty-nine in June, 1993.

Kay Finch Marks

Bank, model of Swiss Chalet, two story w/pastels & brown, Model No. 4628, 6" h. **$450**

Kay Finch Shell-Shaped Bowl

Bowl, 4" l., 2 3/4" h. shell-shaped, three feet, scalloped rim, ivory exterior, dark green interior, ca. 1939-1945, stamp mark "Kay Finch California," Model No. 510 (ILLUS.)..................................... **95**
Bowl, swan-shaped, chartreuse glaze, No. 4956 .... **190**
Candleholder, figure of "Scandie" girl w/round candle support on her head, pale pink body, light blue accents & trim, 5 1/4" h. **175**
Cup, child's, figural cat's head......................... **110**

Kay Finch Bride & Groom Figures

Figure of a bride, black hair w/pink flower, head bent downward, white swirling long dress w/pink accents, blue & pink flowers bouquet w/three blue ribbons trailing down the gown, elbow length white gloves, Model No. 201, 6 1/2" h. (ILLUS. right) **300**
Figure of a child, "P.J.," standing, brown hair in pigtails tied w/big bows, head slightly tilted to left, white ground w/blue accents, Model No. 5002, 5" h. **220**

Figure of a "Godey" woman, standing, head w/hat slightly turned & lowered to left, cape across shoulders, hands just below waist & in a muff, basic glazes of white, green, pink, rose & grey, Model No. 122, 9 1/2" h. **160**

Figure of a groom, standing w/legs slightly apart, black hair, mustache, shoes & jacket w/flower in lapel, grey trousers, Model No. 204, 6 1/2" h. (ILLUS. left previous page)... **300**

Figure of a "Scandie" girl, standing in long white dress w/blue apron & scarf tied around her blonde hair, Model No. 126, 5 1/4" h. **155**

Figures of Sage & Maiden, each on a base, No. 4852-55, pr. **275**

Model of bear, No. 4847, 5" h. **250**

Model of bird, "Mrs. Dove," Freeman-McFarlin item introduced in 1977, Model No. 804, 8 1/2" l., 5 1/2" l. **200**

Model of cat, "Ambrosia," seated on back legs w/front legs straight & together, Model No. 155, pink & white, 10" h. **775**

Model of dog, Yorky standing w/right front leg up, white w/pink fur, Model No. 170, 5" h. **285**

Model of elephant, "Popcorn," Model No. 192, 6 3/4" h. **385**

Model of elephant, seated, white w/pink inside ears, Model No. 4804, 4 1/2" h. **230**

Model of elephant, "Violet," walking position, pastels & flowers, Model No. 190, 17" h. **2,900**

Model of fountain w/attached bird on edge, pink w/white bird, Model No. 5388, 6" h. **175**

Model of hen, yellow & green **200**

Model of hippo, standing w/head up & mouth open, bow tied around neck, pink body w/polka dots & pastel accents, Model No. 5019, 5 3/4" h. **475**

Model of lamb, kneeling, ears out, pink body, white & dark pink accents, Model No. 136, 2 1/2" l., 2 1/4" h. **95**

Model of Mr. Bird, matte teakwood, Model No. 454.. **135**

Model of Mrs. Bird, matte teakwood, Model No. 453... **120**

Model of owl, "Hoot," standing, ears up, ruffled feathers, pastel green & lilac on pink body, black eyes & nose, Model No. 187, 8 1/2" h. **150**

Models of rooster & hen, Butch & Biddy, Model Nos. 176 & 177, pr. **300**

Mug, figural Missouri Mule, yellow glaze, 5" h. **350**

Nativity group, iridescent barn w/gold trim outside, green gloss on inside bottom, brown gloss straw, & blue sky, Model No. 4952, can also be hung as a wall display, marked underglaze, "Kay Finch California," iridescent white w/gold trim, Jesus in a manger w/gold trim on top of manger, iridescent kneeling angel in prayer, iridescent standing white angel w/gold trim, barn, 6" l., 6 1/2" h., Jesus in

manger, 1 1/4" h., kneeling angel, 1 1/2"., standing angel, 2 1/4" h., set of 4 ..... **310**

Planter, "Baby book," pink baby in diaper w/left leg & arm raised & leaning against an open book, relief flower decoration on book, marked "Baby's First from California," Model No. B5143, 6 1/2" h. **125**

Planter, baby's block, Baby's First from California line, 6 1/2" h. **165**

Kay Finch Bear Planter

Planter, model of a bear seated, white gloss w/pink ears, eyes & paws, Model No. 4906, 5 3/4" h. (ILLUS.) **300**

Trinket box, heart-shaped, bird perched on lid, deep green box w/royal blue bird, Model No. B5051, 2 1/2" h. **135**

Vase, 7 1/4" h., 5 1/4" w., straight sides, light & dark green & light & dark brown leaves overall except plain green on recessed 3/4" base, marked "Kay Fiinch California".. **100**

Wall plaque/ashtray, figural, boxer dog, rounded corners, one of many from the Parade of Champions set, Model No. 4955, 4 3/4" sq. **95**

Wall pocket, Santa face, white beard, red mouth, pink cheeks, black eyes & red cap on right side extending to tip of beard, holly sprig on forehead at edge of cap, Model No. 5373, 9 1/2" h. **425**

Wall pocket, Santa face, white beard, red mouth, pink cheeks, black eyes & red cap on right side extending to tip of beard, holly sprig on forehead at edge of cap, w/"Merry Xmas" in gold script at bottom center of beard, Model No. 5373, 9 1/2" h. **450**

LEFTON

The Lefton China Company was the creation of Mr. George Zoltan Lefton who migrated to the United States from Hungary in 1939. In 1941 he embarked on a new career and began shaping a business that sprang from his passion for collecting fine china and porcelains. Though his funds were very limited, his vision was to develop a source from which to obtain fine porcelains by reviving the postwar Japanese ceramic industry, which dated back to antiquity. As a trailblazer, George Zoltan Lefton soon earned the reputation as "The China King".

Counted among the most desirable and sought after collectibles of today, Lefton items such as Bluebirds, Miss Priss, Angels, all types of dinnerware and tea-related items are eagerly acquired by collectors. As is true with any antique or collectible, prices may vary, depending on location, condition and availability.

For additional information on the history of Lefton China, its factories, marks, products and values, readers should consult the Collector's Encyclopedia of Lefton China, Books I and II and The Lefton Price Guide by Loretta DeLozier.

Lefton "Pin Money" Bank

Bank, porcelain, model of a coin purse, white decorated w/rhinestones & applied flowers & marked "Pin Money," No. 90256, 5" h. (ILLUS.) **$60**

Lefton Lion Bank

Bank, model of a lion, wearing glasses, No. 13384, 6" h. (ILLUS.)...................................... **55**
Bank, model of a cat, No. 1564, 6 3/4" h............ **30**
Bowl, 7" l., large shell w/cherub & applied roses, No. 926, rare **600**
Bowl, 9 1/4" l., oval footed form, green bisque w/applied pink roses, No. 773, rare **335**

Various Lefton Christy Items

Box, cov., candy, round footed, Christy decoration, No. 442, 5" (ILLUS. left) **35**
Cake plate, Americana patt., No. 980, 12 1/4" d. **75**
Candleholders, two-light, figural cherub w/musical instrument, pastel green & applied pink flowers, No. 965, each 7" l., pr., rare **175**
Casserole, cov., Americana patt., No. 978 ...... **145**
Cheese dish, cov., Honey Bee, No. 1285.......... **60**

Lefton Brown Heritage Floral Coffeepot

Coffeepot, cov., Brown Heritage Floral patt., No. 062 (ILLUS.) **200**
Coffeepot, cov., Eastern Star patt...................... **75**
Coffeepot, cov., Festival patt., No. 2935 .... **145**
Coffeepot, cov., Forget-Me-Not patt., No. 4174, 6-cup **95**
Coffeepot, cov., Garden Daisy patt., No. 1506 .... **50**
Coffeepot, cov., Green Heritage patt., No. 3065 .... **165**

Lefton Blue Paisley Compote

Compote, open, footed, Blue Paisley patt., lattice edge, No. 2341, 7" (ILLUS.)................ **18**
Cookie Jar, cov., Santa Claus, No. 2097, 7 1/4" **103**
Cookie jar, cov., white, decorated w/relief-molded cookies, No. 102................................. **45**
Cookie Jar, cov., White Holly patt., No. 6054 .... **115**
Creamer & cov. sugar bowl, Black Chintz patt., No. 1934, pr. **95**
Creamer & cov. sugar bowl, Dutch girl, No. 2698, pr. **85**
Creamer & cov. sugar bowl, Eastern Star patt., No. 102, pr. **25**

Figural Cow Creamer & Sugar Bowl

Creamer & cov. sugar bowl, figural
Bossie the Cow, No. 6512, pr. (ILLUS.) **35**
Creamer & cov. sugar bowl, Green Holly,
No. 1355 , pr. **30**
Creamer & cov. sugar bowl, Rose Chintz
patt., No. 912, pr. **75**

Rose Heirloom Creamer & Sugar

Creamer & cov. sugar bowl, Rose Heir-
loom patt., No. 1075, pr. (ILLUS.) **85**
Cup & saucer, Americana patt., No. 963 .... **38**
Cup & saucer, demitasse, Eastern Star
patt. **20**
Cup & saucer, demitasse, Rose Heirloom
patt., No. 1378 .... **34**
Cup & saucer, Eastern Star patt., No. 2337 .... **15**
Cup & saucer, green w/pink roses, No.
801 .... **38**
Dessert set: cake plate & 6 serving plates;
fruit decoration, No. 1133, 7 pcs. **175**
Dish, lemon, Magnolia patt., No 2618 .... **20**

Country Squire Deviled Egg Dish

Dish, deviled egg, Country Squire patt., No.
1601, 12 1/2" d. (ILLUS.) **28**
Egg cup, Elegant Rose patt., No. 2048 .... **40**
Egg cup, figural bluebird, No. 286 .... **60**
Figure group, Bride & Groom in Honey-
moon Boat, white w/pink, No. 990,
6 1/4" h. **175**
Figure group, girls on candy cane, No.
626, 4" h. **70**
Figure group, Provincial Girl w/bird in
cage, No. 5263, 8" h. **135**
Figure group, Rock A Bye Baby in Tree-
top, No. 1104, 8" h. **200**

Figure group, white bisque horses
w/cherub, No. 772, 7 1/2", rare **950**
Figurine, clown, No. 01881, 3 3/4" **22**
Figurine, clown, three kinds, No. 02146,
6 1/4", each **55**
Figurine, flower girl, No. 125, 4 1/2" h. (3
different figures), each **42**
Figurine, Gay Nineties, No. 8574, 8" h. **175**

Gay Nineties Figurine

Figurine, Gay Nineties, white w/gold trim,
No. 1573, 7 1/2" h. (ILLUS.) **150**

Figure of George Washington

Figurine, George Washington, No. 1108,
8" h. (ILLUS.) **85**
Figurine, Infant of Prague, No. 718, 8" h. **150**
Figurine, kewpie, No. 02132, 3" **20**
Figurine, lady, standing wearing blue gown
w/applied flowers, No. 4494, 8" h. **80**
Figurine, Lady w/chintz rose dress, No.
780, 8 1/2" **145**
Figurine, lady w/flowers in apron, blue &
white, No. 5604, 6" h. (ILLUS. next
page) **55**
Figurine, Madonna w/Child, No. 1057,
8 1/2" h. **95**

Lefton Lady Figurine

Victorian Lady with Umbrella and Lefton Waitress Bloomer Girl

Lefton Angel - March

Figurine, March, Angel, No. 1978J (ILLUS.).. **55**

Figurine, Miss January, No. 5146...................... **22**

Figurine, Miss Murray, Old Masters series, No. 3987, 7 1/4" h. **75**

Figurine, Old Mother Hubbard, No. 1105 .... **165**

Figurine, Russian lady, No. 752, 11" h. **225**

Angel in Frame

Figurine, Saturday, square frame, No. 6883, 3 1/4 x 4" (ILLUS.)................................. **28**

Figurine, Sing a Song of Six Pence, nursery rhyme, No. 1254, 6" h. **150**

Figurine, Victorian lady w/umbrella, creamy yellow, white & gold gown, No. 585, 7 1/2" h. (ILLUS. top left)............... **150-250**

Figurine, Waitress Bloomer Girl, No. 10532 (ILLUS. top right)................................ **95**

Figurines, angels, tumbling, No. 80159, 2 3/4" h., 4 pcs. **140**

Lefton Candy Cane Kids

Figurines, Candy Cane Kids, No. 8745, 4 1/2", 3 pcs. (ILLUS.).................................... **60**

Figurines, cherub on tree, grey green bisque, No. 952, rare, 5", pr. **175**

Figurines, Colonial couple, Brian & Hildegard, No. 337, 10", pr. **350**

Lefton Colonial Couple

Figurines, Colonial couple, Norman & Elaine, No. 3045, 7" h., pr. (ILLUS.)............. **150**

Jam jar, cov., Miss Priss, No. 1515 (ILLUS. next page) **110**

Jam jar, cov., orange, teapot-shaped, No. 6973 .... **35**

Jam jar, cov., Pennsylvania Dutch, No. 3612 .... **55**

Jam jar, cov., square w/relief-molded basketweave base, cover w/molded green

leaves, fruit section finial, No. 5108,
5 1/2" h. **12**

Lefton Miss Priss Jam Jar

Jam jar w/spoon, cov., figural pear, No.
1071 .... **15**
Jar, cov., Coffee Girl w/hot coffee, No.
4804 .... **85**
Lady head vase, pink, No. 1343, 6 1/2" h. **22**

*Lefton Hurricane Lamp and Lefton Green
Holly Lantern*

Lamp, hurricane-type, Green Holly, No.
4229, 5 1/2" h. (ILLUS.) **45**
Lantern, Green Holly, No. 2694, 8 1/2" h.
(ILLUS.) **125**

Lefton Country Post Office

Model, Country Post Office, Colonial Vil-
lage series, No. 07341 (ILLUS.) **65**
Model of a bird, Parakeet, No. 395, 5" **35**
Model of a bird, Waxwing, No. 6609,
4 1/2" **18**
Model of a dog, Pekinese, No. 7328, 4" **40**
Model of a duck, Mallard, No. 2070, 4" **35**
Model of a duck, No. 7555, 11 1/2"
(ILLUS.) **125**

Lefton Duck

Model of a hand, bisque, lady's w/applied
porcelain flower bracelet, No. KW2933 .... **45**
Model of a horse, hunter, matte finish, No.
1006, 7" **80**
Model of a horse, No. 547, 4 1/2", three
different figures, each **30**
Model of a horse, white w/wooden base,
No. 352, 5 1/4" **55**
Model of a leopard, No. 6703, 6 1/2" **65**
Model of a quetzal, No. 1054, 9" **180**
Model of a red fox, No. 5058, 5" **50**
Model of a sea gull, No. 02715, 7" **70**
Model of a spaniel, No. 80521 .... **50**
Model of a squirrel, bisque, No. 4749, 5" **30**

Lefton Tiger

Model of a tiger, black, white & gold, No.
8743, 8 1/2" l. (ILLUS.) **85**

Lefton Eagle

Model of an eagle, No. 802, 11" h.
(ILLUS.) **100**
Model of an elephant, w/raised trunk &
tusks, No. 075, original paper label, 5" h. **70**

Models of a poodle, white w/lilacs, No. 157, 5" h., each **40**

Models of swan w/baby, No. 841, 3 1/2", pr. **55**

Mug, Christy decoration, No. 447, 7" h. (ILLUS. right) **8**

Paperweight, glass, figural green apple, No. 2390 .... **40**

Pitcher & bowl, miniature, Paisley Fantazia, No. 6806, 3 1/2", pr. **22**

Planter, bisque, ice pink, No. 1030, 4" **15**

Planter, figural Dutch shoe w/boy, No. 5260 .... **36**

Salt & pepper shakers, stein-shaped, shamrock design, No. 2219. 5" h., pr. **12**

Snack set, Brown Heritage floral patt., No. 1864 .... **32**

Snack set, Elegant Rose patt., No. 2124 .... **30**

Snack set, Misty Rose patt., No. 5690 .... **18**

Snack set, modern design, decal, No. 2121, 8" l. **22**

Snack set, Violet Chintz patt., No. 638 .... **30**

Tea bag holder, Miss Priss, No. 1506 .... **55**

Dainty Miss Tea Bag Holder

Tea bag holder, teapot shape, Dainty Miss w/green polka dots, No. 648 (ILLUS.) **50**

Teapot, cov., Dresden shape, Elegant Rose patt., No. 2032 .... **225**

Teapot, cov., figural Dutch Girl, No. 2699 .... **225**

Teapot, cov., figural Miss Priss, No. 1516 .... **195**

Teapot, cov., Pink Cotillion patt., No. 3186 ...... **110**

Teapot, cov., Yellow Tulip patt., No. 6735 .... **95**

Lefton Violet Chintz Tidbit Tray

Tidbit tray, Single Violet chintz, No. 651 (ILLUS.) **35**

Toothpick holder, Petites Fleurs patt., No. 6436, 4 1/4" h. **20**

Vase, 5 1/2" h., bisque, figural hands w/applied flowers, No. 4198 .... **28**

Vase, 5 1/2" h., flower-shaped, No. 1548 .... **18**

Vase, 6 1/4" h., cylindrical w/Christy decoration & gold trim, No. 438 (ILLUS. center) **15**

Vase, 7" h., pink w/Forget-Me-Not decoration, No. 7633 .... **65-76**

Wall plaque, china, violin w/pink roses, No. 704, 7" d. **55**

Wall plaque, diamond-shaped apple, No. 921 .... **15**

Wall plaque, hot air balloon w/two kittens in basket, tan, white, pink & blue, No. 3709, 4 1/2" **30**

Wall plaque, three mermaids, No. 3107 .... **125**

Lefton Two Piece Wall Plaque

Wall plaques, figural girl w/blond hair, white, pink & blue dress, holding watering can together w/pink & yellow flowers & green leaves in blue flowerpot, No. 2630, girl 7" h., the set (ILLUS.) **125**

Fish with Babies Wall Plaques

Wall plaques, fish w/babies, No. 60419, largest 7" l., the set (ILLUS.) **75**

Wall plaques, ornate scrolled & relief-molded forms w/a boy & a girl leaning on wall above leafy vines w/grape clusters, No. 350, 8 1/2", pr. **100**

Wall plaques, oval, relief-molded w/Colonial boy & girl figures, No. 1753, 11", pr. **150**

Wall plaques, oval w/Colonial figures, No. 5826, 10" d., pr. **135**

Wall pocket, girl w/basket, pink, No. 50264, 7" h. **135**

LENOX

The Ceramic Art Company was established at Trenton, New Jersey, in 1889 by Jonathan Coxon and Walter Scott Lenox. In addition to true porcelain, it also made a Belleek-type ware. Renamed Lenox Company in 1906, it is still in operation today.

Lenox Mark

Busts of a man & woman, Art Deco style, the young man w/short cropped hair, a pointed chin & long neck, the young woman w/a long face & long neck, downcast eyes, her hair in a pony tail combed to one side, each raised on a thick rectangular plinth, glossy ivory glaze, base impressed "A.B.C. O. '35" & green Lenox stamp, 8 3/4" h., pr. **$220**

Figure of a young woman, Art Deco stylized standing lady w/short hair, nude except for a long drapery looped through her arms, looking down at a seated greyhound at her side, on a stepped round base, glossy ivory glaze, base impressed "Lenox - A.B.C. O. '37," 13 1/2" h. **468**

Figure of a young woman, Art Deco style standing lady w/her head turned to one side, holding her long flowing gown out at the sides, glossy ivory glaze, impressed on the base "Lenox - A.B.C.O. '37," 13 3/4" h. **385**

Vase, 8 1/4" h., baluster-form, decorated w/applied & enameled peonies & wildflowers w/gilt trim.. **143**

Vase, 10 1/2" h., baluster-form, creamy ground decorated overall w/silver overlay in a dense vining floral design **201**

LIMOGES

Numerous factories produced china in Limoges, France, with major production in the 19th century. Some pieces listed below are identified by the name of the maker or the mark of the factory. Although the famed Haviland Company was located in Limoges, wares bearing their marks are not included in this listing. Also see HAVILAND.

An excellent reference is The Collector's Encyclopedia of Limoges Porcelain, Second Edition, *by Mary Frank Gaston (Collector Books, 1992).*

Cabinet plate, central printed scene of lovers in a wooded setting, scrolled gilt trim w/enameled floral cartouches, giltwood frame, ca. 1900, 9 1/2" d. **$173**

Chocolate pot, cov., cream, pink & green ground finely decorated w/birds & holly sprigs, 9 1/4" h. **110**

Chocolate pot, cov., swelled base below the wide cylindrical body w/an angled rim w/spout, domed cover w/gold loop handle, long gold C-scroll handle down the back, decorated below the spout w/a narrow panel of small florals, the rest of the body studio-decorated w/long stems of colorful blossoms,10 1/2" h. **173**

Limoges Creamer & Sugar Bowl

Creamer & cov. sugar bowl, bulbous bodies decorated on front & back w/purple & lavender violets & green leaves, violet colored handles, lavish gold trim, "T & V, Limoges, France," creamer 4" d., 3 1/2" h., sugar bowl 4" d., 3 3/4" h. (Tressemann & Vogt), pr. (ILLUS.) **110**

Dessert set: 9 1/2" d. plate & six matching 6" plates; fancy blanks w/gold & floral decoration, 7 pcs.. **121**

Dessert set: rectangular tray & eight dessert plates; decorated w/pairs of cherubs in different poses against a background sky, heavy gold-trimmed scalloped border, the set **1,100**

Dresser tray, decorated w/h.p. yellow flowers, pale pink raised Rococo border, 12" d.. **100**

Fish set: 17 1/2" oval platter & 12 small plates; each w/a different fish & shells & sea life, two different manufacturers of the blanks, ca. 1900, the set **1,035**

Limoges Game Plate

Game plates, one w/center h.p. decoration of pheasant, the other w/a quail, both just above water & near yellow flowers & grasses, pastel pink, blue & cream background & heavy gold irregular & beaded rim, artist-signed, 9 1/2" d., pr. (ILLUS. of one)...................................... **225**

Lettuce bowl w/underplate, decorated w/h.p. violets, 6 1/2" d. **110**

Luncheon plates, 7 3/4" d., each h.p. w/different exotic flower, gold border, set of 12, T & V - Limoges - France **182**

Oyster plates, crescent-shaped w/gilt foliate designs, blue, pink, green & yellow ground, six wells, ca. 1900, set of 18 .... **2,070**

Plaque, pierced for hanging, decorated w/scene of courting couple & sheep, artist-signed, cobalt & gold border, 10 1/2" d. **100**

Limoges Portrait Plaque

Plaques, rectangular, Art Nouveau style enamel bust portrait of female surrounded by large flowers in center circle w/square border decorated w/flowers & scrolling leaves, each set in floral decorated brass frame w/velvet liner, artist-signed "Dorval," ca. 1900, France, 9 1/2 x 12", pr. (ILLUS. of one)................. **8,050**

Plate, 10" d., pierced to hang, bust portrait of a Cavalier smoking against a shaded ground (Coronet) **100**

Plate, 12 1/4" d., pierced to hang, scalloped & scroll-molded gold edge, h.p. center decoration of purple plums, a large orange seed pod & green leaves on a pastel ground, artist-signed **225**

Limoges Punch Bowl & Underplate

Punch bowl & underplate, footed flaring bowl w/serpentine gilt rim, interior & exterior decorated w/h.p. grape clusters & leaves, matching round underplate w/gold rim, ca. 1900, bowl 15" d., underplate 18" d., the set (ILLUS.) **1,495**

Sweetmeat dish, cov., decorated w/roses & green leaves, gold trim, 9" w., 6" h. **110**

Tea set: cov. teapot, cov. sugar bowl, creamer & six cups & saucers; each w/black-printed landscapes within blue enamel medallions & w/blue & gilt trim, late 19th c., teapot 7 3/4" h., the set............. **173**

Vase, 15" h., two-handled, enamel-decorated scene of a female picking flowers, gilt-trimmed, ca. 1900................................... **633**

LIVERPOOL

Liverpool is most often used as a generic term for fine earthenware products, usually of creamware or pearlware, produced at numerous potteries in this English city during the late 18th and early 19th centuries. Many examples, especially pitchers, were decorated with transfer-printed patriotic designs aimed specifically at the American buying public.

Bowl, 8 3/4" d., 3 3/4" h., creamware, a wide footring below deep rounded & gently flaring sides, decorated w/black transfer-printed scene w/ships, sailor & wife reading "When this you see, remember me..." (wear & stains)............... **$715**

Liverpool Mug & Pitcher

Mug, tall cylindrical form, transfer-printed outdoor scene of uniformed soldier on horseback above "George Washington, Esq. General and Commander in Chief of the Continental Army in America," early 19th c., cracks, chips on base & handle, staining, 4 5/8" h. (ILLUS. left)...... **2,185**

Pitcher, milk, 5 1/2" h., Queensware, black transfer-printed oval reserve w/"Lafayette" & "Ben Franklin," eagle & reading "Republicans are not always Ungrateful, Ricd. Hall & Son" (old yellowed repairs to spout, wear & minor damage) **605**

Pitcher, 6 1/4" h., creamware, bulbous body w/wide tapering cylindrical neck & pinched spout, both sides depicting black transfer-printed decoration of an eagle, flag & two women as Peace & Plenty & a circular reserve w/the names of ten states & Boston w/the inscription "Peace, Plenty, and Independence" & under the spout "Success to the Trade of Rhode Island," restoration, minor imperfections **1,610**

Pitcher, 7 1/2" h., jug-form, black transfer-printed design w/one side showing the seasons of spring & autumn, the reverse decorated w/a scenic oval reserve above a related verse, framed by floral swags, scrolls & various devices, spout damage, staining, edge roughness, early 19th c. (ILLUS. right) **633**

Pitcher, 8" h., jug-form, black transfer-printed design on buff ground, one side depicts two portrait busts of John Hancock & Samuel Adams in an oval w/a beehive & horn of plenty & the inscription "The Memory of Washington and the Proscribed Patriots of America, Liberty, Virtue, Peace, Justice, and Equity to All Mankind," the reverse depicts an oval w/a military scene w/hero & cannon, w/ships & farmers plowing in the distance, inscribed "Success to America whose Militiia is better than Standing Armies. May Its Citizens Emulate Soldiers and its Soldiers Heros...," Great Seal of the United States beneath the spout, early 19th c., restoration, chips **2,300**

Washington Liverpool Pitcher

Pitcher, 8 7/8" h., jug-form, black transfer-printed scenes, one side w/"Washington in Glory America in Tears," the reverse w/"The Macedonian & The United States" & a spread eagle below the spout, minor rim nick & glaze wear, base chip, early 19th c. (ILLUS.) **2,300**

Pitcher, 9 3/4" h., jug-form, large oval reserve w/transfer-printed decoration of a three-masted ship flying the American flag & a spread eagle w/American shield & "The Memory of Washington and the Proscribed Patriots of America" around border, polychrome highlights, restoration, minor abrasions to transfers, early 19th c. **1,725**

Pitcher, 9 3/4" h., jug-form, one side decorated w/a black transfer-printed reserve w/a portrait of Washington surrounded by Justice, Liberty & Victory encircled by fifteen stars & the names of the fifteen states, the reverse w/a reserve of "Peace, Plenty and Independence," inscribed under the spout "Philip & Jane Gilkey," early 19th c. (base chip, minor staining, minute rim chip, rim roughness).. **1,725**

Pitcher, 10" h., jug-form, creamware, black transfer-printed scene titled "Washington in His Glory," reverse titled "America in Tears" w/eagle & ship, traces of gold trim (stains & chips).................................. **1,705**

Liverpool Pitcher

Pitcher, 10 1/2" h., jug-form, transfer-printed w/"Washington in Glory American in Tears" & on the reverse Masonic elements w/an eagle & monogram "SOS" within a Masonic reserve, below the spout, staining, old repair to handle, minor hairlines, early 19th c. (ILLUS.) **1,380**

LURAY PASTELS

LuRay Pastels, made by The Taylor, Smith & Taylor Co. of Chester, West Virginia from 1938 until 1961, was a line available in four colors - Windsor Blue, Surf Green, Persian Cream and Sharon Pink. No one original color seems to be more desirable than the others. A fifth color, Chatham Gray, ran from 1949 until 1952. Collectors refer to the early-shaped A/D sets as "Chocolate Sets." Decal-decorated LuRay sets were produced but are very rare. No known examples of the handleless sugar, 7" mini platter or gray salad bowl have been found with the LuRay backstamp. An asterisk (*) indicates an older original mold shape.

Original Style After-Dinner Service

After-dinner coffee cup, four original colors, each (ILLUS. front).......................... **$20-25**
After-dinner coffee cup, gray **75-100**
After-dinner coffeepot, cov., four original colors, each (ILLUS. back)................... **150-200**
After-dinner individual sugar bowl, cov., four original colors, each (ILLUS. right)..... **50-75**

After-dinner inidividual creamer, four
original colors, each (ILLUS. left)
previous page... **45-65**
After-dinner saucer, four original colors,
each (ILLUS. front previous page) **7-12**
After-dinner saucer, gray........................... **15-25**

Various LuRay Bowls

Bowl, 5" d., fruit, four original colors, each
(ILLUS. front)... **5-8**
Bowl, 5" d., fruit, gray............................... **10-15.99**
Bowl, 6 1/4" d., grapefruit, rare, four origi-
nal colors, each (ILLUS. left w/fruit bowl)
.... **350-400**
Bowl, 36's bowl (oatmeal), four original col-
ors, each **50-75**
Bowl, 36's bowl (oatmeal), gray **250-300**
Bowl, coupe soup, flat, four original colors,
each (ILLUS. right w/fruit bowl) **15-20**
Bowl, coupe soup, flat, gray **30-40**
Bowl, cream soup, four original colors,
each **75-95**
Bowl, lug soup (tab cereal), four original
colors, each.. **20-25**
Bowl, lug soup (tab cereal), gray **40-50**
Butter dish, cov., four original colors, each .. **50-75**
Butter dish, cov., gray **150-225**
Cake plate, 11" d., four original colors,
each **65-95**

LuRay Calendar Plate

Calendar plate, 8", 9" or 10" d., each
(ILLUS. of 10" d).. **50-75**
Casserole, cov., four original colors,
each **125-175**
"Chocolate set" A/D creamer*, four origi-
nal colors, each (ILLUS. left) **400-500**
"Chocolate set" A/D cup*, four original
colors, each (ILLUS. front) **75-100**
"Chocolate set" A/D pot*, cov., four origi-
nal colors, each (ILLUS. back) **1,000-1,500**
"Chocolate set" A/D saucer*, four original
colors, each (ILLUS. front) **25-35**

"Chocolate set" A/D sugar bowl*, cov.,
four original colors, each (ILLUS. right)
.... **500-600**

Modern Style "Chocolate Set"

Chop plate, 15" d., four original colors,
each **30-40**
Chop plate, 15" d., gray **350-450**
Coaster (nut dish), four original colors,
each **75-95**

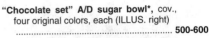

Compartment (Grill) Plate

Compartment (grill) plate, four original
colors, each (ILLUS.) **25-30**
Compartment (grill) plate, gray **100-125**
Cream soup saucer, four original colors,
each **20-25**
Creamer, four original colors, each **10-15**
Creamer, gray **30-45**
Egg cup, double, four original colors, each... **15-25**
Egg cup, double, gray **75-100**
Epergne (flower vase), four original col-
ors, each **125-150**

Various LuRay Jugs

Jug, juice, four original colors, each
(ILLUS. left)... **175-225**
Jug, water, flat, four original colors, each
(ILLUS. right)... **75-95**
Jug, water, footed*, four original colors,
each (ILLUS. center) **100-125**
Mixing bowl, 7" d., four original colors,
each **125-175**
Mixing bowl, 8 3/4" d., four original colors,
each **125-175**
Mixing bowl, 10 1/4" d., four original col-
ors, each **125-175**

Luray Muffin Cover & Plate

Muffin cover, four original colors, each
  (ILLUS.)... **175-225**
Pepper shaker, four original colors, each..... **10-15**
Pepper shaker, gray **20-30**
Pickle (celery) dish, four original colors,
  each **35-45**
Plate, 6" d., four original colors, each............... **4-6**
Plate, 6" d., gray **8-12**
Plate, 7" d., four original colors, each........... **10-15**
Plate, 7" d., gray **20-30**
Plate, 8" d., four original colors, each........... **20-25**
Plate, 8" d., gray **40-50**
Plate, 9" d., four original colors, each........... **10-15**
Plate, 9" d., gray **20-30**
Plate, 10" d., four original colors, each.......... **15-20**
Plate, 10" d., gray... **30-40**
Platter, 7" l., mini size, four original colors,
  each **200-250**
Platter, 11 1/2" l., four original colors, each .. **15-20**
Platter, 11 1/2" l., gray.................................... **45-75**
Platter, 13" l., four original colors, each **15-25**
Platter, 13" l., gray.. **45-75**
Relish dish, four-part, four original colors,
  each **125-175**
Salad bowl, four original colors, each........... **50-75**
Salad bowl, gray **300-400**
Salt shaker, four original colors, each **10-15**
Salt shaker, gray... **20-30**

LuRay Sauceboats

Sauceboat, four original colors, each
  (ILLUS. left on celery tray) **30-40**
Sauceboat, w/fixed stand, four original col-
  ors, each (ILLUS. right) **25-35**
Sugar bowl, cov., four original colors, each.. **15-20**

LuRay Sugar Bowls

Sugar bowl, cov., gray (ILLUS. left).............. **45-60**
Sugar bowl, cov., handleless, four original
  colors, each (ILLUS. right) **75-125**
Tea cup, four original colors, each **7-12**
Tea cup, gray **15-25**
Tea saucer, four original colors, each.............. **3-5**
Tea saucer, gray **7-10**

Teapot, cov., curved spout, four original
  colors, each... **75-95**
Teapot, cov., curved spout, gray.............. **300-400**
Teapot, cov., flat spout*, four original col-
  ors, each **150-200**
Tidbit tray, three-tier, four original colors,
  each **95-125**

Two-tier Tidbit Tray

Tidbit tray, two-tier, four original colors,
  each (ILLUS.) **75-100**
Tidbit tray, two-tier, gray........................ **150-200**

LuRay Tumblers

Tumbler, juice, four original colors,
  3 1/2" h., each (ILLUS. left) **45-65**
Tumbler, water, four original colors,
  4 1/4" h., each (ILLUS. right).................. **75-100**
Vase, bud, four original colors, each **250-350**
Vase, urn-type, four original colors, each .. **250-350**
Vegetable bowl (baker), oval, four original
  colors, each.. **20-25**
Vegetable bowl (baker), oval, gray **60-75**
Vegetable bowl (nappy), round, four origi-
  nal colors, each.. **20-25**
Vegetable bowl (nappy), round, gray.......... **60-75**

LUSTRE WARES

Lustred wares in imitation of copper, gold, silver and other colors were produced in England in the early 19th century and onward. Gold, copper or platinum oxides were painted on glazed objects which were then fired, giving them a lustred effect. Various forms of lustre wares include plain lustre with the entire object coated to obtain a metallic effect, bands of lustre decoration and painted lustre designs. Particularly appealing is the pink or purple "splash lustre" sometimes referred to as "Sunderland" lustre in the mistaken belief it was confined to the production of Sunderland area potteries. Objects decorated in silver lustre by the "resist" process, wherein parts of the objects to be left free from lustre decoration were treated with wax, are referred to as "silver resist."

Wares formerly called "Canary Yellow Lustre" are now referred to as "Yellow-Glazed Earthen- wares."

COPPER

Creamer, yellow band w/white reserves w/purple transfer-printed scene of woman & child in classical attire, poly- chrome enamel, 4 1/8" h. (repairs) **$182**

Pitcher, 5 3/4" h., yellow band w/white reserves w/red transfer-printed scene of badminton players w/blue, yellow & green enamel, minor wear **341**

Copper Lustre Pitcher

Pitcher, 6 3/8" h., flared foot below globular lower section, wide flaring cylindrical neck w/long spout, C-scroll handle, a wide canary band w/white oval reserves printed in black, one w/"Lafayette," the other w/Cornwallis," wear, interior blis- ters & a few exterior blisters in yellow, early 19th c. (ILLUS.) **770**

Pitcher, 7" h., small disk foot supporting a round widely flaring rounded lower body below a short angled shoulder to the tall cylindrical neck w/a figural serpent head rim spout & angled serpent handle, the sections of the body & neck w/blue ground decorated w/applied & poly- chromed basket of flowers near the base & band of flowers on the neck, copper lustre bands around the foot, body & rim & copper lustre spout & handle, ca. 1840..... **413**

Pitcher, 7" h., yellow band w/white reserves & brown transfer-printed scenes of woman & children in garden, yellow & blue enamel (minor wear) **193**

Copper Lustre Punch Bowl

Punch bowl, footed w/slightly flared sides, decorated w/wide white center band w/free-hand pink lustre house design, interior wear, 10 1/4" d., 4 7/8" h. (ILLUS.) **605**

Tea set: cov. 6 1/2" h. teapot, 5" h. cov. sugar bowl, 3 1/2" h. creamer; footed bulbous body, teapot w/swan's neck spout & relief-molded eagle handle, sugar bowl w/shell-shaped shoulder handles, overall copper lustre w/dark tan bands, rare, early set, 3 pcs. **280**

SILVER & SILVER RESIST

Creamer, jug-type, decorated w/silver resist bands of stylized scrolling florals, 3 3/4" h. (damage & repair) **121**

Silver Lustre Creamer & Sugar Bowl

Creamer & cov. sugar bowl, footed, wide cylindrical body, creamer w/arched spout & D-form handle, sugar bowl w/inset cover w/blossom finial, minor stains & sugar bowl w/crow's foot hair- lines, repair to scalloped lip & chips inside lid flange, 5 3/4" h., pr. (ILLUS.) **220**

Mug, cylindrical, pearlware w/relief-molded decoration, wide silver-resist band w/leaf sprigs & red stripes, 3 1/2" h. (small flakes) **110**

SUNDERLAND PINK & OTHERS

Bowl, 10" d., interior sides decorated w/two verses & a sailing ship enclosed in wreath borders w/"Lady Liberty" in the center, color enhanced w/green & red highlights, pink lustre bands on the inte- rior & exterior rims, England, 19th c. (glaze losses, rim & base chip) **489**

Frog mug, cylindrical form, two-handled, overall Sunderland pink splash lustre & black transfer-printed inscriptions, "Sailor's Farewell" & "Sailor's Prayer," interior bottom fitted w/a small figural frog, 19th c., 5 5/8" h. (hairline) **604**

Pitcher, 6 1/4" h., jug-form, pearlware, footed bulbous ovoid body tapering to a short neck w/rim spout, C-scroll handle, the sides molded w/a scene of a stag, doe & fawn highlighted in pink lustre & polychrome enamel on a white ground, first half 19th c. **385**

Jug-type Pitchers

Pitcher, 7 1/8" h., jug-form, white reserves w/black transfer-printed & polychrome enamel decoration of ship, maiden & seaman & appropriate verses, wear & minor enamel flaking, crow's foot hairlines in bottom (ILLUS. left) **715**

Pitcher, 7 1/4" h., jug-form, transfer-printed scene of a life boat, picture of Susan & William & motto **413**

Pitcher, 7 3/8" h., jug-form, pink lustre w/grape clusters & green enamel leaves & scrolling vines (some wear & scratches) **468**

Pitcher, 7 3/4" h., jug-form, pearlware, relief-molded basketweave design w/flowers & vintage, double satyr head at spout, polychrome enamel & pink lustre, minor wear & small chip on spout (ILLUS. right) **660**

Pitcher, jug-form, footed wide bulbous squatty body tapering to a short cylindrical neck w/arched spout, decorated w/black transfer-printed scenes & inscribed "Country Lad and Lass" & "Sailor's Farewell," pink luster & polychrome enamel (wear) **550**

MAJOLICA

Majolica, a tin-enameled glazed pottery, has been produced for centuries. It originally took its name from the island of Majorca, a source of figuline (potter's clay). Subsequently it was widely produced in England, Europe and the United States. Etruscan majolica, now avidly sought, was made by Griffen, Smith & Hill, Phoenixville, Pa., in the last quarter of the 19th century. Most majolica advertised today is 19th or 20th century. Once scorned by most collectors, interest in this colorful ware so popular during the Victorian era has now revived and prices have risen dramatically in the past few years. Also see WEDGWOOD.

Majolica Etruscan Mark

ETRUSCAN

Basket, wicker-handled, Begonia patt. **$660**

Bowl, 8 3/8" d., Shell & Seaweed patt., glazed in pink, brown, bluish grey & green, impressed mark (rim wear, firing marks in glaze) **316**

Butter pat, Leaf on Plate patt. **85**

Cake stand, Shell & Seaweed patt., upright shell-form pedestal, in pink, brown, bluish grey & green glazes, impressed mark, 4 7/8" h. (rim chips) **489**

Compote, shell, triple dolphin-footed (ILLUS.) **4,950**

Compote, Daisy patt. in yellow, pink & blue, mark for Griffen, Smith & Co., hairlines, 9" d., 5 3/8" h. **193**

Shell Dolphin-footed Compote

Rare Etruscan Holy Water Font

Holy water font, domed cylindrical body w/shell decorated cup-shaped top, decorated w/portrait of Virgin Mary, Rose of Sharon & Tree of Life, pat. date Nov. 6, 1883, 6 1/2" h. (ILLUS) **8,800**

Pitcher, 6" h., Shell & Seaweed patt. **195**

Baseball & Soccer Pitcher

Pitcher, 7 3/4" h., jug-type, decorated w/multicolored scene of baseball & soccer players (ILLUS.) **3,025**

Punch set: punch bowl & six matching cups; Lily patt., the set **2,970**

Above: Chintz China 'Joyce-Lynn' pattern teapot $1,295

Right: American Painted Porcelain 8¾" d. plate with orange poppies $50

Russel Wright Casual China pieces
Back: stacking salt & pepper shakers $20-25; redesigned salt shaker & pepper mill $200-300. Front, left to right: tea cup & saucer $10-15; coffee cup & saucer $15-20 and after-dinner cup & saucer $150-175

Above: Shelley China 'Festoons & Fruit' luncheon set $125

Above right: Midwest Potteries, Morton, Illinois model of a fish, 10½" h. $40

Right: Bisque figurine of a seated Dutch girl, 6½" h. $195.

LuRay jugs
Left to right: pink juice jug, $175-200, yellow footed water jug, $100-125, and blue flat-bottomed water jug, $75-95

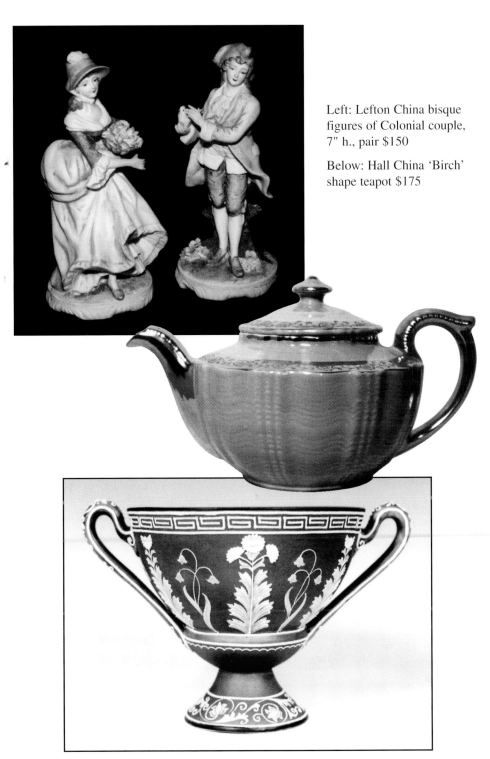

Left: Lefton China bisque figures of Colonial couple, 7" h., pair $150

Below: Hall China 'Birch' shape teapot $175

Nippon Wedgwood-style loving cup, 5½" h. $303

Top left: Noritake China Art Deco cigarette jar $380

Top right: Harker Pottery Kiddo Set: mug, $15, plate $30

Above: Blue & White Pottery 'Windy City' 8½" pitcher $300

Left: Early McCoy Cameo design jardiniere & pedestal. $250-350

Above: Blue & White Pottery printed "Wildflower" advertising salt crock $450

Right: Rookwood Pottery Black Iris glaze vase, 9" h. $7,700

Autumn Leaf Newport shape teapot. $60.

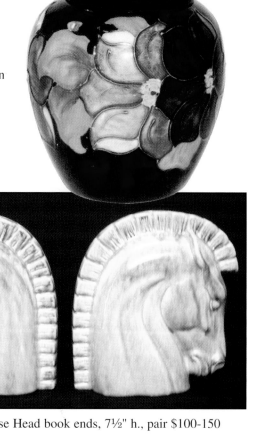

Above: Rare Nippon moon-shaped 'tapestry' basket, 9" h. $1,870

Above right: Royal Bayreuth Poppy mold chocolate pot, 8½" h. $1,300

Right: Moorcroft Clematis pattern ginger jar $870

Gonder Trojan Horse Head book ends, 7½" h., pair $100-150

Left: Early Quimper oval platter, 11¾" l. $150

Below: German Jasper Ware hair receiver, 4" h. $95

Lefton China novelty cow creamer & sugar bowl, pair $35

Above: Torquay Scandy pattern Motto Ware coffeepot, 7" h. $156

Right: McCoy Pottery Christmas Tree cookie jar $800-1,000

White Ironstone 'Fruit Garden' compote, 12" d., 6¾" h. $225-250

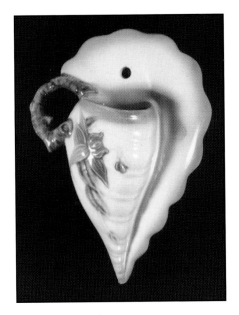

Above left: Hull Pottery Woodland Gloss pattern wall pocket $93

Above right: American Etruscan majolica strawberry tray $1,760

Right: Stoneware two gallon crock with stenciled and painted decoration $413

Very rare Fiesta turquoise blue covered onion soup bowl $11,000

Above left: Shelley China 'Jacobean' pattern 8¾" d. plate $50-60

Above right: Amphora bust of a sultry princess, 14½" h. $3,000-4,000

Left: Uhl Pottery Polar Bear sand jar, 14½" h. $250

Royal Copley models of kittens, 8" h., each $75-85

Above left: Florence Ceramics 'Linda Lou'
figure, 7¾" h. $150-175

Above right: Fine Haviland hand-painted
scenic shell-shaped dish, 9½" l. $1,925

Right: R.S. Prussia Mold 517 tankard pitcher
with LeBrun portrait, 15" h. $3,000-3,500

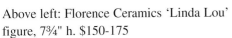

George Jones English majolica empty nest quail game dish $19,250

Right: Schafer & Vater figural novelty ashtray, 3¾" h. $145

Below left: Group of Cowan Pottery pieces: A figural Pan on Toadstool, 9" h. $1,100; a reclining Ram ashtray in green $250; a figural Chicken ashtray $70, and an orange lustre glaze vase, 7½" h. $90

Below right: Warwick Bouquet #2 portrait vase, 10½" h. $245

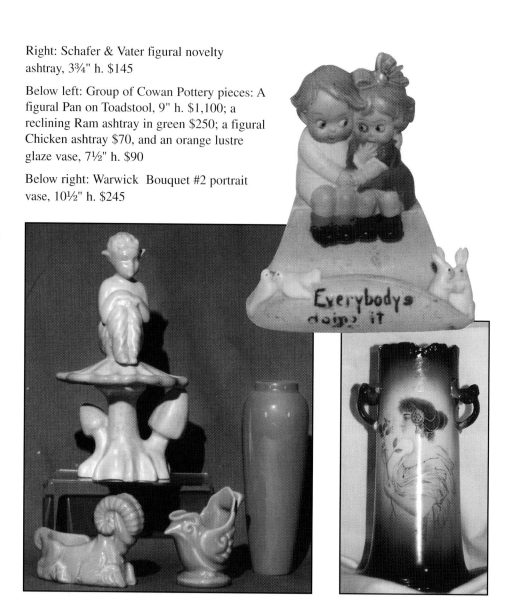

Colorful Noritake Art Deco creamer & sugar, pair $110

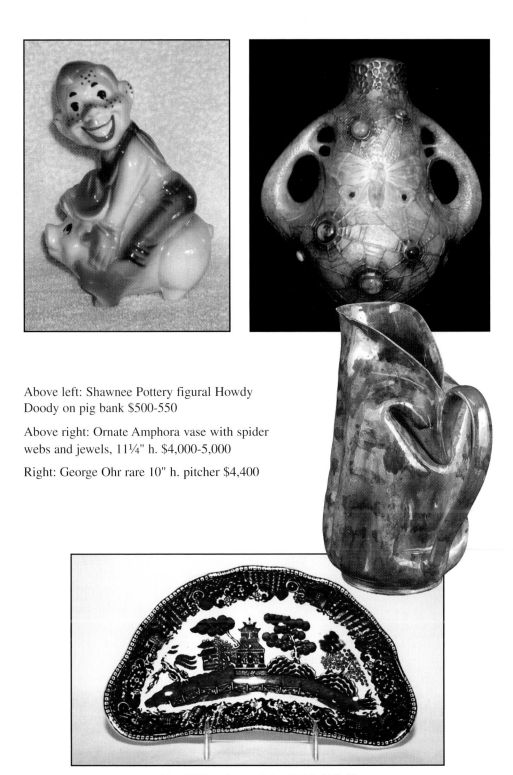

Above left: Shawnee Pottery figural Howdy Doody on pig bank $500-550

Above right: Ornate Amphora vase with spider webs and jewels, 11¼" h. $4,000-5,000

Right: George Ohr rare 10" h. pitcher $4,400

Blue Willow bone dish, 6½" l. $75-80

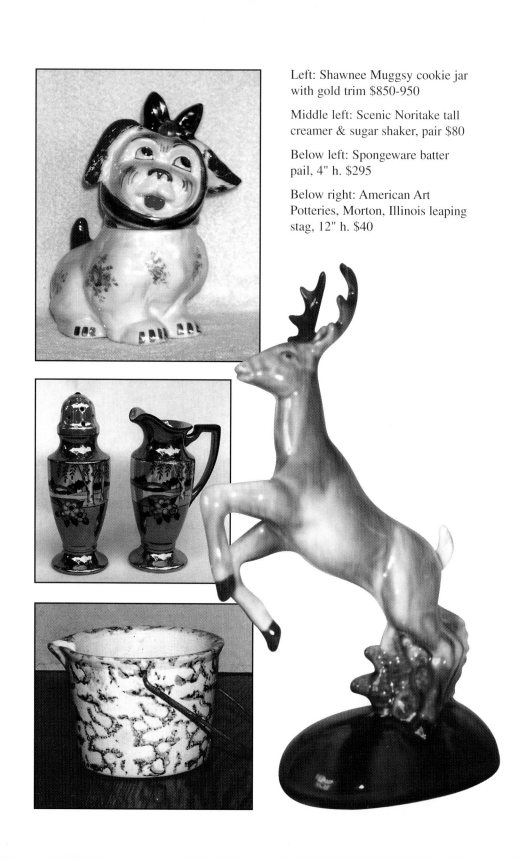

Left: Shawnee Muggsy cookie jar with gold trim $850-950

Middle left: Scenic Noritake tall creamer & sugar shaker, pair $80

Below left: Spongeware batter pail, 4" h. $295

Below right: American Art Potteries, Morton, Illinois leaping stag, 12" h. $40

Above: Blue Willow teapot with gold trim, 6" h. $250-275

Left: Bennington Pottery Flint Enamel-glazed candlestick $385

Below: Ceramic Arts Studio Cinderella & The Prince figurines $150-175

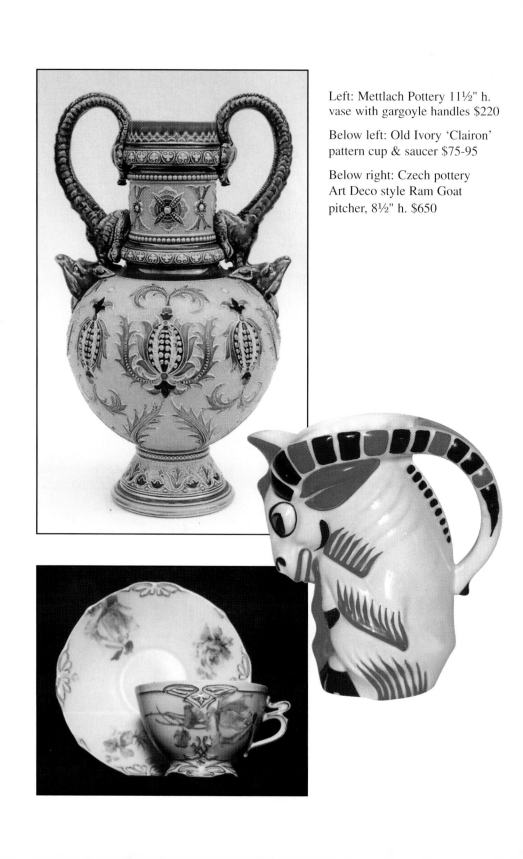

Left: Mettlach Pottery 11½" h. vase with gargoyle handles $220

Below left: Old Ivory 'Clairon' pattern cup & saucer $75-95

Below right: Czech pottery Art Deco style Ram Goat pitcher, 8½" h. $650

Serving tray, spade-shaped dish, Strawberry patt., cobalt blue, missing creamer & sugar bowl **1,760**

Etruscan Soap Dish & Vases

Soap dish, cov., Star of David finial, blue (ILLUS. far right)....................................... **2,200**

Syrup pitcher w/metal lid, Sunflower patt., cobalt blue ground....................................... **495**

Vase, bud, 4" h., Corn patt. (ILLUS. far left)..... **660**

Vase, 4 3/4" h., Oak Leaf & Acorn patt. (ILLUS. second from left) **550**

Vase, 6 1/2" h., flaring foot below baluster-form body w/wide cylindrical neck, cobalt blue & yellow w/brown figural lion head at shoulder, lion leg handles (ILLUS. second from right) **1,210**

Butterfly Wall Pocket

Wall pocket, butterfly-shaped, ivory, yellow, green & cobalt blue (ILLUS.) **3,850**

GENERAL

Bowl, cov., 7 1/4" d., figural artichoke w/attached underplate, bird finial **295**

Box, cov., modeled in the form of a turquoise-glazed cushion tied w/yellow cord & surmounted by a white dog knop, the pink-glazed interior fitted w/three rectangular & two oval wells, George Jones, England, ca. 1870s, 10 5/8" l......... **4,312**

Cake set: 12" handled server & six matching plates; deep red florals on a gold basketweave ground, the set **165**

Candelabrum, three-light, urn-form nozzles supported on a shaped cross bar above a flower-filled urn raised on a fluted pedestal flanked by two scantily-clad cherubs on an oval base raised on four bracket feet, impressed marks, Minton, England, ca. 1869, 16 1/8" h. (seated cherub w/restored leg & foot, small chip to bracket foot at back of base) **5,462**

Centerpiece, modeled as a large turquoise cabbage leaf supported by green ferns flanked by two white & black crouched rabbits, Minton **9,075**

Minton Majolica Centerpiece

Centerpiece, modeled as a basket raised on a clump of reeds & supported by three putti, on shaped Neoclassical base, impressed "Minton" date code for 1863 & design number 874, 11 1/2" h. (ILLUS.)... **4,887**

Charger, center decorated w/polychrome classical scene bordered w/musical instruments, mythological figures & animals, 19th c., Italy, 18" d. **633**

Cheese dish, cov., tall cylindrical cover w/flat top centered by an arched branch handle & molded prunus branches & blossoms, matching large blossoming branches molded around the sides on an argenta ground, Wedgwood impressed mark, ca. 1882, 8 1/4" h. (slight stains) **690**

Compote, open, the pedestal composed of three figural standing herons on a tripartite base, supporting a wide shallow rounded dish composed of a band of large lily pad leaves, late 19th c. **440**

Compote, 7 3/4" h., open, the shaped oval bowl supported by a naturalistically molded oak tree on an oval base applied w/a recumbent hound & a grouse, George Jones, impressed registry mark & indistinct painted design number, ca. 1875 .... **6,569**

Cup & saucer, Bird & Fan patt........................ **195**

Majolica Palissy-style Dish

Dish, oval, Palissy-style, center w/relief-molded Venus & Cupid on mottled grey ground, the rim molded w/eight shallow wells alternating w/satyr & angel masks within ochre strapwork borders, impressed marks, Minton, England, ca. 1875, 19 1/2" l. (ILLUS.) **3,450**

Figurines, figural vintager modeled as a cherub draped in either ivy or ears of wheat, tugging at a rope wrapped around a tall flared basket to one side, a discarded quiver of arrows beneath their feet, impressed marks, Minton, England, ca. 1863 & 1864, one w/incised "405," 10 3/4" h., pr. (one w/minor restoration to edge of basket) **6,037**

George Jones Game Dish

Game dish, cov., two-handled, game bird nestled in grassy setting on cover, the sides decorated w/rabbits amid ferns, George Jones, England, 13" w., 7" h. (ILLUS.) **19,250**

Game tureen, cov., two-handled, basket-form, dark brown bamboo w/relief-molded fish & game on cover surrounded by green leaves, George Jones, England **8,250**

Majolica Garden Seat

Garden seats, Chinese barrel-shaped, decorated w/relief-molded irises & leaves in green glazes on cream ground, ca. 1895, impressed marks, Wardle & Company, 18 1/2" h., pr. (ILLUS. of one) .. **4,600**

Jardiniere, inverted pear shape, molded w/vertical raised straps set w/lion's mask & ring handles & terminating in paw feet, blue ground, the gadrooned rim glazed in green & interior pale pink, impressed

marks, Minton, England, ca. 1871, 14 1/4" h. **2,645**

Jardinieres, lozenge form foot supporting semi-ovoid body w/relief-molded sprays of white dog roses on brown glaze basketweave ground, relief-molded branches at rim & foot, turquoise interior, marked w/painted "2," Staffordshire, ca. 1870, 8 1/2" h., pr. **2,070**

Oyster plates, six-well, bordered by shells & seaweed & glazed in white, alternating w/either pink, turquoise or blue about a central circular well of the same color, set of ten consisting of five turquoise, two pink & three blue, painted cross & four dots mark, English or American, after a Minton design, ca. 1880, 9 1/4" d. (four w/glaze faults or repair, one w/minor chip & one w/minor haircrack) **2,875**

George Jones Butterfly Patch Box

Patch box, cov., modeled as a butterfly, browns, white, yellow & blue lid, green & white floral decoration around sides, George Jones, England (ILLUS.) **6,600**

Pitcher, 8" h., tapering cylindrical form w/C-form handle, greenish blue ground on lower part w/underwater scene of fish, crabs & plant life, dark blue handle & wide band around top w/relief-molded seagulls, George Jones, England **13,200**

Pitcher, 8 1/4" h., Fish on Waves, squatty bulbous body, angled handle **275**

Pitcher, 8 1/4" h., Sharkskin & Floral Bow decoration **85**

Pitcher, 9" h., figural monkey **800**

Pitcher, 9 1/4" h., Birds Nest decoration, bulbous ovoid form w/tree knurls protruding around base, angled branch handle **95**

Pitcher, 10" h., figural, seated cat, green interior, ivory exterior w/brown floral trim above eyes, brown tail forms handle, leafy green base, Minton (ILLUS.) **9,350**

Pitcher, 13" h., jug-form, hinged shell-form pewter lid w/figural jester head knop, modeled as an ivy-clad rustic stone tower w/four dancing figures wearing colorful medieval-style costumes, impressed marks & dated 1869, Minton, England (cover & handle restored) **1,610**

Platter, oval, 25" l., molded in low relief w/a naturalistically-colored salmon resting on a bed of green fern leaves on a turquoise ground, the reeded rim glazed in greyish green, impressed marks, year &

"QIG," painted shape number "M 2164," Wedgwood, England (very minor hair-crack) **4,887**

Minton Figural Cat Pitcher

Sardine box, cov., rectangular, molded w/band of green leaves on turquoise ground, the cover w/three grey sardines on a bed of seaweed, interior & cover w/pink glaze, George Jones, England, ca. 1870, 5 3/4" l. **1,840**

Strawberry server, molded w/strawberry leaves on blue & white napkin ground & fitted w/a creamer & sugar bowl, George Jones, 13" l.. **600**

Sugar bowl, cov., Bird & Fan patt.................... **250**

Tea set: cov. teapot, cov. sugar bowl, creamer & tray; the oblong keyhole-form tray w/a blossom sprig border band, serving pieces of simple ovoid form w/the lower body w/a molded brown basketweave design, the upper body molded w/white blossoms on leafy twigs against a blue ground, George Jones, England, late 19th c., the set..................... **4,400**

Teapot, cov., Chinese man finial...................... **250**

Teapot, cov., figural, naturalistically modeled as a large fish in pale blue & pink & set w/green seaweed handle w/turquoise spout protruding from mouth, Minton, England, molded diamond registration mark, gilt-printed Minton crowned globe mark, 7 3/8" h. (green enamel flaked) **1,495**

Vase, 6 1/2" h., model of a large inverted straw bonnet, leghorn-shape w/basketweave ground molded w/long ribbons, flowers & a feather against the sides w/alternating dark & light bands of color, impressed Wedgwood mark, ca. 1882 (slight hairlines) **575**

Vases, 28" h., "Queen's" footed slender ovoid form tapering to cylindrical neck w/flared rim, molded w/fruiting vine & berried ivy branches on ochre ground beneath twig handles tied w/pale blue ribbon & set on each shoulder w/the head of a cat, green bands of molded fluting around lower body & neck, impressed "1857," Minton, England, repair to one rim & handle, chips to cats'

Minton Majolica "Queen's" Vase

ears, one w/chip to foot, pr. (ILLUS. of one).. **25,875**

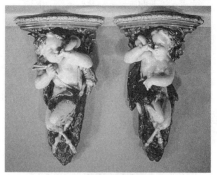

Minton Satyr Wall Bracket Shelves

Wall bracket shelves, conical form w/relief-molded satyr figures, Minton, 18" h., pr. (ILLUS.) **17,600**

MARBLEHEAD

This pottery was organized in 1904 by Dr. Herbert J. Hall as a therapeutic aid to patients in a sanitarium he ran in Marblehead, Massachusetts. It was later separated from the sanitarium and directed by Arthur E. Baggs, a fine artist and designer, who bought out the factory in 1916 and operated it until its closing in 1936. Most wares were hand-thrown and decorated and carry the company mark of a stylized sailing vessel flanked by the letters "M" and "P."

Marblehead Mark

Bowl, 4 1/8" h., tapered spherical form, dark teal blue glaze, impressed mark, early 20th c., ... **$173**

Bowl, 6" d., 3" h., tapering wide squatty bulbous form w/a short wide rolled neck, overall brick red metallic glaze, impressed mark **385**

Bowl, 6 1/4" d., 2 1/4" h., compressed bulbous incurved sides, smooth dark blue glaze w/light blue interior, impressed ship mark **220**

Bowl-vase, wide bulbous body tapering slightly to a wide flat mouth covered in a smooth speckled brown glaze, impressed ship mark, 5 1/4" d., 2 3/4" h. **358**

Bowl-vase, miniature, a squatty bulbous form tapering to a flat rim, overall brown matte glaze, paper label, impressed mark, 3 1/2" d. (burst bubble on side) **198**

Bowl-vase, deep slightly tapering cylindrical sides w/a closed rim, overall yellow matte glaze, impressed mark, 5 1/2" d., 3 1/2" h. **660**

Bowl-vase, deep wide cylindrical form w/wide flaring rim covered in matte mauve glaze, lavender interior, impressed ship mark, 7 1/2" d., 3 3/4" h. **385**

Match safe, cov., octagonal, w/striker inside lid, covered in a fine smooth matte green glaze, impressed ship mark, 2 x 3" (glaze abrasion around rim) **385**

Marblehead Pitcher

Pitcher, 5" h., wide bulbous body w/arched spout & C-form handle, incised decoration of ship at sea, glossy blue glaze, impressed mark (ILLUS.) **330**

Pitcher, 5" h., 6" d., footed bulbous shouldered body w/a short neck w/pointed spout, loop handle, embossed around the neck w/waves, the sides w/rounded medallions around galleons under sail in blue, ochre & green, the waves & handle in blue & the background in cream, semi-matte glaze, impressed ship mark **770**

Rare Marblehead Plate

Plate, 7 1/2" d., border decorated w/a frieze of camels and nomads in blue & yellow on white ground, impressed ship mark (ILLUS.) **1,045**

Tile, square, decorated w/a landscape of trees in dark green reflected in a lake, impressed ship mark & paper label, 4 1/4" sq.(small chip to front & back) **770**

Tile, square, depicting a cluster of trees in dark green under a blue overcast sky, impressed ship mark & paper label, 4 1/4" sq. **880**

Vase, 2 3/4" h., decorated in a teal blue matte glaze, black underglaze visible near rim, narrow mouth on a flared bulbous form, marked on base, ca. 1910 .... **374**

Vase, 3 5/8" h., short flared rim on a squat bulbous body, decorated w/repeating stylized trees, black trunks & blue leaves over a grey ground, impressed mark & initials of Hannah Tutt, ca. 1905 .... **2,415**

Vase, 4 1/4" h., 4 3/4" d., bulbous ovoid body w/a flat mouth, decorated around the mouth w/red & purple stylized blossoms in a band on the semi-matte pink ground, mark under glaze **880**

Vase, cov., 4 1/4" h., 4 3/4" d., wide bulbous ovoid body tapering to a wide flaring rim w/bobeche lid, covered in a smooth matte grey glaze, paper label **660**

Vase, 4 3/4" h., swollen cylindrical form, decorated around the rim w/repeating raised flower & leaf design in faint blue, red & tan on a speckled blue matte ground, by Hannah Tutt, impressed mark & artist's initials, early 20th c. **1,610**

Vase, 6" h., cylindrical, carved & painted around the rim w/alternating blue & brown dragonflies against the medium matte green ground, artist-signed "Hanna Tutt" & impressed mark (small base flake) **1,760**

Vase, 6 1/4" h., 3 3/4" d., bulbous base below a wide cylindrical body w/flat rim, repeated design around rim of brown stylized flowers on long stems, green ground, early ship mark (repair to minor glaze flaking to rim) **2,860**

Vase, 6 1/4" h., 5 1/4" d., flaring rim over a swollen flaring body, matte blue glaze, impressed mark (minor glaze scratches) **460**

Vase, 7" h., tall cylindrical form, dark matte green glaze, impressed company cipher **518**

Vase, 7 3/4" h., gently tapering rounded cylindrical body w/a short flared rim, dark blue matte glaze, impressed mark **805**

Vase, 8 1/2" h., 4" d., tapering cylindrical body w/molded rim, decorated in wax-resist w/stylized peacock feathers in brown on a mottled green ground, impressed ship mark & "W" (ILLUS.) **4,400**

Vase, 8 1/2" h., 8" d., heavy bell-form body w/closed rim, unusual frothy matte bluish green glaze, incised "M" w/sea gull (repair to small drilled bottom side hole) **990**

Vase, 11 3/4" h., wide slightly tapering cylindrical form w/flat rim, blue matte glaze, impressed mark (tight line at rim) **660**

Vase with Peacock Feathers

MARTIN BROTHERS

Martinware, the term used for this pottery, dates from 1873 and is the product of the Martin brothers—Robert, Wallace, Edwin, Walter and Charles—often considered the first British studio potters. From first to final stages, their hand-thrown pottery was completely the work of the team. The early wares may be simple and conventional, but the Martin brothers built up their reputation by producing ornately engraved, incised or carved designs as well as rather bizarre figural wares. The amusing face-jugs are considered some of their finest work. After 1910, the work of the pottery declined and can be considered finished by 1915, though some attempts were made to fire pottery as late as the 1920s.

R.W.Martin & Brothers London & Southall

Martin Brothers Mark

Bowl-vase, footed wide squatty bulbous form tapering to a flat molded rim, faceted sides, covered in a fine red & green lustered crystalline glaze, incised "4-1900 - Martin Bro. - London and Southall," 1900, 7" d., 5" h. **$523**

Martin Brothers Humidor and Floral Vase

Humidor, cov., grotesque bird-shaped body on round base, the cover formed by the head, glazed in brown & black

tones, both parts incised "R.W.Martin Bros. London & Southall - 1903," repair to tip of beak, 7 3/4" h., 3 1/4" d. (ILLUS.).. **2,530**

Spoon warmer, stoneware, modeled as an open-mouthed caninesque face, glazed in green, brown & cobalt blue, applied loop handle, incised "R.W. Martin - London & Southall - 4-3-80," 5 1/2" h. **2,185**

Vase, 4 1/4" h., 3 1/2" d., stoneware, flaring foot supporting a baluster-shaped body w/tall wide neck & flaring rim, incised rings near base & at shoulder, decorated overall w/plumes & blossoms in blue & brown on a greyish green ground, incised "R.W.Martin - 680" (ILLUS.) **220**

Vase, 9" h., 4" d., tall squared ovoid form tapering to short square neck w/molded rim, upturned loop handles at the shoulder, decorated in sgraffito w/a veined pattern on an amber ground, incised "N5-7-1903 - Martin Bros. - London & Southall" **1,100**

Vase, 9 1/4" h., 6 1/4" d., footed bulbous ovoid body tapering to a wide flaring neck, covered in vivid incised & modeled swirls, brown & black matte glaze, incised "1 - 1 - 1903 - Martin Bros. - London Southall" **1,870**

Vases, 9" h., simple ovoid body tapering to a slightly flaring cylindrical neck, decorated w/a large crab on one side & a lobster on the opposite side w/assorted sea creatures in brown against "1903," pr. **1,870**

MCCOY

Collectors are now seeking the art wares of two McCoy potteries. One was founded in Roseville, Ohio, in the late 19th century as the J.W. McCoy Pottery, subsequently becoming Brush-McCoy Pottery Co., later Brush Pottery. The other was also founded in Roseville in 1910 as Nelson McCoy Sanitary Stoneware Co., later becoming Nelson McCoy Pottery. In 1967 the pottery was sold to D.T. Chase of the Mount Clemens Pottery Co. who sold his interest to the Lancaster Colony Corp. in 1974. The pottery shop closed in 1985. Cookie jars are especially collectible today.

A helpful reference book is The Collector's Encyclopedia of McCoy Pottery, *by the Huxfords (Collector Books), and* McCoy Cookie Jars From the First to the Latest, *by Harold Nichols (Nichols Publishing, 1987).*

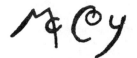

McCoy Mark

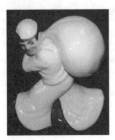

McCoy Seaman's Bank

Bank, figural seaman w/sack over shoulder, white, blue & black, 5 3/4" h. (ILLUS.) **$65**

Basket, hanging-type, Butterfly line, 6 1/2" h. **175-300**

Book end/planter, model of a bird dog, ca. 1955, 5 3/4 x 6", pr. **150-200**

Book end/planter, model of a violin, ca. 1959, 10" h., pr. **100-150**

Book ends, decorated w/swallows, ca. 1956, 5 1/2 x 6" **125-150**

Book ends, Lily Bud line, ca. 1940s, 5 3/4" h., pr. **150-200**

Book ends, model of a bird, ca. 1940s, marked "NM," pr. **175-225**

Book ends, model of a rearing horse, 1940s., 8" h., pr. **100-125**

Cache pot, double w/applied bird **35-45**

Candleholders, Lily Bud line, 5" d., pr. **60-80**

Antelope Centerpiece

Centerpiece, four sections w/center model of antelope, green & tan, ca. 1955, 8 1/2 x 12" (ILLUS.) **250-350**

Coffee serving set: cov. server, stand & eight mugs; El Rancho Bar-B-Que line, 1960, the set **325**

Cookie jar, Asparagus, ca. 1977 .... **40-50**

Cookie jar, Bean pot **55**

Cookie jar, Bobby Baker **53**

Cookie jar, Boy on Baseball, 1978 .... **310**

Cookie jar, Bugs Bunny cylinder, 1971-72 ...... **185**

Cookie jar, Bunch of Bananas, ca. 1948 .. **125-150**

Cookie jar, Burlap Sack **65**

Cookie jar, Cauliflower Mammy **900**

Cookie jar, Christmas Tree, ca. 1959 (ILLUS. top next column) **800-1,000**

Cookie jar, Clown bust, ca. 1943 .... **220**

Cookie jar, Clown in Barrel **60**

Christmas Tree Cookie Jar

Cookie jar, Coffee Grinder **50**

Cookie jar, Covered Wagon (Cookie Wagon), 1959-62 .... **105**

Davy Crockett Cookie Jar

Cookie jar, Davy Crockett head, ca. 1957 (ILLUS.) **575-650**

Cookie jar, Eagle Basket **40**

Cookie jar, Engine, black **175**

Cookie jar, Friendship 7 .... **70**

Cookie jar, Happy Face, ca. 1972 .... **60-80**

Cookie jar, heart-shaped, Hobnail line, ca. 1940 .... **400-500**

Cookie jar, Hound Dog, ca. 1977 .... **25-35**

Cookie jar, House, ca. 1986 (ILLUS.) **300-350**

Cookie jar, Jack-O-Lantern, orange w/green cover **600**

Cookie jar, Kittens (Three) on Ball of Yarn, green **100**

Cookie jar, Leprechaun, red **1,250**

Cookie jar, Liberty Bell **55**

Cookie jar, Love Birds: Kissing Penguins, ca. 1946 .... **75-100**

Cookie jar, Mammy **60**

Cookie jar, Mammy, red polka dot dress, ca. 1930s **375**

Cookie jar, Midge, without freckles (rare) **600**

Cookie jar, Quaker Oats canister **695**

Cookie jar, Rag Doll (Raggedy Ann,) ca. 1972 .... **100-125**

House Cookie Jar

Cookie jar, Rocking Chair (Dalmations), 1961 .... **325-375**
Cookie jar, round, Hobnail line, ca. 1940 .. **100-200**
Cookie jar, Thinking Puppy **40**
Cookie jar, Touring Car **130**

W.C. Fields Cookie Jar

Cookie jar, W.C. Fields, ca. 1972 (ILLUS.) **175-200**
Cookie jar, Windmill **60**
Creamer & open sugar bowl, Sunburst Gold glaze, ca. 1957, original paper inventory tags, pr. **125**
Dog dish, embossed "Man's Best Friend, His Dog," 7 1/2" d. **60-75**
Flower bowl ornament, model of a duck, 4" h. **75-90**
Flower bowl ornament, model of a pea-cock, 4 3/4" h. **100-125**
Flower holder, figural, model of a fish, 4 1/4" l. **100-200**
Flower holder, figural, model of a turtle, 4 1/4" l. **50-100**
Food warmer, model of a chuck wagon w/brass wagon wheels & candleholder, El Rancho line, ca. 1960, 3 qt. (ILLUS.) **225-250**

Chuck Wagon Food Warmer

Iced tea server, El Rancho Bar-B-Que line, ca. 1960, 11 1/2" h. **250-300**
Jardiniere, swallows decoration, 7" h. **85-125**
Jardiniere, fish decoration, ca. 1958, 7 1/2" h. **350-400**
Jardiniere, Spring Wood line, ca. 1960, 10" h. **50-60**
Jardiniere & pedestal base, basketweave design, overall 21", 2 pc. **250-350**

Cameo Design Jardiniere & Pedestal

Jardiniere & pedestal base, cameo design, green, blue & ivory blended gloss glaze, overall 21" h., 2 pcs. (ILLUS.) **250-350**
Jardiniere & pedestal base, holly design, overall 21" h., 2 pc. **250-350**
Jardiniere & pedestal base, quilted design, ca. 1955, overall 21" h., 2 pcs. **200-250**
Mug, "Happy Face," ca. 1971, 4" **15-20**
Mug, Irish Setter decoration **35**
Mug, relief molded scary gorilla face, ca. 1978 .... **30-40**
Oil jar, marked "NM," 12" h. **125-200**
Pitcher, 6" h., round, Hobnail line, 48 oz. **90-125**
Pitcher, 7 3/4" h., figural W. C. Fields head, tan **50-60**
Pitcher, 10" h., Butterfly line **150-225**

Figural Fish Pitcher

Pitcher, model of a fish, ca. 1949
(ILLUS.).. **500-600**
Pitcher-vase, 7" h., figural parrot, ca.
1952 .... **150-200**
Planter, Baa Baa Black Sheep, ca. 1940s,
4 1/2" h.. **45-60**
Planter, banana boat, ca. 1959, 11" l....... **125-175**
Planter, divided, Butterfly line, white,
5 1/2 x 7 1/2" **125-150**
Planter, figural, clown riding pig, white
w/blue & red trim, 8 1/2" l. **80-100**
Planter, figural, Madonna, white, 6" h. **250-300**

Bird Dog with Pheasant Planter

Planter, model of a bird dog w/pheasant,
relief-molded rock base, rail fence &
bush, ca. 1954, 8 1/2 x 12 1/2"
(ILLUS.).. **200-250**
Planter, model of a carriage, ca. 1955,
8 x 9" **150-200**
Planter, model of a cluster of grapes &
leaves, 5 x 6 1/2" **125-150**
Planter, model of a cowboy hat, ca. 1956,
8" l. **35-50**
Planter, model of a duck w/umbrella, ca.
1954, 7 1/4 x 7 1/2" **100-150**
Planter, model of a frog w/umbrella, dark
glaze, 1954... **125-175**
Planter, model of a goose w/cart, 8" l. **35-45**
Planter, model of a lemon, 5 x 6 1/2" **75-100**
Planter, model of a Mary Ann-style shoe,
5" l. **25-40**
Planter, model of a panda & crib, 6" l.......... **75-100**
Planter, model of a rooster on wheel of
wheelbarrow, 10 1/2" l.......................... **100-125**
Planter, model of a scoop w/figural mammy
seated on rim, ca. 1953, 7 1/2" h. **150-200**
Planter, model of a snowman, 4 x 6" **50-60**

Planter, model of a squirrel, ca. 1955,
4 1/2 x 5" **25-30**
Planter, model of a trolley car, ca. 1954,
3 3/4 x 7" **80-100**
Planter, model of a wagon wheel, ca. 1954,
8" h.. **30-40**
Planter, model of a wishing well, ca. 1950,
6" h. or 7" h... **20-30**
Planter, model of a zebras, ca. 1956,
6 1/2 x 8 1/2" **600-700**
Planter, model of flying ducks, green glaze,
No. 760, ca. 1955, 8 1/2 x 10 3/4" **125-175**
Planter, model of pussy at the well, ca.
1957, 7" l. **125-175**

Rabbits & Stump Planter

Planter, model of rabbits & stump, ca.
1951, 5 1/2" h., white w/brown trim
(ILLUS.).. **60-75**
Planter, model of "stretch" dachshund,
8 1/4" l. **175-200**
Planting dish, rectangular, front w/five
relief-molded Scottie dog heads, white,
brown & green, ca, 1949, 8" l. **40-50**
Platter, 14" l., Butterfly line........................ **250-400**
Porch jar, Sand Butterfly design, 20" h..... **450-600**

Sand Jar with Sphinx Design

Sand jar, sphinx design, ca. 1930s, 16" h.
(ILLUS.).. **1,000-1,400**
Spoon rest, Butterfly line, 4 x 7 1/2" **100-150**
Spoon rest, model of a penguin, 5 x 7" **100-150**
Sprinkler, model of a turtle, green w/yellow
trim, ca. 1950, 5 1/2 x 10" **60-80**

Strawberry jar, w/relief-molded peacock,
8" h. **35-50**

Tea set: cov. teapot, creamer & open sugar
bowl; oval shape w/branch handles,
brown & green vine & ivy leaf decoration
on white ground, 3 pcs. **90-110**

Tea set: cov. teapot, creamer & open sugar
bowl; Pine Cone patt., ca. 1946, 3 pcs.... **75-100**

Tray, novelty, model of hands, NM
mark, ca. 1940s, 8 1/2" **100-125**

TV lamp, model of a panther, ca. 1950s,
7 1/2 x 9 1/2" **65-80**

Mermaid & Shell TV Lamp

TV lamp, model of a seashell & mermaid,
yellow & green, 6 x 9 3/4" (ILLUS.) **200-300**

Vase, 6" h., heart-shaped, ca. 1940s **50-70**

Vase, 6" h., Hobnail line, Castlegate
shape **150-200**

Vase, 6 1/2" h., figural lower tulip, ca.
1953 .... **100-125**

Vase, 7 1/2" h., figural Uncle Sam head........ **50-60**

Vase, 8" h., Blossomtime line, pink & green
molded florals on creamy yellow ground........ **45**

Vase, 8 1/4" h., figural magnolia, ca. 1953,
pink, white, brown & green.................... **150-175**

Vase, 8 1/4" h., model of a gloved
hand, ca. 1940s................................... **150-200**

Poppy Vase

Vase, 8 1/2", figural poppy, pink, ca. 1955
(ILLUS.)... **600-800**

Vase, 8 1/2" h., triple lily-form, ca. 1950 .... **50-75**

Ivy Decorated Vase

Vase, 9" h., footed, flaring conical body
w/brown angled branch handles, decorated w/brown vines & green ivy leaves,
white ground (ILLUS.) **90-100**

Vase, 9" h. or 10" h., figural lizard
handles.. **300-400**

Vase, 9" h., petal form w/angled handles,
ca. 1955 .... **150-175**

Vase, 14" h., Antique Curio line, ca. 1962 ... **75-100**

Vase, 14" h., ribbed pattern **200-300**

Vase, 14 1/2" h., fan-shaped, ca. 1954 ..... **150-200**

Vase, 9" h., footed, tapering body w/irregu-
lar rim, relief-molded contrasting leaf
decoration at top **100-125**

Wall pocket, Blossomtime line, 7 3/4" h. ... **95-130**

Wall pocket, Lily Bud line, marked "NM,"
8" l. **200-250**

Wall pocket, model of a bird bath,
5 x 6 1/2" **85-100**

Wall pocket, model of a bunch of
bananas **125-150**

Wall pocket, model of a cuckoo clock,
8" l. **125-150**

Wall pocket, model of a Dutch shoe,
7 1/2" l. **40-50**

Wall pocket, model of a fan, blue,
8 x 8 1/2" **75-90**

Wall pocket, model of a grape cluster **80-100**

Mailbox Wall Pocket

Wall pocket, model of a mailbox, 7" h.
(ILLUS.)... **90-100**

Wall pocket, model of a pear........................ **65-80**

Wall pocket, model of a violin, 10 1/4" h... **100-200**

Wall pocket, model of lovebirds on trivet,
8 1/2" l. **75-90**

MEISSEN

The secret of true hard paste porcelain, known long before to the Chinese, was "discovered" accidentally in Meissen, Germany, by J.F. Bottger, an alchemist working with E.W. Tschirnhausen. The first European true porcelain was made in the Meissen Porcelain Works, organized about 1709. Meissen marks have been widely copied by other factories. Some pieces listed here are recent.

Meissen Mark

Candelabra, four-light, each modeled w/a man or woman seated on high domed base painted w/birds & insects, each figure holding a child on their lap & supporting a scroll-molded candleholder fitted w/three flower-encrusted branches, ca. second half 19th c., underglaze-blue crossed swords mark & incised "D 176" & "D 177," 18 5/8" h., pr. (one damaged, minor chips, losses & restoration to candelabra) **$2,875**

Centerpiece, figural, Blue Onion patt., modeled as a boy & girl figure w/a goat atop a pedestal base, a pierced basket on either side, blue crossed swords mark, No. 1074, late 19th - early 20th c., 18" l., 8 3/4" h. (damages)........................... **978**

Centerpiece, a pierced shallow basket supported on a foliate stem above a rocky base applied w/four dancing figures, shaded pink enamel & gilding, gilt trim, interior w/stylized flower meander, underglaze-blue crossed swords mark, 12 1/8" h. (stem restored & minor crack to basket) **1,725**

Clock, shelf or mantel, a round clock dial w/Roman numerals enclosed in a footed scroll-molded body in pale pink, turquoise & gilding w/four applied figures of putti, each allegorical of one of the Four Seasons, colorful applied flowers & leaves, second half 19th c., underglaze-blue crossed swords, 18 3/8" h. **4,600**

Dessert service: five 8" d. plates w/pierced rims & two compotes; the plates w/basketweave edges w/three pink flower-filled reserves, a large wreath of pink flowers around the center, each compote w/a domed gadrooned round foot & tall ringed pedestal supporting a shallow flaring dish w/a reticulated border & centered by a standing figure of a young boy flower seller or a young girl flower seller, gilt trim, early 20th c., compotes 11 1/2" h., the set **1,840**

Meissen Dish

Dish, deep w/flanged rim, scalloped border, slip decorated w/raised foliate & scrolled cartouches & enameled floral sprays, early 19th c., Germany, 15 1/4" d. (ILLUS.).................................... **1,265**

Ewer, flattened ovoid body, allegorical decoration w/figures & scenes representing the element Water, painted & incised marks, drilled, 19th c., 24" h. **4,600**

Figure group, a shepherdess in 18th c. dress standing & grooming a lamb atop a tree trunk, polychrome decoration, blue crossed swords marks & incised inventory number "F68" & pattern number "61," late 18th c., 5" h. (some early repairs) **518**

Figure group, a tailor in 18th c. dress riding astride a horned goat, one hand aloft holding scissors, finely decorated, incised "73011," on thin rectangular base, early 20th c., 9 1/4" h. **1,840**

Meissen Figure of Exotic Dancer

Figure of a dancer, exotic nude female posed holding her arms out to the sides grasping the sides of a draped cape decorated w/gilt vines, stepping forward on a circular base, her brown hair pulled up into a coiled bun w/gilt head band, early 20th c., underglaze-blue crossed swords mark, incised on base "B256-85" & painted "74," 10 3/4" h. (ILLUS.) **2,185**

Figure of a gardener, standing in 18th c. attire, colored enamel & gilt trim, leaning on a shovel & holding flowers, incised "C69," late 19th c., 7 1/2" h. **575**

Figures, allegorical, representing "Day" & "Night," each a figure of a scantily clad child floating above a gilt hemisphere on an octagonal base, Night in a dark blue flowing cloak & crowned in a tiara w/alternating gilt & platinum stars, Day w/gilt rays emerging from his hair & draped in pale pink & holding a flaming torch & a sprig of roses, blue crossed swords mark, incised numbers "L135" & "L134," late 19th - early 20th c., 20 3/4" h., pr. (minor chips & restorations) **12,075**

Plate, 9 5/8" d., gilt-decorated pink & burgundy border w/an enamel-decorated center scene of a cupid & female in a wooded landscape, titled on back "Lei wiedergut," late 19th c. **489**

Platter, Blue Onion patt., 1814-60, crossed swords mark **250**

Tea Set w/Miner Decoration

Tea set: cov. 3 1/2" h. teapot, cov. 5" h. tea canister, six cups & 4 3/4" d. saucers; each w/scrolled gilt trim & central enamel decorations of miners at work, 18th c., Germany, the set (ILLUS. of part) **13,800**

Teapot, cov., figural, model of a rooster, enamel decoration, late 19th - early 20th c., 6" l. **575**

Tray, oval, raised border of molded laurel leaves & grapes, an ornate gilt-framed central cartouche enamel-decorated w/a detailed landscape w/buildings & 18th c. figures, late 18th - early 19th c., 10 x 13 3/8" **1,840**

Vase, 15 1/2" h., classic baluster-form, a fluted flaring base & pedestal w/rings supporting the ovoid body w/a band of flutes below the wide cobalt blue body band decorated w/large gilt & silver florals, ringed shoulder & short flaring neck w/incurved molded rim flanked by long looped snake handles from rim to shoulder, gilt trim on base & body & new gilt trim on handles, late 19th c. (ILLUS.) **2,300**

Lovely Large Meissen Vase

METLOX POTTERIES

Technically, Metlox Potteries began business in 1921 but it was not until the 1970s that collectors began to take notice of the varied and high quality items produced by them. It was in 1932 that Metlox began producing dishes for everyday use and within two years the now well-known Poppytrail came on the market. Metlox continued to grow, putting out decorated dinnerwares, a very successful line designed by Carl Romanelli called Modern Masterpieces, Nostalgia line and the Poppets group.

When Carl Romanelli, a sculptor, joined Metlox he was the first artware designer Metlox hired. Romanelli was known for his miniature animals, Zodiac series and novelties. However, a majority of artware collectors prefer his nudes and nudes with vases.

Collectors seem to prefer a Metlox "line" rather than a Metlox assortment. The company made a large amount of dinnerware which is still inexpensive today. They also turned out their share of cookie jars. Besides the lines already mentioned, Vernonware has always been a popular collectible. Their giftware line of the 1980s, which is beginning to catch collectors' interest, included animals, clocks (which were difficult to make so few left the factory), flowerpots and so on. American Royal Horses was part of the Nostalgia line and is being noticed by collectors today.

In 1946 Evan Shaw purchased Metlox from Willis Prouty. Shaw had owned the American Pottery which was destroyed by fire just before he bought Metlox. Many researchers credit Evan Shaw with the tremendous success of the company. When he died ih 1980 Kenneth Avery headed the company. Operations ceased in 1989.

METLOX Miniatures
by METLOX
MADE IN
U. S. A.
MANHATTAN BEACH
CALIFORNIA

C Romanelli

Metlox Marks

Incised or stamped mark (top left)
Carl Romanelli's name found on the base rim
of nudes and certain vases (bottom)
Paper label in blue on silver. (top right)

Ashtray, Homestead Provincial patt.,
8 1/4" d. **$60**
Ashtray, Sombrero patt., 2 3/4 x 6" 30
Ashtray, Red Rooster patt., Provincial
shape, 8" sq. 38
Ashtray, Red Rooster patt., Provincial
shape, 10" sq. 65
Bowl, individual soup, 5" d., lug-handled,
California Provincial patt. 45
Bowl, individual soup, 5" d., lug-handled,
Provincial Rose patt. 17
Bowl, individual soup, 5" d., lug-handled,
Red Rooster patt. 23
Bowl, individual soup, 5" d., lug-handled,
Red Rooster patt., Provincial shape.............. 10
Bowl, fruit, 6" d., Red Rooster patt., Provin-
cial shape 5
Bowl, cereal, 7 1/8" d., Vernonware, Della
Robbia shape 10
Bowl, soup, 8 1/8" d., Sculptured Grape
patt. 14
Bowl, 11" d., low flower-type, round w/ruf-
fled rim, No. 736... 27
Bowl, salad, 11 1/8" d., Red Rooster patt.,
Provincial shape.. 75
Butter dish, cov., Provincial Rose patt. 50
Butter dish, cov., Sculptured Grape patt. 45
Butter dish, cov., Vernonware, Della Rob-
bia shape... 60
Candleholder, Provincial Blue patt. 35
Candlestick, Homestead Provincial patt........... 30
Canister, cov., model of broccoli stalks,
"Vegetable" line, green glaze w/darker
green cover, 1 1/2 qt. 130
Canister set, Happy Time patt., Provincial
shape, set of 4 175
Casserole, cov., basketweave base w/fig-
ural chicken lid, Red Rooster patt., Pro-
vincial shape, 1 qt., 10 oz. 150
Casserole, cov., hen on nest, California
Provincial patt., 1 qt., 10 oz.......................... 215
Coffee carafe, cov., & metal warmer, Cali-
fornia Provincial patt., 7 cup, 44 oz. 275
Coffeepot, cov., California Provincial patt.,
green, 42 oz. 90
Coffeepot, cov., Homestead Provincial
patt. 90
Coffeepot, cov., Provincial Blue patt............... 100
Coffeepot, cov., Provincial Rose patt. 70
Coffeepot, cov., Vernonware, Della Robbia
shape 50
Cookie jar, Ballerina Bear............................... 110

Cookie jar, Bear w/Blue Sweater..................... 105
Cookie jar, Chef Pierre 100
Cookie jar, cov., Provincial Blue patt. 225
Cookie jar, cov., Provincial Rose patt. 80

Rare Drummer Boy Cookie Jar

Cookie jar, Drummer Boy (ILLUS.)................. 750
Cookie jar, Parrot, seated on a short brown
tree stump, green & yellow, Model No.
555 425
Cookie jar, Pine Cone w/grey squirrel fin-
ial, Model No. 509, 11" h. 95
Cookie jar, Rex, dinosaur, white...................... 110

Rose Blossom & Tulip Cookie Jars

Cookie jar, Rose Blossom, pale pink
w/green leaves at bottom, Model No.
513, 2 3/4 qt. (ILLUS. right) 380
Cookie jar, Tulip, yellow & green (ILLUS.
left) 425
Creamer, Antique Grape patt., Traditional
shape 17
Creamer, Sculptured Grape patt., Tradi-
tional shape 16
Cruet set, 2 pcs. on wood tray, Red
Rooster patt., Provincial shape, the set 70
Cruet set, 5-piece, Provincial Rose patt........... 150
Cup & saucer, Antique Grape patt., Tradi-
tional shape 10
Cup & saucer, California Provincial patt. 16
Cup & saucer, Heavenly Days patt., Any-
time shape.. 12
Cup & saucer, Pintoria patt., rectangular
shaped saucer w/round depression for
round cup, Poppy Orange gloss, scarce
pattern, set 95
Cup & saucer, Sculptured Grape patt.,
blue fruit w/green leaves & brown twigs,
set 19
Cup & saucer, Sculptured Grape patt.,
Traditional shape.. 10

Grover Poppets Figure

Man & Woman in Surrey

METTLACH

Ceramics with the name Mettlach were produced by Villeroy & Boch and other potteries in the Mettlach area of Germany. Villeroy and Boch's finest years of production are thought to be from about 1890 to 1910.

Mettlach Mark

Plaque, pierced to hang, etched cavalier & bar maid, blue background, castle marked, dated 1900, No. 2322, 14 1/2"d. ... **$795**
Plaque, pierced to hang, round, blue-decorated village landscape on a white ground, titled on the back "Hannover," No. 5036, 17 3/8" d. 259

Mettlach Plaque with Cavalier

Plaque, pierced to hang, round, etched in center w/scene of cavalier seated at table raising a glass of beer in one hand, browns & white on a blue ground w/brown border band, No. 2622, dated 1910, artist-initialed, 7 3/4" d. (ILLUS.) 235

Mettlach Punch Bowl Set

Punch bowl, cover & undertray, bulbous urn-form footed body w/molded double-C scroll handles, flaring foot, low domed cover w/ladle hole & upright scrolled ring handle, printed under glaze w/a decoration of scenes of gnomes working at a wine press & drinking, No. 2339/1028, early 20th c., 7 1/2 liter, 16" h., the set (ILLUS.)...................................... 748

Vase, 9 1/2" h., large ovoid body w/a short slightly tapering neck, the body in dark blue w/an overall latticework design, each diamond segment w/a small molded red dot or florette, the neck in brick red w/a gold zigzag band & white florettes, impressed marks 330
Vase, 10" h., tall square tapering form swelled near the base, incised & painted w/a geometric design w/vertical bands down the sides connecting to a group of graduated squares all in dark green & red on a creamy ground, impressed marks 550

Mettlach Vase w/Gargoyle Handles

Vase, 11 1/2" h., flared foot below wide bulbous body w/ringed cylindrical neck flanked by gargoyle handles, polychrome & gilt decoration on beige ground, impressed mark, No. 1409 (ILLUS.).. 220

STEINS
Mettlach, No. 1154, etched four-panel scenes of hunters, inlaid lid, 1 liter 600
Mettlach, No. 1527, etched, four men drinking, brown background, signed "Warth," inlaid lid, 1 liter 600
Mettlach, No. 1566, etched, man on high-wheel bicycle, signed "Gorig," inlaid lid, 1/2 liter.. 1,000
Mettlach, No. 1786, etched, lid w/relief scene of Munich, St. Floiran putting out fire, dragon handle, ceramic dragon's head thumblift, pewter lid, 1/2 liter 700
Mettlach, No. 1818, etched, tavern scene, pewter lid, signed "Goring," 6 1/5 liters 1,800
Mettlach, No. 1821, relief, musician w/guitar, inlaid lid, 3 1/5 liters 350
Mettlach, No. 1909, colorful transfer-printed design of a man smoking a pipe while sitting at a tavern table w/stein, artist-signed, verse on reverse by B. Auerbach, inlaid pewter lid, 1/2 liter (chip beneath base of thumblift cover) 175
Mettlach, No. 2001A, relief-molded in the form of hand-painted books of law, inlaid pewter lid, 1/2 liter 575
Mettlach, No. 2024, etched 'Berlin' design w/shield of the city of Berlin, inlaid lid, 1/2 liter.. 550

Mettlach, No. 2035, etched Bacchus carousing, inlaid lid, 1/2 liter........................ 450

Mettlach, No. 2038, decorated relief, town of Rodenstein, houses & towers on inlay, inlaid lid, 3 4/5 liters.................................. 3,800

Mettlach, No. 2049, etched, chess stein, chessboard, inlaid lid, 1/2 liter.................. 2,500

Mettlach, No. 2090, etched club stein, man at table w/his club smoking pipe, signed "Schlitt," inlaid lid, 1/2 liter 550

Mettlach, No. 2100, etched, Prosit stein, knight w/stein & man w/fur clothing, signed "Schlitt," inlaid lid, 1/2 liter............. 1,100

Mettlach, No. 2106, decorated relief, monkeys in cage, monkey handle, inlaid lid, 1/2 liter...................... 4,500

Mettlach, No. 2126, etched symphonia stein, composers, signed "Schlitt," pewter lid, 5 1/2 liters.................................... 6,500

Mettlach, No. 2136, etched, Anheuser Busch Brewery, inlaid lid, 1/2 liter 2,500

Mettlach, No. 2219, relief, dancing & musical scenes, three panels, inlaid lid, 3 1/10 liters...... 500

Mettlach, No. 2235, etched scene of a barmaid holding steins, targets in the background, pewter lid, 1/2 liter.......................... 460

Mettlach, No. 2277, etched scene of Nurnberg, inlaid lid, 1/2 liter 525

Mettlach, No. 24, relief, figures on four separate panels, inlaid lid, 1 liter.................. 300

Mettlach, No. 2782, Rookwood-style, h.p. bust portrait of a Cavalier drinking, hinged pewter lid, 17 3/4" h, 4 1/2 liter......... 489

Mettlach, No. 3236, etched Art Nouveau design in blue & white, inlaid lid, 1/2 liter 575

Mettlach, No. 3395, Cameo style, footed spherical body w/a cylindrical neck & rim spout w/mask, molded C-form handle, inlaid lid, the body w/a wide blue band decorated w/white relief peasant figures drinking, ten pin & vine design on blue neckband, 7" d., 12" h. 385

Mettlach, No. 485, relief, musicians & dancers on blue background, inlaid lid, 1 liter 350

Mettlach, No. 5001, faience-type, printed-under-glaze coat of arms, pewter lid, 4.6 liters................................ 850

Mettlach, No. 954 (2176), PUG, knight drinking, signed "Schlitt," pewter lid, 2 1/10 liters.................................... 600

Mettlach Drinking Gnomes

Mettlach, No. 966 (2184), PUG, drinking gonmes, by Schlitt, inlaid lid, 1/2 liter (ILLUS.)....................................... 300

MINTON

The Minton factory in England was established by Thomas Minton in 1793. The factory made earthenware, especially the blue-printed variety and Thomas Minton is sometimes credited with invention of the blue "Willow" pattern. For a time majolica and tiles were also an important part of production, but bone china soon became the principal ware. Mintons, Ltd., continues in operation today. Also see MAJOLICA.

Minton Marks

Cabinet plates, finely enameled white scenes of birds flying & perched amongst blossoming branches on turquoise ground within a gilt acid-etched & pierced fretwork border at the rim, underside center of each plate also enameled in turquoise, together w/a later fitted carrying case, puce printed crowned globe mark, faint impressed "MINTONS," year cyphers & diamond registration mark, painted pattern number G 1859, one w/small area of repair to rim, 9 1/2" d., set of 13 .... $12,650

Dinner service: 21" l. oval well-and-tree platter, five oval platters graduating from 13" to 19 1/2" l., 14" l. cov. soup tureen & undertray, four 11 1/4" l. oval vegetable dishes & three covers, 10 5/8" d. two-handled fruit bowl, 11 7/8" d. plateau dish, 11 1/4" l. oval serving bowl, seventeen 10 1/4" d. soup plates, nineteen 10 1/4" d. plates & twenty-five 9" d. plates; fine earthenware, Italian patt., decorated w/border bands w/leafy scroll bands alternating w/round portrait medallions & palmettes, ca. 1865, the set 1,725

Plates, 9 1/4" d., each w/gilt-decorated embossed floral banding on the turquoise rim band, central scenes of animals in landscapes, ca. 1870, set of 6 489

Plates, 10 1/8" d., w/h.p. scene of bird by William Mussill, each titled on reverse, artist-signed, ca. 1800, England, retailed by T. Goode & Co., London, set of 17 (ILLUS. of one)... 5,175

Plates, 10 1/2" d., each w/a scalloped rim, banded, scrolled & festooned foliate designs within a wide ivory-ground border, printed & impressed marks, 1929, set of 12 2,070

Minton Plate w/Bird

Vase, 10" h., Astra Ware, footed, baluster-form w/flared rim, multicolored crystal-line glaze, ink stamp mark (tight line at rim) 165

Vases, 7 1/2" h., pate-sur-pate, slender ovoid form w/scenes of Diana assisting Cupid in the firing of an arrow, white on olive green ground beneath gilt foliate band at the shoulder, the reverse w/either a group of trophies or a heart pierced by two arrows, artist-signed, printed marks, ca. 1900, pr. 5,175

MOCHA

Mocha decoration is found on basically utilitarian creamware or yellowware articles and is achieved by a simple chemical reaction. A color pigment of brown, blue, green or black is given an acid nature by infusion of tobacco or hops. When this acid nature colorant is applied in blobs to an alkaline ground color, it reacts by spreading in feathery sea-weed designs. This type of decoration is usually accompanied by horizontal bands of light color slip. Produced in numerous Staffordshire potteries from the late 18th until the late 19th centuries, its name is derived from the similar markings found on mocha quartz. In addition to the seaweed decora-tion, mocha wares are also seen with Earthworm and Cat's Eye patterns or a marbleized effect.

Bowl, 7 1/4" d., 4" h., bulbous cylindrical body on a thin footring, the sides taper-ing to flaring rim, blue, white & brown Earthworm patt. on orange ground, dark brown bands on white ground (repairs, glaze wear)... **$230**

Mug, cylindrical, blue, brown & cream Earthworm patt. in vertical configuration on cream & white striped ground, green impressed band, dark brown alternating stripes, white handle w/leaf-impressed ends, 4 3/8" d., 5 7/8" h. (handle & body repaired, cracks, chips) 2,760

Mug, cylindrical body w/applied white han-dle w/leaf-impressed ends, decorated w/a wide band in the Open Chain patt. on pumpkin ground w/upper & lower dark brown bands & white molded base band, 19th c., 6" d., 5 3/8" h. (minor glaze imperfections, small hairline cracks)... 1,955

Various Mocha Items

Mug, cylindrical w/narrow white & dark brown stripes, large cream band w/dark brown seaweed decoration, applied han-dle, chips & base hairlines, 4 5/8" h. (ILLUS. top row, left) 1,100

Mug, cylindrical w/C-form handle, Earth-worm patt., impressed geometric border in dark brown, blue & cream on a pump-kin ground, 19th c., 5 1/2" h. (hairlines, glaze wear, minute rim chips) 518

Mug, cylindrical w/blue, dark brown & orange stripes, center band decorated w/white wavy lines & groups of dots in white slip, embossed green rim band & applied leaftip handle, stains, wear & surface chips, 6" h. (ILLUS. bottom row, left) 2,970

Pepper pot, footed cylindrical form w/domed top, decorated w/blue & white stripes & dark brown band w/white leaves & dots, blue top, chips, 4 3/4" h. 715

Pitcher, 4 7/8" h., barrel-shaped w/arched spout & C-form handle, dark blue sea-weed on burnt orange band w/black & white stripes, embossed green rim band & applied handle w/green leaftips, chips (ILLUS. bottom right)................................. 1,870

Pitcher, 6" h., 4 1/2" d., blue, white & brown Cat's-Eye patt. on tan ground, blue & brown stripes on white ground, white handle w/plain impressed ends (chips to spout, imperfections) 230

Pitcher, 6 1/4" h., 4" d., jug-form, footed ovoid body decorated w/a blue, brown & white Earthworm patt. on brown ground, green impressed bands, brown & white alternating stripes, white handle w/leaf-impressed ends, early 19th c. (cracks, minor chips)... 1,035

Pitcher, 6 1/4" h., 4 1/4" d., dark brown & white Cat's-Eye patt. on bright blue ground, dark brown stripes on white ground, white leaftip handle (small cracks & hairline cracks) 230

Pitcher, 7 1/4" h., 4 3/8" d., jug-form, cream slip undulating band decoration on a dark brown ground, light blue, cream & dark brown Cat's-eye patt. on

ochre ground, green impressed leaf decoration on raised shoulder, light blue &
cream alternating stripes, white handle
w/leaf-impressed ends, first half 19th c.
(spout & neck repairs, crack on handle
bottom) **3,795**

Shaker w/domed top, footed bulbous body
w/tapered neck to the top, yellowware
decorated w/stripes of blue, white &
black, chips, 4 3/8" h. (ILLUS. top row,
right) **578**

Sugar bowl, footed wide cylindrical body
w/small applied rim handles w/tooled
ends, decorated w/balloons in orange,
white & dark brown on deep cream
ground w/dark brown & white stripes, no
lid, wear & damage, 4" d., 3" h. (ILLUS.
top row, center) **1,760**

Mocha Washbowl w/Cat's Eye

Wash bowl, round w/canted sides & flared
rim, ochre, dark brown & white Cat's Eye
decoration bordered by white banding
on rim, similar band on interior without
white banding, blue ground, white leaf
decoration on blue ground on center bottom, the exterior decorated w/white
wavy stripe decoration on dark brown
ground, blue stripe decoration on white
ground, cracks on bottom of bowl, chips,
imperfections, 12" d., 5" h. (ILLUS.) **4,025**

Waste bowl, white w/grey band & dark
brown stripes, Earthworm patt. in blue &
white, 4 3/4" d... **495**

MOORCROFT

*William Moorcroft became a designer for James
Macintyre & Co. in 1897 and was put in charge of
their art pottery production. Moorcroft developed a
number of popular designs, including Florian Ware
while with Macintyre and continued with that firm
until 1913 when they discontinued the production of
art pottery.*

*After leaving Macintyre in 1913, Moorcroft set up
his own pottery in Burslem and continued producing the art wares he had designed earlier as well as
introducing new patterns. After William's death in
1945, the pottery was operated by his son, Walter.*

MOORCROFT

Moorcroft Marks

Bowl, 4" d., Dawn Landscape patt., stylized
design w/trees in matte blue glaze, artist-signed, impressed mark, ca. 1928 .... **$345**

Hibiscus Pattern Covered Bowl

Bowl, cov., 5 1/2" d., 3 1/2" h., bulbous
body, button finial, Hibiscus patt., red &
yellow blossoms on dark blue ground,
incised "Made in England - Moorcroft" &
stamped label "#222 By Appointment W.
Moorcroft Potters to the Queen," artist-
initialed (ILLUS.) **380**

Bowl, 8" d., Poppy patt., the interior tube-
lined w/a garland of large & small
blooms in tones of puce & purple, joined
by scrolling green foliage, the exterior
w/three spiraling stems, all reserved on
a watery cobalt blue ground, impressed
"MOORCROFT" & painted signature, ca.
1928 .... **747**

Ginger jar, cov., Clematis patt, dark blue,
rose & yellow flowers & green leaves on
cobalt blue ground, incised stamp "Made
in England," 6" h. **870**

Jar, cov., wide ovoid body w/a rounded
shoulder to the short cylindrical neck fitted w/a domed cover, Eventide patt.,
decorated w/a landscape scene w/a
band of large mushroom-shaped trees in
brown, yellow & greenish brown against
a shaded yellow & red sunset background w/brown mountains, ink artist-
signature & die-stamped "Made in
England - 760," 8 1/2" d., 11" h. **6,600**

Lamp bases, Poppy patt., baluster-form,
tube-lined w/a continuous band of flowers & foliage colored in tones of yellow,
red, cobalt blue & green on a graduated
mottled blue ground, all washed in a thin
red flambé glaze, ca. 1950, 12 1/4" h.,
pr. **1,035**

Vase, 3 1/2" h., miniature, tapering cylindrical body w/a rounded shoulder centering
a short flaring neck, dark blue ground
w/multi-colored Orchid patt., original
label... **413**

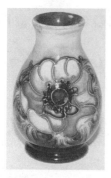

Small Poppy Pattern Vase

Vase, 4 1/8" h., footed bulbous ovoid body tapering to rolled rim, Poppy patt., red blossom, green leaves on cobalt blue shading to green ground, cobalt blue interior, incised "Made in England - Potters H.M. Queen" in blue (ILLUS.) **200**

Vase, 6" h., 5 1/4" d., Landscape patt., footed bulbous ovoid body w/flaring rim, scene of blue trees on a mottled blue & yellow ground, script mark **2,200**

Blackberry Pattern Vase

Vase, 6 1/8" h., footed baluster form w/flared rim, Blackberry patt., purple & red fruit & leaves on shaded dark & light blue & green ground, cobalt blue interior, incised "Made in England - Potter to the Queen" (ILLUS.).. **340**

Vase, 6 1/4" h., 4 1/2" d., Cornflower patt., ovoid body w/cylindrical molded rim, impressed "MOORCROFT - MADE IN ENGLAND - 210" **1,320**

Vase, 6 1/2" h., footed baluster-form, large red six-petaled blossoms & green leaves on a shaded pale green to dark blue ground, impressed & painted marks **358**

Vase, 6 3/4" h., 3" d., slender baluster-form w/short flared neck, decorated overall w/clusters of blue & pink flowers & green leaves on a white ground, Macintyre stamp, Moorcroft signature **1,980**

Poppy Pattern Vase

Vase, 7 1/4" h., footed bulbous ovoid body tapering to flared neck, Poppy patt., red & white blossoms & green leaves on dark blue ground, printed mark "Made in England," artist-initialed (ILLUS.) **700**

Vase, 8 1/2" h., Claremont patt., ovoid body decorated w/large mushrooms in red, green & yellow against a blue ground, impressed & painted marks **2,640**

Vase, 10" h., Poppy patt., wide ovoid body w/slightly flaring rim, red & black ground, die-stamped mark & artist-signed **4,400**

Vase, 12" h., bottle-form, Eventide Landscape patt., the lower body tube-lined w/trees in an undulating landscape, glazed in watery tones of green, ochre & blue against a deep red sky, impressed "MOORCROFT - 156" & painted signature, ca. 1925 (hairline in upper rim) **862**

Moorcroft Trumpet-Form Vase

Vase, 17 1/8" h., trumpet-form, gently flaring cylindrical body tube-lined w/ Poppy patt., reserved on mottled blue & green ground, interior w/mottled dark cobalt blue glaze, impressed "Moorcroft," Cobridge factory mark, W. Moorcroft signature in blue script, applied paper label "Potter to H.M. the Queen," ca. 1920, upper rim w/traces of restoration (ILLUS.)... **2,070**

MORTON POTTERIES

A total of six potteries were in operation at various times in Morton, Illinois from 1877 to 1976. All traced their origins from the Morton Brick and Tile Company begun in 1877 by six Rapp brothers who came to America in the early 1870s to escape forced military service under Kaiser Wilhelm I. Sons, nephews and cousins of the founding fathers were responsible for the continuation of the pottery industry in Morton as a result of buy-outs or the establishment of new and separate operations. The potteries are listed chronologically by beginning dates.

Morton's natural clay deposits were ideal for the Rapp's venture into pottery production. Local clay was used until it was depleted in 1940. That clay fired out to a golden ecru color. After 1940, clay was imported from South Carolina and Indiana. It fired out snow white. The differences in clay allow one to easily date production at the Morton potteries. Only a few items were marked by any of the potteries. Occasionally, paper labels were used, but most of those have long disappeared. Glaze is sometimes a determinant. Early glazes were Rockingham brown, green and cobalt blue, or transparent, to produce yellowware. In the 20s and 30s colorful drip glazes were used. In the later years solid pastel and Deco colors were in vogue.

Most of Morton's potteries were short-lived, operating for twenty years or less. Their products are elusive. However, Morton Pottery Company was in operation for fifty-four years and its products appear regularly in today's secondary market.

Rapp Brothers Brick & Tile Company & Morton Pottery Works (1877-1915) - Morton Earthenware Company (1915-1917)

Baker, deep, yellowware, 10" d. **$100**

Morton Paperweight, Bank & Marble

Bank, figural acorn, w/advertising for "Acorn Stove Company," green (ILLUS. center) **80**
Churn, mottled brown Rockingham glaze, 4 gal. **180**

Morton Jardiniere

Jardiniere, tapering cylindrical form, embossed leaf design, green, 7" d. (ILLUS.) **50**
Marble, mottled brown Rockingham glaze, 4 1/2" d. (ILLUS. right) **40**

Mug, yellowware, 1/2 pt. **75**
Paperweight, model of a bison, advertises Rock Sand Company, brown Rockingham glaze, 2 1/2" l. (ILLUS. with bank) **70**
Pie baker, yellowware, 10" d. **125**

Morton Dutch Pitcher

Pitcher, jug-type, milk (Dutch jug), cobalt blue, 3 1/2 pt. (ILLUS.) **90**

Pitcher with Spatter Bark Design

Pitcher, jug-type, milk, bulbous body w/relief-molded tree bark design, green, brown & yellow spatter, 1 3/4 qt. (ILLUS.) **150**
Stein, barrel-shaped w/"Trinke was klar ist und rede was wahr ist" embossed around rim & base, green, 1 pt. **85**
Teapot, cov., acorn-shaped, mottled brown Rockingham glaze, 3 3/4 cup size **90**

Morton Rebecca at the Well Teapots

Teapot, cov., tapering cylindrical body w/swan's neck spout, leaf-tip handle & bud finial, embossed Rebecca at the Well decoration, yellowware, 7 pt. (ILLUS. right) **185**
Teapot, cov., tapering cylindrical body w/swan's neck spout, leaf-tip handle & bud finial, embossed Rebecca at the Well decoration, mottled brown Rockingham glaze, 8 1/2 pt. (ILLUS. left) **175**

Urinal, shovel-shaped, mottled brown Rockingham glaze **50**

Urinal, shovel-shaped, yellowware (ILLUS. bottom) **65**

Cliftwood Art Potteries, Inc. (1920-1940)

Dolphin-based Pieces

Compote, 5 1/4 x 8 1/2", domed base w/four figural dolphins supporting bowl w/flaring paneled sides, old rose glaze (ILLUS. top) **90**

Console bowl, rectangular w/flared rim supported by four figural dolphins on domed base, old rose glaze, 5 1/4 x 13 1/2" (ILLUS. bottom) **100**

Figural Console Set

Console set: bowl & pr. of candlesticks; figural Viking ship w/dragon head at each end, candlesticks w/cupped socket above figural dragon head w/flared base, matte ivory & turquoise glaze, the set (ILLUS.) **225**

Creamer, figural cow, standing, tail forms handle, chocolate brown drip glaze, 3 3/4 x 6" (ILLUS.) **85**

Flower frog, figural turtle, holes pierced on back, herbage green, 5 1/2" l. **24**

Flower frog, figural woman, "Lorilei," blue mulberry drip glaze, 6 1/2" h. **75**

Model of dog, Scottie, standing, cobalt blue, 5 1/2 x 7 1/2" **60**

Model of elephant, grey, standing, 7 1/4 x 13 1/2" **125**

Figural Cow Creamer

Model of lion, standing, natural color, spray glaze, 9 1/4 x 16" **200**

Model of tiger, standing, natural colors, 5 x 16" **150**

Vase, 10" h., domed base w/four figural dolphins supporting tapering body w/paneled sides, fluted rim, matte ivory & turquoise, No. 224 .... **75**

Vase, 14 1/2" h., flared foot below tall tapering cylindrical body, the narrow shoulder tapering to a waisted cylindrical neck, No. 113, chocolate brown drip glaze **80**

Vase, 16" h., footed baluster-form body w/flat rim, No. 114, bluish grey drip glaze **75**

Vase, 18 1/4" h., urn-form w/figural snakes swallowing fish handles, No. 132, cobalt blue **110**

Morton Waffle Set

Waffle set: cov. batter pitcher & cov. syrup pitcher on tray; cylindrical body w/incurved side under handle, button finials, old rose drip glaze, the set (ILLUS.) **150**

Tree Trunk Form Wall Pocket

Wall pocket, rectangular tree trunk design w/pointed base, three openings at top, chocolate drip glaze, 8" h. (ILLUS.)................ **80**

Morton Pottery Company (1922-1976)

Bank, acorn shape, solid bottom, brown, 3 1/4" h.. **40**

A Variety of Figural Hen Pieces

Bank, figural, hen on nest, white w/red cold painted comb, black feather detail, yellow beak, 4" h. (ILLUS. back row, center).. **50**

Bank, figural, house, shoe-shaped, yellow w/red roof, 6 1/2" h. **30**

Bank, figural, kitten reclining, grey & white, 4 x 6"... **25**

Cookie jar, cov., hen on nest, figural chick finial, white, black trim & cold-painted red comb (ILLUS. back row, right) **130**

Panda Bear Cookie Jar

Cookie jar, cov., panda bear, black & white (ILLUS.)... **95**

Cookie jar, cov., turkey w/poult (chick) finial, brown... **150**

Creamer & sugar bowl, model of chicken & rooster, black & white w/cold-painted red comb, pr. (ILLUS. far left & second from left, front row) **45**

Cuspidor, bulbous body w/wide flaring neck, decorated w/embossed tavern scene, green, 5 1/2" (ILLUS.)......................... **35**

Cuspidor with Tavern Scene

John F. Kennedy, Jr. Figure

Figure of John F. Kennedy, Jr., standing on square base, right hand to head in salute position, grey & beige, 7" h. (ILLUS.)... **95**

Grass grower, bisque, bust of soldier w/"Hi Buddy" embossed on back of collar, 6 3/4" h. **40**

Grass grower, bisque, bust of "Paddy O'Hair," red clay **35**

Head vase, lady w/1920s hair style, wide brim hat, white glossy glaze **60**

Head vase, lady w/1940s hair style, pill box hat, white matte glaze **50**

Head vase, lady w/upswept hair style, white w/red lips, bow in hair & heart-shaped locket **40**

Morton Kerosene Lamp

Lamp, kerosene, brass fixture w/glass chimney, cylindrical body w/ribbed base & relief-molded swag design, white ground (ILLUS.)... 50

Lamp base, female bunny w/umbrella, multicolored.. 50

Dog with Pheasant Lamp Base

Lamp base, model of a black & white dog w/brown pheasant in mouth, relief-molded brown & green grassy base, 5 x 10", 8 1/4" h. (ILLUS.) 75

Lamp base, model of a Teddy bear, heart-shaped nose, pink or blue, each 45

Rocking Horse Lamp/Planter

Lamp base/planter, model of rocking horse, white w/brown, pink & blue trim (ILLUS.)... 40

Boston Terrier Model & Planter

Model of dog, Boston terrier, sitting, black & white, 7" h. (ILLUS. right)........................... 40

Planter, model of Boston terrier, sitting, black & white (ILLUS. left) 30

Salt & pepper shakers, miniature, model of chick, black & white, 1 3/4" h., pr. (ILLUS. front row, right)... 100

Toothpick holder, miniature, model of chick, black & white, 1 3/4" h. (ILLUS. front row, center) 50

CHRISTMAS NOVELTIES

Cigarette box, cov., figural Santa Claus head, hat cover becomes ashtray, cold painted red hat (ILLUS.)............................... 40

Figural Santa Claus Head Cigarette Box

Lollypop tree, w/holes to insert lollypops, green & white glaze, 9 1/4" h. 40

Plate, 8", figural Santa Claus face, white w/blue eyes, pink cheeks, hat cold painted red 40

Plate, 12", figural Santa Claus face, white w/blue eyes, pink cheeks, hat cold painted red 50

Figural Santa Claus Punch Set

Punch set: Punch bowl & 12 punch cups; figural Santa Claus head, white w/pink trim, 13 pcs. (ILLUS. of part) 360

Midwest Potteries, Inc. (1940-1944)

Book end, Art Deco style base w/model of deer, yellow w/gold trim, 8" h. (ILLUS.) 25

Figure of baseball player, batter, grey uniform, 7 1/4" h.. 300

Art Deco Style Book End

Model of elephant, standing, trunk raised, white w/gold trim & "GOP" in gold on side, 6 1/2" h. (ILLUS.) **30**

Model of GOP Elephant

Model of fish, on seaweed base, yellow & brown spray glaze, 10 1/2" h. (ILLUS.) **40**

Model of Fish in Seaweed

Model of mountain goat, natural colors, spray glaze, 9 1/2"... **45**

Model of tiger, stalking position w/open mouth, beige & tan w/h.p. brown stripes, 7 x 12" **50**

Figural Duck Pitcher

Pitcher, model of a duck w/cattail handle, blue & brown spray glaze, 10" h. (ILLUS.).. **38**

Planter, domed base supporting model of sea gull in flight, joined at base w/relief-molded seashell bowl, white & gold, 12" h. **40**

African Woman Wall Mask

Wall mask, African woman w/neck rings, ebony w/gold trim, 8" h. (ILLUS.) **50**

American Art Potteries (1947-1963)

Bottle, crown shape, pink & grey spray glaze, 6" h. **24**

Petal-form Console Set

Console set: bowl & pr. of candleholders; shallow oblong bowl & flower-form candleholders on leaf-shaped base, grey exterior w/pink interior, 3 pcs. (ILLUS.).......... **30**

Vases with Ostrich Feather Decoration

Cornucopia-vase, single relief-molded ostrich feather decoration, shaded grey exterior, yellow interior spray glaze, 10 1/2" h. (ILLUS. left).................................. 35

Doll parts, ceramic, 7 1/2" head w/h.p. face, 4" arms & 4 1/2" legs, 5 pcs. 90

Model of stag, leaping position, domed green base w/relief-molded grasses near back legs, shaded brown & white w/dark brown antlers & hooves, 12" h. 40

Planter, model of a bunny beside log, natural colors spray glaze 20

Jumping Horse TV Lamp

TV lamp, model of a horse jumping over wall, brown & tan spray glaze, 8" h. (ILLUS.)... 40

Afghan Hounds TV Lamp

TV lamp, model of a standing & reclining Afghan hound on oblong base, glossy black glaze, 15" h. (ILLUS.)............................ 60

TV lamp/planter, model of two fish on thick rectangular base w/relief-molded shell design on front, tan, chartreuse & black spray glaze, 3 1/2 x 6 x 9" 30

Small Morton Vase

Vase, 6" h., footed bulbous base tapering to tall slender cylindrical neck w/flat rim, decorated w/embossed leaf design, brown shading to yellow spray glaze (ILLUS.)... 20

Vase, 9" h., flared footed base tapering to cylindrical body w/ruffled tulip-shaped rim, yellow, pink & mauve spray glaze 25

Vase, 10 1/2" h., flared base w/fan-shaped body, double relief-molded ostrich feather arched end handles w/decoration extending down sides to base, brown & tan spray glaze w/yellow interior (ILLUS. right)... 45

MULBERRY

Mulberry or Flow Mulberry ironstone wares were produced in the Staffordshire district of England in the period between 1840 and 1870 at many of the same factories which produced its close "cousin," Flow Blue china. In fact, some of the early Flow Blue patterns were also decorated with the dark blackish or brownish purple mulberry coloration and feature the same heavy smearing or "flown" effect. Produced on sturdy ironstone bodies, the designs were either transfer-printed or hand-painted (Brushstroke) with an Asian, Scenic, Floral or Marble design. Some patterns were also decorated with additional colors over or under the glaze; these are designated in the following listings as "w/polychrome."

Quite a bit of this ware is still to be found and it is becoming increasingly sought-after by collectors although presently its values lag somewhat behind similar Flow Blue pieces. The standard references to Mulberry wares is Petra Williams' book, Flow Blue China and Mulberry Ware, Similarity and Value Guide *and* Mulberry Ironstone - Flow Blue's Best Kept Little Secret, *by Ellen R. Hill.*

ACADIA (Maker Unknown, ca. 1850)
Creamer, 6" h., Classic Gothic shape **$250**

Acadia Plate

Plate, 8" d. (ILLUS.)................................. **100**

AMERILLIA (Podmore, Walker & Co., ca. 1850)
Egg cup **200**
Plate, 9 1/2" **85**
Vegetable dish, cov. **350**

ATHENS (Charles Meigh, ca. 1845)
Creamer, 6", vertical-paneled Gothic shape..... **150**
Cup plate **100**

Athens Pitcher

Pitcher, 6 paneled, 10" h. (ILLUS.) **300**
Punch cup **125**
Sugar, cov., vertical-paneled Gothic shape **200**

ATHENS (Wm. Adams & Son, ca. 1849)
Cup plate **95**
Plate, 8 1/2" d. **55**
Soup Plate, w/flanged rim, 9" d **90**
Sugar, covered, full-paneled Gothic shape **225**
Teapot, cov., full-paneled Gothic shape........... **310**

AVA (T. J. & J. Mayer, ca. 1850)
Cup & saucer, handleless, w/polychrome **80**
Plate, 9 1/2" d., w/polychrome........................... **75**
Plate, 10 1/2" d., w/polychrome **85**
Platter, 16" l., w/polychrome **250**
Sauce tureen, cover & undertray, w/poly-
  chrome, 3 pcs.. **500**

BEAUTIES OF CHINA (Mellor Venables & Co., ca. 1845)
Cup plate **95**
Plate, 7 1/2" d., w/polychrome......................... **65**
Platter, 14" l., w/polychrome **225**
Sauce tureen, cover, ladle & undertray,
  long octagon, 4 pcs. **675**

BOCHARA (James Edwards, ca. 1850)
Creamer, 6" h., full-paneled Gothic shape **150**
Pitcher, 7 1/2" h., full-paneled Gothic
  shape **170**
Plate, 10 1/2" d. **75**

Bochara Teapot

Teapot, cov., pedestaled Gothic style
  (ILLUS.)... **350**

BRUNSWICK (Mellor Venables & Co., ca. 1845)
Plate, 7 1/2" d., w/polychrome............................ **65**
Platter, 16" l., w/polychrome **275**
Relish dish, stubby mitten-shape, w/poly-
  chrome **125**
Sugar, cov., Classic Gothic shape, w/poly-
  chrome **225**

BRYONIA (Paul Utzchneider & Co., ca. 1880)
Cup & saucer, handled..................................... **60**
Gravy boat **150**
Plate, 7 1/2" d.. **50**

Bryonia Plate

Plate, 9 1/2" d. (ILLUS.)..................................... **65**

CEYLON (Charles Meigh, ca. 1840)
Plate, 9 1/2" d. **65**
Plate, 10 1/2" d., w/polychrome......................... **85**
Platter, 14" l., w/polychrome **175**
Vegetable bowl, open, small **125**

CHUSAN (P. Holdcroft, ca. 1850)
Plate, 9 1/2" d. **80**
Potato bowl, 11" d. **250**

CLEOPATRA (F. Morley & Co., ca. 1850)
Basin & ewer, w/polychrome **750**
Plate, 9 1/2" d. **70**
Soap box, cover & drainer, 3 pcs.................. **250**
Soup plate, w/flanged rim, 9" d........................ **90**

COREA (Joseph Clementson, ca. 1850)
Cup & saucer, handleless **75**
Sugar, covered, long hexagon **250**
Teapot, covered, long hexagon........................ **350**

COREAN (Podmore, Walker & Co., ca. 1850)

Cup plate 75
Cup & saucer, handled, large.......................... 125
Relish, mitten-shape 135

Corean Sauce Tureen

Sauce tureen, cover & undertray, 3 pcs.
(ILLUS.)... 475
Sugar, cov., oval bulbous style 350

COTTON PLANT (J. Furnival, ca. 1850)

Creamer, 6 5/8" h., paneled grape shape,
w/polychrome 200

Cotton Plant Teapot

Teapot, cov., cockscomb handle, w/poly-
chrome (ILLUS.)... 650

CYPRUS (Wm. Davenport, ca. 1845)

Cup plate 85

Cyprus Gravy

Gravy boat, unusual handle (ILLUS.) 150
Pitcher, 11" h., 6-sided.................................... 250

DORA (E. Challinor, ca. 1850)

Plate, 9 1/2" d. 65
Teapot, cov., Baltic shape, brush stroke 650

FERN & VINE (Maker Unknown, ca. 1850)

Fern & Vine Creamer

Creamer, 6" h., Classic Gothic style
(ILLUS.)... 225
Plate, 7 1/2" d. 75

FLORA (Hulme & Booth, ca. 1850)

Creamer, 6" h., w/polychrome, grand loop
shape 150

FLORA (T. Walker, ca. 1847)

Cup & saucer, handleless 65
Plate, 7 1/2" d. 75
Plate, 9 1/2" d. 85
Sugar, cov., Classic Gothic shape 250

FLOWER VASE (T. J. & J. Mayer, ca. 1850)

Teapot, cov., w/polychrome, Prize Bloom
shape 560

FOLIAGE (J. Edwards, ca. 1850)

Gravy boat 150

Foliage Plate

Plate, 8" d. (ILLUS.)... 75

GERANIUM (Podmore, Walker & Co., ca. 1850)

Geranium Plate

Plate, 8" d. (ILLUS.).. 65
Waste bowl 135

JARDINIERE (Villeroy & Boch, ca. 1880)
Gravy boat 125
Plate, 7 1/2" d. 55
Plate, 9 1/2" d. 75
Vegetable bowl, open, round 150

JEDDO (Wm. Adams, ca. 1849)
Cup plate 95
Cup & saucer, handleless 75
Relish dish, octagonal 125

Jeddo Sugar Bowl

Sugar, cov., full-paneled Gothic shape
(ILLUS.).. 195
Teapot, cov., full-paneled Gothic shape........... 300

KAN-SU (Thomas Walker, ca. 1847)
Cup & saucer, handleless 75
Plate, 7 1/2" d. 60
Platter, 14" l. 250
Vegetable dish, cov., octagonal 375

MARBLE (A. Shaw, ca. 1850)

Marble Creamer and Teapot

Creamer, 6" h., 10 panel Gothic shape
(ILLUS.).. 200
Invalid feeder, large... 500
Waste bowl 150

MARBLE (Mellor Venables, ca. 1845)
Plate, 9 1/2" d. 75
Teapot, cov., child's, vertical paneled
Gothic.. 350
Teapot, cov., vertical paneled Gothic
shape (ILLUS.) 450

MEDINA (J. Furnival, ca. 1850)
Cup & saucer, handleless 65
Gravy boat 155
Sugar, cov., cockscomb handle 350

NANKIN (Davenport, ca. 1845)

Nankin Pitcher

Pitcher, 8" h., mask spout jug w/poly-
chrome (ILLUS.).. 300
Plate, 8 1/2" d., w/polychrome............................ 75

NING PO (R. Hall, ca. 1840)
Cup & saucer, handleless 65
Plate, 10 1/2" d. 85
Soup plate, w/flanged rim, 10" d. 90

PARISIAN GROUPS (J. Clementson, ca. 1850)
Plate, 7 1/2" d., w/polychrome............................ 60
Plate, 8 1/2" d., w/polychrome............................ 70
Sauce dish, w/polychrome................................. 65
Sauce tureen, cover & undertray, w/poly-
chrome, 3 pcs.. 450

PELEW (Edward Challinor, ca. 1850)
Cup & saucer, handleless, pedestalled 95
Plate, 7 1/2" d. 60
Plate, 10 1/2" d. 90
Punch cup, ring handle...................................... 100

Pelew Teapot

Teapot, cov., pumpkin shape (ILLUS.).............. 395

PERUVIAN (John Wedge Wood, ca. 1850)

Peruvian Cup & Saucer

Cup & saucer, handleless, "double bulge"
(ILLUS.).. 85
Gravy boat 145
Teapot, cov., 16 paneled................................... 400
Waste bowl, "double bulge" 150

PHANTASIA (J. Furnival, ca. 1850)
Creamer, 6" h., w/polychrome, cockscomb handle 325
Cup plate, w/polychrome 95
Plate, 9 1/2" d., w/polychrome.......................... 85
Sugar, cov., w/polychrome, cockscomb handle 400
Teapot, cov., w/polychrome, cockscomb handle 650

RHONE SCENERY (T. J. & J. Mayer, ca. 1850)
Gravy boat 150
Plate, 7 1/2" d. 45
Plate, 10 1/2" d... 65
Sauce tureen, cover & undertray, 3 pcs....... 500
Sugar, cov., full-paneled Gothic shape 200

SCINDE (T. Walker, ca. 1847)
Creamer, 6" h., Classic Gothic shape 150
Plate, 9 1/2" d. 80
Soup plate, w/flanged rim, 9" d......................... 90
Teapot, cov., Classic Gothic shape................. 350

SHAPOO (T. & R. Boote, ca. 1850)
Plate, 8 1/2" d. 75
Sugar, cov., Primary shape............................. 300
Teapot, cov., Primary shape 450
Vegetable dish, cov., flame finial.................... 350

TEMPLE (Podmore, Walker & Co., ca. 1850)
Cup plate 75
Cup & saucer, handled, large........................... 95
Plate, 8 1/2" d. 55
Sugar, cov., Classic Gothic shape 200
Teapot, cov., Classic Gothic shape................. 350

VINCENNES (J. Alcock, ca. 1840)
Compote, Gothic Cameo shape 500
Cup & saucer, handleless, thumbprint 85
Plate, 7 1/2" d. 60
Plate, 10 1/2" d. 80

Vincennes Punch Cup

Punch cup (ILLUS.) 125
Soup tureen, cover & undertray, 10-sided, 3 pcs. 2,000

WASHINGTON VASE (Podmore, Walker & Co., ca. 1850)
Creamer, 6" h., Classic Gothic shape 225
Cup & saucer, handleless 85
Plate, 10 1/2" d. 75
Soup plate, w/flanged rim, 9" d........................ 85
Teapot, cov., bulbous shape 495

WHAMPOA (Mellor Venables & Co., ca. 1845)
Gravy boat 165
Plate, 10 1/2" d... 95

Sauce tureen, cov., long octagon shape, 2 pcs... 300

WREATH (Thomas Furnival, ca. 1850)

Wreath Ewer

Ewer (ILLUS.) 295
Plate, 9 1/2" d. 85

NEWCOMB COLLEGE POTTERY

This pottery was established in the art department of Newcomb College, New Orleans, Louisiana, in 1897. Each piece was hand-thrown and bore the potter's mark & decorator's monogram on the base. It was always a studio business and never operated as a factory and its pieces are therefore scarce, with the early wares being eagerly sought. The pottery closed in 1940.

Newcomb College Pottery Mark

Bowl, 7" d., 2 1/2" h., footed wide squatty bulbous form w/a wide flat mouth, the shoulder decorated w/pairs of large pink blossoms w/yellow centers joined by slender green leaves all against a dark blue ground, matte glaze, impressed mark, "H. Bailey - #IZ31" **$990**

Bowl, 8 1/2" d., 3 1/4" h., low round body w/incurved sides & narrow flat rim, incised stylized white & yellow blossoms on a glossy cobalt & green ground, by Henrietta Bailey, 1904, two hairlines at rim, impressed "NC - HB - ZZ74" **4,950**

Bowl-vase, footed squatty round bulbous body incised around top w/a band of white & yellow roses on a bluish green ground, by Henrietta Bailey, 1914, impressed "NC - HB - GT32 - JM - 256" 31/4 x 6 1/4" **1,870**

Newcomb Bowl-Vase with Crocus

Bowl-vase, decorated w/cobalt blue rim over incised band of repeating crocus above a band of leaves, cream, yellow, pale blue, blue & bluish green over light blue body, interior gloss glazed cream, by Marie H. LeBlanc, 1905, impressed "NC, W - JM - CB54" & artist's cipher, 5 1/2" d., 4 1/4" h. (ILLUS.) **4,025**

Bowl-vase, bulbous body w/deeply-colored landscape scene of a live oak w/Spanish moss w/full moon in background, by Sadie Irvine, ca. 1932, impressed "NC - SI - KS - UB46," 5 1/2" d., 3 3/4" h. **2,090**

Bowl-vase, squatty bulbous body w/short cylindrical neck, decorated w/light blue & yellow daffodils on a faded blue ground, by Sadie Irvine, ca. 1922, impressed "NC - SI - JM - MI38 - 212," 7" d., 4 1/4" h. **1,980**

Mug, slightly tapering waisted form w/loop handle, decorated w/a wide upper band of stylized landscape in bluish green above a wide blue-washed lower band, glossy glaze, painted by Desiree Roman & Marie Delavigne, 1901, impressed "NC - DR - MD - G73X - Q - JM," 5" w., 4" h. **3,575**

Pitcher, 5" h., 4 1/2" d., gently flaring cylindrical body w/a pinched rim spout & loop handle, decorated w/an upper band in the Espanol geometric patt., on a dark blue matte ground, impressed "207" **1,320**

Pitcher, cov., milk, 5 1/4" h., cylindrical body w/pinched spout, flat inset lid & button finial, large loop handle, the top decorated w/a band of incised stylized blossoms in orange, dark blue & bluish green against a light blue ground, orange spout, rim & narrow band on lid, decorated by Charlotte Payne, 1905, impressed "NC - CP - AT44" **3,850**

Vase, 3 1/2" h., wide bulbous ovoid body w/narrow cylindrical neck & closed rim, incised decoration of tall trees w/Spanish moss in shades of blue against a peach sunset background **1,900**

Vase, 4 1/4" h., 4 1/2" d., footed squatty bulbous body, the wide shoulder tapering to cylindrical neck w/flat rim, decorated w/h.p. yellow sunflower petals & blue seeds, outlined in blue, on ivory ground, by S. Massegali, artist-signed & impressed "NC - P," stilt pull to base (ILLUS.) **4,950**

Early Newcomb College Vase

Vase, 4 1/2" h., 2 1/2" d., bud-type, waisted cylindrical form decorated up the sides w/sprigs of wide flowers & green long leaves on a bluish green ground, by Henrietta Bailey, 1915, impressed "NC - KB82 - HB - 212".................................... **1,870**

Vase, 5 1/4" h., bulbous ovoid form w/flat rim, incised w/yellow daisies on an ivory & light blue ground, by Desiree Roman, 1903, impressed "NC - D.R. - JM - Q - JJ79," (two tight hairlines to rim) **7,150**

Vase, 5 1/2" h., bulbous ovoid body tapering to a short cylindrical neck, carved & painted around the shoulder w/a narrow band of pairs of small white blossoms & green leaves & vines against a dark blue matte ground, impressed mark, "#QP91 - A.F. Simpson" **1,320**

Newcomb College Vase w/Sailboats

Vase, 5 3/4" h., 5 3/4" d., wide expanding cylindrical body w/flat rim, carved & decorated w/a continuous band of blue sailboats w/clouds in background, glossy blue, white & green glaze, decorated by Desiree Roman, ca. 1903, impressed "NC - W - D.R. - X37 -JM" (ILLUS.) **13,750**

Vase, 6" h., bulbous body tapering to wide cylindrical neck w/closed rim, decorated w/light blue irises w/green leaves on faded blue ground, by C. Chalaron, ca. 1925, impressed "NC - JM - 26ON33 - CMC".. **2,420**

Vase, 6" h., slightly swelled cylindrical form tapering slightly to a short cylindrical neck, carved & painted around the shoulder w/large light blue flowers w/ivory & green centers & green leaves against a dark blue matte ground, impressed mark, "#OY14 - #19 -Sadie Irvine" **1,320**

Vase, 6 1/2" h., footed wide ovoid body w/a wide shoulder sloping to a small cylindrical neck, carved & painted around the shoulder w/large stylized pale lavender rose blossoms on pale green scrolled leafy stems down the sides against a streaky blue matte ground, impressed mark, "#GC26 - M. Robertson - A.F. Simpson" **4,675**

Vase, 7" h., 5" d., wide ovoid body w/a short cylindrical neck, decorated w/tooled stylized yellow flowers on tall stems & large pointed leaves in celadon green against an ivory ground, by Esther H. Elliott, stamped "NC - EHE - BB10 - Q - JM" **24,750**

Vase, 7 1/2" h., footed wide expanding cylindrical ridged body by Kenneth Smith, covered in semi-matte turquoise glaze, impressed "NC - Kenneth Smith" **605**

Vase, 7 1/2" h., 4 1/2" d., simple ovoid body w/a small tapering neck, decorated around the upper two-thirds w/a paneled band of tall incised stylized birch seed pods in bluish green against an ivory ground, a blue-washed band around the lower section, by Henrietta Bailey, 1904, marked "NC - PP71 - HBailey - JM - Q" .. **15,400**

Vase, 8" h., slender ovoid body w/narrow shoulder tapering to wide cylindrical neck, decorated w/scene of live oaks & Spanish moss w/full moon, green tones, by Sadie Irvine, ca. 1922, impressed "NC - SI - 250 - MW7M4" **3,190**

Floral Newcomb Vase

Vase, 9" h., ovoid body, the rounded shoulder centered by small cylindrical neck w/flared rim, decorated w/ivory & yellow blossoms & leaves outlined in blue, green ground, impressed "NC - JM - N or Z," firing lines & stilt pull under base (ILLUS.) **6,600**

Vase, 9 1/2" h., bulbous w/tapering shoulder & closed rim, decorated w/incised band of stylized light blue flowers on a white ground over a dark blue band & glossy blue base, by Sabrina Wells, 1904, ink mark & "NC - S.E.WELL - SS38" (line inside rim, not through, from firing) **8,250**

Vase, 9 1/2" h., tall slender waisted cylindrical body, the upper half w/an incised & finely painted band of stylized slender upright leaves & spearpoint blossoms in ivory, green & blue above the lower body w/a streaked ivory, green & blue glossy glaze, "C. Payne - J.M. - #YY29" **6,050**

Vase, 10 1/2" h., inverted trumpet-form body w/slightly flared rim, decorated w/pink berries & long green leaves on faded blue ground, by Sadie Irvine, ca. 1920, impressed "NC - KZ21 - 83 - SI" **2,750**

Vase, 12 1/4" h., tall ovoid body decorated w/moonlight scene of live oaks w/Spanish moss, by Sadie Irvine, ca. 1925, impressed "NC - SI - OX28 - JM - 117" **7,700**

NILOAK POTTERY

This pottery was made in Benton, Arkansas and featured hand-thrown varicolored swirled clay decoration in objects of classic forms. Designated Mission Ware, this line is the most desirable of Niloak's production which was begun early in this century. Less expensive to produce, the cast Hywood Line, finished with either high gloss or semi-matte glazes, was introduced during the economic depression of the 1930s. The pottery ceased operation about 1946.

Niloak

Niloak Pottery Mark

Ashtray, Mission Ware, shallow round form w/curved sides & incurved rim, swirled tan & cream clays, 3 1/2" d. **$88**

Ashtray/match holder, Mission Ware, shallow round form w/rim rests centered by cylindrical match holder, swirled brown, orange & cream clays, paper label, 2 1/4 x 4 3/4" **440**

Bowl-vase, Mission Ware, wide flat-bottomed form w/rounded bottom & tapering cylindrical sides to the wide flat mouth, dark brown, beige & dark terra cotta swirled clays, stamped mark, 8" d., 6" h. **440**

Candlestick, Mission Ware, swirled colored clays, 10 1/4" h **250**

Candlesticks, Mission Ware, widely flaring funnel base tapering to a molded cylindrical shaft topped by a wide cupped socket, swirled brown, blue, terra cotta & sand clays, stamped mark, 5" d., 8" h., pr **330**

Chamber pot, child's, Mission Ware, footed squatty bulbous form w/wide flared rim & C-form handle, swirled cream & brown clays, 5 1/2" d. **550**

Chamberstick, Mission Ware, flaring base w/loop handle, swirled tan, brown, orange & cream clays, 4 1/2" h. **253**

Cigarette jar, cov., Mission Ware, cylindrical w/inset lid & bud finial, swirled blue,
cream & brown clays, 4 3/4" h...................... **825**

Compote, open, Mission Ware, flared foot,
shallow, round w/incurved sides & rim,
swirled grey, tan, orange & cream clays,
5" h., 10" d... **825**

Decanter w/original stopper, Mission
Ware, swirled tan, orange, grey & cream
clays, 10 1/2" h. (chips to top of
decanter)... **880**

Figurine, Southern Belle, Hywood Line,
standing, wearing hat, pink & aqua matte
glaze, 7" h. **110**

Flower bowl, Mission Ware, squatty bulbous body w/center opening & pierced
rim, swirled brown, cream & orange
clays, 3 x 5 1/2" (one line, probably in
making) **198**

Niloak Flower Frogs & Umbrella Stand

Flower frogs, Mission Ware, round,
swirled multicolored clays, largest
4 1/2" w., set of 3 (ILLUS. front).................. **121**

Flowerpot w/undertray, Mission Ware,
expanding cylindrical form w/flat rim,
hole in bottom for drainage, swirled
brown, tan, grey & cream clays, 9" d.,
10" h.. **1,045**

Humidor, cov., Mission Ware, wide
waisted cylinder w/inset lid & large round
flat finial, swirled cream, tan & light
brown clays, 6 1/2" h. **1,430**

Jardiniere, Mission Ware, bulbous ovoid
w/collared rim, swirled brown clays,
10" h.. **1,210**

Model of dog, bulldog w/collar, Hywood
Line, red matte glaze, 4" h. **110**

Mug, Mission Ware, cylindrical w/C-form
handle, swirled multicolored clays, 5" h. **253**

Mugs, Mission Ware, tapering cylindrical
form w/C-form handles, swirled light &
dark brown clays, patent pending mark,
4" h., set of 6 .... **990**

Necklace, Mission Ware, alternating small
& tiny stones suspending a pendent consisting of a group of long & round swirled
light clay stones, 18" l. **825**

Pedestal base, Mission Ware, short wide
waisted cylindrical form, swirled cream,

tan, brown & grey clays, 7" h. (bruise to
bottom) **358**

Pitcher, tankard, 10 1/2" h., corseted form,
Mission Ware **495**

Pitcher, 11" h., Mission Ware, tall slender
ovoid body w/rim spout & rim turned up
above large C-form handle, large swirls
of brown, tan, cream & grey clays............. **1,320**

Powder bowl, cov., Mission Ware, footed
bulbous body, flat inset lid w/small button finial, swirled grey, tan & cream
clays, 6" w., 3 1/2" h. **523**

Punch bowl, Mission Ware, pedestal foot,
deep rounded sides w/molded rim,
swirled cream, tan & brown clays, 13" d.,
9" h. **2,640**

Shot glasses, Mission Ware, tapering
cylindrical form, swirled multicolored
clays, 2 1/4" h., set of 6 (one chip) **468**

Tankard set: Mission Ware, cylindrical
10 1/2" h. tankard & twelve 2" h. cylindrical mugs; tan pitcher w/zig-zag swirls in
cream & brown, multicolored swirled
mugs, pitcher w/hairline, two mugs
w/flaws, the set... **1,760**

Tray, Mission Ware, round w/straight sides,
swirled orange, cream, grey & brown
clays, 13" d.. **1,045**

Umbrella stand, Mission Ware, wide cylindrical body w/flared foot & rim, swirled
multicolored clays, 20" h. (firing crack in
base) **2,310**

Umbrella stand, Mission Ware, cylindrical
w/flared foot & rim, swirled cream, tan,
blue & brown clays, crack to base, 21" h.
(ILLUS. w/flower frogs).............................. **1,650**

Vase, 3" h., Mission Ware, heavy short
cylindrical form w/closed rim, swirling
cream, brown, blue & red clays,
impressed mark... **154**

Vase, 4" d., Mission Ware, bulbous ovoid
body w/a thick molded rim, swirled grey,
tan, rust & blue clays, first art mark.............. **69**

Vase, 4 1/4" h., Mission Ware, waisted
cylindrical form, swirled brown, cream,
tan & blue clays... **52**

Vase, 5 3/4" h., 7" d., Mission Ware,
squatty spherical form w/closed rim,
swirled brown, blue, terra cotta & sand
clays, stamped mark & paper label **248**

Vase, 6" h., Mission Ware, bulbous lower
body tapering to a tall waisted neck,
swirled blue, brown & cream clays................ **92**

Vase, 7" h., Mission Ware, fan-type, swirled
orange, grey, blue & cream clays................ **319**

Vase, bud, 7" h., Mission Ware, flared base
tapering to slender cylinder w/flat rim,
swirled multicolored clays **154**

Vase, 8 1/2" h., 4 1/2" d., Mission Ware, tall
trumpet-form body on a flaring disk foot,
swirled brown, blue & terra cotta clays,
stamped mark **165**

Vase, 9 1/2" h., 5" d., Mission Ware, baluster-form w/short flared neck, banded
swirls of brown, blue, terra cotta & sand
clays, stamped mark **303**

Vase, 9 1/2" h., 5 1/2" d., Mission Ware,
footed bulbous base tapering to a tall

wide trumpet neck, swirled brown, blue, terra cotta & purple clays, stamped mark..... **358**

Vase, 10" h., 4 1/2" d., Mission Ware, tall cylindrical body w/flaring foot, swirled brown, blue & reddish terra cotta clays, stamped mark & paper label **385**

Vase, 12" h., 7 1/2' d., Mission Ware, tall ovoid body tapering to a short flaring neck, finely swirled brown, ivory & terra cotta clays, stamped mark & paper label **495**

Vase, 12 1/4" d., 5 1/2" d., Mission Ware, tall slender corseted form, swirled brown, blue, terra cotta & purple clays, stamped mark **330**

Vase, 14" h., 7" d., Mission Ware, tall footed swelled cylindrical form w/a narrow shoulder tapering to a thick molded rim, finely swirled brown, blue, terra cotta & purple clays, stamped mark & paper label **880**

Wall pocket, Mission Ware, conical w/flat rim, swirled brown, orange, grey & cream clays, paper label, 7 1/2" l. **440**

Whiskey jug, Mission Ware, four-sided centered by cylindrical neck w/molded rim, wide shoulder w/loop handle, swirled blue, grey & cream clays, 6" h. **2,750**

NIPPON

"Nippon" is a term which is used to describe a wide range of porcelain wares produced in Japan from the late 19th century until about 1921. It was in 1891 that the U.S. implemented the McKinley Tariff Act which required that all wares exported to the United States carry a marking indicating the country of origin. The Japanese chose to use "Nippon," their name for Japan. In 1921 the import laws were revised and the words "Made in" had to be added to the markings. Japan was also required to replace the "Nippon" with the English name "Japan" on all wares sent to the U.S.

Many Japanese factories produced Nippon porcelains and much of it was hand-painted with ornate floral or landscape decoration and heavy gold decoration, applied beading and slip-trailed designs referred to as "moriage." We indicate the specific marking used on a piece, when known, at the end of each listing below. Be aware that a number of Nippon markings have been reproduced and used on new porcelain wares.

Important reference books on Nippon include: The Collector's Encyclopedia of Nippon Porcelain, Series One through Three, by Joan F. Van Patten (Collector Books, Paducah, Kentucky) and The Wonderful World of Nippon Porcelain, 1891-1921 by Kathy Wojciechowski (Schiffer Publishing, Ltd., Atglen, Pennsylvania).

Ashtray, round flat-bottomed form w/upright low sides & attached rest on rim, the interior painted w/a colorful hand of cards showing a 'full house' of aces & kings against a shaded orangish yellow ground, 4" d. (green "M" in Wreath mark)..... **$35**

Basket, boat-shaped w/a high arched spout at each end, an arched gold handle across the center, the sides painted

w/a lakeside scene w/sailboat & beaded trim, 5 1/2" l. (blue "Rising Sun" mark) **58**

Rare Nippon Tapestry Basket

Basket, "tapestry," moon-shaped, flattened round form w/a large kidney-shaped opening for the handle, on a flat gold base, decorated w/an autumnal landscape w/swans on a lake, 9" h., blue "Maple Leaf" mark (ILLUS.)...................... **1,870**

Candlesticks, squared baluster-form w/flaring base, the sides w/a h.p. sunset scene w/house in meadow, gold socket rim, 5 1/2" h., pr. (green "Kinso Nippon" mark) **81**

Celery dish, oblong w/incurved rim, h.p. decoration of house in meadow scene, 12" l. (green "M" in Wreath mark)................... **66**

Celery dishes, long oval form w/end handles pierced in the form of a Native American chieftain's head, the interior painted w/a lakeside landscape at sunset, 8 1/4" l., pr. (green "M" in Wreath mark) **104**

Center bowl, squatty rounded oval form w/incurved scalloped rim & upright pointed loop end handles, decorated w/large pink blossoms w/yellow centers & green leaves on a moss green ground, moriage trim, 9" l. (blue "Maple Leaf" mark) **173**

Nippon Scenic Chamberstick

Chamberstick, saucer-form base decorated w/scene of house by lake w/trees & mountains, natural colors, 4 1/4" d., 2" h., green "M" in Wreath mark (ILLUS.) **125**

Charger, round, "tapestry," a fine linen finish on a design of large pink roses & green leaves against a shaded tan ground, raised gold rim band, 12" d., blue "Maple Leaf" mark **2,640**

Chocolate pot, cov., tall lobed & waisted body w/a pointed rim spout, forked S-scroll handle & domed cover w/pierced finial, white bands at base & on neck trimmed w/green buttons, the side lobes each w/an oval lavender panel, white on dark green bands on the neck, overall ornate moriage decoration, unmarked, 9" h. **201**

Chocolate set: cov. pot & five cups & saucers; cylindrical w/angled gold handles, each piece w/h.p. lakeside landscape scene w/tall slender leafy trees silhouetted in the foreground, the set (green "M" in Wreath mark) **173**

Condiment set: salt & pepper shakers, cov. mustard jar w/ladle, toothpick holder & tray; each of hexagonal form & decorated w/ornate gold scrolling & cobalt blue bands on white, gold handles, rectangular tray w/angled corners, the set ("RC Nippon" mark) **161**

Condiment set: square form salt & pepper shakers, tapering square form cov. mustard jar & rectangular tray; all decorated w/h.p. dragon motif in green & gold w/gold handles & finial on mustard jar, 4 pcs. **66**

Cracker jar, cov., wide cylindrical form on tiny gold ball feet, gently rounded shoulder supporting a domed cover w/pointed gold finial, h.p. overall w/large purple iris & green leaves on a stippled greenish yellow ground, acanthus leaf brackets molded in relief, 7 1/2" h. (blue "Maple Leaf" mark) **518**

Fernery, footed bulbous form w/deeply scalloped rim, decorated w/h.p. florals & moriage scrolling w/a center scenic transfer of the World Exposition Building, unmarked, 5" h. **286**

Humidor, cov., hexagonal footed form w/inset domed cover & angular button finial, the sides decorated w/pairs of tall pale green & brown upright lily blossoms on stems w/brown leaf bands at the top & bottom, the blossoms dividing a background Egyptian river sunset scene w/sailing ships, matching brown bands on the cover, 6 1/2" h. (green "M" in Wreath mark) **425**

Nippon Wedgwood-style Loving Cup

Loving cup, Wedgwood-style, deep tapering bowl on a flaring funnel foot, long loop handles at the sides, blue ground w/overall white slip decoration including bands of scrolls, Greek key and tall stems of flowers around the body, 5 1/2" h., green "M" in Wreath mark (ILLUS.).. **303**

Mug, cylindrical w/incurved rim & angled gold handle, the center w/a wide red band & round reserve h.p. w/various gambling designs including dice & cards, against a dark charcoal mottled ground, 5" h. (green "M" in Wreath mark) **144**

Nappy, shallow round form w/ring handle & widely flaring rim w/h.p. ornate gold scroll decorated border, 7" d. (blue "Maple Leaf" mark).. **28**

Nut dish, trefoil shape w/three handles, fine moriage decoration w/acorns, 7" d. (green "M" in Wreath mark)......................... **110**

Nut dish, oblong, relief-molded acorns at one end w/large h.p. brown leaves down the center, 8" l. (green "M" in Wreath mark) **69**

Nut dish, octagonal w/two tab handles, h.p. interior decoration of hazel nuts, 8" (green "M" in Wreath mark).............. **83**

Pitcher, 5 1/2" h., tankard-type, h.p. w/a stylized Dutch landscape w/windmill & lake in background & a man stealing geese being chased by other geese in foreground, enameled jewel trim (green "Wreath Studio Handpainted" mark) **115**

Plaque, pierced to hang, round, h.p. desert scene w/three men on camels near an oasis, shaded deep rose to lavender ground w/purple mountains in the distance, beaded rim, 9" d. (green "M" in Wreath mark) **150**

Plaque, pierced to hang, h.p. center portrait of a monk in red surrounded by a stippled gold border w/scrolled medallions, 9 1/2" d., green "M" in Wreath mark **660**

Soap dish, cover & insert, oval, deep sided, the slightly domed cover w/pink-trimmed arched center handle & decorated w/a landscape w/windmill scene, the border of the cover & bottom decorated w/a narrow band of enameling w/jewels, 5" l. (blue "Maple Leaf" mark) **173**

Toothpick holder, footed slightly tapering cylindrical form w/angled rim handles, h.p. landscape scene of a cottage & apple tree, 2 1/4" h. (green "M" in Wreath mark) **69**

Tray, h.p. w/lovely gold-outlined yellow & red primroses w/heavy gold border & rim, marked, 5 1/2 x 12 1/2" **125**

Urn, cov., large baluster-form w/domed & scroll-molded bolted-on foot, the large ovoid body tapering to a trumpet neck & molded rim w/a high domed small cover w/gold knob finial, upright winged scroll gold shoulder handles, the whole w/a dark cobalt blue ground ornately decorated overall w/delicate gold scrolling centering an oval & banded lakeside landscape scene in full color, highlighted w/green jewels, 17 1/2" h. (green "Maple Leaf" mark) **5,520**

Vase, 5" h., footed wide cylindrical body w/short neck, angled handles from shoulder to rim, h.p. cartoon-type outdoor scene w/cottage (green "M" in Wreath mark) **77**

Scenic Nippon Tapestry Vase

Vase, 5" h., "tapestry," wide ovoid body tapering to a short flared neck flanked by small looped shoulder handles, decorated w/a wide h.p. central landscape scene in autumn colors, decorative gold bands around the neck & base, gold handles, green "Maple Leaf" mark (ILLUS.).. **688**

Vase, 5 1/4" h., simple ovoid body w/a short upright scalloped mouth flanked by ornate scroll handles, the body h.p. w/large white apple blossoms & green leaves on a dark to light shaded blue ground, enameled rim & handles (blue "Sendai" mark) **58**

Vase, 7" h., four-footed spherical body w/a narrow short neck flaring into a four-lobed upturned rim, large C-scroll round handles from rim to shoulder, decorated overall w/ornate moriage beading w/white & purple florals & green leaves & rim (blue "Maple Leaf" mark) **350**

Vase, 8 1/2" h., swelled cylindrical body tapering to a tiny neck w/flared rim flanked by scrolling loop handles, the body completely decorated w/colorful large flowers in red, white & pink on a shaded green ground, the neck & handles in white on brown in the Wedgwood style (blue "Maple Leaf" mark) **201**

Vase, 9" h., footed ovoid body w/incurved short neck flanked by twig handles, the sides molded in relief w/large pink roses w/green leaves & stems & trimmed in gold, on a mottled dark green & gold ground, blue "Maple Leaf" mark (ILLUS.)..... **880**

Vase, 11 1/2" h., flaring oblong foot tapering to a slender pedestal continuing to the wide bulbous ovoid shouldered body centered by a short narrow neck w/a widely flaring lobed rim, ring handles on the shoulder, burgundy ground w/a large

central yellow & white reserve w/delicate blue & green vining florals in moriage around the sides, green neck & handles w/further moriage beading, unmarked (minor losses)... **345**

Nippon Vase with Molded Roses

Vase, 12" h., decorated w/colorful h.p. poppies on shaded matte brown ground, delicate slip-trailed decorated neck, handles & base **265**

Vase, 12" h., pillow-style w/flattened ovoid body on a flared scrolling foot, wide rounded shoulders centered by a short flaring deeply ruffled neck, double loop gilt shoulder handles, decorated w/a central reserve showing a mountainous lakeside landscape w/a heavy gold border, ornate gilt scrolling w/turquoise jeweling above & below scene, gilt neck & foot bands & gilt handles, marked "Hand-painted Morimura Nippon" **770**

Vase, 15" h., tall slender swelled cylindrical body w/a rounded shoulder to a small cylindrical gold neck flanked by small gold loop shoulder handles, the wide center band h.p. w/large clusters of purple & green grapes against a shaded yellow ground, the shoulder & base w/gilt-bordered & trimmed bands of large h.p. pink roses, blue blossoms & green leaves (blue "Maple Leaf" mark) **1,380**

Vase, 17 1/2" h., tall slender swelled cylindrical form tapering to a molded rim, a wide continuous finely painted mountainous landscape scene on a satin ground, cobalt blue rim & base bands heavily decorated w/gilt scrolling & turquoise jeweling, blue "Maple Leaf" mark (ILLUS. top next page) **7,480**

Vases, 13 1/2" h., tall slender triangular baluster-form body w/a wide rounded shoulder centering a short widely flaring tricorner mouth, decorated overall w/large h.p. red roses among large heavy gold acanthus leaves, raised on short flaring spade-shaped feet, unmarked, pr. **690**

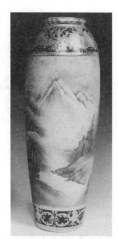

Large Ornate Nippon Landscape Vase

Wall Plaque with Lions

Wall plaque, round, molded in relief w/a lion & lioness in a rocky landscape, natural coloration, 10 1/2" d., green "M" in Wreath mark (ILLUS.) **440**

Wall plaque, round, molded in relief w/a scene of a Native American racing on horseback & pointing a rifle, natural coloration, 10 1/2" d., green "M" in Wreath mark **990**

Nippon Whiskey Jug with Landscape

Whiskey jug w/stopper, wide square form w/slightly flaring sides below the wide rounded shoulder centered by a small cylindrical neck w/rim spout & angled handle, bulbous mushroom stopper, one side w/a valley landscape, other panels w/bands of stylized leafy scrolls on orangish brown against a cream ground, edges, shoulder & neck w/a black or orangish tan ground decorated w/stylized leafy scrolls & classical motifs, 7 1/2" h., green "M" in Wreath mark (ILLUS.).. **770**

Ornate Nippon Whiskey Jug

Whiskey jug w/stopper, wide swelled cylindrical body w/a wide shoulder centered by a small cylindrical neck w/a spout & flared edges, angled handle, decorated w/bands of Egyptian designs on a white ground, gold handle & trim, w/advertising for E.M. Higgins Old Velvet, 6 1/2" h., green "M" in Wreath mark (ILLUS.).. **825**

NORITAKE

Noritake china, still in production in Japan, has been exported in large quantities to this country since early in this century. Though the Noritake Company first registered in 1904, it did not use "Noritake" as part of its backstamp until 1918. Interest in Noritake has escalated as collectors now seek out pieces made between the "Nippon" era and World War II (1921-41). The Azalea pattern is also popular with collectors.

Noritake Mark

Ashtray, center Queen of Clubs decoration, 4" w.. **$40**

Ashtray, figural polar bear, blue ground, 4 1/4" d., 2 1/2" h.. **52**

Ashtray, center Indian head decoration, 5 1/2" w. **215**

Ashtray, figural nude lady seated at edge of lustered flower form tray, 7" w.................. **595**

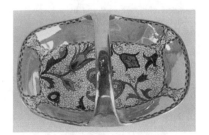

Noritake Basket

Basket, oblong w/center handle, gold lustre ground, interior w/center stylized floral decoration & geometric design in each corner & around rim, 7 3/4" l., 3" h. (ILLUS.) **80**

Basket, Roseara patt. **90**

Basket-bowl, footed, petal-shaped rim, 6 1/2" w. **90**

Basket-vase 7 1/2" h. **110**

Berry set: master bowl & 6 sauce dishes; decal & h.p. purple orchids, green leaves & pods decoration on green ground, 7 pcs. **80**

Bonbon, raised gold decoration, 6 1/4" w. **25**

Bonbon dish, Azalea patt. **40**

Noritake Scenic Bowl

Bowl, 6" sq., flanged rim w/pierced handles, orange lustre ground decorated w/h.p. scene w/large tree in foreground (ILLUS.) **80**

Bowl, 6 1/2" d., 2" h., fluted sides of alternating light & dark grey panels w/pointed rims, center w/Art Deco floral decoration **155**

Bowl, 7" w., square w/incurved sides, three-footed, interior w/relief-molded filbert nuts in brown trimmed w/h.p. autumn leaves **79**

Bowl, 8 3/4" d., 2" h., Art Deco style orange & white checkerboard ground decorated w/stylized dark brown rose buds & leaves outlined in grey & grey stems (ILLUS.) **175**

Noritake Art Deco Bowl

Bowl, 9" d., footed, scenic interior decoration, lustre finish exterior **50**

Bowl, shell-shaped, three-footed, Tree in Meadow patt. **295**

Bowl, soup, Azalea patt. **20**

Butter dish, cover & drain insert, Azalea patt., 3 pcs. **85**

Cake plate, Sheridan patt., 9 3/4" d. **25**

Noritake Cake Plate

Cake plate, rectangular, open-handled, turquoise border w/oval center Oriental scene on black ground, 10" l. (ILLUS.) **110**

Cake plate, open-handled, Tree in Meadow patt. **33**

Cake set: 10" d. handled master cake plate & 6 serving plates; fruit bowl medallions center, blue lustre rims, 7 pcs. **90**

Cake set: 14 x 6 1/4" oblong tray w/pierced handles & six 6 1/2" d. serving plates; white w/pale green & gold floral border, 7 pcs. **90**

Candlesticks, Indian motif decoration, 3 1/4" h., pr. **110**

Candy dish, octagonal, Tree in Meadow patt. **365**

Candy dish, cov., figural bird finial, scalloped rim, blue lustre finish, 6 1/2 x 7 1/4" **120**

Celery set: celery tray & 6 individual salt dips, decal & h.p. florals & butterflies decoration, 7 pcs. **85**

Celery tray, Azalea patt. **45**

Cigarette holder, footed, figural swan, orange lustre w/black neck & head, black outlining on wing feathers & tail, 3" w., 4 1/2" h. **120**

Cigarette holder, bell-shaped w/bird finial, 5" h. **350**

Cigarette Holder w/Golfer Decoration

Cigarette holder/playing card holder, pedestal foot, gold lustre ground decorated w/scene of golfer, 4" h. (ILLUS.) **275**

Art Deco Style Cigarette Jar

Cigarette jar, cov., bell-shaped cover w/bird finial, Art Deco style silhouetted scenic decoration of woman in chair & man standing, both holding cigarettes, 4 3/4" h., 3 1/2" d. (ILLUS.) **380**

Coffee set: cov. coffeepot, creamer, cov. sugar bowl & four cups & saucers; greyish blue butterfly, pink florals & grey leaves decoration, 11 pcs. **225**

Cologne bottle w/flower cluster stopper, Art Deco man wearing checkered cape & lustered sides, 6 3/4" h. **295**

Cologne bottle w/stopper, two-handled, Art Deco lady decoration **375**

Condiment set: cov. mustard jar & pr. salt & pepper shakers on handled tray; blue lustre w/tops decorated w/flowers, 7" w. tray, the set **240**

Condiment set: cov. mustard jar & pr. salt & pepper shakers on handled tray; bulbous blue lustre mustard jar w/red rosebud finial, green leaves, ovoid shakers w/clown head tops, red, blue, orange & white lustre, blue lustre tray, 7" l., the set (ILLUS.) **320**

Figural Condiment Set

Condiment set: cov. mustard jar & pr. salt & pepper shakers on handled tray; lustre borders & tops, 5 1/2" w. tray, the set **60**

Noritake Cracker Jar

Cracker jar, cov., footed spherical body decorated w/a black band w/white swords & shields design & center oval yellow medallion w/scene of white sailboat on lake, white clouds in distance & blue stylized tree in foreground, black & white geometric design bands around rim & cover edge, orange lustre ground, 7" h. (ILLUS.) **250**

Creamer, Azalea patt. **25**

Creamer, Tree in Meadow patt. **20**

Creamer & cov. sugar bowl, Azalea patt., pr. **85**

Creamer & cov. sugar bowl, blue scenic decoration, brown borders, pr. **70**

Art Deco Style Creamer & Sugar Bowl

Creamer & open sugar bowl, Art Deco style checked decoration in black, blue, brown & white, orange lustre interior basket-shaped sugar bowl w/overhead handle, creamer 3" h., sugar bowl 4 1/2" h., pr. (ILLUS.) **110**

Creamer & sugar shaker, berry set-type, decorated w/a scene of a gondola, orange lustre ground, pr. 6 1/2" h. **75**

Berry Set Creamer & Sugar Shaker

Creamer & sugar shaker, berry set-type, orange lustre interior, scenic decoration w/cottage, bridge & trees above floral cluster, blue lustre ground, 6 1/2" h., pr. (ILLUS.).. **80**

Creamer & sugar shaker, berry set-type, raised gold decoration, 5 3/4" h. creamer & 6 1/4" h. sugar shaker, pr........................... **80**

Noritake Cruet Set

Cruet set w/original stoppers, the two conjoined globular bottles set at angles & joined w/a handle at the shoulder, shaded orange lustre ground decorated w/green & yellow clover leaves & stems, 6" l., 3 1/2" h. (ILLUS.) **125**

Cup & saucer, demitasse, Tree in Meadow patt. **35**

Cup & saucer, Tree in Meadow patt. **15**

Desk set: heart-shaped tray w/pen rack at front & two cov. jars w/floral finials; decal & h.p. florals, 6 1/2" w. **275**

Dinner bell, figural Chinaman, 3 1/2" h. **310**

Dish, blue lustre trim, 5" sq. **20**

Dresser box, cov., figural lady on lid, lustre finish, 5" h.. **600**

Figurine, maiden carrying a bundle of sticks on her head **140**

Fish plates, h.p. & decal w/h.p. center fish decoration, gold borders, 8 1/2" d., pr. **110**

Flower holder, model of bird on stump, base pierced w/four flower holes, 4 1/2" h.. **95**

Hair receiver, cov., Art Deco style, geometric design on gold lustre ground, 3 1/2" d. (ILLUS.)... **160**

Humidor, cov., model of an owl w/head as cover, lustre finish, 7" h. **750**

Humidor, cov., relief-molded & h.p. horse head, 7" h. **650**

Art Deco Style Hair Receiver

Humidor, cov., four panels of decal & h.p. yellow roses & black leaves on orange ground within h.p. black oval borders, 7 1/2" h.. **450**

Inkwell, model of an owl, Art Deco style, 3 1/2" h... **240**

Figural Jam Set

Jam jar, cover & underplate, melon-shaped, pink ground w/grey leaves, handle & leaf-shaped underplate, 5 3/4" l., 4 1/4" h., the set (ILLUS.)........................... **115**

Lemon plate, Azalea patt................................... **35**

Lobster set: sauce bowl, underplate & ladle; molded lotus form, petals w/high-lights & lobster decoration on 10 3/4" d. underplate **195**

Marmalade jar, cover, underplate & ladle, flower bud finial, 5 1/4" h. **70**

Mayonnaise set, Azalea patt., 3 pcs. **45**

Night light, figural lady, 9 1/4" h., 2 pc......... **2,000**

Nut bowl, tri-lobed bowl w/figural squirrel seated at side eating nut, 7 1/2" w. **120**

Nut bowl, molded nut shell form w/three relief-molded nuts & side h.p. w/walnuts & green ferns decoration................................ **75**

Nut set: 6" d. bowl shaped like open chestnut & six 2" d. nut dishes; earthtone ground w/h.p. nuts & leaves, the set **150**

Scenic Noritake Plaque

Plaque, pierced to hang, silhouetted Art Deco style scene of woman in gown w/full ruffled skirt, sitting on couch & holding mirror, white lustre ground, 8 3/4" d. (ILLUS.).. 325

Plaque, pierced to hang, relief-molded & h.p. double Indian portraits, 10 1/2" d....... 500

Plate, 6 1/2" d., Azalea patt. 12

Plate, 6 1/2" d., Tree in Meadow patt. 16

Plate, 7 1/2" d., Azalea patt. 13

Plate, dinner, Azalea patt. 35

Platter, 10" l., Tree in Meadow patt.................... 100

Platter, 14" l., Tree in Meadow patt.................... 60

Powder box, cov., figural, an Art Deco style female figure on a chair in colors of orange, black, green, white & brown w/a lustre finish, 1930s, 4 1/4 x 5", 7" h. **2,070**

Powder box, cov., figural bird finial, 3 1/2" d... 110

Powder box, cov., Art Deco decoration, 4" d... 550

Floral-Decorated Power Puff Box

Powder puff box, cov., disk-form, stylized floral decoration in red, blue, white & black on a white iridized ground w/blue lustre border, 4" d. (ILLUS.) 195

Relish dish, Azalea patt., 8" l.............................. 25

Ring holder, model of a hand 40

Salt & pepper shakers, Tree in Meadow patt., pr. 20

Sauce dish, Azalea patt..................................... 15

Shaving mug, landscape scene w/tree, birds & moon decoration 65

Smoke set: handled tray, cigar & cigarette jars & match holder; cigars, cigarettes & matchsticks decoration, the set..................... 325

Spoon holder, double tray-form, oblong shape w/gold angular center handle, orange lustre interior, exterior decorated w/flowers & butterfly on black ground, 6 1/2" l., 2 1/2" h. 95

Sugar bowl, cov., Azalea patt............................ 60

Sugar shaker, lavender & gold decoration, blue lustre trim...................................... 45

Syrup jug, Azalea patt. 60

Tea strainer w/footed rest, cov., Azalea patt. decal & h.p. red roses & gold trim on green ground, 2 pcs. 85

Toast rack, two-slice, blue & yellow decoration 60

Tray, pierced handles, decal & h.p. fruit border, lustre center, 11" w. 85

Tray, rectangular, pierced end handles, floral decoration on white ground, green

edge trim w/brown trim on handles, 17 1/2" l. 95

Scenic Noritake Vase

Vase, 4 1/4" h., 5 1/4" d., footed bulbous body w/figural leaf & grape cluster handles, gold & blue lustre ground decorated w/scene of trees & children (ILLUS.).. 275

Vase, 5 1/2" h., orange & gold rim & handles, h.p. tree & cottage lakeside scene.. 65

Noritake Fan-shaped Vase

Vase, 6 1/2" h., footed, fan-shaped, colorful Art Deco floral design on orange ground (ILLUS.).. 225

Vase, 7" h., fan-shaped w/ruffled rim, fruit & vines decoration, green & blue base.............. 70

Vase, 8" h., footed ovoid body w/squared rim handles, butterfly decoration on shaded & streaked blue & orange ground 195

Stylized Noritake Vase

Vase, 8 1/4" h., 5 1/4" d., footed ovoid body w/scalloped rim & scrolled rim handles, blue interior, exterior base w/blue, brown & black vertical lines on white, black band on upper body decorated w/stylized flowers in yellow, purple, brown & blue w/green & brown leaves (ILLUS.) **550**

Vase, 8 1/4" h., Indian motif & lustre decoration **130**

Vase, 8 1/2" h., bulbous body, Tree in the Meadow patt.................................. **98**

Vegetable bowl, open, round, Tree in Meadow patt................................. **45**

Vegetable dish, cov., round, Azalea patt........... **90**

Wall pocket, double, conical two-part form w/arched backplate, decorated w/an exotic blue & yellow bird among branches of red & blue stylized blossoms against a cream ground, purple lustre rim band, 8" l. **110**

Wall pocket, trumpet-form, wide upper band decorated w/an autumn sunset scene, lavender lustre rim band & base, 8 1/4" l. **72**

Wall pocket, double, relief-molded floral cresting backplate, stylized florals & bird of paradise decoration, lustre border, 8" l. **160**

Wall pocket, single, h.p. tree & cottage lakeside scene on blue lustered ground, 8" h.................. **110**

Waste bowl, Azalea patt. **60**

NORTH DAKOTA SCHOOL OF MINES

All pottery produced at the University of North Dakota School of Mines was made from North Dakota clay. In 1910, the University hired Margaret Kelly Cable to teach pottery making and she remained at the school until her retirement. Julia Mattson and Margaret Pachl were other instructors between 1923 and 1970. Designs and glazes varied through the years ranging from the Art Nouveau to modern styles. Pieces were marked "University of North Dakota - Grand Forks, N.D. - Made at School of Mines, N.D." within a circle and also signed by the students until 1963. Since that time, the pieces bear only the students' signatures. Items signed "Huck" are by the artist Flora Huckfield and were made between 1923 and 1949.

North Dakota School of Mines Mark

Bowl, 6 1/2" d., 2" h., round straight sides decorated w/a h.p. & lightly tooled scene of oxen & covered wagons on the prairie against a blue sky, brown ground, decorated by Julia Mattson, circular ink mark & incised "JM#6 - 121 - Huck." (ILLUS.) . **$1,045**

North Dakota School of Mines Bowl

Bowl-Vase with Coyotes

Bowl-vase, squatty bulbous body decorated w/an embossed band of medium matte green coyotes silhouetted against a darker matte green ground, by Julia Mattson, 1925, circular ink stamp & incised "JM25," stilt pull to base, 3 x 4 1/4" (ILLUS.)..................................... **660**

Charger, the center decorated w/a large stylized flower in polychrome cuerda seca, w/red flower petals at the dark border & centered between the five large flower petals, ink stamp & artist mark, 10" d......................... **770**

Figure of cowboy, bentonite, standing, wearing chaps & large hat, neckerchief & gun & holster, brown & black, by Julia Mattson, incised "JM 13 UND," 3 x 4 3/4"..... **605**

Model of a hawk, bentonite, wings & back decorated w/yellow & black stripes, rectangular base, by Julia Mattson, incised signature, 5" h., 3 3/4" l. **880**

Pitcher, 5" h., 8 1/2" d., footed squatty bulbous body w/embossed frieze of "Red River Ox Carts" by M. Cable, glossy ivory glaze on buff clay body, die-stamped mark, embossed signature & title & "140" **990**

Pitcher, 5 1/2" h., bulbous body w/flaring neck, pinched spout & loop handle, incised decoration of children at play & stylized florals, polychrome matte glaze, decorated by Franc Freeman, ink stamp & incised signature, 1947 .... **605**

Trivet, round, decorated w/large stylized polychrome bird standing on long branch beneath a stylized flower, by Julia Mattson, ink mark & incised "JMattson," couple of small burst bubbles, 6" d. **440**

Vase, miniature, 3 1/4" h., squatty bulbous ovoid body w/green stripes on a mustard ground, by Julia Mattson, ink stamp & "M." **358**

Vase, 3 1/2" h., bentonite, bulbous body w/wide narrow rim, decorated w/a band of black wolves in silhouette on a brick red ground, ink stamp & "ML"..................... **1,100**

Vase, 3 1/2" h., 3 1/2" d., wide bulbous body decorated overall w/painted white snowflakes on a dark blue ground, ink stamp **385**

Vase, 5" h., 6" d., round sharply angled sides w/wide sloping shoulder tapering to short cylindrical neck w/flat rim, decorated w/a repeating incised frieze of bison in matte brown & green on dark brown ground w/dark brown band at mid-body & brown ground on lower body, carved by Margaret Cable, ink stamp & "M. Cable" **5,225**

Vase, 5 1/4" h., 6" d., wide bulbous ovoid form w/wide angled shoulder to flat mouth, molded around the shoulder w/rectangular panels each enclosing a bison in ochre on a brown ground, overall ochre background, by Margaret Cable, circular stamp mark & "Bison - 117A - M.Cable" **1,980**

Vase, 5 1/2" h., ovoid body w/rolled rim, decorated w/polychrome horizontal stripes, by Julia Mattson, ink-stamped & incised mark **495**

Vase, 5 1/2" h., slender ovoid w/ringed shoulder tapering to a short cylindrical neck w/closed rim, decorated w/incised cowboys w/lassos & "Why Not Minot" under a glossy blue glaze, by Julia Mattson, ink mark & incised mark **715**

Vase, 6" h., swelled cylindrical body tapering to wide flaring rim, decorated near the shoulder w/red & white daisies on long green stems, caramel ground, by Hildegarde Fried, 1924, ink stamp & "H.F." **3,300**

North Dakota Vase

Vase, 6 1/4" h., 7" d., spherical body w/wide shoulder band incised w/continuous scene of covered wagons pulled by oxen, shaded matte brown glaze, decorated by Margaret Cable, circular stamp & title "186, M. Cable" (ILLUS.) **2,530**

Vase, 7" h., shouldered slender ovoid body w/slightly flaring rim, decorated w/blue irises & green leaves on a shaded green ground, by Margaret Cable, ink mark & "MKC, 1916," **2,970**

Vase, 7 1/4" h., wide bulbous body tapering to short slightly flaring cylindrical neck, decorated w/large stylized purple flowers w/orange centers & green leaves on a brown ground, hand-carved by Julia Mattson, 1925, ink stamp & incised "M." (ILLUS.) **7,150**

North Dakota School of Mines Vase

Vase, 8 3/4" h., ovoid body tapering to wide cylindrical neck, large stylized excised brown daffodils & leaves on a dark brown ground, by F. Cunningham, 1950, ink stamp & incised signature **1,870**

Vase, 14" h., shouldered ovoid body tapering to a wide flaring neck, decorated w/large trees silhouetted against an orange sky, decorated by Margaret Cable, w/ink stamp mark & "M. Cable 1917" **9,350**

OHR (GEORGE) POTTERY

George Ohr, the eccentric potter of Biloxi, Mississippi, worked from about 1883 to 1906. Some think him to be one of the most expert throwers the craft will ever see. The majority of his works were hand-thrown, exceedingly thin-walled items, some of which have a crushed or folded appearance. He considered himself the foremost potter in the world and declined to sell much of his production, instead accumulating a great horde to leave as a legacy to his children. In 1972 this collection was purchased for resale by an antiques dealer.

GEO. E. OHR

BILOXI, MISS.

Ohr Pottery Marks

Bowl, 3 1/2 x 7 1/2", footed, bisque-fired free-form shape assymetrically pinched & folded, red & ivory marbleized clay, incised signature (one chip to edge) **$4,400**

Bowl, 4 1/2" d., 2 1/4" h., a wide flaring foot supports the squatty rounded body w/a flaring crimped rim, covered in a gunmetal volcanic glaze, die-stamped "G.E. OHR - Biloxi, Miss." **990**

Bowl, 4 3/4" d., 3 1/2" h., free-form collapsed body w/closed-in rim, covered in a speckled black & brown glaze, die-stamped "G.E. OHR - Biloxi, Miss.".......... **2,530**

Bowl-vase, footed squatty bulbous form w/the top sides heavily dimpled & folded toward the center, overall aventurine glaze, impressed "G.E. OHR - Biloxi, Miss.," 4" d., 3" h. **2,310**

Bowl-vase, footed oblong upright sides w/deeply pinched & folded sides, bisque scroddled clay, incised script signature, 6" w., 4" h. **3,190**

Chamberstick, a round cushion base tapering to a short cylindrical stem w/a cupped socket, a low fanned handle on the base, mottled greenish brown glaze, impressed "GEO E OHR Biloxi," 3" h. **460**

Chamberstick, wide footed domed bulbous base w/a deep in-body twist, tapering to a cylindrical neck w/flared rim, applied angular handle from the neck to the base, gunmetal & green exterior glaze, matte ochre interior glaze, incised "G.E. OHR," 3 1/2" d., 4" h. **2,310**

George Ohr Ewer and Pitcher

Ewer, a short flaring pedestal foot supports a ringed spherical base tapering from the round shoulder to a tall cylindrical neck w/wide incurved rim w/small pinched spout, angled handle from below rim to shoulder, covered in a mottled umber & mirrored black glaze, impressed marks "G.E. OHR - Biloxi, Miss." 7 3/4" h., 4 1/2" d. (ILLUS.) **2,750**

Model of a cabin on slats, pitch-roofed structure w/a diamond lattice roof design & a short round chimney, taupe-brown clay, signed "GEO. E OHR Biloxi, Miss.," 3" h. (in-the-making imperfections) **518**

Mug, footed bulbous angled ovoid body w/a squared tab handle pierced w/three openings, brown gunmetal glaze, impressed "G.E. OHR. - Biloxi, Miss.," 5 1/4" w., 3 1/2" h. **2,090**

Mug, Joe Jefferson-type, cylindrical form w/pinched handle, covered in an unusual salmon pink & green glossy glaze, inscribed "Hers (sic) your good health and all your family's - may they all live long and prosper - J.Jefferson," die-stamped "G.E. OHR - Biloxi, Miss. - 8-18-1896," 4" h... **1,210**

Pitcher, 3 1/2" h., 4 3/4" d., footed bulbous body w/flaring rim, pinched spout & C-scroll handle, covered in gunmetal volcanic glaze, die-stamped "G.E. OHR - Biloxi, Miss." (ILLUS.)................................ **1,430**

Pitcher, 6 1/2" h., 4" d., footed bulbous base below a double-funnel form body w/tapering sides below the tall flaring neck w/pinched rim spout, applied looped strap handle, bright pink, green, red & white sponged matte glaze, impressed "G.E.OHR - Biloxi, Miss.".......... **7,700**

Large Ohr Pitcher

Pitcher, 10" h., 7" d., footed tapering ovoid dimpled body w/a folded side & single looped ribbon handle, red, pink, cobalt blue, green, yellow & white sponged glaze, one chip & several minor nicks at rim, one small base chip, impressed "G.E. Ohr - Biloxi, Miss." & script signature (ILLUS.)... **44,000**

Puzzle mug, cylindrical w/large pierced holes around the molded rim above double bands of smaller holes, a pinched & twisted base band, stylized rabbit-form squared handle, mottled brown glaze, impressed "G. E. Ohr Biloxi, Miss.," 3 1/2" h.. **1,150**

Vase, 2 1/2" h., 3 3/4" d., wide squatty bulbous base w/flared & ruffled rim, covered in a dark bottle green & gunmetal glaze w/melt fissures, die-stamped "G.E. OHR - Biloxi, Miss.".................................... **825**

Vase, 4" h., 2 3/4" d., footed tapering cylindrical body w/rounded base, molded rings at neck, covered in a fine & unusual sponged raspberry, red & black matte & glossy glaze, die-stamped " G.E. OHR - Biloxi, Miss" **2,090**

Vase, 4" h., 3 1/4" d., footed, bulbous base w/pinched & folded rim, covered in fine & unusual sponged cobalt, raspberry, ochre & green glossy glaze, die-stamped "G.E. OHR - Biloxi, Miss" (two glaze flecks to rim) **2,970**

Vase, 4 1/4" h., slightly waisted cylindrical body w/upright pinched & scalloped rim & ribbon handles, covered in a rare cobalt blue, green & raspberry mottled glaze, die-stamped "G. E. OHR - Biloxi, Miss.".. **4,675**

Vase, 4 1/2" h., 4" d., footed free-form shape w/collapsed body, dimpled top & torn rim, covered in green & ochre speckled glaze, die-stamped "G.E. OHR - BILOXI" **8,250**

Vase, 4 3/4" h., a crimped rim on a cylindrical body w/thumbprints around the base, mottled black glaze, impressed "G.E. Ohr Biloxi, Miss.".................................... **1,380**

Vase, 5" h., free-form bisque-fired pale clay, a footring below the squatty bulbous body, pierced & dimpled around the sides, a tall neck w/torn & folded rim, early price tag mounted w/new wire, script signature **2,310**

Vase, 5" h., 4" d., bulbous ovoid body below a twisted & crumpled shoulder & a wide upright neck w/ragged-edged torn rim, overall green, mahogany, gunmetal & ochre speckled glaze, impressed "G.E. OHR - Biloxi, Miss." **5,500**

Vase, 6" h., flared foot below bulbous base w/deep in-body twists at shoulder, tapering to wide cylindrical neck, covered in limpid mirrored mahogany speckled glaze, die-stamped "G.E. OHR - Biloxi, Miss" **2,090**

Vase, 6" h., 4" d., footed ovoid body tapering to a wide short cylindrical neck w/a tightly crimped upright rim, raspberry, green, blue & grey sponged glaze, stamped "G.E. OHR - Biloxi, Miss." (touch-ups to nick on two rim tips) **4,400**

Ohr Pinched Neck Vase

Vase, 6 3/4" h., bulbous base w/tall upright tightly pinched neck, covered in a brown & caramel marbleized glossy glaze, die-stamped "G.E. OHR - Biloxi, Miss." (ILLUS.) **2,200**

OLD IVORY

Old Ivory china was produced in Silesia, Germany, in the late 1800s and takes its name from the soft white background coloring. A wide range of table pieces was made with the various patterns usually identified by a number rather than a name.

The following prices are averages for Old Ivory at this time. Rare patterns will command higher prices and there is some variance in prices geographically. These prices are also based on the item being perfect. Cups are measured across the top opening.

Basket, handled, No. U2, Deco patt. **$400**
Berry set: 10 1/2" d. master bowl & six small berries; No. 15, Clairon patt., the set **285**
Berry set: 9 1/2" master bowl & six small berries; No. 84, Empire patt., the set **250**
Bonbon, inside handle, No. 62, Florette patt., rare, 6" l. **450**
Bone dish, No. 16, Worcester patt., rare **400**

Bouillon cup & saucer, No. 16, Clairon patt., 3 1/2" d. **250**
Bowl, 5 1/2" d., No. 7, Clairon patt. **45**
Bowl, 6 1/2" d., No. 22, Clairon patt. **100**
Bowl, 9" d., No. 34, Empire patt. **150**
Bowl, 9" d., No. 69, Florette patt. **200**
Bowl, 10" d., No. 11, Clairon patt. **125**
Bowl, 10" d., No. 16, Clairon patt. **125**
Bun tray, oval w/open handles, No. 122, Alice patt., 10" l. **300**
Butter pat, No. 15, Mignon patt., 3 1/4" d. **150**
Cake plate, open-handled, No. 200, Deco patt., 9 1/2" h. **125**
Cake plate, tab-handled, No. U15, Florette patt., 9 1/2" d. **185**
Cake plate, open-handled, No. 10, Clairon patt., 10 1/2" d. **150**
Cake plate, open-handled, No. 17, Clairon patt., 10 1/2" d. **400**

Florette Cake Plate

Cake plate, tab-handled, No. 75, Florette patt. (ILLUS.) **250-300**
Cake set: 10 1/2" d. cake plate & six small serving plates; No. 69, Florette patt., the set **450**
Celery dish, No. 28, Clairon patt., 11 1/4" l. **150**
Center bowl, No. 84, Deco Variant patt., 12 1/2" d. **500**
Charger, No. 16, Clairon patt., 13" d. **300**

Various Florette Pattern Pieces

Charger, No. 44, Florette patt. (ILLUS. center back) **500-650**
Chocolate pot, cov., No. 44, Florette patt., rare, 9 1/2" h. (ILLUS. far right) **600-700**
Chocolate set: 9 1/2" h. cov. pot & six cups & saucers; No. 53, Empire patt., rare, the set **1,500**

Chocolate set: 9 1/2" h. cov. pot & six cups & saucers; No. 75, Empire patt., the set **900**

Chowder cup & saucer, No. U29, Eglantine patt., 4" d. **300**

Cider cup & saucer, No. 16, Clairon patt., 3" d. **150**

Coffeepot, cov., No. 84, Deco variant patt., 9" h. **1,200**

Empire Pattern Demitasse Coffeepot

Coffeepot, cov., demitasse, No. 123, Empire patt. (ILLUS.) **500-650**

Compote, 9" d., open, No. U11, Alice patt., rare **600**

No. 15 Clairon Cracker Jar

Cracker jar, cov., No. 15, Clairon patt., 8 1/2" h. (ILLUS.) **500**

Cracker jar, No. 44, Florette patt. (ILLUS. far left) **850-1,000**

Creamer & cov. sugar bowl, No. 122, Alice patt., pr. **250**

Creamer & cov. sugar bowl, No. 11, Clairon patt., 5 1/2" h., pr. **175**

Creamer & cov. sugar bowl, No. 202, Deco patt., pr. **185**

Creamer & cov. sugar bowl, service size, No. 84, Deco Variant patt., pr. **400**

Creamer & cov. sugar bowl, service size, No. U17, Eglantine patt., pr. **500**

Creamer & cov. sugar bowl, No. 76, Louis XVI patt., rare, pr. **300-400**

Cup & saucer, cov., bouillon-type, No. 73, Alice patt., rare, 3 1/2" d. **350**

Cup & saucer, No. U30, Alice variant w/Y border **65-75**

Cup & saucer, No. 16, Clairon patt., 3 1/4" d. **75**

Clairon Pattern Cup & Saucer

Cup & saucer, No. 90, Clairon patt. (ILLUS.) **75-95**

Cup & saucer, No. 203, Deco patt., 3 1/4" d. **95**

Cup & saucer, No. 82, Empire patt. **75-95**

Cup & saucer, No. 84, Empire patt., 3 1/4" d. **75**

Cup & saucer, 5 o'clock-type, No. 28, Empire patt., 3" d. **85**

Florette Pattern Cup & Saucer

Cup & saucer, No. 62, Florette patt. (ILLUS.) **150-250**

Demitasse cup & saucer, No. 16, Clairon patt., 2 1/2" d. **125**

Demitasse cup & saucer, No. 22, Clairon patt., 2 1/2" d. **200**

Deco Pattern Cup & Saucer & Teapot

Demitasse cup & saucer, No. 75, Deco Variant patt. (ILLUS. left) **125-140**

Demitasse cup & saucer, No. 5, Elysee patt., rare, 2 1/2" d. **175**

Demitasse pot, cov., No. 73, Clairon patt., 7 1/2" h. **525**

Demitasse pot, cov., No. 33, Empire patt., 7 1/2" h. **500**

Demitasse pot, cov., No. 62, Florette patt.,
    very rare, 7 1/2" h...................... **1,200**
Demitasse pot, No. 44, Florette patt.
    (ILLUS. second from right) **800-900**
Dish, tri-lobed, No. 202, Deco patt., 6" w. 95
Dish, tri-lobed, No. 204, Rivoli patt., 6" w. 175
Dresser tray, No. 90, Clairon patt.,
    11 1/2" l. 250
Dresser tray, No. 34, Empire patt. 250
Egg cup, No. 84, Eglantine patt., very rare,
    2 1/2" h. 500

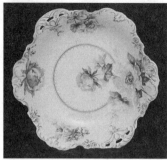

Eglantine Pattern Ice Cream Bowl

Ice cream bowl, No. 6, Eglantine patt.
    (ILLUS.) **300-400**
Jam dish, individual, No. 28, Alice patt. 150
Jam jar, cov., No. 137, Deco patt., 3 1/2" h. 250
Mayonnaise set, No. 10, Empire patt.,
    6 1/2" d., the set 275
Muffineer, No. 73, Louis XVI patt., 4" h. 485

Louis XVI Muffineer & Salt & Peppers

Muffineer, No. 84, Louis XVI patt. (ILLUS.
    left) **350-450**
Mustache cup & saucer, No. 16, Clairon
    patt., 3 1/2" d. 300
Mustache cup & saucer, No. 4, Elysee
    patt., 3 1/2" d. 450
Mustard pot, cov., No. 84, Carmen patt.,
    3 3/4" h. 325
Olive dish, No. 20, Florette patt., rare,
    6 1/2" l. 195
Pickle dish, No. 32, Empire, 8 1/2" l. 75
Pin tray, No. U22, Eglantine patt. 350
Pitcher, water, No. 84, Acanthus patt.
    (ILLUS. top of next column) **1,000-1,200**
Pitcher, 8" h., water, No. 11, Acanthus
    patt. 1,200
Plate, 7 1/2" d., No. 12, Clairon patt. 85
Plate, 8 1/2" d., No. 8, Clairon patt. 85
Plate, 9 1/2" d., dinner, No. 21, Clairon
    patt., rare.................................... 300
Plate, 8 1/2" d., No. 200, Deco patt. 75
Plate, 7 1/2" d., No. 4, Elysee patt.................... 65
Plate, 8 1/2" d., No. 15, Empire patt. 75

Acanthus Pattern Water Pitcher

Platter, 11 1/2" l., No. 22, Clairon patt............. 325
Platter, 13 1/2" l., No. 75, Alice patt. 300
Porringer, No. 82, Empire patt., 6 1/4" d. 175
Powder jar, cov., No. U22, Eglantine patt.,
    rare... 450
Ramekin & underplate, No. 11, Quadrille
    patt., rare, 4 1/2" d., 2 pcs. 500
Salt & pepper shakers, No. 44, Florette
    patt. (ILLUS. second from left) **150-250**
Salt & pepper shakers, No. 15, Louis XVI
    patt., pr. (ILLUS. right)...................... **100-125**
Salt & pepper shakers, No. 76, Louis XVI
    patt., 2 3/4" h., pr........................... 200
Shaving mug, No. 22, Clairon patt., rare,
    3 1/4" h...................................... 1,000
Soup tureen, cov., No. 84, Deco Variant
    patt., rare, 13" l............................. 2,500
Spoon rest, lay-down type, No. 204, Deco
    patt., 8 1/4" l. 250
Spooner, No. 40, Carmen patt., 4" h............... 400
Tazza, No. U2, Rivoli patt., rare, 9" d. 600
Tea cup & saucer, No. 4, Elysee patt.,
    3 1/4" d...................................... 95
Tea tile, No. 15, Alice patt., 6" sq. 225
Teapot, cov., No. 200, Deco patt., 8 1/2" l. 500
Teapot, cov., No. 75, Deco Variant patt.
    (ILLUS. right)............................... **500-600**
Toothpick holder, No. 15, Clairon patt.,
    2 1/4" h...................................... 295
Vase, 5" h., No. 134, Deco Variant patt........... 385
Vegetable dish, cov., No. 15, Clairon patt.,
    10 1/2" l. 1,000
Waste bowl, No. 28, Worcester patt., 5" d. 295

OWENS

*Owens pottery was the product of the J.B.
Owens Pottery Company, which operated in Ohio
from 1890 to 1929. In 1891 it located in Zanesville
and produced art pottery from 1896, introducing
"Utopian" wares as its first art pottery. The company switched to tile after 1907. Efforts to rebuild
after the factory burned in 1928 failed and the company closed in 1929.*

Owens Pottery Mark

Bowl, 3 1/2 x 11", Aborigine line, rounded sides w/flat rim, tan earthenware w/dark brown stripes & light & brown zigzag lines, interior w/dark brown glaze, incised "JBO" & mark No. 10...................... **$150**

Owens Ewer

Ewer, Utopian line, decorated w/yellow roses on a brown, green & amber ground, decorated by Sarah Timberlake, artist-initialed & impressed "Utopia, J.B. Owens, 181," minor crazing, 9 3/8" h. (ILLUS.) **303**

Owens Alpine Line Humidor

Humidor, cov., Alpine line, squatty bulbous body, cover w/molded rim & large domed finial, decorated w/h.p. scene of pipe & bag of tobacco, shaded brown ground, mark No. 13, 5 7/8" h.(ILLUS.)........ **750**
Jardiniere, Art Nouveau line, footed, wide tapering cylindrical body w/flaring rim, under-glaze gold swirl decoration on dark brown ground, impressed "J.B.

Owens" & "Art Nouveau," shape No. 1005, 7 1/2" h. **350**
Jardiniere, Cyrano line, footed waisted cylindrical body, squeeze bag applied filigree designs & beading at rim, dark brown glossy ground, unmarked, 8 1/4" h... **350**

Owens Delft Jardiniere

Jardiniere, Delft line, footed bulbous body w/slightly flaring rim, decorated w/typical Holland scene of a young girl & her mother standing near the water, a ship in the background, shaded blue ground, unmarked, 10 1/2" h. (ILLUS.)...................... **750**
Jug, Aborigine line, squatty bulbous base tapering to cylindrical neck & loop handle, tan & brown earthenware exterior, incised "JBO," shape No. 31, 5 1/8" h. **200**

Corona Line Model of Dog

Model of a dog, Whippet or Greyhound, sitting, wearing collar, glass eyes, shaded grey, Corona line, unmarked (ILLUS.)... **5,000**
Model of a rabbit, sitting animal w/raised ears, glass eyes, shaded grey & tan, Corona line, marked "Corona," shape No. 8873, 13 x 15".................................... **3,500**
Mug, Feroza line, cylindrical body w/C-form handle, molded uneven ground in iridescent deep red, shape No. 1108, 4 7/8" h. **450**
Pitcher, Embossed Lotus line, tapering cylindrical form w/incurved rim, pinched spout & C-form handle, cream ground

decorated w/embossed & slip-painted berries & leaves, marked "Lotus," shape No. X236, mark No. 10, 3" h. **250**

Owens Feroza Line Pitcher

Pitcher, tankard, 11 1/4" h., Feroza line, uneven molded ground w/mottled dark brownish iridescent finish, shape No. 1109 (ILLUS.)... **850**

Pitcher, tankard, 17" h., Onyx line, tapering cylindrical form w/ringed base, long D-form angled handle, shape No. 819, mark No. 8.. **650**

Teapot cov., Lotus line, Aladdin-type, domed cover w/button finial, shaded green w/floral decoration in green, pink & white, marked "Owens" & "Denny," shape No. 1255, 3 1/4 x 7" **450**

Tile, Arts & Crafts style, decoration w/acorns & oak leaves in grey, green & brown on tan ground, impressed Owens," 5 3/8 x 5 7/8"................................. **248**

Umbrella stand, Henri Deux line, baluster-form w/scalloped rim, portrait of woman & tan, white & light blue floral decoration on blue ground, unmarked, 22 1/4" h. **850**

Owens Aqua Verdi Vase

Vase, 3 7/8" h., Aqua Verdi line, short wide tapering cylindrical form w/three thick loop handles from rim to base, relief-molded lizard on textured variegated light to dark green ground (ILLUS.).............. **650**

Vase, 5" h., Onyx line, footed crescent-shaped body, mottled, striated brown, tan & cream ground, unmarked, shape No. 872 .... **250**

Vase, 5 1/2" h., Feroza line, bulbous ovoid body w/tapering shoulder flanked by large loop handles, closed mouth, uneven molded ground in iridescent mottled brownish black, shape No. 1090 ..... **450**

Vase, 5 3/4" h., Art Vellum line, tapering square form w/small molded rim, yellow & orange floral decoration on brown ground, shape No. 112, mark No. 13 .... **350**

Owens Cyrano Line Vase

Vase, 6 1/4" h., Cyrano line, compressed base tapering to wide slightly waisted cylindrical body flanked by large loop handles, decorated w/squeeze bag applied filigree lacy & floral design in white & tan w/beading at the base & rim, dark green glossy ground, unmarked, shape No. 357 (ILLUS.) **850**

Vase, 8 3/4" h., slightly swelled cylindrical body, Embossed Lotus line, dark brown ground decorated w/embossed & slip-painted berries & leaves, marked "Lotus," shape No. X220, mark No. 10 .... **600**

Vase, 9" h., Utopian line, footed tapering ovoid body w/flared rim, "First of Three Pharaoh's Horses," decorated by Hattie Eberlein, impressed Owens Utopian logo, artist's monogram in white slip on foot , shape No. 982,(some evidence of slightly cupped glaze).................................... **358**

Vase, 10" h., Opalesce line, footed bulbous ovoid body tapering to tall slender cylindrical neck w/flared rim, decorated w/Art Nouveau style metallic florals, marked "Owens," shape No. 1124 .... **850**

Owens Aborigine Line Vase

Vase, 8 3/4 x 11", Aborigine line, bulbous shouldered body tapering to wide cylindrical neck w/flat rim, light tan earthen-ware w/rust band & geometric decoration, chocolate brown rim & interior glaze, incised "JBO" (ILLUS.) **600**

Vase, 11 1/4" h., Oriental line, waisted cylindrical form w/rows of white & tan beading at rim & base & center band of lacy squeeze bag design in white & tan, dark brown ground, unmarked, shape No. 863... **350**

Vase, 16 1/2" h., Lotus line, compressed bulbous base tapering to tall cylindrical body w/slightly tapering neck & closed rim, decorated w/irises in rose, pink, purple & yellow w/green leaves against an ivory, grey & peach ground, artist-signed, impressed mark (harmless glaze flaws to top).. **1,540**

Wall pocket, Green Ware line, cornucopia-shaped w/scalloped rim, decorated w/relief-molded flowers & ribbon, marked "Owensart," 11" l. **400**

OYSTER PLATES

Oyster plates intrigue a few collectors. Oysters were shucked and the meat served in wells of these attractive plates specifically designed to serve oysters. During the late 19th century were made of fine china and majolica. Some plates were decorated in the realistic "trompe l'oeil" technique while others simply matched the pattern of a dinner service.

China, five-well, ivory ground w/white seaweed & gilt trim, one w/white ground & gilt seaweed, marked "Brownfields China for Tiffany and Co.," 9 1/4" d., set of 6 .... **$726**

Majolica, four-well, fan-shaped, turquoise w/pink & white wells, mark of George Jones & stamped "J.W. Boteler - June 16, 1874," collection label, 8 1/2 x 9 1/4" (minor glaze loss at rim)............................ **3,740**

Group of Victorian Oyster Plates

Majolica, six-well, one well molded as a large fish head, the others as fat oblong fish, round central well, brown & yellow w/green fish, England, 19th c., 9 3/4 x 10 1/4", pr. (ILLUS. back right) **1,540**

Majolica, six-well, ring of turquoise blue wells separated by molded brown & green seaweed w/a central shell-shaped sauce dish, George Jones, England, 19th c., repair to sauce dish, 10 1/2" d., pr. (ILLUS. back left) **2,860**

Majolica, twelve-well, round w/brown wells in the center surrounded by a flanged

rim w/a green ground & relief decoration of seaweed & shells, blue trim, Longchamp mark, France, late 19th c., minor flakes, 8 1/2" d. (ILLUS. front left) **495**

Majolica, twelve-well, turquoise ground w/ivory wells around the border & green leaves around the central well, probably French, 19th c., 14 3/4" d. (ILLUS. back center) **660**

Majolica, twenty-seven-well, lazy-Susan type, cobalt blue & mottled yellow w/molded green seaweed, three entwined fish finial, incised Mintons mark, England, 19th c., 10 x 12" (restoration to well rims) **13,200**

Porcelain, five-well, large shell form w/five oyster shell-shaped wells w/a small central well, each well decorated w/colorful scenes of birds & flowers w/gilt trim, artist-signed, Kutani ware, Japan, late 19th c., 9 1/4" d. (ILLUS. front right).................... **825**

Porcelain, five-well, ivory ground w/gilt border, Limoges, France, late 19th - early 20th c., 7 1/2" d., set of 4 .... **220**

Porcelain, six-well, pink & yellow w/shell decorations, trimmed in brown, unmarked, 9" d., set of 4 .... **220**

Porcelain, six-well, floral decoration on a white ground, green borders & gilt trim, Austria, late 19th - early 20th c., 8 1/2" d., set of 5 (minor flakes) **330**

Porcelain, six-well, floral-decorated wells on a green ground, incised "Karlsbad - Austria," late 19th - early 20th c., 9" d., set of 5 .... **4,125**

Porcelain, five-well, various shell & seaweed designs, Limoges, France, late 19th - early 20th c., 9" d., set of 6 .... **528**

Porcelain, six-well, solid white ground w/shells & basketweave in relief, marked "Longchamp - France," late 19th - early 20th c., 9 1/4" d., set of 6 (two chipped)....... **198**

Porcelain, five-well, octagonal, multicolored ground w/h.p. seaweed & shells, marked "Oscar Gutherz - Limoges," France, late 19th - early 20th c., 7 3/4" w., set of 7....................................... **1,155**

Porcelain, five-well, white ground w/pink floral decoration, marked "Karlsbad - Austria," late 19th - early 20th c., 8 1/4" d., set of 7 (minor gilt loss)................. **424**

PARIAN

Parian is unglazed porcelain in the biscuit stage, and takes its name from its resemblance to Parian marble used for statuary. Parian wares were made in this country and abroad through much of the last century and continue to be made.

Bust of Captain Matthew Webb, figure shown displaying sporting medals for swimming across the English Channel in 1875, bolted to a Parian pedestal base inscribed on reverse "Published as the Act directs by J.S. Crapper of Hanley & C. Marsh of Wolston, by special consent and assistance of Captain Matthew Webb. December 6th, 1875," 19th c., 25" h. **$460**

Figure group, Naomi and Her Daughter, modeled on an oval base, attributed to John Bell, England, impressed title, no factory mark, 1865, 12 3/4" h. (hand restored, nick to bag, slight loss to ribbon) 57

Figure Group of Civil War Soldiers

Figure group, based on Rogers Group entitled "One More Shot," attributed to Copeland, two Civil War soldiers, one standing & one wounded & wrapping a bandage on his leg, set on a festooned circular base, unmarked, ca. 1865, 20 1/2" h. (ILLUS.).................................... **5,175**

Figure of William Shakespeare

Figure of William Shakespeare, full-bodied figure modeled in traditional pose, standing & resting his right elbow on a pile of books & a script atop a column molded in relief w/theatrical emblems, all on a shaped rectangular base, ca. 1850, minor chips to bows of shoes, 16 3/4" h. (ILLUS.).. **575**

PARIS & OLD PARIS

China known by the generic name of Paris and Old Paris was made by several Parisian factories from the 18th through the 19th century; some of it is marked and some is not. Much of it was handsomely decorated.

Cachepot, cov., tapering cylindrical form w/parcel-gilt & polychrome floral decoration surrounding landscape vignette cartouches, 19th c., 7 3/4" h............................ **$488**

Cachepots, tapering cylindrical body lion's mask handles & decorated w/ gilt floral scrollwork & cartouches on green & white ground, ca. 1840, 7 1/4" d., 8 3/8" h., pr. **1,400**

Cachepots, footed, tapering cylindrical body w/enamel decorated landscape scene of children, 19th c., green ground, 7 3/4" d., 7 1/2" h., pr. **805**

Paris Figural Centerpiece

Centerpiece, round scrolled foot below fan-shaped gilt ground foliate molded body w/scalloped rim & loop end handles, decorated in relief w/male & female figures in a landscape setting, 19th c., 19" w., 11 3/4" h. (ILLUS.)......................... **1,265**

Desk set: graduated cylindrical pots & covers, 2 3/4" h., 3 1/4" h. & 3 1/2" h., on a 7 3/8 x 9 1/2" oval tray; each piece w/heavy gilt borders & covers, each decorated w/early 19th c. figures in landscapes, 19th c., the set **2,070**

Fruit compotes, figural, gilt & green enamel-decorated openwork bowls supported by three cherub figures standing on a triangular base, 10 5/8" h., the pair **10,925**

Luncheon set: 11 5/8" l. cov. oval soup tureen & undertray, 8" d. cov. vegetable bowl, a sauceboat w/attached undertray, cov. sauce tureen w/attached undertray, 4 3/8" h. tazza, 9" h. cov. coffeepot, seven 8 3/8" d. plates, 9 1/2" d. cake plate & 11" l., 13 1/4" l. & 22 1/4" l. oval platters; each enamel-decorated w/butterflies & floral sprays, overall gilt trim, late 19th c., the set...................................... **978**

Sweetmeat baskets, reticulated body & out-curving rim, decorated w/floral sprays, 19th c., 4 1/4" d., pr. **126**

Urns, pedestal foot, two-handled, flared rim, decorated w/floral cartouches, 19th c., 5" d., 6 3/4" h., pr. **475**

Vase, 10 1/2" h., swelled cylindrical lower body tapering to a tall ringed cylindrical neck, the sides w/large oval reserves, one decorated w/the Eiffel Tower, the other w/a bust portrait of a Turkish prince, the neck decorated w/stylized leafy flowering vines, late 19th c. **518**

Vases, 13" h., scrolled handles, pink ground decorated w/colored & gilt-trimmed florals, late 19th c., pr. **288**

Vases, 14 1/2" h., footed baluster-form w/flaring ringed neck, a dark blue ground decorated on the front w/a large oval panel of a couple in 18th c. attire in a garden, the back w/a floral cartouche, a band of gilt florals around the neck & gilt bands at top & base, late 19th c., pr. **2,645**

Vases, 17 1/2" h., footed squatty bulbous wide lower body w/a wide shoulder tapering to a tall slender trumpet neck, each w/a colorful continuous landscape painted around the body & lower neck, one w/a view of the Bospherus, the other a view of the Grand Canal, each w/a gilt beaded ring around the neck below a pink upper section w/ornate white scroll-ing, gilt trim, late 19th c., pr. **6,325**

PAUL REVERE POTTERY

This pottery was established in Boston, Massachusetts, in 1906, by a group of philanthropists seeking to establish better conditions for underprivileged young girls of the area. Edith Brown served as supervisor of the small "Saturday Evening Girls Club" pottery operation which was moved, in 1912, to a house close to the Old North Church where Paul Revere's signal lanterns had been placed. The wares were mostly hand decorated in mineral colors and both sgraffito and molded decorations were employed. Although it became popular, it was never a profitable operation and always depended on financial contributions to operate. After the death of Edith Brown in 1932, the pottery foundered and finally closed in 1942.

Paul Revere Marks

Bowl, 4 1/2" d., 3 3/8" h., swollen form w/glossy green glaze & red-tinted rim, signed "S.E.G. 3.23 - SJM" **$173**

Bowl, 5 1/2" d., 2 1/2" h., squatty rounded sides w/a closed wide rim, the upper half decorated w/a continuous landscape scene w/brown trees outlined in black on a yellow ground & white sky, yellow on the lower half (repaired chips) **495**

Paul Revere Landscape Bowl and Vase with Daffodils

Bowl, 6" d., center medallion design of a stylized landscape scene in cuerda seca, w/brown tree outlined in black, against a blue sky, surrounded by dark blue band, light blue border (ILLUS.) **990**

Center bowl, decorated w/white geese in cuerda seca against a band of yellow & brown, white interior w/matte green exterior, ca. 1912, ink mark, SACB paper label, SEG Bowl Shop label & ink mark, 4 1/2 x 11 3/4" (tight hairline from rim) **4,950**

Charger, round, a narrow rim band decorated w/green trees against a blue sky on an ivory ground, ivory center, signed "S.E.G. - E.T. - 5-17," 1917, 12 1/2" d. (minor inside footring chips) **660**

Creamer, decorated w/incised windmills in matte shades of green & cream, marked "SEG" & faint artist's initials, 3 1/4" h. (hairline) **403**

Paul Revere Plate w/Camel Border

Plate, decorated around the rim w/camel design, marked "S.E.G." (ILLUS.) **1,870**

Plate, 6 1/2" d., border decorated w/h.p. pine cones in brown & green, white matte ground, ink mark "SEG - 8.17" **165**

Plate, 6 1/2" d., the border band w/a decoration of a white hens & chicks spaced around the rim on a wide yellow band, white center, artist-signed, dated "9-13"....... **715**

Tumbler, 3 1/4" d., tapering cylindrical form, decorated below rim w/h.p. frieze of squirrels in blue on white crackled ground, ca. 1912, ink mark "SEG - 91.7.12" (two nicks to rim) **468**

Vase, 3 7/8" h., cylindrical w/flared rim, glossy cobalt blue glaze, impressed mark **144**

Vase, 7 1/2" h., wide bulbous ovoid body tapering sharply to a flat mouth w/closed-in rim, covered in mottled flowing medium green microcrystalline glaze, ink mark & paper label **385**

Vase, 10" h., slightly swelled tapering cylindrical body w/a wide mouth, decorated around the shoulder w/incised & painted daffodils in cream & yellow w/green stems & leaves, light blue sky beneath cream band at top, impressed mark, paper label, artist initialed & dated "4-24" (ILLUS. right) **3,575**

Vase, 10" h., swelled cylindrical body w/wide flat mouth, medium blue semi-matte glaze, die-stamped mark & ink-marked "GM -7.25" **330**

Wall pocket, pocket-form w/slightly flared rim tapering to base, dark sage green glaze, marked "S.E.G." & Paul Revere Pottery paper label, 4" w., 6" l. **288**

PENNSBURY POTTERY

Henry Below and his wife Lee founded the Pennsbury Pottery in Morrisville, Pennsylvania in 1950. The Belows chose the name because William Penn's home was nearby. Lee, a talented artist who designed the well-known Rooster pattern, almost the entire folk art designs and the Pennsylvania German blue and white hand-painted dinnerware, had been affiliated with Stangl Pottery of Trenton, New Jersey. Mr. Below had learned pottery making in Germany and became an expert in mold making and ceramic engineering. He, too, had been associated with Stangl Pottery and when he and Lee opened Pennsbury Pottery, several workers from Stangl joined the Belows. Mr. Below's death in 1959 was unexpected and Mrs. Below passed away in 1968 after a long illness. Pennsbury filed for bankruptcy in October, 1970. In 1971 the pottery was destroyed by fire.

During Pennsbury's production years, an earthenware with a high temperature firing was used. Most of the designs are a sgraffito-type similar to Stangl's products. The most popular coloring, a characteristic of Pennsbury, is the smear-type glaze of light brown after the sgraffito technique has been used. Birds are usually marked by hand and most often include the name of the bird. Dinnerware followed and then art pieces, ashtrays and teapots. The first dinnerware line was Black Rooster followed by Red Rooster. There was also a line known as Blue Dowry which had the same decorations as the brown folk art pattern but the decorations were done in cobalt.

Pennsbury Pennsbury
Pottery Pottery

Pennsbury Pottery Marks

Canister, cov., Black Rooster patt., w/black rooster finial, front reads "Flour," 9" h......... **$185**

Cup & saucer, Black Rooster patt., cup 2 1/2" h., saucer 4" d. **55**

Desk basket, Two Women Under Tree patt., 5" h. **75**

Model of chickadee, head down, on irregular base, model no. 111, signed R.B., 3 1/2" h. **140**

Mug, beer-type, Barber Shop Quartet patt. **35**

Mug, beer, Amish patt., dark brown rim & bottom w/dark brown applied handle, 5" h. **38**

Commemorative Pie Plate

Pie plate, Dutch Haven commemorative, birds & heart in center, inscribed around the rim "When it comes to Shoo-Fly Pie - Grandma sure knew how - t'is the Kind of Dish she used - Dutch Haven does it now," 9" d. (ILLUS.) **125**

Pitcher, 5" h., Delft Toleware patt., fruit & leaves, white body w/fruit & leaves outlined in blue, blue inside **95**

Amish Pattern Pitcher

Pitcher, 7 1/4" h., Amish patt. w/interlocked pretzels on reverse (ILLUS.) **105**

Plaque, commemorative, "What Giffs, what ouches you?," reverse marked "NFB-PWC Philadelphia, PA 1960," drilled for hanging, 4" d. (ILLUS.) **30**

Plaque, Rooster patt., "When the cock crows the night is all," drilled for hanging, 4" d. **40**

Commemorative Plaque

Plaque, shows woman holding Pennsbury cookie jar, marked "It is Whole Empty," drilled for hanging, 4" d. **35**

Plaque with Amish Couple Kissing

Plaque, Amish man & woman kissing over cow, drilled for hanging, 8" d. (ILLUS.)........... **87**
Plate, 6" d., Black Rooster patt. **25**

Plate with Courting Buggy

Plate, 8" d., Courting Buggy patt. (ILLUS.)......... **75**

Plate with Red Rooster Pattern

Plate, 10" d., Red Rooster patt. (ILLUS.) **48**
Relish tray, Black Rooster patt., five-section, each w/different scene, Christmas-tree shape, 14 1/2" l., 11" w **220**

Wall pocket, donkey & clown w/dark green border, ivory center, 6 1/2" sq. **105**

PETERS & REED

In 1897 John D. Peters and Adam Reed formed a partnership to produce flowerpots in Zanesville, Ohio. Formally incorporated as Peters and Reed in 1901, this type of production was the mainstay until after 1907 when they gradually expanded into the art pottery field. Frank Ferrell, a former designer at the Weller Pottery, developed the "Moss Aztec" line while associated with Peters and Reed and other art lines followed. Though unmarked, attribution is not difficult once familiar with the various lines. In 1921, Peters and Reed became Zane Pottery which continued in production until 1941.

Peters & Reed Mark

Ewer, decorated w/lion's head w/grape-vine, 11" h. **$160**
Pitcher, cavalier decoration **125**
Planter, hanging-type, Moss Aztec line, signed "Ferrell," 9 x 13" **325**
Vase, 6" h., tripod base, glossy brown glaze... **160**
Vase, 8" h., Moss Aztec line **95**
Vase, 8 3/8" h., footed bulbous base tapering to slightly flared rim, decorated w/high glaze Chromal landscape scene in rich shades of blue, rust, cream, green & cobalt, unmarked **440**

Moss Aztec Vase & Wall Pocket

Vase, 9 3/4" h., Moss Aztec line, tapering cylindrical body decorated w/relief-molded pine cone decoration on matte brown ground w/green tinting, unmarked (ILLUS. right)... **330**
Vase, 10" h., Moss Aztec line, tall slender waisted cylindrical form w/large heavily embossed triangular Art Nouveau-style blossoms around the top w/vines & leafy vines down the sides & around the bottom, greenish brown overall glaze **385**

Wall pocket, Egyptian line, matte green glaze.. **225**

Wall pocket, sprigged-on floral trim, glossy brown glaze.. **135**

Wall pocket, conical, decorated at the top w/band of relief-molded Art Nouveau style with poppies, matte brown ground w/green tinting, designed by Frank Ferrell & artist-signed, 9 1/4" h. (ILLUS. left)..... **138**

PEWABIC

Mary Chase Perry (Stratton) and Horace J. Caulkins were partners in this Detroit, Michigan pottery. Established in 1903, Pewabic Pottery evolved from their Revelation Pottery, "Pewabic" meaning "clay with copper color" in the language of Michigan's Chippewa Indians. Caulkins attended to the clay formulas and Mary Perry Stratton was artistic creator of forms & glaze formulas, eventually developing a wide range of colors for her finely textured glazes. The pottery's reputation for fine wares and architectural tiles enabled it to survive the depression years of the 1930s. After Caulkins died in 1923, Mrs. Stratton continued to be active in the pottery until her death, at age ninety-four, in 1961. Her contributions to the art pottery field are numerous.

Pewabic Pottery Mark

Bowl, 8 1/2" d., 2 1/2" h., low canted sides w/incurved rim, the sides covered w/embossed lily pads, centered at the shoulder w/ring handles under a flowing matte green glaze, impressed mark........ **$3,300**

Box, cov., rectangular w/flat corners, center of lid w/relief-molded antelope, iridescent cream, yellow & green glaze, impressed "Pewabic Detroit," 4 3/4" w., 1 7/8" h... **358**

Vase, 3 1/2" h., 5 1/4" d., wide bulbous ovoid body w/a wide shoulder tapering to a wide flat molded rim, black, green & lavender lustred glaze, impressed circular mark... **495**

Vase, miniature, 3 3/4" h., 2 1/2" d., ovoid base sharply tapering to wide cylindrical neck, iridescent cobalt glaze, impressed mark.. **385**

Vase, 3 3/4" h., 4" d., baluster-form body w/wide cylindrical neck covered in a lustered striated glaze in purple & green, unmarked.. **825**

Vase, 5" h., 3 3/4" d., bottle-shaped, covered in a lustered celadon & blush glaze, circular die-stamped mark............................. **495**

Vase, 5" h., 4 1/2" d., footed w/angular ovoid sides, tapering shoulder w/flaring neck, covered w/an excellent red metallic luster glaze w/light green lowlights, unmarked.. **550**

Vase, 5" h., 5" d., a cylindrical foot supporting a wide short flaring cylindrical body w/a wide shoulder tapering sharply to a short flared neck, overall purple mirror glaze, impressed circular mark **770**

Vase, 5 1/2" h., 5 1/2" d., bulbous ovoid body w/a rounded shoulder tapering to a wide short flaring neck, overall streaky turquoise & taupe lustred glaze, impressed circular mark **715**

Vase, 6 1/2" h., 4 1/4" d., footed bulbous ovoid body w/a rounded shoulder to the wide, short cylindrical neck w/flaring rim covered in a mirrored purple, lavender & green glaze, circular die-stamped mark **880**

Vase, 8" h., footed spherical lower body below a wide trumpet neck, metallic blue, green & gunmetal overall lustre glaze, impressed mark **605**

Large Pewabic Vase and Ovoid Vase

Vase, 8" h., wide baluster-form body w/a wide flat rim, embossed w/large flowers & leaves under a flowing matte green glaze, impressed mark (ILLUS.)............... **6,325**

Vase, 8" h., 6" d., baluster-form w/the wide shoulder tapering to a short rolled neck, overall lustered dark blue glaze, impressed mark... **825**

Vase, 8 1/2" h., 4 1/2" d., bulbous ovoid body w/short molded rim, lustered burgundy & celadon glaze over a ridged body, circular die-stamped mark, paper label (ILLUS.) **1,650**

PHOENIX BIRD & FLYING TURKEY PORCELAIN

The phoenix bird, a symbol of immortality and spiritual rebirth, has been handed down through Egyptian mythology as a bird that consumed itself by fire after 500 years and then rose again, renewed, from its ashes. This bird has been used to decorate Japanese porcelain designed for export for more than 100 years. The pattern incorporates a blue design of the bird, variously known as the "Flying Phoenix," the "Flying Turkey" or the "Ho-o," stamped on a white ground. It became popular with collectors because there was an abundant supply since the ware was produced for a long period of time. Pieces can be found marked with Japanese characters, with a "Nippon" mark, or a "Made in Japan" mark or "Occupied Japan" mark. Though there are several variations to the pattern and border, we have lumped them together since values seem to be quite comparable. A word of caution to collectors: Phoenix Bird pattern is still being produced.

Bowl, 4 3/4" d. **$5**
Chocolate pot, cov., scalloped shape **125**
Creamer & cov. sugar, 2 3/4" h., pr. **20**
Cup & saucer, demitasse **12**

Phoenix Bird Cup & Saucer

Cup & saucer (ILLUS.) **15**
Egg cup, double **8**
Plate, 6" d. **4**
Plate, 7 1/4" d. **6**
Plate, 8 1/2" d. **10**
Plate, dinner, 9 1/2" d. **45**
Platter, 15" l., oval, dark blue, Nippon mark **110**
Salt & pepper shakers, pr. **11**
Teapot, cov., individual size **24**
Tumbler, 2 5/8" h. **12**

PICKARD

Pickard, Inc., making fine decorated china today in Antioch, Illinois, was founded in Chicago in 1894 by Wilder A. Pickard. The company now makes its own blanks but once only decorated those bought from other potteries, primarily from the Havilands and others in Limoges, France.

Pickard Mark

Bowl, 10" d., h.p. blackberries, raspberries, grapes & blossoms, artist-signed **$495**
Cake plate w/open handles, Classic Ruins by Moonlight patt., 10 1/2" d. **275**
Candlesticks, overall engraved gold florals, 9" h., pr. **250**
Chocolate cup & saucer, Haviland blank, "Raised Gold Daisy," artist-signed, ca. 1905 .... **60**
Coffeepot, cov., tankard-type, tall tapering cylindrical body w/a long gold swan's-neck spout & long gold C-scroll handle, small domed cover w/gold knob finial, the cream body decorated around the top w/two wide gold bands overlapped by long looping green tendrils & small purple blossoms, pearlized finish, signed under spout, ca. 1903-05, 8 3/4" h. **330**
Dish, leaf-shaped, overall gold w/etched gold design, 3 1/2 x 5 1/2" **125**
Lemonade set: pitcher & eight tumblers; the wide waisted cylindrical tankard pitcher w/a rim spout & C-scroll handle,

plain cylindrical tumblers, all decorated overall w/the gold Encrusted Honeysuckle patt., unsigned, the set **1,650**
Pitcher, lemonade, 6 1/4" h., bulbous ovoid body tapering to a flat ring, gold angled handle, large pink carnations on golden stems around the sides on a white ground w/gold bands at the rim & bottom, artist-signed, 1905-10 mark **450**

Fine Early Pickard Lemonade Pitcher

Pitcher, lemonade, 6 1/2" h., squatty bulbous ovoid body tapering to a scalloped rim w/wide arched spout, C-form gold handle, wide gold scrolls & red gooseberries w/green leaves on a white ground, Gooseberries Conventional patt., artist-signed, 1903-05 mark (ILLUS.)... **700**
Vase, 7 1/2" h., floral-decorated in the Art Nouveau style w/enamels & gilt trim, printed mark, ca. 1900 .... **288**

PIERCE (HOWARD) PORCELAINS

Howard Pierce opened a small studio in 1941 in Claremont, California. Having worked with William Manker also of Claremont, it is sometimes possible to see Manker's influence in some of Pierce's early work. Always being a studio potter with a tremendous talent (creating his own designs, making molds, firing and painting the items) collectors felt the loss when Howard Pierce died in February, 1994. Prices for his pieces have escalated far above what anyone would have imagined.

Wildlife and animals played a large part in Howard and Ellen Pierce's life with squirrels coming up to their window to be fed from their hands. They lived surrounded by these and other charming creatures. Many of Howard's creations came from watching them. He made roadrunners, monkeys, raccoons, an assortment of eagles, panthers, seals, geese, and many more.

However, his talent did not stop with wildlife nor animals. Over time he created nativity scenes, vases, bowls, St. Frances figures, three piece angel sets, tiles, advertising items and more. A set of three individual angels had one of the shortest runs of any creation Howard produced. They were difficult to make and time consuming. Naturally, they are valued higher than most pieces because of their scarcity. The angels with black faces are even more difficult to find; fewer of them were made.

Howard used various materials to create his pieces: Polyurethane (which caused him an allergic reaction), Cement, Wedgwood-type Jasperware, Mount St. Helens Ash (use caution not to confuse this treatment with the rough textured pieces), Gold Leaf, Pewter, Copper, and, of course, Porcelain.

Due to Howard's health, Howard and Ellen Pierce destroyed all the molds they had created over fifty years. This occurred in 1992 but it was less than a year before Howard began to make pieces again. In 1993, he purchased a small kiln and began to work on a limited schedule. He created smaller versions of his larger pieces and collectors practically stood in line to buy them. These pieces are stamped simply "Pierce."

Howard Pierce Marks

Bowl, 7 1/4" d., 4 1/4" h., fluted body flaring to a fluted rim, Manker influence, pale & deep blue w/black accents, incised mark, "Pierce 1983" in script **$100**

Howard Pierce Bowl

Bowl, 13" l., 2" h., free-form, black outside, speckled black & white inside, 1950s (ILLUS.).. **75**

Candleholders, comma-shaped, high gloss grey glaze, 2 3/4" h., pr...................... **100**

Figure group, boy standing w/head bent & left arm extended to feed dog seated at his left side, nondescript mottled brown glaze, marked "Howard Pierce," 5" h. **85**

Figure group, three monkeys stacked on top of one another, black, one-piece, Model No. 300P, 15" h. **275**

Pierce Owls in a Tree

Figure group, two owls in a tree, seated on branches, three open branches for small flowers, dull dark brown tree, light & dark brown owls, larger, unusual size for Pierce owls in tree, stamp mark "Howard Pierce," tree, 6" w., 13" h., large owl, 6" h., small owl, 3 1/2" h. (ILLUS.)................. **240**

Figure of native woman, w/long body, short legs, arms behind her back, dark brown glaze w/mottled brown skirt, hard-to-find, 3 1/2" w., 16 1/2" h. **285**

Figures of Hawaiian boy & girl, overall black bodies w/green mottled pants on boy, green mottled grass skirt on girl, both w/hands in Hula dance position, 1950s, boy, 7" h., girl, 6 3/4" h., pr. **185**

Jug, bulbous body w/small pouring spout & small finger hold, brown mottled rough-textured glaze, stamp mark "Howard Pierce," 5 3/4' h. **110**

Magnet, model of a dinosaur, gloss grey glaze, 3" l., 1 1/2" h. **75**

Model of bear, brown, 7" l................................. **85**

Model of circus horse, head down, tail straight, leaping position w/middle of body supported by small, round center base, light blue w/cobalt accents, experimental glaze, 7 1/2" l., 6 1/2" h **185**

Model of hippo, standing, short tail, bulbous body, large nose & mouth, small ears & eyes, very distinct features, dark grey bottom, mottled grey top, 1950s, stamp marked "Howard Pierce Porcelain," 9 3/4" l., 3" h. **185**

Model of panther, pacing position, brown glaze, 11 1/2" l., 2 3/4" h. **250**

Model of skunk, rough textured matte glaze, 6" h. **125**

Models of birds, seated, heads up, nondescript bodies except for eyes & beaks, black satin-matte glaze w/orangish red breasts, stamp mark "Howard Pierce," large, 4 1/2" h., medium, 3" h., small, 1 3/4" h., the set **165**

Howard Pierce Dogs w/Drooping Ears

Models of dogs w/drooping ears, dark & light brown, 8" h., & 6" h., pr. (ILLUS.) **175**

Models of fish, each on a half-circle base, dark brown bodies w/speckled bases & fins, large fish, 6" h., medium fish, 4 3/4" h., small fish, 3" h., the set................ **165**

Models of giraffes, brown & white, 1950s, 9" h., 10" h., pr. **215**

Models of monkeys, grey, pr. **165**

Pencil holder, nude women in relief around outside, tan & brown glaze, one year limited production, 1980, 3 1/2" d., 4 1/4" h. **160**

Planter, half-circle alcove in gold leaf w/white bisque angel holding songbook & standing in alcove, hard-to-find, 7" h. **175**

Howard Pierce Sugar Bowl

Sugar bowl, open, Wedgwood-type white bisque lamb motif, pale blue matte handle & outer edges, produced in 1950s, 2 3/4" h. (ILLUS.).. **60**

Vase, 9" h., tapering body w/a flaring neck & stretched rim, brown bottom half of body & neck, yellow mid-section of body & interior, stamp mark, "Howard Pierce," & copyright symbol, hard-to-find color combination.. **90**

Wall plaque, rectangular, modernistic birds in relief, pale green background w/darker green birds, cement, 19" l., 1/2" deep, 6 1/4" h. **250**

Whistle, bird-shaped w/hole at tail, grey w/white textured glaze, 3 1/2" h. **100**

Whistle, snake crawling w/body forming an "M" shape, brown w/white glaze, 3 1/4" l., 2 3/4" h. **125**

PISGAH FOREST POTTERY

Walter Stephen experimented with making pottery shortly after 1900 with his parents in Tennessee. After their deaths in 1910, he eventually moved to the foot of Mt. Pisgah in North Carolina where he became a partner of C.P. Ryman. Together they built a kiln and a shop but this partnership was dissolved in 1916. During 1920 Stephen again began to experiment with pottery and by 1926 had his own pottery and equipment. Pieces are usually marked and may also be signed "W. Stephen" and dated. Walter Stephen died in 1961 but work at the pottery still continues, although on a part-time basis.

Pisgah Forest Marks

Pisgah Forest Bowl-Vase and Cameo Mug

Bowl, 5 1/4" d., Cameo Ware, round, slightly curved sides, covered wagon scene in white on matte olive green ground, decorated by Walter Stephen, ca. 1953, marked "1953 Cameo Stephen Longpine Ardenne" on base & "Stephen" in white slip on side, 5 1/4" d., 2 1/4" h...................................... **$138**

Bowl-vase, wide squatty bulbous body w/a wide shoulder tapering to a wide rolled rim, covered in white & umber glaze w/white & blue crystals, embossed mark & dated 1941, 6" d., 4 1/2" h. (ILLUS.)......... **440**

Creamer, Cameo Ware, bulbous shape w/small pinched spout & C-form handle, scene of covered wagon pulled by oxen on matte olive green ground, decorated by Walter Stephen, ca. 1953, Longpine Ardenne mark, artist's name in white slip, paper label from Allanstand Mountain Crafts, Asheville, N.C. on bottom, 3 1/8" h. **220**

Mug, Cameo Ware, white relief landscape scene of trees & a cabin in the mountains against a teal blue ground, ca. 1949, embossed "Stephen," 3 1/2 x 4" (ILLUS.)... **303**

Teapot, cov., Cameo Ware, bulbous body w/inset lid w/button finial, short spout & C-form handle, pioneer family & cov. wagon scene in heavy white slip on medium blue ground, decorated by Walter Stephen, ca. 1953, Longpine Ardenne mark & date on bottom, artist's name on side, 5" h. **303**

Vase, 5 1/2" h., 5 1/2" d., wide bulbous body w/short cylindrical neck, celadon & pink glaze w/large blooming crystals, embossed mark, 1949 .... **990**

Vase, 6 1/4" h., trumpet form body, grey & beige glaze w/densely-packed crystals, pink interior, embossed mark (some bubbles to glaze)... **385**

Vase, 7 1/4" h., wide shoulder tapering to the base, extended neck, crystallized blue glaze over a mustard yellow ground, raised mark **546**

Vase, 8 3/4" h., 5 1/2" d., baluster-form w/short cylindrical neck & flaring rim, cream & celadon flambé glaze w/blue & white crystals near base, pink interior, shaved mark.. **715**

Vase, 9" h., baluster-form w/short cylindrical neck & flaring rim, white, celadon & blue crystalline glaze, pink interior, embossed mark & dated 1949 .... **1,100**

QUIMPER

This French earthenware pottery has been made in France since the end of the 17th century and is still in production today. Because the colorful decoration on this ware, predominantly of Breton peasant figures, is all hand-painted and each piece is unique, it has become increasingly popular with collectors in recent years. Most pieces offered today date from about the mid-19th century to the present. Modern potteries continue to operate today and contemporary examples are available in gift shops.

Quimper Marks

Delft-style Bonboniere

Bonboniere (candy dish), cov., long low rectangular form w/cut corners, overall blue on white Delft-style floral & leaf decoration, Henriot Quimper marked in blue, mint, 5 x 10 1/2", 4 1/2" h. (ILLUS.)............ **$500**

Bowls, 5 1/4" d., berry, center decorated w/a traditional peasant man or lady surrounded by a border band of floral sprig garland, HB Quimper cz 176, mint, set of 6 250

Brandy set: 6 1/2 x 7" keg supported on a wooden frame w/six small cups hanging from frame; "Ivoire Corbeille" patt., keg decorated w/a bust portrait of a man one on side & a lady on the other, Henriot Quimper 101, mint, the set.............................. 70

Bust of a baby, Modern Movement, modeled sipping from a bowl, crest of the town of Brest on interior of bowl, Henriot Quimper & C. Maillard marks, mint, 5" w., 2 1/2" h. 160

Butter knife, stainless steel blade, handle decorated w/a peasant lady on one side & a reserve of florals on the other, unsigned, mint, 4 1/2" l. 30

Calottes (flat European soup plates), each decorated in various shades of blue on a cream ground in a geometric "snowflake" style design, Henriot Quimper 90, overall excellent, 9" d., set of 4 100

Figural Quimper Candlesticks

Candlesticks, figural, Modern Movement, each in the form of a standing man posing w/a pot atop his head forming the candle socket, yellow-glazed ground w/green-dotted shirt, HB Quimper France, excellent, 7 3/4" h., pr. (ILLUS.)...... **325**

Charger, wooden, round w/serrated rim, decorated w/an interior cottage scene of a lady making crepes over an open fire, rich Modern Movement colors in traditional Paul Fouillen palette, by Paul Fouillen, excellent, rare large size, 15 3/4" d. **750**

Quimper Faience Charger

Charger, faience central polychrome landscape scene w/figures playing Bocce, floral banded borders, signed "d'apres Deyrolle and Heriot Quimper," ca. 1930, France, 18" d. (ILLUS.) **1,035**

Christmas ornament, round ball decorated w/a peasant lady & florals, dated 1986, HB-Henriot mark, mint......................... 20

Cigarette holder, special commission from "Camel" cigarettes, features a brown camel on each side w/palm trees on the corners, Henriot Quimper France 96, very good, 3 1/2" l., 3" h. (fine hairline) 275

Coffeepot, cov., yellow ground decorated w/a peasant man & lady w/floral sprays, Macy's (in a star) indicating a commissioned piece, 8" h. (finial broken & reglued) 100

Dish, shell-shaped, Demi-Fantasie patt., scene of full-facing man leaning on a walking stick w/floral sprays at either side, HR Quimper mark, 5 x 7 1/2" (small piece off corner reglued)..................... 55

Doll dishes, decorated w/peasants w/florals on either side, HB Quimper France w/ artist's initials, mint, 6" d., set of 6 .... **125**

Doll dishes, each piece w/a pink glaze decorated w/a colorful rooster in the center & a blue sponged rim, unsigned but attributable to Henriot, excellent, set of 9 pcs. **100**

Breton Dancers Figure Group

Figure group, Modern Movement, a young Breton couple dancing the folk dance "gavotte," by artist Micheau-Vernez, Henriot Quimper plus the artist's mark, mint, 12 1/2" h. (ILLUS.) **450**

Figure of boy, Modern Movement, little Breton boy wearing a black hat, blue jacket, black vest, brown pants & yellow clogs, by Berthe Savigny, HB Quimper py F.822 & Savigny signature, mint, 10 1/4" h. **250**

Figure of The Virgin & Child, "Vierge et l'Enfant," Mary standing wearing a crown & cradling the Baby Jesus in her arms & holding a flower in her right hand, unusual & rare mold w/much detail work on the robes, Henriot Quimper France, mint, 11 1/2" h. **500**

Quimper Fish Platter with Couple

Fish platter, oval, "Ivoire Corbeille" patt., center decorated w/busts of a young couple surrounded by swags of blue-sponged circlets, Henriot Quimper 79, pierced to hang, excellent, 10 1/4 x 21" (ILLUS.) **650**

Inkwell, heart-shaped, decorated w/a facing peasant couple w/floral sprays around the sides, complete w/insert & lid, Henriot Quimper, excellent, 3 x 3 1/2" (one tiny rim flake) **250**

Jardiniere, low oval form w/upright sides w/flared rim & base bands supported on four paw feet, figural satyr head end handles, "Decor Riche" patt., front w/oval reserve of a seated courting couple w/blue acanthus panels & border, the reverse w/a reserve w/intricate colored flower blossoms, HB Quimper, excellent, one foot professionally repaired, 8 1/2 x 16", 5 3/4" h. **1,250**

Quimper Triangular Knife Rests

Knife rest, triangular w/flared ends, in the "Bluets" (blue Forget-me-nots) patt., unsigned but attributable to AP, late 19th c., good condition w/some glaze edge wear, 3 1/2" l. (ILLUS. center) **50**

Knife rests, long triangular form w/flared ends, hollow center, one decorated w/a standing peasant man, the other w/a standing peasant woman, florals on the other two sides, HR Quimper, excellent w/a couple of tiny flakes, 3 1/4" l., matched pr. (ILLUS. left & right) **65**

Figural Quimper Lamp

Lamp, table model, figural, Modern Movement, figure of a Breton lady standing w/her arms extended out supporting large shallow baskets of colorful flowers, socket shafts issuing from flowers, on a square foot, by C. Maillard, Henriot Quimper France & C. Maillard mark, 13" h. (ILLUS.) **850**

Pitcher, figural, Modern Movement, model of a peasant man's head, the streamers from his hat forming the handle, his hat brim serving as the spout, Henriot Quimper France w/a.g. 159, mint **250**

Pitcher, 4 3/4" h., bulbous body, decorated w/a traditional peasant lady w/floral sprays, Henriot Quimper France beneath handle, excellent (tiny wear spot on lip).. **100**

Pitcher, 5 1/2" h., cylindrical neck, decorated w/a traditional peasant man & floral sprays, HR Quimper 38 France beneath handle, mint.................................... **125**

Plate, 6 1/2" l., oval w/scalloped rim, Flower patt., brown sponged border trim on a cream-glazed ground, HB Quimper France x.xx, excellent **35**

Porquier-Beau Botanical Plate

Plate, 9 1/4" d., lightly scalloped flanged rim w/yellow edge band, h.p. blackberry canes w/berries, First Period Porquier-Beau Botanical, intersecting PB mark, excellent condition (ILLUS.) **1,000**

Plate, 9 1/4" d., "Scene Breton" design w/a group scene of a family praying at a wayside shrine, First Period Porquier-Beau, intersecting PB mark, mint................ **875**

Plate, 9 1/2" d., colorful rooster on fence center scene, blue, green, brown & white geometric border, unsigned, late 19th c., mint **250**

Plate, 9 1/2" d., "Croisille" patt., center w/a lady holding a basket & facing forward, surrounded by a border which alternates blue criss-cross lattice & a stylized dogwood blossom, Henriot Quimper, very good (dust adhering to glaze from manufacturing) **200**

Plate, 9 1/2" d., Modern Movement, geometric decoration in vibrant colors of cobalt blue, rose, tan, orange & brown w/a stylized star in the center, HB Quimper 176 C.C., mint **125**

Rare Breton Legends Plate

Plate, 10" d., slightly scalloped flanged rim, Breton Legends patt., large color scene of a bagpiper surrounded by goblins

dancing beneath a quarter moon, Henriot Quimper France 117, rare, mint (ILLUS.)... **700**

Plates, 9 1/4" d., traditional decoration, one w/a man standing holding a pipe, the other w/a facing lady standing holding a flower, each figure flanked by colorful bushes all within a brush stroke border garland, HR Quimper beneath the figures, mint, pr. **325**

Early Quimper Oval Platter

Platter, 7 1/2 x 11 3/4", oval w/scalloped rim, central color scene of a native peasant lady seated on a stump w/an "a la touche" floral border, unsigned, mid-19th c., mint (ILLUS.) **150**

Platter, 9 1/4 x 12", oval w/slightly scalloped rim, center decoration of a profiled peasant man w/walking stick surrounded by a floral garland border, HR Quimper beneath the figure, mint **200**

Croisille Pattern Quimper Platter

Platter, 10 1/2 x 13 1/2", oval w/scalloped rim, "Croisille" patt., Demi-Fantasie style peasant couple in the center surrounded by a border of blue criss-cross latticework (croisille) & stylized dogwood flowers, Henriot Quimper 159 in blue w/an impressed 3, excellent w/vibrant colors (ILLUS.)... **900**

Porringer, round bowl, decorated w/traditional peasant man w/floral sprays & blue handles, Henriot Quimper France 42, excellent, overall 5 1/2" l. **35**

Salt basket, figural, double-type w/two kissing swans, black & yellow sponging on necks & bodies w/blue wings, Henriot Quimper, mint, 3 1/2 x 3 1/2".......................... **65**

Salt dip, open, decorated w/a floral garland on the exterior rim, HB Quimper, mint, 2" d. **25**

Salt & pepper cellar, oblong double open chambers w/a central ring handle, "Suject ordinaire" patt., a peasant man & flowers surrounded by yellow & blue concentric bands, Henriot Quimper France 595, mint, 5 1/4" l. **35**

Serving dish, rectangular w/rounded corners & six shallow sections, yellow-glazed ground w/each section decorated w/a peasant or floral cluster, Henriot Quimper France 72, excellent, 9 x 15" **100**

Snuff bottle, figural, model of a small book, decorated w/a rooster & the phrase "Quand ce cog chantera, mon amour finira," reverse sides decorated w/a peasant man, HB only, late 19th c., mint, 3" l. **300**

Tea set, child's: cov. teapot, cov. sugar bowl, creamer & three cups & saucers; white background glaze w/blue sponged trim & "a la touche" flower sprigs w/rose-colored buds & green leaves, unsigned but attributable to Henriot,ca. 1950s-60s, the set (one cup broken & reglued) **75**

Teabag holder, figural, model of a bagpipe, "Bruyere" (pink bleeding heart flower) patt., black & yellow sponged border trim & a pink bow handle, Henriot Quimper 138, mint, 4" l. **20**

Quimper Tray with Ropetwist Handles

Tray, rectangular w/notched corners & ropetwist end handles, Demi-Fantasie patt., center decoration of a peasant woman standing & holding a distaff flanked by tall colorful flowering bushes, dark blue border band & handles, Henriot Quimper France 100, mint, 8 1/2 x 13 1/4" (ILLUS.)............................... **250**

Trivet, footed, yellow ground decorated w/a peasant man w/florals & a red "S" link chain border, Macy's Quimper France x, excellent, 5 3/4" sq. **85**

Vase, 5" h., 7 1/2" w., fan-shaped, decorated w/a traditional peasant couple w/florals & a red lattice fan case w/blue butterfly figural feet, Henriot Quimper France 80, very good (faint 1" hairline) **300**

Vase with Demi-Fantasie Pattern

Vase, 11" h., baluster-form w/flared foot, short cylindrical neck & loop handles from rim to shoulder, h.p. Demi-Fantasie patt., a crest of Brittany on the shoulder band above a color scene of two courting peasants, upper & lower borders festooned w/bleeding hearts & wild gorse, HR Quimper mark, one flat chip of bottom (ILLUS.)` **1,100**

Vase, 12 1/2" h., "Decor Riche" patt., the front w/a color scene of a young couple courting surrounded by bleeding hearts & wild gorse blossoms, the reverse shows the Crest of Brittany, blue acanthus scrolled borders around the rim & base, HenRiot Quimper France 159, mint **550**

Vases, 9" h., 8" d., bulbous flat-bottomed shape tapering to a short rolled neck, "Broderie Bretonne" patt., each w/a cartouche framing a colored scene, one w/a seated peasant lady, the other w/a facing seated man w/pipe, raised yellow detailed wisteria vines on a dark blue ground around the sides, HB Quimper 524 Pi & Pj marks, mint, pr. **2,000**

Fine Quimper Wall Plaque

Wall plaque, rectangular w/cut corners, a large bas-relief courting couple in the center under the words "Au dud névez," & "Ploare"" (their village name) below, zigzag geometric border in terra cotta, black & cream, First Period Porquier-

Beau, signed & w/intersecting PB, late
19th c., superb, 15 x 18 1/4" (ILLUS.) **1,200**

Wall pocket, figural, in the shape of an
open envelope, decorated w/a traditional
peasant man w/floral sprays & blue latticework, one side unglazed w/match
striker, HR Quimper, 4 1/4" w., 4 1/4" h.
(one tiny back corner flake) **175**

Wall pockets, cone-shaped, decorated
w/the "Demi-Fantasie" patt., profiled
peasant lady holding a folded umbrella
on one, the other w/a three-quarters portrait of a facing man w/hand on his hip &
holding a pipe to his lips, HR Quimper
beneath the figures, mint, 10 1/4" l., pr. **350**

REDWARE

*Red earthenware pottery was made in the Amer-
ican colonies from the late 1600s. Bowls, crocks
and all types of utilitarian wares were turned out in
great abundance to supplement the pewter and
handmade treenware. The ready availability of the
clay, the same used in making bricks and roof tiles,
accounted for the vast production. The lead-glazed
redware retained its reddish color though a variety
of colors could be obtained by adding various met-
als to the glaze. Interesting effects occurred accidentally through unsuspected impurities in the clay
or uneven temperatures in the firing kiln which
sometimes resulted in streaks or mottled splotches.*

*Redware pottery was seldom marked by the
maker.*

Apple butter jar, bulbous ovoid body
w/applied handle & tooled lines, brown
splotches on deep orange ground, 5" h. **$578**

Bowl, 5 1/4" d., 2 1/2" h., footed w/rounded
sides & flat rim, dark greenish orange
ground w/brown spots, bottom incised
"B" (minor glaze flakes on interior) **303**

Bowl, 10 1/2" d., 7" h., deep sides w/light
green glaze splotches, 19th c. (chips) **460**

Bust, sculpted unglazed gentleman wearing shirt, bow tie & jacket, on shaped
pedestal, 19th c., 5" h. (some chips &
losses) **287**

Bust of man, full bottomed wig, wheel
thrown & hand-molded & tooled, brown
glaze, 10" h. (minor chips).......................... **770**

Redware Butter Churn

Butter churn, wooden lid & plunger, 19th
c., 28" d., 26" h. (ILLUS.)...................... **300-350**

Chamberstick, cylindrical w/saucer base &
applied handle, brown & green glaze on
orange ground, 3" h. (base glued)............... **176**

Creamer, cylindrical w/reeded base &
applied handle, green & mottled brown
glaze on orange ground, 2 1/8" h. (edge
chips).. **303**

Dish, orange ground w/brown sponged rim,
6 1/2" d. (wear & chips) **440**

Dish, orange glazed interior, exterior & rim
w/black patina, 7 1/2" d. (wear & hair-
line) **303**

Redware Dish

Dish, oblong, shallow canted sides w/flat
narrow rim, orange ground w/brown &
green spots, 11 3/4" l. (ILLUS.) **660**

Doorstop, square form decorated
w/molded starflower, yellow & brown
glaze, 3 x 4 3/4 x 5" **330**

Figure of Uncle Sam, standing full-figure,
polychrome, 4" h. (worn & flaked poly-
chrome) **275**

Flask, ovoid body tapering to small molded
rim, deep orangish ground w/dark brown
splotches, 7" h. (wear & minor chips).......... **385**

Flowerpot w/attached saucer, tapering
cylindrical form, tooled lines at base &
rim, yellow slip & mottled brown, orange
& cream glaze, wear, flakes & short hair-
lines, 5" h. **358**

Flowerpot w/saucer, tapering cylindrical
form w/narrow rolled rim, brown running
glaze on orange ground, impressed
"John W. Bell, Waynesboro, Pa.,"
4 3/8" h. (chips) **385**

Redware Ram-form Footwarmer

Footwarmer, figural recumbent ram, 19th
c., very minor chips, 6 3/4" h., 13 1/2" l.
(ILLUS.).. **518**

Jar, ovoid body w/wide molded rim, greenish mottled glaze w/amber spots,
5 1/2" h. **248**

Jar, footed bulbous ovoid body tapering to a wide slightly flaring rim, dark brown splotches on orange ground w/mottled green glaze, 7 3/8" h. (chips) **825**

Jar, wide cylindrical body w/flared rim, net like pattern of dark brown over burnt orange ground, 7 1/2" h. (wear & small chips)... **523**

Jar, cov., wide cylindrical body w/shoulder tapering to flared rim, inset cover w/tiny cylindrical finial, dark brown daubs on greenish glaze w/mottled amber, yellow & green, 8" h. (chips)................................ **1,485**

Jar, ovoid w/shoulder handles, clear reddish brown w/black splotches, chips, 9 1/2" h.. **220**

Jug, globular w/ribbed strap handle & tooled lines, amber ground w/brown splotches & green mottled glaze, 3 5/8" h... **4,510**

Jug, bulbous ovoid body w/applied ribbed handle, brown flecks on a metallic deep amber ground, 7 1/4" h. (wear & surface & edge chips) **193**

Redware Jug

Jug, globular w/strap handle, brown w/orange spots, 18th c., America, 27" d., 11" h. (ILLUS.)... **50-75**

Jug, bulbous ovoid, brown running glaze on deep orange ground, glazed over handle attachment, 12" h. (wear & old chips)... **110**

Jug, bulbous ovoid body w/applied strap handle, deep reddish tan, 12 1/4" d. (wear & minor glaze flakes)........................ **550**

Model of dog, seated Spaniel w/molded & hand-tooled features including a neck chain & padlock, clear glaze w/brown streaking, 19th c., 8 1/4" h. (edge chips, glaze flakes, old repair, black paint on bottom edge).. **358**

Mold, food, Turk's turban-style, divided & fluted, dark brown glaze wbrown sponged scalloped rim, 7 3/4" d. (small flakes)... **138**

Mold, food, Turk's turban-style, swirled design w/running brown glaze on orange ground, impressed label "John W. Bell, Waynesboro, Pa.," 8 3/4" d., 4 1/8" h. (hairline) **495**

Mug, footed bulbous body w/molded ribs & applied handle, brown sponging w/mottled green glaze on orange ground, 3" h. **275**

Mush mug, footed squatty bulbous body w/applied ribbed handle, dark greenish amber glaze, 3 1/2" h. (chips) **88**

Pepper pot, waisted cylindrical base w/top tapering sharply to mushroom-shaped top pierced w/holes, brown sponging on green & light brown glaze, 5 1/2" h. **495**

Pie plate, brown brushed & sponged design on burnt orange ground, 7 3/8" d. (minor chips & short hairline) **220**

Pie plate, orange glaze w/dark brown splotches, 8 1/4" d. **1,155**

Pitcher, 6 3/4" h., squatty ovoid body tapering to tall slightly flared rim w/pinched spout & applied ribbed strap handle, brown splotches & flecks on lighter brown ground **220**

Pitcher, 7 5/8" h., bulbous ovoid body w/tooled band, gallery rim lip, pinched spout & ribbed strap handle, dark brown splotches & flecks on orange ground (wear & chips) **660**

Pitcher, cov., 9" h., wide ovoid body w/ribbed strap handle, clear glaze w/brown sponging on a red ground (lid is good fit but color varies)............................. **523**

Pitcher, 10 3/4" h., wide ovoid body tapering to a flared rim w/pinched spout, ribbed strap handle, old wooden lid, clear mottled green glaze w/running daubs of yellow slip highlighted w/brown & green, brown glazed interior (minor chips).. **9,900**

Pot, cov., squatty bulbous body w/flared rim, strap handle & pouring spout, dark brown sponged glaze, 5" h. (small chips & mismatched lid).. **110**

Stove leveler, flaring cylindrical form w/molded top, brown splotches on orange ground, 2 3/4" h. (chips)................. **176**

Teapot, cov., cylindrical form w/an engine-turned body in an overall optic block design, straight angled spout, large loop handle, slightly domed cover w/knob finial, impressed pseudo-Chinese mark, England, ca. 1770, 6" h. (restored chip on spout lip, nicks to rims)......................... **748**

RED WING

Various potteries operated in Red Wing, Minnesota from 1868, the most successful being the Red Wing Stoneware Co., organized in 1878. Merged with other local potteries through the years, it became known as Red Wing Union Stoneware Co. in 1894, and was one of the largest producers of utilitarian stoneware items in the United States. After a decline in the popularity of stoneware products, an art pottery line was introduced to compensate for the loss and this was reflected in a new name for the company, Red Wing Potteries, Inc., in 1930. Stoneware production ceased entirely in 1947, but vases, planters, cookie jars and dinnerwares of art pottery quality continued in production until 1967 when the pottery ceased operation altogether.

Red Wing Marks

CONVENTION COMMEMORATIVES

Red Wing Commemorative Acid Pitcher

Acid pitcher, 1986 Red Wing Collectors Society Commemorative, maker produced 1,982 (ILLUS.) **$225**

Bowl, 1980 Red Wing Collectors Society Commemorative, maker produced 400 .... **995**

Buttermilk feeder, & chicken drinking font, 1993 Red Wing Collectors Society Commemorative, maker produced 4,820 .... **95**

Crock, 1977 Red Wing Collectors Society Commemorative, maker produced 250 ..... **2,595**

Jar, pantry, 1991 Red Wing Collectors Society Commemorative, maker produced 3,560 .... **115**

Jug, 1978 Red Wing Collectors Society Commemorative, maker produced 350 ..... **2,195**

Jug, fancy, 1990 Red Wing Collectors Society Commemorative, maker produced 3,550 .... **95**

Red Wing Miniature Jug

Jug, miniature, 1981 Red Wing Collectors Society Commemorative, maker produced 750 (ILLUS.) **445**

Mug, 1982 Red Wing Collectors Society Commemorative, maker produced 697 .... **695**

Planter, giraffe, 1995 Red Wing Collectors Society Commemorative, maker produced 8,186 .... **85**

DINNERWARES & NOVELTIES

Ashtray, wing-shaped, marked "Red Wing Potteries 75th Anniversary, 1878-1953," 7 3/8" **95**

Red Wing Basket

Basket, white & green, marked "Red Wing USA #1275," 9 3/4" l. (ILLUS.) **80**

Basket, yellow & grey, marked "Red Wing USA #348," w/75th Anniversary Stamp, 7" h. **50**

Beverage server, cov., Tampico patt. **85**

Bowl, cereal, Provincial patt. **8**

Bowl, salad, 12" d., Tampico patt...................... **75**

Casserole, cov., French-style w/handle, Town & Country patt., rust glaze, ca. 1946 .... **165**

Casserole, cov., Village Green patt. **33**

Console bowl, Magnolia patt., 12" l................. **115**

Cookie jar, cov., Bob White patt. **95**

Cookie jar, cov., figural French Chef, blue glaze... **250**

French Chef Cookie Jar and Figurine

Cookie jar, cov., French Chef, blue on blue, Red Wing Pottery stamp (ILLUS.) **135**

Cookie jar, cov., green rooster, marked "Red Wing #249," 9 1/4" l. **145**

Cookie jar, cov., yellow grapes, marked "Red Wing USA," 10" h. **80**

Creamer, Provincial patt..................................... **12**

Cup & saucer, Provincial patt. **10**

Figurine, brown beaver w/football, signed "Red Wing Potteries, Red Wing, Minn.," dated 1939, very rare, 2 5/8" h. (ILLUS.) **175**

Figurine, green swan, marked "Red Wing USA #259," 5 1/8" h. **55**

Figurine, green & yellow sitting deer, marked "Red Wing USA #1338," 6" h. **110**

Figurine, grey lined rooster, marked "Red Wing #M-1438," 9 1/4" h. **85**

Marmite, Village Green patt. **9**

Planter, model of a Dachshund dog, blue glaze, No. 1342 .... **95**

Planter, goose, flecked, Nile blue, marked
"Red Wing USA #439," 9 1/2" l. **105**

Log-shaped Planter

Planter, log-shaped, white birch pottery,
unmarked, 11" l. (ILLUS.).............................. **85**

Plate, 6" d., bread & butter, Provincial patt.......... **4**

Plate, 10" d., dinner, Provincial patt. **10**

Salt & pepper shakers, Village Green
patt., pr. **14**

Syrup pitcher, Provincial patt. **15**

Red Wing Trivet

Trivet, Minnesota Centennial 1858-1958,
back signed "Red Wing Potteries,"
6 1/2" d. (ILLUS.)... **95**

Vase, brushed ware w/cattails, stamped
"Red Wing Union Stoneware," rare,
7 3/8" h. **105**

Red Wing Bud Vase

Vase, green bud vase, stamped "Red Wing
Art Pottery," rare, 8 7/8" h. (ILLUS.)............. **150**

STONEWARE & UTILITY WARES

Bean Pot with Christmas Greetings

Bean pot, cov., white & brown glaze,
w/advertising "Christmas Greetings from
Christel's Cash Store, Brillion, Wisc."
(ILLUS.).. **105**

Bean pot, cov., white & brown glaze,
w/advertising "Peter Bootzin, The Corner
Store, Medford, Wisc." **85**

Bean pot, cov., white & brown glaze,
w/advertising "Peterson Department
Store, Clintonville, Wisc." **95**

Bean pot, cov., white & brown glaze,
w/advertising "Sheffield Brick & Tile Co.,
Sheffield, Iowa" **80**

Beater jar, spongeband, w/advertising "It
Pays to Mix with Allen, Herman, Minn." **850**

Beater jar, white glaze w/blue band,
w/advertising "Huemoeller Bros.,
Northrop-Truman, Minnesota " **150**

Beater Jar with Advertising

Beater jar, white glaze w/blue band,
w/advertising "Schulenburg & Thom,
Wells, Minn." **145**

Bowl, 5" d., paneled spongeware.................... **280**

Bowl, 6" d., paneled spongeware, w/adver-
tising "Muscoda, Spring Green, Bosco-
bel, Wisc." **325**

Bowl, 6" d., saffronware, yellowware **140**

Bowl, 7" d., Dunlap bowl, brown & white,
w/advertising "Columbia Metal Products
Co., Chicago, IL." **55**

Butter Crock, white glazed stoneware, bottom signed "Minnesota Stoneware Co.," 10 lbs............ **75**

Butter Crock, white glazed stoneware, bottom signed "Red Wing Stoneware," 10 lbs............ **65**

Christmas tree holder, green glaze............ **425**

Churn, white glazed stoneware, large wing, upside down oval stamp, 2 gal............ **475**

Churn, white glazed stoneware, birch leaf with ski oval mark, 3 gal............ **290**

Churn, salt glazed stoneware, cobalt markings, unsigned, 4 gal............ **845**

Stoneware Churn

Churn, white glazed stoneware, large wing, oval stamp below wing, 5 gal. (ILLUS.)............ **350**

Churn, white glazed stoneware, large wing, oval stamp below wing, 8 gal............ **1,550**

Crock, white glazed stoneware, bottom signed "Minnesota Stoneware, Red Wing, Minn.," 8 3/4" d., 1 gal............ **45**

Four Gallon Stoneware Crock

Crock, white glazed stoneware, two birch leaves, w/Union oval stamp mark, 11" d., 4 gal. (ILLUS.)............ **115**

Crock, white glazed stoneware, two "elephant ears," no oval stamp, eared handles, 11" d., 4 gal.(ILLUS. next column)............ **95**

Crock, white glazed stoneware, 6" wing, Red Wing oval stamp, bail handles, 15 1/4" d., 10 gal............ **135**

Crock w/Elephant Ears Marking

Crock, white glazed stoneware, two birch leaves, Union oval stamp, eared handles, 15 1/2" d., 10 gal............ **145**

Crock, white glazed stoneware, two birch leaves, no oval stamp, eared handles, 16" d., 12 gal............ **125**

Crock, white glazed stoneware, 6" wing, Red Wing oval stamp, no handles, 19 1/4" d., 20 gal............ **125**

Crock, white glazed stoneware, Red Wing & Union oval stamp, bail handles, 20" h., 20 gal............ **121**

Fruit jar, cov., Stone Mason, black label, patent date Jan. 24, 1899, "Union Stoneware" stamp, 1 qt............ **275**

Fruit jar, cov., Stone Mason, black label, patent date Jan. 24, 1899, "Union Stoneware" stamp, 1 gal............ **750**

Pure Leaf Lard Jar

Jar, cov., Hazel Pure Food Co., white glazed stoneware, stamped "Pure Leaf Lard," wire handle, complete with lid, 5 lbs. (ILLUS.)............ **245**

Jar, cov., ball lock, brown & white glazed stoneware, no wing, Red Wing oval stamp, 3 gal............ **135**

Jar, cov., white glazed stoneware, stamped "Red Wing Refrigerator Jar"............ **265**

Jug, beehive-shaped, Albany slip, North Star stoneware, star on base, rare, 1 qt............ **285**

Jug, beehive-shaped, salt glazed stoneware, signed "Minnesota Stoneware
Company," 2 gal. **1,175**

Red Wing Shouldered Jug

Jug, shouldered, white glazed stoneware,
4" wing, Red Wing oval stamp, 3 gal.
(ILLUS.). **165**

Jug, beehive-shaped, white glazed stoneware, two birch leaves, no oval stamp, 4
gal. **550**

Jug, beehive-shaped, white glazed stoneware, 4" wing, Red Wing oval stamp, 5
gal. **385**

Jug, shouldered, brown & white glazed
stoneware, 4" wing, no oval stamp, 5
gal. **450**

Jug, shouldered, white glazed stoneware,
two birch leaves, no stamp, bottom
signed, 5 gal. **195**

"Koverwate," (crock cover-weight
designed to keep the contents sub-
merged under preserving liquid; bottom
& side holes allowed brine to come to
the top), white glazed stoneware,
stamped "Koverwate, Red Wing, Minn.,"
6 gal. size **245**

"Koverwate," white glazed stoneware,
stamped "Koverwate, Red Wing, Minn.,"
25 gal. size **350**

Stoneware Pie Plate

Pie plate, white glazed stoneware, signed
"Minnesota Stoneware Co., Red Wing,
Minn.," rare, 9 3/4" d. (ILLUS.) **145**

Poultry feeder jar, cov., white glazed
stoneware poultry drinking font & buttermilk feeder, bell-shaped, marked "Red
Wing," complete with base, 1 gal. **145**

Three Gallon Stoneware Water Cooler

Water cooler, cov., white glazed stoneware, bailed handles, small wing, 3 gal.
(ILLUS.). **450**

Water cooler, cov., white glazed stone-
ware, bail handles, small wing, 5 gal. **425**

Water cooler, cov., white glazed stone-
ware, bail handles, large wing, 10 gal. **700**

ROCKINGHAM WARES

*The Marquis of Rockingham first established an
earthenware pottery in the Yorkshire district of
England around 1745 and it was occupied after-
wards by various potters. The well-known mottled
brown Rockingham glaze was introduced about
1788 by the Brameld Brothers and became immediately popular. It was during the 1820s that the production of true porcelain began at the factory and
continued to be made until the firm closed in 1842.
Since that time the so-called Rockingham glaze
has been used by various potters in England and
the United States, including some famous wares
produced in Bennington, Vermont. However, very
similar glazes were also used by potteries in other
areas of the United States including Ohio and Indiana and only wares specifically attributed to Bennington should use that name. The following listings
will include mainly wares featuring the dark brown
mottled glaze produced at various sites here and
abroad.*

Flask, flattened ovoid form tapering to a
short molded neck, the front & back
molded in relief w/scenes of hunting
dogs, mottled dark brown glaze,
7 1/4" h. (hairline in bottom) **$330**

Loving cup, large cylindrical form on a
molded base w/large C-form branch
handle on each side, one side relief-
molded w/a drinking scene, the other
side w/a dog fight, molded vintage rim
band, overall dark brown mottled glaze,
6 7/8" h. (bottom rim chips) **248**

Model of a bull, overall mottled brown
glaze, 19th c., 16" l., 12 5/8" h. (minor
losses, restoration) **7,475**

Model of a dog, seated Spaniel facing
viewer, on a thick oblong base, freestanding front legs, molded deer &
hounds around the base mottled dark
brown glaze, 19th c., 10 1/2" h. **399**

Model of a dog, seated Spaniel on thick
irregular-shaped base, freestanding

front legs, mottled dark brown glaze, wear on nose, hairlines in front legs & small chips on base, 10 3/4" h. **330**

Rockingham Lion

Model of a lion, recumbent animal w/curly mane, on rectangular stepped base, mottled dark brown glaze, minor chips on base, 9 3/8" l. (ILLUS.) **880**

Mugs, mottled brown & cream, ca. 1890, 3 1/2" d., 4 1/4" h., set of 6 .... **200**

Pitcher, 9 1/2" h., footed bulbous body w/arched spout & C-form handle, mottled brown glaze w/detailed relief-molded vintage & foliage pinwheels (small chips on spout) **413**

Pitcher, 9 5/8" h., bulbous ovoid body tapering to slightly flaring rim, pinched spout, relief-molded hanging game, mottled brown glaze, figural hound handle **275**

Rockingham Pitcher

Pitcher, 9"h., ovoid body tapering to a wide rolled spout & branch handle, the sides molded w/a scene of a hunter & dog, dark brown mottled brown glaze on yellowware, late 19th c. (ILLUS.) **200**

Snuff jar, figural Mr. Toby, mottled dark brown glaze, 19th c., 4 1/8" h. (minor glaze wear on rim)...................... **374**

Teapot, cov., footed ovoid body w/swan's-neck spout & C-form handle, domed cover w/bud-form finial, mottled brown glaze w/relief-molded scene of Rebecca at the well, early 20th c., Ohio, 8 1/2" h. (ILLUS.).. **200**

Rockingham Teapot

ROOKWOOD

Considered America's foremost art pottery, the Rookwood Pottery Company was established in Cincinnati, Ohio in 1880, by Mrs. Maria Nichols Longworth Storer. To accurately record its development, each piece carried the Rookwood insignia, or mark, was dated, and, if individually decorated, was usually signed by the artist. The pottery remained in Cincinnati until 1959 when it was sold to Herschede Hall Clock Company and moved to Starkville, Mississippi, where it continued in operation until 1967.

A private company is now producing a limited variety of pieces using original Rookwood molds.

Rookwood Mark

Basket, hanging-type, bulbous bullet form, green Matte glaze, No. S1732, 1905, 10" d., 9" l. (minute flakes) **$440**

Basket, gondola-shaped w/curved & pointed ends, decorated w/slip-painted daisies in yellow on a shaded green ground, Standard glaze, No. 374, 1888, K. Shirayamadani, 15 1/2" l., 8" h................ **660**

Book ends, figural, model of a squirrel seated on a log holding up & eating a nut, greyish green Matte glaze, No. 6025, 1928, Sallie Toohey, 4 1/4" h., pr. **748**

Book ends, figural, modeled as a blue jay, w/oak leaves & acorns, creamy Matte glaze, No. 2829, 1929, 5 3/8" h., pr............. **316**

Book ends, figural, one w/Dutch girl dressed in blue & white, the other w/Dutch boy w/blue hat & lavender vest, leaning on dark brown stone wall behind a stand of pink tulips, Matte glaze, No. 6022, 1928, Sallie Toohey, 6" h., pr. **523**

Bowl, 6 1/2" d., porcelain, flared sides w/center decoration of six-pointed star design w/pink, white & red roses painted between star points, blue scroll design border w/gold trim, No. 2239, 1920, W.E. Hentschel (ILLUS.) **495**

Rookwood Bowl

Bowl, 7" w., deep square, slightly rounded body w/indented corners on square foot, Limoges-style decoration w/two butterflies in brown tones soaring against a peach, green & white smeared ground w/gold highlights & black reeds, painted gold accents at rim, kiln mark, No. 166, 1883, N.J. Hirschfeld..................................... **413**

Unusual Rookwood Bowl

Bowl, 12" l., oval w/incurved sides forming openings at each end, decorated w/detailed flowers in green & blue w/white centers against an ivory, light blue & medium blue ground, gold geometric & floral designs, No. 344B, 1887, Kataro Shirayamadani (ILLUS.) **1,540**

Bowl-vase, bulbous body w/incurved rim, the upper body decorated w/pink flowers w/green centers on a light blue ground, the lower body darker blue w/scalloped edge, impressed "V" & signature, No. 214E, 1915, E.H. McDermott, 4 1/2" d. **358**

Card holder, rectangular form on pedestal base, paneled design w/ribbed top, blue crystalline glaze, No. 2952, 1927, 3" w., 3 1/2" h.. **220**

Unusual Rookwood Chalice

Chalice, cone-shaped body supported by three large loop handles from rim

extending into feet w/relief-molded gargoyle heads, body decorated w/orange & yellow flowers & green foliage under a tiger eye glaze, early Standard glaze, No. 350, 1888, artist's signature illegible, 8" h. (ILLUS.).. **605**

Clock, relief-molded panther on base, gunmetal glaze, No. 7039, 1950, 7 1/2" h. **286**

Compote, shallow oblong form w/crimped rim, floral medallion in center, pedestal base, glossy red glaze, No. S2205, 1955, marked w/Rookwood anniversary triangle, 6" d., 4 1/2" h. **231**

Cup & saucer, cylindrical w/D-form handle, painted & incised cherry blossoms on olive ground, saucer 5" d., cup 3" h., No. 208, 1886, Anna M. Bookprinter **275**

Rookwood Silver Overlay Ewer

Ewer, footed, baluster-form w/a widely flaring rolled tricorner rim, slender S-scroll handle, decorated w/yellow blossoms on green leaves trimmed w/silver overlay flowering vines up the sides & beneath the handle w/a silver overlaid rim, handle & base, Standard glaze, No. 510, 1892, silver marked by Gorham Co., No. R198, Harriet R. Strafer, insignificant break in silver & fracture to base not visible from top or outside, 7" h. (ILLUS.) **3,850**

Ewer, squatty bulbous base on a narrow footring tapering to slender cylindrical neck w/flaring rim & pinched spout w/long arched handle, decorated w/yellow dogwood w/black centers on brown stems & green leaves on a dark brown, orange & green ground, Standard glaze, No. 495B, 1899, Mary Nourse, 9" h. **770**

Ewer, oviform w/an elongated neck & floriform spout, in a Standard glaze, decorated w/a mustard yellow & olive green branch of prunus, applied w/a C-scroll handle, No. 450 W, 1892, Albert R. Valentien, 17" h. **1,150**

Flower frog, figural satyr w/turtle, brown Matte glaze, No. 2336, 1921, 7" h............... **468**

Inkwell, flat oval form w/flared rim, decorated w/feather among yellow & green clover, centered w/spherical well adorned w/silver overlay in elaborate scrolled design w/hammered silver top, Standard glaze, No. 586C, 1899, silver marked by Gorham Co., Constance

Baker, 10" l. (minor flaws underneath base, probably in firing)............................ **1,760**

Jar, cov., wide squatty compressed body raised on tiny peg feet, the wide shoulder centered by a low, wide domed cover, incised rectangular panels, fine dark red & dusty green Matte glaze, No. 1349, 1908, 6" d. (minor inner rim flake)...... **413**

Model of an egret, head up & turned to the side, glossy black glaze, No. 6992, 1948, 8 1/2" h... **187**

Native American Portrait Mug

Mug, ovoid body w/wide flat rim, C-form handle, decorated w/bust portrait of Native American brave w/one feather in head band & elaborate beadwork on chest, blue & yellow, Standard glaze, incised "Big Mane," No. 837, 1898, Sadie Markland, 5" h. (ILLUS.)................. **1,870**

Paperweight, figural seated female nude on rectangular base, ivory Matte glaze, impressed signature, No. 2868, 1928, 4" h.. **330**

Pilgrim flask, spherical body w/narrow cylindrical neck, applied handle from neck to shoulder, Limoges-type, decorated w/scene of white geese in flight & white, orange & black water fowl wading in pool against smeared ground in olive green & white w/gold accents & black reeds, 1882, A.R. Valentien, 7" h. **880**

Pin tray, shallow oval form w/rolled rim, figural molded reclining nude female at one end, glossy green glaze, No. 2595, 1949, 4 1/2" w. **176**

Plaque, rectangular, a wide landscape scene of trees along a riverbank, unusual red leaves on brown trunks w/green grass along light blue body of water, Vellum glaze, incised "V" & painted signature, 1915, original frame, E.T. Hurley, 5 1/2 x 9 1/2"........................ **2,860**

Plaque, rectangular, a winter landscape depicting a wind-swept evergreen tree in the snow silhouetted against a pink sky, Vellum glaze, 1915, E.F. McDermott, original wooden frame, 8 1/2 x 11".......... **4,675**

Plaque, rectangular, large landscape of an autumn scene w/birch trees by a pond, Vellum glaze, original molded frame, 1940s, w/paper label & artist's initials, E.T. Hurley, 11 x 13" **11,000**

Plate, 12" d., decorated w/daisies on a sienna ground, Cameo glaze, No. 520, 1890, Harriet E. Wilcox **575**

Rookwood Tea Set

Tea set: cov. 7 1/2" d., 5" h. teapot, 5" d. creamer & 6" d. cov. sugar bowl; each w/squatty bulbous bodies, decorated w/wild roses in salmon & white w/brown stems, thorns & leaves against a peach to ivory ground, Cameo glaze, the creamer w/C-form handle & pinched spout, the sugar bowl w/C-form handles & domed lip w/butterfly finial, the teapot w/swan's-neck spout, domed cover w/butterfly finial & rattan-wrapped swing bail handle, No. 404, 1891, H.E. Wilcox, teapot lid has crack & small flake to creamer, the set (ILLUS. of teapot).............. **660**

Teapot, cov., cylindrical w/domed lid & knob finial, swan's-neck spout & C-scroll handle, decorated w/yellow & orange carnations w/green stems & buds on paneled body, Standard glaze, No. 552, 1894, L.N. Lincoln, 7 1/2" h. **770**

Tile, carved & painted stylized floral design in brown & green w/blue background, framed, 4" sq... **286**

Tile, squeezebag technique decoration of white windmill, dark blue trees against a light blue sky, 1919, artist-signed, framed, 6" sq... **330**

Tray, molded design of a peacock feather, black & blue Matte glaze, No. 1668, 1922, 6 1/2" l. **165**

Rookwood Floral Decorated Urn

Urn, cov., porcelain, wide bulbous ovoid body w/high domed cover w/button finial, decorated w/elaborate overall floral design w/swirling blossoms & leaves in red, green, blue, yellow & brown against an ivory ground, decorated inner lid & decorated & pierced exterior top, No. 2448, 1921, Arthur Conant, harmless line in body, 14 1/2" h. (ILLUS.) **6,600**

Vase, 3" h., bulbous rounded body w/a four-sided wide neck incised w/a band of short pickets, shaded dark blue to moss green Matte glaze, No.1186, 1905 .... **440**

Vase, 6" h., ovoid body w/wide shoulder tapering to short cylindrical neck, painted stylized papyrus decoration in red, yellow & green on a grey ground, yellow leaf design outlined in blue on shoulder, Matte glaze, No. 1926, 1921, C.S. Todd **2,420**

Vase, 6" h., 4 3/4" d., bulbous nearly spherical body tapering to a short flaring trumpet neck, decorated w/white hydrangea on an opalescent dark blue & green ground, Sea Green glaze, No. 402, 1902, Sara Sax **5,225**

Vase, 6" h., 5 1/2" d., Jewel Porcelain, wide bulbous body w/narrow rolled rim, decorated w/Art Deco flowers in pink, green & blue, No. 6180, 1930, Sara Sax **2,310**

Vase, 6 1/2" h., tapering cylindrical body w/slightly flared rim, band near bottom decorated w/scene of boats in cobalt blue against a cream sea & sky, cobalt blue Vellum glaze, incised initials, incised "GV," No. 1658F, 1912, Lenore Asbury **1,320**

Vase, 7 1/2" h., 3 3/4" d., slightly swelled cylindrical form w/a tapering shoulder to the molded rim, scenic design of tall slender trees in a misty landscape in shades of grey, blue & purple, Vellum glaze, No. 2001, 1914, C. J. McLaughlin (minor pitting) **935**

Vase, 8 1/4" h, gently flaring cylindrical body w/flat rim, thickly enameled antelopes & stylized foliage in white & brown under a matte yellow Butterfat glaze, No. 6112, 1929, William Hentschel **4,950**

Vase, 8 1/2" h., shouldered cylindrical body tapering slightly to short neck w/molded rim, decorated w/pink poppies on a shaded grey ground, Vellum glaze, No. 944D, 1907, Elizabeth Lincoln **523**

Vase, 8 3/4" h., 4" d., cylindrical w/incurved rim, decorated w/a wide upper band painted w/pale purple irises & green leaves & stems on an ivory ground, lavender background, Iris glaze, No. 952, 1909, Lenore Asbury **1,980**

Vase, 9" h., footed trumpet form w/handles at base, decorated w/molded design of two ladies & stars, glossy grey glaze, No. 6539, 1935 .... **385**

Vase, 9" h., footed urn-form body w/narrow shoulder tapering to cylindrical neck w/wide flaring rim, decorated w/animal portrait of a growling leopard, Standard glaze, No. 410, 1893, overall crazing, Bruce Horsfall **4,888**

Rare Black Iris Vase

Vase, 9" h., slender ovoid body tapering to a short wide slightly rolled neck, decorated w/broad purple & pink irises w/yellow beards on green to blue stems w/green to blue leaves surrounding vase, two unopened buds in purple & yellow on a ground shading from peach, purple & light green to black, Black Iris glaze, No. 907E, 1907, Constance Baker (ILLUS.) **7,700**

Vase, 9 1/4" h., 3 3/4" d., tall slightly swelled cylindrical body tapering slightly to a short cylindrical neck, decorated w/large pale purple irises & dark green leaves & stems on a dark grey to white ground, Iris glaze, No. 907D, 1906, Sara Sax **4,125**

Vase, 9 1/2" h., 4 3/4" d., Jewel Porcelain, swelled cylindrical body w/a thick molded rim, decorated w/stylized reclining nudes in ivory on a flowing brown & cobalt blue ground, No. 1121C, 1931, Jens Jensen **6,600**

Vase, 10 1/4" h., 5 3/4" d., simple tall ovoid form w/short flared rim, decorated w/an autumnal landscape w/elm trees in yellow, brown & polychrome against cream & blue, Wax Matte glaze, No. 892C, 1938, Mary Helen McDonald **3,850**

Vase, 10 1/2" h., 4" d., tapering cylindrical body decorated w/purple lilacs against a grey to ivory ground, Iris glaze, No. S1771, 1904, Ed Diers (restoration to top) **550**

Vase, 11 3/4" h., 6 1/2" d., footed ovoid body tapering gently to a flaring neck, decorated w/large fleshy magnolias in lavender & white on a pale purple to blue ground, Vellum glaze, No. 827, 1927, Lenore Asbury **6,050**

Vase, 15" h., 7 1/2" d., gently flaring cylindrical form w/a wide flat rim, boldly decorated w/stylized blue iris & green leaves on a pink ground, Wax Matte glaze, No. 1369, 1925, Sallie Coyne **3,575**

Vase, 24 1/2" h., tall tapering cylindrical form, streak effect decoration of finely detailed daylilies & leaves, Standard glaze, No. 865, 1889, crazing, glaze bursts, firing cracks to base & body, Albert R. Valentien **1,725**

Vase, 26" h., 11" d., floor-type, tall ovoid body tapering to a flaring trumpet neck, a wide embossed stylized geometric band in yellow around the neck, overall frothy Matte green glaze, No. 306, 1916... **3,575**

Wall pocket, conical w/flared & scalloped rim, two loop handles near rim, blue Matte glaze, No. 2965, 1928, 6" h. **330**

Rookwood Cicada Wall Pocket

Wall pocket, model of a cicada, green Matte glaze, No. 1636, 1908, short glazed-over firing line, 4 1/2 x 9" (ILLUS.).. **3,080**

Wall sconce, rectangular plaque-form deeply embossed w/a pair of owls under a green & brown Matte glaze, candle socket at the bottom edge, No. 1688, 1910, 6 x 11 1/4" (minor restoration to candleholder & sides).................................. **660**

Water jug, Turkish style, bulbous ovoid body tapering to closed flat mouth w/overhead loop handle, tapering cylindrical spout on one end w/short flaring cylindrical filling spout on the other, die impressed design at top, shoulder & base covered in gold w/gold trim on spouts & handle, body decorated w/two painted butterflies in tones of brown above black reeds & grasses on matte finish ground of cream & shaded blue, No. 41, 1886, Matt Daly, 9 1/2" h. **1,210**

ROSE MEDALLION & ROSE CANTON

The lovely Chinese ware known as Rose Medallion was made through the past century and into the present day. It features alternating panels of people and flowers or insects with most pieces having four medallions with a central rose or peony medallion. The ware is called Rose Canton if florals and birds or insects fill all the panels. Unless otherwise noted, our listing is for Rose Medallion ware.

Basket & undertray, oval reticulated sides on a matching solid undertray, 19th c., basket 9 3/8" l., undertray 9 7/8" l., 2 pcs. (very minor chips, minor gilt & enamel wear) **$920**

Bottle w/cover & basin, Rose Mandarin variant, 19th c., bottle 16" h., basin 15 7/8" d., 4 7/8" h. (chips, minor wear) **1,840**

Rose Medallion Bough Pot

Bough pots, square waisted upright form w/slightly domed top pieces w/holes, figural panels, foliate gilded side handles, minor glaze wear, 19th c., 9" h., pr. (ILLUS. of one) **4,313**

Bowl, 8 3/8" d., Rose Mandarin variant, shallow round form w/tightly scalloped rim, the interior decorated w/four alternating reserves of figures or florals, the exterior decorated w/15 figures, orange peel glaze, 19th c. **523**

Bowl, 10" d., 4 7/8" h., Rose Mandarin variant, four-lobed rounded sides w/notched & down-curved rims, orange peel glaze, 19th c. **1,540**

Bowl, 10 1/2" d., cut-corner bowl, 19th c. (glaze wear) **1,093**

Bowl, 10 5/8" d., 4" h., shallow w/scalloped sides, 19th c. (minor gilt & enamel wear, minute rim chips) **575**

Brush box, cov., rectangular, interior divided into two compartments, 19th c., 2 1/2 x 3 1/2 x 7" (glaze wear)..................... **316**

Cake stand, a wide cylindrical foot supporting a wide shallow dished top decorated on the interior w/alternating floral & figural reserves, 19th c., 8 5/8" d., 3 3/4" h. (minor edge flakes) **468**

Candlesticks, cylindrical shaft above a flaring round foot, 19th c., 7" h., pr. (minor glaze wear) **1,495**

Chamber pot, usual paneled decoration, 19th c., 9 5/8" d. (minute rim chips).............. **633**

Charger, ca. 1860, 14 1/2" d. **728**

Cider jug, cov., Rose Mandarin patt., w/woven double strap applied handle, lid w/foo dog finial, 19th c., 9 1/2" (glaze wear, finial imperfections) **2,990**

Compote, 9 1/2" d., 3 1/2" h., 19th c. **288**

Compote, 11 x 14", 3" h., rounded diamond shape shallow bowl on a low flaring matching foot, 19th c. (imperfections)..... **748**

Dish, Rose Mandarin variant, oblong gently lobed from, figural scene in the center, butterflies around the rim, orange peel glaze, 19th c., 10 3/4" l. (chip on table ring).. **605**

Dishes, almond-shaped, each shallow oblong piece decorated w/alternating figural & floral reserves, orange peel glaze, heavy gilt trim, 19th c., 10 3/4" l., pr. **660**

Fruit basket, reticulated basket with undertray, 19th c. (glaze wear).............................. **748**

Fruit basket & undertray, oval reticulated basket on matching oval undertray, China, 19th c., 8 3/4 x 10", overall 14 1/4" h. **1,610**

Fruit tazza, Rose Mandarin variant, diamond-shaped, 19th c., 12 1/4" d. (minor glaze wear).. **748**

Garden seat, Rose Mandarin variant, barrel-form body, decorated w/a court scene surrounding the central body w/upper & lower bands of butterflies & floral designs, China, 19th c., 18 1/2" h. (chips at interior bottom edge, minor glaze wear).. **2,645**

Garden seats, Rose Mandarin variant, 19th c., 19" h., pr. (minor glaze wear) **4,600**

Mug, Rose Mandarin variant, tall cylindrical form w/decorated rim band above a band of three standing figures, entwined arched strap handle, 19th c., 4 7/8" h. **550**

Pitcher, 7 3/4" h. to top of handle, Rose Mandarin variant, paneled form w/scalloped rim, 19th c. (minor glaze chips, wear) **1,380**

Plate set: six 8 1/2" to 9 3/4" d. dinner plates & four 9 1/8" d. soup plates; 19th c., set of 10 (minor chips, two w/hairlines, minor gilt & enamel wear) **374**

Plates: four 9 5/8" d. dinner plates, eight 8 1/2" d. luncheon plates, eight 6" d. bread & butter plates; 19th c., the set (minor chips, glaze wear) **920**

Platter, 14 3/4" oval, Rose Mandarin variant, 19th c. (gilt & enamel wear, minute rim chips, knife marks) **633**

Platter, 15 3/4" l., oval, Rose Mandarin variant, 19th c. (gilt & enamel wear, minor chips)... **1,093**

Platter, 16 3/4" l., oval, Rose Mandarin variant **880**

Rose Mandarin Punch Bowl

Punch bowl, Rose Mandarin variant, deep rounded sides, interior & exterior decorated w/colorful panels of figures, florals & birds, 19th c., minor base chips, scratches, glaze loss, 13 1/2" d. (ILLUS.).. **1,495**

Punch bowl, Rose Mandarin variant, 19th c., 14 3/4" d. (glaze wear) **2,645**

Punch bowl, Rose Canton variant, large floral panels around the exterior & interior, 19th c., very minor gilt & enamel wea 21" d. **3,450**

Salt dips, low oval waisted cylindrical base supporting an oval dished top, 19th c.,

3 1/4 x 4 1/2", 1 1/2" h., pr. (minor imperfections).. **1,725**

Sauce tureens, cov., gilt finials & handles, 19th c., 6 d., pr. (minor chips to handles, glaze wear)... **1,093**

Serving bowl, shaped edges, 19th c., 9 1/2" d., 4 7/8" h. (very minor chips to base) **1,093**

Serving dish, cov., footed squatty round form w/upturned end loop handles, low domed reversible pierced cover, 19th c., 7 1/8" d. (minute chip to handle, minor gilt & enamel wear) **633**

Shrimp dish, 19th c., 9 1/2" d. (minor glaze chips, wear)... **345**

Shrimp dish, Rose Mandarin variant, 19th c., 10 5/8" l. (enamel loss, gilt wear) **431**

Tea cups & saucers, similar decoration, 19th c., set of 12 (minor chips, restoration, glaze losses) **978**

Tea set: cov. 4 1/2" h. teapot, sugar, creamer, four cups w/saucers; late 19th c. (restoration to teapot spout, glaze wear) **805**

Teapot, cov., Rose Mandarin variant, gilt decorated spout & handle, 19th c., 8 1/4" h. (minor chips, glaze losses) **1,265**

Urn, cov., Rose Mandarin variant, balusterform w/a rounded domed cover w/a gilt seated Foo dog finial, gilt Foo dog mask shoulder handles, 19th c., 16" h. (minor glaze wear)... **1,380**

Vase, 9 7/8" h., Rose Mandarin variant, bottle-form, w/applied kylins & foo dogs, 19th c. (minor gilt & enamel wear) **374**

Vases, 12 3/8" h., 7 3/4" d., Ku-form w/raised acanthus leaf ribbing & gilt archaic dragon design on blue ground, first half 19th c., pr. **3,335**

Vases 15" h., baluster-form, the wide cylindrical neck w/a flaring rim & flanked by a pair of molded foo dog handles, decorated w/panels of Oriental figures, birds & insects, ca. 1850, pr............................. **2,912**

Rose Medallion Covered Vases

Vases cov., 18 1/2" h., footed wide ovoid body tapering slightly to cylindrical neck flanked by figural handles, domed cover w/bud finial, on hardwood stands, gilt & enamel wear, minor chips to one lid, 19th c., pr. (ILLUS.) **2,860**

Vases 24" h., ovoid body tapering to tall cylindrical neck w/flaring rim, decorated around the neck w/applied kylins & foo dogs, 19th c., minor gilt & enamel wear, on hardwood stands, pr. **2,300**

Wash bowl, wide round form w/paneled decoration, on a hardwood stand, 19th c., 16 1/8" d., 4 7/8" h. (minor gilt & enamel wear) **1,265**

Rose Medallion Wash Bowl & Pitcher

Wash bowl & pitcher, 14 3/4" h. bulbous ovoid body w/long slender angled handle, paneled decoration, 16" d. bowl w/deep rounded sides & flared rim, interior & rim w/matching decoration, 19th c. (ILLUS.) **633**

Water bottle, cov., bulbous base w/tall slender cylindrical neck, small domed cover w/blossom finial, on hardwood stand, 19th, minor chips to lid, minor gilt & enamel wear, 15" h. **805**

ROSEMEADE

Laura Taylor was a ceramic artist who supervised Federal Works Projects in her native North Dakota during the Depression era and later demonstrated at the potter's wheel during the 1939 New York World's Fair. In 1940, Laura Taylor and Robert J. Hughes opened the Rosemeade-Wahpeton Pottery, naming it after the North Dakota county and town of Wahpeton where it was located. Rosemeade Pottery was made on a small scale for only about twelve years with Laura Taylor designing the items and perfecting colors. Her animal and bird figures are popular among collectors. Hughes and Taylor married in 1943 and the pottery did a thriving business until her death in 1959. The pottery closed in 1961 but stock was sold from the factory salesroom until 1964.

Rosemeade Mark

Model of bear, solid black glaze, 3" l. **$395**

Salt & pepper shakers, model of Bobwhite quail, pr. **60**

Salt & pepper shakers, model of Brussel sprout, pr. **20**

Salt & pepper shakers, model of duck, yellow glaze, pr. **50**

Salt & pepper shakers, model of elephant, rose, pr. **95**

Salt & pepper shakers, model of Flickertail, pr. **62**

Salt & pepper shakers, model of moccasin, pr. **50**

Salt & pepper shakers, model of pheasant, miniature, pr. **44**

Salt & pepper shakers, model of rose, pr. **33**

Salt & pepper shakers, model of skunk, large, pr. **68**

Salt & pepper shakers, model of skunk, small, pr. **60**

Salt & pepper shakers, model of tulip blossom, pr. **43**

Salt & pepper shakers, model of turkey, small, pr. **83**

Sugar bowl, model of a Mallard duck **75**

ROSEVILLE

Roseville Pottery Company operated in Zanesville, Ohio, from 1898 to 1954 after having been in business for six years prior to that in Muskingum County, Ohio. Art wares similar to those of Owens and Weller Potteries were produced. Items listed here are by patterns or lines.

Roseville

Roseville Mark

APPLE BLOSSOM (1948)
White apple blossoms in relief on blue, green or pink ground; brown tree branch handles.

Basket, hanging-type, green ground, 8" **$220**

Basket, hanging-type, pink ground, 8" **300**

Basket w/low overhead handle, blue ground, No. 310-10", 10" h. **280-285**

Basket w/low overhead handle, green ground, No. 310-10", 10" h. **300-350**

Basket w/overhead handle, blue ground, No. 309-8", 8" h. **315**

Basket w/overhead handle, green ground, No. 309-8", 8" h. **150-200**

Basket w/overhead handle, pink ground, No. 309-8", 8" h. **250**

Book ends, green ground, No. 359, pr. **198**

Book ends, pink ground, No. 359, pr. **260**

Bowl, 6 1/2" d., 2 1/2" h., flat handles, green ground, No. 326-6" **145**

Bowl, 8" d., blue ground, No. 328-8" **125**

Bowl, 8" d., green ground, No. 328-8" **105**

Candlesticks, pink ground, No. 351-2", 2" h., pr. **108**

Candlesticks, blue ground, No. 352-4 1/2", 4 1/2" h., pr. **350**

Console bowl, pink ground, No. 330-10", 10" l. **195**

Console bowl, pink ground, No. 333-14", 14" l. **175**

Cornucopia-vase, blue ground, No. 321-6", 6" h. **60**

Cornucopia-vase, green ground, No. 321-
6", 6 " h.. **68**
Cornucopia-vase, blue ground, No. 323-
8", 8" h.. **160**
Ewer, ovoid, pink ground, No. 316-8", 8" h. **143**
Flowerpot & saucer, pink ground, No.
356-5", 2 pcs. **170**
Jardiniere, blue ground, No. 300-4", 4" h. **140**
Jardiniere, green ground, No. 300-4", 4" h. **135**
Jardiniere, pink ground, No. 300-4", 4" h. **135**
Jardiniere, pink ground, No. 301-6", 6" h. **225**
Jardiniere & pedestal base, pink ground,
No. 303-10", overall 31" h., 2 pcs.............. **1,250**
Teapot, cov., blue ground, No. 371-P **295**
Teapot, cov., pink ground, No. 371-P **260**
Vase, 6" h., two-handled, squatty base,
long cylindrical neck, blue ground, No.
381-6" **145**

Apple Blossom Vase

Vase, 7" h., asymmetrical rim & handles,
green ground, No. 373-7" (ILLUS.) **135**
Vase, 7" h., asymmetrical rim & handles,
pink ground, No. 373-7" **195**
Vase, 7" h., flaring foot w/tapering cylindrical body, asymmetrical rim & handles,
pink ground, No. 382-7" **90-100**
Vase, 7" h., flaring foot w/tapering cylindrical body, asymmetrical rim & handles,
blue ground, No. 382-7" **130**
Vase, 8 1/4" h., flaring foot w/ovoid body &
wide flaring rim, pointed handles from
shoulder to middle of neck, blue ground,
No. 385-8" **150-175**
Vase, 8 1/4" h., flaring foot w/ovoid body &
wide flaring rim, pointed handles from
shoulder to middle of neck, pink ground,
No. 385-8" **185**
Vase, 9 1/2" h., 5" d., asymmetrical han-
dles, cylindrical w/disc base, green
ground, No. 387-9"...................................... **245**
Vase, 10" h., wide flaring foot w/base han-
dles, trumpet-form body, blue ground,
No. 388-10" **175-250**
Vase, 10" h., wide flaring foot w/base han-
dles, trumpet-form body, green ground,
No. 388-10" **297**
Vase, 10" h., wide flaring foot w/base han-
dles, trumpet-form body, pink ground,
No. 388-10" **350-400**
Vase, 10" h., swelled cylindrical body
w/shaped rim, base handles, green
ground, No. 389-10"..................................... **187**
Vase, 10" h., swelled cylindrical body
w/shaped rim, base handles, pink
ground, No. 389-10"..................................... **185**

Vase, 12 1/2" h., base handles, pink
ground, No. 390-12" **295**
Vase, 15" h., floor-type, double base han-
dles, short globular base, long cylindrical
neck, pink ground, No. 392-15"................... **512**
Wall pocket, conical w/overhead handle,
blue ground, No. 366-8", 8" h...................... **215**
Wall pocket, conical w/overhead handle,
brown ground, No. 366-8", 8" h. **190**
Wall pocket, conical w/overhead handle,
green ground, No. 366-8", 8" h.................... **185**
Window box, end handles, blue ground,
No. 368-8", 2 1/2 x 10 1/2" **185**
Window box, rectangular, blue ground,
No. 369-12", 12" l. **195**
Window box, rectangular, green ground,
No. 369-12", 12" l. **160**

BANEDA (1933)
*Band of embossed pods, blossoms and leaves
on green or raspberry pink ground.*

Candleholders, raspberry pink ground, No.
1088-4", 4 1/2" h., pr. **575**
Candlesticks, raspberry pink ground, No.
1087-5", 5" h., pr. **750**
Console bowl, raspberry pink ground, No.
233-8", 10" l... **395**
Console bowl, six-sided, w/handles from
base to rim, green ground, No. 234-10",
11" l... **523**
Jardiniere, two-handled, green ground,
4" h., No. 626-4" **385**
Jardiniere, two-handled, green ground,
No. 626-7", 7" h.. **413**
Jardiniere, two-handled, green ground,
No. 626-7", 7" h... **1,540**
Jardiniere, two-handled, raspberry pink
ground, No. 626-10", 10" h........................ **1,800**
Jardiniere & pedestal base, raspberry
pink ground, No. 626-8", 8" h., 2 pcs......... **1,870**
Jardiniere & pedestal base, green
ground, No. 626-10", jardiniere marked
"1 spot" & "9," pedestal unmarked, overall 28" h., 2 pcs. (two tight, short lines at
rim of jardiniere) **4,290**
Urn, small rim handles, bulbous, green
ground, No. 235-5", 5" h.............................. **545**
Urn, small rim handles, footed bulbous
body w/flat rim, raspberry pink ground,
No. 606-7", 7" h.. **770**
Vase, 4" h., footed bulbous body
w/incurved flat rim, flat shoulder han-
dles, raspberry pink ground, No. 587-4"....... **220**
Vase, 4" h., footed bulbous body
w/incurved flat rim, flat shoulder han-
dles, green ground, No. 587-4" **275**
Vase, 4" h., footed, wide squatty bulbous
base tapering sharply to small molded
mouth, tiny rim handles, raspberry pink
ground, No. 603-4"....................................... **495**
Vase, 5" h., footed, pear-shaped w/small
loop handles near rim, green ground,
No. 601-5".. **550**
Vase, 6" h., two-handled, footed, bulbous
base w/wide cylindrical neck, raspberry
pink ground, No. 589-6" **550**
Vase, 6" h., footed, slender ovoid body
w/short collared neck, loop handles from

shoulder to rim, raspberry pink ground, No. 602-6" **400-450**

Vase, 6" h., footed, slender ovoid body w/short collared neck, loop handles from shoulder to rim, green ground, No. 602-6", original black paper label **650**

Vase, 6" h., raspberry pink ground, No. 605-6", original label.................................... **564**

Vase, 7" h., footed swelled cylindrical body tapering to a short, wide cylindrical neck flanked by small down-curved loop handles, green ground, No. 590-7" **525**

Vase, 7" h., footed wide cylindrical body tapering to short wide cylindrical neck, small loop handles, green ground, No. 592-7" **1,650**

Vase, 7" h., trumpet-shaped w/handles from base to mid-section, green ground, No. 604-7" **350-400**

Vase, 7" h., trumpet-shaped w/handles from base to mid-section, raspberry pink ground, No. 604-7" **700**

Vase, 7" h., footed wide cylindrical body w/wide collared rim, small loop handles from shoulder to rim, green ground, No. 610-7"... **660**

Vase, 8" h., footed, globular w/shoulder handles, raspberry pink ground, No. 595-8"... **880**

Vase, 9" h., cylindrical w/short collared neck, handles rising from shoulder to beneath rim, raspberry pink ground, No. 594-9"... **825**

Vase, 9" h., cylindrical w/short collared neck, handles rising from shoulder to beneath rim, green ground, No. 594-9"........ **893**

Vase, 9" h., bulbous body tapering to short wide cylindrical rim, handles from mid-base to below rim, green ground, No. 596-9"... **853**

Vase, 10" h., footed bulbous body tapering to closed rim, two handles rising from shoulder to beneath rim, raspberry pink ground, No. 597-10" **995**

Baneda Vase

Vase, 12" h., trumpet-form on flaring foot, base handles, green ground, No. 598-12" (ILLUS.).. **880**

Vase, 12" h., expanding cylinder w/small rim handles, green ground, No. 599-12" .. **1,540**

Vase, 12" h., expanding cylinder w/small rim handles, raspberry pink ground, No. 599-12" (repairs to rim, handles & base)...... **770**

Vase, 15" h., floor-type, bulbous ovoid body w/flat rim, shoulder handles, green ground, No. 600-15" **4,400**

BLACKBERRY (1933)
Band of relief clusters of blackberries with vines and ivory leaves accented in green and terra cotta on a green textured ground.

Console bowl, rectangular w/small handles, No. 228-10", 3 1/2 x 13"...................... **427**

Jardiniere, two-handled, No. 623-4", 4" h....... **235**

Jardiniere, two-handled, No. 623-5", 5" h...... **358**

Jardiniere, two-handled, No. 623-9", 9" h..... **1,010**

Jardiniere & pedestal base, 28" h., 2 pcs. .. **3,400**

Vase, 4" h., two-handled, bulbous, No. 567-4".. **313**

Vase, 4" h., 6" d., squatty bulbous form w/small angled shoulder handles, No. 568-4"... **447**

Vase, 5" h., tiny rim handles, canted sides, No. 565-5" **445**

Vase, 5" h., two handles at midsection, bulbous base & wide neck, No. 570-5" **457**

Vase, 6" h., bulbous ovoid w/wide rim, small shoulder handles, No. 571-6" **550-600**

Vase, 6" h., No. 572-6".................................... **626**

Vase, 6" h., two handles at midsection, No. 573-6".. **564**

Blackberry Vase

Vase, 6" h., globular w/tiny rim handles, No. 574-6" (ILLUS.)..................................... **660**

Vase, 8" h., handles at mid-section, slightly globular base & wide neck, No. 575-8" **940**

Vase, 12 1/2" h., ovoid w/loop handles from shoulder to rim, No. 578-12" (minor chip to bottom) **1,320**

Wall pocket, basket-shaped w/narrow base & flaring rim, No. 1267-8" 6 3/4" w. at rim, 8 1/2" h. **925-975**

BLEEDING HEART (1938)
Pink blossoms and green leaves on shaded blue, green or pink ground.

Basket, pink ground, No. 359-8", 8" h. **325**

Basket w/circular handle, blue ground, No. 360-10", 10" h. **250**

Basket w/circular handle, pink ground, 360-10", 10" h., w/gold foil label **331**

Basket w/pointed overhead handle, w/flower frog, green ground, No. 361-12", 12" h., 2 pcs. **358**

Book ends, book-shaped, pink ground, No. 6, pr. **385**

Bowl, 8" w., hexagonal, pink ground, No. 380-8"... **110**

Candleholders, pink ground, No. 1140-2", pr. **165**

Candlesticks, pink ground, 1139-4 1/2",
   4 1/2" h., pr... 165
Console bowl, blue ground, No. 382-10",
   10" l... 295
Console bowl, pink ground, No. 382-10",
   10" l... 250
Console bowl, pink ground, No. 383-14",
   14" l... 450
Cornucopia-vase, pink ground, No. 141-
   6", 6" h.. 165
Ewer, green ground, No. 963-6", 6" h. **200-225**
Ewer, pink ground, No. 972-10", 10" h. 275
Flower frog, round base, scalloped edge,
   overhead handle, pink ground, No. 40,
   3 1/2" h. 110
Flower frog, round base, scalloped edge,
   overhead handle, blue ground, No. 40,
   3 1/2" h. 220
Jardiniere, small pointed shoulder han-
   dles, blue ground, No. 651-3", 3" h. 100
Jardiniere, small pointed shoulder handles, green ground, No. 651-3", 3" h. 110
Jardiniere & pedestal base, pink ground,
   jardiniere 8" h., No. 651-8", 2 pcs. **1,045**
Jardiniere & pedestal base, blue ground,
   jardiniere 10" h., No. 651-10", 2 pcs. **3,500**

Bleeding Heart Pitcher

Pitcher, 8" h., asymmetrical w/high arched
   handle, pink ground, No. 1323 (ILLUS.)....... 399
Plate, 10 1/2" w., hexagonal, pink ground,
   No. 381-10" 110
Urn-vase, pink ground, No. 377-4", 4" h. 135
Vase, 5" h., blue ground, No. 962-5" 115
Vase, 6 1/2" h., base handles, blue ground,
   No. 964-6"... 175
Vase, 6 1/2" h., base handles, pink ground,
   No. 964-6"... 75
Vase, 8" h., green ground, No. 139-8"............. 325
Vase, 8" h., pillow-type, pink ground, No.
   968-8" 275
Vase, 9" h., pillow-type, blue ground, No.
   970-9"... 300
Vase, 12" h., expanding cylinder w/small
   handles at shoulder, blue ground, No.
   974-12"... 660
Vase, 15" h., two-handled, flaring hexago-
   nal mouth, pink ground, No. 976-15"............ 775

Vase, 18" h., floor-type, blue ground, No.
   977-18".. **1,200**

BUSHBERRY (1948)
*Berries and leaves on blue, green or russet
bark-textured ground; brown or green branch handles.*

Ashtray, blue ground, No. 26.......................... 195
Basket, hanging-type w/original chains,
   blue ground, No. 465-5", 7"........................... 375
Basket, hanging-type w/original chains,
   green ground, No. 465-5", 7"......................... 275
Basket, blue ground, No. 370-8", 8" h. 265
**Basket w/asymmetrical overhead han-
   dle,** blue ground, No. 369-6 1/2",
   6 1/2" h.. 195
**Basket w/asymmetrical overhead han-
   dle,** russet ground, No. 369-6 1/2",
   6 1/2" h.. 180
Basket w/low overhead handle, russet
   ground, No. 357-10", 10" h......................... 280
Basket w/low overhead handle, asym-
   metric rim, blue ground, No. 372-12",
   12 h. 420
Beverage set: 8 3/4" h. pitcher w/ice lip &
   six 3 1/2" h. mugs; blue ground, pitcher
   No. 1325, mugs No. 1-3 1/2", 7 pcs. **1,500**
Bowl, 4" d., two-handled, russet ground,
   No. 411-4"... 110
Bowl, 6" d., russet ground, No. 412-6"............ 195
Bowl, 10" d., russet ground, No. 1-10" 195
Console bowl, two-handled, blue ground,
   No. 414-10", 10" d....................................... 180
Console bowl, end handles, blue ground,
   No. 385-10", 13" l. 154
Cornucopia-vase, blue ground, No. 153-6" 135
Cornucopia-vase, double, green ground,
   No. 155-8", 6" h.. 100
Cornucopia-vase, double, russet ground,
   No. 155-8", 6" h.. **100-150**
Cornucopia-vase, double, blue ground,
   No. 155-8" 215
Ewer, green ground, No. 1-6, 6" h................... 150
Ewer, russet ground, No. 1-6, 6" h. 185
Ewer, blue ground, No. 2-10", 10" h. 300
Ewer, green ground, No. 2-10", 10" h. 275
Jardiniere, two-handled, No. 657-3" 100
Jardiniere, two-handled, russet ground,
   No. 657-4", 4" h... 100
Jardiniere & pedestal base, two-handled,
   green ground, No. 657-10", 2 pcs. (chip
   to rim, sm. chip to base & one handle of
   pedestal) **1,045**
Jardiniere & pedestal base, two-handled,
   russet ground, No. 657-8", 2 pcs........... **500-600**
Jardiniere & pedestal base, two-handled,
   blue ground, No. 657-8", overall 24" h., 2
   pcs. 798
Mug, green ground, No. 1-3 1/2", 3 1/2" h........ 135
Pitcher, 8 3/4" h., blue w/green branch
   handle, No. 1325 427
Sand jar, green ground, No. 778-14",
   14" h.. **1,400**
Tea set: cov. teapot, creamer & sugar
   bowl; blue ground, No. 2, No. 2C, No.
   2S, 3 pcs. **550-575**
Tea set: cov. teapot, open creamer &
   sugar; russet ground, No. 2, No. 2C &
   No. 2S, 3 pcs... 650

Umbrella stand, double handles, blue
ground, No. 779-20", 20 1/2" h.................... 985
Vase, 6" h., two-handled, green ground,
No. 30-6"... 90-100
Vase, 6" h., angular side handles, low foot,
globular w/wide neck, blue ground, No.
156-6".. 165
Vase, 6" h., angular side handles, low foot,
globular w/wide neck, russet ground, No.
156-6".. 95
Vase, 7" h., footed cylindrical body w/asym-
metrical handles, blue ground, No. 32-7"..... 275
Vase, bud, 7" h., asymmetrical base handles, cylindrical body, blue ground, No.
152-7"... 160

Bushberry Vase

Vase, 8" h., footed tapering squared body
w/flaring rim flanked by down-turned
forked branch handles, green ground,
No. 33-8" (ILLUS.).. 295
Vase, 9" h., two-handled, ovoid, blue
ground, No. 35-9"... 205
Vase, 12 1/2" h., large asymmetrical side
handles, bulging cylinder w/flaring foot,
russet ground, No. 38-12".................... 225-250
Vase, 12 1/2" h., large asymmetrical side
handles, bulging cylinder w/flaring foot,
blue ground, No. 38-12".............................. 375
Vase, 14 1/2" h., blue ground, No. 39-14"........ 605
Vase, 18" h., floor-type, blue ground, No.
41-18" (short tight line to rim, restoration
to one handle).. 550
Vase, 18" h., floor-type, green ground, No.
41-18" (grinding chips to base)................... 880

CARNELIAN I (1910-15)

*Matte glaze with a combination of two colors or
two shades of the same color with the darker dripping over the lighter tone or heavy and textured
glaze with intermingled colors and some running.*

Bowl, 8" d., 3" h., deep green & light green,
No. 163-8"... 88
Bowl, 9 1/2" d., wide squatty bulbous sides
tapering sharply to a wide molded rim,
deep green & light green................................ 69
Candleholder, green ground, No. 1059-
2 1/2", 2 1/2" h... 70
Candleholders, simple disc base w/incised
rings at base of candle nozzle, deep
green & light green, No. 1063-3",
2 1/2" h., pr... 110
Console bowl, footed low oval form
w/canted sides & ornate scrolled end
handles, light & dark green, No. 152-8",
10 3/4" l., 4" h.. 165

Console bowl, hexagonal, blue & green,
No. 170-14", 14" l., 4" h................................. 83
Console bowl, footed shallow oval form
w/angled end handles, light & dark
green, No. 157-14", 16" l., 2 3/4" h............... 248
Console set: 9 1/2" l. 3 1/2" h. octagonal
bowl & pair of 3" h. candleholders; pink
& blue, Nos. 164-3" & 1064-3", 3 pcs........... 103
Ewer, footed wide compressed globular
body w/wide shoulder to the pointed &
arched spout, scrolled C-form handle
from the neck to lower base, dark & light
blue, No. 1314-8", 8" h................................. 220
Flower frog, blue & grey ground, 6 1/4" w.,
2 1/2" h... 120
Flower frog, green ground, 4 1/2" h................ 175
Vase, pillow-type, green & turquoise............... 160

Carnelian I Double Bud Vase

Vase, double bud, 5" h., gate-form, olive
green & mustard yellow, No. 56-5"
(ILLUS.)... 83
Vase, 6" h., pillow-type, light blue & dark
blue.. 75-100
Vase, 6" h., footed fan-shaped body, mus-
tard yellow over light green, No. 52-6".......... 83
Vase, 7" h., footed wide ovoid base w/wide
shoulder to short collared neck, ornate
handles from mid-section to rim, light &
dark blue, No. 271-7"................................... 110
Vase, 7" h., double gourd-form w/wide neck
& flaring rim, ornate pointed & scrolled
handles from mid-section of base to
below rim, light & dark green, No. 310-7"..... 138
Vase, 8" h., footed wide compressed bulbous body w/wide collared neck, ornate
scroll handles from center of base to rim,
light & dark green & mustard yellow, No.
318-8".. 138
Vase, 9" h., cylindrical w/wide collared
neck, dark blue & light blue, No. 313-9"....... 250
Vase, 10" h., semi-ovoid base & long wide
neck w/rolled rim, ornate handles, grey &
mauve, black label, No. 337-10".................. 413
Vase, 12" h., bulbous ovoid body w/wide
cylindrical neck, scrolled shoulder handles, grey & mauve, No. 338-12"................. 440
Wall pocket, ornate side handles, flaring
rim, turquoise blue & aqua, 8" h.................. 450
Wall pocket, ornate side handles, flaring
rim, mustard over light green, No. 1249-
9", 9" h.. 245

CARNELIAN II (1915)

Intermingled colors, some with a drip effect.

Bowl, footed, six-sided, w/drip glaze in shades of rose, grey, green & tan, small separation at the rim, 4 x 15" 330

Bowl, 10" d., low faceted body, mottled pink & green glaze 495

Bowl, 10 1/2 x 3 1/2", footed w/curved end handles, semi-matte drip glazes in purple & green intermingled w/maroon 468

Bowl, 14" d., short pedestal foot below compressed round body w/incurved sides & wide flaring rim, scrolled handles, mottled pink & green glaze 550

Candleholders, aqua & lilac glaze, No. 1059-2 1/2", 2 1/2" h., pr. 150

Console set: 9 3/4" d., bowl & pair of 3 5/8" h. candleholders; shades of green over blue textured glaze, the set 413

Ewer, pink, mauve, green & black mottled matte glaze, 15" h. 1,760

Lamp base, footed spherical body w/wide cylindrical neck & scrolling angled handles, raspberry & green mottled matte glaze, metal fittings, 8" h. (bruise to one handle) 330

Urn, squatty bulbous body w/wide flaring rim, scrolled handles, 5" h. 303

Urn, globular body tapering to flaring rim, scrolled shoulder handles, rose, green & grey ground, 6" h. 660

Urn, footed, compressed globular form w/short molded neck, ornate scrolled handles, mottled pink, yellow & green glaze, 7" h. 358

Urn, bulbous body w/wide cylindrical neck, ornate scrolled handles from shoulder to rim, mottled pink, yellow & green glaze, 9 3/4" h. 770

Vase, large bulbous handled form, pink & purple ground 550

Carnelian II Vase

Vase, 5" h., fan-shaped body on round disc foot, scrolled handles from base to mid-section, intermingled green & pink glaze (ILLUS.) 138

Vase, bud, 6" h., footed trumpet-form w/ornate handles from base to mid-section, blue ground 90

Vase, bud, 6" h., footed trumpet-form w/ornate handles from base to mid-section, intermingled shades of raspberry pink 135

Vase, 7" h., compressed globular base w/short wide neck, large handles, purple & rose 225

Vase, 8" h., tapering cylindrical body w/short cylindrical neck, mottled pink & green glaze 250-300

Vase, 9" h., bulbous ovoid body w/short collared mouth, angled shoulder handles, mottled pink, yellow & green glaze 715

Vase, 10" h., compressed globular form w/angled handles from mid-section to rim, mottled rose & green glaze 1,100

Vase, 10" h., footed wide tapering cylindrical body w/wide slightly flaring neck, mottled pink & green glaze 523

Vase, 12" h., bulbous ovoid body w/wide flaring rim flanked by buttressed handles, rose, mauve & green mottled glaze, No. 445-12" (restoration to drill hole at base) 1,650

Vase, 12" h., flaring foot below wide bulbous body w/shoulder tapering to wide flaring cylindrical neck, rose, yellow, blue, violet & green mottled matte glaze, No. 446-12" 2,860

Vase, 18" h., floor-type, tall ovoid body w/ringed base and flaring foot, molded rim & scrolled shoulder handles, mottled pink & green glaze 1,815

Wall pocket, slender fanned body flanked by double-scroll handles, shaded green ground, 8" h. 250

CHERRY BLOSSOM (1933)
Sprigs of cherry blossoms, green leaves and twigs with pink fence against a combed blue-green ground or creamy ivory fence against a terra cotta ground shading to dark brown.

Bowl, 4" h., two-handled, canted sides, terra cotta ground 275

Candlesticks, brown ground, pr. 400

Jardiniere, squatty bulbous body, two-handled, terra cotta ground, No. 627-4", 4" h. 450

Jardiniere, shoulder handles, terra cotta ground, 6" h., No. 627-6" 358

Lamp base, footed globular base tapering to short cylindrical neck flanked by small loop handles, terra cotta ground, shape No. 625-8", overall 9" h. 770

Planter, rectangular w/two small handles, terra-cotta ground, No. 240-8", 3 x 11", 7" l. 303

Vase, ball-shaped, blue-green ground 535

Vase, 4" h., compressed squatty bulbous body w/a short slightly flared neck flanked by small loop handles, blue-green ground, No. 617-3 1/2" 468

Vase, 5" h., two-handled, globular w/wide mouth, blue-green ground, No. 627-5" 275

Vase, 6" h., bulbous body, shoulder tapering to wide molded mouth, small loop shoulder handles, terra cotta ground, No. 621-6 354

Vase, 6" h., bulbous body, shoulder tapering to wide molded mouth, small loop shoulder handles, blue-green ground, No. 621-6 605

Vase, 7" h., terra cotta ground, No. 622-7" 525

Vase, 7" h., ovoid body w/tiny shoulder handles, No. 623-7" 660

Vase, 7 1/2" h., two-handled, footed cylindrical body, terra cotta ground, No. 620-7" 343

Vase, 8" h., handles at midsection, terra
cotta ground, No. 624-8" **468**

Cherry Blossom Vase

Vase, 8" h., two-handled, globular, terra
cotta ground, No. 625-8" (ILLUS.)......... **600-700**

Vase, 10" h., slender ovoid body w/wide
cylindrical neck, loop handles from
shoulder to middle of neck, terra cotta
ground, No. 626-10"..................................... **595**

Vase, 15" h., floor-type, bulbous ovoid
w/wide molded mouth, small loop shoulder handles, blue-green ground, No.
628-15" (few minute flecks to decoration,
glazed-over chip to branch & few minor
chips to base)... **3,575**

CLEMATIS (1944)

*Clematis blossoms and heart-shaped green
leaves against a vertically textured ground — white
blossoms on blue, rose-pink blossoms on green
and ivory blossoms on golden brown.*

Basket, hanging-type, blue ground, No.
470-5", 5" h. **225**

Clematis Hanging-Type Basket

Basket, hanging-type, brown ground, No.
470-5", 5" h. (ILLUS.) **175**

Basket, hanging-type, green ground, No.
470-5", 5" h. **175-200**

Basket, waisted cylindrical body, green
ground, No. 387-7" **134**

Basket, blue ground, No. 388-8" **160**

Basket w/ornate circular handle, waisted
cylindrical body, brown ground, No. 387-
7", 7" h.. **170**

Basket w/overhead handle, pedestal
base, blue ground, No. 389-10", 10" h. **195**

Basket w/overhead handle, pedestal
base, green ground, No. 389-10", 10" h
. ... **175-200**

Bowl, 10" d., green ground, No. 6-10" **250**

Candleholders, bulbous w/tiny pointed
handles, brown ground, No. 1158-2",
2" h., pr.. **98**

Candleholders, bulbous w/tiny pointed
handles, green ground, No. 1158-2",
2" h., pr.. **165**

Console bowl, blue ground, No. 461-14",
14" l. **200**

Cookie jar, cov., brown ground, No. 3-8",
8" h... **427**

Cookie jar, cov., green ground, No. 3-8",
8" h... **550**

Cornucopia-vase, blue ground, No. 193-
6", 6" h. **85**

Creamer, blue ground, No. 5C **80**

Creamer, green ground, No. 5C......................... **75**

Creamer & open sugar bowl, green
ground, No. 5S & 5C, pr. **155**

Ewer, green ground, No. 16-6", 6" h. **145**

Ewer, blue ground, No. 17-10", 10" h. **173**

Ewer, green ground, No. 17-10", 10" h............. **245**

Ewer, blue ground, No. 18-15", 15" h. **365**

Flower frog, green ground, No. 192-5",
5" h. **115**

Flowerpot w/saucer, blue ground, No.
668-5", 5 1/2" h...................................... **120-140**

Jardiniere, blue ground, No. 667-8", 8" h. **322**

Tea set: cov. teapot, creamer & open sugar
bowl, green ground, No. 5, 3 pcs. **325**

Teapot, cov., green ground, No. 5 .... **200**

Vase, 6" h., two-handled, green ground,
No. 102-6" **55**

Vase, 6" h., two-handled, blue ground, No.
103-6".. **110**

Vase, 6" h., two-handled, brown ground,
No. 103-6"... **85**

Vase, 6" h., two-handled, urn-form, blue
ground, No. 188-6" **95**

Vase, 7" h., brown ground, No. 105-7" **150**

Vase, bud, 7" h., angular handles rising
from flared base to slender neck, green
ground, No. 187-7" **150**

Vase, 8" h., two-handled, blue ground, No.
107-8".. **90-100**

Vase, 8" h., two-handled, globular base
w/high collared neck, green ground, No.
108-8" **90**

Vase, 8" h., footed baluster-form w/flaring
mouth & angled shoulder handles, blue
ground, No. 122-8" **185**

Vase, 9" h., blue ground, No. 109-9" **225**

Vase, 10" h., two-handled, brown ground,
No. 111-10" **210**

Wall pocket, angular side handles, brown
ground, No. 1295-8", 8 1/2" h...................... **138**

Wall pocket, angular side handles, green
ground, No. 1295-8", 8 1/2" h....................... **200**

CORINTHIAN (1923)

*Deeply fluted ivory and green body below a con-
tinuous band of molded grapevine, fruit, foliage and
florals in naturalistic colors, narrow ivory and green
molded border at the rim.*

Basket, hanging-type w/chains, 8" d. **260**

Bowl, 7" d. **75**

Flower frog, No. 14-3 1/2", 3 1/2" h. **50**

Jardiniere, 8" h., No. 601-8" **325**

Jardiniere, 9" h., No. 601-9" **185**

Vase, double bud, 4 1/2" h., 7" w., gate-
form, No. 37-7".. **138**

Vase, bud, 6 1/4" h. **195**

Corinthian Vase

Vase, 7" h., footed, baluster-form tapering
to wide cylindrical neck, No. 215-7"
(ILLUS.).. **138**
Vase, 7" h., waisted cylindrical body, No.
235-7 .... **138**
Vase, 8 1/2" h. **90**
Wall pocket, No. 1232-8", 8" h. **275**
Wall pocket, conical base tapering to wide
neck w/flaring rim, No. 1228-10", 10" h. **325**

COSMOS (1940)
*Embossed blossoms against a wavy horizontal
ridged band on a textured ground — ivory band
with yellow and orchid blossoms on blue, blue band
with white and orchid blossoms on green or tan.*

Basket, hanging-type, handles rising from
midsection to rim, blue ground, No. 361-
5", 7" h.. **295**
Basket, blue ground, No. 357-10", 10" h.......... **363**
Basket w/pointed overhead handle, ped-
estal base, blue ground, No. 358-12",
12" h. **485**
Bowl, 4" d., blue ground, No. 375-4".............. **185**
Bowl, 4" d., tan ground, No. 375-4"................. **165**
Bowl, 8" d., blue ground, No. 370-8".............. **195**
Bowl, 8" d., tan ground, No. 370-8"................. **110**

Cosmos Candleholder

Candleholders, loop handles above flat
disc base, slender candle nozzle, blue
ground, No. 1136-2", 2 1/2" h., pr.
(ILLUS. of one).. **179**
Console bowl, green ground, No. 370-8",
8" l. **163**
Flower frog, pierced globular body
w/asymmetrical overhead handle, blue
ground, No. 39, 3 1/2" h............................... **145**
Flower frog, pierced globular body
w/asymmetrical overhead handle, tan
shaded to green ground, No. 39,
3 1/2" h. **125**

Flower frogs, pierced globular body
w/asymmetrical overhead handle, blue
ground, No. 39, 3 1/2" h., pr. **248**
Jardiniere, two-handled, blue ground, No.
649-3" **100**
Jardiniere, two-handled, tan ground, No.
649-4", 4" h.. **100-125**
Jardiniere, two-handled, blue ground, No.
649-6", 6" h... **150-225**
Planter, réctangular w/shaped rim, blue
ground, No. 381-9", 9" l. **320**
Rose bowl, two-handled, blue ground, No.
375-4", 4" h.. **175**
Rose bowl, two-handled, green ground,
No. 375-4", 4" h.. **135**
Urn-vase, blue ground, No. 135-8", 8" h. **275**
Urn-vase, green ground, No. 135-8", 8" h........ **250**
Vase, 7" h., globular base w/long slender
neck w/cut-out rim, large loop handles
rising from midsection of base to middle
of neck, green ground, No. 948-7" **193**
Vase, 8" h., footed bulbous base w/wide
cylindrical neck w/scalloped rim, large
loop handles, No. 135-8"............................... **248**
Vase, 8" h., two-handled, cut-out top edge,
tan ground, No. 950-8" **225**
Vase, 9" h., handles rising from midsection
of ovoid body to neck, tan ground, No.
952-9".. **175**
Vase, 9" h., tapering cylinder w/shaped flar-
ing mouth, curved handles at midsec-
tion, green ground, No. 953-9"...................... **250**
Vase, 10" h., trumpet-shaped w/slender
curved handles from base to midsection,
tan ground, No. 954-10" **245**
Vase, 10" h., trumpet-shaped w/slender
curved handles from base to midsection,
green ground, No. 954-10" **375**
Wall pocket, fanned conical shape w/high
arched handle across the top, blue
ground, No. 1285-6", 6 1/2" h........................ **518**
Wall pocket, double, tan ground, No. 1286-
8", 8 1/2" h.. **400**
Window box, tan ground, No. 381-
9 x 3 x 3 1/2", 9" l. **242**

DAHLROSE (1924-28)
*Band of ivory daisy-like blossoms and green
leaves against a mottled tan ground.*

Basket, hanging-type w/original chain, No.
343-6", 7 1/2" d... **278**
Bowl, 8" d., footed squatty bulbous body
tapering to a wide flared rim, angular
end handles from rim to shoulder, No.
180-8".. **210**
Bowl, 10" l., oval, footed sharply canted
sides w/a low molded rim w/angular end
handles from rim to shoulder, No. 179-8"..... **150**
Bowl, 10" d., 3 1/2" h., spherical
w/incurved sides & molded rim,
unmarked **275**
Candleholders, angular handles rising
from low slightly domed base, No. 1069-
3", 3" h., pr.. **135**
Jardiniere, No. 614-4", 4" h. **250-350**
Jardiniere, tiny rim handles, No. 614-7",
7" d., 4" h... **122**
Jardiniere, squatty bulbous form w/tiny rim
handles, No. 614-6", 6" h. **165**

Jardiniere & pedestal base, No. 614-10",
10" h., 2 pcs. (re-glued base chip to jar-
diniere) **935**

Dahlrose Triple Bud Vase

Vase, triple bud, 6" h., a domed round base
w/a swelled cylindrical central shaft
joined by floral panels to outcurved
squared side holders, No. 76-6" (ILLUS.)..... **350**

Vase, double bud, 6" h., gate-form, No. 79-
6", black paper label............................. **145-175**

Vase, 6" h., cylindrical w/small pointed handles at the shoulder, No. 363-6"................... **139**

Vase, 6" h., squatty bulbous body tapering
to wide rolled rim, tiny angled handles
from shoulder to rim, No. 364-6" **224**

Vase, bud, 7" h., a ringed oblong domed
base supports at one side a slender
swelled cylindrical vase w/a flaring rim, a
long, high arched handle runs from one
side of vase down to a forked juncture
w/the base, a smaller down-curved
angular handle joins the two sides, No.
77-7 .... **275**

Vase, bud, 8" h., slender swelled body
w/flaring base & rolled rim, angled buttress side handles w/blossoms, No. 78-
8" **235**

Vase, 8" h., footed bulbous ovoid, No. 365-
8" **413**

Vase, 8" h., footed ovoid body w/flared rim,
angled handles from shoulder to rim, No.
366-8"... **275**

Vase, 10" h., footed tapering square form,
paper label **330**

Vase, 10" h., two-handled, ovoid w/wide
flaring rim, No. 369-10" **380**

Vase, 12" h., footed wide ovoid w/wide flaring rim, angled handles from shoulder to
rim, No. 370-12" **523**

Wall pocket, conical w/molded rim, tiny rim
handles, No. 1258-8", 8" h. **550**

Candleholders, angular handles rising
from low slightly domed base, 3 1/2" h.,
pr. **95**

FERELLA (1931)

*Impressed shell design alternating with small
cut-outs at top and base; mottled brown or turquoise and red glaze.*

Ferella Bowl

Bowl, 12" d., canted sides, low foot, mottled brown glaze, No. 212-12" (ILLUS.)........ **523**

Candleholders, chalice-form w/a low pedestal base supporting a wide deep
pierced rounded cup centered by a cylindrical candle socket, mottled brown
glaze, No. 1078-4", 4 1/2" h., pr. (profes-
sional repair to one) **413**

Console bowl w/attached flower frog,
deep flaring sides, mottled brown glaze,
No. 87-8", 8" d... **498**

Urn-vase, compressed globular form w/tiny
handles at midsection, reticulated foot &
rim, turquoise & red glaze, No. 505-6",
6" h. **468**

Vase, 4" h., angular handles, short narrow
neck, mottled brown glaze, No. 497-4" **429**

Vase, 4" h., angular handles, bulbous, turquoise & red glaze, No. 498-4" **300-350**

Vase, 5" h., footed wide ovoid form w/flar-
ing rim, long side handles, turquoise &
red glaze, No. 500-5" **523**

Vase, 5" h., two-handled, flaring rim, mottled brown glaze, No. 503-5" **400**

Vase, 6" h., large semi-circular handles,
turquoise & red glaze, No. 499-6" **575**

Vase, 6" h., handles rising from shoulder of
compressed globular base to beneath
the rim of the long tapering neck, mottled
brown glaze, No. 502-6" **550**

Vase, 6" h., bulbous base w/canted shoulder flanked by small angular handles,
wide cylindrical neck, & turquoise & red
glaze, No. 505-6"... **700**

Vase, 8" h., slightly ovoid, turquoise & red
glaze, No. 508-8".................................. **650-700**

Vase, 8" h., spherical body on low foot
w/wide slightly flared cylindrical neck,
arched handles from mid-section to
shoulder, turquoise & red glaze, No.
509-8".. **1,100**

Vase, 9 1/4" h., 5 1/4" d., footed slender
ovoid body tapering to a short flaring
neck, low arched handles down the
sides, stylized green & yellow blossoms
on reticulated bands, mottled brown
glaze, No. 507-9".................................. **550-600**

Vase, 10" h., 6" 1/4" d., ovoid body on flaring foot & tapering to a widely flaring
mouth, low angular handles down the
sides, the foot pierced w/a band of small
squares, the mouth pierced w/two bands
of small rectangles, brown glaze, No.
511-10".. **935**

Vase, 10" h., 6" 1/4" d., ovoid body on flaring foot & tapering to a widely flaring

mouth, low angular handles down the sides, the foot pierced w/a band of small squares, the mouth pierced w/two bands of small rectangles, turquoise & red glaze, No. 511-10".................................... **1,650**

Wall pocket, half-round basket-form w/widely flaring rim & high shaped & arched backplate w/hanging hole, turquoise & red glaze, No. 1266-6 1/2", 6 1/2" h... **1,200**

FLORANE I (1920s)
Terra cotta shading to either dark brown or deep olive green on simple shapes, often from the Rosecraft line.

Florane Basket

Basket, footed, ovoid body w/flaring rim, overhead handle, terra cotta shading to olive green, 8 1/4" h. (ILLUS.)...................... **358**

Bowl, 8" d., low, dark brown............................. **110**

Bowl, 8" d., rounded w/upright sides & slightly scalloped rim, No. 62-8" **50**

Vase, double-bud, 5" h., gate-form................... **125**

Vase, 5 5/8" h., footed swelled cylindrical body w/short collared neck, terra cotta shading to olive green................................. **110**

Vase, 6" h., cylindrical body w/short squared handles rising from shoulders to mouth, dark brown **165**

Vase, 6 5/8" h., footed, wide ovoid body w/flat flared rim, terra cotta shading to olive green.. **193**

Vase, 8" h., footed, cylindrical body w/wide flaring rim, squared handles, terra cotta shading to olive green **165**

Vase, bud, 8" h., dark brown **80**

Vase, 12" h., slender ovoid form, terra cotta shading to olive green ground, No. 64-12" **100**

Wall pocket, two-handled, ovoid w/fan-shaped top, terra cotta shading to olive green, 9 3/4" h... **330**

FLORENTINE II (after 1937)
Similar to the ivory Florentine, but with lighter backgrounds, less decoration and without cascades on the dividing panels.

Basket w/pointed overhead handle, footed, bulbous body w/flared rim, No. 321-7", 7" h. **138**

Florentine II Vase

Vase, 12" h., ovoid body tapering to wide cylindrical neck w/flaring rim, angled handles from shoulder to rim, No. 234-12" (ILLUS.)... **303**

FOXGLOVE (1940s)
Sprays of pink and white blossoms embossed against a shaded matte-finish ground.

Basket, hanging-type, blue ground, No. 466-5", 6 1/2" h...................................... **300-350**

Basket, hanging-type, green ground, No. 466-5", 6 1/2" h...................................... **250-300**

Basket w/circular overhead handle, conical body w/asymmetric & shaped rim on round disc base, No. 373-8", 8" h................ **225**

Basket w/circular overhead handle, footed conical body w/widely flaring rim, green ground, No. 374-10", 10" h................ **495**

Basket w/circular overhead handle, footed conical body w/widely flaring rim, pink ground, No. 374-10", 10" h. **220**

Basket w/circular overhead handle, footed fan-shape w/shaped rim, pink ground, No. 375-12", 12" h........................... **330**

Book ends, blue ground, No. 10, pr............... **250**

Foxglove Book Ends

Book ends, pink ground, No. 10, minor glaze nick back edge of one, pr. (ILLUS.)..... **308**

Candleholders, disk base, conical w/angled handles from midsection to base, pink ground, No. 159-5", 5" h., pr. **193**

Console bowl, boat-shaped w/angled end handles, blue ground, No. 421-10", 10" l...... **141**

Console bowl, boat-shaped w/angled end handles, green ground, No. 421-10", 10" l. **210**

Console bowl, boat-shaped w/angled end handles, pink ground, No. 421-10", 10" l...... **205**

Console bowl, oval w/cut-out rim & pointed end handles, blue ground, No. 422-10", 10" l. **160**

Cornucopia-vase, snail shell-type, pink ground, No. 166-6" **135**

Cornucopia-vase, green ground, No. 164-8", 8" h. **275**

Ewer, pink ground, No. 4-6 1/2", 6 1/2" h. **218**

Ewer, blue ground, No. 5-10", 10" h. **270**

Flower frog, cornucopia-shaped, pink ground, No. 46, 4" h. **165**

Jardiniere, two-handled, blue ground, No. 659-3", 3" h. **100**

Jardiniere, two-handled, green ground, No. 659-5", 5" h. **160**

Jardiniere, two-handled, blue ground, No. 659-8", 8" h. **220**

Model of a conch shell, green ground, No. 426-6", 6" l. **225**

Model of a conch shell, pink ground, No. 426-6", 6" l. **175**

Pedestal base, large, blue ground **385**

Tray, single open handle, leaf-shaped, green ground, 8 1/2" w. **100-125**

Tray, open rim handles, shaped oval, blue ground, 11" l. **150**

Urn-vase, pink ground, No. 162-8", 8" h. **248**

Vase, 4" h., squatty bulbous base w/wide cylindrical neck, angular side handles, pink ground, No. 42-4" **110**

Vase, 4" h., squatty bulbous base w/wide cylindrical neck, angular side handles, blue ground, No. 42-4" **145**

Vase, 5" h., three-section pillow-type, pink & green, No. 165-5" **180**

Vase, 6 1/2" h., ovoid body w/flared rim, double angled handles from base to rim, pink ground, No. 44-6" **125-150**

Vase, 7" h., semi-ovoid w/long slender angled side handles, blue ground, No. 45-7" **231**

Vase, 7" h., semi-ovoid w/long slender angled side handles, green ground, No. 45-7" **165**

Vase, 7" h., semi-ovoid w/long slender angled side handles, pink ground, No. 45-7" **138**

Vase, 14" h., conical w/flaring mouth, four short handles rising from disc base, blue ground, No. 53-14" **660**

Vase, 15" h., footed ovoid body, two-handled, green ground, No. 54-15" **468**

Vase, 15" h., footed ovoid body, two-handled, pink ground, No. 54-15" **895**

Vase, 16" h., pear-shaped body w/closed rim, angled handles from lower body to shoulder, green ground, No. 55-16" **605**

Vase, 18" h., floor-type, two-handled, footed baluster-form w/narrow flared rim, blue ground, No. 56-18" **725-750**

Wall pocket, conical w/flaring rim, loop handles, green ground, No. 1292-8", 8" h. **400**

FREESIA (1945)

Trumpet-shaped blossoms and long slender green leaves against wavy impressed lines — white and lavender blossoms on blended green; white and yellow blossoms on shaded blue or terra cotta and brown.

Basket, hanging-type, blue ground, No. 471-5" **300**

Basket, hanging-type, terra cotta ground, No. 471-5" **259**

Basket, green ground, No. 390-7", 7" h. **220**

Basket, terra cotta ground, No. 390-7", 7" h. **160**

Basket, terra cotta ground, No. 392-10", 10" h. **275**

Basket w/low overhead handle, green ground, No. 310-10", 10" h. **250**

Basket w/overhead handle, terra-cotta ground, No. 391-8", 8" h. **143**

Book ends, blue ground, No. 15, 5 1/4" h., pr. **248**

Bowl, 6" d., green ground, No. 464-6" **135**

Bowl, 11" d., two-handled, terra cotta ground, No. 465-8" **135**

Candleholders, tiny pointed handles, domed base, green ground, No. 1160-2", 2" h., pr. **90**

Candlestick, disc base, cylindrical w/low handles, green ground, No. 1161-4 1/2", 4 1/2" h. **75**

Candlesticks, disc base, cylindrical w/low handles, blue ground, No. 1161-4 1/2", 4 1/2" h., pr. **150**

Candlesticks, disc base, cylindrical w/low handles, green ground, No. 1161-4 1/2", 4 1/2" h., pr. **125**

Candlesticks, disc base, cylindrical w/low handles, terra cotta ground, No. 1161-4 1/2", 4 1/2" h., pr. **120-130**

Console bowl, oval w/angled end handles, green ground, No. 7-10", 10" **250**

Console bowl, low, round, green ground, No. 465-8", 8" d. **175**

Cookie jar, cov., bulbous ovoid body w/angled shoulder handles, slightly domed lid w/knob finial, terra cotta ground, No. 4-8", 8" h. **438**

Cookie jar, cov., bulbous ovoid body w/angled shoulder handles, slightly domed lid w/knob finial, blue ground, No. 4-8", 8" h. **550**

Creamer, green ground, No. 6C **100**

Ewer, blue ground, No. 19-6", 6" h. **139**

Ewer, terra cotta ground, No. 19-6", 6" h. **260**

Ewer, blue ground, No. 20-10", 10" h. **300**

Ewer, terra cotta ground, No. 20-10", 10" h. **160**

Jardiniere, rim handles, blue ground, No. 669-8", 8" h. **425**

Jardiniere & pedestal base, green ground, No. 669-8", 2 pcs. **805**

Jardiniere & pedestal base, terra cotta ground, No. 669-8", 2 pcs. **1,000**

Pitcher, 10" h., tankard, footed slender ovoid body w/wide spout & pointed arched handle, terra cotta ground, No. 20-10".. **150-200**

Pitcher, 10" h., tankard, footed slender ovoid body w/wide spout & pointed arched handle, green ground, No. 20-10".. **450**

Freesia Teapot

Tea set: cov. teapot, creamer & open sugar bowl; blue ground, Nos. 6, 6C & 6S, 3 pcs. (ILLUS. of teapot) **605**

Tea set: cov. teapot, creamer & open sugar bowl; Nos. 6, 6C & 6S, terra cotta ground, 3 pcs. **450**

Teapot, cov., terra cotta ground, No. 6 .... **200**

Urn-vase, two-handled, bulbous body tapering to wide cylindrical neck, green ground, No. 196-8", 8" h............................... **209**

Vase, bud, 7" h., handles rising from compressed globular base, long slender tapering neck, terra cotta ground, No. 195-7"... **83**

Vase, 6" h., footed squatty bulbous base w/wide cylindrical neck, large angled handles, terra cotta ground, No. 118-6" **88**

Vase, 6" h., two-handled, wide fan-shaped body, terra cotta ground, No. 199-6"............ **135**

Vase, 7" h., base handles, long cylindrical neck, terra cotta ground, No. 119-7" **75-125**

Vase, bud, 7" h., handles rising from compressed globular base, long slender tapering neck, green ground, No. 195-7" **95-100**

Vase, 7" h., two-handled, fan shaped, blue ground, No. 200-7"..................................... **150**

Vase, 8" h., footed ovoid body flanked by D-form handles, terra cotta ground, No. 121-8"... **150**

Vase, 8" h., globular base & flaring rim, handles at midsection, blue ground, No. 122-8".. **125-150**

Vase, 9" h., two angular handles at base, cylindrical top w/flaring rim, blue ground, No. 124-9" **190**

Vase, 9 1/2" h., a short ringed pedestal base supporting a flaring half-round base w/an angled shoulder tapering slightly to a tall, wide cylindrical neck, down-curved angled loop handles from center of neck to rim of lower shoulder, terra cotta ground, No. 123-9"..................... **180**

Freesia Vase

Vase, 10" h., two-handled, spherical base w/wide cylindrical neck & flat rim, terra cotta ground, No. 126-10" (ILLUS.).............. **165**

Vase, 10" h., two-handled, spherical base w/wide cylindrical neck & flat rim, blue ground, No. 126-10".................................... **230**

Vase, 10 1/2" h., two-handled, trumpet-form body, green ground, No. 125-10" (professional repair) **175**

Vase, 15" h., tall slender ovoid body tapering to narrow cylindrical neck w/wide flaring rim, pointed shoulder handles, blue ground, No. 128-15" **660**

Vase, 18" h., floor-type, tall slender ovoid body w/slightly flared rim, angled shoulder handles, green ground, No. 129-18" **550**

Wall pocket, waisted long body w/small angled side handles, terra cotta ground, No. 1296-8", 8 1/2" h..................................... **295**

Window box, two-handled, green ground, No. 1392-8", 10 1/2" l................................. **150**

Window box, two-handled, terra cotta ground, No. 1392-8", 10 1/2" l..................... **125**

Candleholders, tiny pointed handles, domed base, terra cotta ground, No. 1160-2", 2" h., pr. **100**

FUCHSIA (1939)
Coral pink fuchsia blossoms and green leaves against a background of blue shading to yellow, green shading to terra cotta or terra cotta shading to gold.

Basket, hanging-type, green ground, No. 359-5", 5" h.. **350-450**

Basket, hanging-type, terra cotta ground, No. 359-5", 5" h..................................... **375-450**

Basket, a short pedestal foot supports a wide squatty half-round body w/small half-round tabs on two sides of the incurved rim, a high round handle joins the two other edges, terra cotta ground, No. 350-8", 8" h... **358**

Basket, w/rounded overhead handle & flower frog, green ground, No. 350-8", 8" h.. **695**

Basket, w/overhead handle, blue ground, No. 351-10", 10" h...................................... **248**

Basket, w/overhead handle, terra cotta ground, No. 351-10", 10" h.......................... **220**

Basket w/flower frog, a short pedestal foot supports a wide squatty half-round body w/small half-round tabs on two sides of

Fuchsia Vase

Vase, 15" h., slender ovoid body w/wide cylindrical neck & large C-form handles, terra cotta ground, No. 904-15"............ **550-600**

Vase, 15" h., slender ovoid body w/wide cylindrical neck & large C-form handles, green ground, No. 904-15"........................ 840

Vase, 18" h., 10" d., floor-type, a disc foot supports a tall baluster-form body w/long low C-form handles down the sides, green ground, No. 905-18"...................... 1,500

Vase, 18" h., 10" d., floor-type, a disc foot supports a tall baluster-form body w/long low C-form handles down the sides, blue ground, No. 905-18"............................... 1,650

Vase, 18" h., 10" d., floor-type, a disc foot supports a tall baluster-form body w/long low C-form handles down the sides, terra cotta ground, No. 905-18"............... 1,200

Wall pocket, green ground 850

Wall pocket, two-handled, green ground, No. 1282-8", 8 1/2" h................................ 475

FUTURA (1928)

Varied line with shapes ranging from Art Deco geometrics to futuristic. Matte glaze is typical although an occasional piece may be high gloss.

Futura Basket

Basket, hanging-type, wide sloping shoulders, sharply canted sides, terra cotta & brown w/embossed stylized pastel foliage, No. 344-5", 5" h. (ILLUS.) 248

Bowl, 5" h., square w/flared rim, raised on four feet, tan, green & blue glaze, No. 198-5".. 990

Bowl, 6" d., 5" h., raised on squared feet, slightly canted sides, yellow & green glaze, No. 197-6"...................................... 660

Bowl, 8" w., 4" h., five flaring sides on square base, orange & green glaze, No. 188-8".. 537

Bowl w/flower frog, 8" d., collared base, shaped flaring sides w/relief decoration, rose glaze, Nos. 187-8" & 15-3 1/2", 2 pcs. (professional repair to rim)................... 207

Candleholders, stepped tapering cylindrical base w/wide flaring foot & flaring shallow socket, mottled green glaze, No.

1075-4", 4" h., black paper label on one, pr. (professional repair to one) 990

Console bowl w/flower frog, footed shallow flaring form, shaded green glaze, No. 195-10", 10" d., 2 1/2" h., 2 pcs. 1,045

Console bowl w/flower frog, cut-out base, sharply canted sides w/embossed stylized design, No. 196, 3 1/2 x 5 x 12".......... 317

Jardiniere, angular handles rising from wide sloping shoulders to rim, sharply canted sides, pink & grey ground, No. 616-6", 6" h..................................... 248

Jardiniere, angular handles rising from wide sloping shoulders to rim, sharply canted sides, aqua & green w/pink leaves, No. 616-6", 6" h............................. 275

Jardiniere & pedestal base, angular handles rising from wide sloping shoulders to rim, sharply canted sides, brown ground, No. 616-10", 10" h., unmarked, 2 pcs.. 1,100

Planter, square w/low flat base, sides decorated w/relief stylized tree w/sparse foliage, cream w/green highlights, No. 191-8", 7" sq... 330

Vase, 4" h., square mounted cone-shaped body w/four vertical supports extending down from mid-point of sides to corners of square disc base, striated blue, green & yellow, No. 430-9"............................. 450-500

Vase, 7" h., sharply canted base, handles rising from shoulder to below rim of long cylindrical stepped neck, grey-green & tan, No. 382-7" 425-450

Vase, 7" h., spherical top w/large pointed dark blue & green leaves curving up the sides, resting on a gently sloped rectangular foot, shaded blue & green blue ground, No. 387-7" 650-700

Vase, 8" h., bottle-shaped w/stepped back bands, green & pink, No. 384-8" 468

Vase, 8" h., upright rectangular form on rectangular foot, stepped neck, long square handles, grey & pink ground, No. 386-8", unmarked................................. 550-650

Vase, 8 1/4" h., 5" d., conical body on flat disc base, buttressed sides, orange w/green buttresses & blue base, No. 401-8"... 509

Vase, 9" h., triangular shaped body tapering to stepped round base, leafy branch design, light & dark blue, No. 388-9"............ 732

Vase, 9" h., "Emerald Urn," angular handles rising from bulbous base to rim, sharply stepped neck shaded dark to light green high gloss glaze, No. 389-9", unmarked 923

Futura Vase

Vase, 9" h., footed bulbous base w/canted sides to wide sloping shoulder w/tapering stepped cylindrical neck, angled handles from shoulder to neck, green ribbed leaf design on shaded tan to brown ground, No. 409-9" (ILLUS.).......................... 745

Vase, 10" h., wide nearly spherical body raised on a small cylindrical foot, the steeply stepped round neck w/narrow mouth, swirled black flame-like design around the lower half, green, No. 391-10"............. 853

Vase, 10" h., four flat vertical handles at flaring collared neck, cylindrical body, brown & yellow, No. 432-10"........................ 880

Vase, 10" h., large spherical body on a small footring, the neck composed of stepped bands, flame-form molded design around the lower half, No. 391-10"............. 900

Vase, 12 1/4" h., 5 1/2" d., tall flaring column rising from four spheres & resting on a square base, grey & peach, No. 393-12"............. 1,320

Vase, 14" h., 5 1/2" d., two large handles at lower half, squat stacked base & faceted squared neck, matte glaze in three shades of brown, No. 411-14"................... 3,190

Vase, 15" h., footed tapering cylindrical body w/wide flaring neck, long slender handles, thistle decoration in green on terra cotta & gold ground, No. 438-15" (professional repair of base chip)............. 1,155

Wall pocket, canted sides, angular rim handles, geometric design in blue, yellow, green & lavender on brown ground, No. 1261-8", 6" w., 8 1/4" h.................. 550-650

Wall pocket, canted sides, angular rim handles, geometric design in blue, yellow, green & lavender on brown ground, No. 1261-8", 6" w., 8 1/4" h......................... 400

Window box, rectangular, Art Deco-type shaped rectangular strapwork on sides & ends, grey-blue shading to tan, No. 376-15, 15 1/2" x 5" (small flat base chip)............. 825

IMPERIAL I (1916)

Pretzel-twisted vine & stylized grape leaves decorate rough-textured background in green and brown. Style of modeling is rather crude.

Basket, tall tapering cylindrical form w/circular overhead handle, 12 1/2" h., unmarked...................... 495
Bowl, 7" d., No. 71-7".. 85
Bowl, 8" d., No. 71-8".. 125
Bowl, 8" d., No. 71-8"... 95
Bowl, 9" d., two-handled.................................. 80
Jardiniere & pedestal, 2 pcs. 1,300
Vase, 8" h., bulbous w/pierced handles at shoulder... 145
Vase, triple bud, 8" h., No. 25-8"...................... 140
Vase, bud, 9" h., cylindrical w/flaring base, long pierced side handles, No. 31-9".......... 165

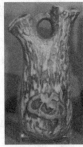

Imperial I Wall Pocket

Wall pocket, double, the two openings joined by slender bridge, No. 1222-9", 10" h. (ILLUS.)...................................... 250-300

IMPERIAL II (1924)

Much variation within the line. There is no common characteristic, although many pieces are heavily glazed, and colors tend to run and blend.

Bowl, 4 1/2" d., ivory ground 75
Bowl, 8" d., 5 1/2" h, squatty gourd-shape, mottled green glaze over smooth sky blue base, No. 203-5".................................. 660

Imperial II Vase

Vase, 4 1/2" h., hemispherical w/flat shoulders & short neck, mauve & turquoise glaze, No. 200-4 1/2", wblack paper label (ILLUS.) 413
Vase, 5" h., wide squatty bulbous body w/a wide shoulder to the short rolled neck, embossed designs around the rim, blue flambé ground, marked w/gold foil label & incised "9" 220

Vase, 5" h., tapering ovoid ringed body, tan shading to green, No. 467-5" **200-225**
Vase, 5" h., tapering ovoid ringed body, yellow ground, No. 467-5" **275**
Vase, 5 1/2" h., tapering cylinder w/horizontal ribbing above base, mottled green ground, No. 468-5" **185-200**
Vase, 6" h., purple & yellow ground, No. 469-6" **250**
Vase, 7" h., globular w/horizontal ribbing at neck, mottled rose glaze, No. 471-7" **650-750**
Vase, 7" h., No. 472-7" **192**
Vase, 7" h., hemispherical w/sloping shoulder & short collared neck, No. 474-7" **425**
Vase, 7" h., 8" d., turquoise & yellow **425**
Vase, 8" h., fan-shaped, two handles from base to midsection, intermingled shades of blue & green **150**
Vase, 8" h., barrel-shape w/horizontal ribbing around upper portion, wide shoulder & small molded rim, mottled cobalt & turquoise glaze, No. 473-7 1/2" **715**
Vase, 10" h., baluster form w/short wide cylindrical neck, cobalt blue ground, No. 477-9 1/2" **1,320**
Vase, 11" h., tapering ovoid body with short wide rim, blue ground **795**

IRIS (1938)
White or yellow blossoms and green leaves on rose blending with green, light blue deepening to a darker blue or tan shading to green or brown.

Basket, tan ground, 10" d., 8 1/2" h. **295**
Basket w/pointed overhead handle, compressed ball form, blue ground, No. 354-8", 8" h. **303**

Iris Basket

Basket w/semicircular overhead handle, rose ground, No. 355-10", 9 1/2" h. (ILLUS.).. **468**
Bowl-vase squatty bulbous body w/stepped shoulder handles, blue ground, No. 357-4", 4" h. **110**
Bowl-vase squatty bulbous body w/stepped shoulder handles, rose ground, No. 357-4", 4" h. **105**
Candlesticks, flat disc base, cylindrical nozzle flanked by elongated open handles, rose ground, No. 1135-4 1/2", 4 1/2" h., pr. **175**
Console bowl, 8" d., tan ground, No. 361-8" **150**
Cornucopia-vase, blue ground, No. 130-4", 4" h. **75**
Cornucopia-vase, rose ground, No. 131-6", 6" h., silver foil label **138**

Ewer, rose ground, No. 926-10", 10" h. **225-275**
Flower frog, blue ground, No. 38 .... **125**
Flower frog, rose ground, No. 38 .... **130**
Flowerpot, brown ground, No. 648-5" **90**
Jardiniere, two-handled, rose ground, No. 647-3", 3" h. **70**
Jardiniere, two-handled, rose ground, No. 647-4", 4" h. **154**
Jardiniere, two-handled, pink ground, No. 647-5", 5" h. (shallow spider-line at base, not thru) **380**
Rose bowl, rose ground, No. 356-6", 6" h. **185**
Vase, 4" h., base handles, tan ground, No. 914-4" **110**
Vase, 5" h., ovoid body on flat circular base, rim handles, blue ground, No. 915-5" **125**
Vase, 6" h., tan ground, No. 917-6" **165**
Vase, 6 1/2" h., two handles rising from shoulder of globular base to midsection of wide neck, rose ground, No. 917-6" .. **150-175**
Vase, 6 1/2" h., two handles rising from shoulder of globular base to midsection of wide neck, blue ground, No. 917-6" **152**
Vase, 6 1/2" h., two handles rising from shoulder of globular base to midsection of wide neck, rose ground, No. 917-6" **160**
Vase, 6 1/2" h., two handles rising from shoulder of globular base to midsection of wide neck, tan shading to brown ground, No. 917-6" **225**
Vase, bud, 7" h., two-handled, blue ground, No. 918-7" **231**
Vase, 7" h., blue ground, No. 919-7" **175**
Vase, 8" h., bulbous base w/short shoulder tapering to wide cylindrical neck & flat rim, handles from shoulder to middle of neck, tan shading to brown ground, No. 921-8" **175**
Vase, 8" h., tan ground, No. 923-8" **225**
Vase, 8" h., urn-form w/pedestal base, tan ground, No. 923-8" **215**
Vase, 10" h., two-handled, rose ground, No. 924-9" **344**
Vase, 10" h., rose ground, No. 927-10" **475**
Vase, 12 1/2" h., semi-ovoid base w/two handles rising from shoulder to beneath rim of short, wide mouth, brown ground, No. 928-12" **350**
Vase, 15" h., two large handles rising from shoulder to rim, blue ground, No. 929-15" **950**
Wall shelf, rose ground, No. 2, 8" h. **450**

JONQUIL (1931)
White jonquil blossoms and green leaves in relief against textured tan ground; green lining.

Bowl, 3" h., large down-turned handles, No. 523-3" **200-250**
Bowl, 4 x 12" **145**
Bowl-vase, bulbous nearly spherical body w/downward looped shoulder handles, 4" h. **115**
Candleholders, No. 1082-4", 4" h., pr. **400**
Crocus pot w/attached saucer, No. 96-7", 7" h. **475**
Jardiniere, No. 621-4", 4" h. **220**
Jardiniere, two-handled, No. 621-8", 8" h. **445**
Jardiniere, No. 621-10", 10" h. **1,200**

Strawberry jar, No. 95-6 1/2", 6 1/2" h. **495**
Vase, 4" h., bulbous spherical form, loop
   handles from mid-section to rim **165**
Vase, 4 1/2 h., two-handled, No. 539-4" **110**
Vase, 5" h., No. 525-5" **231**

Jonquil Vase

Vase, 6 1/2" h., wide bulbous body tapering
   to flat rim, C-form handles, No. 543-
   6 1/2" (ILLUS.) **371**
Vase, 7" h., bulbous base tapering slightly
   to flat mouth, No. 527-7" **413**
Vase, 7 1/5" h., two-handled, trumpet form,
   handles from foot to mid-section, No.
   541-7" **300-325**
Vase, 8" h., tapering cylinder w/elongated
   side handles, No. 528-8" **350-400**
Vase, 8" h., bulbous ovoid body w/short
   collared neck, closed handles from
   shoulder to rim, terra cotta ground, No.
   672-8" **413**
Vase, 9 1/2" h., bulbous base tapering
   slightly to wide cylindrical neck, loop
   handles at midsection, No. 544-9" **550**
Vase, 10 1/2" h., cylindrical w/narrow
   shoulder, asymmetrical, branch handles,
   white ground, No. 583-10" **225**

JUVENILE (1916 ON)
*Transfer-printed and painted on creamware with
nursery rhyme characters, cute animals and other
motifs appealing to children.*

Cup & saucer, Sunbonnet Girl, cup 2" h.,
   saucer 3" d., pr. **125**
Feeding dish w/rolled edge, "Baby's
   Plate" around rim, five chicks around
   interior, 7" d. **195**

Rabbits "Baby's Plate"

Feeding dish w/rolled edge, "Baby's
   Plate" around rim, four rabbits around
   interior, 7" d. (ILLUS.) **195**
Feeding dish w/rolled edge, sitting rab-
   bits, 7" d. **145**

Feeding dish w/rolled edge, chicks deco-
   ration, 8" d. **121**
Feeding dish w/rolled edge, dogs, 8" d. **187**
Feeding dish w/rolled edge, nursery
   rhyme, "Bye Baby Bunting," w/cat, 8" d. **110**
Feeding dish w/rolled edge, nursery
   rhyme, "Little Bo Peep," 8" d. **265**
Feeding dish w/rolled edge, Santa Claus,
   8" d. **750**
Feeding dish w/rolled edge, sitting rab-
   bits, 8" d. **138**
Feeding dish w/rolled edge, Sunbonnet
   girl, 8" d. **165**
Feeding dish w/rolled edge, three ducks,
   8" d. **195**
Mug, chicks, 3" h. **95**
Mug, duck w/hat, 3" h. **150**
Mug, standing rabbit, 3" h. **75-175**
Mug, two-handled, rabbits, 3" h. **195**
Pitcher, 3" h., chicks **115**
Pitcher, 3" h. rabbits **175**
Pitcher, 3 1/2" h., chicks **286**
Pitcher, 3 1/2" h., duck w/hat **145**
Pitcher, 3 1/2" h., fat puppy **85**
Pitcher, 3 1/2" h., side pour, chicks................ **140**
Pitcher, 3 1/2" h., side pour, rabbits **145**
Pitcher, rabbit design, 3 1/2" h. **413**
Plate, 8" d., chicks **185**
Plate, 8" d., Sunbonnet girl **200**

LAUREL (1934)
*Laurel branch and berries in low relief with
reeded panels at the sides. Glazed in deep yellow,
green shading to cream or terra cotta.*

Bowl, 6" d., squatty bulbous body
   w/incurved rim & angled shoulder han-
   dles, yellow ground, No. 250-6 1/4" **248**
Bowl, 6" d., 3 1/2" h., green ground **193**
Bowl, 7" d., shallow, green ground **121**
Candlestick, green ground, 4 1/2" h. **895**

Laurel Urn

Urn, bulbous base w/ringed neck, closed
   shoulder handles, green ground, No.
   250-6 1/4", 6 1/2" h. (ILLUS.) **468**
Urn, deep yellow, No. 250-6 1/2", 6 1/2" h. **265**
Vase, 6" h., No. 239-6" **130**
Vase, 6" h., tapering cylinder w/wide
   mouth, closed angular handles at shoul-
   der, deep yellow, No. 667-6" **231**
Vase, 6" h., angular shoulder handles,
   green ground, No. 668-6" **358**
Vase, 6 1/4" h., green ground, No. 250-
   6 1/4" **450**
Vase, 6 1/2" h., green, No. 669-6 1/2" **185**

LUFFA (1934)

Relief-molded ivy leaves and blossoms on shaded brown or green wavy horizontal ridges.

Luffa Vase

MAGNOLIA (1943)

Large white blossoms with rose centers and black stems in relief against a blue, green or tan textured ground.

Magnolia Ewer

Tea set: cov. teapot, creamer & sugar bowl; blue ground, Nos. 4, 4C & 4S, 3 pcs. (very shallow & small chip to bottom of lid, minor bruise to base of creamer & petal on sugar bowl) **220**

Teapot, cov., green ground, No. 4 .... **330**

Vase, 5" h., blue ground, No. 182-5" **121**

Vase, 7" h., bud, green ground, No. 179-7" **155**

Vase, 8" h., globular w/large angular handles, green ground, No. 91-8" **263**

Vase, 8" h., blue ground, No. 92-8" **165**

Vase, 9" h., two-handled, tan ground, No. 93-9" (chipped) **110**

Wall pocket, overhead handle w/pointed ends, brown ground, No., 1294-8 1/2", 8 1/2" h. **222**

Wall pocket, overhead handle w/pointed ends, blue ground, No. 1294-8 1/2", 8 1/2" h. **375**

MODERNE (1930s)

Art Deco-style rounded and angular shapes trimmed with an embossed panel of vertical lines and modified swirls and circles, white trimmed with terra cotta, medium blue with white and turquoise with a burnished antique gold.

Bowl, 7 x 11", 4" h., pleated body, blue ground, No. 301-10" **83**

Bowl, 7 x 11", 4" h., pleated body, turquoise, No. 301-10" **200**

Candleholders, triple, blue ground, No. 1112-5 1/2", 5 1/2" h., pr. (fleck to rim of one) **440**

Compote, 5" h., open stem, white & tan, No. 295-6 .... **170**

Console bowl, blue ground, No. 302-14", 14" l. **450**

Vase, 6" h., a round foot tapering to a narrow short stem supporting a tall conical body, two small curved handles from foot to lower body, white ground, No. 788-6" (ILLUS.) **160**

Vase, 6" h., a round foot tapering to a narrow short stem supporting a tall conical body, two small curved handles from foot to lower body, turquoise & gold ground, No. 788-6" **385**

Moderne Vase

Vase, 8" h., expanding cylinder, small loop handles at shoulder, white ground, No. 797-8" **193**

MONTACELLO (1931)

White stylized trumpet flowers with black accents on a terra cotta band, light terra cotta mottled in blue, or light green mottled and blended with blue backgrounds.

Basket w/pointed overhead handle, tall collared neck, green ground, No. 332-6", 6 1/2" **605**

Montacello Basket

Basket w/pointed overhead handle, tall collared neck, terra cotta ground, No. 332-6", 6" h. (ILLUS.) **605**

Console bowl, low squatty bulbous oblong form w/flat rim & small round end handles, blue ground, No. 225-9", 13" l., 3" h. **385**

Console bowl, low squatty bulbous oblong form w/flat rim & small round end handles, terra cotta ground, No. 225-9", 13" l., 3" h. **422**

Jardiniere, two-handled, terra cotta ground, No. 559-5", 5" h. **537**

Vase, 4" h., two-handled, terra cotta ground, No. 555-4" **358**

Vase, 5" h., two-handled, conical, terra cotta, black paper label **427**

Vase, 5" h., two handles at mid-section, blue ground, No. 556-5" (small chip to bottom ring) **303**

Vase, 5" h., two handles at mid-section, terra cotta ground, No. 556-5" **358**

Vase, 6" h., ovoid w/large ring shoulder handles, terra cotta ground, No. 560-6" **413**

Vase, 7" h., two-handled, slightly ovoid, wide mouth, blue ground, No. 561-7" (very minor glaze flaws) **413**

Vase, 7" h., spherical base tapering to wide collared neck w/flat rim, loop handles from shoulder to mid-neck, terra cotta ground, No. 562-7" **633**

Vase, 8 1/2" h., small loop handles at shoulder, cylindrical w/flared lip, terra cotta ground, No. 563-8" **495**

Vase, 9" h., bulbous ovoid w/flat rim, loop handles, blue ground, No. 564-9"................. **880**

Vase, 10" h., footed trumpet-form w/base handles, terra cotta ground, No. 565-10" .. **1,760**

MOSS (1930s)

Green moss hanging over brown branch with green leaves; backgrounds are pink, ivory or tan shading to blue.

Bowl, 6" d., footed w/rounded sides, small angled side handles, pink ground, No. 291-6"... **165**

Bowl, 7" d., footed w/rounded sides & small angled side handles, pink ground, No. 291-7" **143**

Bowl, 8" d., footed, round sides & small angled handles, pink shading to blue, No. 291-8"... **143**

Bowl, 10" l., oblong w/end handles, No. 293-10"... **210**

Bowls, 5" d., footed, round sides & small angled handles, pink shading to blue, No. 291-5", pr. **358**

Candleholders, flat disc base, ball-shaped, pink ground, No. 1109-2", 2" h., pr.............. **220**

Moss Console Bowl

Console bowl, oval w/shaped rim & angled end handles, tan shading to blue ground, No. 293-10", 10 1/2" l., 3" h. (ILLUS.) **193**

Rose bowl, footed spherical body w/angled side handles, pink shading to blue ground, No. 289-4", 4" h............................. **182**

Vase, 6" h., footed, expanding cylinder w/angled handles, pink shading to blue, No. 775-6" (restored small chip to bottom ring) **220**

Vase, 7" h., stepped bulbous base tapering to slightly flaring cylindrical neck, angular side handles, pink ground, No. 777-7"..... **275**

Vase, triple bud, pink ground, No. 1108, 7" h... **358**

Vase, 8" h., ovoid w/slightly flaring rim, ornate angular side handles, blue ground, No. 780-8" (pin-head size glaze nick on one handle)..................................... **220**

Vase, 8" h., ovoid w/slightly flaring rim, ornate angular side handles, pink ground, No. 780-8" **330**

Vase, 8 1/2" h., flared foot, bulbous body w/wide flaring rim, blue ground, No. 779-8" **220**

Vase, 10" h., two-handled, footed ovoid body w/flaring rim, tan shading to blue, No. 784-10" **660**

Vase, 12" h., ivory ground, ... **750**

Vase, 12" h., pink ground, No. 785-12"(minor bruises)....................................... **523**

PANEL (1920)

Background colors are dark green or dark brown; decorations embossed within the recessed panels are of natural or stylized floral arrangements or female nudes.

Vase, 6" h., fan-shaped, female nudes, dark green ground...................................... **825**

Vase, 6" h., pillow-shaped, dark brown ground... **358**

Vase, 7" h., brown ground w/dandelions **200**

Vase, 7" h., footed ovoid body w/short cylindrical neck, embossed flowers & leaves on dark green ground **358**

Vase, 8" h., fan-shaped, nude in panel, dark green ground...................................... **605**

Vase, 8" h., fan-shaped w/nudes decoration in orange, brown ground **1,100**

Panel Vase

Vase, 8" h., footed, wide, slightly expanding cylindrical body w/short rolled rim, floral panels, dark green ground, No. 191-8" (ILLUS.).. **413**

Vase, 8" h., compressed bulbous base tapering to wide cylindrical neck, handles from base to mid-section of neck, blue ground, No. 842-8", 8" h. (small chip to base)... **275**

Vase, 8 1/4" h., 5 1/4" w., flattened fan-shaped bowl on a short knob pedestal on flaring round foot, light green on dark green **715**

Vase, 10 1/4" h., 4 1/4" d., tall ovoid body w/widely flaring rim, female nudes, dark green ground, No. 296-10" (small glaze chip to base, possibly in making) **1,430**

Vase, 11" h., footed conical form. nude in panel, dark brown ground, No. 298-11" (drill hole to bottom) **605**

Vase, 11" h., footed conical form. nude in panel, dark green ground, No. 298-11"..... **1,870**

Vase, 12" h., embossed flowers & leaves on dark green ground, No. 299-12 .... **1,045**

Wall pocket, conical form, curved backplate w/pointed center w/hanging hole, nude, green ground, 9" h............................. **297**

Wall pocket, conical form, curved backplate w/pointed center w/hanging hole, nude, brown ground, 9" h. **675**

PINE CONE (1931)

Realistic embossed brown pine cones and green pine needles on shaded blue, brown or green ground. (Pink is extremely rare.)

Ashtray, blue ground, No. 499, 4 1/2" l........... **225**
Ashtray, green ground, No. 499, 4 1/2" l. **116**
Basket, hanging-type, squatty bulbous body tapering slightly toward the base, w/a short wide cylindrical neck flanked by tiny branch hanging handles, brown ground, No. 352-5", 7" d., 5 1/2" h. **450**
Basket, w/overhead branch handle, asymmetrical body, brown ground, No. 408-6", 6" h. **347**
Basket, w/overhead branch handle, disc base, flaring rim, blue ground, No. 338-10", 10" h.. **550-650**
Basket, brown ground, No. 353-11", 11" h....... **475**
Bowl, 4" d., bulbous spherical body w/incurved rim, blue ground, No. 278-4"...... **270**
Bowl, 4" d., bulbous spherical body w/incurved rim, brown ground, No. 278-4" (pin prick glaze nick at mid-body) **138**
Bowl, 6" d., blue ground, No. 261-6" (tight hairline) **176**
Bowl, boat-shaped, 8" l., brown ground, No. 427-8" **325**
Bowl, boat-shaped, 10" l., brown ground, No. 429-10" **500**
Bowl, 11" l., green ground............................... **325**
Bowl-vase, two handles, green ground, No. 400-4" **176**
Candleholders, green ground, No. 451-4", 4" h., pr.. **185**
Candlesticks, green ground, No. 1099-4 1/2", 4 1/2" h., pr. **200**
Console bowl, blue ground, No. 322-12", 12" l. **385**
Console bowl, green ground, No. 322-12", 12" l. **268**
Cornucopia-vase, brown ground, No. 128-8", 8" h. **165**
Cornucopia-vases, blue ground, No. 126-6", 6" h. pr. **385**
Dish, footed, sweeping boat-shaped, one end handle in the form of pine needles & cone, brown ground, No. 432-12", 12 3/4" l. **289**
Dish, divided w/tall center handle, blue ground, No. 462, 6 1/5 x 13" **550**
Ewer, blue ground, No. 851-15", 15" h., ... **2,200**
Ewer, brown ground, No. 851-15", 15" h., ... **1,045**
Flowerpot, blue ground, No. 633-5", 5" h. **319**
Fruit bowl, footed bulbous form w/side handles, one extending over rim, blue ground, No. 262-10" **880**
Jardiniere, blue ground, No. 632-3", 3" h. **222**
Jardiniere, brown ground, No. 632-3", 3" h....... **162**
Jardiniere, brown ground, No. 839-6", 6" h....... **175**
Jardiniere, blue ground, No. 632-8", 8" h. **1,450**
Jardiniere, green ground, No. 632-9", 9" h. **187**
Jardiniere, green ground, No. 403-10", 10" h.. **600**
Jardiniere, brown ground, No. 632-12", 12" h.. **1,760**
Jardiniere & pedestal base, brown ground, No. 632-8", 8" h, 2 pcs., (small nick to rim of jardiniere)............................ **1,760**

Jardiniere & pedestal base, blue ground, large spherical form w/slightly flared rim, applied branch handles, unmarked, 34" overall... **4,025**
Match holder, green ground, No. 498, 3" h...... **220**
Mug, brown ground, No. 960-4", 4" h. **275**
Pitcher, 9" h., blue ground, No. 415-9" **823**
Pitcher, 9" h., green ground, No. 415-9" **358**
Pitcher, 9 1/2" h., ovoid, small branch handle, green ground, No. 708-9" **440**
Pitcher w/ice lip, 8" h., footed wide spherical body w/curved rim & squared spout, brown ground, No. 1321............................... **581**
Planter, brown ground, No. 457-7", 4 1/2" h. **225**
Planter, boat-shaped, blue ground, No. 455-6", 6" l. **273**
Planter, boat-shaped, brown ground, No. 455-6", 6" l., 3" h., ... **200**
Rose bowl, brown ground, No. 261-6", 6" d. **385**
Sand jar, green ground, No. 776-14", 14" h... **1,500**
Tray, blue ground, No. 430-12", 12" l. **330**
Umbrella stand, blue ground, No. 777-20", 20" h. **3,565**
Umbrella stand, brown ground, No. 777-20", 20" h.. **2,334**
Urn, green ground, No. 745-7", 7" h. **275**
Urn-vase, asymmetrical handles, footed, brown ground, No. 121-7", 7" h. **233**
Urn-vase, brown ground, No. 908-8", 8" h. **355**
Vase, 5" h., a deep cup-shaped bowl set off-center on an oval foot w/a pine cone & pine needle handle extending from base to rim, another sprig on pine needles molded into the lower body, brown ground, No. 124-5" **200-250**
Vase, 6" h., bulbous base w/wide cylindrical neck, handles from shoulder to midsection of neck, blue ground, No. 839-6" **385**
Vase, 6" h., fan-shaped, brown, No. 427-6" **325**

Pine Cone Fan Vase

Vase, 6" h., fan-shaped w/single handle, green ground, No. 472-6" (ILLUS.) **303**
Vase, 6" h., footed tapering cylindrical body w/asymmetric handles, green ground, No. 748-6" **303**
Vase, 6" h., wide cylindrical body w/flaring rim, asymmetrical handles, brown ground, No. 838-6" **178**
Vase, 6" h., bulbous base w/wide cylindrical neck, handles from shoulder to midsection of neck, brown ground, No. 839-6".. **182**
Vase, 6" h., trumpet-shaped, brown ground, No. 906-6" **150-200**

Vase, bud, 7" h., blue ground, No. 112-7" 243
Vase, bud, 7" h., brown ground, No. 112-7" 246
Vase, 7" h., two-handled, footed wide cylinder, brown ground, No. 704-7" 220
Vase, 7" h., two-handled, footed wide cylinder, green ground, No. 704-7".................... 203
Vase, triple bud, 8" h., blue ground, No. 113-8".. 405
Vase, triple bud, 8" h., brown ground, No. 113-8".. 330
Vase, 8" h., double, brown ground, No. 473-8".. 275-350
Vase, 8" h., footed cylindrical form w/flaring rim, asymmetric handles, brown ground, No. 746-8 330
Vase, 8" h., compressed bulbous base tapering to wide cylindrical neck, handles from base to mid-section of neck, blue ground, No. 842-8", 8" h. 413
Vase, 8" h., blue ground, No. 844-8" 650
Vase, 8" h., brown ground, No. 908-8" 335
Vase, 8 1/2" h., horn-shaped w/fanned & pleated rim, pine needles & cone-form handle from base of oval foot to mid-section, brown ground, No. 490-8" 248
Vase, 9" h., slender conical body on wide flaring foot, blue ground, No. 705-9" 350-400
Vase, 9" h., slender conical body on wide flaring foot, brown ground, No. 705-9" 220
Vase, 9" h., footed ovoid body w/wide flared rim, asymmetrical handles, blue ground, No. 707-9"....................................... 220
Vase, 9" h., blue ground, No. 846-9" 395
Vase, 9" h., brown ground, No. 846-9" 475
Vase, 10" h., expanding cylinder, brown ground, No. 709-10".................................... 453
Vase, 10" h., expanding cylinder, green ground, No. 709-10".................................... 345
Vase, 10" h., footed cylindrical body w/flaring rim, branch handles from midsection to base, brown ground, No. 804-10" 303
Vase, 10" h., footed, two-handled bulbous body tapering to wide tall cylindrical neck w/irregular cut-out rim, brown ground, No. 848-10"... 458
Vase, 10" h., footed, two-handled bulbous body tapering to wide tall cylindrical neck w/irregular cut-out rim, blue ground, No. 848-10".. 743
Vase, 10" h., brown ground, No. 910-10" 500
Vase, 10 1/2" h., flaring foot beneath an expanding conical body flanked by long handles from base to mid-section in the form of pine needles & pine cone, blue ground, No. 747-10" 450-525
Vase, 12" h., corseted form w/asymmetric branch handles, blue ground, No. 712-12".. 355
Vase, 12" h., corseted form w/asymmetric branch handles, green ground, No. 712-12".. 522
Vase, 15" h., two-handled, ovoid w/waisted neck & flaring mouth, brown ground, No. 807-15"... 800
Vase 18" h., floor-type, footed ovoid body tapering to flaring cylindrical neck, shoulder handles, brown ground, No. 913-18" .. 1,870
Wall pocket, triple, brown ground, No. 466, 8 1/4" h.. 605

Wall pocket, double, two flaring conical containers joined by an arched pine cone & needle top handle, brown ground, No. 1273-8", 8 1/2" h............... 400-425
Wall pocket, double, two flaring conical containers joined by an arched pine cone & needle top handle, green ground, No. 1273-8", 8 1/2" h. 440
Wall shelf, brown ground, No. 1-5 x 8", 5" w., 8" h. (1/8" no show chip at back edge)... 432
Window box, brown ground, No. 488-8"......... 225
Window box, rectangular w/shaped rim & low center handle, brown ground, No. 468-8", 8 3/4" l., 3 3/4" h. 247
Window box, brown ground, No. 516-10", 10" l. 250
Window box, rectangula w/low center handle, blue ground, No. 469-12", 12" l. (fleck to base & under rim (in making) & to handle) 385

POPPY (1930s)
Shaded backgrounds of blue or pink with decoration of poppy flower and green leaves.

Basket, green ground, No. 348-12", 12" h. 385
Bowl, 6", pink ground, No. 335-6" 123
Bowl, 10" l., blue ground, No. 338-10" 158
Console bowl, oval, pink ground, No. 138-10", 10" l.. 148
Console bowl, green ground, No. 340-14", 14" l... 225
Ewer, green ground, No. 876-10", 10" h. 325
Flower frog, pink ground, No. 35, 3 1/2" h....... 110
Jardiniere, tiny handles at rim, pink ground, No. 642-4", 4" h.............................. 128
Jardiniere, 5" h., tiny handles at rim, globular, pink ground, No. 642-5", 5" h. 110
Jardiniere, blue ground, No. 642-6", 6" h. 220
Jardiniere, & pedestal base, green ground, No. 642-8", 8" h., 2 pcs. (wpider line to base of jardiniere, not thru, couple of nicks & one shallow bruise to petals, small flat chip to bottom ring., hairline to edge of pedestal) 440
Urn, green handled, 6" h. 200
Vase, 6" h., footed trumpet-form w/base handles, green ground, No. 866-6" 132

Poppy Vase

Vase, 8" h., footed, wide cylindrical form w/C-form handles, green ground, No. 871-8" (ILLUS.) 165
Vase, 9" h., two-handled, ovoid w/wide mouth, green ground, No. 872-9"............... 264

Vase, 9" h., bulbous base w/wide cylindrical neck, small scrolled handles, pink
ground, No. 873-9" **300**

Vase, 9" h., bulbous base w/wide cylindrical neck, small scrolled handles,green
ground, No. 873-9" **303**

ROSECRAFT PANEL (1920)

*A line of common shapes decorated with panels
of nudes, florals, fruit, and vines in orange, green,
ivory, pink or lavender. Matte finish of dark green or
brown.*

Bowl, 8" d., 2 3/8" h., shallow round form
w/rolled rim, orange floral decoration on
brown ground **138**

Candleholders, decorated w/purple flow-
ers on dark green ground, 2" h., pr. **165**

Vase, 6" h., cylindrical, decorated w/purple
flowers on dark green ground **248**

Vase, 8" h., wide bulbous body w/a round
shoulder to the molded neck, decorated
w/vines, leaves & fruit in orange on
brown ground, No. 293-8" **358**

Rosecraft Panel Vase

Vase, 9" h., baluster-form body w/trumpet-
form neck, orange floral decoration on
dark brown ground, No. 294-8" (ILLUS.)...... **248**

Wall pocket, conical form w/ruffled rim
flanked by cut-out panels, nude decora-
tion in orange, dark brown ground, 7" h. **825**

ROZANE (1900)

*Dark blended backgrounds; slip decorated
underglaze artware.*

Vase, 4" h., bulbous base tapering to wide
cylindrical neck w/flaring neck, yellow
daisy decoration, No. 844-4" **193**

Vase, 4 5/8" h., bulbous base w/tall cylindrical neck & flared rim, shaded brown
ground w/Art Nouveau-style silver overlay flowers, impressed "Rozane 923
RPCo," "E" & "4," silver impressed
"999/1000" (ILLUS.) **523**

Vase, 4 5/8" h., footed bulbous base tapering to wide cylindrical neck w/flaring rim,
rose hip decoration, Greek key handles
from shoulder to rim, No. 847 (repair to
foot) **165**

Rozane Vase with Silver Overlay

Vase, 11 1/4" h., slender cylindrical body
tapering to narrow cylindrical neck
w/flaring rim, brown, green & orange
ground w/decoration of wild roses, artist-
signed **385**

RUSSCO (1930s)

*Octagonal rim openings, stacked handles, nar-
row perpendicular panel front and back. One type
glaze is solid matte color; another is matte color
with lustrous crystalline over glaze, some of which
shows actual grown crystals.*

Urn-vase, angular handles, blue, No. 108-
6, 7" h. **128**

Urn-vase, angular handles, crystalline
green to gold glaze, No. 108-6, 7" h............ **220**

Urn-vase, footed, bulbous base w/small
buttressed handles, wide tapering cylindrical neck w/slightly flaring rim, gold
crystalline glaze, partial paper label, No.
109-8", 8 1/2" h... **187**

Vase, 6" h., two-handled, footed globular
body w/wide shoulder tapering to flared
rim, turquoise glaze, No. 259-6", silver
foil label **83**

Russco Snowflake Crystalline Vase

Vase, 6" h., two-handled, footed globular
body w/wide shoulder tapering to flared
rim, snowflake crystalline yellow over
green glaze, No. 259-6", silver foil label
(ILLUS.)... **220**

Vase, 8 1/2" h., maroon **95**

Vase, 8 1/2" h., flared foot, slender trumpet
form w/curved base handles, cream
w/green crystalline overglaze, No. 695-
8"... **242**

Vase, 10" h., footed baluster form w/flaring
rim & slender scrolled handles, orange
glaze, No. 700-10".. **358**

SILHOUETTE (1952)

Recessed area silhouettes nature study or female nudes. Colors are rose, turquoise, tan and white with turquoise.

Basket, flaring cylinder w/pointed overhead handle, florals, turquoise blue, No. 708-6", 6" h. **83**
Basket, curved rim & asymmetrical handle, florals, rose ground, No. 710-10", 10" h. **183**
Basket w/overhead handle, tan, No. 708-6", 6" h. **113**
Planter, florals, rose ground, No. 769-9", 9" l. **210**
Planter, florals, turquoise ground, footed long rectangular form, No. 756-5", 5" h. **75**

Silhouette Urn

Urn, four wing-shaped feet on disc base, reclining female nudes, turquoise ground, No. 763-8", 8" h. (ILLUS.) **440**
Vase, 5" h., florals, white ground, No. 779-5" **125**
Vase, 7" h., fan-shaped, female nudes, rose ground, No. 783-7" **385**
Vase, 9" h., double, base w/canted sides supporting two square vases w/sloping rims, joined by a stylized branch-form center post, florals, orange shading to brown ground, No. 757-9" **165**
Vase, 12" h., florals, rose ground, No. 788-12" **253**
Vase, 12" h., florals, white ground, No. 788-12" **99**
Vase, 14" h., globular base w/expanding cylindrical neck w/fluted rim, foliage, rose ground, No. 789-14", each **460**

SNOWBERRY (1946)

Brown branch with small white berries and green leaves embossed over spider-web design in various background colors (blue, green and rose).

Basket, w/asymmetrical overhead handle, shaded rose ground, No. 1BK-8", 8" h. **149**
Basket w/curved overhead handle, disc base, shaded green ground, No. 1BK-10", 10" h, ... **165**
Book ends, shaded green ground, No. 1BE, pr. **231**
Candleholders, squatty w/angular handles at shoulder, shaded rose ground, No. 1CS1-2", 2" h., pr. **115**
Console bowl, shaded rose ground, No. 1BL1-10", 10" l. **138**
Console bowl, shaded rose ground, No. 1BL-8", 11" l. **115**

Console bowl, boat-shaped, pointed end handles, shaded rose ground, No. 1BL2-12", 15" l. **148**
Ewer, shaded green ground, No. 1TK-6", 6" h. **118**
Ewer, shaded rose ground, No. 1TK-6", 6" h. **127**
Ewer, shaded green ground, No. 1TK-10, 10" h. **240**
Ewer, flaring base, oval body, shaded rose ground, No. 1TK-15", 16" h. **319**
Jardiniere, two-handled, shaded green ground, No. 1J-4", 4" h. **150**
Jardiniere, two-handled, shaded rose ground, No. 1J-4", 4" h. **104**
Tea set: cov. teapot, open sugar bowl & creamer; shaded green ground, Nos. 1TP, 1S & 1C, 3 pcs. **360**
Tea set: cov. teapot, open sugar bowl & creamer; shaded blue ground, Nos. 1TP, 1S & 1C, the set **303**
Tray, long leaf-shaped, shaded rose ground, No. 1BL1-12", 14" l. **104**
Vase, 6" h., shaded rose ground, No. 1V-6" **125**
Vase, 6 1/2" h., pillow-type, shaded blue ground, No. 1FH-6" **110**
Vase, 7" h., two-handled, shaded blue ground, No. 1V1-7" **145**
Vase, 7" h., two-handled, shaded rose ground, No. 1V1-7" **103**

Snowberry Vase

Vase, 8" h., ovoid w/flat shoulder & flaring rim, small pointed shoulder handles, shaded green ground, No. 1V2-8" (ILLUS.) **176**
Vase, 9" h., shaded green ground, No. 1V2-9" **185**
Vase, 10" h., shaded rose ground, No. 1V2-10" **242**
Vase, 15" h., floor-type, shaded green ground, 1V1-15" **450**
Vase, 18" h., shaded blue ground, No. 1V-18 ...... **450**
Vase, 18" h., shaded rose ground, No. 1V-18" **440**
Wall pocket, wide half-round form tapering to a pointed base, low angled handles along the lower sides, shaded blue ground, No. 1WP-8", 8" w., 5 1/2" h. **250-300**
Wall pocket, wide half-round form tapering to a pointed base, low angled handles along the lower sides, shaded rose ground, No. 1WP-8", 8" w., 5 1/2" h. **237**

SUNFLOWER (1930)

Tall stems support yellow sunflowers whose blooms form a repetitive band. Textured background shades from tan to dark green at base.

Basket, hanging-type, 8" d., 5" h...................... 935
Bowl, 3 5/8" h., flaring sides, slender loop
 handles.. 715
Bowl, 5" d., No. 208-5"...................................... 748
Jardiniere, No. 619-8", 8" h., unmarked
 (two hairlines from rim, straight 1" & T-
 shaped 1/1/2")... 1,100
Jardiniere, No. 619-10", unmarked (resto-
 ration to opposing hairlines, small chip to
 edge of leaf) 1,045
Jardiniere, No. 619-12" (minor scrape
 inside rim, stress fracture to base) 2,530
Umbrella stand, footed cylindrical form,
 No. 770-20", unmarked, 20" h................... 7,425
Urn-vase, nearly spherical w/tiny rim han-
 dles, 4" h. 506
Vase, 5" h., swelled cylindrical body w/long
 side handles & closed rim 558
Vase, 5" h. 382
Vase, 6" h., swelled cylindrical body
 w/short cylindrical neck flanked by small
 loop handles, No. 485-6"............................. 724
Vase, 6" h., squatty bulbous body, wide
 shoulder w/short cylindrical neck, No.
 488-6" (bruise to rim, abrasion to one
 flower) 770
Vase, 7" h., bulbous base below expanding
 cylindrical neck w/wide flaring flat rim
 (crack from rim) 413
Vase, 7" h., waisted cylindrical form w/wide
 flaring mouth, No. 487-7" 990

Sunflower Vase

Vase, 8" h., bulbous base, wide tapering
 cylindrical neck, No. 490-8" (ILLUS.) 1,115
Vase, 9" h., bulbous base w/wide cylindrical neck, small loop handles, No. 493-9"
 (repair to top)... 953
Vase, 10" h., tall swelled cylindrical body
 tapering slightly to a wide flat mouth
 flanked by tiny loop handles, No. 494-
 10" (nearly invisible flat chip off base)....... 1,375
Window box, 3 1/2 x 11"............................... 1,500

TEASEL (1936)

Embossed decorations of long-stems gracefully curving with delicate spider-like pods. Colors and glaze treatments vary from monochrome matte to crystalline. Colors are beige to tan, medium blue

highlighted with gold, pale blue and deep rose (possibly others).

Bowl, 4" d., pale blue ground, No. 342-4" 187
Bowl, 8" d., blue ground, No. 344-8".............. 175
Candleholders, shaded blue ground, No.
 1131, 2" h., pr.. 165
Jardiniere, brown ground, footed squatty
 bulbous body w/a wide cylindrical neck,
 small angled shoulder handles, No. 644-
 4", 4" h... 150
Jardiniere, peach matte ground, footed
 squatty bulbous body w/a wide cylindrical neck, small angled shoulder handles,
 No. 644-4", 4" h... 165
Jardiniere, footed spherical body w/a wide
 closed rim & small tab shoulder handles,
 blue ground, No. 343-6", 6" h....................... 178
Rose bowl, footed spherical body w/a wide
 closed rim & small tab shoulder handles,
 beige shading to tan ground, No. 343-6",
 6" h... 132
Vase, 6" h., closed handles at midsection,
 cut-out rim, beige shading to tan ground,
 No. 881-6".. 150
Vase, 6" h., closed handles at midsection,
 cut-out rim, mottled blue ground, No.
 881-6"... 165
Vase, 6" h., closed handles at rim, beige
 shading to tan ground, No. 882-6" 176
Vase, 6" h., closed handles at rim, deep
 rose, No. 882-6" 138

Teasel Vase

Vase, 8" h., closed handles at shoulder,
 low foot, blue ground, No. 884-8"
 (ILLUS.)... 193
Vase, 8" h., blue ground, rectangular foot
 below flaring rectangular body
 w/stepped rim ends, shaped low but-
 tress side handles, No. 885-8" 190
Vase, 9" h., closed handles at base, flaring
 mouth, beige shading to tan, No. 886-9"...... 330

TOURMALINE (1933)

Although the semi-gloss medium blue, high-lighted around the rim with lighter high gloss and gold effect, seems to be accepted as the standard Tourmaline glaze, the catalogue definitely shows this and two other types as well. One is a mottled overall turquoise, the other a mottled salmon that appears to be lined in the high gloss but with no over run to the outside.

Bowl, 7" d., shallow w/sharply canted sides, intermingled blue crystalline mat glaze, No. 152-7 495

Bowl, 7" d., shallow w/sharply canted sides, mottled blue semi-gloss glaze, No. 152-7 165

Candlesticks, flared ribbed base, flaring nozzle, mottled blue ground, gold labels, No. 1089-4 1/2", 4 1/2" h., pr 165

Urn-vase, compressed globular base w/short collared neck, mottled blue, No. A-200-4", 4 1/2" h. 253

Vase, 5 1/2" h., globular w/loop handles rising from midsection to rim, mottled turquoise blue, No. A-517-6" 112

Vase, 6" h., pillow-type, mottled blue glaze 75

Vase, 6" h., mottled blue ground, No. A517-6" 175

Vase, 7" h., cylindrical w/low flaring foot, slightly flared rim, mottled blue, No. 308-7" 121

Vase, 7" h., shaded orange glaze, No. 318-7" 143

Tourmaline Vase

Vase, 8" h., hexagonal twisted form, mottled pink & green semi-gloss glaze, large gold foil label (ILLUS.) 220

Vase, 8" h., twisted paneled effect, mottled blue, No. A-425-8" 385

Vase, 9" h., flared foot below buttressed base, trumpet-form body, mottled turquoise glaze, No. A-429-9" 413

Vase, 10" h., squatty bulbous base w/wide cylindrical neck w/horizontally ribbed lower half & slightly flaring rim, mottled blue mat over blue-yellow glossy glaze, gold foil label 468

VELMOSS (1935)

Characterized by three horizontal wavy lines around the top from which long, blade-like leaves extend downward. Colors are green, blue, tan and pink.

Jardiniere, footed spherical body w/short wide neck & pointed shoulder handles, mottled blue glaze, No. 264-5", 5" h. 198

Vase, 6" h., swelled cylindrical body w/pointed shoulder handles, mottled raspberry red glaze, No. 714-6", gold foil label 235

Vase, bud, 7" h., rose ground, No. 115-7" 154

Velmoss Bud Vase

Vase, double bud, 8" h., triangular base w/tall conical form joined to shorter cylindrical form by figural leaf cluster, mottled blue, No. 116-8" (ILLUS.) 223

Vase, 12" h., ovoid body tapering to wide cylindrical neck w/wide flat rim, angled handles, mottled raspberry red, No. 721-12", gold foil label 468

VISTA (1920)

Embossed green coconut palm trees & lavender blue pool against grey ground.

Basket, hanging-type, wide low-sided cylindrical form w/three low strap handles along the sides, 8" d., 4" h. (abrasion to bottom, glaze scaling to edge & rim, tough-up to a couple of points) 385

Basket w/pointed overhead handle, tapering square form w/pointed side rim, 5 1/2 x 6 1/2" 454

Bowl, 7" d., 3 1/2" h., deep, few minor flakes 300

Vista Bowl

Bowl, 8 3/8" d., 4" h., cylindrical form w/flat rim, unmarked (ILLUS.) 220

Jardiniere, 9" h. 465

Jardiniere & pedestal base, 12" h., jardiniere, overall 36" h., 2 pcs. (two glaze flakes to rim & "T"-shaped hairline to base of jardiniere which crawls up side & spreads 4" 2,200

Planter, rectangular w/curved sides & end handles, 4 1/2 x 11 1/2", 6" h. (bruise to corner of base, shallow line to bottom that does not go through, small chip to inner rim, minor glaze scaling) 715

Vase, 9 3/4" h., cylindrical body tapering to flared base, round shoulder w/flat molded mouth, unmarked 660

Vase, 10" h., bulbous base tapering to cylindrical neck flanked by buttressed handles (restoration to rim chip).................. **523**

Vase, 10" h., tapering cylindrical body w/flaring base **660**

Vase, 12" h., ovoid body tapering to round base **660**

Vase, 12" h., wide cylindrical form expanding slightly at top flanked by buttressed handles... **823**

Vase, 12" h., 4 3/4" d., footed, bulbous base tapering to tall wide cylindrical neck w/flat rim.. **715**

Vase, floor-type, 14" h., footed tapering cylindrical form **915**

Vase, 15" h., tall tapering cylindrical body w/flaring foot & bulbous top w/closed rim (bruise to rim) **1,100**

WINCRAFT (1948)

Revived shapes from older lines such as Pine Cone, Bushberry, Cremona, Primrose and others. Vases with animal motifs, contemporary shapes in high gloss of blue, tan, lime and green.

Basket, hanging-type, lime green ground, 8" h.. **175**

Basket, hanging-type, tan ground, 8" h........... **165**

Basket, footed half-round form w/arched rim & angled overhead handle, lime green ground, No. 208-8", 8" h. **190**

Basket, footed half-round form w/arched rim & angled overhead handle, tan ground, No. 208-8", 8" h............................. **154**

Cigarette box, cov., shaded blue ground, No. 240, 4 1/2" l.................................... **121**

Console bowl, rectangular foot supporting a long, low serpentine bowl w/pointed ends, green ground, No. 227-10", 13 1/2" l., 4" h. **49**

Cornucopia-vase, florals in relief on shaded green ground, No. 222-8", 8" h.......... **95**

Ewer, bell-form body below a tall neck w/upright tall spout & angled shoulder handle, chartreuse ground, No. 216-8", 8" h.. **115**

Flowerpot, blue ground, No. 265-5", 5" h. **80**

Jardiniere, pink ground, No. 635-6", 6" h. **330**

Teapot, cov., brown & yellow ground, No. 271-P.. **265**

Vase, 6" h., asymmetrical fan shape, pine cones & needles in relief on lime ground, No. 272-6".. **115**

Vase, 8" h., blue ground w/arrow leaf design, No. 273-8".. **125**

Vase, 8" h., flowing lily form w/asymmetrical side handles, tulip & foliage in relief on glossy green & yellow ground, No. 282-8".. **150**

Vase, 10" h., cylindrical, tab handles, black panther & green palm trees in relief on blue ground, No. 290-10" **605**

Vase, 12" h., yellow, No. 275-12" **605**

Vase, 12" h., fan-shaped, glossy gold ground, No. 287-12" **99**

Wall pocket, tan ground, No. 267-5".............. **295**

Wall pocket, rectangular box-like holders w/horizontal ribbing & ivy leaves as rim handle, brown ground, No. 266-4", 8 1/2" h.. **250**

WINDSOR (1931)

Brown or blue mottled glaze, some with leaves, vines and ferns, some with a repetitive band arrangement of small squares and rectangles in yellow and green.

Windsor Bowl

Bowl, 10 5/8" l., 3 1/2" h., angular end handles, slightly canted sides, geometric design against mottled terra cotta ground (ILLUS.).. **413**

Vase, 5" h., No. 545-5" **535**

Vase, 6" h., canted sides, handles rising from shoulder to rim, geometric design against mottled terra cotta ground, No. 546-6".. **440**

Vase, 6" h., canted sides, handles rising from shoulder to rim, geometric design against mottled blue ground, No. 546-6"...... **440**

Vase, 7" h., large handles, globular base, stylized ferns against mottled terra cotta ground, No. 548-7" (restoration to base chip) **330**

Vase, 7" h., large handles, globular base, stylized ferns against mottled blue ground, No. 548-7"....................................... **715**

Vase, 7" h., trumpet-shaped w/long loop handles from rim to midsection, green leaves on terra cotta ground, NO. 550-7"..... **495**

Vase, 8" h., two-handled cylindrical body, decorated w/floral sprays in green on terra cotta ground, No. 552-8", black paper label & old sales room label w/price **660**

WISTERIA (1933)

Lavender wisteria blossoms and green vines against a roughly textured brown shading to deep blue ground, rarely found in only brown.

Bowl-vase, squatty bulbous form tapering sharply to a flat mouth flanked by small loop handles, brown ground, No. 242-4", 4" h. **382**

Bowl-vase, squatty bulbous form tapering sharply to a flat mouth flanked by small loop handles, blue ground, No. 242-4", 4" h... **463**

Urn, bulbous body w/wide flat mouth, small loop shoulder handles, brown ground, 8" h.. **880**

Urn-vase, small rim handles, straight sides, No. 632-5", 5" h... **550**

Urn-vase, small rim handles, straight sides, No. 632-5", 5" h. (glaze scrape to base, few minor flecks to decoration) **330**

Vase, 4" h., squatty, angular handles on sharply canted shoulder, blue ground, No. 629-4", silver foil label............................ **550**

Vase, 4" h., squatty, angular handles on sharply canted shoulder, brown ground, No. 629-4", silver foil label............................ **315**

Vase, 6" h., ovoid body tapering to short cylindrical neck flanked by small loop handles, blue ground, No. 631-6"................ **560**

Vase, 6 1/2" h., 4" d., bulbous ovoid body w/a wide shoulder tapering up to a small mouth, small angled shoulder handles, mottled blue & brown ground, No. 630-6"..... **504**

Vase, 7" h., bulbous waisted ovoid body w/small pointed shoulder handles, brown ground, No. 634-7" **547**

Vase, 8" h., pear-shaped body w/short cylindrical neck & tiny angled shoulder handles, blue ground, No. 636-8"................ **870**

Vase, 8 1/2" h., bulbous ovoid body tapering to a short cylindrical neck w/a wide flat rim, pointed angled handles from the neck to the shoulder, blue ground............. **2,090**

Vase, 8 1/2" h., slender base handles, conical body bulging slightly below rim, brown ground, No. 635-8" **509**

Vase, 8 1/2" h., slender base handles, conical body bulging slightly below rim, blue ground, No. 635-8" **867**

Vase, 9 1/2" h., cylindrical ovoid body w/angular handles rising from shoulder to midsection of slender cylindrical neck, brown ground, No. 638-9", partial paper label... **523**

Vase, 10" h., cylindrical body w/closed rim, angled shoulder handles, brown ground, No. 639-10" **605**

Vase, 10" h., cylindrical body w/closed rim, angled shoulder handles, blue ground, No. 639-10" **1,870**

Tall Wisteria Vase

Vase, 12" h., two-handled, expanding cylinder w/flaring rim, brown ground, No. 640-12" (ILLUS.) **1,650**

Vase, 15" h., bottle-shaped w/angular handles at shoulder, blue ground, No. 641-15" (restoration to rim & handles, small flakes to a few petals) **2,310**

ZEPHYR LILY (1946)

Tall lilies and slender leaves adorn swirl-textured backgrounds of Bermuda Blue, Evergreen and Sienna Tan.

Basket, hanging-type, terra cotta ground, No. 472-5", 5" h. **175**

Basket, footed half-round body w/curled-in rim tabs & high arched handle, terra cotta ground, No. 393-7", 7" h. **188**

Basket, hanging-type, terra cotta ground, No. 472-5", 7 1/2" h. **175**

Basket, hanging-type, green ground, No. 472-5", 7 1/2" w. **253**

Book ends, terra cotta ground, No. 16, 5 1/2" h., pr. **231**

Bowl, 6" d., terra cotta ground, No. 472-6"........ **95**

Console bowl, end handles, terra cotta ground, No. 479-14", 16 1/2" **99**

Cookie jar, cov., blue ground, No. 5-8", 10" h. **358**

Ewer, footed flaring lower body w/angled shoulder tapering to a tall forked neck w/upright tall spout, long low arched handle, blue ground, No. 23-10", 10" h. **183**

Flowerpot w/saucer, blue ground, No. 672-5", 5" h. **225**

Jardiniere, terra cotta ground, No. 671-8", 8" h. **193**

Jardiniere, two-handled, green ground, No. 679-9", 9" h. **385**

Tea set: cov. teapot, creamer & open sugar bowl; terra cotta ground, 3 pcs. **413**

Vase, 7" h., blue ground, No. 132-7" **160**

Vase, 8" h., two-handled, terra cotta ground..... **195**

Vase, 8 1/2" h., a disc foot & short pedestal support a tall slightly swelled cylindrical body w/a thin-rolled rim, low curved handles from mid-body to the base of the pedestal, green ground, No. 133-8" **175**

Vase, 9" h., conical w/flaring buttressed base, blue ground, No. 136-9" **110**

Zephyr Lily Vase

Vase, 12 1/2" h., handles rising from shoulder of compressed globular base to middle of slender neck w/flaring mouth, blended blue ground, No. 140-12" (ILLUS.) **207**

Vase, 12 1/2" h., handles rising from shoulder of compressed globular base to middle of slender neck w/flaring mouth, green ground, No. 140-12"........................... **295**

ROYAL BAYREUTH

Good china in numerous patterns and designs has been made at the Royal Bayreuth factory in Tettau, Germany since 1794. Listings below are by the company's lines, plus miscellaneous pieces. Interest in this china remains at a peak and prices continue to rise. Pieces listed carry the company's blue mark except where noted otherwise.

Royal Bayreuth Mark

CORINTHIAN

Cake plate, classical figures on black ground, 10" d....................................... **$125-150**

Corinthian Candlestick

Candlestick, classical figures on black ground, tall (ILLUS.) 195

Creamer, classical figures on green ground....... 50

Creamer & cov. sugar bowl, classical figures on black ground, pr. 100

Pitcher, milk, classic figures on green ground 125

Pitcher, tankard, 6 7/8" h., 3 3/4" d., orange inside top, classical figures on black satin ground gold bands w/black & white geometric design around neck & base 125

Planter, classical figures on red ground........... 100

Toothpick holder, classical figures on black ground, 2 1/4" h. **175-200**

DEVIL & CARDS

Ashtray 150

Ashtray, two cards 325

Ashtray w/match holder 250

Candleholder 550

Creamer, figural red devil, 3 1/2" h............ **300-400**

Devil & Cards Creamer

Creamer (ILLUS.)...................................... **150-225**

Creamer, 3 3/4" h. **250-325**

Creamer, figural red devil, 4 1/2" h............ **375-475**

Match holder, hanging-type, 4" w., 5" h. **500-600**

Mug, 4 3/4" h. **400-500**

Mug, w/blue rim 395

Pitcher, milk, 5" h. **450-600**

Devil & Cards Pitcher

Pitcher, water, 7 1/4" h. (ILLUS.) **700-850**

Plate, 6" d. 500

Salt dip, master size 325

Salt shaker 175

Stamp box, cov., 3 1/2" l. 595

Sugar bowl, cov. 400

Sugar bowl, open, short 350

MOTHER-OF-PEARL

Ashtray, Murex Shell patt. 80

Basket, reticulated rim, ornate handle, rose decoration, 3 3/4 x 4" oval, 4 1/4" h.............. 150

Bowl, 3 1/2" octagonal, white w/green highlights, pearlized finish..................................... 65

Bowl, 5 1/2" d., grape cluster mold, pearlized white finish... 150

Bowl, 6 1/2 x 9", oak leaf-shaped, footed, pearlized finish w/gold trim.......................... 850

Bowl, 10" oval, handled, figural poppy mold, apricot satin finish............................... 600

Cake plate, decorated w/roses, 10 1/2" d. 125

Compote, open, 4 1/2" d., 4 1/2" h., reticulated bowl & base, decorated w/delicate roses, pearlized finish 140

Compote, open, decorated w/roses, pearlized finish, small... 49

Creamer, grape cluster mold, pearlized white, 3 3/4" h... **175**

Creamer, Murex Shell patt., white pearlized finish, 4 1/2" h. **150-200**

Creamer, boot-shaped, figural Spiky Shell patt., 4 3/4" h.................................... **250-275**

Creamer, Murex Shell patt., spiky form.............. **95**

Creamer & cov. sugar bowl, grape cluster mold, pearlized yellow, colorful foliage, pr... **375**

Cup & saucer, demitasse, footed, figural Spiky Shell patt., pearlized finish **150**

Cup & saucer, demitasse, Oyster & Pearl mold **350**

Dish, cov., Murex Shell patt., large **175**

Hatpin holder, figural poppy mold, pearlized white finish.. **575**

Humidor, cov., Murex Shell patt. **850**

Mustard jar, cov., Murex Shell patt. white pearlized finish, 3 1/2" h. **200-250**

Nappy, grape cluster mold, pearlized white finish, 6" x 7" **175**

Nappy, handled, figural poppy mold, pearlized satin finish.................................... **150-250**

Pitcher, milk, boot-shaped, figural Spiky Shell patt., pearlized finish, 5 1/2" h............. **375**

Sugar bowl, cov., footed, figural Spiky Shell patt., pearlized finish, 3 1/2" h............. **325**

Toothpick holder, Murex Shell patt................. **110**

Toothpick holder, Murex Shell patt., pearlized finish **175**

Wall pocket, figural grape cluster, pearlized finish, 9" h. **400-600**

ROSE TAPESTRY

Basket, two-color roses, 3" h. **350**

Basket, two-color roses, 4 1/4" w., 3 3/4" h...... **450**

Basket, yellow roses, 3 3/4 x 4 1/4" **363**

Basket, miniature, rope handle, tiny pink roses frame the rim, small bouquet of yellow roses on each side & yellow roses on the interior, shadow green leaves, 2 1/2 x 4 1/4 x 4 1/2" **325**

Basket, three-color roses, 4 3/4 x 5 1/4" **425**

Basket, miniature, two color roses on yellow ground, braided decoration around rim **375**

Bell, pink American Beauty roses, 3" h. **450-550**

Bell, gold loop handle, three-color roses, 3 1/4" h.. **400**

Rose Tapestry Bowl

Bowl, 10 1/2" d., gently scalloped rim w/four shell-molded gilt-trimmed handles, three-color roses (ILLUS.) **900-1,100**

Bowl, 10 1/2" d., shell- & scroll-molded rim, three-color roses **995**

Box, w/domed cover, three-color roses, 4 1/2" d., 2 3/4" h.. **400**

Box, cov., shell-shaped, 3 x 5 1/2" **375**

Cake plate, three-color roses, free-form fancy rim w/gold beading, 9 1/2" w.............. **425**

Cake plate, pierced gold handles, three-color roses, 10 1/2" d. **450-500**

Candy dish, three-color roses, 8" oval............. **350**

Chamberstick, a shaped & flattened base centered by a waisted cylindrical short standard supporting the dished socket w/three rim points, an ornate C-scroll handle down the side, three-color roses, 4 1/4" h.. **850-950**

Chocolate set: cov. chocolate pot w/four matching cups & saucers, three-color roses, 9 pcs.................................... **2,000-2,400**

Clock, table-model, three-color roses, upright rectangular case w/a flaring base & domed top.. **1,000**

Creamer, wide cylindrical body slightly flaring at the base & w/a long buttress spout & gilt angled handle, two-color roses on a rose ground, 3" h...................................... **385**

Creamer, swelled cylindrical body w/a long pinched spout, angled loop handle, 4" h. **250-325**

Creamer, two-color roses, 3 1/2" d., 4" h. **375**

Creamer, pinched spout, two-color roses......... **355**

Creamer & cov. sugar bowl, pink & white roses, pr. **675**

Creamer & cov. sugar bowl, two-color roses, pr. **575**

Cups & saucers, demitasse, three-color roses, 2 sets.. **300**

Dessert set: large cake plate & six matching small serving plates; three-color roses, 7 pcs... **1,100**

Dish, three-color roses, 2" w., 4 1/2" l, 1 1/2" h.. **195**

Dish, handled, clover-shaped, decorated w/yellow roses, 5" w. **225**

Dish, leaf-shaped, three-color roses, 5" l. . **225-250**

Dresser box, cov., kidney-shaped, double pink roses, 2 x 5 1/4"............................ **375-400**

Flowerpot & underplate, three-color roses, 3 x 4", 2 pcs..................................... **295**

Rose Tapestry Hair Receiver

Hair receiver, cov., footed, two-color roses, 4" d., 2 1/2" h. (ILLUS.)..................... **375**

Hatpin holder, two-color roses, scroll-molded reticulated gilt-trimmed foot below the baluster-form body w/a flaring gilt-trimmed rim, 4 1/2" h. **550-650**

Match holder, hanging-type, three-color roses **460**

Model of a high-top lady's shoe, pink roses w/a band of green leaves around top, 3 1/2" h. **500-700**

Model of a shoe, decorated w/pink roses & original shoe lace **450-475**

Nappy, open-handled, three-color roses, 5" d. **225**

Nut set: master footed bowl & six small footed bowls; decorated w/pink roses, 7 pcs.. **1,250-1,275**

Pitcher, 5" h., wide cylindrical body tapering slightly toward rim, three-color roses, 24 oz. **375**

Rose Tapestry Planter

Planter, squatty bulbous base below wide gently flaring sides w/a ruffled rim, small loop handles near the base, three-color roses, 2 3/4" h. (ILLUS.)............................... **280**

Plaque, pierced to hang, large pink roses **575**

Plate, 6" d. **200-250**

Plate, 7" d., three-color roses **275**

Plate, 7 1/2" d., round w/slightly scalloped rim & four sections of fanned ruffles spaced around the edge, three-color roses **300-400**

Plate, 10 1/2" d., overall colorful roses w/four gilded scrolls around the rims **175-200**

Powder box, cov., footed, three-color roses, 4" d., 2 1/2" h. **350-450**

Powder jar, cov., footed squatty rounded base w/a squatty domed cover, three-color roses, 3" d., 2 1/2" h. **425-525**

Relish dish, open-handled, three-color roses, 4 x 8" **300-350**

Relish dish, oblong w/gilt-trimmed scalloped rim, decorated w/large pink roses, 4 3/4" w., 8" l. **325-375**

Salt dip, ruffled rim, 3" d............................... **280**

Salt & pepper shakers, three-color roses, pr... **495**

Salt shaker, pink roses **250**

Sugar bowl, cov., two-handled one-color rose, 3 1/2" d., 3 1/4" h........................... **350**

Vase, 4 1/4" h., footed swelled base tapering to cylindrical sides, two-color roses........ **345**

Vase, 4 1/2" h., decorated w/American Beauty roses.. **375**

Vase, 4 3/4" h., slightly swelled slender cylindrical body w/a short rolled neck, three-color roses in pink, yellow & white **288**

Vase, 6 1/2" h., decorated w/roses & shadow ferns... **350-425**

Vase, 7" h., bulbous ovoid body tapering to a short tiny flared neck **300-375**

Wall pocket, three-color roses, 5 x 9"........... **1,300**

SUNBONNET BABIES

Ashtray, babies cleaning **275**

Bell, babies fishing **400-450**

Bell, babies sewing, unmarked **400-450**

Candlestick, babies washing, 5" d., 1 3/4" h.. **275**

Sunbonnet Babies Creamer

Creamer, babies fishing (ILLUS.)..................... **250**

Creamer, babies ironing, 3" h.......................... **250**

Creamer & open sugar bowl, babies sewing, pr. **475**

Creamer & open sugar bowl, boat-shaped, babies fishing on sugar, babies cleaning on creamer, pr. **500**

Cup & saucer, babies washing........................ **350**

Dish, diamond-shaped **200**

Dish, heart-shaped... **200**

Sunbonnet Babies Hair Receiver

Hair receiver, cov., babies washing, 2 3/4" h. (ILLUS.)....................................... **400**

Mug, babies washing...................................... **350**

Pitcher, milk, 4 1/4" h., babies washing **325**

Plate, 6" d., babies washing **250-325**

Saucer, babies fishing....................................... **75**

Tea set, child's **700-800**

Toothpick holder, babies mending **450-550**

Vase, 3" h., babies fishing **235**

TOMATO ITEMS

Tomato bowl, berry.. **50**

Tomato bowls, 5 3/4" d., set of 4..................... **145**

Tomato box, cov., large.................................... **45**

Tomato box, cov., w/green & brown finial, 3" d. **45**

Tomato creamer, cov., large **200**

Tomato creamer, cov., small...................... **45-50**

Tomato Creamer & Sugar Bowl

Tomato creamer & cov. sugar bowl, creamer 3" d., 3" h., sugar bowl 3 1/2" d., 4" h. pr. (ILLUS.) 125

Tomato cup & saucer, demitasse 125

Tomato mustard jar, cov. 125

Tomato mustard jar, cov. w/leaf-shaped underplate, the set 75

Tomato mustard jar, cover & figural leaf spoon, 3 pcs. 125

Tomato pitcher, milk, 4 1/2" h. 250-350

Tomato pitcher, water, 6" h. 500

Tomato plate, 4 1/4" d., ring-handled, figural lettuce leaf 19

Tomato plate, 5 1/2" d., ring-handled, figural lettuce leaf w/molded yellow flowers 29

Tomato plate, 7" d., ring-handled, figural lettuce leaf w/molded yellow flowers 38

Tomato salt & pepper shakers, pr. 150

Tomato sugar bowl, cov. 110

Tomato tea set, cov. teapot, creamer & cov. sugar bowl, 3 pcs. 325

Tomato teapot, cov., small 350

MISCELLANEOUS

Ashtray, figural elk 275

Ashtray, figural lobster 150

Ashtray, figural, oyster & pearl design, 4" l. 275-325

Ashtray, stork decoration, artist-signed, 4 1/2" l. 60

Ashtray, figural shell, 4 1/2 x 4 1/2" 45

Ashtray, stork decoration on yellow ground, 3 1/4 x 5", 1 1/4" h. 125

Ashtray, mountain goat decoration, 5 1/2" l. 350-450

Ashtray, scenic decoration of Dutch lady w/basket, 5 1/2" d. 60

Basket, miniature, scene w/cows, unmarked 59

Basket, "tapestry," footed, bulbous body w/a ruffled rim & ornate gold-trimmed overhead handle, portrait of lady w/horse, 5" h. 595

Basket, handled, boy & donkey decoration, artist-signed, 5 3/4" h. 175

Basket w/reticulated handles, decorated w/white roses, 7 3/4" l., 3 1/2" h. 125

Bell, musicians scene, men playing a cello & mandolin 275-325

Bell, nursery rhyme decoration w/Jack & the Beanstalk 400-450

Berry set: 9 3/4" d. bowl & four 5" d. sauce dishes; decorated w/musicians scene, 5 pcs. 350-450

Berry set: 9 1/2" d. bowl & six 5" d. sauce dishes' portrait decoration, 7 pcs. 650-750

Bowl, 5 3/4" d., nursery rhyme scene w/Jack & Jill 125

Bowl, 6" d., figural conch shell 75

Bowl, 6 7/8" d., 2 1/2" h., footed, shallow slightly scalloped sides, Cavalier Musicians decoration, gold trim on feet 110

Bowl, 8" l., 4" h., figural lobster 250

Bowl, 6 1/4 x 8 1/2", shell-shaped 400-450

Bowl, 10 1/2" d., floral decoration, blown-out mold 250-300

Bowl, 10 1/2" d., "tapestry," decorated w/Colonial scene 1,100-1,300

Box, cov., four-footed ring base, scenic decoration of Dutch children 125

Box, cov., shell-shaped, nursery rhyme scene, Little Boy Blue decoration 225

Box w/Desert Scene

Box, cov., square, desert scene decoration on cover, Arabs w/camels on background colors of pink & brown, unmarked, 2 x 2 1/2", 1 3/4" h. (ILLUS.) 65

Royal Bayreuth Heart-shaped Box

Box, cov., heart-shaped decorated w/scene of two brown & white cows & trees in pasture, green & yellow background, unmarked, 2 x 3 1/4", 1 1/2" h. (ILLUS.) 65

Box, cov., scene of woman on horse, woman & man w/rake watching, 4 1/4" d., 2 1/4" h. 200-225

Box, cov., figural turtle, 2 3/4 x 5" 1,500

Cake Plate with Polar Bears

Cake plate, decorated w/snowy scene & two polar bears, gold trimmed scalloped border (ILLUS. previous page)........ **1,700-2,200**

Candleholder, penguin decoration **335**

Candlestick, figural bassett hound, brown, 4" h. **500-550**

Candlestick, decorated w/scene of cows, 4" h. **75-100**

Candlestick, w/match holder, figural clown, 7" h. **1,300**

Candlestick, oblong dished base w/a standard at one edge flanked by downswept open handles, tulip-form socket w/flattened rim, interior of dished base decorated w/scene of hunter & dogs **275-325**

Candy dish, figural lobster.............................. **125**

Candy dish w/turned over edge, nursery rhyme scene w/Little Miss Muffet................. **125**

Celery dish, figural lobster.............................. **150**

Chamberstick, wide deeply dished, round pinched sides, central cylindrical socket w/flattened rim, S-scroll handle from side of dish to socket, dark brick red ground, decorated w/"Dancing Frogs" & flying insects, rare **1,200-1,500**

Cheese dish, miniature, scenic decoration **400-500**

Poppy Pattern Chocolate Pot

Chocolate pot, cov., figural poppy, tall pink blossom w/ruffled rim, figural poppy on cover, light green & white leafy footed base & large leaf & stem handle, 8 1/2" h. (ILLUS.)............................ **1,400-2,000**

Cracker jar, cov., figural lobster...................... **600**

Cracker jar, cov., figural poppy, 6" h......... **700-900**

Creamer, Arab scene decoration **95**

Creamer, Brittany Girl decoration **75**

Creamer, cobalt blue, Babes in Woods decoration (unmarked)................................ **250**

Creamer, decorated w/man in fishing boat scene **145**

Creamer, figural alligator, 4 1/2 " h............ **350-400**

Creamer, figural apple............................... **150-225**

Creamer, figural black cat **250-300**

Creamer, figural bull, brown **275-325**

Creamer, figural bull, grey........................ **250-325**

Creamer, figural bull head, 4" h................ **175-225**

Creamer, figural butterfly, open wings **350-450**

Creamer, figural cat handle, 4" h. **400-450**

Creamer, figural chimpanzee, 4" h........... **400-450**

Creamer, figural cockatoo, 4" h................ **400-500**

Creamer, figural crow, black, 4 1/2" h. **150-200**

Creamer, figural crow, black & white......... **150-200**

Creamer, figural crow, brown beak **150-200**

Creamer, figural crow, brown bill & eyes (rare) **250**

Creamer, figural dachshund **300-400**

Creamer, figural duck...................................... **315**

Creamer, figural eagle, grey **400-450**

Creamer, figural elk.. **153**

Creamer, figural fish head, grey **250**

Creamer, figural flounder, 4 1/4" h. **600-800**

Creamer, figural frog **160-175**

Creamer, figural geranium, 4" h. **450-550**

Creamer, figural girl w/basket, 4 1/4" h. **550-650**

Creamer, figural girl w/pitcher, red **895**

Creamer, figural grape cluster, light green **128**

Creamer, figural ibex head w/trumpet-form bowl, stirrup-type, 4 1/4" h. **700-800**

Creamer, figural lady bug, 4" h.............. **900-1,100**

Creamer, figural lamplighter **250-300**

Creamer, figural lemon **200-225**

Creamer, figural leopard **3,200-3,600**

Figural Lobster Creamer

Creamer, figural lobster (ILLUS.) **125-175**

Creamer, figural Man of the Mountain, 3 1/2" h. **110-125**

Creamer, figural maple leaf, 4" h............... **250-325**

Creamer, figural milk maid, red dress, 4 3/4" h. **700-800**

Creamer, figural monk, brown, 4 1/2" h..... **600-800**

Creamer, figural monkey, brown **425-450**

Creamer, figural oak leaf, white w/orchid highlights **275**

Creamer, figural orange **200-250**

Creamer, figural pansy, purple, 4" h......... **250-300**

Creamer, figural parakeet **350-500**

Creamer, figural parakeet, green **275-325**

Creamer, figural pear **535-550**

Creamer, figural pig, blue **775**

Creamer, figural pig, grey........................ **550-600**

Creamer, figural pig, red, 4 1/4" h. **600-800**

Creamer, figural platypus, 4" h........... **1,000-1,200**

Creamer, figural poodle, grey **300-375**

Creamer, figural poodle, red, 4 1/2" h. **500-600**

Creamer, figural poppy **200-250**

Creamer, figural poppy, peach iridescent........ **425**

Creamer, figural red parrot handle **700**

Creamer, figural robin, 4" h. **175-225**

Creamer, figural rooster **400-450**

Creamer, figural rose, pink, 3" h................ **350-400**

Creamer, figural Santa Claus, attached handle, red, 4 1/4" h....................... **3,200-3,600**

Creamer, figural seal **325-400**

Water Buffalo Creamer

Creamer, figural water buffalo, black &
white (ILLUS.) **175**

Creamer, figural water buffalo, souvenir of
Portland, Oregon **300**

Creamer, figural watermelon **395**

Creamer, flow blue, Babes in Woods deco-
ration **325**

Creamer, miniature, "tapestry" scene of girl
& horse **275**

Creamer, scene of girl w/basket, salmon
color **800-1,000**

Creamer, stirrup-type, figural ibex head **625**

Creamer, "tapestry," Scottish highland
goats scene **350**

Creamer, figural seashell, boot-shaped,
3 3/4" h. **195**

Creamer, "tapestry," footed ovoid body
tapering to a wide rounded & flaring
neck w/a pinched spout & small C-scroll
handle, sheep in the meadow decora-
tion, 3 3/4" h. **300-350**

Creamer, pinched spout, "tapestry," goats
decoration, 4" h. **350**

Creamer, crowing rooster & hen decora-
tion, 4 1/4" h. **125**

Creamer, figural elk head, shades of brown
& cream, 3 1/2" d., 4 1/4" h. **225**

Creamer, figural lamplighter, green,
4 1/2" h. **275**

Creamer, figural crow, black, 4 3/4" h. **225**

Creamer, "tapestry," wide ovoid body w/a
flaring foot & a long pinched spout,
ornate gilt D-form handle, "The Bathers"
landscape scene, 3 1/2" h. **375-425**

Creamer & cov. sugar bowl, figural apple,
pr. **350-400**

Creamer & cov. sugar bowl, figural grape
cluster, purple, pr. **225**

Creamer & cov. sugar bowl, figural pansy,
lavender, pr. **375**

Creamer & open sugar bowl, each decorated w/a mountain landscape w/a boy &
donkey, 3" h., pr. **250-350**

Creamer & open sugar bowl, figural grape
cluster, pr. **320**

Creamer & open sugar bowl, figural
poppy, pr. **400-500**

Creamer & open sugar bowl, figural
poppy, white satin finish, pr. **525**

Creamer & open sugar bowl, figural
rooster, creamer w/multicolored feathers
& sugar bowl in black, pr. **1,200**

Creamer & open sugar bowl, figural
strawberry, unmarked, pr. **500-600**

Creamer & open sugar bowl, "tapestry,"
barrel-shaped, the creamer w/a long
pinched spout, creamer w/goose girl

scene, sugar w/Alpine village scene,
sugar bowl 3 7/8" h., creamer 4 1/4" h.,
pr. **675**

Cup & saucer, figural rose **150-200**

Cup & saucer, floral decoration on the
inside & outside, gold handle on cup,
scalloped standard saucer, ca. 1916 .... **35-75**

Cup & saucer, scene of man w/turkeys **125**

Cup & saucer, "tapestry," floral
decoration **200-250**

Cup & saucer, demitasse, Castle scene
decoration, artist-signed **140**

Dish, leaf-shaped, "tapestry," scenic Lady
& Prince decoration **125**

Dresser tray, rectangular, "tapestry," Lady
& Prince scenic decoration, 7 x 9 1/4"... **450-550**

Dresser tray, rectangular w/rounded corners, scene of boy & three donkeys in
landscape, 8 x 11" **175-250**

Dresser tray, rectangular w/rounded corners, "tapestry" decoration of a young
courting couple wearing early 19th c.
attire, 11 1/2" l. **500-600**

Dresser tray, decorated w/hunting scene. **200-275**

Ewer, scene of hunter w/dog, 4 1/2" h. **225**

Ewer, cobalt blue, Babes in Woods decora-
tion, 6" h. **650**

Royal Bayreuth Flower Holder

Flower holder, bulbous ovoid body
w/domed flower holder top w/holes,
color Hunt Scene decoration, 3 3/4" h.
(ILLUS.) **200-250**

Flower holder w/frog-style cover, hunt
scene decoration, 3 3/4" h **200-225**

Gravy boat w/attached liner, decorated
w/multicolored floral sprays, gadrooned
border, gold trim, cream ground **45**

Gravy boat & underplate, figural poppy,
satin finish, 2 pcs. **250**

Hair receiver, cov., decorated w/scene of
boy & donkey **125-150**

Hair receiver, cov., "tapestry," scene of
farmer w/turkeys **300**

Hatpin holder, footed baluster-form body
w/a scalloped rim & top pierced w/holes,
"tapestry" design of a youth & maiden in
early 19th c. costume, 4 1/2" h. **450-575**

Hatpin holder, hexagonal shape, decorated w/pink & white roses, green leaves
& gold trim on rim, satin finish **350**

Humidor, cov., figural elk **950**

Humidor, cov., figural gorilla, black **1,750**

Humidor, cov., tapering cylindrical body
w/elk head handles, figural antlers on lid,
brown, 6 1/4" h. **600-800**

Humidor, cov., 7 3/4" h. **900-1,200**

Lamp base, "tapestry," slender ovoid body decorated w/"The Chase" scene, hounds after stag in water, raised on a metal ring support w/four short legs w/paw feet, set on an octagonal metal base w/molded swirled leafy stems, fitted for electricity, overall 21" h. (ILLUS.) **900-1,100**

Royal Bayreuth Lamp Base

Match holder, hanging-type, figural elk **575**
Match holder, hanging-type, figural shell .. **275-325**
Match holder, hanging-type, figural spiky shell **275**
Match holder, hanging-type, stork decoration on yellow ground **325-350**
Match holder, hanging-type, "tapestry," sheep in landscape scene, 4 1/2" l **485**

"Shadow Trees" Scenic Match Holder

Match holder w/striker, decorated water scene w/brown "Shadow Trees" & boats on orange & gold ground, unmarked, 3 1/4" d., 2 1/2" h. (ILLUS.) **65**
Mint dish, ruffled, w/Dutch girl decoration, 4 1/2" d. **125**
Model of a man's high top slipper **250**
Model of a man's shoe, black oxford **150**
Mug, beer, figural elk **400-450**
Mug, figural clown **550**
Mug, candle lady decoration, 5" h. **300-375**
Mug, beer, figural elk, 5 3/4" h. (ILLUS.) **650**
Mustard jar, cov., figural grape cluster, yellow **175**
Mustard jar, cov., figural lobster **225**
Mustard jar, cov., figural rose **550**
Mustard jar, cov., figural shell **100-160**
Mustard jar, cov., figural pansy, 3 1/4" h. .. **400-600**

Figural Elk Beer Mug

Mustard jar, cover & spoon, figural poppy, red, green spoon, 3 pcs **300**
Nappy, handled, figural poppy **150**
Nut set: large pedestal-based open compote & six matching servers; each decorated w/a colorful pastoral scene w/animals, 7 pcs **450**
Pin dish, decorated w/Arab scene **75-100**
Pin tray, triangular, "tapestry" portrait decoration of lady wearing large purple plumed hat, 5 x 5 x 5" **250**
Pincushion, figural elk head **350**
Pipe holder, figural Bassett hound, black .. **450-550**
Pitcher, 2 1/2" h., scene w/cows **170**

Royal Bayreuth Pitcher & Vase

Pitcher, 3 1/8" h., 2 3/8" w., squared waisted body w/short, wide spout & angled gilt handle, scene of Arab on horse (ILLUS. right) **125**
Pitcher, 3 1/4" h., 2" d., decorated w/Cavalier scene, two Cavaliers drinking at a table, grey & cream ground, unmarked **55**
Pitcher, 3 1/2" h., nursery rhyme scene w/Little Boy Blue **210**
Pitcher, 3 1/2" h., scenic decoration of Arab on horse **95**
Pitcher, 3 1/2" h., 2 1/4" d., scene of musicians, one playing bass & one w/mandolin, unmarked **55**
Pitcher, 3 3/4" h., corset-shaped, Colonial Curtsey scene w/a couple **165**
Pitcher, miniature, 4 1/2" h., scene of a skiff w/sail **125**
Pitcher, squatty, 5" h., 5" d., decorated w/hunting scene **100**
Pitcher, 5 1/4" h., pinched spout, "tapestry," scene of train on bridge over raging river **550**
Pitcher, 6" h., decorated w/hunting scene **125-150**

Pitcher, 6 3/4" h., wide ovoid body w/a flaring lightly scalloped base & a long pinched spout, "tapestry" finish w/a color landscape "Don Quixote" scene **525-575**

Pitcher, lemonade, 6 3/4" h., wide ovoid body w/flat foot & long pinched spout, ornate D-shape handle, dark brick red ground w/green "Dancing Frog" & flying insects decoration **1,200-1,500**

Pitcher, milk, figural lobster **250**

Pitcher, milk, figural oak leaf **500**

Pitcher, milk, figural poppy **350**

Pitcher, milk, figural red & white parrot handle **550**

Pitcher, milk, figural St. Bernard dog, unmarked **400**

Pitcher, milk, Goose Girl decoration **150**

Pitcher, milk, musicians decoration **150**

Pitcher, milk, 3" h., figural shell w/lobster handle **150**

Pitcher, milk, 4" h., figural St. Bernard **450-600**

Pitcher, milk, 4 1/4" h., figural rose **600-800**

Pitcher, milk, 5" h., figural dachshund **600-700**

Pitcher, milk, 5" h., figural fish head.......... **450-500**

Pitcher, milk, 5" h., figural owl, brown **400-600**

Pitcher, milk, 5 1/4" h., figural elk............. **275-325**

Pitcher, milk, 5 1/2" h., figural fish head........... **300**

Pitcher, milk, 5 1/2" h., figural lamplighter, green **400-500**

Pitcher, milk, tankard, 9 1/2" h., h.p. pastoral cow scene **200-250**

Pitcher, water, 6" h., figural apple **700-900**

Pitcher, water, 6" h., figural pelican **700-900**

Pitcher, water, 6" h., figural Santa Claus, red **7,000-9,000**

Figural Sunflower Pitcher

Pitcher, water, 6 1/2" h., figural sunflower (ILLUS.)... **4,500-5,000**

Pitcher, water, 6 3/4" h., figural lobster **395**

Pitcher, water, 6 3/4" h., figural robin **800-900**

Pitcher, water, 7" h., figural coachman **800**

Pitcher, water, 7" h., figural duck **800-1,000**

Pitcher, water, 7" h., figural elk **500-700**

Pitcher, water, 7" h., figural orange........... **800-900**

Pitcher, water, 7 1/4" h., pinched spout, scenic decoration of cows in pasture **257-300**

Pitcher, water, 7 1/2" h., figural conch shell, brownish amethyst & yellow mottled body, orange angled coral handle **500-700**

Pitcher, water, 7 3/4" h., 6" d., figural lobster, red shaded to orange w/green handle **525**

Pitcher, decorated w/scene of hunter & dog **125-175**

Pitcher, sheep scene **150**

Royal Bayreuth "Tapestry" Plaque

Plaque, pierced to hang, "tapestry," round w/a scroll-molded gilt-trimmed border, center portrait of woman leaning on horse, 9 1/2" d. (ILLUS.)...................... **775-825**

Plate, 5 1/4" d., leaf-shaped, decorated w/small yellow flowers on green ground, green curved handle **38**

Plate, 6" d., decorated w/soccer scene **175-200**

Plate, 6" d., handled, figural leaf & flower........... **85**

Plate, 7" d., decorated w/scene of girl walking dog **100**

Plate, 7 1/2" d., nursery rhyme scene w/Little Bo Peep.. **125**

Plate, 8" d., decorated w/pink & yellow flowers, gold rim, pink ground, blue mark.. **50-75**

Plate, 8" d., scene of man hunting................... **125**

Plate, 8 1/2" d., scene of man fishing.............. **125**

Plate, 8 1/2" d., scene of man hunting............. **125**

Plate, 9" d., candle girl decoration............. **150-175**

Plate, 9 1/2" d., scroll-molded rim, "tapestry," toasting Cavalier scene........................ **825**

Plate, 9 1/2" d., "tapestry," lady w/horse scene **770-800**

Plate, 9 1/2" d., "tapestry," landscape scene w/deer by a river **250**

Playing card box, cov., decorated w/a sailing ship scene **195-250**

Powder box, cov., Cavalier Musicians scene... **175**

Powder box, cov., round, "tapestry," scenic Lady & Prince decoration **150-175**

Powder jar, figural pansy, 4 1/4" h. **500-600**

Relish dish, open-handled, footed, ruffled edge, cow scene decoration, 8" l. **175**

Relish dish, figural cucumber, 5 1/4 x 12 1/2" **150-250**

Relish dish, figural Murex Shell **200-300**

Salt & pepper shakers, figural conch shell, unmarked, pr. **100**

Salt & pepper shakers, figural ear of corn, pr. **600-800**

Salt & pepper shakers, figural grape cluster, purple, pr. **150-175**

Salt & pepper shakers, figural poppy, red, pr. **300-400**

Stamp box, cov., "tapestry," Cottage by Water Fall scene **225**

String holder, hanging-type, figural rooster head **550-650**

Sugar bowl, cov., Brittany Girl decoration **100**

Sugar bowl, cov., figural lemon (small finial flake) **175**

Sugar bowl, cov., figural pansy, purple (tiny rim flake).. **225-250**
Sugar bowl, cov., figural poppy, red **225-250**
Sugar bowl, cov., figural rose **300-400**
Sugar bowl, cov., figural shell w/lobster handle **200**
Sugar bowl, cov., figural lobster, 3 3/4" h... **110-150**
Tea strainer, figural pansy, 5 3/4" l........... **350-400**
Tea strainer, figural red poppy, 5 3/4" l..... **350-400**
Teapot, cov., child's, decorated w/a scene of hunters, 3 3/4" h. **125**
Teapot, cov., child's, boy & donkey decoration, green, unmarked, 4" h. **225**
Teapot, cov., demitasse, decorated w/scene of rooster & hen **250-300**
Teapot, cov., figural orange, 6 1/2" h. **425-500**
Toothpick holder, Bird of Paradise decoration **225-250**
Toothpick holder, decorated w/scene of girl w/two chickens **100**
Toothpick holder, figural bellringer, 3 1/2" h... **175-225**
Toothpick holder, figural elk head, 3" h... **225-250**
Toothpick holder, figural Murex Shell............. **175**
Toothpick holder, figural poppy, red............ **300**
Toothpick holder, man hunting turkeys scene... **200**
Toothpick holder, "tapestry," scene of woman w/pony & trees, 2 2/5" h............. **450-550**
Toothpick holder, three-handled floral decoration, 2 1/4" h. **175-200**
Toothpick holder, three-handled, Harvest scene decoration.. **150**

Toothpick Holder with Hunt Scene

Toothpick holder, three-handled, Hunt scene decoration, 3" h. (ILLUS.) **265**
Toothpick holder, three-handled, scene of horse & wagon **150**
Tray, decorated w/scene of girl w/geese, molded rim w/gold trim, 9 x 12 1/4" **425**
Tray, "tapestry," scene of train on bridge over raging river, 7 3/4 x 11" **800**
Vase, miniature, 2 3/4" h., conical body on three tab feet, tapering to a short flaring neck, small knob handles at shoulders, decorated w/a scene of cows...................... **125**
Vase, 3" h., basket-shaped w/overhead handle, square rim, Babes in Woods decoration **325-350**
Vase, 3" h., scene of children w/St. Bernard dog **125**
Vase, 3 1/4" d., footed, baluster-form body w/angled shoulder handles, short cylin-

drical silver rim, Cavalier Musicians scene on grey ground **75-125**
Vase, 3 1/4" h., 1 7/8" d., footed, conical body tapering to a silver rim, small tab handles, decorated w/scene of white & brown cows w/green & brown ground (ILLUS. left, with pitcher)......................... **75-125**
Vase, 3 1/2" h., Cavalier Musicians decoration **125**
Vase, 4" h., two-handled, decorated w/long-tailed Bird of Paradise **225-300**
Vase, 4 1/2" h., sailing scene decoration... **135-150**
Vase, 4 1/2" h., "tapestry," courting couple decoration **525**
Vase, bud, 4 1/2" h., two handles, Babes in Wood scene, cobalt blue & white **225-325**
Vase, 4 3/4" h., handled, Babes in Woods decoration, girl holding doll **500-550**
Vase, bud, 4 3/4" h., "tapestry," rounded body w/a thin tall neck, Lady & Prince scenic decoration **120-200**
Vase, 5" h., "tapestry," bulbous ovoid body tapering to a short slender flaring neck, cottage by a waterfall landscape **295-350**
Vase, 5 1/2" h., portrait decoration **250-300**
Vase, 5 1/2" h., teardrop-shaped, colorful floral decoration.. **125**
Vase, 6" h., "tapestry," decorated w/a scene of an elk & three hounds in a river..... **475**
Vase, 7" h., decorated w/Arab scene **125-150**
Vase, 7" h., decorated w/portrait of a lady.. **275-350**
Vase, 7" h., "tapestry," a bulbous ovoid body w/the rounded shoulder centering a tiny flared neck, a shaded pastel ground centered on one side w/a three-quarters length portrait of a lady in 18th c. attire w/a large feathered hat & large muff, the reverse w/a landscape scene **550-650**
Vase, 8 1/4" h., footed squatty bulbous bottom tapering to a tall waisted base w/a gently scalloped flaring rim, polychrome boy & two donkeys decoration **250-300**
Vase, 8 1/4" h., "tapestry," slender ovoid body w/a short cylindrical flaring neck, "The Bathers" landscape scene **435-550**
Vase, 9" h., tall slender waisted cylindrical body w/a gently scalloped flaring rim, three long green scroll & bead loop handles down the sides, the top body w/a band decorated w/a toasting Cavaliers scene in color on one side & "Ye Old Bell" scene on the other, the lower body all in dark green, ca. 1902 .... **250-300**
Vase, 9 1/2" h., peacock decoration, openwork on neck & at base, ornate scroll handles, lavish gold trim **740**
Vase, 11 1/2" h., polar bear scene **850**
Vase, double-bud, ovoid body w/two angled short flaring necks joined by a small handle, scene of Dutch children **125**
Vase, miniature, ball-shaped, footed, silver rim, Arab scene decoration **150**
Vases, 2 1/2" h., decorated w/sunset scene of a ship, pr. **100-125**

Small Royal Bayreuth Vases

Vases, 3 1/8" h., 2 5/8" d., squatty bulbous lower body below the tall tapering sides ending in a ringed neck & flanked by loop handles, one w/scene of Dutch boy & girl playing w/brown dog & the other w/scene of Dutch boy & girl playing w/white & brown dog, green mark, pr. (ILLUS.) **110**

Wall pocket, figural grape cluster, purple **350**

Wall pocket, figural grape cluster, yellow **350**

Wall pocket, depicts a jester & "Many Kiss the Child for the Nurses SAKE," green ground, signed "NOKE," 9" h. **750**

Wall pocket, figural red poppy, 9 1/2" l. **650-700**

ROYAL BONN & BONN

Bonn and subsequently Royal Bonn china were produced in Bonn, Germany, in a manufactory established in 1755. Later wares made there are often marked Mehlem or bear the initials FM or a castle mark. Most wares were of the hand-painted type. Clock cases were also made in Bonn.

Royal Bonn & Bonn Mark

Ewer, earthenware 'aesthetic movement,' pear-form body & attenuated gently curved spout painted w/finch perched on a flowering orchid plant w/gilt clouds & moon in distance on a cream ground, shoulders applied w/angular gilt handle, red printed & impressed factory marks, painted numeral 1807/4, late 19th c., 12" h. **$115**

Urn, tall classical form w/gilt mask-form handles, the body painted w/a floral still life, on paw feet resting on a shaped base, ca. 1900, 15 1/2" h. **316**

Vase, 11 1/2" h., two-handled, ivory ground w/gilt & enameled flower garden scenes, late 19th c. **115**

Ornate Royal Bonn Vase

Vase, 14" h., baluster-form w/a wide shoulder below the short flaring neck, bright pink ground decorated on the front w/an oval reserve w/a color bust portrait of a lovely long-haired lady, the back w/another reserve w/a landscape, ornate gold banding & scrolls highlighted w/green leafy vines & yellow sprigs (ILLUS.) **1,200-1,300**

ROYAL COPLEY

Royal Copley was a trade name used by the Spaulding China Company of Sebring, Ohio during the 1940s and 1950s for a variety of ceramic figurines, planters and other decorative pieces. Similar pieces were also produced under the trade name "Royal Windsor" as well as the Spaulding China mark.

The Spaulding China Company stopped producing in 1957 but for the next two years other potteries finished production of their outstanding orders. Today these originally inexpensive wares are developing a dedicated collector following.

Ashtray, heart-shaped w/two love birds sitting at top of heart, signed "Royal Copley," rose w/blue or yellow w/blue, 5 1/2", each **$35-50**

Bank, model of a pig, standing & smiling, two small holes in bottom, bank must be broken to retrieve money, 4 1/2" h. **35-50**

"Farmer Pig" Bank

Bank, model of a pig, "Farmer Pig," standing & wearing neck scarf, brown w/tan
scarf, pink w/blue scarf, blue w/green
scarf & brown & green w/brown scarf,
two small holes in bottom, bank must be
broken to retrieve money, brown
w/green scarf is hardest to find, pink is
most desirable color, 5 1/2" h., each
(ILLUS.)... **75-125**

Teddy Bear Bank & Planters

Bank, model of Teddy bear, white w/black
& gold trim, red bow at neck, two small
holes in bottom, bank must be broken to
retrieve money, 7 1/4" h. (ILLUS. left)....**175-200**
Bank, model of rooster, one, two, three or
four small holes in bottom, bank must be
broken to retrieve money, three colora-
tions available, 7 1/2" h., each **75-85**
Bank, model of Teddy bear, brown, two
small holes in bottom, bank must be bro-
ken to retrieve money, 7 1/2" h. **150-160**
Creamer & sugar bowl, w/leaf handles,
yellow & brown, grey & pink or tricolored,
marked "Royal Copley" on bottom, tricolored & grey & pink are equally hard to
find, 3" h., pr., each set **50-75**

Figure of Dancing Lady

Figurine, dancing lady, wearing hat & long
full-skirted dress, one hand holding her
hat in place while wind blows at her
dress, four colorations, unmarked, 8" h.,
each (ILLUS.) **135-150**
Head vase planter, "Island Lady," jet black
w/white turban, earrings, signed "Royal
Windsor" on back, three runners on bot-
tom of base, 8" h. **100**

Lamp base, model of pig, decorated w/pink
or blue stripes, factory-drilled on top &
bottom, unmarked, extremely hard to
find, pink is easier to locate, 6 1/2" h.,
each **200-225**

Figural Cocker Spaniel Lamp Base

Lamp base, model of a dog, Cocker Spaniel, sitting in begging position, brown or
black, black is more rare than brown,
10" h. (ILLUS.)...................................... **125-150**
Model of bear, Teddy bear, eyes closed &
playing concertina, brown, unmarked,
7 1/2" h. (hard to find in mint condition)... **90-100**
Model of bird, Swallow w/extended wings,
cobalt, rose or yellow, blue is hardest,
choicest & priciest coloration, 7" h.,
each **75-150**
Model of bird, Hunt's Swallow, female flying toward
ground, male flying upward, four colorations,
some are hand-decorated, cobalt pair & females
hardest to find, 8" h., pr. **150-250**
Model of bird, Jay bird, various colors,
Spaulding mark, hand-decorated birds
bring higher prices, 8" h. **75-100**
Model of cockatoo, signed "Royal Cop-
ley," rose or green, 8 1/4" h., each **45-50**
Model of dog pulling wagon, sitting dog,
brown w/black & white spots, wagon
imprinted "FLYER" on side, unmarked,
5 1/4" h. **35-50**

Model of Royal Windsor Gadwell

Model of drake & duck, Gadwells, Game
Bird series, signed "A.D. Priollo" on
base, Royal Windsor mark, series consists of Gadwells, Teals & Mallards,
Gadwells & Teals are hardest to find,
sizes vary, pr. (ILLUS. of drake)............ **150-250**
Model of hen & rooster, black & white
w/red trim, green base, 5 1/2" h. & 6" h.,
pr. (rooster is harder to find).................. **350-400**

Model of hen & rooster, teal breast, Royal Windsor mark, 10" h. & 10 1/4" h., pr. (hens are harder to find)........................ **350-400**

Model of kitten, brown to brown grey, 8" h., each (colors hard to match) **100-125**

Model of rooster, all-white, 10" h. **129**

Models of birds, Kingfishers, one on leaf base w/wings extended, the other flying downward, blue, rose or yellow, blue is hardest to find, rose pairs are hard to match, 5" h., pr., each **100-150**

Models of kittens, black & white w/red bow at neck, sitting, one looking up & one looking down, one shown on left is harder to find, 8" h., each **75-85**

Pitcher, 8" h., Pome Fruit patt., stamped or incised "Royal Copley" on bottom, five colorations, each (blue is most popular & priciest)... **45-85**

Planter, figure of Madonna w/side planter, marked w/raised letters on bottom, Royal Windsor mark, pale blue, pale rose or solid white, 6 1/4" h., each (solid white is most difficult color to locate)......... **40-55**

Planter, model of Cocker-type dog standing on a log & playing a large bass fiddle, unmarked, 7" h. (premium item, very difficult to find)..................................... **165-175**

Figural Poodle Planter

Planter, model of dog, recumbent Poodle wearing collar, grey, pink or white, grey is hardest to find, pink is most common color, 8 1/2" l., 6 1/2" h., each (ILLUS.) **60-85**

Planter, model of puppy w/mailbox, black & white, runners on underside, unmarked, 8 1/2" h. (premium item)......................... **75-100**

Rooster Planter

Planter, model of rooster on wheelbarrow, 8" h. (ILLUS.)....................................... **100-125**

Planter, model of Teddy bear w/basket on back, brown w/blue, pink or yellow basket, runners on bottom, unmarked, 6 1/4" h., each **65-75**

Planter, model of Teddy bear, white w/black trim & red bow at neck, 6 1/4" h. (ILLUS. right).. **45-55**

Planter, model of Teddy bear, white w/black trim & red bow at neck, 8" h. (ILLUS. center)... **75-85**

Planter, model of two Siamese cats, one sitting & one recumbent, white w/black trim, blue eyes, green or rust woven basket, green is more desirable, 8" h., each **175-200**

Planter/book ends, model of ram's head, pr. **55**

Vase, 8 1/2" h., figural, model of mare nuzzling her foal, signed "Royal Copley," medium rusty brown.................................. **35-50**

Vase, 10" h., pink & green floral decal decoration on butterscotch or white ground, three distinct classic styles, marked "Spaulding" in gold on underside, each (collectors prefer butterscotch finish) **75-100**

Wall pocket, model of rooster, full figure walking bird, black & white w/green background or brown w/green background, signed "Royal Copley," 5 1/2" h., each (black & white version is more prized by collectors) **45-60**

Wall pocket, figural, "Pigtail Girl," bust of girl w/ruffled collar & bonnet, grey, deep red, turquoise, pink & deep blue, marked "Royal Copley," deep red & blue are the most desired & therefore harder to find & costlier, 7" h., each **75-125**

Wall pocket, figural, full face pirate head w/ruddy complexion, grey or red bandanna, signed "Royal Copley," 8" h., each **45-60**

Wall pockets, figural, head of old man & old woman w/grey hair & old-style hat, deep rose & miscellaneous other colors, signed "Royal Copley," 8" h., each pr...... **80-100**

ROYAL DUX

This factory in Bohemia was noted for the figural porcelain wares in the Art Nouveau style which were exported around the turn of the century. Other notable figural pieces were produced through the 1930s and the factory was nationalized after World War II.

Royal Dux Marks

Centerpiece, figural, modeled in high-relief as branches & foliage in a buff glaze, the heads of four maidens incorporated into the upwardly flowing form ending in large leaves forming a bowl, marked "Royal Dux Bohemia" & w/a large "E" in

a triangle, impressed "333 13," 18 1/2" h. (restoration)... **$748**
Figure group, a young boy w/a Setter dog, enameled & gilt-trimmed, Czechoslovakia mark, early 20th c., 13 1/4" h.................. **288**

Detailed Royal Dux Figure Groups

Figure groups, one w/a shepherd playing pipes w/sheep around his feet & standing next to an Ionic column, the other w/a shepherdess w/a staff standing w/goats at her feet, also beside an Ionic column, fine enameled decoration, late 19th - early 20th c., 16 1/2" h., pr. (ILLUS.).. **748**
Serving dish, figural, a maiden & a pair of lovebirds on an open shell dish, ca. 1900, 8 1/2" h... **230**
Vases, 19" h., Art Nouveau design w/an ivory ground decorated w/stylized leaves & berries in relief, raised "Czechoslovakia" mark, early 20th c., pr........................... **978**

ROYAL VIENNA

The second factory in Europe to make hard paste porcelain was established in Vienna in 1719 by Claud Innocentius de Paquier. The factory underwent various changes of administration through the years and finally closed in 1865. Since then, however, the porcelain has been reproduced by various factories in Austria and Germany, many of which have also reproduced the early beehive mark. Early pieces, naturally, bring far higher prices than the later ones or the reproductions.

Royal Vienna Mark

Cabinet plate, 9 1/2" d., finely painted in the center w/the birth of Venus, the young beauty nude & recumbent on the waves w/five cupids hovering above her, staring down or blowing conch shells, within an elaborately gilt foliate scroll & trelliswork border reserved on a cream ground within a gilt edged rim, shield mark painted in blue, impressed factory marks & letters, title painted in red script, ca. 1900 .... **$1,495**
Cabinet plate, 9 5/8" d., finely painted in the center w/portrait of Bianca, the young maiden w/long curly brown hair, wearing a pearl necklace & white chemise, within a gilt foliate frame & cobalt ground border gilt w/interlinking arched panels, shield factory mark in underglaze blue, faint impressed numeral & title in black script, signed Hamer, ca. 1900 .... **747**

Royal Vienna Cabinet Plates

Cabinet plate, 9 1/2" d., h.p. center scene of maiden clad in white drapery standing in a garden below falling blossoms, pale blue & maroon border gilt w/vignettes of animals & scrollwork panels, ca. 1900, artist-signed, underglaze-blue shield mark, small ground out chip to rim (ILLUS. right)............................... **805**
Cabinet plate, center free-form enamel decorated panel depicting a nude female in landscape, border w/gilt foliate design on deep burgundy ground, late 19th c., 9 1/2" d. **1,840**
Cabinet plate, central figural scene "Mione & Amor," gilt foliate design on cobalt border, late 19th c., 9 1/2" d. **518**
Cabinet plate, 9 5/8" d., h.p. center portrait of Angelina, a young dark-haired woman wearing an off the shoulder gown, a flower in her hair, within a maroon, yellow, pink & green ground border gilt w/foliate scrollwork, shield mark in underglaze-blue, artist-signed & title painted in black on reverse (ILLUS. center).. **1,380**
Cabinet plate, 9 3/4" d., h.p. center scene of maiden guiding two soldiers towards a woodland lake w/blue ground border decorated w/stylized foliage & flower medallions, gold trim, late 19th c., underglaze-blue shield mark (ILLUS. left)............ **690**
Cabinet plates, 9 1/2" d., each decorated in center w/scene of three maidens or a young woman w/a cupid, each on a terrace and within a gilt scroll cartouche, reserved on cobalt ground & surrounded by three panels of cupids amongst clouds separated by tooled gilt oblong panels & foliate scrollwork within a gilt edged rim, shield marks in underglaze-blue, titles in black script, signed Mohau, early 20th c., the pair................................. **1,495**

Charger, round, the center decorated w/a large colorful scene of Roman soldiers under canopy in the forest being served by a kneeling maiden, gilt scrolled & floral border w/red & blue panels, titled on the reverse "Vortigern and Rovena," overglaze blue beehive mark on back, 16" d. **1,725**

Figural group, modeled as an amorous man wearing a pale yellow hat, buff jacket & breeches, seated beside a fashionable lady wearing a floral decorated dress, accompanied by a young boy seated on the grass behind them, all beneath a tree on a domed shaped base, shield factory mark in underglaze-blue, impressed letter "P", 19th c., 9" h. **287**

Royal Vienna Portrait Plaque

Plaque, round w/central enamel decorated bust portrait depicting Queen Elizabeth of England, scrolled gilt foliate decorated ruby red border, titled in German on reverse, 19th c, 16 1/2" d. (ILLUS.) **2,300**

Plate, 9 1/2" d., cabinet-type, the decorated cobalt blue border around a central h.p. figural scene, titled on back "Soll ich?," underglaze-blue beehive mark, ca. 1900 ..... **518**

Plate, 10 1/8" d., gilt-trimmed cobalt blue border, center w/a colored enamel bust portrait of a female, late 19th c **316**

Plates, 11 1/2" d., the center decorated w/colorful scene of seated woman & man standing near, titled "Maiden and Shepard Boy," gilt designs on wide green ground, ca. 1864, beehive mark under glaze & over glaze **1,200**

Urn, cov., cylindrical body painted w/continuous scene of classical figures on stippled gilt ground, raised on three fluted column supports w/paw feet on stepped circular base, all decorated in gilding on a cobalt ground, removable waisted neck & cover w/similar decoration, pseudo shield factory mark in underglaze-blue, titles in blue script, 17 1/2" h. .. **3,220**

Royal Vienna Covered Urn

Urn, cov., decorated w/two continuous figural scenes, one titled "Hector Abschied" & the other "Alexander und die Familie des Darius" on a gilt ground flanked by loop handles, raised on a circular base w/figural panels, pseudo shield mark in blue enamel & decorator mark of Dorfl Franz, late 19th c., 21" h. (ILLUS.) **4,887**

ROYAL WORCESTER

This porcelain has been made by the Royal Worcester Porcelain Co. at Worcester, England, from 1862 to the present. For earlier porcelain made in Worcester, see WORCESTER. Royal Worcester is distinguished from wares made at Worcester between 1751 and 1862 that are referred to as only Worcester by collectors.

Royal Worcester Marks

Basket, scrolled sides, ivory ground w/yellow & orange tinting & gilt trim, No. 1483, 1892, 10 3/8" l., 9 1/4" h. **$489**

Bowl, 7 1/2 x 8 1/2", 4" h., basketweave exterior, open gold handles, interior w/multicolored flowers, beige bisque ground, ca. 1903 .... **295**

Cabinet plates, 10 1/2" d., each w/a different English rural scene within a narrow acid-etched gilt border, artist-signed, printed mark, ca. 1929, set of 12 (ILLUS. of part) **5,750**

Candlestick, figural, a young woodsman w/an ax over his shoulder standing to one side of a tall slender tree trunk topped by the candle socket, a large ovoid wicker basket standing on the other side of the tree, a green & cream colored ground w/gilt trim, Shape 1793, ca. 1895, printed mark, 11 7/8" h. **633**

Royal Worcester Scenic Plates

Cups & saucers, cream-colored ground w/gilt highlighted enameled floral designs, ca. 1900, saucers 5 3/8" d., two extra saucers, set of 10.............................. 374

Equestrian group, George Washington on horseback, modeled by Bernard Winskill, number 80 from a limited edition of 750, black printed, painted & incised factory marks, w/wooden base, ca. 1975, overall 17 7/8" h. 402

Royal Worcester Ewer

Ewer, bottle-form, Patent Metallic-type, bulbous body tapering to a tall cylindrical neck w/a pointed rim spout, a long curling gilt figural lizard handle, decorated in color w/a large sprig of blossoms against a creamy ground, ca. 1886, chip, 8 3/4" h. (ILLUS.)... 230

Ewer, bulbous basketweave-molded body w/tall neck, applied w/a realistic gilt lizard wrapped around the sides & forming the handle, late 19th c., 6" h......................... 460

Ewer, Chelsea-style, large ovoid body raised on a short round pedestal on a square foot, a short ringed cylindrical neck flaring to a long arched ruffled & crimped spout & continuing into a high looped handle ending in a satyr mask, gilt neck, handle & base, the ivory body

decorated w/a large color-enameled leafy blossom branch trimmed w/gilt, Shape 1144, ca. 1892, 10 3/4" h................. 575

Ewer, classical baluster-form, a ringed & stepped round pedestal base supporting a wide ovoid body w/a wide shoulder tapering to a short ringed neck w/a rolled tricorner rim continuing into an ornate scrolled arched handle from rim to triple-branched ends at the shoulder, cream ground decorated on the sides w/large green & gilt ferns w/heavy gilt trim on the neck, spout, handle & base, Shape 1309, ca. 1890, printed mark, 10 1/2" h. 633

Ewer, compressed spherical body beneath attenuated gently flaring cylindrical neck w/gently curving gilt spout, decorated in colored enamels & gilt w/floral sprays on cream ground, upper rim & C-scroll handle pierced w/foliate scrollwork, puce printed factory mark w/year letter, impressed factory marks & numerals, painted letters & numerals, ca. 1887, 14 3/4" h. 468

Ewer, footed tapering melon-lobed body w/a flaring neck w/shell-scalloped rim, large gilt twig handle & small gilt twig handles around the waist, decorated w/multicolored foliage on the cream ground, No. 1507, 1902, 9" h. 316

Figure, "June," barefoot boy playing harmonica, his dog by his side, No. 3456, designed by F. Doughty, 1949 125

Figure, Sabrina, terra cotta & turquoise glazed figure, finely modeled as a classical maiden partly covered by a voluminous billowing drape, tied around her middle w/a belt, holding an inverted vase & standing barefoot on a manganese glazed drum-shaped base, all on a turquoise glazed cylindrical column molded w/foliate borders heightened in gilding, impressed factory mark, ca. 1880, 25 3/8" h. (small chips to headdress & fingers on left hand) 1,610

Figure group, "Hide and Seek," modeled as a young boy & girl hiding amid three tree stump-form vases, set on an oval rockwork base, Shape 825, printed mark, ca. 1881, 6 1/2" h. (gilt wear, line in base) 489

Figure group, Parian, allegorical group of Peace blessing the Arts, colored & glazed figures modeled as three classical maidens, each wearing a long flowing robe, center maiden w/laurel wreath in her right hand, standing w/arms outstretched & hands on the heads of the other two maidens sitting flanking her, all surrounded by discarded mallet, sword, shield & anvil on an oblong base, impressed factory mark & clay mark "R," ca. 1880, 11 1/2" h. 632

Inkstand, figural, a fluted round well & domed cover w/a seated putto finial, the sides w/applied seaweed, supported by a stand w/three shell-form dishes alternating w/three nude female sphinx figures, enameled decoration, ca. 1877,

printed mark, 7 1/4" h. (restored headdress, hairline in one shell dish, gilt rim
wear) **920**

Jardiniere, Oriental-style, wide bulbous
spherical body w/a low wide ring neck,
raised on scrolled-under legs & pierced
scrolls in gilt & bronze enamel, the sides
molded in bold relief w/lily pads in
bronze enamel & gilt leaves, cream
ground, ca. 1882, printed mark, 6 1/2" h.
(gilt wear) **374**

Plate, 10 3/4" d., round w/irregular border,
decorated overall w/a landscape of the
village of Tewkesbury done in natural
colors, gilt rim band, artist-signed, dated
1953 .... **225**

Plates, 9 1/4" d., blue enamel & gilt floral
trim w/bird centers, ca. 1886, set of 10 .... **259**

Vase, 3 1/4" h., double-walled, ovoid body
w/a short rolled neck, the outer cellwork
body pierced around lobed cartouches
decorated w/gilt-decorated landscapes
on the inner body wall, gilt jeweling on
the outer cellwork, printed mark, ca.
1887 .... **1,150**

Vase, cov., 9 1/4" h., bulbous ovoid body
tapering to a short flared neck, fitted
domed cover w/molded gilt scroll band &
gilt pointed finial, the base & neck
molded w/gilt foliate designs & pierced
lattice panels around the neck, ornate
gilt scrolled shoulder handles, ca. 1892 ...... **403**

Vase, 11 5/8" h., gilt square base below
ovoid body w/flared rim, decorated on
front w/a colorful spray of flowers within
a gilt square frame & flanked by burnished gilt scroll handles, cobalt ground
between gilt borders & pedestal foot, top
of pedestal & corner of base restored,
some crackling to glaze & wear to gilding, factory mark in iron red script
(ILLUS.).. **1,082**

Royal Worcester Vase

Vase, 14 1/4" h., classical baluster-form, a
short ringed pedestal base supporting
the tall ovoid body tapering to a slender
waisted neck w/rolled rim, griffin head
figural shoulder handles, large side panels decorated in color w/scenes of polar
bears & ice-capped mountains, molded
trim on cream ground w/gilt trim, Shape
1764, ca. 1903 (missing cover) **16,100**

Vases, 4 1/4" h., 3" d., Sabrina Ware,
inverted pear-shaped body, decorated
w/fish & seaweed in light blue on deep
blue ground, ca. 1909, pr. (ILLUS.)............. **375**

Vases, 6 7/8" h., bud-type, a ringed &
domed round foot w/a beaded net decoration below the short beaded ring stem
below the tall slender cylindrical body
w/a flared, swirled scroll-molded scalloped rim, ornate scrolling foliate gilt
handles at the lower body, a pink
shaded to yellow ground w/delicate floral
decoration & gilt trim, ca. 1900, pr.
(slight rim chip restored).............................. **690**

Royal Worcester Sabrina Ware Vases

Vases, 7 1/4" h., figural, one modeled as a
boy & girl w/a waterpot, the other w/a
boy playing a horn as a girl looks on, artist-signed, impressed marks, ca. 1880,
pr. (gilt wear) **1,035**

R.S. PRUSSIA
& RELATED WARES

*Ornately decorated china marked "R.S. Prussia"
and "R.S. Germany" continues to grow in popularity. According to the Third Series of Mary Frank
Gaston's* Encyclopedia of R.S. Prussia, *these
marks were used by the Reinhold Schlegelmilch
porcelain factories located in Suhl in the Germanic
region known as Prussia prior to World War I, and
in Tillowitz, Silesia which became part of Poland
after World War II. Other marks sought by collectors include "R.S. Suhl," R.S." steeple or church
marks, and "R.S. Poland."*

*The Suhl factory was founded by Reinhold
Schlegelmilch in 1869 and closed in 1917. The
Tillowitz factory was established in 1895 by Erhard
Schlegelmilch, Reinhold's son. This china custom-
arily bears the phrase "R.S. Germany" and "R.S.
Tillowitz." The Tillowitz factory closed in 1945, but it
was Tillowitz factory closed in 1945, but it was re-
opened for a few years under Polish administration.
The "R.S. Poland" mark is attributed to that later
time period.*

*Prices are high and collectors should beware of
the forgeries that sometimes find their way to the
market. Mold names and numbers are taken from
Mary Gaston's books on R.S. Prussia.*

*The "R.S. Prussia" mark and the "R.S. Suhl"
mark have been reproduced, so buy with care.*

Collectors are also interested in the porcelain products made by the Erdmann Schlegelmilch factory. This factory was founded by three brothers in Suhl in 1861. They named the factory in honor of their father, Erdmann Schlegelmilch. A variety of marks incorporating the "E.S." initials were used. The factory closed ca. 1935. The Erdmann Schlegelmilch factory was an earlier and entirely separate business from the Reinhold Schlegelmilch factory. The two were not related to each other.

R.S. GERMANY

R.S. Prussia & Related Wares — A

Berry set: 9" master bowl & six matching 5 1/2" sauce dishes, Iris mold, decorated w/large red roses, 7 pcs. **$500-550**

Bowl, 8" h., handled, decorated w/scene of two colorful parrots, green highlights 275-325

Bowl, 10" d., decorated w/wild roses, raspberries, & blueberries, glossy glaze 125-175

Bowl, 10 1/2", handled, Lebrun portrait, Tiffany finish, artist's palette, paintbrush.. 1,800-2,000

Bowl, large, Lettuce mold, floral decoration. lustre finish 300-350

R.S. Germany Cake Plate

Cake plate, double-pierced small gold side handles, decorated w/a scene of a maiden near a cottage at the edge of a dark forest, 10" d. (ILLUS.)................... 275-325

Cheese server, a slightly dished round plate centered by a short pedestal supporting a small dished plate, each section decorated w/large blossoms joined by green tendrils on a shaded ground, 8 1/2" d. 39

Chocolate set: cov. pot & five cups & saucers; white flower decoration, blue mark, the set 500-550

Coffeepot, cov., demitasse, Ribbon & Jewel mold, rose garland decoration 400-450

Creamer, Mold 640, decorated w/roses, gold trim on ruffled rim & ornate handle 35-50

R.S. Germany Cup & Saucer

Cup & saucer, decorated w/blue, black & white bands on beige lustre ground, cup w/center silhouette of Art Deco lady in blue dancing w/blue scarf, cup 3 1/2" d., 2 1/4" h., saucer 5 3/4" d. (ILLUS.)........ 100-150

Cup & saucer, demitasse, ornate handle, eight-footed 75-100

Gravy boat w/underplate, poppy decoration 75-100

Mustard jar, cov., calla lily decoration......... 65-100

Pitcher, 9" h., Mold 343, floral decoration w/overall gilt tracery on cobalt blue (red castle mark)... 700-800

Plate, 7 1/4" d., poppy decoration 30-50

Plate, 8" d., decorated w/scene of colorful parrots, gold rim 250-300

Plate, 11 1/4" d., smooth round form w/gold rim band, white, green & pink lilac clusters between curved panels of small gold leaves on a pale green ground 125

Salad set, 10 1/2" d. lettuce bowl & six 8" d. matching plates, Mold 12, Iris decoration on pearl lustre finish, 7 pcs. 300-350

Toothpick holder, two-handled, decorated w/roses & gold trim, artist-signed... 75-125

Tray, handled, decorated w/large white & green poppies, 15 1/4" l. 275-300

R.S. PRUSSIA

Bell, tall trumpet-form ruffled body w/twig handle, decorated w/small purple flowers & green leaves on white ground, unmarked, 3 1/2" l. 300-350

Berry set: master bowl & six sauce dishes; five-lobed, floral relief rim w/forget-me-nots & water lilies decoration, artist-signed, 7 pcs. 400-450

Ribbon & Jewel Melon Eaters Berry Set

Berry set: master bowl & six sauce dishes; Ribbon & Jewel mold w/Melon Eaters decoartion, 7 pcs. (ILLUS) 3,500-3,800

Bowl, 7" d., decorated w/roses, satin finish **150-200**

Bowl, 9 3/4" d., Iris variant mold, rosette center & pale green floral decoration **250-300**

Bowl, 10" d., floral decoration in black & gold **150-175**

Bowl, 10" d., Icicle mold (Mold 7), red & gold border around the creamy satin interior decorated w/large gold roses ... **450-525**

Bowl, 10" d., Iris mold, Spring Season portrait decoration **2,200-2,400**

Bowl, 10" d., Mold 202, gold beaded rim, double swans center scene in shades of beige & white, unmarked **200-225**

Summer Season Portrait Bowl

Bowl, 10" d., Mold 85, Summer Season portrait w/mill scene in background (ILLUS.) **2,000-2,400**

Bowl, 10 1/4" d., center decoration of pink roses w/pearlized finish, border in shades of lavender & blue w/satin finish, lavish gold trim (unlisted mold) **400-450**

Bowl, 10 1/4" d., Mold 251, apple blossom decoration, satin finish **250-300**

Bowl, 10 1/2" d., Countess Potocka portrait decoration, heavy gold trim **4,000-4,300**

Bowl, 10 1/2" d., decorated w/pink roses & carnations on white shaded to peach ground, iridescent Tiffany finish **595**

Bowl, 10 1/2" d., decorated w/scene of Dice Throwers, red trim **850-1,000**

Bowl, 10 1/2" d., handled, four-lobed, decorated w/Art Nouveau relief-molded scrolls & colorful sprays on shaded green ground **200-250**

Bowl, 10 1/2" d., Iris mold, poppy decoration **350-400**

Bowl, 10 1/2" d., Mold 101, Tiffany finish around rim, orchid & cream trim on molded border blossoms, central bouquet of pink, yellow & white roses w/green leaves **250-300**

Bowl, 10 1/2" d., Point & Clover mold (Mold 82), decorated w/forget-me-nots & roses, satin finish, artist-signed **300-350**

Bowl, 10 1/2" d., Point & Clover mold (Mold 82), decorated w/pink roses & green leaves w/shadow flowers & a Tiffany finish **250-300**

Bowl, 10 3/4" d., Mold 217, "tapestry" center mill scene, gilt scroll border **1,100-1,400**

Bowl, 11" d., 3" h., Sunflower mold, satin finish **450-500**

R.S. Prussia Swans Decorated Bowl

Bowl, 11" d., Icicle mold (Mold 7), Swans decoration w/clouds & autumn foliage in the background (ILLUS.) **600-700**

Bowl, 11" d., Mold 155, Sheepherder scene decoration in shades of green w/gold & pink **350-400**

Bowl, 11" d., Mold 22, four large jewels, satin finish **250-300**

Bowl, 11" d., Mold 96, pink roses & white snowballs decoration on a pale creamy yellow ground w/shaded dark green & white rim panels w/shadow flowers **400-450**

Bowl, 11" d., 3" h., Fishscale mold, decorated w/white lilies on purple & orange lustre ground, artist-signed **325-375**

Bread tray, Mold 428, wide oval form w/low flared sides w/a narrow flanged rim, pierced end rim handles, decorated w/a large cluster of roses in peach, pink & green, traces of gold edging, 9 x 12 1/2" **175-225**

Butter dish, cover & insert, Mold 51, floral decoration, unmarked **200-250**

Floral Decorated Cake Plate

Cake plate, open handled, decorated w/pink & white flowers, green leaves, pink & yellow ground, gold trim, 9 3/4" d. (ILLUS.) **195**

Cake plate, open-handled, Fleur-de-Lis mold, Spring Season portrait, 9 3/4" d. **1,300-1,600**

Cake plate, open-handled, Mold 155, hanging basket decoration, 10" d. **325-350**

Cake plate, open-handled, Mold 259, decorated w/pink & yellow roses, pearl button finish, 10" d...................................... **350-400**

Cake plate, open-handled, Fleur-de-Lis mold, decorated w/a castle scene in rust, gold, lavender & yellow, 10 1/4" d. ... **1,000-1,300**

Cake plate, open-handled, Medallion mold, center Flora portrait, Tiffany finish w/four cupid medallions, unmarked, 10 1/2" d.. **900-1,000**

Cake plate, Iris mold, yellow poppy decoration, 11" d. **250-300**

Cake plate, open-handled, Carnation mold (Mold 28), dark pink roses against teal & green w/gold trim, 11" d. **250-300**

Cake plate, open-handled, modified Fleur-de-Lis mold, floral decoration, beaded, satin finish, artist-signed, 11" d. **175-225**

Cake plate, Hidden Image mold, light blue highlights, 11 1/2" d............................. **450-500**

Cake plate, open handles, Mold 256, satin ground decorated w/flowers in blue, pink & white w/gold trim, 11 1/2" d. **120-150**

Cake plate, open-handled, Mold 330, decorated w/snapdragons on pastel ground, artist-signed, 11 1/2" d. **350-375**

Cake plate, open-handled, Mold 343, Winter figural portrait in keyhole medallion, cobalt blue inner border, gold outer border, 12 1/2" d....................................... **400-450**

Cake plate, Bow-tie mold, pink & gold **500-600**

Cake plate, open-handled, Carnation mold, decorated w/multicolored roses **300-350**

Celery dish, Carnation mold, carnations & pink roses decoration on white shaded to peach ground, iridescent Tiffany finish, 9" **375**

Celery dish, Hidden Image mold, colored hair, 5 x 12" **400-450**

Celery dish, Mold 25, oblong, pearlized finish w/Surreal Dogwood blossoms w/gold trim, 6 x 12 1/4" **75-125**

Celery tray, Mold 254, decorated w/green & pink roses, lavish gold tracery, artist-signed, 12" l...................................... **275-325**

Celery tray, Ribbon & Jewel mold (Mold 18), pink roses & white snowball blossoms within a wide cobalt blue border w/gilt trim, 12" l. **250-300**

Celery tray, Mold 255, decorated w/Surreal Dogwood decoration, pearlized lustre finish, artist-signed, 12 1/4" l. **200-225**

Celery tray, open-handled decorated w/soft pink & white flower center w/lily-of-the-valley, embossed edge of ferns & pastel colors w/gold highlights, 12 1/2" l. **200-250**

Centerpiece bowl, Carnation mold, decorated w/pink & yellow roses, 15 1/2" d....................................... **2,000-2,500**

Chocolate cup & saucer, decorated w/Castle scene **125-150**

Chocolate cup & saucer, footed, egg-shaped cup, pink & white poppies decoration **100-150**

Chocolate pot, cov., Hidden Image mold image on both sides, light green, 9 3/4" h. **1,000-1,100**

Chocolate pot, cov., peacock & pine trees decoration **650-750**

Chocolate pot, cov., Swag & Tassel mold, decorated w/scene of sheepherder & swallows.. **900-1,000**

Chocolate set, cov. pot & four cups & saucers, sunflower decoration, the set **700-750**

Chocolate set: 10" h. cov. chocolate pot & four cups & saucers; Mold 729, pansy decoration w/gold trim, the set **900-975**

Chocolate set: 10" h. cov. chocolate pot & four cups & saucers; Ribbon and Jewel mold, scene of Dice Throwers decoration on pot & single Melon Eater scene on cups, the set............................... **4,500-5,000**

Chocolate set: tankard-style covered pot & six cups & saucers; Mold 510, laurel chain decoration, the set **1,000-1,300**

Lebrun-decorated Chocolate Set

Chocolate set: 10" h., cov. chocolate pot & six cups & saucers; Mold 517, Madame Lebrun portrait decoration, the set (ILLUS.)... **7,200-8,000**

Coffeepot, cov., Mold 517, raised floral designs as part of border, unmarked **250-300**

Cracker jar, cov., Mold 540a, beige satin ground w/floral decoration in orchid, yellow & gold, 9 1/2" w. handle to handle, overall 5 1/2" h. **300-350**

Cracker jar, cov., Mold 634, molded feet, surreal dogwood blossoms decoration on pearlized lustre finish, 8" d., 6 1/2" h. **250-300**

Cracker jar, cov., Mold 704, grape leaf decoration, 7" h. **450-500**

Cracker jar, cov., decorated w/hanging basket of flowers, satin finish, 6 x 9 1/2" **325-375**

Cracker jar, cov., Hidden Image mold, image on both sides, green mum decoration **900-1,000**

Cracker jar, cov., Lebrun portrait decoration, no hat, satin finish **1,500-2,000**

Creamer & cov. sugar bowl, floral decoration, green highlights, pr............................. **125-150**

Creamer & cov. sugar bowl, Mold 505, pink & yellow roses, pr. **125-175**

Creamer & cov. sugar bowl, Ribbon & Jewel mold, single Melon Eaters decoration, pr. (ILLUS. next column) **1,500-1,800**

Creamer & cov. sugar bowl, satin finish, Tiffany trim, pr. **175-200**

Cup & saucer, decorated w/pink roses, peg feet & scalloped rim, cup 1 3/4" h., saucer 4 1/4" d., pr. **125-175**

Dessert set: 9 1/2" d. cake plate & six 7" d. individual plates; Carnation mold, decorated w/carnations, pink & white roses,

iridescent Tiffany finish on pale green,
the set **995**

Melon Eaters Creamer & Sugar

Dessert set: pedestal cup & saucer, creamer & sugar bowl, two 9 3/4" d., handled plates, eleven 7 1/4" d. plates, nine cups & saucers, oversized creamer & sugar bowl, plain mold, decoration w/pink poppies w/tints of aqua, yellow & purple, all pieces are matching, the set **2,200-2,500**

Dresser tray, decorated w/mill scene, shaded green ground, 7 x 11" **350-450**

Dresser tray, Icicle mold, scenic decoration, Man in the Mountain, 7 x 11 1/2"... **600-700**

Dresser tray, rectangular w/pierced end handles, Mold 404, decorated w/pink & white roses, Tiffany border w/gold clover leaves **250-300**

Ferner, six vertical ribs, scalloped, decorated w/lilies-of-the-valley on shaded pastel ground, artist-signed, 3 7/8 x 8 1/4" **200-250**

Hair receiver, cov., Mold 814, Surreal Dogwood decoration **150-175**

Match holder w/striker, floral decoration.. **100-125**

Model of a lady's slipper, embossed scrolling on instep & heel & embossed feather on one side of slipper, a dotted medallion w/roses & lily-of-the-valley on the other, shaded turquoise blue w/fancy rim trimmed w/gold, 8" l...................... **250-300**

Mug, Lily mold, Lebrun portrait decoration (no hat)... **200-250**

Mug, rose decoration on pink satin finish .. **125-175**

Mustache cup, Mold 502 .... **250-300**

Mustard pot, cov., Mold 509a, decorated w/white flowers, glossy light green ground.. **150-175**

Mustard pot, cov., Mold 521, pink rose decoration, satin finish **150-200**

Nut bowl, footed, Point & Clover mold, decorated w/ten roses in shades of salmon, yellow & rose against a pink, green & gold lustre-finished bround, 6 1/2" d.. **150-200**

Nut dish, Carnation mold (Mold 28), floral decoration w/pearlized finish **200-250**

Pin dish, cov., Hidden Image mold, floral decoration, 2 3/4 x 4 3/4" **350-450**

Pitcher, cider, 7" h., iris decoration w/green & gold background **250-300**

Pitcher, lemonade, 6" h., Mold 501, relief-molded turquoise blue on white w/pink Surreal blossoms & fans around scalloped top & base, unmarked **250-300**

Pitcher, tankard, 10" h., Mold 584, decorated w/hanging basket of pink & white roses **700-750**

Pitcher, tankard, 11" h., Carnation Mold, overall decoration of pink poppies & carnations, white ground, iridescent Tiffany finish... **1,100**

R. S. Prussia Tankard Pitchers

Pitcher, tankard, 12" h., Mold 538, decorated w/Melon Eaters scene (ILLUS. left) **3,500-4,000**

Pitcher, tankard, 13" h., decorated w/poppies.. **600-650**

Pitcher, tankard, 13" h., decorated w/scene of Old Man in Mountain & swans on lake (ILLUS. right) **4,000-4,500**

Pitcher, tankard, 13 1/4" h., Stippled Floral mold (Mold 525), roses decoration, unmarked **625-675**

Pitcher, tankard, 13 1/2" h., Carnation Mold, pink poppy decoration, green ground.. **750-850**

Pitcher, tankard, 15" h., Mold 517, bronzed finish rim & base bands centering a Le-Brun II portrait against a shaded brown & green ground, gold handle **3,000-3,500**

Pitcher, water, 8 3/4" h., Carnation mold **660**

Plaque, decorated w/scene of lady w/dog, 9 1/4 x 13" **2,000-2,500**

Plate, 7" d., Fleur-de-Lis mold, Summer Season Portrait decoration.................... **450-500**

Plate, 7 1/2" d., Carnation mold, decorated w/pink roses, lavender ground, satin finish... **200-250**

Plate, 7 1/2" d., Carnation mold, decorated w/pink roses, pink ground, unmarked **175**

Plate, 8 1/2" d., Gibson Girl portrait decoration, maroon bonnet **500-550**

Plate, 8 1/2" d., Medallion mold (Mold 14), Reflecting Lilies patt. **125-150**

Plate, 8 1/2" d., Mold 263, pink & white roses decoration................................... **175-200**

Plate, 8 1/2" d., Mold 300, beaded gold band around the lobed rim, Old Mill Scene decoration in center against a shaded dark green to yellow & blue ground **150-200**

Plate, 8 3/4" d., Mold 278, center decoration of pink poppies on white ground, green border.. **150-175**

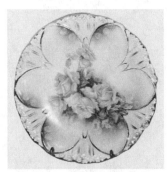

Mold 91 Rose-decorated Plate

Plate, 8 3/4" d., Mold 91, yellow roses decoration on pink ground, shiny yellow border (ILLUS.)... **150-200**

Plate, 9" d., Mold 343, spring figural scenic decoration in keyhole medallion, iridescent Tiffany purple finish at base of figure, gold finish around portrait decoration w/small pink roses **1,800-2,100**

Plate, 9 3/4" d., Icicle mold, swan decoration **800-900**

Plate, 11" d., decorated w/carnations & roses w/gold trim, white shading to peach ground, iridescent Tiffany finish (slight gold wear).. **250**

Plate, 11" d., Point & Clover mold, Melon Eater decoration................................. **900-1,100**

Plate, dessert, Mold 506, branches of pink roses & green leaves against a shaded bluish green to white ground w/shadow flowers & satin finish **100-125**

Relish dish, Fleur-de-Lis mold, basket of flowers decoration w/shadow flowers, 8" l.. **100-125**

Relish dish, scene of masted ship, 4 1/2 x 9 1/2" **250-300**

Relish dish, Icicle mold, scene of swans on lake.. **450-500**

Relish dish, Mold 82, decorated w/forget-me-nots & multicolored carnations, six jeweled domes **125-175**

Shaving mug, Hidden Image mold, floral decoration **175-225**

Spooner/vase, Mold 502, three-handled, decorated w/delicate roses & gold trim, unsigned, 4 1/4" h. **75-100**

Syrup pitcher, Mold 512, dogwood & pine decoration **175**

Syrup pitcher & underplate, Mold 507, white & pink roses on a shaded brown to pale yellow ground, 2 pcs...................... **200-250**

Tea set: child's, cov. teapot & four cups & saucers; decorated w/roses, the set **650-700**

Tea set: cov. teapot, creamer & cov. sugar bowl; floral decoration, the set **300-350**

Tea set: cov. teapot, creamer & cov. sugar bowl, mill & castle scene, shaded brown ground, 3 pcs. **900-1,000**

Tea set: cov. teapot, creamer & cov. sugar bowl; pedestal base, scene of Colonial children, 3 pcs. **600-700**

Tea strainer, floral decoration................... **200-250**

Toothpick holder, ribbed hexagonal shape w/two handles, decorated w/colorful roses **265-300**

Toothpick holder, Stippled Floral mold (Mold 23), white floral decoration **150-175**

Toothpick holder, three-handled, decorated w/white daisies on blue ground, gold handles & trim on top **150-175**

Toothpick holder, urn-shaped, floral decoration, molded star mark **150-175**

Tray, pierced handles, Mold 82, decorated w/full blossom red & pink roses, 8 x 11 1/8" (gold Royal Vienna mark).... **250-300**

Tray, rectangular, pierced handles, Mold 404, decorated w/pink & white roses, Tiffany border w/gold clover leaves........... **250-300**

Vase, 4" h., salesman's sample, handled, Mold 914, decorated w/large lilies & green foliage, raised beading around shoulder, gold handles, shaded green ground, artist-signed **150-175**

Vase, 4 1/2" h., Mold 910, decorated w/pink roses, satin finish w/iridescent Tiffany finish around base................................... **250-275**

Vase, 5 1/2" h., cottage & mill scene decoration, cobalt trim................................... **550-650**

Vase, 6 1/4" h., castle scene decoration, brown tones w/jewels **450-500**

Vase, 6 1/4" h., decorated w/brown & cream shadow flowers **75-100**

Vase, 6 1/4" h., decorated w/mill scene, brown w/jewels..................................... **450-500**

Vase, 8" h., cylindrical body w/incurved angled shoulder handles, decorated w/parrots on white satin ground, unmarked **2,200-2,600**

R.S. Prussia Vases

Vase, 8" h., ovoid body w/wide shoulder tapering to cylindrical neck w/flared rim, decorated w/scene of black swans (ILLUS. left) **1,200-1,500**

Vase, 10" h., ovoid body decorated w/scene of two tigers, pastel satin finish (ILLUS. right) **5,000-6,000**

Vase, two handled, tall slender ovoid body w/colorful scene of two parrots, shaded brown foliage, unmarked **1,800-2,000**

Vases, 11 3/4" h., Mold 901, footed slightly tapering cylindrical body w/a high flaring cupped deeply fluted neck w/jewels, beading & jewels around the shoulder &

Rare Melon Eaters Vases

foot, ornate scrolled gilt handles, Melon Eaters decoration against a shaded dark green ground, pr., each (ILLUS.) **1,800-2,000**

OTHER MARKS

Bowl, 10" d., Cabbage mold w/center rose decoration (R.S. Tillowitz) **250-300**

Bowl, 10" d., Irregular Border mold, colorful magenta border band around gold-bordered pointed dark green panels, the center w/a round reserve w/a colorful romantic scene w/18th c. lovers, Prov. Saxe **150-175**

Bowl, 10" d., shallow w/very ornate, large Flora portrait, front pose past waist, floral garland, veiling, four different cameo portraits of Flora, wide Tiffany border, lavish gold (E.S. Prov. Saxe) **1,100-1,300**

Chocolate pot, cov., Art Nouveau decoration, glossy finish (R.S. Tillowitz - Silesia) **55**

Chocolate pot, cov., lemon yellow ground w/Art Deco decoration & gold trim (R.S. Tillowitz - Silesia) **150**

Coffee set: 6 5/8" l., 3 1/4" d., cov. ovoid coffeepot & two cups & saucers; each piece decorated w/a color oval reserve w/a different romantic scene within a thin gilt border & a deep burgundy panel against a creamy white ground trimmed w/gilt scrolls, a wide red & narrow dark green border band on each, saucers 2 3/4" d., cups 2 1/4" h., blue beehive & R.S. Suhl marks, the set **650**

Coffee set: cov. coffeepot, cov. sugar bowl, creamer & six cups & saucers; the tall ovoid pot w/a long swan's-neck spout, domed cover w/flame finial & ornate scrolled handle, each piece decorated w/an oval color central reserve w/a classical scene based on Angelica Kauffmann, borders in dark burgundy & green on white w/scattered delicate gold trim, coffeepot 9" h., R.S. Suhl, the set (ILLUS. of coffeepot) **1,800-2,000**

R.S. Suhl Coffeepot from a Set

Cup & saucer, deep bell-form cup w/ornate pierced scrolling handle, the sides decorated w/an oval reserve w/a color scene of an 18th c. courting couple, within a maroon panel w/deep red & green border bands, overall delicate gilt trim, saucer 4 7/8" d., cup 2 1/4" h., R.S. Suhl (ILLUS.)... **100-150**

R.S. Suhl Ornate Cup & Saucer

Fernery, pedestal base, decorated w/pink & white roses, mother-of-pearl finish (R.S. Poland)... **450**

Match holder, hanging-type on attached backplate decorated w/a scene of a man w/mug of beer & pipe (E.S. Prov. Saxe) **175-200**

Plate, 7" d., scene of girl w/rose, trimmed w/gold flowers, beading & a burgundy border **100-125**

Plate, 7 3/4" d., Sunflower mold, rose pink & yellow roses w/Tiffany finsih (Wheelock Prussia).. **125-150**

Plate, 8" d., peafowl decoration (R.S. Tillowitz - Silesia) **150-200**

Plate, 10 1/2" d., lovely center portrait of Madame DuBarry, four cameos in different poses on a deep burgundy lustre border band (E.W. Prov. Saxe) **500-600**

Relish dish, woman's portrait w/shadow flowers & vine border on green ground, 8" l. (E.S. Germany Royal Saxe)........... **100-125**

Server, center handle w/three loops, dished paneled base w/a lightly scalloped rim, lavender & pink roses & green leaves on a pale creamy green ground & gilt border trim, 11" d., 8" h., R.S. Poland **500-550**

E. Schlegelmilch Handled Server

Server, center-handled, decorated w/orange, white & pink poppies on a shaded bluish grey ground, w/a narrow gilt border band, 8 1/2" d., 3 3/4" h., E. Schlegelmilch - Thuringia (ILLUS.) **100-150**

Serving dish, center-handled, decorated w/lavender & pink roses, gold trim, 11" d. (R.S. Poland) **500-550**

Tray, rectangular, open-handled, bright colored bird decoration, 5 x 14" (R.S. Tillowitz) **75-100**

Vase, miniature, 3 1/2" h., cylindrical body w/a rounded shoulder tapering to a tiny rolled neck, decorated w/a colored scene of crowned cranes (R.S. Poland) **375-425**

Vase, 6" h., simple ovoid body w/flaring rim, decorated in color w/golden pheasants against a dark green shaded forest background, R.S. Tillowitz - Silesia **275-325**

Melon Eaters Vase

Vase, 6 3/8" h., 3" d., wide ovoid shouldered body tapering to slender flaring cylindrical neck, Melon Eater decoration surrounded by gold border w/reverse decorated w/heart-shaped area w/dainty pink roses on pastel ground, two-thirds of vase covered in purplish lustre w/fine gold leaves & flowers overall, neck in off white w/fine gold floral decoration, artist-signed in gold, Red Crown "Viersa" mark, Suhl or Tillowitz (ILLUS.) **350-400**

Vase, 7" h., footed urn-form w/scrolled handles, decorated w/scene of two geese, R.S. Poland **1,500-1,800**

Vase, 7 1/2" h., wide squatty bulbous base tapering sharply to a tall slender cylindrical neck w/an upturned four-lobed rim, long slender gold handles from rim to shoulder, decorated w/a center reserve of a standing Art Nouveau maiden w/her hands behind her head & a peacock behind her framed by delicate gold scrolls & beading & floral bouquets all on a pearl lustre ground (Prov. Saxe - E.W. Germany) **375-425**

Vase, 9" h., 3" d., tall slender ovoid body tapering to a tall slender trumpet neck, a wide band around the body decorated w/a colored scene of "The Melon Eaters" between narrow gold & white bands, the neck & lower body in deep rose decorated w/gilt leaf sprigs (R.S. Suhl) **800-1,000**

Vase, 9 1/4" h., gently tapering cylindrical body w/a wide cupped scalloped gilt rim, pierced gold serpentine handles from rim to center of sides, decorated around the body w/large blossoms in purple, pink, yellow & green on a shaded brownish green ground (Prove. Saxe) **125-150**

Vase, 9 1/2" h., portrait of "Lady with Swallows," gold beading, turquoise on white ground (Prov. Saxe - E.S. Germany) ... **500-550**

Vase, 10" h., gold Rococo handles, scene of sleeping maiden w/cherub decoration (E.S. Royal Saxe)................................. **350-400**

Vase, 13 1/2" h., portrait of "Lady with Swallows," gold beaded frame, green pearl lustre finish w/gold trim" (Prov. Saxe - E.S. Germany) **600-650**

Vase, 13 1/2" h., twisted gold handles, portrait of "Goddess of Fire," iridescent burgundy & opalescent colors w/lavish gold trim (Prov. Saxe, E.S. Germany).......... **650-700**

R.S. Poland Landscape Vase

Vases, 10" h., gently swelled body tapering to narrow rounded shoulders & a short flaring scalloped neck, ornate C-scroll gilt shoulder handles, gold neck band, the body decorated w/a colored scene of a sheepherder leading his flock toward a mill in the background, trees overhead, the second identical except w/a cottage scene, R.S. Poland, pr. (ILLUS. of one)
.... **1,350-1,400**

RUSSEL WRIGHT DESIGNS

The innovative dinnerwares designed by Russel Wright and produced by various companies beginning in the late 1930s were an immediate success with a society that was turning to a more casual and informal lifestyle. His designs, with their flowing lines and unconventional shapes, were produced in many different colors which allowed the hostess to arrange a creative table.

Although not antique, these designs, which we list below by line and manufacturer, are highly collectible. In addition to dinnerwares, Wright was also known as a trend-setter in the design of furniture, glassware, lamps, fabric and a multitude of other household goods.

Russel Wright Marks

AMERICAN MODERN
(Steubenville Pottery Co.)

Baker, cov., glacier blue, small $55
Baker, cov., granite grey, small 30
Bowl, child's, black chutney 85
Bowl, child's, chartreuse 60
Bowl, fruit, lug handle, cedar green 20

Group of American Modern Pieces

Bowl, fruit, lug handle, chartreuse (ILLUS. left) 20
Bowl, fruit, lug handle, glacier blue 28
Bowl, salad, cedar green 85
Bowl, salad, white 165
Bowl, soup, lug handle, bean brown 22
Butter dish, cov., granite grey 255
Butter dish, cov., white 365
Carafe, granite grey (no stopper) 185
Carafe w/stopper, bean brown 500
Casserole, cov., stick handle, black chutney 45

Black Chutney Celery Tray

Celery tray, black chutney, 13" l. (ILLUS.) 30
Coaster, granite grey 15
Coaster, white 30
Coffee cup cover, black chutney 175
Coffee cup cover, coral 110
Coffeepot, cov., black chutney 265
Coffeepot, cov., cedar green 200

Coffeepot, seafoam blue 185
Coffeepot, cov., demitasse, chartreuse 95
Coffeepot, cov., demitasse, coral 118
Coffeepot, cov., demitasse, granite grey 235
Creamer, cedar green 20
Creamer, white 30
Cup & saucer, coffee, cantaloupe 15-20
Cup & saucer, coffee, seafoam blue 15
Cup & saucer, demitasse, cantaloupe 50
Cup & saucer, demitasse, chartreuse 25
Gravy boat, chartreuse 20
Hostess plate, chartreuse 75
Hostess plate & cup, cedar green, pr. 95

American Modern Hostess Set

Hostess plate & cup, white, pr. (ILLUS.) 200
Ice box jar, cov., black chutney 225
Ice box jar, cov., coral 185
Mug (tumbler), black chutney 125
Mug (tumbler), cedar green 85
Pickle dish, seafoam blue 18
Pickle dish, white 28
Pitcher, cov., water, cedar green 235
Pitcher, cov., water, white 325
Pitcher, water, 12" h., bean brown 150
Pitcher, water, 12" h., granite grey 105
Pitcher, water, 12" h., seafoam blue 110
Plate, bread & butter, 6 1/4" d., coral 6
Plate, salad, 8" d., seafoam blue 12
Plate, salad, 8" d., white 20
Plate, dinner, 10" d., cantaloupe 20
Plate, dinner, 10" d., granite grey 10
Plate, chop, 13" sq., chartreuse 25
Plate, chop, 13" sq., seafoam blue 50
Plate, child's, coral 60
Plate, child's, seafoam blue 75
Platter, 13 3/4" l., oblong, granite grey 40
Platter, 13 3/4" l., oblong, white 65
Ramekin, cov., individual, bean brown 250
Ramekin, cov., individual, granite grey 188
Relish dish, divided, raffia handle, coral 175
Relish dish, divided, raffia handle, white 300
Relish rosette, granite grey 175
Relish rosette, seafoam blue 225
Salad fork & spoon, coral, pr. 135
Salad fork & spoon, white, pr. 275
Sauce boat, bean brown 75
Sauce boat, coral 40
Shaker, single, chartreuse 6
Shaker, single, glacier blue 12
Stack server, cov., cedar green (ILLUS. back, with fruit bowl) 100-120
Stack server, cov., chartreuse 170

Stack server, cov., granite grey 300
Sugar bowl, cov., chartreuse 8
Sugar bowl, cov., granite grey 10
Teapot, cov., cedar green 150
Teapot, cov., seafoam blue 135
Tumbler, child's, cedar green 85
Tumbler, child's, granite grey 60
Vegetable bowl, cov., cedar green, 12" l 75
Vegetable bowl, cov., coral, 12" l. 63
Vegetable dish, open, divided, black chut-
  ney 105
Vegetable dish, open, divided, cedar
  green (ILLUS. right front, with fruit bowl) 95
Vegetable dish, open, oval, cantaloupe,
  10" l. 45
Vegetable dish, open, oval, granite grey,
  10" l. 25

CASUAL CHINA
(Iroquois China Company)

Bowl, 5" d., cereal, redesigned 15
Bowl, 5" d., cereal, ripe apricot 15
Bowl, 5 1/2" d., fruit, ice blue, 9 1/2 oz. 15
Bowl, 5 3/4" d., fruit, redesigned, oyster
  grey 16
Bowl, 10" d., salad, pink sherbet, 52 oz. 40
Butter dish, cov., brick red, 1/4 lb. 1,000
Butter dish, cov., white, 1/2 lb. 150
Butter dish, cov., pink sherbet 95
Carafe, cov., charcoal 265
Carafe, cov., oyster grey 300
Casserole, cov., lettuce green, 8" d., 2 qt. 45
Casserole, deep tureen, lemon yellow 250
Casserole, deep tureen, white 260
Coffeepot, cov., nutmeg brown 150

Casual Creamer, Pitcher & Coffeepot

Coffeepot, cov., oyster grey (ILLUS.
  right) 125-150
Coffeepot, cov., sugar white 200
Coffeepot, cov., demitasse, avocado yel-
  low 135
Coffeepot, cov., demitasse, lemon yellow 125
Cover for casserole, oyster grey, 4 qt. 30
Cover for cereal/soup bowl 25
Cover for vegetable bowl, open/divided 35
Cover for water pitcher 50
Creamer, family-style, oyster grey (ILLUS.
  left) 40-45
Creamer, family-style, pink sherbet 58
Creamer, stacking-type, ice blue 20
Cup & saucer, coffee, oyster grey (ILLUS.
  front center) 15-20
Cup & saucer, redesigned, avocado yellow 18
Cup & saucer, tea, charcoal 15
Cup & saucer, tea, lemon yellow 25

Cup & saucer, tea, lemon yellow (ILLUS.
  left front) 10-15

Casual Cups & Saucers & Shakers

Cup & saucer, demitasse (after dinner),
  avocado yellow (ILLUS. front right) 150-175
Cup & saucer, demitasse (after dinner),
  pink sherbet 200
Cup & saucer, demitasse (after dinner),
  sugar white 175
Gravy, redesigned w/cover which becomes
  stand, ripe apricot 185
Gravy, redesigned w/cover which becomes
  stand, sugar white 200
Gravy bowl, 5 1/4", 12 oz. 25
Gravy stand, ice blue 20
Gravy stand, oyster grey 30
Gravy w/attached stand, avocado yellow 75
Gravy w/attached stand, nutmeg brown 100
Gumbo soup bowl, handled, cantaloupe,
  21 oz. 20
Gumbo soup bowl, handled, charcoal, 21
  oz. 45
Gumbo soup bowl, handled, ice blue, 21
  oz. 40
Hostess set: plate w/well & matching cup;
  sugar white, 2 pcs. 75-85
Mug, pink sherbet, 13 oz. 85
Mug, restyled, aqua 135
Mug, restyled, ice blue 55
Mug, sugar white, 13 oz. 90
Party (hostess) plate w/cup, pr., each 115
Pepper mill, lemon yellow 300
Pitcher, cov., charcoal, 1 1/2 qt. 175
Pitcher, cov., ice blue, 1 1/2 qt. 155
Pitcher, redesigned, nutmeg brown 185
Pitcher, redesigned, ripe apricot (ILLUS.
  center with coffeepot) 150-200
Plate, bread & butter, 6 1/2" d., lettuce
  green 8
Plate, salad, 7 1/2" d. 15
Plate, luncheon, 9 1/2" d., pink sherbet 10
Plate, dinner, 10" d., oyster grey 15
Plate, chop, 13 7/8" d., ice blue 55
Plate, chop, 13 7/8" d., parsley green 60
Platter, 10 1/4" oval, individual, lettuce
  green 85
Platter, 12 3/4" oval, brick red 55
Platter, 12 3/4" oval, parsley green 35
Platter, 14 1/2" oval, sugar white 45
Salt & pepper shakers, stacking-type, ice
  blue, pr. 25
Salt & pepper shakers, stacking-type,
  parsley green & oyster grey , pr. (ILLUS.
  left rear, with cups) 20-25
Salt & pepper shakers, stacking-type,
  parsley green, pr. 30
Salt shaker, single, redesigned 200

Salt shaker & pepper mill, redesigned,
lemon yellow, pr. (ILLUS. right rear, with
cups) **200-300**
Soup, 11 1/2 oz. **22**
Soup, redesigned, 18 oz. **25**
Sugar, redesigned, aqua.................................. **350**
Sugar, stacking-type, brick red......................... **450**
Sugar, stacking-type, pink sherbet..................... **20**
Sugar, stacking-type, sugar white, family
size.. **40**
Teapot, cov., restyled, aqua......................... **2,000**
Tumbler, ice tea, Pinch patt., seafoam
blue, Imperial Glass Co., 14 oz. **45**
Tumbler, water, Pinch patt., brick red,
Imperial Glass Co., 11 oz............................. **110**
Vegetable dish, open, cantaloupe, 10" d.......... **14**
Vegetable dish, open, cantaloupe, 81/8",
36 oz. **55**
Vegetable dish, open, nutmeg brown,
81/8", 36 oz. **35**
Vegetable dish, open or divided (casse-
role), 10", sugar white **50**

IROQUOIS CASUAL COOKWARE
Casserole, 3 qt.. **225**
Dutch oven **500**
Fry pan, cov. **500**
Sauce pan, cov. **500**
Serving tray, electric, 12 3/4 x 17 1/2".......... **2,000**

SASCHA BRASTOFF

Sascha Brastoff dedicated his life to creating
works with a flair all his own. He was a costume
designer for major movie studios, a dancer, a window dresser and a talented painter. The creator in
Sascha put him on the path to ceramics early in life
when he was awarded a scholarship to the Cleveland Art School; however, he also worked with
watercolors, charcoals, pastels, resin, fabrics,
ceramics and metal sculptures, and enamels. Nelson Rockefeller, Brastoff's friend, understood the
uniqueness of his talents and, in 1953, he built a
complex in Los Angeles, California to house the
many creations Sascha was able to produce.

A full line of hand-painted china with names
such as Allegro, La Jolla, Roman Coin and Night
Song was created. Surf Ballet was a popular dinnerware line and was achieved by dipping pieces of
blue, pink or yellow into real gold or platinum. Also
highly popular was Sascha's line of enamels on
copper. Many collectors do not know that Sascha
dabbled in textiles. A yard of cloth in good condition
might command several hundred dollars on today's
market. His artware items included patterns such
as Star Steed, a leaping-fantasy horse and Rooftops, a series of houses where the roofs somehow
seemed to be the prominent feature. Even then, as
well as today, these pieces were and are, two of the
most highly collectible Sascha artware patterns.

Sascha Brastoff also created a line of Alaskan-
motif items. Many collectors confuse Matthew
Adams pieces with those of Sascha. Even though
Adams worked for Brastoff for a period of time, his
pieces are not nearly as sought after as those that
Sascha created.

Brastoff's crystal ball served him well during his
lifetime. In the late 1940s and early 1950s he cre-

ated a series of Western motif cachepots which
excites any collectors when found today. Almost a
decade before the poodle craze in the 1950s,
Sascha created a line of poodle products. In the
1950s, cigarette smoking was at an all-time high
and Sascha was there with smoking accessories.

From 1947-1952 pieces were signed "Sascha
B." or with the full signature, "Sasha Brastoff." After
1953 and before 1962, during the years of his fac-
tory-studio, pieces done by his employees showed
"Sascha B." and more often than not, also included
the chanticleer back stamp. Caution should be
taken to understand that the chanticleer with the full
name "Sascha Brastoff" below it is not the "full signature" mark that elevates pieces to substantial
prices. The chanticleer mark is usually in gold and
will incorporate Sascha's work name in the same
color. Sascha's personal full signauture is the one
commanding the high prices.

Health problems forced Sascha to leave his
company in 1963. After 1962 pieces were marked
"Sascha B." and also included the 'R' in a circle
trademark. Ten years later the business closed.

Sascha Brastoff died on Feburary 4, 1993. The
passing of this flamboyant artist, whose special
character was well reflected in his work, means that
similar creations will probably never be achieved
again.

Sascha Brastoff

Sascha B.

Brastoff Marks

Ashtray, floral decoration, No. 110AC **$45**
Ashtray, round, leaf decoration, full signa-
ture, large **350**
Ashtray, Western scene w/covered wagon,
rare promotional piece, 14" w....................... **175**
Bowl, 8" d., footed, abstract design................... **38**
Box, cov., Jewel Bird decoration, No. 020........ **70**
Candleholder, resin, green or blue, 6" h.,
each **65**
Cigarette box, cov., Rooftops patt., No.
021, 8" l. **70**
Cigarette box, cov., "Star Steed" decora-
tion **145**
Compote, polar bear decoration, No. 085......... **65**
Dish, horse decoration on green ground,
6 1/2" sq. **30**
Dish, three-footed, fish-shaped (flounder),
house decoration, 8 1/4 x 8 1/2".................... **90**
Lamp base, mosaic tile, 27" h......................... **210**
Model of polar bear, blue resin, 10" h............. **400**
Model of rooster, mosaic design, 15" h. **515**
Plate, square, vegetable decoration, full
signature **275**
Plate, 9" d., Merbaby patt. **65**

Sascha Brastoff Horse Salt Shaker

Salt shaker, model of a horse, white, produced in 1947-1948, 5 1/4" l, 3 1/4" h. (ILLUS.).. 85

Tray, floral decoration, marked "Sample" under glaze, 7" sq. 95

Vase, 5" h., Provincial Rooster patt., No. F20.. 400

Wall pocket, Rooftops patt., No. 031, 20" h. 415

SATSUMA

These decorated wares have been produced in Japan since the end of the 18th century. The early pieces are scarce and high-priced. Later Satsuma wares are plentiful and, with prices rising, as highly collectible as earlier pieces.

Charger, round, Thousand Flowers patt., Satsuma mon in gold on brown, signed, early 20th c... $403

Tea bowl, deep rounded sides, finely decorated on the interior w/clamshell-shaped reserves enclosing landscapes, courtiers & a central panel of the underwater palace of the dragon king, the exterior decorated w/room interiors & landscapes, the above entirely enclosed in brocade grounds, late 19th c., 4 3/4" d. 1,840

Urn, cov., wide baluster-form body, domed cover w/gilded foo dog finial, decorated w/pastel enameled scenes w/flowers & butterflies, late 19th c., 18 3/4" h................... 83

Large Satsuma Vase

Vase, 18" h., domed foot below tall square-shaped body, the narrow shoulder tapering to a short wide cylindrical neck w/slightly flared rim, overall design of Buddhist Immortals, highlighted w/heavy gilt trim, late 19th c. (ILLUS.)........................ 575

SCHAFER & VATER

Founded in Rudolstadt, Thuringia, Germany in 1890, the Schafer and Vater Porcelain Factory specialized in decorative pieces of porcelain usually in white or colored bisque. They produced many novelty figural items such as creamers, toothpick holders, boxes and hatpin holders and also produced a line of jasper ware with white relief decoration in imitation of the famous Wedgwood jasper wares. The firm also decorated whiteware blanks.

The company ceased production in 1962 and collectors now seek out their charming pieces which may be marked with a crown over a starburst containing the script letter "R."

Schafer & Vater Mark

Ashtray, figural, jasper ware, grotesque man's head, open mouth w/small holes above simulated whiskers, reads "I Want To Be Shaved" & illegible writing below mouth, 3 1/2" $95

Schafer & Vater Ashtray

Ashtray, figural, little boy in white & little girl in dark blue w/green hair ribbon, white rabbits on one corner, white doves on other, inscribed on front "Everybody's doing it," unmarked, 2 1/2 x 3 1/2", 3 3/4" h. (ILLUS.) 145

Dresser box, cov., jasper ware, egg-shaped, cameo medallion top w/double silhouettes, lavender, 3 x 3 x 4" 95

Flask, figural Santa in white coat, 6" h. 265

Pitcher, 3" h., jasper ware, Victorian cameo side medallion, light green w/gold trim 45

Toothpick holder, figural, model of a human skull 25

SCHOOP (HEDI) ART CREATIONS

Hedi Schoop escaped from Germany in 1930 then immigrated to Hollywood, California in 1933.

She began producing ceramics of her own designs in 1940. Schoop turned out as many as 30,000 pieces per year once her production was running smoothly. A fire destroyed the pottery in 1958 and Hedi did free-lance work for several California companies. She retired from working full-time in the early 1960s but her talents would not let her quit completely. She died in 1996 and had painted, although sparingly, until then.

There were a variety of marks ranging from the stamped or incised Schoop signature to the hard-to-find Hedi Schoop sticker. The words "Hollywood, Cal." or "California" can also be found in conjunction with the Hedi Schoop name. You can find items with a production number, artists' names or initials.

Schoop was imitated by many artists especially some decorators who opened businesses of their own after working with Schoop. Mac and Yona Lippen owned Yona Ceramics and Katherine Schueftan owned Kim Ward Studio. They used many of Schoop's designs and today they have their own following among collectors. There were others but Schueftan lost a lawsuit Hedi had brought against her in 1942 for design infringements. It is important to buy pieces marked Hedi Schoop or buy from a reputable dealer if you want to be sure you have the real thing.

Considering the number of products created, it would be easy to assume that Schoop pieces are plentiful. This would be an erroneous assumption. Collectors will indeed be fortunate to find any Schoop figurines for less than $100.00 and to amass many of her products takes dedication and determination.

Pick up marks from Ceramics PG Vol. 2

Candleholder, figural, a mermaid holding a single candle socket in each hand above her head, rare, ca. 1950, 13 1/2" h............. **$600**

Figure of a ballerina dancer, on a thin round base, long skirt flared upward revealing right foot, right arm extended & holding up skirt, left arm extended forward w/head turned to front, bluish grey w/silver overtones, impressed mark "Hedi Schoop," 9 1/4" h. 110

Hedi Schoop Chinese Woman Figure

Figure of a Chinese woman, standing on a round black base, white floor-length skirt, black, white & green blouse w/long

sleeves flaring at wrists, a white flower in black hair above each ear, right fingers bent to hold a pot w/black cloth handle & in same colors as blouse, right leg bent at knee, woman 9" h., pot 2 1/2" h., 2 pcs. (ILLUS.) 125

Figure of a clown, standing w/one leg crossed over the other, one hand to head, other hand to mouth, bucket & mop at his side, 10 1/2" h. 155

Figure of a girl, standing & holding hand-made flowers in both arms, "Debutante," rough textured finish, ca. 1943, 12 1/2" h... 185

Figure of a girl, standing on cobalt blue-glazed round base, legs slightly apart, arms stretched out to sides, hands folded to hold jump rope, rough textured black hair w/pigtails out to sides & held in place w/cobalt blue glossy ties, light blue long sleeved shirt, cobalt blue over-blouse w/straps, rough textured cobalt blue short skirt & socks, inkstamp on unglazed bottom, "Hedi Schoop Hollywood, Cal.," 8 1/2" h..................................... 165

Schoop Jardiniere with Chinese Scene

Jardiniere, cylindrical, incised stylized design of a kneeling Chinese woman w/ming trees & animals, base & design in gold glaze on a light green body, 7" h. (ILLUS.)... 125

Lamp, figural, TV-type, Comedy & Tragedy masks on a base w/full Comedy, part Tragedy conjoined, dark green w/gold trim, ca. 1954, 10 3/4" l., 12" h. 275

Model of a cat lying down, head up, tail wrapped around side, paws tucked under body, brown collar around neck w/two yellow bells & two small brown pots attached, white rough textured body, inkstamp under glaze, "Hedi Schoop Hollywood, Cal.," 6 3/4" l., 6 1/2" h. 115

Planter, model of a horse, rough textured mane & tail, white glossy glazed body w/mint green face accents, saddle, bows in assorted areas & scalloped edging at the base, inkstamp mark "Hedi Schoop," 7 1/2" h. 100

Figural Hedi Schoop Tray

Tray, figural, divided w/irregular leaf-shaped raised edges, the rim mounted w/the figure of a cherub on her knees, arms outstretched beside her, head tilted, beige & gold tray interior, beige w/pink-tinged cherub, gold wings, rose on left wrist, belt of roses around her waist w/rose-glazed bowl exterior & rose hair, bottom of tray also in a glossy rose, incised "Hedi Schoop," 11 1/2" l., overall 6" h. (ILLUS.) **135**

Vase, 9" h. at highest point, 4 1/2" h., at lowest point, 9" l., seashell-form, footed oval base, fluted edge rising from the low end to the higher end, dark green base w/dark green & gold fading to light green, rim trimmed in gold, transparent textured glossy glaze, marked w/a silver label w/red block letters, "Hedi Schoop Hollywood, Calif." on two lines **85**

SÈVRES & SÈVRES-STYLE

Some of the most desirable porcelain ever produced was made at the Sèvres factory, originally established at Vincennes, France, and transferred, through permission of Madame de Pompadour, to Sèvres as the Royal Manufactory about the middle of the 18th century. King Louis XV took sole responsibility for the works in 1759 when production of hard paste wares began. Between 1850 and 1900, many biscuit and soft-paste pieces were made again. Fine early pieces are scarce and high-priced. Many of those available today are late productions. The various Sèvres marks have been copied and pieces listed as "Sèvres-Style" are similar to actual Sèvres wares, but not necessarily from that factory. Three of the many Sèvres marks are illustrated below.

Sevres Marks

Box, cov., Sevres-style, rectangular w/fluted corners, enamel & gilt-decorated w/floral sides & a landscape w/dogs & cats on the cover, late 19th c., 3 3/8" l. **$230**

Center bowl, the sides painted w/reserves of a courting couple & a landscape, on a cobalt blue ground, artist-signed, gilt-metal mounts, ca. 1900, 12 3/4" l. **403**

Bronze-mounted Sevres Centerpiece

Centerpiece, a gilt-bronze mounted porcelain bulbous body w/continuous putto decorated figural band within 'jewel' & gilt decorated borders on a bleu celeste ground flanked by angular handles fitted w/winged putti, on a drapery-cast reeded base, late 19th c., lacking lid, 14 1/2" h. (ILLUS.) **8,625**

Cup & saucer, cobalt blue ground w/gilt framed oval cartouche on the cup, enamel-decorated w/flowers, 19th c., cup 3 1/8" h. **230**

Cup & saucer, the cup finely painted w/three royal portraits within a border of red jewels reserved on a deep blue ground gilt & jewelled w/foliate scrollwork, the saucer h.p. w/a coat-of-arms within a similarly decorated border, second half 19th c., pseudo Sevres marks in blue, the cup w/painted titles "Gabrielle d' Estrées," "Marguerite de Navarre" & "Henri IV," minor losses to jewelling, cup 3" h. **2,587**

Dresser box w/hinged cover, oval cartouche-shaped, the low domed cover h.p. w/a large reserve in color of two lovers in a floral garden, framed by gilt scrolling on the cobalt blue ground, cobalt ground base w/further gilt trim, gilt-metal hinged mounts at the rim, the cover opening to reveal an interior h.p. w/florals, artist-signed, base marked "Chateau de Touceneies" w/a blue overglaze ribbon mark, late 19th c., 12" l. **1,150**

Sevres Huntsman Figure

Figure of a huntsman, bisque, finely modeled as a young man standing before a tree stump on a shaped base & blowing a large hunting horn, 19th c., impressed factory mark & incised "AD98," horn & right hand restored, 15" h. (ILLUS.) **920**

Jewelry box, cov., rectangular w/serpentine sides, the slightly domed cover painted w/a large figural scene titled "L'Accord des Violons" framed by ornate gilt scrolling on a cobalt blue ground, the sides w/various color landscape vignettes within gilt scroll borders on a cobalt blue ground, signed illegibly, mid-19th c., 10 1/2 x 15", 5" h. **5,175**

Sevres Lamp Base

Lamp base, the wide ovoid body raised on a bronze grooved & draped pedestal, enamel decorated figural & floral cartouches on blue ground, late 18th - early 19th c., 13 1/4" h. (ILLUS.)........................ **1,840**

Patch box, cov., the cover decorated w/a Napoleonic scene in color, the sides w/landscape panels, all on a cobalt blue ground, gilt scroll trim, late 19th c., 6" l. **978**

Plaque, round, decorated w/scene depicting a Napoleonic battle within a tied laurel band on a bleu celeste ground, marked w/interlacing "Ls" in red enamel, late 19th c., mounted in a round wood frame, 21" d. **3,220**

Platter, 19" l., oval, mounted in a narrow gilt-metal frame w/pierced scroll end handles & supported on pierced scroll legs, the center of the platter h.p. w/an oval reserve w/a colorful 18th c. courtship scene w/a couple in a landscape, the wide border band in cobalt blue w/ornate gilt scrolling, artist-signed, marked on base w/overglaze blue ribbon mark, late 19th c..................................... **2,300**

Urns, circular gilt-decorated foot w/square base supporting a swelled pear-shaped body w/tall cylindrical neck, berried laurel wreath shoulder handles, each decorated w/opposing figural & landscape panels within gilt-decorated foliate borders reserved on a gilt-trimmed cobalt blue ground, marked w/interlacing "Ls" enclosing the letter B in underglaze-blue, late 19th c., missing lids, 20 1/2" h., pr. **6,325**

Vanity set, porcelain, comprising wash basin & pitcher, scent bottle w/stopper, cup & cov. rectangular box, each h.p. w/scene of courting couples within silver overlaid cartouches, ca. 1860, 5 pcs. **3,450**

Vase, 24" h., wide ovoid body w/narrow shoulder tapering to short wide cylindrical neck flanked w/long slender ornate handles, bronze pedestal & shaped foot, decorated w/gilt-scrolled foliate framed rectangular panels h.p. w/classical figures & floral bouquet on a cobalt blue ground, artist-signed, 19th c. (ILLUS.) **2,760**

Sevres Vase

Vases, cov., tall urn-form bodies, a slender pedestal base on a scrolled ormolu foot tapering to a ormolu connector ring to the tall tapering urn-form body, ormolu scroll rim mount continuing to ornate scrolled & arched handles, the tapering domed cover w/a gilt pineapple finial, a soft green ground, the body decorated w/a large full-length color portrait of an Art Nouveau maiden between large flowers all trimmed w/ornate gilt highlights, further gilt trim on the cover & base, ca. 1900, pr. **6,875**

SHAWNEE

The Shawnee Pottery Company of Zanesville, Ohio opened its doors for operation in 1936 and, sadly, closed in 1961. The pottery was inexpensive for its quality and was readily purchased at dimestores as well as department stores. Sears-Roebuck, Butler Bros., Woolworths and S. Kresge were just a few of the companies that were long-time retailers of this fine pottery.

Shawnee Pottery Company had a wide array of merchandise to offer from knick-knacks to dinnerware, though Shawnee is quite often associated with colorful pig cookie jars and dazzling "Corn King" line dinnerware. Planters, miniatures, cookie jars & corn line are much in demand by today's avid collectors. Factory seconds were purchased by outside decorators and trimmed with gold, decals and unusual hand painting which made those pieces extremely desirable in today's market and also enhances the value considerably.

Shawnee Pottery has become the most sought-after pottery in today's collectible market.

Reference books available are Mark E. Supnick's book, Collecting Shawnee Pottery, The Collector's Guide to Shawnee Pottery by Duane and Janice Vanderbilt or Shawnee Pottery — An Identification & Value Guide by Jim and Bev Mangus.

Shawnee
U.S.A.
Shawnee Mark

Shawnee Figural Banks

Bank, figural Bulldog, 4 1/2" h., unmarked (ILLUS. left) **$175-200**
Bank, figural Tumbling Bear, unmarked, 4 3/4" h. (ILLUS. right) **175-200**

Figural Howdy Doody Bank

Bank, figural, Howdy Doody riding a pig, marked "Bob Smith U.S.A.," 6 3/4" h. (ILLUS.) **500-550**
Bank - cookie jar, figural Winnie Pig, orange trim **350**
Bank - cookie jar, figural Winnie Pig, chocolate or butterscotch, marked "Patented: Smiley Shawnee 60 U.S.A." or "Patented: Smiley Shawnee 61 U.S.A." 10 1/2" h., each **450-500**
Book ends, figural dog head, Setter, marked "U.S.A.," 3 3/4" h., pr. **65-75**

Shawnee Figural Book Ends

Book ends, figural, full-figure of a man at potter's wheel, brown, marked "Crafted by Shawnee Potteries Zanesville, Ohio 1960," 9" h., pr. (ILLUS.) **400-500**
Butter dish, cov., Corn King line, No. 72, 1/4 lb. **60**
Casserole, cov., Corn King line, No. 74, 1 1/2 qt. **55**
Casserole, cov., Corn King patt., No. 74 .... **85**
Cigarette box, cov., embossed Indian arrowhead on lid, brown, marked "Shawnee," 3 1/4 x 4 1/2" **400-500**
Coffeepot, cov., Pennsylvania Dutch patt., marked "U.S.A. 52," 42 oz.................... **195-225**
Coffeepot, cov., Sunflower patt, marked "U.S.A.," 42 oz...................................... **195-225**

Valencia Line Coffeepot

Coffeepot, cov., Valencia line, tangerine glaze, 7 1/2" h. (ILLUS.) **95-125**
Cookie jar, figural Cottage, marked "U.S.A. 6," 7" h.. **800-1,000**
Cookie jar, embossed Little Chef patt............... **70**
Cookie jar, figural Cinderella, unmarked......... **125**
Cookie jar, figural Drum Major, marked "U.S.A. 10," 10" h. **275-300**
Cookie jar, figural Dutch Boy (Jack) **225**
Cookie jar, figural Dutch Boy (Jack), paint under glaze, striped pants, marked "U.S.A.," 11" h. **125-150**
Cookie jar, figural Dutch Girl (Jill) **50**

Cookie jar, figural Dutch Girl (Jill), paint under glaze, marked "U.S.A.," 11 1/2" h. **125-150**

Cookie jar, figural Dutch Girl, tulip decoration & gold trim **298**

Cookie jar, figural ear of corn, Corn King line, No. 66, 10 1/2" h. **265-275**

Cookie jar, figural elephant, pink **50**

Cookie jar, figural Fruit Basket **88**

Great Northern Boy Cookie Jar

Cookie jar, figural Great Northern Boy, marked "Great Northern U.S.A. 1025," 9 3/4" h. (ILLUS.).................................. **350-400**

Cookie jar, figural Great Northern Girl, marked "Great Northern U.S.A. 1026," 10" h. **375-425**

Cookie jar, figural Jo-Jo the Clown, marked "Shawnee U.S.A. 12," 9" h. **275-350**

Jumbo (Lucky) Elephant Cookie Jar

Cookie jar, figural Jumbo (Lucky) Elephant, decal decoration & gold trim (ILLUS.)... **700-800**

Muggsy Cookie Jar

Cookie jar, figural Muggsy Dog, blue bow, gold trim & decals, marked "Patented Muggsy U.S.A.," 11 3/4" h. (ILLUS.) **850-950**

Cookie jar, figural Owl **108**

Cookie jar, figural Owl, gold trim & hand-decoration **150**

Cookie jar, figural Puss 'n Boots, color & long tail marked "Patented Puss N Boots U.S.A.," **225-300**

Cookie jar, figural Smiley Pig, w/clover blossom, marked "Patented Smiley U.S.A.," 11 1/2" h. **500-575**

Cookie jar, figural Winnie Pig, clover blossom decoration, marked "Patented Winnie U.S.A.," 12" h................................. **500-575**

Creamer, ball-type, Dutch Style, decorated w/red feather, marked "U.S.A. 12," 4 1/2" h. **95-125**

Pennsylvania Dutch Creamer & Sugar Bowl

Creamer, ball-type, Pennsylvania Dutch patt., marked "U.S.A. 12," 4 1/2" h. (ILLUS. right)... **75-95**

Creamer, ball-type, Sunflower patt., marked "U.S.A.," 4 1/2" H.......................... **45-65**

Creamer, Corn King patt., No. 70...................... **31**

Creamer, figural Smiley Pig, decorated w/embossed peach flower, marked "Patented Smiley U.S.A.," 4 1/2" h. **125-150**

Creamer, "King Corn" line, marked "Shawnee U.S.A. 70," 5" h. **35-45**

Creamer, Lobster Ware, figural lobster handle, charcoal grey, marked "U.S.A. 909," 4 1/2" h... **65-85**

Valencia Line Dealer's Display Sign

Dealer's display sign, figural Spanish dancers, "Valencia" embossed across base, tangerine glaze, 11 1/4" h. (ILLUS.)... **400-450**

Head vase Polynesian woman, marked "Shawnee U.S.A. 896," 5 3/4" h. **75-95**

Lamp base, figural Deer, 4 1/2" h., unmarked **35-45**

Lamp base, figural Mother Goose,
6 1/2" h., unmarked **75-85**

Lamp base, figural Rabbit eating ear of
corn, 6 1/2" h., unmarked **75-85**

Matchbox holder, embossed Fern patt.,
marked "U.S.A.," 5 1/2" h. **75-100**

Mixing bowl, Corn King line, marked
"Shawnee 6," 6" d.. **50**

Mixing bowl, Corn King line, marked
"Shawnee 8," 8" d.. **65**

Pitcher, ball-type, 7" h., Valencia line,
marked "U.S.A." **45-65**

Pitcher, ball-type, 7 1/4" h., Pennsylvania
Dutch patt., marked "U.S.A." **95-125**

Pitcher, ball-type, 7 1/4" h., Sunflower
patt., marked "U.S.A." **95-125**

Figural Boy Blue Pitcher

Pitcher, 7 1/2" h., figural Boy Blue, gold
trim, marked "Shawnee U.S.A. 46"
(ILLUS.)... **200-245**

Pitcher, 7 1/2" h., figural Chanticleer
Rooster, marked "Patented Chanticleer
U.S.A." **75-85**

Pitcher, 7 1/2" h., igural Bo Peep, marked
"Shawnee U.S.A. 47" **95-125**

Pitcher, 7 3/4" h., figural Smiley Pig, peach
flower decoration, marked "Patented
Smiley U.S.A." **165-185**

Fox & Bag Planter

Planter, model of a fox & bag, marked
"U.S.A.," 4 1/2" h. (ILLUS.)...................... **50-75**

Planter, model of a highchair & kitten, pink
or blue, marked "U.S.A. 727," each.......... **75-85**

Planters, models of train engine, coal car,
boxcar & caboose, white, decorated,
Nos. 550, 551, 552, 553, 4 pcs. **85-125**

Flower & Fern Salt Box

Salt box, cov., Flower & Fern patt., yellow,
marked "U.S.A.," 4 3/4" h. (ILLUS.)......... **95-125**

Large Corn King Salt & Pepper

Salt & pepper shakers, figural, Corn King
line, No. 77, large range size, 5 1/4" h.,
pr. (ILLUS.)... **40**

Salt & pepper shakers, figural Corn King,
No. 77, pr. **37**

Salt & pepper shakers, figural Cottage,
pr. **275-325**

Salt & pepper shakers, figural Duck, pr....... **45-55**

Salt & pepper shakers, figural Flower
Clusters, pr.. **45-55**

Salt & pepper shakers, figural Milk Can,
pr. **75-95**

Figural Smiley & Winnie Shakers

Salt & pepper shakers, figural Smiley Pig
& Winnie Pig, clover blossom decora-
tion, small, pr. (ILLUS.) **75-95**

Salt & pepper shakers, figural Smiley Pig
& Winnie Pig, heart decoration, large,
pr. **100-125**

Salt & pepper shakers, figural Smiley Pig
& Winnie Pig, heart decoration, small, pr...... **45-55**

Salt & pepper shakers, Valencia line, pr...... **20-25**

Snack jar/bean pot, cov., tab-handled,
Lobster Ware, figural lobster finial on lid,
marked "Kenwood U.S.A. 925." 8" h. **375-400**

Sugar bowl, cov., "Corn King" line, No. 78,
5 1/4" h. **55-65**

Sugar bowl, cov., figural Cottage, marked
"U.S.A. 8," 4 1/2" h. **375-425**
Sugar bowl, open, Pennsylvania Dutch
patt., marked "U.S.A.," 2 3/4" h. (ILLUS.
left w/creamer) **85-95**
Teapot, cov., Clover Bud embossed deco-
ration, marked "U.S.A.," 6 1/2" h. **200-275**
Teapot, cov., "Corn King" line, marked
"Shawnee 75," 30 oz. **75-95**

Shawnee Cottage Teapot

Teapot, cov., figural Cottage, marked
"U.S.A. 7," 5 1/2" h. (ILLUS.) **375-450**
Teapot, cov., figural Granny Ann, peach &
blue, marked "Patented Granny Ann,
U.S.A.," 8" h. **100-125**
Teapot, cov., figural Piper's Son, marked
"Tom the Piper's Son patented U.S.A.
44," 7" h. **100-125**
Teapot, cov., Pennsylvania Dutch patt.,
marked "U.S.A. 18," 18 oz......................... **65-85**
Utility basket, cov., oval, marked "U.S.A.,"
4 3/4" h. **85-95**
Utility bucket, cov., marked "U.S.A.," 5" h. .. **45-55**
Wall pocket, model of a birdhouse, No.
830, brown & tan w/gold trim......................... **30**

Scotty Dog Wall Pocket

Wall pocket, Scotty Dog head, 9 1/2" h.,
unmarked (ILLUS.).................................... **65-95**
Wall pocket, Sunflower patt., marked
"U.S.A.," 6 3/4" h. **35-45**
Wall pocket, Tropical Fruit, pink, marked
"U.S.A.," 6 1/2" h. **35-45**

SHELLEY CHINA

Members of the Shelley family were in the pottery business in England as early as the 18th century. In 1872 Joseph Shelley formed a partnership
with James Wileman of Wileman & Co. who operated the Foley China Works. The Wileman & Co.
name was used for the firm for the next fifty years,
and between 1890 and 1910 the words "The Foley"
appeared above conjoined "WC" initials.

Beginning in 1910 the Shelley family name in a
shield appeared on wares, although the firm's offi-
cial name was still Wileman & Co. The company's
name was finally changed to Shelley in 1925 and
then Shelley China Ltd. after 1965. The firm
changed hands in the 1960s and became part of
the Doulton Group in 1971.

At first only average quality earthenwares were
produced but in the late 1890s new shapes and
better quality decorations were used.

Bone china was introduced at Shelley before
World War I and these fine dinnerwares became
very popular in the United States and are increasingly popular today with collectors. Thin "eggshell
china" teawares, miniatures and souvenir items
were widely marketed during the 1920s and 1930s
and are sought-after today.

Shelley Mark

Ashtray, advertising-type, "Greer's O.V.H." ... **$100**
Ashtray, Dainty Blue patt. **50**
Ashtray-match holder, advertising-type,
horseshoe-shaped, "White Horse" **125**
Backbar water pitcher, "White Horse" **500**
Bowl, berry, Blue Rock patt.............................. **30**
Bowl, 8" w., lustre glaze, signed "Walter
Slater".. **800**
Breakfast set: two-cup cov. coffeepot,
creamer, open sugar bowl, two 8" d.
plates, two 6" d. plates, two 5 1/2" d.
bowls & one cov. pancake dish; Stocks
patt., Dainty shape, the set **875**
Butter dish, cov., Dainty White patt.................. **48**
Butter dish, cov., round, Blue Rock patt.......... **175**
Cake set: 10" handled cake plate & six
6" d. plates; Wild Flower patt., the set.......... **210**
Candlestick, Art Deco-style, orange glaze,
2 1/2" h.. **150**

Cloisonné Pattern Candlestick

Candlestick, flaring round base below the
tapering shaft & bulbed candle socket,
down-curved handle from socket to
base, Cloisonné patt., 6 1/2" h. (ILLUS.)...... **200**
Candy dish, Dainty Pink patt., 4 1/2" l. **65**

Coffeepot, cov., Bluebells patt., Vincent shape **200**

Coffeepot, cov., Campanula patt., tall tapering ovoid body w/domed cover, 7" h. **300**

Dainty Blue Coffee, Tea & Water Pots

Coffeepot, cov., Dainty Blue patt., Dainty shape (ILLUS. right) **600**

Coffeepot, cov., Dainty patt. **435**

Coffeepot, cov., Syringa patt., Regent shape **350**

Coffeepot, cov., Violets patt., Mayfair shape **325**

Creamer & open sugar bowl, Dainty Blue patt., Dainty shape, pr. **130**

Creamer & open sugar bowl, Floral patt., Dainty shape w/floral-molded handle, pr. **300**

Creamer & open sugar bowl, Wileman & Co., pr. **150**

Creamer, open sugar bowl & tray, Blue Rock patt., 3 pcs. **165**

Creamer & sugar bowl, Blue Rock patt., pr. **110**

Creamer & sugar bowl, Harebell patt., pr. **85**

Creamer & sugar bowl, Maytime patt., pr. **175**

Cup & saucer, Ashbourne patt., Gainsborough shape (ILLUS.) **200**

Ashbourne Pattern Cup & Saucer

Cup & saucer, Begonia patt., six-flute shape **78**

Cup & saucer, Black Dainty patt., Dainty shape, rare **800**

Chinoiserie Pattern Cup & Saucer

Cup & saucer, Chinoiserie patt., Ripon shape (ILLUS.) **200**

Cup & saucer, Countryside (Chintz style) patt., gold foot & scroll handle **204**

Cup & saucer, Countryside patt., Queen Anne shape **185**

Cup & saucer, Countryside patt., various Chintz shapes, each.................................... **200**

Cup & saucer, Dainty Black patt., Dainty shape, rare **800**

Dainty Cup & Saucer w/Floral Handle

Cup & saucer, Dainty shape, lavender & cream w/floral-molded handle (ILLUS.)........ **175**

Cup & saucer, Dainty shape, solid color........... **60**

Cup & saucer, demitasse Acacia patt., Regent shape **100**

Floral-Handled Cup & Saucer

Cup & saucer, Floral patt., Queen Anne shape w/floral-molded handle (ILLUS.)........ **400**

Cup & saucer, Floral patt., Vogue (Art Deco style) shape **300**

Cup & saucer, Green Daisy patt., Henley (Chintz) shape... **150**

Cup & saucer, Harebell patt. **52**

Cup & saucer, Japan patt., Alexandra shape, Wileman & Co. **100**

Cup & saucer, miniature, Lily of the Valley patt., Westminster shape **325**

Cup & saucer, Morning Glory patt. **62**

Cup & saucer, Polka Dot Black patt., Henley shape.. **135**

Cup & saucer, Polka Dot patt. **58**

Cup & saucer, Primrose patt., various
Chintz shapes, each..................................... **120**

Cup & saucer, Regency patt., Dainty
shape **60**

Cup & saucer, Rock Garden patt., footed
Oleander shape... **170**

Cup & saucer, Wildflower patt. **52**

Cup & saucer, Woodland patt. **55**

Cup & saucer, demitasse, Forget-Me-Not
patt. **48**

Cup & saucer, demitasse, Pansy patt. **48**

Cup & saucer, demitasse, Rose Spray
patt. **48**

Cups & saucers, demitasse, footed, pink
w/aqua dots, gold lined, 6 each, 12 pcs. **350**

Cups & saucers, Crochet patt., pink & blue
flower w/gold trim, set of 6 .... **290**

Demitasse pot, cov., Wildflowers patt.,
Dainty shape **300**

Dessert set: cup & saucer & dessert plate;
Campanula patt., 3 pcs. **165**

Dessert set: cup & saucer & dessert plate;
Rosebud patt.. **125**

Dessert set, cup & saucer & dessert plate,
Rock Garden patt., 3 pcs. **110**

Egg cup, Dainty Shamrock patt. **55**

Hot water pot, cov., Dainty Blue patt.,
Dainty shape (ILLUS. center)...................... **600**

Invalid feeder, Floral patt. **250**

Jam pot, cov., Dainty Blue patt. **200**

Jam pot w/metal cover & holder, Bridal
Rose patt., the set.. **175**

Jelly mold, French shape, large **75**

Jelly mold, model of a large white chicken **200**

Loving cup, Bermuda commemorative,
"1609-1959," 4 1/2 x 7"................................ **100**

Luncheon set, 8" d. plate, cup & saucer,
Blue Daisy patt., Chintz shape, 3 pcs. **160**

Luncheon set: cup, saucer & two plates:
Jungle Print patt., Daisy shape, Wileman
& Co., the set **175**

Luncheon set, 8" plate, cup & saucer,
Harebell patt., 3 pcs. **65**

Luncheon set, 8" plate, cup & saucer,
Stocks patt., 3 pcs.. **65**

Blue Iris Luncheon Set

Luncheon set (trio): cup, saucer & plate:
Blue Iris patt., Queen Anne shape, the
set (ILLUS.) **200**

Luncheon set (trio): cup, saucer & plate:
Countryside (Chintz) patt., Oleander
shape, the set **350**

Luncheon set (trio): cup, saucer & plate:
Crackle patt., Queen Anne shape, the
set **190**

Luncheon set (trio): cup, saucer & plate:
Dainty Black patt., Dainty shape, the set .. **1,075**

Luncheon set (trio): cup, saucer & plate:
Daisy Cluster patt., Empire shape, Wile-
man & Co., the set **125**

Gladiolus Luncheon Set

Luncheon set (trio): cup, saucer & plate:
Gladiolus patt., Eve (Art Deco style)
shape, the set (ILLUS.) **250**

Luncheon set (trio): cup, saucer & plate:
Hollyhocks patt., Regent shape, the set....... **135**

Luncheon set (trio): cup, saucer & plate:
Japan patt., Fairy shape, Wileman &
Co., the set **200**

Luncheon set (trio): cup, saucer & plate:
Japan patt., Queen Anne shape, Wile-
man & Co., the set **175**

Luncheon set (trio): cup, saucer & plate:
Lines & Shades patt., Eve (Art Deco
style) shape, the set.................................... **250**

Thistle Pattern Luncheon Set

Luncheon set (trio): cup, saucer & plate;
Thistle patt., Alexandra shape, Wileman
& Co., the set (ILLUS.) **125**

Mint dish, Dainty Blue patt................................ **72**

Shelley Model of a Drake

Model of a drake duck, brown head, grey
& black body, Bird Series #12, 4 1/2" h.
(ILLUS.)... **500**

Model of a parrot, Bird Series #3, 7 1/2" h. **500**

Mug, decorated w/the coat-of-arms of Wales, 3" h. 100

Napkin ring, Harmony patt. 100

Nut dish, Old England patt., signed by Eric Slater 75

Pitcher, water, jug-form, Blue Dragon patt. 500

Plate, bread & butter, Blue Rock patt. 30

Plate, dinner, Blue Rock patt. 95

Plate, dinner, Harebell patt. 45

Plate, Festoons & Fruit patt., Roseberry shape 50-100

Art Deco Floral-decorated Plate

Plate, Pattern No.11752, florals & butterflies, Art Deco-style shape (ILLUS.) **100-125**

Plate, square, Maytime patt. 125

Plate, 6" d., Rock Garden patt. 25

Plate, 8" d., Dainty Blue patt. 65

Jacobean Pattern Plate

Plate, 8 3/4" d., Jacobean patt. (ILLUS.) **50-60**

Plate, 11" d., dinner, Blue Rock patt. 85

Platter, 10 x 13", meat, Blue Rock patt. 140

Platter, 14 1/2" l., Harebell patt. 150

Reamer & base, Harmony patt., streaky mottled pink & green glaze, 2 pc. 350

Shaving mug, Harmony patt. 175

Sugar bowl, open, square, Rock Garden patt. 59

Tea set, Blue Gladiolus patt., Eve (Art Deco style) shape, 21 pcs. **2,100**

Tea set, Green Lines & Bands patt., Eve (Art Deco style) shape, 21 pcs. **2,000**

Red Blocks Art Deco Tea Set

Tea set, Red Blocks patt., Mode (Art Deco style) shape, teapot & 22 pcs. (ILLUS. of part) **3,200**

Tea set, Sun-Ray patt., Vogue (Art Deco style) shape, 21 pcs. **2,500**

Tea set, Yellow Phlox patt., Regent shape, teapot & 37 pcs. **1,800**

Teapot, cov., Begonia patt. 475

Teapot, cov., Countryside (Chintz-type) patt., Eve (Art Deco style) shape 800

Teapot, cov., Dainty Blue patt., Dainty shape (ILLUS. left) 600

Teapot, cov., Dainty Blue patt., large 495

Teapot, cov., Harebell patt. 325

Harmony Drip-Ware Teapot

Teapot, cov., Harmony Drip-Ware, Cambridge shape (ILLUS.) 600

Teapot, cov., Hollyhocks patt., Regent shape 350

Rare Laburnum Pattern Teapot

Teapot, cov., Laburnum patt., Eve (Art Deco style) shape (ILLUS.) 650

Teapot, cov., Wildflower patt., Dainty shape 450

Toast rack, Harmony Ware patt. 150

Umbrella stand, advertising-type, columnar form w/molded pilasters flanking arched niches around the side, dark blue ground printed in white w/"Shelley China - Potters to The World," 27" h. (ILLUS.) **2,500**

Rare Shelley Umbrella Stand

Vase, 4 1/2" h., Melody patt............................. 200
Vase, 5" h., Balloons & Flashes patt. 125
Vase, 5" h., Cloisonné patt. 200
Vase, 6" h., New Violettes patt. 100

Harmony Ware Moresque Vase

Vase, 6" h., tall waisted shape, Harmony
   Ware, Moresque patt., stylized blossoms
   in orange, pale & dark blue & brown
   (ILLUS.).. 150
Vase, 6 1/2" h., New Fruit patt. 150
Vase, 7" h., Jazz Circles patt., black & yel-
   low design 175
Vegetable bowl, open, oval, Harebell patt.,
   9 1/2" l. 145

NURSERY WARE BY MABEL LUCIE ATTWELL

Baby feeding plate, color scene inscribed
   "Fairy Folk with Tiny Wings..."...................... 350
Child's set: cup, saucer & plate; scene of
   an airplane & Boo-Boos, the set 500
Cruet set: three mushroom-shaped cov-
   ered pots & figural shaker on four-lobed
   tray; Boo-Boo set (ILLUS.) 1,000

Boo-Boo Cruet Set

Figurine, Boo-Boo with knapsack 900
Figurine, Boo-Boo with mushroom 900

Rare Diddums Figurine

Figurine, Diddums (ILLUS.) 2,200
Figurine, Golfer... 2,200
Figurine, I's Shy... 2,200
Figurine, Little Mermaid 2,500
Mug & saucer, color duck scene inscribed
   "Quacky the Sailor," the set........................ 375
Mug & saucer, color scene of Mother Rab-
   bit & baby Rabbity, inscribed "When
   Rabbity fell...," the set 375
Mug & saucer, inscribed "If the Fairies
   came to Tea," the set 375
Platter, 8" w., duck scene inscribed
   "Quacky the Sailor" 180

Child's Platter with Duck Scene

Platter, 8" l., squared shape w/molded handles, color scene of mother duck & children, inscribed "Will Somebody Kindly
   Tell..." (ILLUS.)... 300

Boo-Boo Figural Tea Set

Tea set: cov. teapot, creamer & open
   sugar; Boo-Boo set w/mushroom-
   shaped open sugar & mushroom house-
   shaped teapot w/figural Boo-Boo
   creamer, the set (ILLUS.)......................... 2,500

INTARSIO ART POTTERY (1997-99)

Intarsio Art Pottery Clock

Clock, table model, Art Nouveau-style
   upright case w/a brown border around a
   colored central panel w/a dial above a
   scene of a Medieval couple by a sundial

above the inscription "The Days May Come - The Days May Go..."(ILLUS.) **1,500**

Intarsio Art Pottery Cracker Jar

Cracker jar, cov., footed bulbous body w/silver plate rim, cover & bail handle, wide color band decorated w/scenes from Shakespeare plays, 6" h. (ILLUS.) **850**

Caricature Teapot of Lord Salisbury

Teapot, cov., caricature of Lord Salisbury, dark green, black, tan & brown (ILLUS.) ... **1,000**
Teapot, cov., Cornflower patt., blue ground .. **1,200**
Teapot, cov., Oriental shape, wide squatty base centered by an urn-form neck w/domed cover, upright shaped spout & C-scroll handle, dark brown ground decorated w/stylized deep rose & green blossoms & leaves on yellow bands, lighter brown spout & handle **1,400**
Toby mug, "The Irishman," 7 1/2" h. **850**

Rare Intarsio Umbrella Stand

Umbrella stand, cylindrical w/flared foot, Flowers patt., white storks flying into a large rising sun in a blue sky, dark water & water lilies around the bottom, 25" h. (ILLUS.) **8,500**

Vase, 8 1/2" h., bulbous body centered by a wide cylindrical neck w/four curved handles from neck to shoulder, decorated w/a central band of brown & white chickens on a blue & green ground, bands of brown scrolls on a green ground above & below & a dark blue neck w/white & yellow flowers & green leaves, green handles **1,800**

Wash bowl & pitcher set, Art Nouveau design w/large stylized flowers in yellow & shaded blue to white on green swirled leafy stems on a dark green & black ground, bowl 18" d., the set (ILLUS.) **2,200**

Intarsio Art Nouveau-style Wash Set

SLIPWARE

This term refers to ceramics, primarily redware, decorated by the application of slip, or semi-liquid paste made of clay. Such wares were made for decades in England and Germany and elsewhere on the Continent, and in the Pennsylvania Dutch country and elsewhere in the United States. Today, contemporary copies of early Slipware items are featured in numerous decorator magazines and offered for sale in gift catalogs.

Bowl, 6 3/4" d., 3" h., redware, wide shallow sides w/molded edge, a band of white slip squiggle design below rim, mottled greenish glaze w/brown flecks & amber spots **$275**

Bowl, 14 3/4" d., 3 1/2" h., shallow, squiggly white slip decoration on dark brown glaze (wear & old edge chips) **1,980**

Slip-Decorated Redware Bread Tray

Bread tray, redware, glazed oblong dish w/notched rim, decorated w/abstract patterns in yellow slip, 19th c., 11 1/2 x 18 1/2" (ILLUS.) **2,070**

Charger, redware, coggle wheel rim w/yellow slip squiggles & inscription "Pony up the Cash," attributed to Day Pottery, Norwalk, Connecticut, 14" d. (wear, hairline & old rim chips) **18,700**

Dish, rectangular redware decorated w/a slip-trailed inscription "Chicken Pottry (sic)," American, 19th c., 9 3/4 x 14 1/2" (chips) **460**

Loaf dish, redware, rectangular w/coggle wheel rim, yellow three-quill slip decoration, 14" l. (some glaze flaking & edge chips)... **715**

Loaf dish, redware, rectangular w/coggle wheel rim, yellow four-quill zigzag slip decoration in center & on each side, 14 1/4" l. (wear, glaze flakes & chips) **770**

Mold, food, Turk's turban-style, orange ground w/dark brown splotches & flecks & yellow slip rim, 9" d., 3" h. (wear & small chips) **330**

Pie plate, w/coggled rim, three-line yellow slip decoration w/green, 7 7/8" d. (minor wear & small chip)....................................... **550**

Pie plate, w/coggled rim, yellow slip decoration highlighted in brown & green on greyish amber ground, 7 7/8" d. (wear)........ **550**

Pie plate, redware w/coggled rim w/three-line slip decoration, 8" d. (wear, hairline & small rim chips)... **605**

Pie plate, redware w/coggled rim, dark brown & green flecked glaze w/white slip wavy lines, attributed to Stahl Pottery, Powder Valley, Lehigh County, Pennsylvania, 8 3/8" d. (minor glaze flakes on rim) **550**

Pie plate, redware w/coggled rim, decorated w/large yellow slip bird on branch, 10" d. (wear & hairlines) **3,410**

Pie plate, redware w/coggled rim, yellow triple-quill slip decoration, 10" d. **468**

Pie plate, w/coggled rim, yellow slip Seaweed design on blue glaze, 10 1/2" d. (minor wear, edge chips & short hairlines) **1,623**

Pie plate, redware w/coggle wheel rim, yellow slip flourish decoration, 12" d. (slip worn & flaked) **880**

Plate, 11 1/2" d., redware w/crimped rim & inscribed "Lafayette" in yellow slip w/yel-

low slip scrolls above & below inscription, 19th c., Pennsylvania **6,900**

SPATTERWARE

This ceramic ware takes its name from the "spattered" decoration, in various colors, generally used to trim pieces hand-painted with rustic center designs of flowers, birds, houses, etc. Popular in the early 19th century, most was imported from England.

Related wares, called "stick spatter," had free-hand designs applied with pieces of cut sponge attached to sticks, hence the name. Examples date from the 19th and early 20th century and were produced in England, Europe and America.

Some early spatter-decorated wares were marked by the manufacturers, but not many. 20th century reproductions are also sometimes marked, including those produced by Boleslaw Cybis.

Creamer, bulbous body w/C-form handle & arched spout, Rose patt., free-hand flower in red, green & black in center w/blue spatter ground, 3 5/8" h. (stains & flakes on table ring & chips on rim) **$303**

Spatterware Creamer

Creamer, bulbous body w/C-form handle & pinched spout, Peafowl patt., free-hand bird in blue, yellow & black, overall strawberry or thumbprint red, green & blue spatter, professional repair, 4" h. (ILLUS.)... **5,170**

Creamer, footed squatty bulbous base w/tapering wide cylindrical neck, long pinched spout & large C-form handle, red, green & black Holly Berry patt. band around base w/overall blue spatter above, 4" h. **660**

Various Spatterware Items

Creamer, bulbous body w/C-form handle & arched spout, Rooster patt., free-hand bird in yellow ochre, red, blue & black, blue border, professional repair, 4 1/2" h. (ILLUS. right)................................. **880**

Creamer, footed paneled bulbous body w/arched spout & angled C-form handle,

Peafowl patt., free-hand bird in blue, green, red & black, blue spatter border, 4 1/2" h. **798**

Creamer, footed bulbous body w/high arched spout & scrolled C-form handle, Tree patt., free-hand tree in green & black, purple spatter border, 5" h. (stains & base of handle glued) **990**

Creamer, footed bulbous paneled body w/scrolled C-form handle & high arched spout, Peafowl patt., free-hand red, blue, green & black bird w/red spatter, 5 1/2" h. **1,375**

Creamer, footed paneled bulbous body w/arched spout & angled C-form handle, Clipper Ship patt., free-hand ship in green, red & black, blue spatter border, 5 5/8" h. (ILLUS. left) **4,840**

Cup, handleless, free-hand Gooney bird in blue, teal green, red & black, blue spatter ground (flakes on table ring) **220**

Cup plate, Peafowl patt. in black, blue & green w/unusual black breast, red spatter background, impressed mark "Opaque Porcelain - Holden," 4" w. (chip on table ring, minor stains) **550**

Cup & saucer, handleless, Acorn & Oak Leaves patt. in two shades of green, brown & black, dark red spatter border (saucer slightly lighter in color & professional repair to cup) **1,100**

Spatterware Cup & Saucer

Cup & saucer, handleless, Dove patt., free-hand bird in yellow ochre, blue, green & black, blue spatter border (ILLUS.) **2,750**

Cup & saucer, handleless, Drape patt., Rainbow spatter in red & blue **2,090**

Spatter Handleless Cups & Saucers

Cup & saucer, handleless, Forget-Me-Not patt., free-hand flower in blue, red, green & black, blue spatter border in shape of six-point star on saucer, impressed anchor mark on saucer (ILLUS. bottom row, right) **3,190**

Cup & saucer, handleless, Fort patt., free-hand fort in blue, black, red & green, red spatter border... **1,980**

Cup & saucer, handleless, Fort patt., free-hand fort in green, black & red, blue spatter border (ILLUS. top row, center)........ **660**

Cup & saucer, handleless, Gooney Bird patt. in red, blue, green & black, blue spatter border, cup w/paneled sides (minor pinpoints on rim of cup) **1,320**

Cup & saucer, handleless, Guinea Hen patt. in red, blue, green & black, red spatter border (professional repair to saucer, red varies slightly) **1,540**

Cup & saucer, handleless, Mourning Tulip patt., free-hand flower in yellow, green & black, blue spatter border (pinpoint flakes).. **4,290**

Cup & saucer, handleless, Pansy patt. in red, blue, green & black, blue spatter border (pinpoints on saucer rim) **3,850**

Cup & saucer, handleless, Peacock patt., free-hand bird in yellow, blue, green, red & black, overall light green spatter (ILLUS. top row, right) **1,650**

Cup & saucer, handleless, Peacock patt., free-hand bird in yellow, blue, green, red & black, overall lilac spatter (ILLUS. top row, left) **2,310**

Cup & saucer, handleless, Rainbow spatter border, alternating blue & green **1,485**

Cup & saucer, handleless, Rainbow spatter border, alternating blue & yellow (cup slightly lighter in color & has pinpoint flakes).. **2,090**

Cup & saucer, handleless, Rooster patt., free-hand blue, red, yellow & black bird on an overall blue spatter ground (ILLUS. bottom row, left) **974**

Cup & saucer, handleless, Rose patt. in red, green & black, Rainbow spatter border in black & brown (hairline in saucer) **495**

Cup & saucer, handleless, Schoolhouse patt., red, green & black, blue spatter border, scalloped border on cup, chips on saucer table ring, repair to cup (ILLUS. bottom row, center) **990**

Pitcher, 6 1/2" h., paneled body w/blue transfer-printed Eagle & Shield patt. w/red spatter (wear, crazing & dark stains)... **468**

Pitcher, 8" h., paneled body, angled handle, arched pinched spout over molded fan, Peafowl patt., free-hand bird in blue, green, red & black, blue spatter border (professional repair) **990**

Pitcher, water, 10 5/8" h., tall tapering paneled body w/high arched spout & D-form handle, overall light blue spatter on white ground (chips & hairline on spout) **220**

Plate, 6 1/8" d., Adams Rose patt. in red & green, rainbow spatter border in red, blue & green, impressed "Adams" (minor crow's foot & scratches) **935**

Plate, 6 1/2" d., Peafowl patt., free-hand bird in blue, yellow, green & black, red & blue spatter rim **880**

Plate, 6 1/2" d., Wigwam patt., wigwams flanked by blue spatter trees **440**

Plate, 7 1/4" d., Pomegranate patt. in red, blue, black & green, blue spatter border, impressed "F.G. Meakin" (wear & professional repair) **440**

Plate, 7 3/4" d., Peafowl patt., free-hand blue, black, red & pale yellow, overall green spatter.. **1,650**

Plate, 8 5/8" d., Rooster Peafowl patt., free-hand bird in dark blue, pale yellow, red & black, overall dark blue spatter **2,860**

Plate, 9 3/8" d., plaid spatterware design in purple, red, blue & green (pinpoint edge flakes).. **5,170**

Plate, 9 1/2" d., Bull's Eye patt., blue & green spatter border (crazing & light scratches).. **1,430**

Plate, 9 1/2" d., Clover patt. in red, green & black, embossed rim (minor stains) **4,070**

Sugar bowl, cov., Rooster patt., free-hand bird in yellow, blue, red & black, blue spatter border, professional repair, 4 1/4" h. (ILLUS. center with creamers) **880**

Sugar bowl, cov., Rainbow spatter in yellow & black, 4 1/2" h. (lid slightly oversize & professionally restored chip, minor crazing) **1,210**

Teapot, cov., footed bulbous body w/flaring rim, C-form handle & swan's-neck spout, inset stepped & pointed cover w/blossom finial, Tree patt., free-hand tree in green & black, purple spatter border, 6" h. (professional repair).......................... **1,980**

Teapot, cov., creamware, an upright oval cylindrical body w/tapering shoulder to a fitted domed cover w/knob finial, swan's-neck spout, C-form handle, Rainbow spatter in vertical narrow bands of yellow, goldenrod, blue, green & dark brown, early 19th c., 6 1/2" h. (chips, lid repaired).. **6,710**

Teapot, cov., bulbous body w/narrow shoulder tapering to wide cylindrical neck, C-form handle & swan's-neck spout, domed cover w/button finial, Parrot patt., free-hand bird in red, green & black, blue spatter border, 6 3/4" h. (minor stains & wear, lid professionally repaired) **2,530**

Toddy dish, round, Primrose patt., free-hand flower in red, yellow, green & black, blue spatter border, 5" d. **633**

Toddy dish, Wigwam patt., wigwams flanked by blue spatter trees, 5 1/8" d. **495**

Vegetable dish, open, footed cartouche-form w/flanged rim & molded end handles, Rose patt. in red, green & black, blue spatter border, 11 1/4" l. (stains, wear, glued foot chip)................................. **468**

Waste bowl, Fort patt. in black, red, yellow & green, blue spatter border, 4 1/4" d. **495**

Waste bowl, Fort patt. in red, green, black & yellow, blue spatter border, 5 3/8" d., 3 1/8" h. (wear & stains w/pinpoint edge flakes).. **1,155**

STICK & CUT SPONGE

Stick Spatter Shallow Bowl

Bowl, 14 1/2" d., 3" h., border decorated w/stick spatter floral design in red, blue, green, yellow & purple, marked "Maastricht" (ILLUS.)... **88**

Plate, 8 3/4" d., ironstone w/blue design stick spatter border & purple transfer-printed eagle w/shield, English registry mark w/"Gem. R. Hammersley".................... **165**

Plate, 9 1/2" d., Rabbit patt., black transfer-printed border band w/six rabbits & three frogs trimmed in yellow & green, free-hand decorated center w/ring of cut-sponge flowers & red striping....................... **633**

Plate, chop, 16 1/4" d., decorated w/free-hand blue flowers & red & green cut-sponge blossoms & leaves, "Villeroy & Boch" **413**

Wash bowl & pitcher, 10 3/4" h. pitcher, ovoid body w/arched spout & C-form handle, center design of large stylized four-petal flower in red & green, overall blue sponging, 12 5/8" d. bowl w/same center design & bordered by blue sponging, the set (chip on back edge of bowl rim) **1,375**

SPONGEWARE

Spongeware's designs were spattered, sponged or daubed on in colors, sometimes with a piece of cloth. Blue on white was the most common type, but mottled tans, browns and greens on yellowware were also popular. Spongeware generally has an overall pattern with a coarser look than Spatterwares, to which it is loosely related. These wares were extensively produced in England and America well into the 20th century.

Spongeware Pig Bank

Bank, figural pig, teal green & tan sponging on cream ground, glaze wear on ears & shallow flake on one foot, 6" l. (ILLUS.) **$275**

Batter pail, cylindrical w/molded rim & rim spout, wire bail handle, blue sponging on white, 5 1/4" d., 4" h. **295**

Bean pot, bulbous flat-bottomed body tapering to a flat mouth, small loop handle at shoulder, wide spiral bands of blue sponging on white, marked "3 qt.," 6 1/2" h. (lid missing) **165**

Green Spongeware Birdhouse

Birdhouse, cylindrical w/conical roof w/knob finial for hanging, overall mottled dark green sponging, 7 1/4" h. (ILLUS.) **300**

Bowl, 3 1/4" d., cov., miniature, flaring sides w/domed cover & button finial, wire bail w/wooden handle, blue sponging on white (hairline & chips) **468**

Bowl, 10 1/4" d., 5" h., blue & white w/two blue accent bands, ca. 1880, (two minor exterior rim chips).. **143**

Butter crock, low wide cylindrical form w/molded rim, blue on white w/blue printed "Butter" on front, 9" d., 6" h. **303**

Canister, barrel-shaped w/blue sponged bands at top & bottom & thin blue bands flanking center sponging & the name "Rice," 5 3/4" h. **500**

Jar, bulbous ovoid body tapering slightly to flared rim, blue on white, 4 1/4" h. (pinpoint rim flakes)... **798**

Jar, cov., ovoid w/molded rim, brown, blue & green sponging on white w/black transfer-printed label reading "Spaulding's Pure Fresh Cookies," 9 1/4" h. (chip on bottom edge) **220**

Fine Spongeware Jardiniere

Jardiniere, wide bulbous form w/flared rim, embossed rings of small scrolls trimmed

w/rings of blue sponging on white, 9" d., 7 1/2" h. (ILLUS.).. **500**

Jug, semi-ovoid body w/wire bail & wooden handle, labeled "Grandmother's Maple Syrup of 50 Years Ago" & "Mfg'd by F.H. Weeks, Akron, O" on bottom, blue sponging on white, 8" h. (chips) **1,375**

Mixing bowl, footed, deep slightly flared sides, blue sponging on white, 10" d., 5" h. (glaze wear on rim & internal hairline) **220**

Mixing bowl, footed, deep flaring sides, bold repeating bands of blue sponging on white at base & below rim w/blue strips around center, chips on foot, 11 1/4" d., 5" h. **275**

Mixing bowls, yellowware, nesting-type w/overall blue sponging, 3 1/2" to 9 1/4" d., set of 5 (largest does not ring) **295**

Mug, cylindrical w/molded C-form handle, blue sponging on white, 3 5/8" h. (slight crow's foot in bottom) **138**

Pitcher, 6" h., ovoid body w/C-form handle & pinched spout, blue on white w/brown slip interior (chips on lip & wear) **330**

Pitcher, 6 3/4" h., cylindrical w/D-form handle, blue sponging on white w/center horizontal stripe (minor flake on table ring) **605**

Blue & White Spongeware Pitcher and Bulbous Water Pitcher

Pitcher, 7" h., blue & white, ca. 1880, few minor glaze flecks at interior rim (ILLUS.)..... **330**

Pitcher, 7 1/4" h., footed bulbous nearly spherical body tapering to a wide flat flaring neck, thick C-scroll handle, overall heavy blue sponging w/a wide blue band around the bottom flanked by two white bands & two thin blue bands (small chips, hairlines) **330**

Pitcher, 9" h., tall slightly tapering cylindrical body w/pinched spout & C-form handle, relief-molded rose decoration, blue sponging on white **495**

Pitcher, 12" h., water, bulbous, blue & white w/three blue accent bands, ca. 1880, one minor glaze fleck at spout (ILLUS. right)....................................... **358**

Plates, 9" d. w/flanged scalloped rim, yellowware w/overall fine brown sponging, England, late 18th - early 19th c., pr. (rim chips, one w/rim repair).............................. **440**

Platter, 9 3/4 x 13 3/4", oblong, blue sponging on white **193**

Pot, cylindrical w/pouring spout, wire bail & wooden handle, blue on white, 5 1/4" d., 4" h. (small rim chips)................................... **385**

Ramekins/custard cups, blue on white, 3 1/4" d., 2 1/4" h. set of 6 (pieces are similar).. **385**

Salt crock, cov., embossed Basketweave and Grapes patt., overall bold blue sponging on white **375**

Salt crock, cylindrical w/hinged wooden lid, overall brown & greyish sponging, faint worn gilt label "Salt," 6" h. **137**

Soap dish, rectangular w/rounded corners, blue w/a bit of red sponging on white, 4 x 6 1/2" (small chips).................................. **72**

Teapot, cov., miniature, squatty bulbous body w/C-form handle, swan's-neck spout & inset cover w/blossom finial, blue on white, 4 1/8" h. (minor chips).......... **853**

Wash bowl & pitcher, yellowware 15" d. bowl w/flaring sides & 11 3/4" h. bulbous pitcher, overall blue sponging, 2 pcs. (bowl w/repair & additional damage, worn gilding) **275**

STAFFORDSHIRE FIGURES

Small figures and groups made of pottery were produced by the majority of the Staffordshire, England potters in the 19th century and were used as mantel decorations or "chimney ornaments," as they were sometimes called. Pairs of dogs were favorites and were turned out by the carload, and 19th century pieces are still available. Well-painted reproductions also abound and collectors are urged to exercise caution before investing.

Calf, recumbent figure w/brush-stroked orange spots on molded greenish brown base, 3" d., 2 1/2" h. (small chip on one ear & light wear) **$308**

Camel, recumbent figure, brownish tan w/red line on base, 3 1/4" d., 3 1/4" h. (few minute spots of wear) **616**

Cat, recumbent animal on embossed scrolled base, black over yellow sponge decoration w/some red on base, 3 1/2" d., 2 3/4" h. (tiny chip on left ear) **448**

Cat, seated, black & brown sponging on white, glazed over crack at seam, 4 1/2" h. **275**

Dog, pearlware, hollow-molded, stylized creature w/head turned to the right & painted w/random patches of brown, blue & ochre, lying on a domed natural-istic base, ca. 1790-1810, 4 1/8" h. (hair crack to hind quarters) **460**

Dog, seated Mastiff w/open front legs, head turned to the side, boldly spotted fur, on a rectangular enameled pillow base, early 19th c., 4 5/8" h. (chip on pillow corner)... **633**

Dog, seated whippet facing the viewer, on an oval base, decorated w/overall small black dots, black ears & polychrome facial features & neck chain, mid-19th c., 7" h. (wear, chips on base, roughness on nose) **330**

*Staffordshire Spaniel Figure
and Staffordshire Figure of Pug*

Dog, Spaniel in seated position, molded fur & chain, large copper lustre spots & trim w/painted facial details, embossed numbers on bottom, 19th c., 10" h. (ILLUS.)....... **225**

Dogs, Pug in seated position w/ears erect, yellow eyes, black & red painted facial details, wearing black collar w/gilt pad-lock, second half 19th c., 10 1/4" h., pr. (ILLUS. of one)... **1,265**

Dogs, Spaniel seated on his haunches, looking to his right & left respectively & wearing a collar w/lock, glazed in white w/gilt highlights, w/black & pink face markings, mounted as table lamps, late 19th c., 12 1/2" h., pr. (one glass eye missing).. **402**

Dogs, Whippets in standing position, each w/a rabbit in its mouth, painted in beige & red, 19th c., 11" h., pr. (minor chips)........ **748**

Figure, earthenware, rider on horseback, ca. 1880, 11 1/2" h..................... **123**

Figure group, a young girl in early Victo-rian costume & wearing a hat reclining against an oversized recumbent dog, decorated in red & white w/blue, pink & black trim, mid-19th c., 6 1/2" h. (craz-ing) **1,595**

Figure group, Scottish couple standing on oval base, polychrome trim, 19th c., 7 7/8" h. (very minor chip & losses)............. **230**

Figure group, 'The Death of Nelson,' showing the dying admiral seated between two officers, the back modeled as his ship the Victory, polychrome dec-oration, rectangular base, mid-19th c.......... **518**

Figure of a youth, standing wearing 18th c. peasant attire, beside a tree trunk, decorated w/overglaze colored enamels, impressed mark, possibly Ralph or Enoch Wedgwood, ca. 1800, 10" h. (restored neck, shallow chip on plinth)......... **690**

Figure of Dan O'Connell, minister wearing a green scarf & black coat w/gilt trim, standing beside a column covered w/blue & orange drape on a grassy oval base w/gilt title, ca. 1900, 17 1/2" h............. **575**

Pearlware Figure of Hercules

Figure of Hercules, pearlware, muscular bearded male wearing red, yellow & black loin cloth, resting on one knee on a black marbled square base w/his head lowered as he supports a pierced pale yellow globe representing the world on his shoulders, early 19th c., possibly by Obadiah Sherrat, minute chips, 11 3/8" h. (ILLUS.)....................................... 575

Figure of The Duke of Wellington, standing wearing a cape atop a square marbleized pedestal, gilt trim, ca. 1840, 13 1/4" h. (restoration to back of shoulders)... 345

Figure of "The Lion Slayer," standing bearded man wearing a Scottish kilt & feathered hat, a dead lion beside him, polychrome trim, 19th c., 15 3/4" h. (some worn gilt).. 220

Figures of Milton and Shakespeare

Figures of Milton & Shakespeare, pearlware, each modeled holding a quill pen & standing beside a stack of books & manuscripts on & beside a column on a black marbled square base w/green top, ca. 1810-20, chip to upper rim of Milton's base, both w/minor losses & some flaking to enamels, 15 1/2" h., pr. (ILLUS.)... **1,495**

Figures of Prudence & Fortitude, pearlware, each modeled as a young classical maiden wearing a long floral gown,

green & yellow or puce & yellow drape & sandals, standing on a black marbled square base, Prudence holding a torch in her left hand & w/a green serpent wrapped around her right wrist, Fortitude leaning against a column, Prudence w/restoration at left shoulder & right wrist, Fortitude w/hairline crack running through the middle, minor flaking to enamels, ca. 1820, 21" h., pr. **4,600**

Horses, modeled w/right or left front leg raised & looking straight ahead, supported on an oval bright green base, the animals in cream w/black spots, mane & facial markings, mid-19th c., 5 1/4" l., pr. .. **1,035**

Lion, recumbent animal facing viewer, undecorated, oval base, late 18th c., 4" l. (slight chips) **863**

Match/spill holder, figural fox w/a swan in his mouth in foreground, colorfully decorated in yellow green, black & orange enamels, 9 3/4" h. (few spots of glaze wear) **672**

Model of a castle, squared form w/center tower, Gothic windows & red door flanked by green vines w/pink flowers, blue roofs, two chimneys, cole slaw decoration, 10 3/4" h. (small area of restoration to cole slaw decoration on tower).......... **476**

Rabbit, recumbent animal w/black sponge decoration, green & black line on base, 3 3/4" d., 2 1/2" h. (few small spots of wear) **476**

STAFFORDSHIRE TRANSFER WARES

The process of transfer-printing designs on earthenwares developed in England in the late 18th century and by the mid-19th century most common ceramic wares were decorated in this manner, most often with romantic European or Oriental landscape scenes, animals or flowers. The earliest such wares were printed in dark blue but a little later light blue, pink, purple, red, black, green and brown were used. A majority of these wares were produced at various English potteries right up till the turn of the century but French and other European firms also made similar pieces and all are quite collectible. The best reference on this area is Petra Williams' book Staffordshire Romantic Transfer Patterns - Cup Plates and Early Victorian China (Fountain House East, 1978).

Cake stand, footed, Wild Rose patt., blue on white, mid-19th c., 12" d., 2 1/2" h. (crazing) **$403**

Staffordshire Chamber Pitcher

Chamber pitcher, wide cylindrical body decorated on both sides w/green transfer-printed vignette of a steam packet in choppy seas above an Irish patriotic emblem titled "City of Dublin Steam Packet Company," floral device under the spout, handle & border, minor crazing & wear, 8" d., 8 1/2" h. (ILLUS.) **978**

Coffeepot, cov., footed bulbous baluster-form body w/domed cover, long angled handle & swan's-neck spout, overall design of large roses & other flowers, dark blue, small chips, ca. 1830, 11" h. **825**

Coffeepot, cov., footed bulbous ovoid body w/ringed & waisted neck w/molded rim & inset domed cover w/knob finial, swan's-neck spout & C-scroll handle, dark blue transfer of an English farmyard scene, ca. 1830, 11 1/4" h. (chips, spider crack, finial reglued) **523**

Cup & saucer, handleless, dark blue transfer of a boy fishing w/an English country house in the background, ca. 1830 (chip on foot) **165**

Cup & saucer, handleless, scene of horse-drawn sleigh, dark blue, ca. 1830 (some edge glaze flakes) **275**

Gravy boat, Winter patt., pink, 6" l. **55**

Loving cup, wide cylindrical body w/three loop handles, black transfer-printed medallions trimmed in polychrome, one titled "Autumn," one w/the farmer's arms & the third w/"Industry Produceth Wealth," early 19th c., 6" h. (stains, light crazing, spider crack in bottom) **220**

Pepper shaker, baluster-form w/domed cap, floral transfer w/an English landscape scene w/a church & fisherman, dark blue, ca. 1830, 4 5/8" h. (chips on cap) **385**

Pitcher, 7 1/2" h., bulbous ovoid body w/a shoulder tapering to a short wide flaring cupped neck w/high arched rim spout, C-scroll handle, decorated w/haying scenes, green, impressed "Adams," ca. 1840 .... **385**

Plate, 6" d., Palestine patt., pink **33**

Plate, 8" d., Canova patt., pink, T. Mayer **50**

Plate, 8" d., Carolina patt., purple, R. Hall **22**

Plate, 8 1/4" d., Palestine patt., pink **39**

Plate, 8 1/2" d., Asiatic View patt., pink, marked "FD" **28**

Plate, 9" d., Asiatic Scenery patt., pink, marked "Jacksons" **50**

Plate, 9" d., Lozere patt., light blue, Challinor **44**

Plate, 9 1/4" d., Canova patt., pink, T. Mayer **66**

Plate, 10" d., lightly scalloped flanged rim, the center w/a black transfer scene of Victorian men & women riding safety-style bicycles, titled around scene "Les Sports No. 11 - Bicyclettes," dark blue floral & stem band border trim, back marked "Terre de Fer France," ca. 1900 .... **44**

Plates, 7 1/2" d., Tyrolean patt., pink, WR & Co., pr. **66**

Platter, 11 5/8" l., oval, floral border w/fruit center, dark blue (light crazing, surface flake) **495**

Platter, 12 3/4" l., oval, floral border w/central scene of East Indian scenery w/elephant, dark blue, impressed "Rogers," ca. 1830 (pinpoint edge flakes).. **385**

Platter, 14 5/8" l., oval, scrolling foliate border w/reserves of manor houses, a center reserve of game birds, dark blue, ca. 1840 (very minor rim chips & knife marks) **633**

Platter, 15 1/2" l., two-color decorated, red floral border w/blue central reserve depicting a rural scene of an early train crossing an aqueduct w/a hillside village in the distance, England, late 19th c. (glaze crazing)... **374**

Early Staffordshire Platter

Platter, 16 1/2" l., oval, scrolling foliate border w/reserves of manor houses, a center reserve of game birds, dark blue, ca. 1840, wear & crazing (ILLUS.) **935**

Platter, 17 1/2" l., oval, medium blue transfer-printed center scene of fleet of ships, wide border decorated w/shells & seaweed, John Rogers & Sons (wear & scratches, small rim chips) **1,650**

Platter, 16 1/4 x 19", decorated w/central reserve depicting an American eagle carrying a patriotic banner in flight above a distant group of sailing vessels w/rays of the rising sun in the background, scrolled foliate border, teal green, England, mid-19th c. (minor staining, glaze wear)... **460**

Platter, 20 1/2" l., oval, center reserve w/fruits, wide floral border, dark blue, impressed "Stubbs" (wear w/stains & scratches) **1,430**

Platter, 22" l., Chinese Views patt., light blue, R & W **83**

Shaving mug, Asiatic Scenery patt., light blue, 3" h. **55**

Teapot, cov., creamware, globular form w/leaf-molded handle & spout printed in black on one side w/a scene titled "Harlequin and Columbine Discovered in an Arbor by Pierrot," the reverse w/animals in a barnyard scene, England, ca. 1770, 5" h. (chips on spout, teapot & cover rims) **633**

Undertray, round, Italian Flower Garden patt., embossed rim & handles, 9" d. **77**

STANGL POTTERY

Johann Martin Stangl, who first came to work for the Fulper Pottery in 1910 as a ceramic chemist and plant superintendent, acquired a financial interest and became president of the company in 1926. The name of the firm was changed to Stangl Pottery in 1929 and at that time much of the production was devoted to a high grade dinnerware to enable the company to survive the Depression years. One of the earliest solid-color dinnerware patterns was their Colonial line, introduced in 1926. In the 1930s it was joined by their Americana pattern. After 1942 these early patterns were followed by a wide range of hand-decorated patterns featuring flowers and fruits with a few decorated with animals or human figures.

Around 1940 a very limited edition of porcelain birds, patterned after the illustrations in John James Audubon's "Birds of America," was issued. Stangl subsequently began production of less expensive ceramic birds and these proved to be popular during the war years, 1940-46. Each bird was hand-painted and each was well marked with impressed, painted or stamped numerals which indicated the species and the size.

All operations ceased at the Trenton, New Jersey plant in 1978.

Two reference books which collectors will find helpful are The Collectors Handbook of Stangl Pottery by Norma Rehl (The Democrat Press, 1979), and Stangl Pottery by Harvey Duke (Wallace-Homestead, 1994).

Stangl Mark

BIRDS

Bird of Paradise, No. 3408, 5 1/2" h. **$134**

Stangl Broadbill Hummingbird

Broadbill Hummingbird, No. 3629, 4 1/2" h. (ILLUS.).. **165**
Cardinal, revised, No. 3444, 6 1/2" h. **220**
Cockatoo, No. 3405, 6" h................................. **54**
Cockatoo, medium, No. 3580, multi-colored, 8 7/8" h.. **120**
Cockatoo, No. 3584, 11 3/8" h...................... **325**
Cockatoos, double, No. 3405-D, 9 1/2" h. **167**
Duck, standing, No. 3431, 8" h...................... **385**
Evening Grosbeak, No. 3813, 5" h. **100**
Gray Cardinal, (Pyrrhuloxia), No. 3596, 4 3/4" h.. **65**
Hummingbirds, No. 3599D, 3 x 10 1/2", pr.. **300**
Parrot, No. 2449 .... **169**
Rieffers Hummingbird, No. 3628, 4 1/2" h.. **141**
Rufous Hummingbird, No. 3585, 3" h. **75**
Wilson Warbler, No. 3597, 3 1/2" h. **60**
Yellow Warbler, (Prothonatary), No. 3447, 5" h... **65**

DINNERWARES & ARTWARES
Ashtray, Caribbean patt...................................... **50**

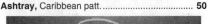

Stangl Beverage Set

Beverage set w/stand: two qt. ribbed spherical pitcher & six handleless mugs; pitcher in matte cream glaze, mugs in matte aqua glaze, nested in conforming aluminum stand, 9 1/2" h., 21" l., impressed maker's mark on base, mid-20th c., one mug w/nick, one w/hairline, minor crazing (ILLUS.) **115**
Bowl, Caribbean patt... **6**
Candleholders, Caribbean patt., pr. **30**
Coaster, Country Life patt. **25**
Cup, Country Life patt. **30**
Cup & saucer, Country Life patt. **40**
Cup & saucer, demitasse, Ranger patt........... **125**
Cup & three-part dish, Mealtime Special patt., Kiddieware line **145**
Dish, fruit, 5 1/2", Country Life patt., rooster decoration **35**
Lamp base, Fruit patt.. **250**

Mug, Golden Blossom patt. 12

Plate, 11" d., Country Life patt., farmer baling hay decoration 200

Plate, "Pony Trail" patt., h.p. boy on pony, Kiddieware line 225

Plate, 6" d., bread & butter, Country Life patt. 15

Plate, 8" d., Country Life patt., pig at fence decoration 100

Plate, 12 1/2" d., chop, Country Life patt., farmhouse decoration 275

Plate, 14 1/2" d., chop, Country Life patt.......... 300

Salt & pepper shakers, Star Flower patt., pr. 20

Vase, 13" h., model of a horse head, No. 3611 475

STONEWARE

Stoneware is essentially a vitreous pottery, impervious to water even in its unglazed state, that has been produced by potteries all over the world for centuries. Utilitarian wares such as crocks, jugs, churns and the like, were the most common productions in the numerous potteries that sprang into existence in the United States during the 19th century. These items were often enhanced by the application of a cobalt blue oxide decoration. In addition to the coarse, primarily salt-glazed stonewares, there are other categories of stoneware known by such special names as basalt, jasper and others.

Batter pail, w/bail handle, unusual cobalt blue slip-quilled tree stump design, "6" in blue script, probably Whites Utica, unsigned, ca. 1860, 6 qt., 11 3/4" h. (chips at spout & two through lines extending from rim) **$660**

Betty lamp stand, waisted cylinder w/flared foot & rim, dark greenish brown glaze, attributed to Zanesville, 3 1/2" h. (minor chips & one large chip on lip)............ 138

Bottle, cylindrical body w/a conical shoulder tapering to a swelled lip w/cobalt blue trim, impressed mark "F. Gleason - 1853," 9 5/8" h.. 193

Bottle, cylindrical body w/narrow shoulder tapering to wide, slightly flared neck, brown pebble glaze w/embossed eagle, impressed label "Vitreous Stone Bottle...American Bottle Co. Middlebury, O.," lime coated interior, 5 1/4" h................. 165

Bottle, dark brown Albany slip w/matte finish, impressed label "S. Routson, Wooster, O.," 9 1/8" h. 605

Butter churn, w/eared handles, thick brushed cobalt blue paddletail design, "N.A. White & Son, Utica, NY," ca. 1885, 5 gal., 16 1/2" h. (thick blue w/silvery black cast, in making & minor surface chip at rim) 1,705

*Butter Churn w/Double Flower Design
Five Gallon Cake Crock w/Dog*

Butter churn, swelled cylindrical form, slip-quilled cobalt blue top to bottom double flower, double "6" gal. designation in blue slip-quill, includes original dasher guide, "A.O. Wittemore Havana, NY," ca. 1870, through line on back extending from rim & small line at right ear, 18" h. (ILLUS.) 2,750

Butter churn, ovoid body tapering to a cylindrical neck w/molded rim & flanked by eared handles, slip-quilled cobalt blue large scrolling foliate cluster at the front, Worcester, Massachusetts, 19th c., 5 gal., 18 1/4" h. (minor chips, hairlines)........ 460

Butter crock, cylindrical w/molded rim, cobalt blue stenciled label "Hamilton & Jones, Greensboro, Pa.," 6 3/8" d., 5" h. (chips) 303

Cake crock, cov., cylindrical, slip-quilled cobalt blue large standing dog amid extensive ground cover, rare form & design, "West Troy Pottery," 5 gal., ca. 1880, short tight line on back & few minor interior surface chips, 13" d.,12" h. (ILLUS.).. 2,750

Stoneware Crock

Crock, slightly tapering cylindrical body w/molded rim, slip-quilled cobalt blue floral decoration, zigzag blue lines & "L.R. Potts - Captina.O.," 2 gal. (ILLUS.) 413

Crock, cylindrical w/molded rim, cobalt blue stenciled label arched at the top "Thomas Medford - Stoves - Queensware - etc. - Huntington, W. Va.," freehand blue squiggle band at top & plain band around base, late 19th c., 8 1/4" d., 6 3/4" h. 440

Bennington Stoneware Crock

Crock, cylindrical w/molded rim & applied eared handles, decorated w/a slip-quilled cobalt blue house flanked by fencing & a tree, impressed "J & E Norton, Bennington, Vermont," 1850-61, 7 1/4" h. (ILLUS.)...................... **2,760**

Crock, ovoid w/applied & open handles, impressed & tooled design around rim, incised & blue accented double scalloped design in front, blue accents at name & handles, "S. Amboy, New Jersey," ca. 1805, almost invisible through line in front, 9 1/2" h. **2,530**

Early Stoneware Crock

Crock, ovoid w/wide cylindrical neck, applied loop handles, decorated w/a slip-quilled cobalt blue blooming flower on one side & a wave design on the other, mid-19th c., cracks, minor chips, 4 gal., 14 1/2" h. (ILLUS.) **173**

Cylindrical Crock w/Swan Design

Crock, cylindrical w/molded rim & eared handles, brushed blue swan design, ca. 1870, unsigned, attributed to Pottery

Works, Little West 12th St., NY, 1 gal., 7 1/2" h. (ILLUS.)...................................... **1,045**

Crock, ovoid w/molded rim, blue accent stripes & gallon designation in blue brush strokes, "R.T. Williams, New Geneva, PA," ca. 1860, 1 1/2 gal., 9" h. **303**

Crock, cylindrical w/molded rim & eared handles, brushed cobalt blue flower design, "A.O. Whittemore, Havana, NY," ca. 1870, 2 gal., 8 1/2" h. (kiln burn/stack mark at base in making) **165**

Crock, w/molded rim & eared handles, simple slip-quilled flower design & "2", "Geddes, NY," ca. 1860, 2 gal., 9" h. (rim chip & short through line on back, some design fry) **143**

Crock, cylindrical w/molded rim & eared handles, slip-quilled cobalt blue chicken pecking corn on ground cover, chicken heading downhill, "New York Stoneware Co., Fort Edward, NY," ca. 1880, 2 gal., 9 1/2" h. **1,210**

Crock, cylindrical w/molded rim & eared handles, slip-quilled cobalt blue decoration of a traveler viewing a direction sign reading "11 miles to Hartford," marked by Seymour Bosworth, Hartford, Connecticut, 3 gal., 10" h. (chips, prefiring dent) **690**

Crock, cylindrical w/molded rim & eared handles, slip-quilled cobalt blue bird & stylized "3" design, "S. Hart Fulton," ca. 1877, glaze spider on back, 3 gal., 10 1/2" h. **578**

Crock, cylindrical w/eared handles, brushed flower decoration w/signature, very early, ca. 1850, short-lived Buffalo maker, "P. Mugler & Co., Buffalo, NY," 3 gal., 11" h. (one very minor surface chip at base) **330**

"N. Clark & Co., Mt. Morris" Crock

Crock, ovoid w/eared handles, brushed "3" & accent plume design, very uncommon maker, "N. Clark & Co., Mt. Morris," ca. 1840, few minor rim chips & minor interior lime staining, 3 gal., 12 1/2" h. (ILLUS.).. **303**

Crock, cylindrical w/molded rim & eared handles, thick brushed cobalt blue hops vine design, "J. Fisher & Co., Lyons, NY," ca. 1880, 4 gal., 11 1/2" h. **440**

Crock, cylindrical w/eared handles & slip-quilled cluster of grapes framed w/large leaves & vine, uncommon size for this potter, "W.A. MacQuoid & Co., Pottery

Works Little West St., NY," ca. 1865, 5 gal., 12" h. (hairline at ear on right side) ... **1,320**

Crock, cylindrical w/molded rim & eared handles, slip-quilled cobalt blue large bird on plume design, "Reidinger & Caire, Pokeepsie, NY," ca. 1870, 5 gal., 12" h. **908**

Rare Stoneware Flask

Flask, salt-glazed flattened ovoid body tapering to a short neck w/molded mouth, the sides incised "New York July th4 (sic) 1789" & "I. McKINZIE (sic) July 1789," flanked by cobalt blue leafy branches, one w/flower, attributed to Henry Remmey, New York, ca. 1789 (ILLUS.).. **12,650**

Inkwell, figural bust of old woman wearing bonnet, tan glaze w/brown highlights, 2 1/4" h. (wear & small chips)...................... **275**

Jar, cov., swelled cylindrical form w/eared handles, unique cobalt blue eyedropper application to form petals on this flower design, "Clark & Co., Rochester, NY," ca. 1850, 1 gal., 9 1/2" h. (rim chip in front) **413**

Jar, ovoid body w/thick molded rim & applied eared handles, cobalt blue slip-quilled polka dot bird looking backwards, impressed label "W. Roberts, Binghamton, N.Y. 2," 9 1/2" h...................................... **688**

Jar, semi-ovoid body w/applied shoulder handles, cobalt blue brushed floral design w/tulip on one side & flowering tree on the other, impressed "S. Bell 1/1/2," 10 1/4" h. (chips) **1,210**

Jar, semi-ovoid w/molded rim & eared handles, cobalt blue stenciled label "Knox, Haught & Co., Shinnston, W.Va." above leafy sprig w/further free-hand blue leafy bands around the top & "3" at the bottom, late 19th c., 3 gal., 12 3/4" h............. **1,018**

Jar, slightly ovoid w/heavy molded rim & applied eared handles, stenciled cobalt blue front label for "Williams & Reppert, Greensboro, Pa." above a free-hand "3," free-hand blue bands at top & base, late 19th c., 3 gal., 14" h. (rim chips).................. **248**

Three Gallon Jar w/Brushed Cherries

Jar, swelled cylindrical form w/eared handles, brushed cobalt blue cherries w/two large leaves & stem design & "3," marked "W.A. MacQuoid & Co. Pottery Works Little W. 12th St. NY," ca. 1870, age spiders on back, 3 gal., 14" h. (ILLUS.)... **1,375**

Jar, cov., eared handles, unsigned, advertising, slip-quilled w/large dotted bird on top of flower, long tail & filled wing, impressed "Hiram Partridge & Son, #8 Court St. Indigo Paste," attributed to Crafts Factory, Whatley, Mass., ca. 1860, 4 gal., 15 1/2" h. (professional restorations to two tight lines extending from rim).. **798**

Jug, miniature unglazed handled form w/Albany slip interior, pencil or pen scribed on base but difficult to make out, ca. 1870, 3" h **72**

Jug, bold ovoid body tapering to a small short tooled neck, applied strap shoulder handle, impressed label "Charlestown," grey salt glaze w/olive bands, early 19th c., 10 1/4" h. (minor edge chips on base, surface chips).. **220**

Jug, semi-ovoid w/blue slip-quilled cobalt blue inscription "S.F. Eagan 141 Seneca St. Buffalo N.Y.," J. Fisher, Lyons, NY, ca. 1880, 1 gal., 10 1/2" h. (glaze drip in front in making & large rust color stain on back) **132**

Jug, ovoid w/brushed flower design & very deeply incised w/double snake design, "H. & G. Nash, Utica, NY," ca. 1835, 1 gal., 11" h. extremely rare (minor glaze spider on back) **1,000**

Jug, ovoid w/brushed decoration, "D. Roberts & Co., Utica," ca. 1828, 2 gal., 12" h. (overall staining & glaze spiders at spout) **330**

Jug, ovoid w/brushed cobalt blue flower design, "N. White Utica," ca. 1840, 2 gal.,13" h. (glaze burn & stack marks in making) **275**

Jug, ovoid w/incised leaves & blue accented cluster of cherries, blue accents at handle, New York City origin, ca. 1820, unsigned, stack mark/kiln burn in making, 2 gal., 13 1/2" h., rare **880**

Jug, semi-ovoid, slip-quilled cobalt blue "2" & "Lyons", marked "J. Fisher, Lyons, NY," ca. 1880, 2 gal., 13 1/2" h. (surface chip at spout)..................................... **715**

Jug, semi-ovoid w/cobalt blue signature sunflower design, well-proportioned, "John Burger, Rochester," ca. 1865, 2 gal., 13 1/2" h. (very tight spider line on side) **908**

Jug, semi-ovoid w/cobalt blue slip-quilled bird on foliage, scrolls, impressed "Lack & Van Arsdale, Cornwall, C-2," 14" h. (minor chips, stains) **385**

Jug, ovoid, impressed w/a spread-winged eagle atop a cannon & "Charlestown," Charlestown, Massachusetts, 19th c., 14 1/2" h. (chips, kiln burns)........................ **374**

Jug, semi-ovoid w/small molded mouth & applied handle, cobalt blue brushed floral design & impressed label "Cowden & Wilcox, Harrisburg Pa 3," 3 gal., 14 3/4" h. (minor lip chips)............................ **275**

Jug w/Wooden Stopper

Jug, w/carved wooden stopper, semi-ovoid, cobalt blue leaf & vine design, top to bottom, "Edmands & Co.," ca. 1870, stone ping & long glaze spider lines on side, kiln burn on front in making, 3 gal., 15" h. (ILLUS.)... **220**

Jug, ovoid, incised & blue-trimmed flower at top, blue accents at name & handle, extremely rare mark, "P. Cross, Hartford," ca. 1805, 2 gal., 16" h. (professional restoration to age lines throughout & surface chips at the spout) **990**

Jug, tapering cylindrical body w/applied shoulder handles, cobalt blue brushed vintage below Xs & dots, impressed "4," 4 gal., 16" h. (hairlines) **303**

Jug, ovoid, two handled, cobalt blue brushed tree design, "I. Seymour Troy Factory," very early maker's mark, ca. 1810, 4 gal., 18" h. (professional restoration to freeze cracks up from base in front) **715**

Meat tenderizer, dated 1877, original handle, 9" l. **110**

Milk bowl, deep slightly flaring cylindrical sides w/wide molded rim, cobalt blue stenciled label "A.P. Donaghho, Parkersburg, W.Va.," 12 3/4" d., 6 1/2" h. (professional repair, slight rim chip)................... **308**

Milk pan, brushed cobalt blue three-leaf decoration, rim pouring lip, ca. 1850, unsigned, two minor glaze separations in making & small surface chip at rim, 1 gal., 4" h. (ILLUS.)....................................... **275**

Gallon Milk Pan

Model of a lamb, relief-molded reclining lamb, blue accents highlight ears, blue accent at the front foot, hand-incised detailed facial features, found in & attributed to Lyons, NY, ca. 1860, unsigned, extremely rare, 2" h., 2 1/2" l., ... **825**

Pitcher, 8 1/2" h., unglazed grey clay w/brushed brown Albany slip-quilled decoration, New Geneva Pottery, unsigned, ca. 1860, 1 qt.............................. **853**

Slip-quilled Ovoid Pitcher

Pitcher, 9" h., ovoid, slip-quilled cobalt zigzag, lines & dot decoration, unsigned, probably Albany pottery, ca. 1850, surface chip at base in front and tight line at rim, on side, 1 gal. (ILLUS.) **523**

Pitcher, 10" h., brushed cobalt blue tulip decoration, "Burger & Lang, Rochester, NY," 1 gal., ca. 1870 (some surface wear & chips along the rim from use)........... **605**

Pitcher, 11" h., handled, w/three beautiful roses on front & blue accents around base and top, Pottery Works, Little West 12th Street NY, unsigned, ca. 1870, 1 gal. **2,530**

Pitcher, 11 1/2" h., bulbous ovoid body w/tall cylindrical neck w/pinched rim spout & applied strap handle, colbalt blue brushed foliage design, impressed label "M. & T. Miller, Newport, Pa." (chips) **1,540**

Pitcher, 13 1/4" h., bulbous ovoid body w/a tall cylindrical neck w/pinched rim spout, applied strap handle, brushed cobalt blue large blossoms, leafy twigs & impressed "2," 2 gal. **880**

Preserving jar, cylindrical tapering slightly to a molded rim, cobalt blue stenciled label for A.P. Donaghho, Fredericktown, Pa. above a large spread-winged eagle, 9 1/2" h. **935**

Preserving jar, swelled cylindrical form, brushed thick cobalt blue flower design & blue accents at ears, "Penn Yan," ca. 1860, 1 gal., 9 1/2" h. (very minor surface chip at rim) **198**

Preserving jar, swelled cylindrical body w/cobalt blue stenciled flowers & "Jas Hamilton & Co., 2," 11" h. (crooked & hairlines) **248**

Preserving Jar with Wreath Design

Preserving jar, cov., swelled cylindrical form w/eared handles, thick brushed cobalt blue wreath design & "2," marked "T. Harrington, Lyons," ca. 1860, 2 gal., 11 1/2" h. (ILLUS.) **633**

Preserving jar, w/original lid, eared handles, stenciled sign of friendship - a handshake in thick blue, "Somerset Potters Works," ca. 1880, few rim chips & small tight line over right ear, 4 gal., 14 1/2" h. **413**

Stove leveler, flaring pedestal below a wide cupped rim, brushed cobalt blue leaf bands, 4 1/2" h. (hairline, chips) **440**

Water Cooler with Bird on Plume

Water cooler, cov., slip-quilled bird on plume design, body has blue accented deep incised lines, "New York Stoneware Co.," ca. 1870, 4 gal., 15 1/2" h. (ILLUS.) **1,155**

Ornate Salt Glazed Filter

Water filter, cov., marked "Perfection Filter Manufactured by the Central NY Pottery Utica NY," in relief & blue accented, opposite side w/embossed leaf design accented in blue, relief-molded cupids holding banner around the name, gargoyle handles, age line throughout base & one very tight 3" through line at rim, 10" h. (ILLUS.) **688**

TECO POTTERY

Teco Pottery was actually the line of art pottery introduced by the American Terra Cotta and Ceramic Company of Terra Cotta (Crystal Lake), Illinois in 1902. Founded by William D. Gates in 1881, American Terra Cotta originally produced only bricks and drain tile. Because of superior facilities for experimentation, including a chemical laboratory, the company was able to develop an art pottery line, favoring a matte green glaze in the earlier years but eventually achieving a wide range of colors including a metallic lustre glaze and a crystalline glaze. Though some hand-thrown pottery was made, Gates favored a molded ware because it was less expensive to produce. By 1923, Teco Pottery was no longer being made and in 1930 American Terra Cotta and Ceramic Company was sold. A book on the topic is Teco: Art Pottery of the Prairie School, by Sharon S. Darling (Erie Art Museum, 1990).

Teco Mark

Bowl, 4 1/2" d., 2 1/2" h., low squatty wide bulbous sides w/throwing ridges, a wide shoulder curving up to a closed rim, deep raspberry matte finish, impressed mark (short hairline) **$220**

Bowl, 8 1/2" d., 2 1/2" h., a wide flat-bottomed squatty bulbous lower body curving upward to a wide flat mouth, upper portion w/a green matte glaze shading into a heavy charcoal glaze, impressed mark **385**

Bowl, 9" d., 2" h., wide flat bottom w/shallow rounded sides & closed molded wide mouth, overall green matte glaze, impressed marks **605**

Ewer, bulbous tapering ovoid body w/the wide shoulder centered by a short small neck w/a deeply folded tricorner rim & loop handle from rim to shoulder, unusual matte brown glaze, 4" h. (stilt chips) **154**

Jardiniere, wide ovoid body tapering to a short flaring neck, molded around the lower body w/eight lily pads below a row of water lily blossoms alternating w/pointed arrowroot leaf buttress-form open handles attaching to the neck rim, smooth matte green glaze, stamped mark, 9 3/4 x 10" (some restoration) **12,100**

Pitcher, 9" h., corseted-form w/an organic wishbone handle & an undulating rim, matte green glaze, impressed marks **1,100**

Vase, 4" h., 4" d., squatty bulbous ovoid body tapering to a small flared neck, smooth matte green glaze, stamped mark **2,640**

Vase, 4 3/4" h., compressed bulbous base w/wide horizontally ribbed cylindrical neck & flat rim, green matte glaze, marked twice on base **495**

Vase, 6 1/4" h., 5" d., bulbous ovoid body, the rounded shoulder tapering to a short cylindrical neck w/slightly flaring rim, matte green glaze, tight hairline from rim, stamped mark **303**

Vase, 6 1/2" h., 2 1/4" d., slender cylindrical body tapering to a flaring rim, buttressed handles down the sides, rich yellow matte finish, impressed mark **1,045**

Vase, 7 1/4" h., tall tapering cylindrical form w/flared & molded rim, four squared buttress handles from the rim to the edge of the base, seafoam green glaze, impressed twice w/mark, ca. 1910 .... **1,840**

Vase, 9" h., tall swelled cylindrical body tapering slightly to the widely flaring neck, small squared shoulder handles, overall dark green matte glaze w/heavy charcoaling, impressed mark **770**

Vase, 11" h., tall slender swelled cylindrical body tapering at the shoulder to a slender flaring trumpet neck, overall terra cotta-colored matte glaze, impressed mark **495**

Vase, 11 1/4" h., footed bulbous base tapering to a tall cylindrical neck w/flared rim, four whiplash handles from base to below rim, matte green glaze (restoration to small chip at base & on two handles) **1,870**

Vase, 11 3/4" h., a large cupped tulip blossom framed by four heavy buttress leaf-molded supports forming the squared body, matte green glaze, designed by Fernand Moreau, stamped "Teco" (invisible repair to small chip at rim) **4,125**

Tall Teco Vase with Leaves

Vase, 11 3/4" h., footed wide cylindrical body w/trumpet-form neck, body covered w/relief-molded narrow leaves & forming handles, smooth matte green glaze, stamped "TECO" (ILLUS.) **16,500**

Vase, 13" h., 6 1/4" d., footed swelled cylindrical body w/a narrow shoulder to the short flaring neck, smooth matte green glaze, impressed mark **1,100**

TEPLITZ - AMPHORA

In the late 19th and early 20th centuries numerous potteries operated in the vicinity of Teplitz in the Bohemian region of what was Austria but is now the Czech Republic. They included Amphora, RStK, Stellmacher, Ernst Wahliss, Paul Dachsel, Imperial and lesser-known potteries such as Johanne Maresh, Julius Dressler, Bernard Bloch and Heliosine.

The number of collectors in this category is growing while availability of better or rarer pieces is shrinking. Consequently, prices for all pieces are appreciating, while those for better and/or rarer pieces, including restored rare pieces, are soaring.

The price ranges presented here are retail. They presume mint or near mint condition or, in the case of very rare damaged pieces, proper restoration. They reflect such variables as rarity, design, quality of glaze, size, and the intangible "in-vogue factor." They are the prices that knowledgeable sellers will charge and knowledgeable collectors will pay.

Teplitz-Amphora Marks

Bowl, 10 1/4" w., 5 1/4" h., consisting of two wonderfully detailed high-glazed fish swimming around the perimeter, each executed in the Art Nouveau style w/flowing fins & tails, tentacles drip from their mouths, high-relief w/gold & reddish highlights, rare theme, impressed in ovals "Amphora" & "Austria" w/a crown... **$3,500-4,000**

Bowl, 14 1/2" w., 4 3/8" h., an exotic Paul Dachsel design of calla lilies growing out of stems which originate at the bottom & gracefully extend around the sides to fully developed calla lilies at each end, in the center on each side are several 'jewels' w/abstract leaves of high-glazed green w/gold overtones,mottled texture w/'jeweled' greenish gold embellishments, stamped over glaze w/intertwined "PD - Turn-Teplitz," handwritten over glaze "0/45" **4,500-5,500**

Bust of a Sultry Princess

Bust of a woman, perhaps Sarah Bernhardt in the role of a sultry princess, magnificently finished w/plentiful gold & bronze glazes w/without excessive fussiness, mounted on a base featuring a maiden on a horse in a forest setting, the bust seemingly supported by stag horns protruding from each side, impressed "Amphora" & "Austria" in a lozenge w/a crown, 1431 & "A" in blue, 13 1/2" w., 18 1/4" h. (ILLUS.)........................... **3,000-4,000**

Bust of Richard Wagner, the somber looking composer mounted on a pedestal emblazoned "Wagner" on the front, the head w/a beautiful soft flesh-toned Amphora glaze, the pedestal w/a shriveled tan & white glaze w/shades of olive green highlights, one of a rare series of composers, impressed "Amphora" & "Austria" in ovals w/a crown, a circle w/"Imperial Amphora" & "250 -1," 19 3/4" h. **2,000-2,500**

Candlestick, rare Amphora piece w/many of their special characteristics including jewels, spider webs, butterflies & wonderful soft muted Amphora glazes w/reds, blues & gold, a large handle extends from near the top of the socket,

four smaller handles extend up & outward from the base, eleven jewels of various sizes & colors, impressed "Amphora" in an oval & a crown & "28," 14" h. **3,500-4,000**

Centerpiece, an expansive bowl w/a 'jeweled' effect along the rim, supported by two seated male lions w/fine details, a round base w/a 'jeweled' effect, the underside of the bowl suggests a tropical jungle, a better example of a design featuring animals supporting a bowl, multicolored 'jewels,' lion in a natural brownish glaze, stamped "Amphora - Made in Czecho-slovakia" in an oval, "734 - 261" in black ink, 12" w., 9 5/8" h. **1,000-1,500**

Clock, table model, a fantasy stork, similar to Martin Bros. birds, stands next to a clock dial framed by Art Nouveau-style leaves, fine detailing, soft brownish tan glaze, rare, raised rectangle w/factory logo & "AK-Turn," impressed "319," 13" h. (ILLUS.)................................ **3,500-4,000**

Fantasy Stork Clock

Ewer, an Art Nouveau design w/extraordinary detail combining a reticulated handle suggesting Paul Dachsel & varied circles on the body suggesting Gustav Klimt, a reticulated top, many 'jewels' of different colors & sizes randomly located over the body suggesting a spectrum of stars in the milky way, unusual gold bud spout, high-glazed blue garlands randomly draped about the body, heavy gold trim on the upper part of the handle, top & spout, a subdued gold trim extends down the handle to & around the bottom where there is an abstract tree design, very difficult to produce, rare, impressed "Amphora" in a circle & "40 -537," 14" h. **4,000-5,000**

Ewer, gilt-trimmed ivory ground w/enamel-decorated birds in the paneled sides, Teplitz mark, Czechoslovakia, early 20th c., 10 5/8" h. **345**

Figure group, a small fine scenic figural group w/a rooster & hen perched side by side overlooking a pond, a small gold frog climbing into the pond, gives a barnyard feeling, soft muted shades of tan w/highlights of gold, a realistic theme & valuable because of the small size, impressed "Amphora" in an oval & illegible numbers, 6 1/2" w., 7 3/4" h. **750-1,000**

Humidor, cov., figural, a fantasy piece featuring a large globe representing the world being shot from a tiny canon & caught by a jester lying on his back, the jester reputedly represents a prime minister of the time, a hat at the top of the globe forms the handles, soft muted grey Amphora glaze, rare, impressed "Amphora" in an oval & "4216," 14" w., 9" h. (ILLUS.)................................. **3,000-4,000**

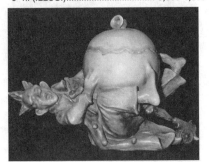

Unique Figural Humidor

Humidor, cov., figural, a massive Native American theme composed of three Indian heads w/high-glazed pink & green feathered headdresses, 'jeweled' & draping beaded necklaces on two, a draping necklace of animal teeth on the third, high-glaze green & cobalt blue finial handle on a decorative mixed glazed top, basic color of Campina brown w/much contrasting high-glaze in green, pink, brown & blue, rare, impressed ovals w/"Amphora" & "Austria," a crown & "Imperial - Amphora - Turn" in a circle & "S-1633-46," 10 1/2" h. **2,000-3,000**

Pitcher, 12" h., cov., footed, modeled as a stylized fish, ribbed body decorated w/gilt outlined yellow flowers, fish scale texture near rim, spout & lid form mouth w/splashes of water at top of lid, stamped "R S + K, Turn-Teplitz, made in Austria" **316**

Plaque, a large oval shape centered by an Art Nouveau lady in high-relief attired in a luminescent pink dress blowing a double-horned musical instrument. She is seated on a rocky ledge. The border of the plaque consists of garlands of flowers & leaves in high-relief, especially the buds, basic color of seafoam green, the surrounding florals in greens & tans, impressed "Ernst Wahliss," 17 x 19 1/2" **1,400-1,800**

Plaque, terra cotta rectangular form depicting a very stylized beautifully coiffed Art Nouveau lady in profile in high-relief, her unique elegance suggesting a lady of high social stature, the borders are garlanded leaves & buds in high-relief, organic mossy shades of green, soft pur-

ples, tans & warm browns, impressed marks "Ernst Wahliss - Made in Austria - Turn - Wien - 157," 11 3/4 x 17" **1,200-1,500**

Vase, 5 3/4" h., figural, elegantly executed Paul Dachsel creation w/a greenish cast & numerous vertical ribs extending up from the base, four intertwined gold-bodied dragonflies form a reticulated top, immediately below a series of smaller dragonflies encircle the vase, two multi-layered handles within handles complete the design, stamped over glaze w/intertwined "PD - Turn - Teplitz," impressed "104".. **2,000-2,500**

Vase, 7 1/2" h., a playful expression of Amphora w/a pink snake draped around the body of the bulbous vase & extending to the top where its delicate tongue protrudes, a subtle leaf design extends around the bottom, the pink color of the snake distinguishes this piece from more drab versions, impressed in ovals "Amphora" & "Austria," & "4114 - 52".................................... **1,500-1,800**

Vase, 7 3/4" h., round bulbous shape, decorated w/a profile of a young girl w/long flowing brownish hair full of numerous multicolored high-glazed flowers w/gold touches, all surrounded by a brownish tan forest scene, finely executed, impressed "Amphora - 663," overglaze red mark "RStK - Turn - Teplitz - Made in Austria".. **1,700-2,200**

Vase, 8 3/4" h., four-paneled high-shouldered squared form w/a front-faced Mucha-style Art Nouveau princess portrait, elaborate gold enameling against a landscape decorated w/blue & purple trees w/gold highlights above a base decorated w/Paul Dachsel-style abstract red flowers in a green base, impressed "Amphora" in oval & "579-40," red "RStK Austria" overglaze mark, artist mark "Fr" in gold overglaze **3,000-3,500**

Vase, 9" h., a bulbous Paul Dachsel forest scene w/reticulated gold top & varied reddish mushrooms in high-relief encircling the bottom, a production mold but hand-painted to produce a uniquely different forest scene, stamped over the glaze w/intertwined "PD - Turn - Teplitz," impressed "1106 -2," blue overglaze "094".. **3,000-4,000**

Rare Amphora Cat Head Vase

Vase, 9" h., wide bulbous tapering form, rare form suggesting an inverted Tiffany lamp shade, four large Persian cat heads molded in full relief & projecting from the sides w/a forest of abstract trees w/160-170 opal-like translucent 'jewels' symbolizing fruits, the jewels in various sizes & shades of opal blue mounted in gold surrounds, heavy gold rim, the tree branches extending to the jewels on a background of Klimt-like subtle gold circles, holes behind the jewels permit candlelight or an electric bulb to illuminate the jewels, cat heads finished in a soft pinkish gold w/traces of green & gold highlights on the ears, impressed "Amphora - Austria" in a lozenge, a crown & "8183 - 28" (ILLUS.)...................................... **12,000-14,000**

Vase, 9 7/8" h., a Paul Dachsel abstract design w/a reticulated geometric top & a reticulated handle within a reticulated handle sweeping in an arc from the top to the bottom w/abstract tendrils extending around the bottom of the body & back of the handles, several high-glazed green pods resembling teardrops of various sizes hang from the abstract handle, vines & a center funnel, the top rim & top of handle finished in gold, rare, stamped over glaze w/intertwined "PD - Turn - Teplitz" **3,500-4,000**

Vase, 10" h., a Paul Dachsel abstract architectural style w/a geometric design consisting of a rounded bottom from which four handles begin flush & extend to the top of the rim where they flare open, each handle suggests an abstract candelabrum w/charcoal flames rising from each, finished in iridescent gunmetal grey w/charcoal black sheen touches, gold wash on top, moderne in all respects even though produced in the 1904-10 period, rare form, stamped over glaze w/intertwined "PD - Turn - Teplitz," impressed "1049" **4,500-5,500**

Vase, 10 5/8" h., figural, in the form of a prancing male lion, snarling open mouth, standing on a broad base narrowing at the top, numerous concentric circles form bands around the top & bottom, lion reflects an iridescent gold, green & rose combination of color, body of base in metallic green w/undertones of blues & splotches of reds, impressed "Amphora" & "Austria" in oval, a crown & "500-52," handwritten in black ink over glaze "CB - 613417," estimated value without jewels, $1,500 to 2,000, value w/jewels **2,500-3,500**

Vase, 11" h., four gold Persian cat heads adorn a center-pillared body w/four surrounding gold 'jeweled' arms extending from each cat head to the base, metallic blue w/a gold wash, cobalt blue 'jewels,' rare design, more common versions have cabochons inside animal heads, marked "Amphora" & "Austria" in ovals, a crown & impressed "Imperial" circle mark & "11677 - 51" **2,000-3,000**

Vase, 11 1/4" h., tapering lobed ovoid form of exceptional Art Nouveau design w/numerous 'jewels,' spider webs & two butterflies w/heavy pierced extended handles suggesting a larger butterfly, 17

'jewels' in varying sizes & colors, red abstract circles drape from the gold-edged top, soft muted tan, red, blue & green glazes w/gold iridescence, impressed "Amphora" & "Austria" in ovals, a crown & "8551 -42," red "RStK Austria" overglaze mark (ILLUS.).... **4,000-5,000**

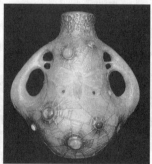

Ornate Jeweled Art Nouveau Vase

Vase, 11 1/2" h., wicker basket-form w/round loop handles extending up from the rim, large relief-molded iridescent white blossoms, rose leaves & green buds on front w/rose band at rim & base, shaded tan ground w/touches of fired-on gold, impressed marks & "Austria Amphora - 115 - 37" **550**

Vase, 12" h., figural, three standing cockatoos, fully feathered, extend around the body of the vase, their plumes rising over the rim, very detailed w/glossy glaze, subtle color mix of blues, greens & tans w/brown streaks, semi-rare, impressed "Amphora" & "Austria" in ovals, a crown & Imperial circle & "11986 - 56".. **1,500-2,000**

Vase, 12 3/4" h., elegant form consisting of four beautifully veined tall leaves forming the funnel of the vase w/the stem of each leaf forming a handle extending into the bottom, each stem issues an additional flat leaf extending across the bottom, leaves finished in a mottled orange w/touches of greens & yellows w/gold overtones, although marked by Ernst Wahliss the design indicates the work of Paul Dachsel who worked at various Amphora factories, rare, stamped over glaze "EW" red mark, impressed "9491," "9786a - 10" in ink over the glaze... **3,000-3,500**

Vase, 13" h., wide-shouldered tapering cylindrical body, a fantasy design by Paul Dachsel worthy of the description "enchanted forest," the design consists of slender molded abstract trees extending from the narrow base to the bulbous top, lovely heart-shaped leaves extend in clusters from the various branches, trees in muted green, the leaves in pearlized off-white w/gold framing, the symbolic sky in rich red extending between the trees from the bottom to the top, rare, intertwined "PD" mark rubbed off (ILLUS.) **5,500-6,500**

Dachsel "Enchanted Forest" Vase

Vase, 14" h., figural, a fantasy dragon featuring two flaring wings, one extending practically from the top to the bottom of the body, the other well above & beyond the rim, creature w/a convoluted tail, spine & teeth, the head w/open mouth positioned at top of the vase, bluish green gold iridescence, glazes vary from a flat tan to a variety of very iridescent colors, made in 14" & 17" size, impressed "Amphora" in oval, illegible numbers, large size w/better glazes, $6,500, 14" size w/drab glazes **3,000**

Vase, 14 5/8" h., a figural fantasy piece, a different variety of dragon vase but not highly glazed, the dragon is mostly brown but it features a well-defined head, body, clawed feet & tail, a snake tongue drapes from the mouth, hideously beautiful, the body contrasts nicely w/the metallic greenish blue iridescence of the mottled background, found in various glazes, impressed "Amphora" & "Austria" in oval, a crown & "C 4543" **3,000-4,000**

Vase, 15 1/2" h., cascades of golden grapes stream down on all sides between four funnel necks, the central funnel projecting skyward, this funnel design suggests Paul Dachsel, especially desirable because the piece is viewable from any angle, metallic purplish glaze w/metallic gold highlights containing numerous little gold circles, marked "Amphora" & "Austria" in ovals, a crown & "3680" **1,500-2,000**

Vase, 16" h., bulbous ovoid body tapering to a slender flaring lobed reticulated neck, outswept loop handles at the lower sides, shimmering burnished gold ground w/red touches, adorned randomly w/twenty large variously colored 'jewels,' one handle in red, the other in gold, overall molded vertical ribbing, rare form, impressed "Amphora" in an oval, crown, old "RStK" mark & "3349" (ILLUS.) **7,500-8,000**

Rare Jeweled Amphora Vase

Vase, 16 1/2" h., a massive fantasy piece w/a large golden iridescent octopus around the bottom, its tentacles extending around the sides & up to the top where they grab a large swimming sea horse, a particularly rare style of octopus w/only one known at present, impressed "Amphora" & "Austria" in ovals, a crown & "4597 - 50" **6,000-7,000**

Vase, 16 1/2" h., fine Paul Dachsel creation in an undulating free-form design consisting of several abstract trees extending from the bottom to the top where a branch wraps around the top & then down dividing into other branches w/a series of red-glazed leaves, numerous white 'jewels' suggesting seeds & seed pods attached to the branches & trunks, red leaves w/gold-tinged ends, very rare form, stamped over the glaze w/intertwined "PD - Turn - Teplitz," impressed "1115" **5,000-6,000**

Vase, 17" h., massive bulbous bottle-form w/four finely detailed gold-finished owl heads projecting from the sides surrounded by brambles, leaves & many clusters of berries & numerous 'jewels' of various sizes & colors interspersed among the brambles, unusual & complicated design, some similar pieces w/other animal heads exist but few survive intact, rare, impressed "Amphora" in oval, a crown & "8160" (ILLUS.) **8,500-9,500**

Rare Owl Head Vase

Vase, 17 1/8" h., tall Art Nouveau form gradually tapering to a narrower top, the bottom w/seven delicate female heads w/long flowing hair emerging from a swirling ocean, tan w/highlights of gold & green, a similar example found in a Berlin museum, marks include a raised Art Nouveau girl's head & "Amphora" in a raised rectangle, red "RStK Austria" mark over the glaze, impressed illegible numbers, handwritten "1081 - L - 372" over the glaze **2,000-3,000**

Rare Reticulated Amphora Vase

Vase, 17 1/2" h., an important reticulated piece composed of a basket-like vase within a vase elaborately entwined w/swooping gold handles joined in the middle, numerous varied colored 'jewels' around the sides, viewed through the reticulation a high-glazed blue swirly design w/gold highlights is seen, the exterior w/a metallic bluish green w/gold wash & gold highlights, high-glazed gold rim, only one known so far, impressed "Amphora" & "Austria" in ovals, a crown & "3791 -45" (ILLUS.).................. **12,000-14,000**

Vase, 18 1/4" h., a fantasy piece w/a coiling beast not really a dragon, snake nor octopus but w/characteristics of each, finished in a golden color w/gold highlights, the head extends above the top, the body entwines down around the sides, mottled metallic purplish blue background, impressed "Amphora" & "Austria" in ovals, a crown & "4539 -50," values vary w/the glaze (ILLUS.) **3,500-4,500**

Amphora Dragon Vase

Vase, 20" h., footed tall wide cylindrical body w/squatty bulbous base & closed-in rim, mottled mauve glaze w/relief-molded dragon figure in yellow, tan & gilt glaze conforming entirely around body & rim, minor restorations to chips, impressed "AMPHORA" in a lozenge, a crown & "4548 50" (ILLUS.) **5,750**

Vase, 20" h., tall slightly tapering cylindrical form w/a widely flared base, boldly molded pine cones hang around the top section from symbolic green trees divided by red indented vertical panels, a Paul Dachsel Secessionist design, rare, stamped over the glaze w/intertwined "PD - Turn - Teplitz" & impressed "2038 - 6" **7,000-8,000**

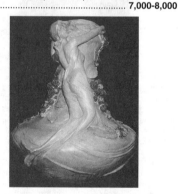

Massive Amphora Mermaid Vase

Vase, 21 1/2" h., portrait-type, a very large profiled Sarah Bernhardt portrait inspired by Gustav Klimt featuring a majestic bird headdress w/eleven 'jewels' of various sizes & colors, the figure w/long flowing hair streaming from under the headdress to her shoulders, below her neck is a jeweled butterfly, on one side a golden sun rises from the ocean emitting numerous golden rays, bluish green metallic background w/heavy gold detail, impressed "Amphora" & "Austria" in a lozenge, a crown & "02047 - 28".................... **14,000-16,000**

Somber, Eerie Dragon Vase

Vase, 22" h., figural, a somber swampy-green dragon encircles the tall body several times, his wings spread like a cobra's hood, leering down hungrily at a frog restrained by his tail at the base, this piece can be found finished in other colors including red & tan, this eerie somber look compensates for what the glaze may lack, impressed "Amphora" & "Austria" in ovals, a crown & "4536 - 6" (ILLUS. previous page) **4,000-5,000**

Vases, 10 1/2" h., footed bulbous ovoid body tapering to a slender cylindrical neck w/a flattened disk rim, painted in shades of purple, pink, green, blue, black & gilt w/the bust of a young maiden wearing a voluminous hood surmounted by a Byzantine crown surrounded by a gilt aura, a lower border of roses, the crown & roses w/applied bosses, one printed w/mark "Turn - Teplitz - Bohemia - R. St. - Made in Austria," the other impressed "Amphora," each impressed "2014 -28," pr. **6,900**

Amphora Sea Life Vases

Vases, 19 1/2" h., tapering cylindrical form w/cushion foot & spiky rim, applied w/a realistically modeled octopus capturing a crab, covered in a sponged blue, white & yellow glaze, the creatures in beige & burnt orange, printed in blue "AMPHORA - Made in Czecho-Slovakia" & impressed numbers, pr. (ILLUS.).......... **2,875**

TIFFANY POTTERY

In 1902 Louis C. Tiffany expanded Tiffany Studios to include ceramics, enamels, gold, silver and gemstones. Tiffany pottery was usually molded rather than wheel-thrown, but it was carefully finished by hand. A limited amount was produced until about 1914. It is scarce.

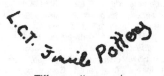

Tiffany pottery mark

Tiffany Bowl-Vase

Bowl-vase, footed wide bulbous body w/wide molded rim, decorated w/low relief-molded flowers & vines, matte tan glaze, inscribed on base "LCT," 9 1/4" h. (ILLUS.).. **$863**

Vase, 6" h., bulbous base w/shoulder tapering to short wide cylindrical neck w/flat rim, molded w/stylized leaves & berries, covered in a mottled sea green & cobalt glaze, ca. 1910, unsigned **3,450**

Tiffany Pottery Vase

Vase, 8 3/4" h., cylindrical body w/flared foot & slightly swelled top, decorated w/molded & reticulated arrowroot plants under blue & green lustered glaze, irregular rim formed by leaftips & blossoms, three very short, very tight hairlines from rim, incised "LCT - acid-etched L.C. Tiffany - Favrile Pottery" (ILLUS.) **15,400**

Rare Tiffany Organic Vase and Tiffany Vase with Narcissus

Vase, 9 1/2" h., base w/an Art Nouveau design consisting of four long relief-molded lobes, the body swelling slightly at the top w/an undulating rim, covered in an unusual glossy metallic black & green finish, incised "LCT" (ILLUS. previous page) **7,700**

Vase, 14 1/2" h., stepped disk foot supporting a bulbous ovoid body tapering to a wide cylindrical neck w/flat rim, decorated w/raised narcissus & leaves swirling around the body under a fading brown, dark blue & khaki matte glaze, chip on base, inscribed "LCT" (ILLUS. previous page) **1,380**

TORQUAY POTTERY

In the second half of the 19th century several art potteries were established in the South Devon region of England to take advantage of a belt of fine red clay. The coastal town of Torquay gives its name to this range of wares which often featured incised sgraffito decoration or colorful country-style decoration with mottos.

The most notable potteries operating in the Torquay area were the Watcombe Pottery, The Torquay Terra-cotta Company and the Aller Vale Art Pottery, which merged with Watcombe Pottery in 1901 and continued production until 1962. Other firms whose wares are collectible include Longpark Pottery and The Devonmoor Art Pottery.

Early wares feature unglazed terra cotta items in the Victorian taste including classical busts, statuary and vases and some painted and glazed wares including examples with a celeste blue interior or highlights. In addition to sgraffito designs other decorations included flowers, Barbotine glazes, Devon pixies framed in leafy scrolls and grotesque figures of cats, dogs and other fanciful animals produced in the 1890s.

The dozen or so potteries flourishing in the region at the turn of the 20th century introduced their most popular product, motto wares, which became the bread and butter line of the local industry. The most popular patterns in this line included Cottage, Black and Colored Cockerels and Scandy, based on Scandinavian rosemaling designs. Most of the mottoes were written in English with a few in Welsh. On early examples the sayings were often in Devonian dialect. These motto wares were sold for years at area seaside resorts and other tourist areas with some pieces exported to Australia, Canada and, to a lesser extent, the U.S.A. In addition to standard size teawares and novelties some miniatures and even oversized pieces were offered.

Production at the potteries stopped during World War II and some of the plants were destroyed in enemy raids. The Watcombe Pottery became Royal Watcombe after the war and Longpark also started up again, but produced simpler patterns. The Dartmouth Pottery started in 1947 and produced cottages similar to those made at Watcombe and also developed a line of figural animals, banks and novelty jugs. The Babbacombe Pottery (1950-59) and St. Marychurch Pottery (ca. 1962-69) were the last two firms to turn out motto wares but these later designs were painted on and the pieces were lighter in color with less detailing.

Many books on the various potteries are available and information can be obtained from the products manager of the North American Torquay Society.

Torquay Pottery Marks

Ashtray, Motto Ware, Colored Cockerel patt., "A place for ashes," Longpark, 1910, 3 1/2" d. **$56**

Ashtray, Motto Ware, Cottage patt., "Who burnt the Tablecloth," Royal Watcombe, 3" d. **35**

Bank, figural, model of an owl in brown, nice detailing, Dartmouth, 1960s, 8" h. **63**

Basket, B2 Scroll patt., colored scrolls on green, painted by H.M. Exeter, 1930, 3 1/2" h. **113**

Basket, hanging-type, Persian patt., decorated overall & one the base, Aller Vale white clay, rare, ca. 1890s, unmarked, 2 5/8" h.(small restoration) **167**

Basket, Motto Ware, Colored Cockerel patt., twisted handle, "No life can be dreary when work's a delight," Watcombe, ca. 1901-20 mark, 3 1/4" h. **129**

Bowl, 8" d., advertising-type, Kingfisher patt., "National Association of Master Bakers, Confectioners & Caterers Conference - Torquay 1931" on blue, Watcombe **239**

Butter tub, two-handled, Motto Ware, Cottage patt., "Du'ee 'ave zum butter," Watcombe, ca. 1925-35, 4 3/4" w. **90**

Miniature Motto Ware Pieces

Candlestick, miniature, Motto Ware, Scandy patt., "The night is long that never finds a day," Longpark, ca. 1910, expert restoration, 2 1/2" h. (ILLUS. left) **110**

Candlestick, Motto Ware, Colored Cockerel patt., "He who would thrive must rise at five," Longpark Torquay, ca. 1903-09, 8" h. **156**

Candy bowl, cov., advertising-type, "The Stationers Association Conference - Torquay 1930," decoration of an inkwell

& quill pen in white on blue, Longpark, 6 1/2" h. **222**

Cauldron pot, Motto Ware, Scandy patt., "Well paid, well satisfied," Watcomb, 2 1/2" h. **64**

Chamberstick, Motto Ware, Scandy patt., " 'Tis the mind that makes the body rich - Shakespeare, Taming of the Shrew," Aller Vale, ca. 1915, 5 1/4" h. **123**

Cheese dish, cov., Motto Ware, Cottage patt., "Don't worry and get wrinkles - Smile and have dimples," also "Cheese," Watcombe, ca. 1930, 6 1/2" d. base, 3 3/4" h. **150**

Coaster, advertising-type, "Camwal Table Waters," Watcombe, 1920, 3 7/8" d. **116**

Coffeepot, cov., Motto Ware, Cottage patt., "Sow a character, reap a destiny," Watcombe, 8 3/4" h. **218**

Coffeepot, cov., Motto Ware, Scandy patt., "Gude things be scarce, take care of me," Watcombe, 7" h. (ILLUS.) **156**

Scandy Motto Ware Coffeepot

Condiment pot, side handle, Motto Ware, Cottage patt., "Better tae sit still than rise tae fall," Aller Vale, ca. 1902-24, 2 1/4" h. **89**

Condiment pot, side-handled, Motto Ware, Cottage patt., "Waste not, Want not," Longpark Torquay England mark, ca. 1930s, 2 1/4" h. **65**

Condiment set: salt & pepper shakers, cov. mustard pot & center-handled holder, Motto Ware, Cottage patt., mottos on all pieces except the holder, Watcombe, ca. 1920, the set **167**

Creamer, souvenir, Heather patt., "Hastings," white heather on mauve ground, 3 1/4" h. **62**

Torquay Crocus Vase

Crocus vase, Motto Ware, Cottage patt., spherical body, "Gather the roses while ye may" & "Old time is still a flying," 3" d., 3 3/4" h. (ILLUS.) **95**

Cup & saucer, Motto Ware, Cottage patt., footed flaring cylindrical cup, inscribed "Have another cup full," saucer 5 3/8" d., cup 3 3/8" d., 3" h. **75**

Dish, figural fish, Motto Ware, Colored Cockerel patt., "A pla(i)ce for ashes," Longpark Torquay, ca. 1904-18, 3 3/4 x 5 3/4" **95**

Dish, figural fish, Motto Ware, Cottage patt., "A pla(i)ce for ashes," Longpark, ca. 1930s, 3 3/4 x 5 1/2" **98**

Dresser tray, Motto Ware, Colored Cockerel patt., "A place for everything," Longpark Torquay, ca. 1903-09, uncommon, 7 1/2 x 10 3/4" **360**

Dresser tray, Motto Ware, Cottage patt., Devon dialect, "Dinna lie in yer bed an lippen tae yer neebor," Watcombe, 1920s, 7 1/2 x 10 3/4" (restored) **210**

Egg cup, Motto Ware, Cottage patt., "Fresh today," Longpark Torquay, ca. 1930, 2 1/2" h. **53**

Egg cup, Motto Ware, Cottage patt., "New laid," Royal Watcombe, ca. 1950, 2 3/4" h. **42**

Egg cup, Motto Ware, Black Cockerel patt., inscribed "Just laid," 1 1/2" d., 1 3/4" h. **45**

Torquay Footed Egg Cup

Egg cup, footed, Motto Ware, Cottage patt., "Laid to day," 3 1/4" h., 3 1/2" d. (ILLUS.) **45**

Ewer, cov., Floral patt., white floral spray on front & reverse on a tan ground, silver plated cover w/"J.A.R." silversmith's mark, Watcombe, ca. 1890s, 8 1/2" h. **310**

Hatpin holder, footed dished base centered by hourglass-shaped holder, Motto Ware, Scandy patt., "A present from Arnside," Longpark Torquay, ca. 1910-20, 4 5/8" h. (ILLUS. next page) **133**

Hot water or coffeepot, cov., bulbous ovoid body tapering to a flaring neck w/rim spout, inset cover w/knob finial, Motto Ware, Cottage patt., "Never put off till tomorrow what can be done today - Newquay," Watcombe, 1925-35 mark, 6" h. **137**

Scandy Pattern Hatpin Holder

Hot water or coffeepot, cov., Motto Ware, "Life is mostly froth and bubble...," scarce motto, Watcombe, ca. 1925-35 mark, 7 3/4" h. 202

Hot water pot, cov., Motto Ware, Colored Cockerel patt., "Two men look through prison bars - One sees the mud and the other the stars," Longpark, ca. 1910-20, 5 1/2" h. 169

Inkwell, Motto Ware, Shamrock patt., "The chosen leaf of Bard and Chief," Aller Vale, ca. 1902-10 mark, 3" h. 105

Jardiniere, B2 Scroll patt., colored scrolls on a green ground, H.M. Exeter Pottery, ca. 1910, 5 1/2" h. 285

Jardiniere, faience, Lantern patt., a lantern in branches on blue ground, Barton Pottery mark, ca. 1920s, small, 3 1/2" h. 84

Jardiniere, Motto Ware, Passion Flower patt., flowers on a blue ground, motto in cream, "For every evil under the sun...," unmarked, Exeter, ca. 1925, 6 1/4" h. 385

Model of a frying pan, Motto Ware, Black Cockerel patt., "I cum frum Totnes - Waste not, want not," Torquay Pottery Co., ca. 1918-24, 4 1/8" l. plus handle 69

Mug, child's, Motto Ware, Cottage patt., "Mary had a little lamb," St. Marychurch, 1960s, 3" h. 68

Mug, child's, Motto Ware, Scandy patt., "Hold me tight and don't be clumsy or you'll break this mug from Romsey," Watcombe, ca. 1902-15, 2 1/4" h. 80

Mustard pot, cov., Motto Ware, Cottage patt., w/"Lands End" on front & "I improve everything" on back, 2 1/4" d., 2 3/4" h. 55

Mustard pot, cov., Motto Ware, Cottage patt., "Soft words win hard hearts," 2 1/2" d., 3" h. 55

Pin tray, Motto Ware, Cottage patt., "Don't Grouse - Work like Helen B. Merry - Ilfracombe," Watcombe, ca. 1901-10 mark, 3 1/4" sq. 52

Pin tray, Motto Ware, Scandy patt., "Tell truth and shame the Devil - Port Arthur Canada," Watcombe, ca. 1910-27, 3 1/4 x 5" 56

Pitcher, 1 3/4" h., miniature, Motto Ware, Cottage patt., "Little and good - Brixham," Royal Watcombe................................. 55

Pitcher, 1 3/4" h., miniature, Motto Ware, Cottage patt., "Little Jack Horner - Runswick Bay" 65

Pitcher, 2 1/2" h., miniature, Motto Ware, Scandy patt., "Demsher Craim tak an try it," Aller Vale... 60

Pitcher, 4 1/8" h., Motto Ware, Colored Cockerel patt., "Success comes not by wishing but hard work bravely done," Aller Vale, ca. 1891-1901 133

Pitcher, 4 1/8" h., Shakespeare's House patt., faience, rendering of Shakespeare's House w/green sprayed borders, Watcombe, ca. 1910-20 96

Pitcher, 4 1/2" h., Sgraffito patt., band of leafy scrolls & flowers on glazed terra cotta, Q1 pattern code, Aller Vale, 1890s....... 88

Torquay Cottage Pattern Pitcher

Pitcher, 5" h., 4" d., Motto Ware, Cottage patt., bulbous body w/tall cylindrical neck, "If you can't be aisy Be as aisy as you can" (ILLUS.) 110

Pitcher, 5 1/4" h., 4 1/2" d., Motto Ware, Cottage patt., spherical base tapering slightly to wide cylindrical neck, "Help yourself don't be shy" 100

Pitcher, 5 1/2" h., pierced rim, handle passes through, Motto Ware, Scandy patt., "If it be so so it is you know...," Aller Vale, ca. 1900 185

Pitcher, 5 3/4" h., Motto Ware, Forget-me-not patt., "From Launceston," white script on dark blue, light blue forget-me-nots on white band w/trellis, Exeter, 1920 123

Pitcher, 6" h., Motto Ware, Black Cockerel patt., "It's an ill wind that blows nobody good," Longpark, ca. 1918-30 142

Scandy Pattern Motto Ware Pitcher

Pitcher, 7 3/4" h., Motto Ware, Scandy patt., "Little duties still put off may end in never done...," Aller Vale, ca. 1891-1910 (ILLUS.) **199**

Plate, 4 1/4" d., miniature doll size, Motto Ware, Scandy patt., "Gude folks be scarce take care of me," colored border, Longpark, ca. 1920 .... **75**

Plate, 4 3/8" d., miniature doll size, Motto Ware, Cottage patt., "A rolling stone gathers no moss," Royal Watcombe, ca. 1950 .... **65**

Black Cockerel Motto Plate

Plate, 6" d., Motto Ware, Black Cockerel patt., "Good morning," Aller Vale, 1891-1910 (ILLUS.) **125**

Plate, 7 1/4" d., Motto Ware, Cottage patt., "Be a little deaf and blind, Happiness you'll always find," Watcombe DMW mark, ca. 1918-27 .... **80**

Plate, 7 1/4" d., Motto Ware, Scandy patt., "A fellow feeling makes us wondrous kind...," Aller Vale, ca. 1891-1902 mark **120**

Plate, 8 1/8" d., Motto Ware, Scandy patt., "As I was going to St. Ives - I met a man with seven wives...," long motto, Watcombe, ca. 1925-35 .... **235**

Motto Ware Puzzle Jug

Puzzle jug, Motto Ware, Colored Cockerel patt., "May you find that all life's troubles after all are only bubbles," Longpark Tormohun ware, ca. 1910, 4" h. (ILLUS.) **182**

Puzzle jug, Motto Ware, Scandy patt., "Within this jug there is good liquor...," Aller Vale, ca. 1910, 4 1/2" h. **175**

Salt & pepper shakers, Motto Ware, Cottage patt., "Waste not, want not" & "A necessity of life," Watcombe, 1920s, 2 3/4" h., pr. **55**

Scent bottle, Devon Violets patt., unmarked Longpark, ca. 1930, 2 1/4" h. **32**

Scent bottle, marked "Genuine Devon Lavender," small silver paper label under name, Watcombe - Made in England mark, ca. 1930 .... **62**

Scent bottle, Somerset Violets patt., ink-well-shaped, Longpark, ca. 1930, 2"h. **54**

Scent bottle w/old brass crown stopper, Devon Violets patt., "Torquay" under green band, Longpark, ca. 1930, 4 1/2" h. **98**

Sugar bowl, cov., Motto Ware, Ivy patt., "Sweeten for yourself," Aller Vale, ca. 1910, 3 1/4" h. **62**

Sugar bowl, open, round tapering sides, Mottto Ware, Black Cockerel patt., "Be aisy with tha sugar," 3 1/4" d., 1 3/4" h. **65**

Torquay Sugar Bowl

Sugar bowl, open, pedestal base, Motto Ware, Black Cockerel patt., "Be aisy with tha sugar," 5 1/4" d., 4 1/4" h. (ILLUS.) **85**

Supper dish, three-part w/handle, Cottage patt., marked "Butter - Cheese - Biscuits," Watcombe Torquay, ca. 1930, 8 x 8 1/2" **165**

Supper dish, three-part w/handle, Scandy patt., marked "Jam - Butter - Cream," Watcombe Torquay, ca. 1901-20, 8 x 9"...... **139**

Tankard, Motto Ware, Scandy patt., "Every blade of grass...," Aller Vale, ca. 1910, 4" h. **78**

Teapot, cov., miniature, Motto Ware, Scandy patt., "Droon yer sorrows in a cup a Tay," Longpark Torquay, ca. 1918-30, 2 3/4" h. (ILLUS. center w/candlestick) **124**

Molded Cottage Teapot

Teapot, cov., Molded Cottage patt., cottage-shaped, inscribed "Old Uncle - Tom Cobley's - Cottage - Widdecombe," Torquay Pottery Co., ca. 1920, 4 7/8" h. (ILLUS.).. **139**

Teapot, cov., Motto Ware, Cottage patt., "Fair is he that comes but fairer he that brings," Made in England - Watcombe mark, ca. 1930s, overall 7 1/4" l., 4 1/4" h. **89**

Torquay Teapot

Teapot, cov., bulbous body, Motto Ware, Cottage patt., "From Torquay" on front & "Du'ee Drink a cup a tay," 4 1/2" d., 3 3/4" h. (ILLUS.) **110**

Toast rack, Motto Ware, Cottage patt., center handle, three tines, "Take a little toast," Watcombe, ca. 1920, 3 1/2" h. **129**

Trivet, round, Motto Ware, "Cottage patt., "Except the kettle boiling B Filling the tpot spoils the T" & Mablethorpe," 5 1/2" d. (ILLUS. next column) **55**

Vase, 1 7/8" h., miniature, Motto Ware, Scandy patt., "Niver say die - Up man and try," Longpark **65**

Vase, 2" h., miniature, tri-corner pinched top, blue flower on white clay ground, Aller Vale, ca. 1900 .... **80**

Torquay Trivet

Vase, 2 1/4" h., miniature, Motto Ware, Scandy patt., "Du'ee think tis yer dooty? Then du et," Longpark, ca. 1910 .... **109**

Vase, 4 1/2" h., D1 Scroll patt., colored scrolls on a blue ground, Aller Vale, rare **164**

Vase, 4 1/2" h., faience, Tintern Abbey patt., abbey ruins in a landscape, cloud-filled sky, Longpark, ca. 1910...................... **149**

Stork Pattern Vase

Vase, 4 5/8" h., faience, waisted shape w/bulbed top pierced w/holes, Stork patt., white & black stock against green ground w/reeds, Crown Dorset, ca. 1910 (ILLUS).. **219**

Vase, 5 7/8" h., Butterflies patt., spherical body w/four flared necks at top, two butterflies on a streaky mauve ground, Longpark, ca. 1904-18 .... **142**

Vase, 7 1/2" h., two-handled, Motto Ware, Scandy patt., "Take fortune as you find her...," H.M. Exeter, ca. 1920 (professional restoration).. **154**

Vase, 7 3/4" h., footed tapering cylindrical form, B2 Scroll patt., colored scrolls on a dark green ground, Longpark, ca. 1909 (ILLUS. top next page)................................. **143**

Vase, 8" h., artware, Wild Rose patt., roses on a black lattice, cream ground, Watcombe Pottery, ca. 1901-20 mark................ **194**

Longpark Scroll Pattern Vase

UHL POTTERY

Original production of utilitarian wares began at Evansville, Indiana in the 1850s and consisted mostly of jugs, jars, crocks and pieces for food preparation and preservation. In 1909, production was moved to Huntingburg, Indiana where a more extensive variety of items was eventually produced including many novelty and advertising items that have become highly collectible. Following labor difficulties, the Uhl Pottery closed in 1944.

Unless it is marked or stamped, Uhl is difficult to identify except by someone with considerable experience. Marked pieces can have several styles of ink stamps and/or an incised number under glaze on the bottom. These numbers are die-cut and impressed in the glazed bottom. Some original molds were acquired by other potteries. Some production exists and should not be considered as Uhl. These may have numbers inscribed by hand with a stylus and are usually not glazed on the bottom.

Many examples have no mark or stamp and may not be bottom-glazed. This is especially true of many of the miniature pieces. If a piece has a 'Meier's Wine' paper label, it was probably made by Uhl.

While many color variations exist, there are about nine basic colors including blue, white, black, rose or pink, yellow, teal, purple, pumpkin and browns/tans. Blue, pink, teal and purple are currently the most sought after colors. Animal planters, vases, liquor/wine containers, pitchers, mugs, banks, kitchenware, bakeware, gardenware and custom-made advertising pieces exist.

Similar pieces by other manufacturers do exist. When placed side by side, a seasoned collector can recognize an authentic example of Uhl Pottery.

A Variety of Uhl Marks

Ashtray, acorn-shaped, brown, marked "Rustic Tavern" on reverse **$780**

Ashtray, advertising Shell Oil, marked "Dale, Indiana" **525**

Ashtray, figural, dog & fireplug, No. 199, brown **525**

Ashtray, marked "American Legion, Post 221, Huntingburg, Indiana" **140**

Bank, figural pig, blue, medium unmarked **375**

Bank, figural pig, white, large, unmarked **400**

Bank, model of a jug, blue, unmarked **185**

Bean pot, "Boston Baked Beans," brown & tan, unmarked **40**

Bottle, hand-turned, green ground **400**

Bowl, soup, No. 6, pink **40**

Buttermilk feeder/chicken waterer, acorn marked (ILLUS. left) **90-100**

Uhl Buttermilk Feeder & Pitcher

Uhl Canteen

Canteen, footed circular form w/short cylindrical neck, loop handle, blue (ILLUS.) **160**

Uhl Canteen & Miniature Jugs

Canteen, miniature, jug-shaped, teal, unmarked (ILLUS. bottom row, right) **40**

Casserole, handled, No. 200, pink, unmarked **75**

Casserole, No. 175, blue, unmarked **50**

Churn, white, 3 gal. **175**

Cookie jar, miniature, brown, unmarked **45**

Cookie jar, pink **135**

Cookie jar, miniature, globe-shaped, marked "Indiana State Fair 1940," pink ground, 4" h. **625**

Creamer & sugar bowl, pink, pr. **75**

Cup & saucer, blue **70**

Jar, cov., cylindrical, blue, 6 oz. (ILLUS. bottom) **50**

Jar, cov., semi-ovoid body, clamp closure type, blue (ILLUS. center right) add $25.00 for clamp **50**

Jar, white, acorn mark, 1 gal. **37**

Jar, white, acorn mark, 2 gal. **42**

Jar, white, acorn mark, 5 gal. **55**

Jar, Evansville oval mark, 15 gal. **225**

Jar, cov., white & blue, marked "Flour" **300**

Jar, Orange Blossom, No. 118, pink **70**

Various Jars & Jugs

Uhl Old Ivory Jardiniere

Jardiniere, old ivory, 14 or 16 1/2" h., each (ILLUS.) **60**

Athenian Jardiniere

Jardiniere, Athenian patt., green, 16 1/2" h. (ILLUS.) **65**

Jardiniere, Roman patt., terra cotta or old ivory, 19" h., each **95**

Jug, handled bulbous body, red glaze, 1 pt. (ILLUS. middle row, left previous column) **20**

Jug, "1939 Merry Xmas," brown & white **175**

Jug, "1942 Merry Christmas," brown & white **200**

Jug, miniature, "Acorn Wares," acorn-shaped (ILLUS. bottom row, center previous column) **30-60**

Jug, miniature, baseball-shaped, white, unmarked, paper label (ILLUS. middle row, left previous page) **56**

Jug, miniature, bulbous ovoid body, paper label (ILLUS. top row, far right previous page) **30-60**

Jug, miniature, football-shaped, brown, unmarked, paper label (ILLUS. middle row, right previous page) **40**

Jug, miniature, globe-shaped, purple, unmarked **90**

Jug, miniature, "Grecian," blue, unmarked **40**

Jug, miniature, Prunella, blue, unmarked (ILLUS. top row, second from right previous page) **60**

Jug, miniature, semi-ovoid body, loop shoulder handles, Meier's label (ILLUS. top row, far left previous page) **60**

Jug, miniature, shouldered, "Grandpa Meiers" label, brown & white, unmarked (ILLUS. middle row, center previous page) **60**

Jug, miniature, square, blue, unmarked, paper label (ILLUS. top row, second from left previous page) **40**

Jug, miniature, two-handled, blue, unmarked **55**

Jug, miniature, two-handled, "Curacoa" (demijohn), paper label, 2 oz. (ILLUS. bottom row, left previous page) **30-60**

Jug, "Polar Bear," flat-sided, blue **325**

Jug, refrigerator-type, flat-sided, No. 190, blue **110**

Jug, refrigerator-type, globe-shaped, pink **90**

Jug, two-handled, Evansville oval mark, 10 gal. **250**

Jug, w/advertising, hand-turned, Evansville mark, 3 gal. **275**

Jugs, handled, bulbous body, blue glaze, numbered 175, 176, 177 (ILLUS. top row, left & right previous page) **20-35**

Medallion, relief-molded "Uhl Pottery," brown **225**

Mixing bowl, 4" d., blue (one of nine sizes) **80**

Model of a turtle, large, unmarked **700**

Model of lady's slipper, miniature, blue, pr. **140**

Model of lady's slipper, miniature, white, unmarked pr. **80**

Mug, barrel-shaped, "Big Boonville Fair 1927," tan & brindle **100**

Mug, miniature, barrel-shaped, pink **130**

Pitcher, cov., squatty body, blue **270**

Pitcher, cov., tapering wide cylindrical body, Grape patt., blue, unmarked **200-250**

Pitcher, Grape patt., blue, 3 qt. **190**

Uhl Barrel-shaped Pitcher

Pitcher, barrel-shaped, blue ground w/white interior (ILLUS.) **68**

Pitcher, barrel-shaped, plum **45**

Pitcher, bulbous body, blue & white sponged, No. 2 size **375**

Pitcher, bulbous body, Grape patt., No. 181, pink **90**

Pitcher, jug-type, "Creme De Coffee," No. 164, pumpkin **35**

Pitcher, Lincoln profile, blue & white, unmarked, No. 2 size **275**

Pitcher, miniature, pink, unmarked **80**

Uhl Grape Pattern Pitcher

Pitcher, squatty tapering cylindrical body, Grape patt., blue ground w/white interior (ILLUS.) **160**

Pitcher set: 3 qt. pitcher & six 16 oz. steins; barrel-shaped, blue w/white interior, No. B-3, the set **800-1,000**

Pitcher set: flagon-type pitcher & six mugs; blue, unmarked, the set............................... **180**

Planter, model of a donkey, white, unmarked **185**

Planter, model of an elephant w/wrinkled
skin, white, unmarked 140
Plate, chop, blue.. 80
Plate, hand-turned, blue 90
Roaster, blue.. 140
Salt & pepper shakers, pink, unmarked,
pr. 60

Polar Bear Sand Jar

Sand jar, wide cylindrical body, Polar Bear
patt., old ivory, 12 1/4" d., 14 1/2" h.
(ILLUS.).. 250
Teapot, cov., No. 131, blue 135
Teapot, cov., No. 132, yellow............................ 65
Vase, bud, No. 516, blue 85
Vase, hand-turned, pink 75
Vase, No. 114, pink 65
Vase, No. 123, blue 70
Vase, No. 158, pink 90

ADVERTISING ITEMS

Various Uhl Advertising Items

Jug, miniature, brown & white glaze
(ILLUS. top row, left) 125
Jug, miniature, two-handled, yellow glaze
(ILLUS. top row, center).............................. 125
Model of a shoe, baby shoe w/tie, brown
glaze (ILLUS. center row, left)....................... 60
Mug, barrel-shaped, yellow glaze (ILLUS.
bottom, far left) 85
Mug, yellow glaze (ILLUS. top row, right)........... 85
Pitcher, miniature, barrel-shaped w/adver-
tising, red glaze (ILLUS. center row,
right) 125-175

Pitcher, tapering cylindrical form, w/adver-
tising for Dillsboro Sanitarium, white
glaze, no recorded sale, one other
believed to exist, estimated price
(ILLUS. bottom, far right)................. 1,800-3,000

ART POTTERY VASES

Various Art Pottery Vases

Vase, cylindrical body w/flaring rim, white
glaze (ILLUS. bottom row, left)................. 30-60
Vase, bulbous body w/closed rim, blue
glaze (ILLUS. center) 30-60
Vase, footed bulbous body w/trumpet-form
neck, white glaze (ILLUS. top row left)...... 30-60
Vase, footed flattened bulbous body w/flat-
tened flaring neck, yellow glaze (ILLUS.
top row, right) 30-60
Vase, tall waisted cylindrical body, red
glaze (ILLUS. bottom row, right) 30-60

CATALOGUE ILLUSTRATIONS

Uhl Butters

Butters, Kansas City, glazed all-white or
blue inside & outside,1, 1 1/2 & 2 lb.,
each (ILLUS. right) 20-30
Butters, low, glazed all-white or blue inside
& outside, 1to 20 lb., each (ILLUS. left) 20-30
Churns, glazed all-white inside & outside, 2
to 6 gal., each 85-200
Harvest jug, 1 gal. w/stoneware handle
intact (ILLUS. top right, next column).... 400-600

Various Uhl Jugs

Ice water jar, cov., nickled faucet, 3 to 10 gal., each **80-125**

Ice Water Keg

Ice water keg, cov., blue banded, nickled faucet, 3 to 10 gal., each (ILLUS.) **150-250**

Various Jars

Jar, without bail, glazed all-white inside & outside, 1/4 to 6 gal., each **25-50**

Jar, 7 gal., extremely rare .... **500+**
Jar, 8 to 12 gal., each **50-100**
Jar, 15 to 30 gal., each **100-250**
Jar, 40 to 60 gal., each (ILLUS.) **250-300**

Kraut weights, glazed white, 10" d. to 13 1/2" d., each (ILLUS.)........................... **10-20**

Various Uhl Pitchers

Pitcher, barrel-shaped, glazed Old Hickory brown outside, white inside, 3 qt. **40-60**

Pitcher, bellied, glazed blue stipple, 1/2 & 1 gal., each (ILLUS. left) **175-300**

Pitcher, Lincoln bust, 5 sizes, each (ILLUS. right) **175-700**

Uhl Pitcher Sets

Pitcher set: 2 qt. pitcher & six 12 oz. steins; Grape patt., glazed Mahogany outside, white inside, No. G-1, marked, 7 pc. set **100-125**

Pitcher set: 2 qt. pitcher & six 12 oz. steins; Grape patt., glazed Periwinkle blue, white inside, No. G-1, marked, 7 pc. set **400-500**

Pitcher set: 2 qt. squatty pitcher & six 12 oz. steins; Grape patt., glazed Mahogany outside, white inside, No. G-2, marked, 7 pc. set **110-135**

Pitcher set: 2 qt. squatty pitcher & six 12 oz. steins; Grape patt., glazed Periwinkle blue outside, white inside, No. G-2, marked, 7 pc. set **400-500**

Pitcher set: 3 qt. pitcher & six 16 oz. steins; barrel-shaped, glazed Old Hickory brown outside, white inside, No. B-3, marked, 7 pc. set 125

Pitcher set: 3 qt. pitcher & six 16 oz. steins; Grape patt., glazed Mahogany outside, white inside, No. G-4, marked, 7 pc. set (ILLUS. previous page)............. 110-135

Pitcher set: 3 qt. pitcher & six 16 oz. steins; Grape patt., glazed Periwinkle blue outside, white inside, No. G-4, marked, 7 pc. set 425-525

Polar jar, cov., nickled faucet, blue tint over white or dark green outside, white inside, 1 to 10 gal., each 250-600

Preserve/mustard jar, cov., 1/2 to 3 gal., each 60

Shoulder jugs, 1/4 to 5 gal., each 25-75

Shoulder jugs, glazed white outside, dark inside, 1 gal. (ILLUS. prev. page, top left) 100-125

Sorghum jug, w/or without faucet hole, 8 & 10 gal., each (ILLUS. prev. page, bottom right) 90-125

Squat bailed jug, 1/2 & 1 gal., each (ILLUS. prev. page, bottom left) 125

Steam table insets, glazed all-white, for 8 1/2 or 10 1/2" opening, each 40-60

MINIATURE ADVERTISING ITEMS

Various Uhl Miniature Advertising Items

Bottle, miniature, advertising, brown glaze, ca. 1933 (ILLUS. top row left) **400-600**

Canteen, miniature, advertising, white glaze, ca. 1933 (ILLUS. top row, center) **400-600**

Jug, miniature, advertising, two-handled, green & brown glaze, ca. 1939 (ILLUS. center row, right) **175-225**

Jug, miniature, advertising, two-handled, green & brown glaze (ILLUS. bottom row, left) **225-300**

Jug, miniature, advertising, white & brown glaze, ca. 1933 (ILLUS. top row, right) **400-600**

Jug, miniature, advertising, white & brown glaze, ca. 1939 (ILLUS. center row, left previous page)................................ **175-225**

Jug, miniature, advertising, white & brown glaze, ca. 1939 (ILLUS. center row, center previous page) **175-225**

Jug, miniature, advertising, white & brown glaze (ILLUS. bottom row, center previous page) **225-300**

MISCELLANEOUS PITCHERS

Various Uhl Pitchers

Creamer, Lincoln profile, blue glaze (ILLUS. right).. **190**

Pitcher, barrel-shaped, blue glaze (ILLUS. top) **60**

Pitcher, bulbous body, blue glaze (ILLUS. far right)... **90-120**

Pitcher, miniature Egyptian jug-type, yellow glaze (ILLUS. center, second from left) **30-40**

Pitcher, miniature, jug-type, brown & white glaze, 1" h. (ILLUS. center, second from right)... **75-100**

Pitcher, miniature modified Egyptian jug-type, yellow glaze (ILLUS. center far right)... **30-40**

Miscellaneous Uhl Pitchers

Pitcher, Egyptian jug-type, black glaze (ILLUS. top left) **30-60**

Pitcher, jug-type, "Creme De Coffee," blue glaze (ILLUS. center) **35**

Pitcher, modified Egyptian jug-type, black or red glaze, each (ILLUS. right top & bottom) **30-60**

Pitchers, cov., Egyptian jug-type, blue glaze (ILLUS. bottom left previous page).. **30-60**

VAN BRIGGLE

The Van Briggle Pottery was established by Artus Van Briggle, who formerly worked for Rookwood Pottery, in Colorado Springs, Colorado at the turn of the century. He died in 1904 but the pottery was carried on by his widow and others. From 1900 until 1920, the pieces were dated. It remains in production today, specializing in Art Pottery.

Van Briggle Pottery Mark

Bowl, 5 1/2" d., 2" h., squatty bulbous body w/a wide tapering shoulder to the wide flat mouth, embossed w/holly under a fine speckled matte green glaze, the brown clay showing through, ca. 1906, incised "AA - Van Briggle - Colo Spgs. - 1906" **$880**

Bowl-vase, wide rounded squatty lower body below a wide angled & sloping shoulder to the wide flat mouth, molded w/large, wide pointed leaves around the sides, overall maroon & blue matte glaze, post-1920s, 9 1/2" d., 5" h. **330**

Bowl-vase, very wide squatty bulbous form w/the upper sides tapering to a flat mouth, embossed around the mouth w/a wide band of mistletoe berries & leaves down the sides, sheer mottled mauve glaze, Shape No. 387, dated 1905, incised mark, 11" d., 5" h. **4,125**

Bowl-vase, wide bulbous body w/molded rim, covered in a fine matte green glaze, incised "AA - VAN BRIGGLE - Colo. Spgs. - 1910," 1910, 4 x 5 1/2".................... **440**

Mug, ovoid form w/thick C-form handle from rim to base, matte green glaze, incised "AA - COLO SPRINGS - 1907 - 28B," 4 1/2" d., 5" h. **358**

Paperweight, figural, modeled as a horned toad on a thin oval base, the toad in a yellowish amber glaze on a matte green base, unmarked, ca. 1914, 3 1/4 x 4 1/2"..... **990**

Plate, 8 1/4" d., molded w/a cluster of purple grapes & large leaves against a textured turquoise ground, incised mark, 1907-11 .... **605**

Van Briggle Plate with Poppies

Plate, 8 1/2" d., crisply incised w/poppies & covered in a bright green glaze, incised "AA - Van Briggle - 1902 - III" (ILLUS.) **1,540**

Plate, 8 1/2" d., heavily embossed w/large grapes & leaves under a deep burgundy & blue matte glaze, incised marks ca. 1907-12 .... **231**

Vase, 2 1/2" h., 3" d., small bulbous form w/a closed rim, three spread-winged finely carved dragonflies around the rim, overall mustard yellow matte glaze, ca. 1907-12 .... **880**

Vase, 4 x 4 1/4", wide cylindrical base tapering to rounded shoulder & flat mouth, molded poppies under a fine speckled matte green glaze, the brown clay showing through, ca. 1903, incised "AA - Van Briggle - 1903 - 204 - III" **2,200**

Vase, 4 1/4" h., squatty bulbous form, sharply canted sides to flat rim, decorated w/stylized relief-molded flowers & stems, mulberry & blue glaze, incised marks & "U.S.A." & "NP" in rectangle, ca. 1922-26 .... **523**

Vase, 4 1/2 x 5", spherical body w/slightly rolled lip, molded stylized design under a matte green glaze, ca. 1904, incised "AA - Van Briggle - 1904 - V - 148" (restored lines to body) **413**

Vase, 5" h., waisted cylindrical body slightly swelled near the top then tapering to a wide flat mouth, decorated w/embossed iris blossoms on swirling vertical stems & leaves under a matte raspberry pink glaze, Shape No. 26, 1907-11 .... **660**

Vase, 6" h., simple ovoid body tapering to a small mouth flanked by relief-molded blue trefoils & small in-body handles, light matte green ground, Shape No. 165 .. **1,623**

Vase, 6 1/2" h., slightly flaring cylindrical body w/a bulbed top w/closed mouth, molded around the top w/tulip blossoms, the stems down the sides, ivory w/light green matte glaze, incised marks, ca. 1905 (tight line at top) **358**

Vase, 7" h., cylindrical body w/small loop handles & relief-molded design at base, leathery green matte glaze, shape No. 535, incised marks & partially obscured date, 1907 (grinding chips off base)............. **715**

Vase, 7" h., 3 1/2" d., slender cylindrical form w/a swelled shoulder & short tapering neck, embossed around the top w/jonquils on tall stems, dark purple dead-matte glaze, incised mark & dated 1902 .... **2,750**

Van Briggle Vase

Vase, 7 1/2" h., bulbous ovoid body w/a narrow cylindrical neck & flat rim, embossed w/wide triangular ribbed leaves w/ruffled edges & flowers, the leaves covered in an unusual brown matte glaze against a robin's-egg blue ground, Shape No. 797, 1907-11 (ILLUS.)... **1,430**

Vase, 7 3/4" h., bulbous base tapering to long slender cylindrical neck w/flaring rim, embossed around base w/papyrus leaves under a matte robin's-egg blue glaze, Shape No. 734, 1907-11 .... **770**

Vase, 8" h., ovoid body tapering to base, decorated w/four large molded leaves, matte yellowish green glaze, dated 1902.... **2,415**

Vase, 8 1/2", 7" d., bulbous ovoid body tapering to a flat-rimmed neck, embossed around the neck & shoulder w/green-washed leaves & red berries w/an overall rich matte raspberry glaze, incised mark, Shape No. 164, dated 1904 .... **3,300**

Vase, 9" h., bulbous base tapering to a tall cylindrical neck, molded around the neck w/flower blossoms on tall stems down the neck & wide pointed leaves around the bottom, two-tone blue shaded to dark green matte glaze, incised marks, ca. 1907-12 .... **770**

Early Rare Van Briggle Vase

Vase, 9" h., 6" d., wide tapering cylindrical body w/a bulbous swelled shoulder tapering slightly to an incurved rim, decorated around the shoulder w/embossed poppy pods & leaves on long stems, covered in a mottled red, blue & mauve matte glaze w/the brown clay body showing through, incised "AA   VAN BRIGGLE - 1902 - III" (ILLUS.) **15,600**

Vase, 9 1/2" h., trumpet-form, the sides molded w/a horizontal vine w/large & small pointed leaves up & down around the sides, turquoise blue ground w/blue overspray, ca. 1930s.................................... **230**

Vase, 10" h., 8" d., wide ovoid body tapering to a cylindrical neck flanked by small loop shoulder handles, molded w/stylized desert flowers & leaves, dark matte green & burgundy glaze, incised mark, dated 1904 .... **2,475**

Vase, 10 3/4" h., tall cylindrical body w/low buttress-type handles flanking the flat mouth, molded w/morning glories under a rare matte yellow glaze, ca. 1903, incised "AA Van Briggle - 1903 - 228" (repair to small base chip) **4,400**

Vase, 14" h., slightly waisted cylindrical body gently swelled at the top w/a closed rim, embossed w/a design of stylized lilies & leaves atop wide stems, matte dark purple glaze, incised "AA - VAN BRIGGLE - 1903 - III- 3," 1903 (minor grind at base from in-fire stilt pull) .. **5,225**

VERNON KILNS

The story of Vernon Kilns Pottery begins with the purchase by Mr. Faye Bennison of the Poxon China Company (Vernon Potteries) in July 1931. The Poxon family had run the pottery for a number of years in Vernon, California, but with the founding of Vernon Kilns the product lines were greatly expanded.

Many innovative dinnerware lines and patterns were introduced during the 1930s, including designs by such noted American artists as Rockwell Kent and Don Blanding. In the early 1940s items were designed to tie in with Walt Disney's animated features "Fantasia" and "Dumbo." Various commemorative plates, including the popular "Bits" series, were also produced over a long period of time. Vernon Kilns was taken over by Metlox Potteries in 1958 and completely ceased production in 1960.

Vernon Kilns Mark

"BITS" SERIES

Plate, 8 1/2" d., Bits of Old New England Series, The Whaler **$38**

Plate, 8 1/2" d., Bits of the Middle West Series, Fourth of July **35**

Plate, 8 1/2" d., Bits of the Old Southwest Series, San Juan Bautista Mission 35
Plate, 8 1/2" d., Bits of the Old Southwest Series, San Juan Capistrano Mission 40
Plate, 8 1/2" d., Bits of the Old West, The Barfly 25

CITIES SERIES - 10 1/2" d.
Plate, "Fort Worth, Texas" 18
Plate, "Greensboro, North Carolina" 18
Plate, "Los Angeles, California" 20

DINNERWARES
Bowl, chowder, tab-handled, Tam O'Shanter patt. 12
Bowl, flower petal-shaped, green, No. 139 50
Bowl, salad, Organdie patt. 60
Bowl, fruit, 5 1/2" d., May Flower patt. 8
Bowl, fruit, 5 1/2" d., Organdie patt. 5
Bowl, salad, 10 1/2" d., Winchester '73 (Frontier Days) patt. 325
Butter dish, cov., Tam O'Shanter patt., 1/4 lb. 28
Casserole, cov., Tam O'Shanter patt................ 48
Casserole, cov., Tickled Pink patt...................... 55
Casserole, cov., Chintz patt., 8" d.................... 140
Chicken baker, cov., Organdie patt. 30
Coaster, Homespun patt. 25
Coffeepot, cov., Tickled Pink patt., 8 cup 60
Comport, footed, Tweed patt. (T-504), 9 1/2" h. 75
Creamer & cov. sugar bowl, Organdie patt., pr. 18

Coronado Creamer & Sugar Bowl

Creamer & open sugar bowl, Coronado patt., orange (ILLUS.) 45
Cup & saucer, demitasse, Organdie patt. 25
Cup & saucer, demitasse, Spanish Court-yard decal patt. 30

Frontier Days Pattern Cup & Saucer

Cup & saucer, Frontier Days (Winchester 73) patt. (ILLUS.) 65

Cup & saucer, Homespun patt. 15
Cup & saucer, Homespun patt., oversize 155
Cup & saucer, Organdie patt. 6
Egg cup, Homespun patt. 20
Gravy boat, Chintz patt. 40
Gravy boat, Organdie patt. 18
Mixing bowl, Gingham patt., 5" d. 16
Pepper mill, Winchester '73 (Frontier Days) patt. 145
Pitcher, Organdie patt., jug-type, 1 pt. 28
Pitcher, 2 qt., jug-type, Winchester '73 (Frontier Days) patt. 295
Pitcher, large, Tam O'Shanter patt. 60
Pitcher, water, Organdie patt. 30
Plate, bread & butter, 6 1/2" d., Homespun patt. 5
Plate, dinner, 9 1/2" d., Winchester '73 (Frontier Days) patt. 75
Plate, dinner, 9 3/4" d., Homespun patt............. 18
Plate, dinner, 10 1/2" d., Organdie patt. 6
Plate, 10 1/2" d., Santa Claus decoration........... 35
Plate, luncheon, May Flower patt. 12
Plate, salad, Organdie patt. 4
Plate, chop, 12" d., Chintz patt. 70
Plate, chop, 12" d., Frontier Days (Win-chester 73) patt. 120
Plate, chop, 12" d., Monterey patt. 30
Plate, chop, 12 1/2" d., Ultra California patt., (carnation) pink or ice green 45
Plate, chop, 14" d., Winchester '73 (Frontier Days) patt. 295
Platter, 12" d., Winchester '73 (Frontier Days) patt. 225
Platter, 14" d., round, Winchester '73 (Frontier Days) patt. 325
Salt & pepper shakers, Homespun patt., pr. 12
Salt & pepper shakers, Organdie patt., pr. 25
Soup plate w/flanged rim, Organdie patt., 8" d. 15
Sugar bowl, cov., Organdie patt. 10
Teapot, cov., Vernon's 1860 patt. 75
Tray, round, Homespun patt., 12" d. 25
Trio buffet server, Country Cousin patt............. 50
Tumbler, Heavenly Days patt., 14 oz................. 16
Tumbler, Tickled Pink patt., 14 oz..................... 18
Vegetable bowl, Homespun patt., 9" d. 15
Vegetable bowl, open, Tam O'Shanter patt. 15
Vegetable bowl, open, divided, Tam O'Shanter patt. 28
Vegetable bowl, open, oval, divided, Fron-tier Days (Winchester 73) patt. 120
Vegetable bowl, open, oval, May Flower patt. 20

DISNEY "FANTASIA" & OTHER ITEMS
Bowl, 10 1/2" d., Sprite, No. 125, blue 260
Figure of Dumbo 225
Figure of Hippo, dancing w/arms out, 5 1/2" h. 450
Figure of Nubian Centaurette, No. 24, 7 1/2" h. 1,050
Figure of Unicorn, sitting, white, No. 14, 5" h. 600
Vase, 7 1/2" h., 12" l., Winged Pegasus patt., a wide flat-sided tapering form w/curved ends & a long rectangular flat

mouth, lightly molded w/the winged horse in a landscape, a white ground h.p. in green, brown, yellow & black, glossy glaze, ca. 1941, marked..................... **600-1,200**

Vase, 10 1/2" h., Goddess patt., footed flattened ovoid form w/a low scalloped rim, relief-molded standing figure of a nude female shooting a bow & arrow, blue... **700-1,200**

DON BLANDING DINNERWARES

Bowl, 5 1/2" d., individual salad, Lei Lani patt. 45
Charger, Lei Lani patt., 17 1/2" d. 200
Cup, Coral Reef patt., maroon 60

Hawaiian Flowers Cup & Saucer

Cup & saucer, Hawaiian Flowers patt., maroon (ILLUS.).. 45
Cup & saucer, Lei Lani patt. 50
Gravy boat, Lei Lani patt. 165
Nappy, 9" d., Lei Lani patt. 165
Plate, 7" d., Lei Lani patt. 27
Plate, 9" d., Hawaiian Flowers patt., maroon 50
Plate, 9" d., Lei Lani patt. 50
Plate, bread & butter, Lei Lani patt. 32
Plate, dinner, Lei Lani patt................................. 45
Plate, chop, 12" d., Hawaiian Flowers patt., maroon 132
Plate, chop, 14" d., Hawaiian Flowers patt., maroon 150
Plate, chop, 14" d., Lei Lani patt., Ultra line 195
Plate, chop, 17" d., Lei Lani patt...................... 200
Salt & pepper shakers, Hawaiian Flowers patt., maroon, pr. 50
Sugar bowl, cov., Lei Lani patt. 50

MISCELLANEOUS COMMEMORATIVES

Plate, "Abraham Lincoln"..................................... 18
Plate, "Badlands, South Dakota" 18
Plate, "Chicago Fair" 18
Plate, "Fort Riley, Texas"..................................... 18
Plate, Mission San Gabriel, multicolored............ 35
Plate, Mission Santa Barbara, multicolored 35
Plate, "United States Map," blue 18
Plate, "University of Chicago"............................. 18

ROCKWELL KENT DESIGNS

Bowl, 9" d., "Our America" series, scene of New York City piers....................................... 100
Cup & saucer, demitasse, Moby Dick patt., blue 75

Jam jar w/notched cover, Moby Dick patt., maroon 200
Mug, Moby Dick patt., maroon........................... 80
Plate, 9 1/2" d., Moby Dick patt., Ultra shape, blue... 69
Plate, 9 1/2" d., "Our America" series, Ultra shape, blue... 69
Plate, 9 1/2" d., Salamina patt. 135

Salamina Plate

Plate, 10 1/2" d., Salamina patt. (ILLUS.)......... 155
Plate, 12" d., Salamina patt. 275
Plate, chop, 12 1/2" d., Salamina patt. 225
Plate, chop, 14" d., "Our America" series, "Down on the Levee"...................................... 110
Plate, chop, 17" d., "Our America" series 300
Sugar bowl, cov., Moby Dick patt. 75
Teapot, cov., Moby Dick patt., blue, 6-cup 160
Tumbler, Moby Dick patt., brown & white 195

STATES SERIES - 10 1/2" d.

Plate, "Illinois".. 18
Plate, "Louisiana" 18
Plate, "New York" 15
Plate, "North Carolina".. 15
Plate, "Tennessee" 20
Plate, "Texas".. 18
Plate, "Washington - The Evergreen State"........ 15

WARWICK

Numerous collectors have turned their attention to the productions of the Warwick China Manufacturing Company that operated in Wheeling, West Virginia, from 1887 until 1951. Prime interest would seem to lie in items produced before 1914 that were decorated with decal portraits of beautiful women, monks and Indians. Fraternal Order items, as well as floral and fruit decorated items, are also popular with collectors. Donald Hoffmann has prepared the following listing and for more information on his books and video see our Special Contributors section.

Warwick Mark

Pitcher, 6 1/2" h., Lemonade shape, brown shaded to brown ground, color floral decoration, No. A-27 .... **$145**

Lemonade Shape Pitcher with Lady

Pitcher, 9 3/4" h., Lemonade shape, overall pink ground w/color "Aunt Hilda" type bust portrait of a young woman w/dark hair in a bouffant style & holding purple flowers, No. H-1 (ILLUS.) 300

Vase, 4" h., Parisian shape, overall charcoal ground, color nude portrait signed "Carreno," No. C-1 275

Vase, 4 1/2" h., Dainty shape, brown shaded to brown ground, colored floral decoration, No. A-27 280

Vase, 6" h., Narcis #3 shape, brown shaded to brown ground, decorated w/a fisherman wearing a yellow slicker, No. A-35.. 240

Vase, 6 1/2" h., Clytie shape, tan shaded to brown ground w/beechnut decoration, matte finish, No. M-2 320

Vase, 6 1/2" h., Den shape, brown shaded to brown ground, pine cone decoration, No. A-64 400

Vase, 6 3/4" h., Narcis #2 shape, overall red ground, color portrait of Princess Potaka, No. E-1.. 260

Vase, 8" h., Chicago shape, brown shaded to brown ground w/red & green floral decoration, No. A-40 300

Vase, 8" h., Rose shape, overall red ground w/color portrait of Madame Recamier, No. E-1....................................... 230

Vase, 8 1/4" h., Narcis #1 shape, overall white ground w/color bird decoration, No. D-1.. 250

Vase, 9 1/4" h., Windsor shape, brown shaded to brown ground, acorn decoration, No. A-67 325

Penn Vase with Acorn Decoration

Vase, 9 1/2" h., Penn shape, brown shaded to brown ground, acorn decoration, No. A-64 (ILLUS.) 195

Vase, 9 1/2" h., Penn shape, overall green color w/no decoration, matte finish, No. M-6 270

Vase, 9 1/2" h., Verbenia #1 shape, brown shaded to brown ground, color floral decoration, No. A-6 165

Vase, 10" h., Henrietta shape, brown shaded to brown ground, color portrait of a semi-nude young woman, No. A-30 325

Vase, 10" h., Roberta shape, brown shaded to brown ground, portrait of a monk, No. A-36 290

Vase, 10" h., Royal #2 shape, brown shaded to brown ground, floral decoration, No. A-27 295

Warwick Bouquet #2 Portrait Vase

Vase, 10 1/2" h., Bouquet #2 shape, brown shaded to brown ground, portrait of a young woman w/dark hair holding a branch w/white flowers, No. A-17 (ILLUS.)... 245

Vase, 11" h., Royal #1 shape, brown shaded to brown ground w/colored floral decoration, No. A-40 295

Vase, 11 1/2" h., Bouquet #1 shape, brown shaded to brown ground, portrait of young woman wearing a pearl necklace, No. A-17.. 265

Vase, 11 1/2" h., Chrysanthemum #3 shape, brown shaded to brown ground, color floral decoration, No. A-6.................... 160

Vase, 11 1/2" h., Hibiscus shape, brown shaded to brown ground, large color scene of red & black & white setter dogs hunting, No. A-50 375

Vase, 11 1/2" h., President shape, tan shaded to tan ground, acorn decoration, matte finish, No. M-4 260

Vase, 11 3/4" h., Egyptian shape, brown shaded to brown ground, red floral decoration, No. A-27 (ILLUS.).............................. 325

Vase, 12 1/2" h., Alexandria shape, brown shaded to brown ground w/color floral decoration, No. A-40 300

Egyptian Shape Vase with Flowers

Vase, 15" h., A Beauty shape, white ground w/red rose (American Beauty) decoration, No. D-2 .... **325**

Vase, 15 1/2" h., Chrysanthemum #1 shape, overall red ground w/a Madame LeBrun child portrait, No. E-1 .... **225**

DINNERWARES

Cup & saucer, Pattern No. 9572, Silver Poppy decoration **10**

Cup & saucer, Pattern No. 9903, Grey Blossom decoration.. **18**

Pitcher, 8" h., buttermilk-type, white ground w/floral decoration of small pink flowers.. **45**

Pitcher, 8" h., milk-type, white ground w/floral decoration of blue forget-me-nots **35**

Plate, 6 1/2" d., bread & butter, Pattern No. 9437-M, Windsor Maroon decoration............. **10**

Plate, 9" d., Pattern AB-9231 .... **8**

Plate, 10" d., dinner, Pattern No. 9584, Bird of Paradise decoration w/single bird **10**

Plate, 10" d., Pattern No. 2098, Venetian Rose decoration... **10**

Vegetable bowl, cov., Pattern No. 2001 .... **40**

COMMERCIAL CHINA

Cup, white w/"Johnny's" logo **25**

Cup & saucer, brown wave decoration, Santone finish **45**

Cup & saucer, white w/"Duckwall's" logo **40**

Cup & saucer, white w/Crestwood pattern **25**

Cup & saucer, white w/Dakota pattern **20**

Mustard jar, cov., white w/"Duckwall's" logo (ILLUS.).. **28**

Warwick "Duckwall's" Mustard Jar

Syrup pitcher, cov., white w/"Johnny's" logo **40**

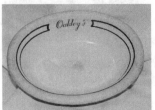

"Oakley's" Oval Vegetable Dish

Vegetable dish, individual, oval, white w/"Oakley's" logo (ILLUS.) **18**

WATT POTTERY

Founded in 1922, in Crooksville, Ohio, this pottery continued in operation until the factory was destroyed by fire in 1965. Although stoneware crocks and jugs were the first wares produced, by 1935 sturdy kitchen items in yellowware were the mainstay of production. Attractive lines like Kitch-N-Queen (banded) wares and the hand-painted Apple, Cherry and Pennsylvania Dutch (tulip) patterns were popular throughout the country. Today these hand-painted utilitarian wares are "hot" with collectors.

A good reference book for collectors is Watt Pottery, An Identification and Value Guide, by Sue and Dave Morris (Collector Books, 1933)

Watt Pottery Mark

Baker, cov., Cherry patt., No. 53, 7 1/2" d...... **$110**

Baker, cov., Apple patt., No. 601, 8" d. **120**

Baker, cov., Apple patt., No. 67, 8 1/4" d. **125**

Baker, cov., Autumn Foliage patt., No. 110, 8 1/2" d. **75**

Baker, cov., Cherry patt., No. 54, 8 1/2" d........ **110**

Baker, cov., Open Apple patt., No. 110, 8 1/2" d. **295**

Baker, Apple patt., rectangular, No. 85, 9" w. **1,000**

Bean cup, Tear Drop patt., No. 75, 3 1/2" d. 2 1/4" h.. **15**

Bean pot, cov., Apple patt., No. 76, 6 1/2" h.. **150**

Bean pot, cov., Dutch Tulip patt., No. 76, 6 1/2" h.. **275**

Bean pot, cov., Rooster patt., No. 76, 6 1/2" h.. **350**

Watt Pottery Apple Pattern Bowls

Bowl, 4" d., 1 1/2" d., Apple patt., No. 602
(ILLUS. far left)... **125**

Bowl, 4 1/4" d., 2" h., Apple patt., No. 04........... **50**

Bowl, 4 1/4" d., 2" h., Double Apple patt.,
No. 04.. **100**

Bowl, 5" d., 2" h., Apple patt., No. 603
(ILLUS. center left previous page) **100**

Bowl, 5 1/4" d., 2 1/2" h., Tear Drop patt.,
No. 05.. **40**

Bowl, 5 1/2" d., 2" h., Reduced Decoration
Apple patt., No. 74 .... **30**

Bowl, 6" d., 2 1/2" h., Apple patt., No. 604
(ILLUS. center previous page) **90**

Bowl, 6" d., 2 1/2" h. Tulip patt., No. 604 .... **150**

Bowl, 6 1/4" d., 2 1/4" h., Cherry patt., No.
52.. **35**

Bowl, 7" d., 3" h., Apple patt., No. 600
(ILLUS. center right page)............................. **50**

Bowl, 7" d., 3" h., Tulip patt., No. 600 .... **125**

Bowl, 7 1/4" d., 3" h., Apple patt., No. 07........... **50**

Bowl, 7 1/4" d., 3" h., Double Apple patt.,
No. 07.. **70**

Bowl, 8" d., 3 1/2" h., Apple patt., No. 601
(ILLUS. far right previous page) **60**

Bowl, 8" d., 3 1/2" h., Tulip patt., No. 601 .... **125**

Bowl, 9 1/2" d., 4" h., Open Apple patt., No.
73 .... **250**

Bowl, 10" d., 3" h., Autumn Foliage patt.,
No. 106.. **85**

Bowl, 11" d., 4" h., Starflower patt., No. 55........ **40**

Bowl, spaghetti, 13" d., 3 1/2" h., Autumn
Foliage patt., No. 39..................................... **135**

Bowl, spaghetti, 13" d., 3 1/2" h,. Dogwood
patt., No. 39 .... **135**

Bowl, spaghetti, 13" d., 3 1/2" h., Dutch
Tulip patt., No. 39 .... **400**

Bowl, spaghetti, 13" d., 3 1/2" h., Open
Apple patt., No. 39 .... **800**

Canister, cov., Apple patt., No. 82, 5" d........... **400**

Canister, cov., Starflower patt., No. 82,
5" d. **300**

Canister, cov., Dutch Tulip patt., No. 81,
6 1/2" d. **400**

Watt Canister, Rio Rose Pattern

Canister, cov., Rio Rose patt., No. 72,
7 1/4" d. (ILLUS.)... **300**

Canister, cov., Apple patt., No. 80,
8 1/2" d. **900**

Canister, cov., Rooster patt., No. 80,
8 1/2" d. **600**

Watt Carafe and Assorted Pitchers

Carafe, cov., Autumn Foliage patt., No.
115, 9 1/2" h. (ILLUS. far left)...................... **200**

Carafe, cov., Brown banded, No. 115,
10 1/2" **350**

Casserole, cov., Apple patt., No. 18, 5" d....... **175**

Casserole, cov., Dogwood patt., No. 18,
5" d. **125**

Casserole, cov., French handled, Apple
patt., No. 18, 5" d. **225**

Casserole, cov., French handled, Rooster
patt., No. 18, 5" d. **200**

Assorted Watt Autumn Foliage Pattern

Chip-n-Dip set, Autumn Foliage patt., No.
110 & 120 bowls, the set (ILLUS. center)..... **150**

Chip-n-Dip set, Double Apple patt., No. 96
&120 bowls, the set....................................... **350**

Churns, stoneware, Eagle or Acorn patt.,
various sizes **100-150**

Cookie jar, cov., "Goodies," No. 76, 6 1/2"
h.. **150**

Cookie jar, cov., Apple patt., No. 21, 7 1/2"
h.. **400**

Cookie jar, cov., Rio Rose patt., No. 21,
7 1/2" h. **150**

Cookie jar, cov., happy/sad face, wooden
lid, No. 34, 8" h.. **150**

Cookie jar, cov., Starflower patt., No. 503,
8" h. **350**

Cookie jar, cov., Tulip patt., No. 503, 8" h. **350**

Cookie jar, cov., Morning Glory patt.,
cream, No. 95, 10" h. **600**

Cookie jar, cov., "Cookie Barrel," wood
grain, 10 1/2" h. **50**

Cookie jar, cov., figural, Policeman,
10 1/2" h., rare **1,100**

Creamer, Apple (three-leaf) patt., No. 62,
4 1/4" h.. **90**

Creamer, Apple (two-leaf) patt., No. 62,
4 1/4" h.. **150**

Creamer, Autumn Foliage patt., No. 62,
4 1/4" h. (ILLUS. left w/Chip-n-Dip set) **250**

Creamer, Dutch Tulip patt., No. 62,
4 1/4" h.. **275**

Creamer, Morning Glory patt., cream, No.
97, 4 1/4" h. **400**

Assorted Watt Pottery, Starflower Pattern (Five-petal)

Creamer, Starflower patt., five-petal, No. 62, 4 1/4" h. (ILLUS. far right) **200**

Assorted Watt Pottery, Starflower Pattern (Four-petal)

Creamer, Starflower patt., four-petal, No. 62, 4 1/4" h. (ILLUS. second from left) **250**
Creamer, Tulip patt., No. 62, 4 1/4" h. **225**

Watt Pottery Crocks

Crocks, stoneware, Eagle or Acorn patt., various sizes (ILLUS. of two) **25-50**
Cruet set, cov., Apple patt., 7 1/2" h. **1,500**
Cruet set, cov., Autumn Foliage patt., 7 1/2" h. **300**
Grease jar, cov., Apple patt., No. 47, 5" h. **400**
Grease jar, cov., Autumn Foliage patt., No. 01, 5" h. **200**
Grease jar, cov., Starflower patt., No. 01, 5" h. **275**
Ice bucket, cov., Autumn Foliage patt., No. 59, 7" h. **200**
Ice bucket, cov., Dutch Tulip patt., No. 59, 7" h. **400**
Ice tea keg, cov., brand name, 11" h. (ILLUS.) **110**
Ice tea keg, cov., plain, 11" h. (ILLUS.) **60**
Mixing bowl, Reduced Decoration Apple patt., deep, No. 61 .... **125**
Mixing bowl, Reduced Decoration Apple patt., Nos. 5, 6, 7, & 9, 5" to 9" d., each **60**
Mixing bowl, Morning Glory patt., 5" d. **125**

Watt Pottery Ice Tea Kegs

Mixing bowls, nesting-type, Apple patt., Nos. 5, 6, 7, & 9, 5" to 9" d., each **60**
Mixing bowls, nesting-type, Apple patt., ribbed, Nos. 5, 6, 7, & 9, 5" to 9" d., each **70**
Mixing bowls, nesting-type, Morning Glory patt., Nos. 6, 7, 8, & 9, 6" to 9" d., each **80**
Mixing bowls, nesting-type, Open Apple patt., Nos. 5, 6, 7, & 8, 5" to 8" d., each **150**
Mixing bowls, nesting-type, Starflower patt., Nos. 5, 6, 7, 8, & 9, 5" to 9" d., each **35**
Mug, Apple patt., No. 121, 3" h. **175**
Mug, Apple patt., No. 501, 4 1/2" h. **275**
Mug, Autumn Foliage patt., No. 501, 4 1/2" h. **125**
Pie plate, Apple patt., No. 33, 9" d. **150**
Pie plate, Rooster patt., No. 33, 9" d. **400**
Pie plate, Starflower patt., five-petal, No. 33, 9" d. **200**
Pitcher, 5 1/2" h., Autumn Foliage patt., No. 15 (ILLUS. far right) **75**
Pitcher, 5 1/2" h., Cross Hatch patt., No. 15 .... **250**
Pitcher, 5 1/2" h., Dutch Tulip patt., No. 15 ...... **300**
Pitcher, 5 1/2" h., Silhouette patt., No. 15 .... **200**
Pitcher, 5 1/2" h., Starflower patt., five-petal, No. 15 (ILLUS. second from right w/creamer) **65**
Pitcher, 5 1/2" h., Starflower patt., four-petal, No. 15 (ILLUS. center w/creamer) **125**
Pitcher, 5 1/2" h., Tulip patt., No. 15 .... **450**
Pitcher, 6 1/2" h., Autumn Foliage patt., No. 16 (ILLUS. second from right) **85**
Pitcher, 6 1/2" h., Cherry patt., No. 16 .... **135**
Pitcher, 6 1/2" h., Double Apple patt., No. 16 .... **200**
Pitcher, 6 1/2" h., Rio Rose patt., No. 16 .... **200**
Pitcher, 6 1/2" h., Silhouette patt., No. 16 .... **75**
Pitcher, 6 1/2" h., Starflower patt., five-petal, No. 16 (ILLUS. second from left w/creamer) **85**
Pitcher, 6 1/2" h., Starflower patt., four-petal, No. 16 (ILLUS. second from right w/creamer) **85**
Pitcher, 7" h., Raised Rose patt., old style **225**
Pitcher, 7" h., Rio Rose, old style **150**
Pitcher, 8" h., Apple patt., refrigerator, No. 69 .... **450**
Pitcher, 8" h., Apple patt., w/ice lip, No. 17 ...... **225**

Pitcher, 8" h., Autumn Foliage patt., No. 17
(ILLUS. second from left page 343) **100**
Pitcher, 8" h., Eagle patt., No. 17..................... **400**
Pitcher, 8" h., Morning Glory patt., No. 96 .... **300**
Pitcher, 8" h., Rio Rose patt., No. 17 .... **250**
Pitcher, 8" h., Starflower patt., four-petal,
No. 17 .... **135**
Pitcher, 8" h., Starflower patt., refrigerator,
No. 69 .... **500**
Pitcher, 8" h., Tear Drop patt., four-petal,
refrigerator, No. 69 .... **500**
Plate, 6 1/2" d., Rio Rose patt. **20**

Watt Moonflower Plate & Platter

Plate, 10" d., Moonflower patt. (ILLUS.
right) **60**
Platter, 12" d., Cherry patt., No. 49
Platter, 12" d., Rio Rose patt., No. 49 .... **75**
Platter, 15" d., Apple patt., No. 31 .... **300**
Platter, 15" d., Autumn Foliage patt., No.
31 .... **100**
Platter, 15" d, Moonflower patt., No. 31
(ILLUS. left) **80**
Platter, 15" d., Starflower patt., No. 31 .... **110**
Salt & pepper shakers, barrel-shaped,
Starflower patt., five-petal, 4" h., the set **200**
Salt & pepper shakers, barrel-shaped,
Tear Drop patt., 4" h., the set **300**
Salt & pepper shakers, hourglass-shaped,
Autumn Foliage patt., 4" h., the set
(ILLUS. far right w/Chip-n-Dip set) **160**
Salt & pepper shakers, hourglass-shaped,
Rooster patt., 4" h., the set........................... **375**
Sugar bowl, cov., Morning Glory patt., No.
98, 4 1/4" h.. **250**
Sugar bowl, cov., Autumn Foliage patt.,
No. 98, 4 1/2" h. (ILLUS. far left w/Chip-
n-Dip set page 343)...................................... **275**

Watt Pottery Teapots

Teapot, cov., Apple patt., No. 505, 5" h.
(ILLUS. left) **2,800**

Teapot, cov., Apple (three-leaf) patt., No.
112, 6" h. (ILLUS. right)............................ **1,500**
Teapot, cov., Autumn Foliage patt., No.
112, 6" h. **1,000**

WEDGWOOD

*Reference here is to the famous pottery estab-
lished by Josiah Wedgwood in 1759 in England.
Numerous types of wares have been produced
through the years to the present.*

WEDGWOOD

Wedgwood Mark

BASALT

Bowl, 5 3/4" d., footed wide rounded form
w/flat rim, applied classical figural relief
designs above an engine-turned band,
impressed mark, late 18th c. **$403**
Bust of Cicero, mounted on a waisted circular socle, impressed title & Wedgwood
and Bentley mark, ca. 1775, 10" h.
(chips to socle rim) **2,300**
Bust of Garrick, miniature, mounted on a
waisted circular socle, impressed mark,
19th c., 3 7/8" h. **431**

Basalt Bust of George Washington

Bust of George Washington, mounted on
a waisted circular socle, impressed title
& mark, 19th c., 19 3/4" h. (ILLUS.) **6,038**
Bust of King George II, shown wearing a
long wig & parade armor, after a carving
by John Michael Rysbrack, on a raised
square plinth, impressed lower case
marks, ca. 1780, 9" h. **1,093**
Bust of Newton, mounted on a waisted cir-
cular socle, impressed mark, 19th c.,
9 1/4" h. **431**
Candlesticks, figural, model of a large
seated griffin w/a tall candle socket atop
the head, on a rectangular platform
base, traces of later gilding, impressed
mark of Wedgwood and Bentley, ca.
1775, one w/wings restored & small rim
chips on socket & plinth, one w/socket

restored at join & small chips on socket rim & wings, 12 1/2" h., pr. (ILLUS.) **19,550**

Coffeepot, cov., wide baluster form w/swan's-neck spout, C-form handle & domed cover w/knob finial, decorated overall w/large clusters of polychromed flowers, impressed mark, ca. 1840, 8 3/4" h. **690**

Cracker jar, cov., the engine-turned body below a band of children playing in relief, silver plate rim, cover & bail handle, impressed mark, late 19th c., 5 1/2" h. **516**

Creamer, helmet-form, short pedestal base below the inverted helmet-form body w/a wide arched spout & D-form loop handle, a continuous relief scene of bacchana-lian boys at play above an engine-turned band, impressed mark of Wedgwood and Bentley, early 19th c., 4 3/8" h. **518**

Crocus pot, figural, the top modeled as a large rounded hedgehog pierced w/holes, in a fitted oblong dished base, impressed marks, 1975, 9 1/2" l. **546**

Basalt Crocus Pot

Crocus pot & undertray, domed woven basketweave beehive-form top w/loop handle pierced overall w/holes, resting on a dished matching tray, impressed mark, early 19th c., 7 1/4" h. (ILLUS.) **1,265**

Figure of a faun playing flute, a nude youth standing & leaning against a fur-draped tree trunk, on a rounded rectan-gular base, impressed title & mark, 19th c., 17 1/4" h. (slight chip restored on instrument) **2,645**

Figure of Aphrodite, nude young woman seated atop a wave-crested base & gaz-ing up at a small seashell she holds in one hand, impressed title & mark, late 19th c., 10 3/8" h. **920**

Basalt Figure of Mercury

Figure of Mercury, the naked youth stand-ing wearing his winged helmet, leaning against a tall tree stump, round base, impressed mark & title, 19th c., 12 1/2" h. (ILLUS.) **2,070**

Figure of Voltaire, standing wearing a long wig, a waistcoat, kneebreeches & a long coat, one arm extended holding a book, after the marble figure by Jean-Claude Rosset, mounted on a free-form circular base, impressed title & mark, 19th c., 10 3/4" h. (footrim chip) **1,610**

Lamp bases, tall classical urn-form w/the sides molded in relief w/oval eagle medallions between foliate festoons ter-minating at lion mask handles, slender pedestal w/round foot on a square stepped base, 20th c., 21" h., pr. **2,645**

Medallion, oval, embossed bust profile portrait of Benjamin Franklin, titled & impressed mark of Wedgwood and Bentley, ca. 1780, 1 3/4 x 2" **1,035**

Medallion, oval, embossed profile bust portrait of George Washington, set in a brass frame, titled & impressed mark of Wedgwood and Bentley, ca. 1775, 2 1/2 x 3 1/4" (edge flakes) **1,725**

Model of a bear, animal walking on all fours, by Ernest Light, ca. 1915, impressed mark, 2 1/2" h. **489**

Mug, cylindrical w/silver-mounted rim band, sides relief-molded w/classical children representing Spring & Winter, impressed lower case mark, D-form handle, late 18th c., 3 1/2" h. (handle restored) **805**

Pitcher, 5 7/8" h., bottle-form, a footed bul-bous ovoid body tapering to a waisted cylindrical neck w/a flaring flattened mouth, arched grapevine handle ending in a bacchus head, the body molded in high-relief w/figure groups representing the Four Seasons, impressed mark, 19th c. **748**

Pitcher, 6 1/2" h., jug-type, "Egyptian" patt., club-form, decorated in iron-red, black & white w/a sphinx at either side of a bird in flight, impressed mark, ca. 1854 (rim chip) **690**

Plant pot & underplate, acanthus leaf borders on a trellis-molded body, impressed mark, 19th c., 2 7/8" h., 2 pcs. (rim nick) **460**

Basalt Plaque with Classical Scene

Plaque, oval, molded in relief w/figures of a classical lady carrying stems of poppies, a cupid walking in front, titled "Night Shedding Poppies," impressed mark of Wedgwood & Bentley, ca. 1777, hairline, 13 1/4 x 17 3/4" (ILLUS.)............................ **6,038**

Punch pot, cov., an engine-turned band below the shoulder, impressed early 19th c. mark, 7 1/2" h. (slight shoulder chips)... **460**

Ring, intaglio-type, oval portrait of the Duke of Gloucester, white gold mounting, impressed mark & numbered 283, Wedgwood and Bentley, intaglio 3/4 x 7/8" **518**

Sugar bowl, cov., cylindrical body tapering in at the bottom, fitted engine-turned domed cover w/rim band & figural sibyl finial, the sides molded w/a scene depicting Domestic Employment, impressed mark, late 18th c., 5" h. **748**

Teapot, cov., cylindrical oval form w/straight angled spout & angled C-form handle, domed cover w/figural Sybil finial, enameled w/palmette, leaf, leaf & berry banding, impressed mark, early 19th c., 8" l. (chip on cover)....................... **3,450**

Vase, cov., classical urn-form, the tall ovoid body w/a angled shoulder tapering to a cylindrical neck w/rolled rim, small domed cover w/knob finial, bacchus head handles from rim to side of shoulder, slender waisted pedestal on a square plinth foot, the sides w/oval relief molded medallions of classical figures, impressed lozenge mark of Wedgwood and Bentley, shape No. 1, ca. 1775, handles restored, replaced cover, 10 1/4" h. (ILLUS.).................................... **1,725**

Vase, 5" h., disk foot & short stem below the bulbous ovoid body tapering slightly to a wide, short rolled neck, the side cast

in relief w/a continuous scene of bacchanalian boys at play, 19th c., impressed mark **575**

Classical Basalt Covered Vase

Vase, cov., 10 1/2" h., classical urn-form, square plinth w/patterned edges supporting a short flaring engine-turned pedestal below the tall ovoid urn-form body w/a wide shoulder tapering to an engine-turned waisted neck w/flared rim & small domed cover w/knob finial, slender ropetwist loop handles from rim to edge of shoulder ending w/a lion mask, the body w/a relief-molded procession of classical figures, acanthus & laurel leaf borders, impressed mark of Wedgwood and Bentley, ca. 1775 (slight rim flakes on plinth) **3,738**

CANEWARE

Creamer, molded w/bamboo leaves, enamel-decorated, impressed lower case mark, 18th c., 2 1/2" h...................... **1,265**

Game dish, cov., low oval form w/insert ring, piecrust-molded rim, low domed cover w/applied radiating acanthus leaves & zigzag & loop border bands, short cylindrical small opening at center of cover, impressed mark, early 19th c., 14" l. (stains, rim chips to ring) **920**

Game dish & cover, oval form, the high cylindrical cover molded in relief around the sides w/leafy vines & dead game, a figural recumbent hare finial, impressed mark, ca. 1871, 7" l. (missing insert dish)..... **575**

Inkstand, modeled as a long narrow boat-form basket w/molded basketweave exterior & central arched handle, applied rosso antico foliate trim, molded wells at each end & holding two covered cylindrical pots w/further trim, impressed mark, late 18th c., overall 8 3/4" l., the set (inkwell stained, interior collar rim chip on one cover, slight rim lines on pots)........... **2,645**

Teapot, cov., spherical bamboo-molded body w/a bamboo-molded spout & loop handle, domed cover w/bamboo twig handle, trimmed w/dark blue banding &

dots, impressed lower case mark, 18th c., 4 1/4" h. (chips on spout) **2,760**

Vase, 7" h., trumpet-form w/flared foot & ringed & widely flaring mouth, applied black classical figures in relief between floral & leaf w/berry bands, impressed mark, early 19th c. (disk lid missing) **690**

JASPER WARE

Basket, basketweave sides w/molded loop handle, dark blue ground applied w/white relief openwork cells, impressed mark, early 19th c., 4 1/2" h. (slight relief loss) **431**

Book case, rectangular flattened oak case w/brass hardware, mounted w/seven round light blue jasper medallions w/white relief portraits or classical designs, the case including five leather-bound journals, marked "Howell, James & Co. - Regent Street, London," no visible marks on medallions, ca. 1900, 3 3/8 x 8 1/4", 5" h. **1,610**

Bowl, 5 7/8" d., black ground decorated w/a white relief figural decoration of the Dancing Hours, impressed mark, 20th c. **489**

Black Jasper Ware Bowl

Bowl, 10 1/8" d., deep footrim supporting deep curved sides, classical white relief figures representing Dancing Hours on a black ground, impressed mark, 20th c. (ILLUS.) **460**

Box, cov., round short cylindrical form w/fitted flattened cover, dark blue ground decorated in white slip w/scrolling stems & blossoms on the cover & leaf-tips around the base rim, artist-signed by Harry Barnard, impressed mark, ca. 1900, 2 3/4" d. (shallow rim chip on cover) **633**

Box, cov., square w/rounded corners, crimson red ground decorated on the slightly domed top & around the sides w/white relief classical figure groups surrounded by flowering bands & corner scrolls on the base, impressed mark, ca. 1920, 4" w. **1,150**

Brooch, oval, blue ground decorated in white relief w/a classical scene of the marriage of Cupid & Psyche, set in a wide scalloped cut-steel mount, no visible mark, ca. 1800, 2 1/2" l. **489**

Busts of Pindar & Aristophanes, solid white, each on a waisted circular socle, impressed marks & titles, Wedgwood and Bentley, ca. 1775, one w/footrim chip, 4" h., pr. **3,335**

Candleholder, stepped cylindrical form, dark blue ground decorated w/white relief classical figures & foliage designs, impressed mark, mid-19th c., 4" h **575**

Candlesticks, columnar standard on a wide flaring round foot, deeply cupped candle socket, black ground decorated around the standard w/white relief classical figures & around the foot w/a scrolling foliate band, a thin leaf band under the socket, impressed mark, 19th c., 8" h., pr. **863**

Candlesticks, cylindrical shaft w/a widely flaring base & topped by a swelled ring below the tall tulip-form candle socket, yellow ground decorated w/black relief classical figures & arabesque scroll border on the shaft & leaf bands on the socket, impressed mark, ca. 1930, 6" h., pr. **690**

Cheese dish, cov., wide cylindrical domed cover w/flat top centered by a button finial, dark blue ground decorated w/white relief classical figures & trees around the sides & radiating leaves & a foliate band around the finial, the matching dished base w/a flanged flat rim w/white relief foliate band, impressed mark, mid-19th c., 4 3/4" h. **345**

Clock, arched pediment w/white relief central winged classical figure flanked by "Tempus Fugit," above the narrow rectangular upright cast w/a round dial w/Arabic numerals above two white relief groups of women & children, white relief leaf bands up the sides & scrolls above the dial, on dark blue, impressed mark, ca. 1900, 8" h. (ILLUS.) **863**

Blue Jasper Ware Clock

Clock case, rectangular w/dark blue ground decorated w/white relief classical figures & foliate designs, impressed mark, ca. 1900, 6" h. **173**

Coffee cup & saucer, cylindrical cup, black ground decorated w/white relief classical trophies & medallions between fruiting festoons terminating at rams' heads, mid-19th c., saucer 5 1/4" d. (restored rim chip to saucer) **690**

Three-Color Jasper Coffee Mug

Coffee mug & saucer, cylindrical w/loop handle, deep dished saucer, white relief Diceware design & yellow quatrefoils on a black ground, impressed mark, mid-19th c., saucer 5 1/4" d. (ILLUS.) **2,530**

Blue Jasper Cracker Jar

Cracker jar, cov., cylindrical w/wide waisted body, the center molded in relief w/white classical figures on a dark blue ground, upper & lower border bands in light blue, silver plate rim, flat cover w/urn finials & swing bail handle, impressed mark, 19th c., 5" h. (ILLUS.) **288**

Cracker Jar with Dancing Hours

Cracker jar, cov., footed wide waisted cylindrical form w/upright scroll handles at the sides, low domed cover w/pointed knob finial, the body w/white relief classical figures representing Dancing Hours w/floral swags around the rim & on the cover, geometric relief bands at the bottom & around the foot, on a green ground, impressed factory mark &

"McVitie and Price 1906," handle restored, 8" h. (ILLUS.) **633**

Cracker jar, cov., low rounded base below the tapering cylindrical sides supporting a low domed cover w/button finial, black ground decorated w/a wide white relief central band of stylized Egyptian figures & designs between narrow florette border bands, white relief starburst around the finial, impressed factory mark & mark of retailer W.T. Lamb & Sons, ca. 1911, 6 1/4" h. (rim nick) **1,265**

Creamer, jug-form, ovoid body w/wide mouth & rim spout, C-scroll handle, black ground decorated w/heavy fruit festoons between rams' heads, classical & trophy designs, impressed mark, mid-19th c., 2 3/4" h. **748**

Earrings, almond-shaped medallions in blue decorated w/white relief classical figure, in a narrow cut-steel frame set w/rhinestones, short chain & screw-on clips, impressed marks, 19th c., 1 3/8" l., pr. **374**

Flowerpot, hanging-type, dark blue ground decorated w/white relief classical figures & foliate designs, unmarked, late 19th c., 6 1/2" h. **403**

Jardiniere, wide footrim below the wide cylindrical body w/a rounded base & flat rim, white relief classical figures of Muses below a band of fruiting grapevine swags suspended from lion masks, narrow border band, on a crimson ground, impressed mark, ca. 1920, 7 1/4" h. (slight surface flake) **2,415**

Small Jasper Jardiniere & Undertray

Jardiniere & undertray, cylindrical pot w/flaring rim molded in white relief w/classical figures on a crimson ground, matching dished undertray w/white relief floral band, impressed mark, ca. 1920, 3 1/2" h. (ILLUS.) **1,840**

Fine Jasper Ware Kerosene Lamp

Lamp, kerosene table model, the large baluster-form base w/white relief classical figures alternating w/upright scrolls over a band of tall acanthus leaves on a dark blue ground, fitted on a gilt brass footed base, brass collar & burner supporting a large spherical glass shade decorated w/a dark blue ground & white classical swags & ribbons, ca. 1900, electrified, overall 22 1/2" h. (ILLUS.) **1,955**

Lantern, candle-type, brass & jasper ware, the domed brass frame w/arched leaf bands around the top over a reticulated band above the open sides w/four oval brass frames enclosing light blue jasper plaques w/white relief classical figures of the Muses, the round base w/a solid band above the reticulated bottom band, no visible marks, 19th c., 11" h. **633**

Letter box, cov., rectangular oak case w/hinged domed cover, the top set w/an oval light blue jasper medallion w/white relief classical figures, cord-form brass trim loops across the cover & down the front & back, bright-cut brass corner plaques & butterfly keyhole escutcheon, late 19th c., 9 1/4" l. **2,070**

Letter opener, a flat oblong pointed wood blade w/a flat ormolu handle set w/a large & small oval blue jasper medallion each w/white relief classical figures, late 19th c., 11 3/4" l. **345**

Medallion, oval, blue ground decorated in white relief w/a standing classical nude female w/drapery, viewed from behind, impressed mark of Wedgwood and Bentley, ca. 1775, 2 5/8 x 3 1/4" **2,070**

Medallion, oval, blue ground decorated w/a white relief bust profile portrait of William Pitt, impressed title "Chatham," impressed mark, narrow brass frame, Wedgwood and Bentley, ca. 1778, 2 5/8 x 3 1/4" (blemish spots on surface) .. **1,610**

Model of "The Hands of the Potter," terra-cotta jasper, a pair of large human hands turning a vessel at the wheel, modeled by Colin Melbourne, No. 3 or 500, 1982, impressed mark, 6 3/4" h. **1,610**

Mustard jar, cov., rounded form in yellow applied w/black fruiting grapevine festoons terminating in lion mask, silver cover, impressed mark, 20th c., 3 3/8" h., ... **316**

Pen tray, narrow thin rectangular wood base w/a beaded ormolu border band & scrolled upright pen rests, the center set w/a rectangular medallion in light blue w/white relief classical scene of the marriage of Cupid & Psyche, a metal-framed round jasper medallion w/classical figures on each side, late 19th c., overall 8 1/4" l. **575**

Perfume bottle w/stopper, blue ground applied w/white relief floral festoons framing portraits possibly depicting Frederick I & Richard Molesworth, jasper stopper & silver screw lid, unmarked, late 18th c., 2 1/2" l. **805**

Early Wedgwood Jasper Pitcher

Pitcher, cov., 8 5/8" h., jug-form, lobed body w/two rows of white relief classical figures arranged in the lobes, domed cover, C-scroll handle, impressed mark, 18th c., rim chips under cover edge (ILLUS.) **920**

Pitcher w/hinged pewter cover, 6 1/8" h., three-color, cylindrical w/ropetwist handle, dark blue ground w/relief-molded yellow trellis & white foliate banding, impressed mark, mid-19th c. (minor relief loss) **633**

Pitchers, 7 1/2" h., 6 1/4" h., 5 1/4" h., set of slightly tapering cylindrical pieces w/small rim spouts & ropetwist handles, olive green ground w/white relief medallion bust portraits of George Washington within a leaf-tip frame w/a fruiting grapevine border around the rim, impressed marks, ca. 1920, the set (footrim chips) **575**

Plaque, oval, white relief scene of Bacchanalian Boys after a design by Lady Diana Beauclerk, on a dark blue ground, impressed mark, matted & framed, 19th c., 3 3/4 x 5 3/4" **748**

Plaque, oval, white relief classical scene of "The Apotheosis of Virgil," on a light blue ground, framed, 19th c., plaque 15 1/4 x 24 1/2" (ILLUS. next page) **4,313**

Plate, 8 1/2" d., blue ground decorated in white relief w/a classical figural scene, impressed mark, ca. 1861 .... **633**

Portland Vase, black ground molded in white relief w/a continuous classical figural scene, half-length figure wearing a Phrygian cap under base, unmarked, late 18th c., 10 1/8" h. (relief loss, surface blister).. **4,600**

Large Jasper Ware Plaque

Portland Vase, 10" h., wide ovoid body tapering to a trumpet neck flanked by arched handles, black ground w/white relief classical figural scene, impressed mark, late 19th c....................................... **2,415**

Potpourri, cov., a wide shallow bowl w/a low domed cover pierced w/a large top hole surrounded by smaller holes, raised on a ringed flaring pedestal on a thick square foot, dark blue ground decorated around the bowl w/large white relief arabesque scroll band, gadroon band, vertical stripes & lappet band on pedestal w/urn & scrolls on the foot, quatrefoils on the cover, early 19th c., impressed mark, 6 3/4" h. **1,725**

Scent bottle w/silver cap, flattened oval form, dark blue ground decorated in white relief w/a classical female figure within an oval framed by a ribbon, leaf & floral wreath, no visible mark, early 19th c., 3 1/4" l. **1,035**

Urn, three-color two-handled urn on pedestal, of shield shape sprigged in lilac & green on a white ground w/oval portrait medallion reserves w/classical maidens suspended between floral swags beneath an upper border of zodiac symbols, base & pedestal foot w/acanthus lappets, cylindrical pedestal w/a continuous scene of putti at play above a fluted lower section, acanthus & key-fret border, impressed "WEDGWOOD," early 19th c., 18 3/4" h. **1,150**

Vase, 3" h., trumpet-form w/loop handles, brown ground decorated w/white relief classical figures & foliate bands, impressed mark, late 19th c. **978**

Vase, cov., 7" h., trumpet-form, the large flaring bowl on a slender flaring pedestal base, dark blue ground w/the bowl decorated w/a white relief band of large

scrolling arabesque florals & foliage over a wide band of delicate leafage, white interior, impressed mark, late 18th - early 19th c. (interior damage, shallow chips on pierced cover) **633**

Vase, 9 3/4" h., classical urn-form w/a short pedestal base & a tall waisted neck w/rolled rim flanked by loop handles, undecorated light green ground, ca. 1900 .... **690**

Gilt-decorated Jasper Ware Vase

Vase, 9 3/4" h., light blue ground decorated w/ornate h.p. raised gilt large flowers & leafy stems, impressed mark, 19th c. (ILLUS.).. **2,875**

Jasper Urn-form Vase

Vase, 10 1/4" h., tall classical urn-form w/waisted neck flanked by arched handles, rolled rim, short domed pedestal base, the body w/a wide panel of white relief classical figures, classical white relief trophies on the neck, white relief leaf band around shoulder, white relief leaves around the base & foot, impressed mark, late 19th c. (ILLUS.).......... **748**

Vase, cov., 13 1/8" h., a tall square plinth supporting a classical tall urn-form vase w/a tall waisted cover w/domed tip & knob finial, green ground decorated around the plinth w/a white relief classical figure on each side, the vase body w/white relief classical figure groups separated by lattice bands below a twisted ribbon top band, the cover w/white relief long lappets, impressed mark, late 19th c.. **2,185**

Vase, 14 3/4" h., trophy-style, classical urn-form on a domed round foot, the waisted neck w/a rolled rim, arched handles from side of neck to shoulder, dark blue ground w/white relief classical figures around the body w/ribbons & trophies around the neck & foliate borders around the shoulder & base, impressed mark, ca. 1900 .... **978**

Vases 7 3/4" h., footed bulbous ovoid body w/a wide shoulder tapering to the flaring trumpet neck, upright loop handles at edge of shoulder, dark blue ground decorated w/white relief classical figure groups alternating w/slender foliate vertical bands, leaf band around the center of the neck, impressed mark, early 20th c., pr. **575**

Large Classical Jasper Vases

Vases, 14" h., classical urn-form, tall ovoid body tapering to a short waisted neck w/a wide rolled rim, arched scroll handles from rim to shoulder, raised on a ringed pedestal on an octagonal plinth, the body w/a wide band of white relief figures of the nine Muses w/gadroon & foliate borders, on a black ground, impressed marks, early 19th c., restorations to handles of each, also one plinth, missing covers, pr. (ILLUS.) **2,415**

Wine cooler, wide ovoid body w/a wide flat rim, figural swan head handles w/wings spread, Dice Ware design w/center panels of a classical "Roman Banquet" scene in white relief on green, applied yellow quatrefoils in the dice design, impressed mark, 19th c., restoration to handle, lower body & base, 10 1/2" h. (ILLUS.)... **4,600**

Rare Jasper Dice Ware Wine Cooler

PEARLWARE

Figure group, a standing boy wearing kneebreeches & a floral-decorated drapery beside a tree stump w/a small spotted dog reclining on the top, plinth base, impressed mark, possibly Ralph or Enoch Wedgwood, ca. 1800, 7 1/4" h. (hairline, restoration at neck)....................... **374**

Figure of Venus, standing woman in classical dress leaning on an upright dolphin, a figure of Cupid behind her, impressed mark, titled on the square plinth, possibly Ralph or Enoch Wedgwood, ca. 1800, 7 3/4" h. (chip to end of thumb)................... **575**

Figures of boys, overglaze enamel-decorated figures on cut-corner rectangular bases, one figure reclining holding a cross, the other reclining with one arm outstretched, impressed mark, cross restored, hairline & footrim chip on base, other w/restorations to base & figure, hairline in base at back, bird missing from hand, ca. 1800, possibly Ralph or Enoch Wedgwood, 7 3/8" h., pr................ **2,185**

Early Pearlware Foot Bath

Foot bath, deep oval form w/upright sides, molded rim & angled loop end handles, blue transfer-printed design showing scenes of the Tower of London, impressed mark, hairlines in base, early 19th c., 19 1/4" l. (ILLUS.) **1,955**

Lazy Susan, gilt & enamel-decorated in panels w/insects & foliage, impressed mark, ca. 1863, 18 5/8" d. **374**

Plate, 9 3/8" d., lightly scalloped flanged rim painted in underglaze-blue w/wavy bands, the interior painted w/a self-portrait of Therese Lessore, artist-signed, impressed mark, ca. 1921 .... **518**

Tea infuser, Beanes Patent model, gilt trim & polychrome decorated transfer-printed foliate design, scrolled handles, brass spigot, impressed mark, ca. 1863, 13 1/4" h. (missing inserts) **316**

QUEEN'S WARE

Bowl, 5 1/2" d., footed deep rounded & flaring sides w/rolled rim, h.p. in silver lustre & puce enamel w/a stylized continuous landscape scene w/female bathers disrobing, artist-signed by Therese Lessore, impressed factory mark, ca. 1920 .... **1,150**

Queen's Ware Breakfast Set

Breakfast set: cov. teapot, cov. sugar bowl, cov. creamer, waste bowl, a cup & saucer & oblong tray; each bulbous piece enamel-decorated w/flowers & insects, tray 16 7/8" l., teapot 4 1/4" h., impressed marks, some restorations, ca 1868, the set (ILLUS.) **1,035**

Bust of Penelope, stylized half-length bust of a Grecian lady, undecorated, modeled by Arnold Machin, printed mark, ca. 1940, 11" h. **374**

Dish, boat-form w/bearded mask head handles on the oval body fitted w/two circular cups, enamel-decorated w/fruiting grapevine decoration, impressed & printed marks, late 19th c., 13 1/4" l. **316**

Dish, oval shell-shape painted on the interior w/colorful cherubs, signed by Emile Lessore, impressed mark, ca. 1860, 13" l. **546**

Figure of Helen, standing Grecian lady wearing a long gown, one arm to her side, one arm across her waist, undecorated, modeled by Arnold Machin, printed marks, ca. 1940, 14" h. **748**

Model of bull, stylized standing Ferdinand, undecorated, modeled by Arnold Machin, impressed mark, ca. 1940, 12 1/4" l. **288**

Orange bowl, cov., low round pedestal foot supporting a wide rounded bowl w/a wide lobe-fluted flaring rim, the high domed cover pierced w/long tapering ovals framed by molded scroll lattice & floral designs, impressed mark, 20th c., 9 1/2" h. **633**

Plate, 9 7/8" d., polychrome decorated black transfer of a sailing ship centering a floral border, titled "Welvaren 1779" & "D'Maria & Adriana Leendert Steur," lower case mark, ca. 1779 (rim nicks) **805**

Pot, cov., kettle-form, three straight tapering angled legs supporting the wide kettle-form body w/slightly flaring cylindrical sides & pointed loop rim handles, a low domed cover w/low arched open handle, decorated by Emile Lessore w/enameled figural landscapes, artist-signed & impressed marks, ca. 1870, 5 1/4" h. (one foot stained) **748**

Sweetmeat baskets, each w/scalloped rim on a pierced body, impressed mark, early 19th c., 5" h., pr. **2,415**

Wash bowl & pitcher, black transfer-printed designs of Venetian-style subjects, printed marks, ca. 1900, bowl 15 3/4" d., pitcher 11" h., the set (bowl w/light general surface wear on interior) **144**

ROSSO ANTICO

Biggin, cov., a squatty bulbous teapot-form base w/long spout & C-scroll handle, molded overall w/floral scrolls & arabesques, the upper slightly flaring cylindrical section molded w/a band of palmette, the slightly domed cover w/a figural spaniel finial, impressed mark, ca. 1840, 5 3/4" h. (insert strainer w/rim chip) **518**

Jardiniere, wide swelled cylindrical form w/wide flat molded rim, molded ribbed band around the top above a wide panel of black basalt applied classical designs, early 19th c., impressed mark, 6 1/2" h. (ILLUS.) **1,150**

Rosso Antico Jardiniere

Oil lamp, antique-style, low oblong boatshape w/upright tightly curled end handle & upturned end spout, enameled around the sides w/floral sprigs, impressed mark, mid-19th c., 4 7/8" l. **518**

Pitcher, 5 3/4" h., jug-form, pear-shaped w/black basalt reeds & foliage in relief, impressed mark, early 19th c. (spider crack in body) **403**

Plate, 7" d., the flared rim band applied w/a white relief design of hieroglyphs & stylized designs, impressed mark, early 19th c. **690**

Potpourri jar, cover & insert, small footring supporting a large spherical body w/upright loop shoulder handles, pierced domed cover w/knob finial, overall floral enamel decoration, impressed mark, ca. 1830, rim chips on cover, 14 3/4" h., three pieces **3,335**

MISCELLANEOUS

Bank, glazed earthenware, modeled as a cylindrical brick building & inscribed on the footrim "Wedgwood - Etruria 1769 - The Round House," brown glaze, ca. 1969, 4 3/4" h. **201**

Bird feeder, majolica, cylindrical w/large open arched panels around the sides below a narrow angled shoulder & wide flat mouth, overall green glaze, impressed mark, ca. 1870, 2 3/4" h. **230**

Bird feeder, majolica, small barrel-shaped object w/the sides pierced w/large vertical rectangular openings w/arched tops, dark green glaze, impressed mark, ca. 1871, 3 7/8" h. **259**

Wedgwood Art Deco Book Ends

Book ends, earthenware, Art Deco style, each a quarter-round arch w/stepped curved bands above lower fanned ribs, a small stylized figure seated at the top, overall red glaze, designed by Erling Olsen, impressed mark, ca. 1932, 6 5/8" h., pr. (ILLUS.) **1,840**

Bottle, cover & underplate, the bottle w/a small short pedestal foot supporting a wide sharply tapering conical body banded w/silver plate & ending in a tall ringed cylindrical neck fitted w/a silver plate rim & flat cover w/a figural sphinx finial, the matching underplate w/a silver plate rim, all w/a mottled brown & green glaze, impressed marks, ca. 1875, overall 10 1/4" h., the set (bottle w/slight rim lines & glaze loss) **1,035**

Bowl, 4 1/2" d., Fairyland Lustre Nizami design, shallow round form, deep green lustre ground exterior & interior, the center w/a Persian scene of a figure in a garden landscape, Pattern Z5494, printed mark, ca. 1920 (very slight interior gilt wear) **3,335**

Bowl, 8 3/4" d., Amherst Pheasant Imperial Lustre, a thick footring supporting a deep rounded bowl, banded exterior design w/colorful pheasants against a light ground flanked by dark bands, a bird in a

hoop interior design on a mottled orange & red ground, Pattern Z5264, "KR" monogram w/horseshoe, printed mark, ca. 1920 (slight interior glaze scratches)... **2,300**

Bowl, 8 3/4" w., Fairyland Lustre, deep rounded octagonal body, the exterior w/"Leapfrogging Elves" against a night sky, the interior w/"Fairy in a Cage" against a daylight sky, Pattern Z4968, printed mark, ca. 1920 (interior glaze wear) **4,600**

Bowl, 10 1/2" d., Dragon Lustre, deep rounded upright sides on a thin footring, the mottled ruby red & blue exterior w/gilt dragons, the mottled mother-of-pearl interior w/butterflies surrounding a central floral medallion, printed mark, ca. 1920 .... **1,265**

Bread tray, majolica, rectangular w/curved-out sides, a flat flanged rim band molded w/waves, an argenta ground, the bottom inside molded w/a lattice of strapwork & coral branches, impressed mark, ca. 1880, 12 3/4" l. (surface wear) **546**

Center bowl, antique-style, short wide pedestal w/a widely flaring round foot, supporting a deep, wide bell-form bowl w/widely rolled rim, the matte black exterior w/printed floral sprigs, the white interior printed w/colorful flowers & gilt trim, printed mark, ca. 1925, 8 5/8" d. (exterior glaze scratches)..................................... **575**

Charger, Caneware, large round & slightly dished form h.p. w/a wide outer band of undulating vine w/large serrated leaves in a purple lustre glaze, a large single leaf in the center, attributed to Millicent Taplin, printed mark, ca. 1930, 12 1/2" d...... **374**

Cheese dish, cov., majolica, Bird & Fan patt., domed cover & conforming underplate, argenta ground, impressed mark, ca. 1880, 9 5/8" h. (slight staining to bottom rim of cover, base restored) **374**

Chess figure, Drabware, a figure of the Queen standing w/long hair looking over her shoulder, wearing a long dress, her arms crossed over her chest, raised socle plinth, impressed mark, early 19th c., 3 7/8" h. **489**

Fine Wedgwood Bone China Clock

Clock case, bone china, D-shaped w/a flat top w/shaped edges overhanging the upright case w/raised pilasters & reeded block feet, a central round dial w/Arabic numerals & a brass bezel, the paneled body decorated overall w/gilt cherubs & flowers & gilt trim on a dark ground, printed mark, late 19th c., top surface worn, 8 3/4" h. (ILLUS.)............................. **1,035**

Wedgwood Majolica Cracker Jar

Cracker jar, cov., majolica, barrel-shaped, silver plated bands around the sides on the marbleized glazed ground, silver plate rim, domed cover & angular swing bail handle, impressed mark, ca. 1878, 6 1/2" h. (ILLUS.).. **288**

Crocus pot & undertray, stoneware, blue smear glaze, domed basketweave bee-hive-form, the top pierced overall w/large holes, matching dished round tray, impressed mark, mid-19th c., 6 1/2" h., 2 pcs.. **575**

Cup, Fairyland Lustre, Nizami York-type, a central design of deer grazing in a land-scape, printed mark, ca. 1920, 3 1/2" d..... **2,530**

Dish, bone china, Chantilly patt., deep round sides w/scallops, enamel-deco-rated w/a swirled border & floral center & rim, the brass-mounted edge in a scrolled foliate design, pseudo-Chantilly & printed factory mark, late 19th c., 8 1/2" d. **259**

William de Morgan-Designed Dish

Dish, earthenware, deep dished round form, crimson lustre-decorated w/a large bird in the center, pale enamel leaves & oranges in the background, designed by William de Morgan, artist-signed "CP" for Charles Passenger & "W.D.M. Fulham" & impressed factory mark, ca. 1900,

slight rim hairline, framed, dish 10 1/4" d. (ILLUS.).. **1,955**

Dish, majolica, large slightly dished round form, a small central circle w/six radiat-ing bands forming panels w/an argenta ground, each panel molded w/a large colorful chrysanthemum-style flower on a stippled ground, the outer rim band w/a radiating glaze design, impressed mark, ca. 1875, 12 1/4" d. **460**

Figure group, Carrara Ware, all-white, titled "The Interpretation" & also called Joseph Before the Pharaoh, the Pha-raoh, a female by his side & young Joseph standing before him on an oval base, modeled by William Beattie, impressed mark, ca. 1860, 19 1/2" h. (chip on underside & footrim, restoration to Joseph's neck & one hand & lower body of Pharaoh)....................................... **1,725**

Carrara "Poor Maria" Figure Group

Figure group, Carrara Ware, "Poor Maria," a seated young woman wearing classi-cal attire, her hair hanging loose, leaning on a tree stump & looking down at a small dog, impressed mark, mouthpiece of horn damaged, second half 19th c., 11 1/2" h. (ILLUS.)...................................... **1,495**

Wedgwood Bone China Figurine

Figure of a ballerina, a young girl seated atop a raised plinth, modeled by Kath-leen Goodwin, artist-signed, impressed & printed marks, ca. 1931, 9" h. (ILLUS.)..... **575**

Figures of Cupid & Psyche, earthenware w/turquoise enamel glaze, each modeled seated on a raised rocky base, impressed mark, ca. 1860, 7 3/4" h., pr. .. **1,093**

Fish platter, majolica, oval w/slightly scalloped rim, a yellow ground molded w/a large salmon atop ferns & leaves, impressed mark, ca. 1880, 25 1/4" l. (light staining) **5,463**

Game dish, cov., majolica, high cylindrical cover w/flat top molded w/dead game & a recumbent rabbit handle, the sides molded w/grapevines & clusters of dead game, mottled dark glaze, impressed mark, ca. 1880, 6 7/8" l. (glaze scratches, no liner) **805**

Jardiniere, majolica, circular form w/overall blue glaze on the molded body w/paneled sides of scrolled flower & urn designs, framed in scrolled strap feet w/foliate relief, printed & impressed marks, ca. 1891, 11" h. **920**

Jug w/stopper, earthenware body of wide ovoid form tapering slightly to a flat bottom, ring shoulder handle, the brown glaze incised & slip-decorated w/a motto within a foliate framed ribbon, motto reads "Who lives a good life is sure to live well," a sterling silver cylindrical neck w/wide arched spout & matching bulbous inverted pear-form silver stopper, impressed mark, artist-signed by Harry Barnard, ca. 1900, 8" h. **575**

Lithophanes, bone china, brass-framed oval forms w/a black-glazed surface revealing white classical relief designs, printed mark, late 19th c., 3 5/8" l., pr. (one w/hairline) **288**

Match holder, majolica, figural, model of a high-topped man's shoe w/a brown glaze, impressed mark, ca. 1882, 2 5/8" h. **978**

Medallion, stoneware, oval, molded profile bust portrait of George Washington, white ground, titled & w/impressed mark of Wedgwood and Bentley, ca. 1777, slight rim nicks & at neckline of portrait, 2 3/4 x 3 3/8" **1,955**

Model of a nuthatch, bone china, based on an original wood sculpture by Walt Ruch, No. 103 of 500, printed mark, modern, 6 1/4" h. **460**

Mortar & pestle, Mortarware, flat white mortar & pestle w/tapering hardwood handle, impressed mark on mortar, ca, 1780, 2 3/4" d., 2 pcs. **978**

Mug, earthenware, cylindrical, h.p. w/a stylized tropical bird on a lustrous yellow ground, impressed mark, ca. 1930, 4" h. **144**

Mussel plate, majolica, the six-lobed scale-molded dish w/twelve circular fish-molded wells, impressed mark. ca. 1866, 11 1/4" d. (rim chip restored) **1,380**

Fine Earthenware Pedestal

Pedestal, earthenware, tall cylindrical form w/a stepped round foot & top, enamel-decorated overall w/large blossoms on tall leafy stalks, impressed mark, surface wear, ca. 1862, 35" h. (ILLUS.)` **1,840**

Pilgrim flask, long oval foot supporting a large flattened disk-form body w/a tiny top flared neck flanked by tiny loop shoulder handles, moonstone glaze w/raised button border, Norman Wilson design, printed & impressed mark, ca. 1950, 8 3/4" h. **518**

Pitcher, 6 1/4" h., figural jug-form, Rockingham-glazed bust portrait of Elihu Yale, impressed mark, ca. 1933................. **230**

Pitcher, 6 1/4" h., majolica, Bird & Fan patt., argenta ground, impressed mark, ca. 1860 .... **345**

Bird & Fan Majolica Pitcher

Pitcher, 6 3/8" h., jug-form, majolica, footed tapering cylindrical form in Bird & Fan patt., twig handle, argenta ground, impressed mark, ca. 1878 (ILLUS.) **345**

Pitcher, 7 1/4" h., jug-type, Cane-glazed earthenware, rounded tapering cylindrical sides w/a ropetwist molded band at the base of the short flared cylindrical neck round bamboo-form handle, U.S.

Centennial model, decorated w/brown transfer printed scenes of the Philadelphia Exhibition on each side, one showing Independence Hall, the other Memorial Hall, molded narrow star band around the mouth, impressed mark, ca. 1876 .... **345**

Plaque, earthenware, rectangular, relief-molded w/a long hunt scene w/horses & riders trimmed in colored enamels, impressed mark, ca. 1930, 6 3/8 x 15 1/4" **863**

Plaques, earthenware, rectangular, embossed bust portraits, one an elderly man w/long beard representing Old Age & a long-haired young maiden representing Youth, brown overall wash, impressed marks, mid-19th c., framed, impressed marks, 7 3/4 x 12 1/2", pr........... **633**

Plate, 10 1/4" d., Fairyland Lustre, "Imps on a Bridge" patt., a Roc center reserve, the rim decorated w/a variety of fruits & flowers, the center w/blue water, violet imps on the bridge & coral enamel on the black Roc bird, Pattern W 1050, printed mark, ca. 1920 .... **7,475**

Plates, 8 5/8" d., majolica, round w/openwork border & mottled enamel colors in the center, impressed mark, ca. 1872, pr. **173**

Plates, 10 5/8" d., bone china, sporting designs, each w/a powder green border around enamel-painted subjects of a golfer & a tennis player, printed marks, mid-20th c., pr. **230**

Modern Wedgwood Bone China Plates

Plates, 10 5/8" d., modernistic geometric designs, limited edition series titled "Variations on a Geometric Theme," printed marks, complete w/original Lucite box, Paolozzi-designed, limited edition of 200, ca. 1987, set of 6 (ILLUS. of part).. **2,530**

Glazed Portland Vase

Portland Vase, glazed ware, classic form w/cobalt blue ground w/white relief classical scenes, glossy glaze, impressed mark, shallow footrim chip, 10" h. (ILLUS.).. **2,990**

Punch bowl, Celtic Lustre design, a wide low pedestal base supporting a very wide gently flaring bowl, the matte black exterior decorated w/gold Celtic ornaments, a mottled orange & red interior w/armagh center, Pattern Z5265, printed mark, ca. 1920, 10 7/8" d. (exterior surface scratches, interior glaze wear) **805**

Fine Fairyland Lustre Punch Bowl

Punch bowl, Fairyland Lustre, deep wide rounded bowl on a wide flaring round base, Poplar Tree patt., the exterior decorated w/a black sky behind a tree-filled landscape, the interior w/the Woodland Elves patt. w/a daylight sky, No. Z4968, printed mark, ca. 1920, interior surface wear, 10 3/4" d. (ILLUS.)........................... **7,475**

Spill vase, Victoria Ware, footed slightly flaring cyindrical form, gilt-trimmed iron-red ground w/white relief classical drapery framing blue ground oval portrait medallions, impressed mark, ca. 1880, 2 3/4" h. **374**

Strawberry set: a small cov. sugar bowl, small creamer & matching tray; majolica, the oblong tray molded on the interior w/large strawberry leaves & blossoms, two small rounded wells at the end hold the sugar & creamer w/matching designs, impressed mark, ca. 1871, tray 10 1/8" l., creamer 1 3/4" h., sugar 1 7/8" h., the set **1,725**

Tea set: 4 1/2" h. cov. teapot, 2 1/2" h. cov. creamer, 3 1/4" h. cov. sugar bowl, two cups & saucers; bone china w/red trans-fer-printed stylized flower & foliage design w/gilt trim, impressed & printed marks, late 19th c., the set (light gilt wear) **489**

Tile, majolica, square, molded in low-relief in the center w/a fox head within a small circle surrounded by large scrolled oak leaves framed w/a plain outer band, mot-tled glaze, impressed mark, 1875, 8" w. (rim nicks).. **201**

Vase, 3 1/2" h., Caneware, New Hispano-Moresque decoration, a footed squatty bulbous form tapering to a short rolled neck, decorated in pink & copper lustre glazes w/a wide band of upright feath-ered devices below a neck band of small overall loops, impressed mark, ca. 1925...... **489**

Vase, 4 1/8" h., Fairyland Lustre, Firbolgs patt., footed baluster-form w/wide short flared neck, shape 2351, a ruby lustre ground, Pattern Z5200, printed mark, ca. 1920 .... **1,380**

Vase, 5" h., bone china, figural, modeled as two lady's hands w/ruffled cuffs tying the lace on a high-topped shoe, on a rectan-gular platform base w/gilt & enamel floral decoration, printed mark, ca. 1900.............. **690**

Vase, 6 3/4" h., Veronese Ware, wide bal-uster-form w/a short molded neck, pale red ground decorated w/stylized flowers & trim in silver lustre, impressed mark, ca. 1935 .... **259**

Wedgwood Lindsay Ware Vases

Vase, 6 7/8" h., Lindsay Ware, bulbous tapering body w/a bulbed neck & flat rim, long angular handles, dark ground deco-rated overall w/enameled butterflies & leafage, printed mark, ca. 1910 (ILLUS. left) **1,380**

Vase, 7 1/4" h., bone china, figural, mod-eled as a spiky shell supported on a branching coral stem on a round waisted foot, undecorated, printed mark, ca. 1895 .... **546**

Vase, 8" h., Agate Ware, classical urn-form, a square black basalt plinth sup-porting the deep urn-form body on a pedestal, the wide shoulder centered by a waisted cylindrical neck w/a wide flat-tened rim, gilt arched scroll handles from the rim down to the shoulder edge termi-nating in goat head masks, swirled

agate-colored overall glaze, impressed lozenge mark of Wedgwood and Bentley, ca. 1775 (restoration to handle & socle, chips to underside of rim & shoulder, gilt wear)................................... **2,875**

Wedgwood Veronese Ware Vase

Vase, 8 1/2" h., Veronese Ware, footed tapering ovoid body w/a flared rim, green ground w/overall silver lustre stylized flo-ral design w/band of lustre ribbing around the neck, impressed mark, ca. 1935 (ILLUS.)... **144**

Vase, 9" h., bone china, a square foot w/notched corners below a slender ped-estal supporting a wide bulbous inverted pear-form body topped by a tall, slender trumpet neck, gilt upright scroll shoulder handles, the cream-colored ground dec-orated w/cobalt blue trim & enameled floral panels within raised gilt frames, printed mark, late 19th c............................... **489**

Vase, 9" h., Lindsay Ware, bulbous base tapering to a large widely flaring trumpet neck, large loop handles from base of neck to bottom of lower body, dark ground enamel-decorated overall w/but-terflies & leafage, printed & impressed mark, ca. 1910, restored rim chip, asso-ciated hairline (ILLUS. right)..................... **1,093**

Marsden's Art Ware Vases

Vase, 9 5/8" h., Marsden's Art Ware, wide ovoid body tapering to a short wide cylin-drical neck, slip-decorated flowers & leaves on a buff ground, impressed mark, ca. 1890, slight glaze scratches (ILLUS. right).. **374**

Vase, cov., 10 3/8" h., Porphyry Ware, classical urn-form, square black basalt plinth supporting a short pedestal under the banded cylindrical body w/a wide shoulder centering a short waisted neck w/a small domed cover & knob finial, blue & brown speckled overall glaze w/upright inwardly-scrolled creamware shoulder handles & long cream laurel swags around the sides connecting the handles, impressed lozenge mark of Wedgwood and Bentley, ca. 1775 (hairline & small chips in cover, one handle restored, nicks in shoulder & plinth) **5,175**

Vase, 11 1/4" h., stoneware, wide bulbous beehive-shape tapering to a flared club-form spout, brown body w/glazed top band & white spout, impressed potter's monogram for J. Dermer & factory mark, mid-20th c. **863**

Wedgwood Golconda Ware Vase

Vase, cov., 22" h., Golconda Ware, large ovoid body w/large upright loop shoulder handles flanking the fitted flat cover w/baluster-form finial, raised on a domed pedestal foot, glazed cane ground w/raised slip leaf & floral overall designs, impressed mark, chip to cover rim, minor slip loss (ILLUS.) **575**

Vases, 6 1/2" h., bone china, tapering cylindrical form w/flared base & wide rolled rim, yellow-glazed w/bands of enameled colorful Oriental landscapes, No. Z5239, printed mark, ca. 1915, pr. **431**

Vases, 7 3/4" h., Fairyland Lustre, Butterfly Women patt., trumpet-form w/stepped round foot, black background w/mother-of-pearl overlay, mother-of-pearl interior w/floating fairies, Shape No. 2810, No. Z4968, printed marks, ca. 1920 (ILLUS. of one) **11,500**

Vases, 7 3/4" h., Victoria Ware, tall baluster-form vase raised on a tall cylindrical plinth, gilt-trimmed iron-red & teal blue ground w/applied white relief classical swags, classical design bands & leaves w/oval medallions on the sides, impressed mark, ca. 1880, gilt wear, pr. .. **1,725**

Vases, 8" h., Ivory Vellum ware, ovoid body tapering to a tall slender flaring neck, the ivory ground decorated w/colored enamel & gilt-trimmed birds perched on branches, a dark brown band w/gilt around the bottom, printed & impressed marks, late 19th c., pr. (light gilt wear) **546**

Fairyland Lustre Trumpet-form Vase

Vases, 14 3/4" h., Marsden's Art Ware, tall ovoid body tapering to a cylindrical neck, slip-decorated floral design on a buff ground, impressed marks, ca. 1885 (ILLUS. of one).. **805**

Fine Early Wedgwood Porphyry Vase

Vases, cov., 18" h., Porphyry Ware, classic urn-form on a square plinth, creamware body w/mottled greenish blue & brown glossy glaze, high-relief oval classical medallions between drapery swags, acanthus leaf footrim, mounted on a square black basalt plinth, pierced cover w/acorn finial, raized lozenge mark of Wedgwood and Bentley, covers restored, one w/chip restored on footrim, chip & edge nicks on plinth, other w/restoration to top rim & socle, edge nicks on plinth, each w/firing lines in relief, ca. 1770, pr. (ILLUS. of one).......................... **9,200**

WELLER

This pottery was made from 1872 to 1945 at a pottery established originally by Samuel A. Weller at Fultonham, Ohio, and moved in 1882 to Zanesville. Numerous lines were produced and listings below are by the pattern or lines.

Reference books on Weller include The Collectors Encyclopedia of Weller Pottery by Sharon & Bob Huxford (Collector Books, 1979) and All About Weller by Ann Gilbert McDonald (Antique Publications, 1989).

WELLER Weller Pottery

Weller Marks

ARDSLEY (1928)
Various shapes molded as cattails among rushes with water lilies at the bottom. Matte glaze.

Planter, pillow-form, overall incised leaves w/irregular rim formed by leaf tips & irises, 7 x 7"... **$358**

Vase, 7 1/2" h., bud-type, gently flaring cylindrical form w/molded green & brown cattails w/white blossoms around the bottom **110**

Ardsley Vase

Vase, double, 9 1/2" h., connected by a pointed branch handle, marked w/half kiln ink stamp logo (ILLUS.) **138**

Vase, 11" h., tall slightly flaring cylindrical form w/flaring base molded w/large blossoms.. **121**

Wall pocket, double, conical sections embossed w/cattails & leaves & joined by figural water lily blossom, 9 1/2 x 11 1/2" **468**

AURELIAN (1898-1910)
Similar to Louwelsa line but brighter colors and a glossy glaze. With bright yellow/orange brush-applied background along with brown and yellow transparent glaze.

Vase, 6" d., 4" h., compressed spherical form painted w/yellow roses on a black & mahogany ground (minimal crazing) **358**

Vase, 9" h., 8" d., very bulbous body w/tiny cylindrical rim, decorated w/red carnations on shaded brown & yellow ground, artist-initialed **880**

BALDIN (About 1915-20)
Rustic designs with relief-molded apples and leaves on branches wrapped around each piece.

Bowl, 4" d., brown ground (unusual high gloss)... **175**

Lamp base, footed metal base w/squatty bulbous body tapering to wide closed rim, decorated w/red & yellow apples, green leaves, brown branches on blue ground, metal fittings, 12 1/2" h.................. **880**

Pedestal base, twisted tapering cylindrical base w/curved branch handles, decorated w/red apples & green leaves on brown & green ground, 28 1/2" h. **286**

Baldin Vase

Vase, 9 1/2" h., wide cylindrical body flaring at base & rim, apple decoration in rose & yellow, green & yellow ground, marked "Weller" in large block letters (ILLUS.) **248**

Vase, 10" h., wide bulbous base tapering slightly to flat rim (firing line to bottom)......... **605**

Wall pocket, unmarked, 11 1/4" l. **440**

BLUE & DECORATED HUDSON (1919)
Hand-painted lifelike sprays of fruit blossoms and flowers in shades of pink and blue on a rich dark blue ground.

Vase, 7 3/4" h., bulbous ovoid body decorated w/a band of flowers & leaves (stilt-pulls to base)... **385**

Vase, 9 3/4" h., bulbous ovoid w/closed rim, decorated w/band of flowering cherry branches, artist's mark & impressed "Weller" **440**

Vase, 10" h., bulbous base tapering to wide cylindrical neck w/flat rim, light & dark pink band w/multicolored flowers around base, dark blue ground, impressed mark..... **286**

Vase, 10 3/4" h., waisted cylinder w/flared foot & widely flaring rim, decorated w/a band of cherry branches **330**

Vase, 11 1/2" h., decorated w/two large sprays of blue & white lilacs, impressed "Weller" in large block letters & probably original Weller sales room label (small burst glaze bubble on rim)........................... **660**

Rare Blue Decorated Vase

Vase, 11 5/8" h., deeply incised h.p. grape cluster decoration in shades of pink & blue, green leaves & brown vine, signed "McLaughlin" on side & impressed "Weller" in large block letters, w/probably original Weller paper showroom label (ILLUS.).. **2,090**

BONITO (1927-33)
Hand-painted florals and foliage in soft tones on cream ground. Quality of artwork greatly affects price.

Vase, 5 1/2" h., ovoid body tapering to a low fanned mouth flanked by small C-scroll handles, a band of delicate blossoms around the center on the ivory ground, marked... **144**
Vase, 6" h., footed widely flaring bulbous ovoid body w/a squared diamond-shaped wide mouth flanked by two small tab rim handles, painted w/a leafy swag centered by blossoms, signed in script **144**

Bonito Vase

Vase, 11" h., footed ovoid body w/slightly flaring rim, shoulder handles, decorated w/orange & lavender flower & bud & green leaves, incised "Weller Pottery" & "N" in brown slip, dark craze line at rim (ILLUS.).. **165**
Vase, 11" h., footed wide ovoid body w/round shoulder & short wide cylindrical neck, small ornate shoulder handles, decorated w/stylized floral spray tied w/a

ribbon bow & green lines around foot & neck, marked & initialed "N. Walsch" **358**

BRIGHTON (1915)
Various bird or butterfly figurals colorfully decorated and with glossy glazes.

Flower frog, model of a Flamingo standing in rushes, head turned facing backward, marked, 6" h. **288**
Flower frog, model of a Kingfisher, perched on open arched twig, 6 1/2" h......... **173**

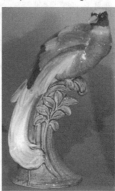

Brighton Bird of Paradise

Model of bird of paradise, rose, black, yellow, green, grey, orange, teal & brown on green & brown stand, impressed "Weller" in large block letters, 10 3/8" h. (ILLUS.) **2,310**
Model of Kingfisher, blue, brown, black & white on green & brown stand, impressed "Weller" in large block letters, 8 1/2" h. (bubble on bird's back) **248**
Model of "Mad Parrot," blue, lavender, red & yellow on green & brown stand, impressed "Weller" in large block letters, 8" h. **715**

CHASE (late 1920s)
White relief fox hunt scenes usually on a deep blue ground.

Chase Hunting Scene Vase

Vase, 8" h., footed bulbous ovoid body w/flaring rim, blue ground (ILLUS.) **275**

Vase, 9" h., footed, flattened, rounded pillow-form body w/three slightly flaring
cylindrical necks at the top, a larger central one flanked by two smaller angled
ones, matte blue ground, marked **288**

Vase, 12" h., footed baluster-form w/flat
rim, mottled green ground decorated
w/sterling silver deposit hunt scene,
marked on base **288**

COPPERTONE (late 1920s)
*Various shapes with an overall mottled bright
green glaze on a "copper" glaze base. Some pieces
with figural frog or fish handles. Models of frogs
also included.*

Bowl, 3 1/2 x 12", flaring sides w/down-
curved rim, incised "Weller Handmade" **605**

Candleholders, model of a turtle beside a
water lily blossom, 3" h., pr. **660**

Center bowl & flower frog, shallow form
w/flaring sides, embossed w/lilypads &
buds, flower frog w/figural frog emerging
from open lily blossom, bowl 3 x 12"
w/paper label, frog 4 x 5", 2 pcs. **990**

Center bowl & flower frog, shallow leaf-
shaped w/figural frog perched on edge
of rim next to water lily blossom, bowl
4 x 15 1/2", 2 pcs.. **825**

Fountain, figural frog, 5 1/2 x 6 1/2"................. **715**

Jardiniere, large nearly spherical body w/a
closed rim, large arched eared shoulder
handles, covered w/a fine green & rust
mottled matte glaze, incised signature,
8 1/2" d., 7" h... **660**

Model of a turtle, incised "Weller Pottery,"
1 1/4 x 4 1/4" **303**

Planter, miniature, figural frog holding a
water lily blossom, incised "Weller Pot-
tery," 4 x 4" **303**

Vase, 6" h., tapering ovoid body w/a wide
closed flat rim, overall vivid mottled
green over dark brown glaze, unmarked...... **550**

Vase, 6 1/2" h., slender gently flaring cylindrical body, mottled heavy green over a
blackish brown ground, incised mark **161**

Vase, 7" h., 9" d., spherical body w/closed
handles... **425**

Vase, 8" h., footed, bulbous base w/wide
flaring neck, large C-form handles from
mid-base to just below rim, mottled dark
green glaze, marked w/incised "M" **385**

Coppertone Vase

Vase, 8 1/4" h., 9" w., fan-shaped top
molded w/reeds above a low squatty bulbous base composed of lily pads &

molded w/a pair of figural frogs on the
shoulder, stamp mark & artist-initialed
(ILLUS.).. **1,045**

Vase, bud, 9" h., 3 1/4" d., slender body
w/flaring irregular rim, frog crawling up
the side, mottled green & brown glaze......... **505**

Vase, 12 1/2" h., waisted cylinder w/flaring
rim, mottled green & brown glaze,
inscribed "Weller Handmade".................... **604**

Vase, 15 1/4" h., footed trumpet-form body... **1,540**

DICKENSWARE 1st LINE (1897-98)
*Underglaze slip-decorated designs on a brown,
green or blue ground. Glossy glaze.*

Jug, footed spherical body w/overhead
handle & small cylindrical spout, decorated w/African-American face on dark
blue ground, 6 1/4" h. (reglued chips to
spout) **385**

Mug, h.p. Virginia creeper decoration by
Sarah Reid McLaughlin, monogrammed
in brown slip on side, impressed "Dickens Ware Weller" & "327," w/semicircu-
lar logo, 6 3/4" h. **248**

Mug, decorated w/floral design, impressed
mark, 7" h.. **99**

Vase, 12 1/4" h., cylindrical body decorated
w/yellow & orange chrysanthemums on
shaded brown ground, decorated by
Eugene Roberts, artist-initialed **605**

Vase, 17" h., baluster form w/monk decoration in orange & yellow on shaded green
ground, impressed mark (restoration) **468**

DICKENSWARE 2nd LINE (early 1900s)
*Various incised "sgraffito" designs usually with a
matte glaze. Quality of the artwork greatly affects
price.*

Humidor, cov., figural, model of a Chinese
man's head, realistic coloring, 5 1/2" h......... **518**

Jug, footed spherical body w/overhead
handle & small cylindrical spout, scene
w/trees & bridge, incised "The Mt. Vernon Bridge Co. Mt. Vernon, O.," 6" h.
(glaze flake to handle, pin-sized fleck to
spout) **440**

Mug, footed, waisted cylindrical body w/C-
form handle, decorated w/incised &
embossed fish on shaded green & tur-
quoise ground, 5" h. **275**

Mug, tapering cylinder w/C-form handle,
incised w/bust of an Indian brave on a
shaded brown & green ground by
Anthony Dunlavy, artist-signed, 5 1/4" h. **413**

Pitcher, tankard, 12" h., portrait of monk,
orange ground (repaired) **275**

Vase, 6 1/2" h., footed, bulbous body
w/flaring rim, incised decoration of monk
in profile (two minute glaze flecks to
base **330**

Vase, 6 3/4" h., footed three-sided form
w/three tiny loop shoulder handles,
scene of fish in water on green ground **495**

Vase, 9 1/2" h., baluster-form body
w/closed rim, scene of two Spanish galleons on stormy seas, polychrome
glaze, decorated by Carl Weigelt **1,540**

Dickensware Scenic Vase

Vase, 9 3/4" h., ovoid body decorated w/forest scene of semi-nude woman holding a bunch of flowers, green trees, dark brown glossy ground, impressed w/"Dickens Ware Weller" semi-circular logo & what appears to be "578" (ILLUS.) **330**

Vase, 10" h., bottle-shaped form w/scene of man playing golf, polychrome matte glaze on a shaded brown & green ground, artist-initialed **1,430**

Vase, 10" h., cylindrical, decorated w/incised portrait of Native American, "Chief White Man," by L.J. Burgess **1,100**

Vase, 10" h., squatty bulbous base tapering to cylindrical body w/slightly flared rim, scene of woman playing golf in polychrome matte glaze on shaded brown & green ground, artist-initialed **1,760**

Vase, 15" h., baluster form w/sgraffito decoration of man w/staff between two trees, impressed mark (restored chips) **468**

Vase, 17 1/2" h., 5 1/2" d., tall slender ovoid form w/incised decoration of a man holding a bird saying "A Bird in the Hand is Worth Two in the Bush," brown, blue, pink, yellow & white, decorated by Edwin L. Pickens, incised "Dickens, Weller, E.L. Pickens" (minute glaze nicks to inside rim) **805**

DICKENSWARE 3rd LINE (1904)
Similar to Eocean line. Various fictional characters molded and slip-painted against pale background colors. Glossy glaze.

Vase, 6 3/4" h., tapering cylindrical body w/incised full figure titled "The Fat Boy," by E.Q **495**

Vase, 10 1/4" h., cylindrical body w/incised full-figured portly gentleman, "Mr. Pickwick - Pickwick Papers," by Lily Mitchell **880**

EOCEAN AND EOCEAN ROSE (1898-1925)
Early art line with various hand-painted flowers on shaded grounds, usually with a clear glossy glaze. Quality of artwork varies greatly.

Candlesticks, widely flaring domed foot supporting a swelled tapering slender standard below the tall socket w/a wide flattened rim, large pink & yellow blossoms around the center of the standard w/dark charcoal above & light lavender below, 10 1/2" h., pr. **316**

Jardiniere, h.p. red roses, leaves & branches decoration on green/grey to white ground, 9" d., 7 1/2" h. **253**

Pitcher, 8" h., bulbous ovoid body w/figural fish handle (firing lines) **1,980**

Vase, 5" h., bulbous base tapering to flat rim, decorated w/pink & white floral spray on shaded green ground (minor scratches) **413**

Vase, 5" h., short wide cylinder w/round shoulder tapering to wide neck w/flat rim, h.p. mushroom decoration in burgundy, lavender & white on grey ground, incised & painted mark **1,210**

Vase, 6 1/2" h., bulbous body tapering to cylindrical neck w/flat rim, white clover on bluish grey ground **330**

Vase, 7" h., swelled cylindrical body w/flat shoulder tapering to wide incurved rim, white dogwood decoration on shaded lavender ground, artist-signed **523**

Vase, 8" h., 7 1/4" d., footed bell-shaped body centered by collared neck, four slender handles from rim to shoulder, decorated w/berries & leaves by Tot Steele **1,100**

Vase, 8 1/4" h., baluster-form body decorated w/pink cherry blossoms on a brown to grey shaded ground **385**

Vase, 8 1/4" h., bulbous ovoid body w/closed rim, purple gooseberries & celadon leaves on a shaded green to pink ground **440**

Vase, 10 1/2" h., slender ovoid body w/burgundy & pink flowers on celadon leaves, shaded green ground **523**

Vase, 11" h., bulbous ovoid body w/short shoulder tapering to incurved rim, decorated around upper body w/pink & lavender roses, shaded grey, white & pink ground **1,045**

Eocean Vase with Egrets and Eocean Vase with Blossoms

Vase, 11" h., wide tapering cylinder decorated w/two finely detailed fluffy egrets in white, lavender, orange & red on green, cream & lavender ground, incised signature, impressed mark (ILLUS.) **2,750**

Vase, 11 1/2" h., bulbous ovoid body w/cupped rim, decorated w/snapdragons in red & celadon on shaded grey ground (overglaze slightly overfired causing minute bubbles) **880**

Vase, 12" h., tall tapering cylindrical form decorated w/yellow narcissus on celadon & lavender leaves, shaded grey ground, stamped "Weller" **1,100**

Vase, 12 1/2" h., expanding cylindrical body w/six open handles rising from narrow shoulder to flared rim, decorated pink & burgundy flowers w/yellow & green leaves, buds & stems against a glossy pale blue to green ground (ILLUS. right) **1,650**

Vase, 12 1/2" h., tall ovoid body tapering to molded rim, decorated w/branches of raspberries w/blossoms & fruit in purples & celadons on shaded ground **1,100**

Vase, 13" h., bulbous base tapering to tall cylindrical neck, red poppies on shaded green ground, unmarked............................ **358**

Vase, 14 3/4" h., baluster-form body w/six loop shoulder handles, decorated w/lavender & grey dogwood blossoms on a shaded purple ground **2,200**

Vase, 18" h., footed slender ovoid body w/flared rim, berries & leaves in pastel tones on shaded black to lavender ground, stamped "Weller" (shallow glaze flake to rim) **990**

FOREST (mid-teens to 1928)
Realistically molded and painted forest scene.

Basket, footed, flaring conical shape w/overhead handle, unmarked, 7 x 10" (small bruise to bottom)............................... **220**

Jardiniere, 3 1/4" h., unmarked **55**

Planter, tub-shaped w/rim handles, 6 1/2" d., 4 1/4" h.. **83**

Vase, 8" h., cylindrical w/slightly flared rim, marked "12" in black slip (tiny glaze nick off base) **110**

Forest Vase

Vase, 8" h., waisted cylinder w/flaring rim, marked "H-" in black slip (ILLUS.) **165**

Vase, 8" h., waisted cylinder w/flaring rim (minute flake to foot) **132**

Vase, 11 1/2" h., tall footed expanding cylindrical body w/flaring rim **358**

Wall pocket, w/copper liner, conical w/owl peering out of tree trunk, die-stamped "Weller," 5 1/2 x 11" (mold firing line, small chip to hanging hole, couple of minor nicks to high points) **303**

GLENDALE (early to late 1920)
Various relief-molded birds in their natural habitats, lifelike coloring.

Candleholders, flared base tapering to cupped socket, chickadees among flowering cherry branches, 2 1/2" h., pr. (restoration to base of one) **275**

Console bowl, decorated w/molded sea gulls in yellow, blue, brown & green, 15" d., ... **413**

Console set: 16" d. bowl w/flowerfrog & pr. of 5 1/2" d. candleholders; embossed w/flying chickadees among flowering cherry branches, the set (opposing hairlines to base of frog)................................ **880**

Vase, 4 1/2" h., bulbous body, wooded scene of wren in nest, unmarked **220**

Vase, 6 1/2" h., footed bulbous ovoid w/flared rim, embossed w/polychrome marsh scene of rook & nest (firing line to base) **715**

Vase, double bud, 4 3/4 x 8", gate-form, square shape, wren & grapevine decoration **303**

Vase, 8 1/2" h., ovoid body, decorated w/bridge scene & wrens in a nest, polychrome glazes... **880**

Vase, 9" h., flaring cylindrical body w/narrow angled shoulder to the flat mouth, molded w/two love birds in color on a leafy tree branch, stamped mark................. **776**

Vase, 11 1/2" h., bulbous base tapering to cylindrical neck & flat rim, embossed polychrome glaze decoration of a quail & nest in gladed thicket, fleck to manufacturing defect at base) **825**

Glendale Vase

Vase, 11 7/8" h., baluster-form w/trumpet neck, decorated w/h.p. scene of a goldfinch on a nest, butterflies, thistles & daisies, artist-signed "Dorothy England" & marked w/the circular "Weller Ware" ink stamp logo (ILLUS.) **1,210**

Vase, 12 7/8" h., ovoid body w/short cylindrical neck, w/scene of nesting bird w/eggs in a swampy, cattail-filled area, impressed "Weller" in large block letters ... **2,310**

Wall pocket, half round bulbous form w/sharply pointed backplate w/hanging hole, two finches on a cherry branch, 7" h. **440**

Wall pocket, conical, polychrome decoration w/wrens on a branch, unmarked, 5 x 8 3/4" (firing line to rim) **358**

Wall pocket, cornucopia-form w/curved tall, arched & scalloped backplate pierced w/a hanging hole, the base molded w/a wren & its young on a flowering cherry blossom branch, unmarked, 6 1/2 x 12 1/2" **385**

HUDSON (1917-34)
Underglaze slip-painted decoration, "parchment-vellum" transparent glaze.

Lamp base, footed, spherical base w/tall square-form body, molded pink pansy at top of each panel, white & grey ground, 13" h. (restored original lamp base) **319**

Hudson Winter Scenic Vase

Vase, 6 3/8" h., bulbous base on narrow foot ring, wide cylindrical neck w/slightly flaring rim, decorated w/detailed scene of a two-story house in a pine forest, nestled in deep snow, snow-covered trees blow in the wind, artist-signed "Timberlake" on side in black slip, base is incised w/"31" & "Weller Pottery" (ILLUS.) **6,325**

Hudson Winter Landscape Vase

Vase, 8" h., bulbous ovoid body w/rolled rim, decorated w/a colorful winter landscape scene w/a fox standing beside a blue stream & near nicely detailed snow-

covered conifers & deciduous trees, by Hester Pillsbury w/"Pillsbury" in black slip, incised "43" & "Weller Pottery" (ILLUS.) **7,425**

Vase, 8" h., footed bulbous ovoid body tapering to a short wide cylindrical neck w/molded rim, loop handles from shoulder to rim, decorated w/branches of flowering cherry blossoms in white on a shaded brown ground, by Mae Timberlake, ink-stamped "Weller Ware" **770**

Vase, 8" h., 5" d., footed bulbous spherical body w/flaring rim, loop shoulder handles, decorated w/blossoming branches in pink tones against a shaded ground, by Mae Timberlake, artist-initialed, kiln mark **990**

Vase, 9 1/2" h., bulbous base w/wide cylindrical neck & flat rim, decorated w/water lilies & leaves on shaded grey ground, stamped "Weller" **385**

Vase, 9 1/2" h., footed cylinder w/h.p. blue & white iris w/green leaves, decorated by Mae Timberlake, artist-signed & incised "Weller Pottery" **1,760**

Vase, 15 1/4" h., 6 1/2" d., ovoid, white & blue iris & green leaves on shaded blue & pale pink matte ground, decorated by Sarah McLaughlin, artist-signed & incised "Weller" (glaze flake at base, minor glaze scrape to shoulder) **1,100**

Vase, 15 1/2" h., ovoid body w/wide flaring rim, h.p. large yellow, pink & purple irises on shaded blue ground, decorated by Mae Timberlake, drilled base, artist-signed & stamped "Weller" **2,310**

Wall pocket, conical, decorated w/pink & white wild roses on a shaded blue matte ground, die-stamped "Weller" 7 1/4 x 2 1/2" (minor nick to back) **550**

JAP BIRDIMAL (1904)
Stylized Japanese-inspired figural bird or animal designs on various solid colored grounds.

Hair receiver, decorated w/four Norse sailing ships, dark blue ground, artist's initials "VH," 4" w., 2" h. **209**

Jardiniere, bulbous body w/wide flat rim, decorated landscape scene of blue trees, yellow moon, grey ground, 8" h. (hairline crack) **275**

Vase, 4 1/2" h., spherical body on three outswept knob feet, tricorner rounded rim, bluish grey ground decorated w/two white geese in flight **265**

Vase, bud, 5 1/2" h., cylinder w/bulbous top, decorated w/stylized peacock feathers on a dark green ground **990**

Vase, 6" h., bulbous body w/wide shoulder & short molded rim, decorated w/a scene of a Japanese maiden under a stylized tree, green ground, (glazed stilt-pull to base) **605**

Vase, 6" h., shouldered ovoid body w/molded rim, decorated in squeezebag w/swimming blue carp on a green ground, unmarked **1,100**

Vase, 7" h., ovoid shouldered body tapering to flat mouth, decorated w/geisha girl w/stringed musical instrument, gold, cream, brown, black & green, outlined by slip trailing w/green & yellow leaf decoration around shoulder & green stems around base, impressed "804" & "5" & incised artist's initials "C.M.M." (small line in base, possibly in the making) **1,320**

Vase, 11 3/4" h., ovoid body w/tapering shoulder, short neck w/flaring rim, squeezebag decoration w/geisha playing shamisen under stylized trees, tan, blue & red on brown ground, incised "Weller - Rhead Faience" (couple of shallow scratches to body, two glazed-over glaze flecks to rim, stilt-pull chip to base) **1,045**

JEWELL & CAMEO JEWELL (about 1910-15)

Similar to the Etna line but most pieces molded with a band of raised oval 'jewels' or jewels and cameo portraits in color against a light or dark shaded ground.

Vase, 7 1/2" h., ovoid body, decorated front & back w/incised design of fern fronds w/swirling blue jewels on a blue, green & light pink ground, impressed mark **770**

Jewell Vase

Vase, 11" h., ovoid, decorated w/relief-molded vine & leaf design w/red flowers & jewels, impressed mark (ILLUS.) **880**

KNIFEWOOD (late teens)

Pieces feature deeply molded designs of dogs, swans, and other birds and animals or flowers in white or cream against dark brown grounds.

Tobacco jar, cov., barrel-shaped, w/low domed cover w/button finial, the sides molded in relief w/a continuous scene of a hunting dog & wild fowl in shades of dark & light brown, impressed mark, 6 1/2" h. **920**

Knifewood Vase

Vase, 5" h., squatty bulbous body w/wide flat rim, decorated w/molded goldfinches on branches of wisteria, impressed "Weller" in large block letters (ILLUS.) **770**

Vase, 6" h., squatty bulbous body w/wide flat rim, decorated w/molded blue & yellow birds sitting on branches w/cherries, impressed "Weller" in large block letters **495**

Vase, 7 1/4" h., ovoid body embossed w/daisies & butterflies on a textured ground, unmarked **275**

Vase, 11 1/2" h., waisted cylindrical body, peacock among trees & roses in pale polychrome on a green ground, unmarked **660**

L'ART NOUVEAU (1903-04)

Various figural and floral-embossed Art Nouveau designs.

Cane stand, bamboo stalk-shaped, embossed w/climbing sunflowers, matte green & yellow, unmarked, 34 1/2" h. (several glaze flakes & one large chip to base) **1,430**

Unusual L'Art Nouveau Vase

Vase, 8" h., slender four-sided body w/molded florals at the top, decorated on one side w/embossed figure of young woman & floral decoration on the other side, semi-gloss glaze of rose to blue to cream, marked "Weller" in small block letters, unobtrusive stilt pulls on bottom (ILLUS.) **248**

Vase, 11" h., two-handled, footed pillow-form body w/flared scalloped rim, embossed w/flowers **385**

Vase, 12" h., tall cylindrical body swelled at the top & tapering to a closed rim, molded at the top w/large peach & brown irises against a shaded green & tan ground, matte glaze, impressed mark **825**

Vase, 12" h., tapering four-sided body w/scalloped rim & shaped base, embossed flowers near rim **220**

Vase, 12 3/4" h., four-sided tapering vase embossed w/fruits & flowers, scalloped rim (minor glaze scaling to rim, nick to leaf, burst blemish) **440**

LASA (1920-25)
Various landscapes on a banded reddish and gold iridescent ground. Lack of scratches and abrasions important.

Vase, 3 1/2" h., bulbous body w/short rolled rim, decorated w/stylized green flowers & geometric designs on reddish & gold iridescent ground, unmarked (ILLUS.) **275**

Lasa Stylized Floral Vase

Vase, 3 5/8" h., wide bulbous body w/short rolled rim, decorated w/h.p. yellow flowers w/green leaves & stems on gold iridescent ground w/reddish rim **248**

Vase, 6" h., footed wide ovoid body decorated w/a frieze of foliage & berries, gold, green & magenta glaze, unmarked **660**

Vase, 6 1/4" h., footed, tapering cylindrical body decorated w/landscape scene w/oak trees on iridescent ground (two very small glaze flakes, light wear) **165**

Vase, 6 1/2" h., ovoid body tapering to rolled rim, decorated w/scene of mountain lake sunset, iridescent glaze, signed "Weller - Lasa" **393**

Vase, 10" h., footed, wide ovoid body tapering to a flat mouth, decorated w/scene of pine trees & water, gold iridescent ground **468**

Vase, 12" h., wide flaring foot tapering to slender cylindrical body & flat rim, decorated w/a scene of twisted trees on shoreline, red, green & gold, artist-signed (worn glaze) **198**

LOUWELSA (1896-1924)
Hand-painted underglaze slip decoration on dark brown shading to yellow ground; glossy yellow glaze.

Candlestick, squatty bulbous base w/narrow cylindrical neck, spout-shaped candle cup & ornate D-form handle, floral decoration, artist-initialed, impressed mark, 6" h. **286**

Louwelsa Humidor

Humidor, cov., bulbous body decorated w/h.p. matches & pipes, decorated by Lizabeth Blake, artist-initialed & impressed "Louwelsa Weller" & "X 176 6," lid chips repaired, tiny glaze nicks off rim, 6 1/2" h. (ILLUS.) **550**

Louwelsa Banquet Lamp

Lamp base, banquet-type, trumpet-shaped body w/narrow flat shoulder & short rolled neck, lily decoration done by Minnie Mitchell, artist's name on side & impressed "Louwelsa Weller," "K 617" & half circle logo inside base, metal sleeve for oil font fits inside rim, ca. early 1900s, 26 5/8" h. (ILLUS.) **3,300**

Pitcher, 12" h., tankard-type, cavalier decoration, artist-signed (repaired) **385**

Pitcher, 16 3/4" h., tankard-type, a flaring ringed base below the tall slender & slightly tapering body w/a rim spout & a C-form handle halfway down the side, decorated w/dark yellowish brown clusters of grapes on leafy vines against a dark shaded ground, artist-signed & marked on base **518**

Vase, 6 1/2" h., slightly tapering cylindrical body, carnation decoration, impressed "Louwelsa Weller 525 K" **165**

Vase, 9 1/2" h., pillow-form, footed, hollyhock decoration, artist-initialed, impressed mark (minor scratches) **358**

Vase, 12" h., tall slender ovoid w/loop handles from shoulder to rim, green leaf & berry decoration (minor scratches to rim)..... **385**

Vase, 15" h., 11" d., wide bulbous body tapering to short cylindrical neck w/flared rim, large h.p. roses on shaded brown ground, decorated by Hester Pillsbury **3,080**

Vase, 19 3/4" h., squatty bulbous base w/trumpet-form neck, wild rose decoration, base impressed "Weller Louwelsa, 9, 8, X 271," decorated by Sarah Reid McLaughlin & artist-signed just below flower (scuff marks & glaze flakes off rim) **468**

MUSKOTA (1915 - late 1920s)

Figural pieces with human figures, birds, animals or frogs. Matte glaze.

Bowl, 5 1/2 x 10", shallow round form w/leaf-shaped rim & center branch handle, figural squirrel w/nut on one end, die-stamped "Weller" **413**

Centerbowl w/attached flower frog, figural turtle w/water lily flower frog, stamped "Weller," 4 3/4 x 10" (restoration to small chip on edge of lilypad & to two feet) **413**

Muskota Flower Frog

Flower frog, figural frog emerging from a lotus blossom, unmarked, 4 1/2" h. (ILLUS.)... **220**

Flower frog, figural geese on round footed base, 7" h. x 7" d. **350**

Model of split rail fence, green & charcoal matte glaze, unmarked, 5" h. **220**

Vase, 7" h., 5 1/2" d., bulbous ovoid body tapering to wide slightly flared rim, decorated w/relief-molded frog & water lily on shaded green matte glaze, stamped "Weller" **880**

ROMA (1912-late '20s)

Cream-colored ground decorated with embossed floral swags, bands or fruit clusters.

Humidor, cov., octagonal, inset cover w/large knob finial, marked, 7" h. **109**

Vase, 7" h., cylindrical body w/panels of pine cone decoration in brown & green **143**

Vase, 9" h., tapering cylinder w/molded ring rim, floral decoration, marked "Weller" in large block letters **110**

Roma Vase

Vase, 10" h., tapering cylindrical body w/a wide flattened rim, embossed rings around lower body w/paneled decoration of pink dogwood blossoms & leaves, unmarked (ILLUS.)....................................... **110**

SABRINIAN (late '20s)

Seashell body with sea horse handle. Pastel colors. Matte finish. Middle period.

Console bowl, 2 1/2 x 9" **195**
Wall pocket, stamp in label **725**

SELMA (Ca. 1923)

Knifewood line with a high-gloss glaze. Occasionally with peacocks, butterflies, and daisies. Middle period.

Selma Vase

Vase, 4" h., squatty bulbous body w/wide flat rim, decorated w/molded daisies & butterflies, marked "Weller" in large block letters & "F" in black slip (ILLUS.) **193**

Vase, 5" h., bulbous body w/flat rim, decorated w/goldfinches among wisteria blossoms, impressed "Weller " in large block letters & "C" painted in brown slip **248**

Vase, 5" h., cylindrical w/flat rim, decorated w/white & yellow daisies............................. **110**

SICARDO (1902-07)

Various shapes with iridescent glaze of metallic shadings in greens, blues, crimson, purple or coppertone decorated with vines, flowers, stars or freeform geometric lines.

Vase, 3 1/2 x 5 3/4", squatty bulbous body w/wide shoulder tapering to short wide cylindrical neck, iridescent gold abstract flowers & leaves, green & purple ground **770**

Sicardo Lobed Vase

Vase, 4" h., three-lobe form, signed "Sicard," impressed mark (ILLUS.)............ **1,100**

Vase, 4 1/2" h., bell-shaped body decorated w/leaves & berries against a bronze, blue, green, rose & purple iridescent ground, signed "Sicard Weller".......... **1,380**

Vase, 4 1/2" h., bulbous four-sided body w/square molded rim, decorated w/flowers in green & red iridescent glaze.............. **880**

Vase, 4 3/4" h., gourd-shaped body, decorated w/chrysanthemum blossoms in iridescent green & purple glaze (glaze drips from rim) **605**

Vase, 5" h., bulbous base below gently tapering conical sides, floral decoration in green & gold iridescent glaze, artist-signed **413**

Vase, 5" h., tapering four-sided form, floral decoration in iridescent highlights of gold, purple & rose, signed "Weller Sicard".. **550**

Vase, 6" h., bulbous cylindrical body w/swelled shoulder tapering to closed rim, decorated w/berries & leaves in iridescent green & bronze glaze **990**

Vase, 6 1/4 x 9 1/2", pillow-form, wide rectangular body w/scalloped rim & side ribbon handles, decorated w/arabesques & curlicues, iridescent green ground **2,090**

Vase, 10 1/2" h., tapering ovoid body w/flaring rim, iridescent floral decoration of gold mums w/green highlights against a purple, blue & red ground, signed "Weller Sicard" **1,870**

Vase, 12" h., twisted-form tapering ovoid body w/flat rim, floral decoration in gold, green & blue w/gold, blue & purple iridescent highlights, signed "Weller Sicard" **2,090**

Vase, 14 1/2" h., footed four lobed ovoid body w/twisted cylindrical neck & floriform rim, painted w/daisies in gold on a lustered purple & green ground (restoration to rim) **2,530**

SILVERTONE (1928)

Various flowers, fruits or butterflies molded on a pale purple-blue matte pebbled ground.

Silvertone Basket

Basket, fan-shaped w/overhead gnarled branch handle, decorated w/cranberry colored flowers & green leaves, marked w/half kiln ink stamp logo & "3" in black slip, 8 1/2" h. (ILLUS.) **303**

Vase, 6 1/2" h., footed squatty bulbous body w/wide flaring rim, decorated w/pink & lavender poppies & green leaves against a purple ground, ink mark..... **413**

Vase, 7" h., gently tapering cylindrical sides w/D-form handles from rim to center of the sides, molded flowers, marked.............. **320**

Vase, 7 1/2" h., footed ovoid fan-shaped w/widely flaring rim, swirled clusters of flowers.. **345**

Vase, 8 1/4" h., 7 3/4" d., footed, spherical body w/scalloped rim, C-form shoulder handles, embossed w/pink poppies on lavender "hammered" ground...................... **275**

Vase, 10" h., bulbous base w/wide cylindrical neck w/molded rim, D-form handles rising from base to rim, decorated w/red & white embossed flowers on a purple, pink & white ground, original labels............. **550**

Vase, 11 3/4" h., slender trumpet-form, calla lily decoration in white w/green leaves, pale purple ground, marked & paper label **605**

Wall pocket, conical w/molded floral decoration on multicolored ground, stamp mark, 10" h. (minute bruise to top) **385**

SOUEVO (1907-10)

Unglazed redware bodies with glossy black interiors. The exterior decorated with black & white American Indian geometric designs.

Basket, hanging-type, w/original chains, 9 1/2" h. **198**

Pitcher, tankard, tall tapering cylindrical body w/a flaring cylindrical neck & rim spout, long D-form handle, decorated down the sides w/stripes of graduated triangles.. **285**

Souevo Vase

Vase, 7" h., bulbous ovoid body w/short cylindrical neck, decorated w/Native American designs under a cranberry glaze, impressed "Weller" in large block letters (ILLUS.) **413**
Candleholders, pr.. **143**

WOODCRAFT (1917)

Rustic designs simulating the appearance of stumps, logs and tree trunks. Some pieces are adorned with owls, squirrels, dogs and other animals. Matte finish.

Basket, hanging-type, unmarked, 9" d., 4" h... **220**

Woodcraft Basket

Basket, figural acorn w/overhead branch handle, marked "Weller" in large block letters, 9 1/2" h. (ILLUS.)............................. **358**
Bowl, 5 1/2 x 7", shallow bulbous form w/oak leaves & acorns around the rim & figural squirrel seated on rim eating a nut, ink stamp mark "Weller Ware," full kiln logo & "H" in black slip, two small chips to oak leaves **220**
Candlelamps, footed tree trunk-form w/red berry decoration, branch handles & molded leaves around top, brown & green ground, original candlelamp holder & old bulbs, overall 17" h., pr. (one w/tiny chip to leaf) **825**
Compote, deep rounded & flaring sides supported by figural branches on tree trunk-form pedestal, molded leaves around rim, earth tones w/red berries, impressed mark, 10" h. **468**
Flower frog, figural crab, 5" l., 1 3/8" h. (small nick on left hind leg).......................... **110**

Model of dogs, two brown to yellow hunting dogs in grasses, base in earth tones & green, impressed block mark, 11" l., 7" h.. **715**
Planter, log-form w/molded leaf & narrow strap handle at top center, 11" l., 4 1/4" h. **110**

Woodcraft Double Bud Vase

Vase, double bud, 8" h., cylindrical tree trunk-forms connected by an arch of branches & molded red berries & green leaves (ILLUS.) **165**
Vase, 9" h., chalice shape w/three branch handles rising from base, impressed mark **187**
Vase, bud, 10" h., cylindrical tree trunk form w/relief-molded branch, apple & leaves down the front **95**
Wall pocket, relief-molded purple plums & green leaves against cylindrical tree branch body, openings at ends of branches, 9" l. **495**

ZONA (about 1920)

Red apples and green leaves on brown branches all on a cream-colored ground; some pieces with molded florals or birds with various glazes. A line of children's dishes was also produced featuring hand-painted or molded animals. This is referred to as the "Zona Baby Line."

Pitcher, 8" h., wide cylindrical form w/flat rim & high arched spout, squared handle, Kingfisher decoration, blue & grey **358**
Plate, 8 7/8" d., Apple patt., pairs of red apples & green leaves around the border on brown branches against the ivory ground **44**

WILLOW WARES

This pseudo-Chinese pattern has been used by numerous firms throughout the years. The original design is attributed to Thomas Minton about 1780 and Thomas Turner is believed to have first produced the ware during his tenure at the Caughley works. The blue underglaze transfer print pattern has never been out of production since that time. An Oriental landscape incorporating a bridge, pagoda, trees, figures and birds, supposedly tells the story of lovers fleeing a cruel father who wished to prevent their marriage. The gods, having pity on them, changed them into birds enabling them to fly away and seek their happiness together.

BLUE

Ashtray, figural whale, ca. 1960, Japan...... **$50-55**
Ashtray, unmarked, American **20**

Bank, figural, stacked pigs, ca. 1960, Japan, 7" h. **50-55**
Bone dish, ca. 1890, unmarked, England **40-50**

Blue Willow Bone Dish

Bone dish, Buffalo Pottery, 6 1/2" l. (ILLUS.)... **75-80**
Bowl, berry, Allertons, England.................... **12-15**
Bowl, berry, Japan **7**
Bowl, berry, milk glass, Hazel Atlas **15**
Bowl, individual, 5 1/4" oval, J. Maddock **20**
Bowl, soup, 8" d., Japan **18-20**
Bowl, 6 1/2 x 8 1/4", Ridgways, England **50-55**
Bowl, salad, 10" d., Japan................................. **75**
Butter dish, cov., Ridgways, England **150-175**
Butter dish, in wood holder, 6" d. **50-75**
Butter dish, cov., 8" d., England..................... **100**
Butter pat, Buffalo Pottery **30**
Butter pat, Wood & Sons................................. **25**
Cake plate, Green & Co., 8" sq..................... **40-45**
Cake stand, child's, Shellware, England, 2 1/2" h.. **75-100**
Cake stand, unmarked, England, 10" d. ... **200-225**

Blue Willow Tin Canister

Canister, cov., round, tin, 5 3/4" h. (ILLUS.).. **20-25**
Canister set: cov., "Coffee," "Flour," "Sugar," "Tea," barrel-shaped, ca. 1960s, Japan, the set........................... **350-400**
Cheese dish, cov., rectangular, unmarked, England.. **175**
Condiment cruet set: cov. oil & vinegar & mustard cruet, salt & pepper; carousel-type base w/wooden handle, Japan, 7 1/2" h., the set **200-225**
Cracker jar, cov., silver lid & handle, Minton, England, 5" h. (ILLUS.).................... **200**
Creamer, Allerton, England................................. **60**
Creamer, individual, Shenango China Co. **25**
Creamer, John Steventon **40**

Blue Willow Cracker Jar

Creamer w/original stopper, figural cow standing on oval base, mouth forms spout & tail forms handle, ca. 1850, unmarked, England, 7" l., 5" h. (ILLUS.).................. **700-800**

Blue Willow Figural Cow Creamer

Cruets w/original stoppers, oil & vinegar, Japan, 6" h., the set **65**
Cup & saucer, "A Present from Towyn," unmarked, England **55-65**
Cup & saucer, Booth **40-45**
Cup & saucer, Buffalo Pottery **35-45**
Cup & saucer, child's, ca. 1900, unmarked, England.. **50**
Cup & saucer, demitasse, Copeland, England **40**
Cup & saucer, "For Auld Lang Syne," W. Adams, England, oversized **100-125**
Cup & saucer, Japan.................................... **10-15**
Drainer, butter, ca. 1890, England, 6" sq. **75**
Egg cup, Booths, England, 4" h. **45-50**
Egg cup, Japan, 4" h.................................... **20-25**
Egg cup, Allerton, England, 4 1/2" h. **40-45**
Ginger jar, cov., Japan, 5" h. **30**
Ginger jar, cov., Mason's, 9" h...................... **60-75**
Gravy boat, Buffalo Pottery **75-85**

Blue Willow Gravy Boat

Gravy boat, ca. 1890, unmarked, England, 7" l. (ILLUS.)... **60-65**

Gravy boat w/attached underplate, double-spouted, Ridgways, England............... **75-85**

Hot pot, electric, Japan, 6" h. **75**

Invalid feeder, ca. 1860, unmarked, England **175-200**

Knife rest, ca. 1860, unmarked, England **85-95**

Ladle, pattern in bowl, unmarked, England, 6" l. **125-135**

Ladle, pattern in bowl, floral handle, unmarked, England, 12" l. **185-200**

Lamp, w/ceramic shade, Japan, 8" h. **75**

Lamp, w/reflector plate, Japan, 8" h. **85-95**

Lamp, Wedgwood, England, 10" h. **200-225**

Mug, "Farmer's," Japan, 4" h. **15-20**

Mustache cup & saucer, Hammersley & Co. **150-175**

Mustard pot, cov., ca. 1870, unmarked, England, 3" h. **100-125**

Pastry stand, three-tiered plates, Royal China Co., Sebring, Ohio, 13" h. **50-60**

Blue Willow Pepper Pot

Pepper pot, ca. 1870, England, 4" h. (ILLUS.) **100-125**

Blue Willow Pitcher

Pitcher, 5 1/2" h., Ridgway, England (ILLUS.) **85-95**

Buffalo Pottery Blue Willow Pitcher

Pitcher, cov., 5 1/2" h., Buffalo Pottery (ILLUS.) **200-225**

Pitcher, 6" h., Royal Corona Ware, S. Hancock & Sons **100-125**

Pitcher, 6" h., scalloped rim, Allerton, England **125-150**

Blue Willow "Chicago Jug"

Pitcher, 7" h., "Chicago Jug," ca. 1907, Buffalo Pottery, 7"h., 3 pt. (ILLUS.) **200-225**

Pitcher, 8" h., glass, Johnson Bros., England **35-40**

Pitcher w/ice lip, 10" h., Japan **100**

Placemat, cloth, 12 x 16" **18-20**

Plate, bread & butter, Allerton, England **12-15**

Plate, bread & butter, Japan **5-7**

Plate, child's, 4 1/2" d., Japan **10-15**

Plate, dinner, Booth's, England **40-45**

Buffalo Blue Willow Dinner Plate

Plate, dinner, Buffalo Pottery (ILLUS.) **30-35**

Plate, dinner, ca. 1870, unmarked, England .. **40-50**

Plate, dinner, flow blue, Royal Doulton.......... **75-85**

Plate, dinner, Holland **18-20**

Plate, dinner, Japan **10-15**

Plate, dinner, Mandarin patt., Copeland, England **40-50**

Plate, dinner, modern, Royal Wessex **6-8**

Plate, dinner, Paden City Pottery **30-35**

Plate, dinner, restaurant ware, Jackson **15-20**

Plate, dinner, Royal China Co. **10-15**

Plate, dinner, scalloped rim, Allerton, England **30-35**

Plate, grill, Allerton, England **45-50**

Plate, luncheon, Wedgwood, England **20-25**

Plate, luncheon, Worcester patt. **40-45**

Plate, 7 1/2" d., Arklow, Ireland **20**

Plate, 10" d., tin, ca. 1988, Robert Steffy **10-12**

Plate, grill, 10" d., Japan................................. **18-20**

Plate, 10 1/4" d., paper, Fonda........................... **1-2**

Plate, grill, 10 1/2" d., Holland **18-20**

Platter, 9 x 11" l., rectangular, Wedgwood
& Co., England **100-125**
Platter, 8 1/2 x 11 1/2" l., oval, scalloped
rim, Buffalo Pottery.............................. **100-125**
Platter, 9 x 12" l., oval, American **15-18**
Platter, 9 x 12" l., oval, Japan **25-30**
Platter, 9 x 12" l., rectangular, Allerton,
England **150-200**
Platter, 11 x 14" l., oval, Johnson Bros.,
England **85-100**
Platter, 11 x 14" l., rectangular, Buffalo
Pottery... **150-200**
Platter, 11 x 14" l., rectangular, ca. 1880s,
unmarked, England **150-200**
Platter, 15 x 19" l., rectangular, well &
tree, ca. 1890, unmarked, England **350-400**
Pudding mold, England, 4 1/2" h. **45-55**
Punch cup, pedestal foot, ca. 1900,
unmarked, England **50-75**
Relish dish, leaf-shaped, ca. 1870,
England **100-125**

Blue Willow Salt Box

Salt box, cov., ca. 1960, wooden lid,
Japan, 5 x 5" (ILLUS.) **175-225**
Salt dip, master, pedestal base, unmarked,
England, 2" h....................................... **100-125**

Blue Willow Salt Dip w/Silver Rim

Salt dip, open, silver rim, ca. 1890,
unmarked, England, 2" h. (ILLUS.) **50-75**
Salt & pepper shakers, Japan, pr. **40-45**
Sauce tureen, ladle & underplate,
cov., ca. 1880s, England...................... **250-275**
Sauce tureen w/underplate, cov., pedes-
tal base, ca. 1890, unmarked, England,
6 1/2" h. (ILLUS. next column) **250-275**
Soup tureen, cov., ca. 1880, unmarked,
England **400-450**
Spoon rest, Japan **40-50**
Sugar bowl, cov., Japan **20-30**
Sugar bowl, cov., Ridgway, England............ **50-75**
Syrup pitcher, cov., frosted, Hazel Atlas,
6" h.. **40-45**
Tablecloth, Simtex...................................... **75-85**
Tea set, child's, Japan, service for six in
box **250-300**

Blue Willow Sauce Tureen w/Underplate

Tea set, child's, tin, Ohio Art Co., Bryan,
Ohio, service for four............................. **150-175**
Tea tile, ca. 1900, unmarked, England, 6" sq. .. **75**
Tea tile, Minton, England, 6" sq. **75**
Teapot, cov., ca. 1890, Royal Doulton **300-350**
Teapot, cov., child's, Japan.......................... **40-45**
Teapot, cov., Homer Laughlin **100**
Teapot, cov., round, Allerton, England...... **250-275**
Teapot, cov., Royal Corona Ware, S. Hancock &
Sons **225-250**
Teapot, individual, Moriyama, Japan,
4 1/2" h. **75-100**
Teapot, cov., Sadler, 4 3/4" h...................... **40-45**

Teapot w/Bamboo Handle

Teapot, cov., bamboo handle, "Semi
China," gold trim, 6" h. (ILLUS.) **250-275**
Teapot, cov., enamel, unmarked, 7" h. **100**

"Yorkshire Relish" Tip Tray

Tip tray, "Yorkshire Relish," England, 4" d.
(ILLUS.)... **50-75**
Toothbrush holder, Wedgwood, England,
5 1/4" h. **95**
Tray, round, brass, 6" d. **50**

Vegetable bowl, cov., rectangular, Buffalo Pottery **175-200**

Vegetable bowl, cov., square, ca. 1900, England **150-175**

Vegetable bowl, open, Japan, 10 1/2" oval **35**

Vegetable bowl, open, Shenango China, 8" d. **30-40**

Vegetable bowl, cov., ca. 1930, England, 9" d. **125**

Vegetable bowl, open, Japan, 9" d **30-35**

Wash pitcher & bowl, ca. 1890, unmarked, England, the set **500-600**

Wash pitcher & bowl, Royal Doulton, the set **700-900**

OTHER COLORS

Butter pat, red, Japan **20**

Charger, brown, Buffalo China, 11" d. **50-60**

Coffeepot, cov., ca. 1890, brown, unmarked, England, 8 3/4" h. **200-225**

Cup & saucer, red, ca. 1930, Buffalo China.. **30-35**

Egg cup, red, England, 4 1/2" h. **35-40**

Plate, 6" d., restaurant ware, brown, Buffalo China **15**

Plate, 9" d., purple, Britannia Pottery **35-40**

Plate, dinner, red, Japan **15-20**

Plate, bread & butter, 6" d., green, Japan **18-20**

Plate, 9" d., ca. 1890, brown, John Meir & Son **20-25**

Plate, 9" d., Mandarin patt., red, Copeland ... **35-40**

Plate, grill, 11 1/4" d., green, Royal Willow China **30-35**

Platter, 9 1/4 x 11 1/4", rectangular, red, Allerton, England **175-200**

Platter, 11 x 19" l., rectangular, green, John Steventon & Sons **125-150**

Sugar bowl, red, Japan **25-35**

Teapot, cov., purple, Britannia Pottery **200-225**

Vegetable bowl, cov., round, green, Victoria Porcelain **100-125**

WORCESTER

The famed English factory was established in 1751 and produced porcelains. Earthenwares were made in the 19th century. Its first period is known as the "Dr. Wall" period; that from 1783 to 1792 as the "Flight" period; that from 1792 to 1807 as the "Barr and Flight & Barr period. The firm became Barr, Flight & Barr from 1807 to 1813; Flight, Barr & Barr from 1813 to 1840; Chamberlain & Co. from 1840 to 1852, and Kerr and Binns from 1852 to 1862. After 1862, the company became the Worcester Royal Porcelain Company, Ltd., known familiarly as Royal Worcester, which see. Also included in the following listing are examples of wares from the early Chamberlains and early Grainger factories in Worcester.

Worcester Marks

Bowl, 6" d., footed deep wide & gently flared body, the exterior enameled in polychrome w/Chinese figures, the interior rim w/underglaze-blue foliate banding, unmarked, 18th c. (glaze wear) **$403**

Bowl, 9 1/4" d., wide shallow form w/wide oval loop reticulated border decorated w/blue florettes, the center w/a floral cluster w/pine cones, further florettes on the exterior, Dr. Wall crescent mark, 18th c. **908**

Creamer, bulbous ovoid body molded w/cabbage leaves below the cylindrical neck w/a mask spout, ornate scroll handle, h.p. blue floral sprig decoration, Dr. Wall crescent mark, 18th c., 5 7/8" h. **633**

Mug, cylindrical, floral-decorated in underglaze-blue, open crescent mark, 18th c., 3 3/8" h. **230**

Plates, 8 1/4" d., scalloped rim w/molded basketweave border, underglaze-blue Chantilly Sprig patt., shaded crescent marks, 18th c., one w/rim chip, pr. **259**

Platter, 8 1/8 x 11 1/2", rectangular w/angled corners & molded rim, underglaze-blue Pine Cone patt., shaded crescent mark, 18th c. **460**

Sauceboat, molded body w/panels of underglaze-blue flowers & a cell border, open crescent mark, 18th c., 5 1/4" l. **288**

Teapot, cov., footed spherical body w/short cylindrical neck & domed cover w/floral finial, C-form handle & short angled spout, underglaze-blue Waiting Chinaman patt., open crescent mark, 18th c., 5 5/8" h. (slight spout nick, chips to finial, line under base) **863**

Tureen, cover & undertray, deep tapering oval body decorated w/an underglaze-blue pine cone design, shell scroll end handles, stepped & domed cover w/artichoke finial, matching oval undertray, shaded crescent mark, 18th c., one tureen handle restored, interior rim flake, chip on handle of tray, tureen 10 1/2" l., the set **805**

YELLOW-GLAZED EARTHENWARE

In the past this early English ware was often referred to as "Canary Lustre," but recently a more accurate title has come into use.

Produced in the late 18th and early 19th centuries, pieces featured an overall yellow glaze, often decorated with silver or copper lustre designs or black, brown or red transfer-printed scenes.

Most pieces are not marked and today the scarcity of examples in good condition keeps market prices high.

Model of a cradle, decorated w/relief-molded interlocking circle design, 4 5/8" l. (wear) **$303**

Mug, child's, cylindrical, black transfer-printed decoration of scene titled "Come Up Donkey," second quarter 19th c., 2" h. (minor rim chips, hairline) **374**

Floral-decorated Yellow-Glazed Pitcher

Pitcher, 6 1/2" h., footed bulbous body decoration w/enameled flowers in red, green, blue & pink lustre on yellow ground, wear & crazing w/hairline in spout (ILLUS.) **605**

Teapot, cov., bulbous body w/arched neck, inset domed cover, swan's-neck spout & C-form handle, black transfer-printed reserves of three musicians, early 19th c., 5 1/2" h. (restoration to cover finial, minor chips) **403**

YELLOWWARE

Yellowware is a form of utilitarian pottery produced in the United States and England from the early 19th century onward. Its body texture is less dense and vitreous (impervious to water) than stoneware. Most, but not all, yellowware is unmarked and its color varies from deep yellow to pale buff. In the late 19th and early 20th centuries bowls in graduated sizes were widely advertised. Still in production, yellowware is plentiful and still reasonably priced.

Bank, figural standing pig, marbleized glaze in brown, green & cream, 6 1/4" l. (wear, glaze flakes) **$83**

Yellowware Dog Bank

Bank, model of a seated dog, facing front, on a rectangular base w/coin slot, green & brown running glaze, chips on base & coin slot, 7 1/2" h. (ILLUS.) **1,045**

Beverage set: 8" h. pitcher & six 4 3/4" h. mugs; all decorated w/blue stripes at rim & base & impressed "100% Buckeye Pure," the set (slight variation in color & size, one mug w/hairline & pitcher w/small chip) **550**

Yellowware Flask and Toby Bottle

Bottle, figural standing Mr. Toby w/fiddle, crazing w/possible hairline in base, chip on hat brim, 8 1/2" h. (ILLUS. right).............. **715**

Bowl, 7" d., 3 1/2" h., cov., cylindrical, decorated w/blue bands & stripes (crazing & stains).. **220**

Dish, rectangular, brown & green sponging, 8 1/2" l. (minor wear) **193**

Flask, decorated w/relief-molded morning glories & an eagle, chips, 7 3/8" h. (ILLUS. left) **1,210**

Food molds, figural rabbit, 9" & 9 1/2" l., pr. (one w/hairline) **248**

Inkwell, figural dog, green & brown running glaze, 6 1/8" l. **440**

Mixing bowl, footed, deep rounded sides w/rim spout, white center band w/blue mocha seaweed decoration, flanked by narrow blue stripes, probably East Liverpool, Ohio, 9 1/4" d., 4 1/2" h. (wear, hairlines in spout & chips) **468**

Mug, cylindrical w/C-form handle, blue stripes w/white sanded band, 2" h.............. **182**

Pitcher, jug-type, 5" h., strap handle & spout w/strainer, decorated w/blue stripes (flakes)... **578**

Yellowware Pitcher

Pitcher, 5 1/4" h., footed bulbous body tapering slightly to wide cylindrical neck w/flared rim, high arched rim spout & C-form ribbed handle w/leaf, light blue & white horizontal stripes around midbody, faint hairline at base of handle (ILLUS.)... **358**

Pitcher, jug-type, 6 1/8" h., w/strap handle, decorated w/white bands & black stripes... **688**

Pitcher, jug-type, 8 1/2" h., w/ribbed handle, decorated w/white band, repair on spout **550**

Pitcher, 8 7/8" h., footed cylindrical body w/flared lip, ornate handle, Gothic design w/relief-molded Mary, John the Baptist & Jesus, light blue cartouche label w/registry mark & "Charles Meigh, Nov 12, 1846, York Minster Jug," England 495

Soap dish, round w/drain holes, 5 5/8" d. (some wear) 550

Vegetable dish, open, oval, impressed mark "Fire Proof," 13 3/8" l. (pinpoint surface flakes)... 495

ZSOLNAY

This pottery was made in Pecs, Hungary, in a factory founded in 1862 by Vilmos Zsolnay. Utilitarian earthenware was originally produced but by the turn of the century ornamental Art Nouveau style wares with bright colors and lustre decoration were produced and these wares are especially sought today. Currently Zsolnay pieces are being made in a new factory.

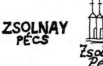

Zsolnay Marks

Basket, egg-shaped, reticulated, yellow, blue & pink, 6 1/2 x 8 1/2" **$795**

Bowl-vase, round footring below the squatty rounded body w/incurved sides pinched in at the rim on one side & molded in relief w/a large moth in iridescent green, gold, purple & blue on a deep red glossy ground, molded factory mark & "6383 - M" on the base, ca. 1901, 3" h. **1,610**

Pitcher, cov., the pierced body enamel-decorated & molded in relief w/flowers & leaves, early 20th c., 12 1/4" h. **403**

Vase, 10 1/4" h., Art Nouveau style, elongated ovoid form w/extended neck & handle, the surface in brilliant orangish red, fiery purples & gold w/floral & leaf designs & a sunset over a tree-lined landscape, raised round stamp trademark, impressed "5572 M 23," ca. 1900 ... **1,610**

GLOSSARY OF SELECTED CERAMIC TERMS

Abino Ware—A line produced by the Buffalo Pottery of Buffalo, New York. Introduced in 1911, this limited line featured mainly sailing ship scenes with a windmill on shore.

Agate Ware—An earthenware pottery featuring a mixture of natural colored clays giving a marbled effect. Popular in England in the 18th century.

Albany slip—A dark brown slip glaze used to line the interiors of most salt-glazed stoneware pottery. Named for a fine clay found near Albany, New York.

Albino line—A version of Griffen, Smith and Hill's Shell & Seaweed majolica pattern with an off-white overall color sometimes trimmed with gold or with pink or blue feathering.

Albion Ware—A line of majolica developed by Edwin Bennett in the 1890s. It featured colored liquid clays over a green clay body decorated with various scenes. Popular for jardinieres and pedestals.

Bas relief—Literally "low relief," referring to lightly molded decorations on ceramic pieces.

Bisquit—Unglazed porcelain left undecorated or sometimes trimmed with pastel colors. Also known as bisque.

Bocage—A background of flowering trees or vines often used as a backdrop for figural groups which were meant to be viewed from the front only.

Bone china—A porcelain body developed in England using the white ashes of bone. It has been the standard English porcelain ware since the early 19th century.

Coleslaw—A type of decoration used on ceramic figurines to imitate hair or fur. It is finely crumbled clay applied to the unfired piece and resembling coleslaw cabbage.

Crackled glaze—A glaze with an intentional network of fine lines produced by uneven contracting of the glaze after firing. First popular on Chinese wares.

Crazing—The fine network of cracks in a glaze produced by uneven contracting of the glaze after firing or later reheating of a piece during usage. An unintentional defect usually found on earthenwares.

Creamware—A light-colored fine earthenware developed in England in the late 18th century and used by numerous potters into the 19th century. Josiah

Wedgewood marketed his version as Queensware.

Crystalline glaze—A glaze containing fine crystals resulting from the presence of mineral salts in the mixture. It was a popular glaze on American art pottery of the late 19th century and early 20th century.

Eared handles—Handles applied to ceramic pieces such as crocks. They are crescent or 'ear' shaped, hence the name.

Earthenware—A class of fine-grained porous pottery fired at relatively low temperature and then glazed. It produces a light and easily molded ware that was widely used by the potteries of Staffordshire, England in the late 18th and early 19th century.

Faience—A form of fine earthenware featuring a tin glaze and originally inspired by Chinese porcelain. It includes early Dutch Delft ware and similar wares made in France, Germany and other areas of Europe.

Fairyland Lustre—A special line of decorated wares developed by Susannah 'Daisy' Makeig-Jones for the Josiah Wedgewood firm early in the 20th century. It featured fantastic or dreamlike scenes with fairies and elves in various colors and with a mother-of-pearl lustre glaze. Closely related to **Dragon Lustre** featuring designs with dragons.

Flambé glaze—A special type of glaze featuring splashed or streaked deep reds and purple, often dripping over another base color. Popular with some American art pottery makers but also used on porcelain wares.

Flint Enamel glaze—A version of the well known brown mottled Rockingham pottery glaze. It was developed by Lyman Fenton & Co. of Bennington, Vermont and patented in 1849. It featured streaks and flecks of green, orange, yellow and blue mixed with the mottled brown glaze.

Glaze—The general term for vitreous (glass-like) coating fired onto pottery and porcelain to produce an impervious surface and protect underglaze decoration.

Hard-paste—Refers to 'true' porcelain, a fine, white clay body developed by the Chinese and containing **kaolin** and **petuntse** or china stone. It is fired at a high temperature and glazed with powdered feldspar to produce a smooth, shiny glaze.

Lead glaze—A shiny glaze most often used on cheap redware pottery and produced using a dry powdered or liquid lead formula. Since it would be toxic, it was generally used on the exterior of utilitarian wares only.

Lithophane—A panel of thin porcelain delicately molded with low-relief pattern or scenes which show up clearly when held to light. It was developed in Europe in the 19th century and was used for decorative panels or lamp shades and was later used in the bottom of some German and Japanese steins, mugs or cups.

Majolica—A type of tin-glazed earthenware pottery developed in Italy and named for the island of Majorca. It was revived in Europe and America in the late 19th century and usually featured brightly colored shiny glazes.

Married—A close match or a duplicate of the original missing section or piece, such as a lid.

Mission Ware—A decorative line of pottery developed by the Niloak Pottery of Benton, Arkansas. It featured variously colored clays swirled together and was used to produce such decorative pieces as vases and candlesticks.

Moriage—Japanese term for the sliptrailed relief decorations used on various forms of porcelain and pottery. Flowers, beading and dragon decoration are typical examples.

Pâte-sur-pâte—French for 'paste on paste,' this refers to a decorative technique where layers of porcelain slip in white are layered on a darker background. Used on artware produced by firms like Minton, Ltd. of England.

Pearlware—A version of white colored creamware developed in England and widely used for inexpensive eathenwares in the late 18th and early 19th century. It has a pearly glaze, hence the name.

Pillow vase—A form of vase designed to resemble a flattened round or oblong pillow. Generally an upright form with flattened sides. A similar form is the **Moon vase** or **flask**, meant to resemble a full moon.

Porcelain—The general category of translucent, vitrified ceramics first developed by the Chinese and later widely produced in Europe and America. Hard-paste is 'true' porcelain, while soft-paste is an 'artifcial' version developed to imitate hard-paste using other ingredients.

Pottery—The very general category of ceramics produced from various types of clay. It includes redware, yellowware, stoneware and various earthenwares. It is generally fired at a much lower temperature than porcelain.

PUG—An abbreviation for "printed under glaze," referring to colored decorations on pottery. Most often it is used in reference to decorations found on Mettlach pottery steins.

Relief-molding—A decorative technique, sometimes erroneously referred to as "blown-out," whereby designs are raised in bold relief against a background. The reverse side of such decoration is hollowed-out, giving the impression the design was produced by 'blowing' from the inside. Often used in reference to certain Nippon porcelain wares.

Rocaille—A French term meaning 'rock-work.' It generally refers to a decoration used for the bases of ceramic figurines.

Salt-glazed stoneware—A version of stoneware pottery where common rock salt is thrown in the kiln during firing and produces hard, shiny glaze like a thin coating of glass. A lightly pitted "orange peel" surface is sometimes the result of this technique.

Sanded—A type of finish usually on pottery wares. Unfired pieces are sprinkled or rolled in fine sand, which, when fired, gives the piece a sandy, rough surface texture.

Sang-de-boeuf—Literally French for "ox blood," it refers to a deep red glaze produced with copper oxide. It was first produced by the Chinese and imitated by European and American potters in the late 19th and early 20th century.

Sgrafitto—An Italian-inspired term for decorative designs scratched or cut through a layer of slip before firing. Generally used on earthenware forms and especially with the Pennsylvania-German potters of America.

Slip—The liquid form of clay, often used to decorate earthenware pieces in a process known as **slip-trailing** or **slip-quilling**.

Soft-paste—A term used to describe a certain type of porcelain body developed in Europe and England from the 16th to late 18th centuries. It was used to imitate true hard-paste porcelain developed by the Chinese but was produced using a white clay mixed with a grit or flux of bone ash or talc and fired at fairly low temperatures. The pieces are translucent, like hard-paste porcelain, but are not as durable. It should **not** be used when referring to earthenwares such as creamware or pearlware.

Sprigging—A term used to describe the ornamenting of ceramic pieces with applied relief decoration, such as blossoms, leaves or even figures.

Standard glaze—The most common form of glazing used on Rookwood Pottery pieces. It is a clear, shiny glaze usually on pieces decorated with florals or portraits against a dark shaded background.

Stoneware—A class of hard, high-fired pottery usually made from dense grey clay and most often decorated with a salt glaze. American 19th century stoneware was often decorated with slip-quilled or hand-brushed cobalt blue decorations.

Tapestry ware—A form of late 19th century porcelain where the piece is impressed with an overall linen cloth texture before firing. The Royal Bayreuth firm is especially known for their fine "Rose Tapestry" line wherein the finely textured ground is decorated with colored roses.

Tin glaze—A form of pottery glaze made opaque by the addition of tin oxide. It was used most notably on early Dutch Delft as well as other early faience and majolica wares.

Underglaze-blue—A cobalt blue produced with metallic oxides applied to an unfired clay body. Blue was one of the few colors which does not run or smear when fired at a high temperature. It was used by the Chinese on porcelain and later copied by firms such as Meissen.

APPENDIX I

CERAMICS CLUBS
& ASSOCIATIONS
For Ceramic Collectors

Abingdon Pottery Club
210 Kllnox Hwy. 5
Abingdon, IL 61410

American Art Pottery Association
P.O. Box 525
Cedar Hill, MO 63016

American Ceramic Circle
419 Gate Lane
Philadelphia, PA 19119

Pottery Lovers Reunion
4969 Hudson Dr.
Stow, OH 44224

Bauer News
P.O. Box 91279
Pasadena, CA 91109-1279

Belleek Collectors Society, The
c/o Reed & Barton Co.
144 West Britannia St.
Taunton, MA 02780

Blue & White Pottery Club
224 12th St., NW
Cedar Rapids, IA 52405

Blue Ridge Collectors Club
Rte. 3, Box 161
Erwin, TN 37650

Carlton Ware International
P.O. Box 161
Sevenoaks
Kent Tn15 6GA England

Ceramic Arts Studio Collectors
P.O. Box 46
Madison, WI 53701-0046

Chintz China Collector (The)
P.O. Box 6126
Folsom, CA 95630

Clarice Cliff Collector's Club
Fantasque House
Tennis Drive, the Park
Nottingham NG1 1AE England

The Dedham Pottery Collectors
Society Newsletter
248 Highland St.
Dedham, MA 02026-5833

Heartland Doulton Collectors
P.O. Box 2434
Jolliet, IL. 60434

Mid-America Doulton Collectors
P.O. Box 483
McHenry, IL 60050

Fiesta Club of America
P.O. Box 15383
Loves Park, IL 61115

Fiesta Collectors Club
P.O. Box 361280
Strongsville, OH 44136

Flow Blue International Collectors'
Club
2774 E. Main St., Suite 136
St. Charles, IL 60174

Frankoma Pottery Collectors Club
5632 N.W. 58th Terrace
Oklahoma City, OK 73122

Gonder Collectors Club
P.O. Box 21
Crooksville, OH 43731

Goss Collectors Club
4 Khasiaberry
Walnut Tree
Milton Keynes MK7 7DP England

Hall Collector's Club
P.O. Box 360488
Cleveland, OH 44136

National Autumn Leaf Collectors
Club
Rt. 16, Box 275
Tulsa, OK 74131-9600

Haviland Collectors Internationale
Foundation
P.O. Box 11632
Milwaukee, WI 53211-0632

Head Vase Society
P.O. Box 83H
Scarsdale, NY 10583-8583

Hull Pottery News (Newsletter)
466 Foreston Place
St. Louis, MO 63119-3927

Hull Pottery *Newsletter*
11023 Tunnell Hill NE
New Lexington, OH 43764

Foundation for Historical Research
of Illinois Potteries
2108 Church St.
Streator, IL 61364-3831

Collectors of Illinois Pottery &
Stoneware
1527 East Converse St.
Springfield, IL 62702

Homer Laughlin
Newsletter: *The Laughlin Eagle*
1270 - 63rd Terrace So.
St. Petersburg, FL 33705

Majolica International Society
1275 First Ave., Stuite 103
New York, NY 10021

Our McCoy Matters (Newsletter)
P.O. Box 14255
Parkville, MO 64152-7255

Arkansas Pottery Collectors Society
(Niloak and Camark Pottery)
P.O. Box 7617
Little Rock, AR 72217

New England Nippon Collectors
Club
64 Burt Rd.
Springfield, MA 01118

Long Island Nippon Collectors Club
145 Andover Pl.
West Hampstead, NY 11552

Lakes & Plains Nippon Collectors
Club
4305 W. Beecher Rd.
P.O. Box 230
Peotone, IL 60468

International Nippon Collectors
Club
112 Oak Ave. N.
Owatonna, MN 55060

Noritake Collectors' Society
1237 Federal Ave., East
Seattle, WA 98102-4329

North Dakota Pottery Collectors
Society
P.O. Box 14
Beach, ND 58621-0014

Old Ivory Newsletter
P.O. Box 1004
Wilsonville, OR 97070-1004

Phoenix Bird Collectors of America
685 S. Washington
Constantine, MI 49042-1325

Pickard Collectors Club
300 E. Grove St.
Bloomington, IL 61701-5232

Purinton Pottery
Newsletter: *Purinton Pastimes*
P.O. Box 9394
Arlington, VA 22219

Red Wing Collectors Society, Inc.
P.O. Box 184
Galesburg, IL 61402-0184

Roseville's of the Past Pottery Club
P.O. Box 656
Clarona, FL 32710-0656

Royal Bayreuth International
Collectors' Society
P.O. Box 325
Orrville, OH 44667-0325

Royal Copley
Newletter: *The Copley Courier*
1639 N. Catalina St.
Burbank, CA 91505-1605

International Association of R.S.
Prussia Collectors Inc.
14215 Turtle Rock
San Antonio, TX 78232

Shawnee Pottery Collectors Club
P.O. Box 713
New Smyrna Beach, FL
32170-0713

Shelley China
  Newletter: *Shelley Group Newsletter*
  12 Lilleshall Rd.
  Clayton Newcastle - Under-Lyme
  Staffordshire ST5 3BX England

Southern Folk Pottery Collectors
Society
  1224 Main St.
  Glastonbury, CT 06033

Stangl/Fulper Collectors
Association
  P.O. Box 64-M
  Changewater, NJ 07831

American Stoneware Association
  208 Cresent Ct.
  Mars, PA 16066-3308

Susie Cooper Collectors Group
  P.O. Box 7436
  London, England N12 7QF

Tea Leaf Club International
Membership
  P.O. Box 377
  Belton, MO 64012

Tile Heritage Foundation
  P.O. Box 1850
  Healdsburg, CA 95448

North American Torquay Society
  604 Orchard View Dr.
  Maumee, OH 43537

Torquay Pottery Collectors Society
  P.O. Box 373
  Schoolcraft, MI 49087-0373

Uhl Collectors Society
  233 E. Timberlin Lane
  Huntingburg, IN 47542

Vernon Views Newsletter
  P.O. Box 945
  Scottsdale, AZ 85252

Watt Collectors Association
  Box 184
  Galesburg, IL 61401

Watt Pottery Collectors
  P.O. Box 26067
  Fairview Park, OH 44126

Wedgwood Society
  The Roman Villa
  Rockbourne, Fordingbridge
  Hants SP6 3PG England

Wedgwood Society of New York
  5 Dogwood Ct.
  Glen Head, NY 11545

International Willow Collectors
  P.O. Box 13382
  Arlington, TX 76094-0382

APPENDIX II

Museums & Libraries
with Ceramic Collections

BENNINGTON

Bennington Museum, The
    W. Main St.
    Bennington, VT 05201

CERAMICS (AMERICAN)

Everson Museum of Art of Syracuse
    & Onondaga County
    401 Harrison St.
    Syracuse, NY 13202

Museum of Ceramics at East
    Liverpool
    400 E. 5th St.
    East Liverpool, OH 43920

CERAMICS (AMERICAN ART POTTERY)

Cincinnati Art Museum
    Eden Park
    Cincinnati, OH 45202

Newcomb College Art Gallery
    1229 Broadway
    New Orleans, LA 70118

Zanesville Art Center
    620 Military Rd.
    Zanesville, OH 43701

CHINESE EXPORT PORCELAIN

Peabody Museum of Salem
    East India Square
    Salem, MA 01970

COWAN POTTERY CO.

Cowan Pottery Museum at the
    Rocky River Public Library
    1600 Hampton Rd.
    Rocky River, OH 44116-2699

DEDHAM

Dedham Historical Society
    612 High St.
    Dedham, MA

PENNSYLVANIA GERMAN

Hershey Museum
    170 W. Hersheypark Dr.
    Hershey, PA 17033

GENERAL COLLECTIONS

The Bayou Bend Collection
    #1 Wescott
    Houston, TX

Greenfield Village and Henry Ford
    Museum
    Oakwood Blvd.
    Dearborn, MI 48121

Jones Museum of Glass &
    Ceramics
    Douglas Hill Rd.
    East Baldwin, ME 04024

Museum of Early Southern
    Decorative Arts
    924 Main St.
    Winston-Salem, NC 27101

Abby Aldrich Rockefeller Folk Art
    Collection
    England St.
    Williamsburg, VA 23185

The Margaret Woodbury Strong
    Museum
    700 Allen Creek Rd.
    Rochester, NY 14618

Henry Francis DuPont Winterthur
    Museum
    Winterthur, DE 19735

APPENDIX III

References to Pottery
and Porcelain Marks

DeBolt's Dictionary of American Pottery Marks—Whiteware & Porcelain
Gerald DeBolt
Collector Books,
Paducah, Kentucky, 1994

Encyclopaedia of British Pottery and Porcelain Marks
Geoffrey A. Godden
Bonanza Books,
New York, New York, 1964

Encyclopedia of Marks on American English and European Earthenware, Ironstone and Stoneware, 1780-1980
Arnold A. Kowalsky &
Dorothy E. Kowalsky
Schiffer Publishing, Ltd.
Atglen, Pennsylvania

Kovel's New Dictionary of Marks, Pottery & Porcelain, 1850 to the Present
Ralph & Terry Kovel
Crown Publishers,
New York, New York, 1986

Lehner's Encyclopedia of U.S. Marks on Pottery, Porcelain & Clay
Lois Lehner
Collector Books,
Paducah, Kentucky, 1988

Marks on German, Bohemian and Austrian Porcelain, 1710 to the Present
Robert E. Röntgen
Schiffer Publishing, Ltd.,
Atglen, Pennsylvania

APPENDIX IV

English Registry Marks

Since the early nineteenth century, the English have used a number of markings on most ceramic wares which can be very helpful in determining the approximate date a piece was produced.

The 'registry' mark can be considered an equivalent of the American patent number. This English numbering system continues in use today.

Beginning in 1842 and continuing until 1883, most pottery and porcelain pieces were printed or stamped with a diamond-shaped registry mark which was coded with numbers and letters indicating the type of material, parcel number of the piece and, most helpful, the day, month and year that the design or pattern was registered at the Public Record Office. Please note that a piece may have been produced a few years after the registration date itself.

Our Chart A here shows the format of the diamond registry mark used between 1842 and 1867. Accompanying it are listings of the corresponding month and year letters used during that period. In a second chart, Chart B, we show the version of the diamond mark used between 1868 and 1883 which depicts a slightly different mark arrangement. Keep in mind that this diamond registry mark was also used on metal, wood and glasswares. It is important to note that the top bubble with the Roman numeral indicates the material involved; pottery and porcelain will always be Numeral IV.

After 1884, the diamond mark was discontinued and instead just a registration number was printed on pieces. The abbreviation "Rd" for "Registration" appears before the number. We list here these design registry numbers by year with the number indicating the first number that was used in that year. For instance, design number 494010 would have been registered sometime in 1909.

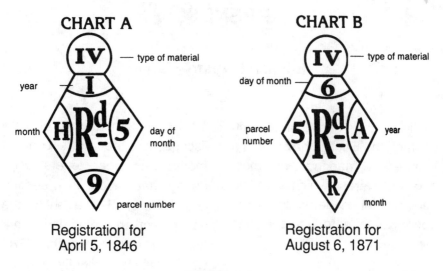

CHART A

— type of material

year

month

day of month

parcel number

Registration for
April 5, 1846

CHART B

— type of material

day of month

parcel number

year

month

Registration for
August 6, 1871

LIST 1

Month of the Year of Registration

C—January
G—February
W—March
H—April
E—May
M—June

I—July
R—August
D—September
B—October
K—November
A—December

LIST 2

Year of Registration—1842-1867

1842—X	1851—P	1860—Z
1843—H	1852—D	1861—R
1844—C	1853—Y	1862—O
1845—A	1854—J	1863—G
1846—I	1855—E	1864—N
1847—F	1856—L	1865—W
1848—U	1857—K	1866—Q
1849—S	1858—B	1867—T
1850—V	1859—M	

LIST 3
Year of Registration—1868-1883

1868—X	1874—U	1879—Y
1869—H	1875—S	1880—J
1870—C	1876—V	1881—E
1871—A	1877—P	1882—L
1872—I	1878—D	1883—K
1873—F		

LIST 4
DESIGN REGISTRY NUMBERS—1884-1951

Jan. 1884—1	1907—493900	1929—742725
1885—20000	1908—518640	1930—751160
1886—40800	1909—535170	1931—760583
1887—64700	Sep. 1909—548919	1932—769670
1888—91800	Oct. 1909—548920	1933—779292
1889—117800	Jan. 1911—575817	1934—789019
1890—142300	1912—594195	1935—799097
1891—164000	1913—612431	1936—808794
1892—186400	1914—630190	1937—817293
1893—206100	1915—644935	1938—825231
1894—225000	1916—635521	1939—832610
1895—248200	1917—658988	1940—837520
1896—268800	1918—662872	1941—838590
1897—291400	1919—666128	1942—839230
Jan. 1898—311677	1920—673750	1943—839980
1899—332200	1921—680147	1944—841040
1900—351600	1922—687144	1945—842670
1901—368186	1923—694999	Jan. 1946—845550
1902—385180	1924—702671	1947—849730
1903—403200	1925—710165	1948—853260
1904—424400	1926—718057	1949—856999
1905—447800	1927—726330	1950—860854
1906—471860	1928—734370	1951—863970

INDEX